THE PAPERS OF
WOODROW WILSON
VOLUME 54
JANUARY 11-FEBRUARY 7, 1919

SPONSORED BY THE WOODROW WILSON
FOUNDATION
AND PRINCETON UNIVERSITY

# THE PAPERS OF

# WOODROW WILSON

ARTHUR S. LINK, *EDITOR*

DAVID W. HIRST, *SENIOR ASSOCIATE EDITOR*

JOHN E. LITTLE, *ASSOCIATE EDITOR*

FREDRICK AANDAHL, *ASSOCIATE EDITOR*

MANFRED F. BOEMEKE, *ASSOCIATE EDITOR*

DENISE THOMPSON, *ASSISTANT EDITOR*

PHYLLIS MARCHAND AND MARGARET D. LINK,
*EDITORIAL ASSISTANTS*

Volume 54
January 11-February 7, 1919

PRINCETON, NEW JERSEY
PRINCETON UNIVERSITY PRESS
1986

# INTRODUCTION

THIS volume opens on January 11, 1919, with the first meeting of the Council of Ten—the heads of government and foreign ministers of the five great victorious powers assembled in Paris to determine the fate of the world. During the following days, they discuss the organization of and representation in the peace conference about to open, its official language, the degree of publicity to be given to its proceedings, and other such procedural matters. The latter having been settled after tedious debate, President Poincaré opens the first Plenary Session with great fanfare in the Peace Rooms in the Ministry of Foreign Affairs on January 18.

During the period to the end of this volume (February 7), Wilson and his colleagues in the Council of Ten discuss, debate, and wrangle over two major questions—the future of former German colonies around the world and the problem of Russian representation. On the former, Wilson stands squarely against all Allied claims to outright annexation. He engages in often bitter debate, particularly with Prime Minister Hughes of Australia, Prime Minister Massey of New Zealand, and Generals Botha and Smuts of the Union of South Africa. When it appears that the conference is near the point of rupture, General Smuts saves the day by proposing that the former German colonies be entrusted to various British Dominions and other powers, but only under a system of three-tiered mandates to be strictly supervised by a league of nations. Wilson accepts Smuts' compromise proposal on January 30, and the first of many crises of the conference is resolved.

Equally troubling and more difficult is the problem of Russia's representation. As early as January 12, Marshal Foch proposes to send Allied troops to Poland to check the advance of Bolshevism into Central Europe. This suggestion sets off a violent controversy in the Council of Ten about how to deal with the Russian problem in general. French spokesmen adamantly oppose any contacts with the Bolshevik "criminals." Lloyd George, on grounds of expediency, and Wilson, on grounds of principle, insist upon at least an all-Russian representation in Paris. They also display an understanding of the causes of the Russian revolution and of the urgent necessity of coming to terms with it. The French finally yield and agree to Wilson's and Lloyd George's suggestion that representatives of all the Russian factions be invited to meet on the island of Prinkipo in the Sea of Marmara, off Constantinople, agree to an armistice in the civil war, and select delegates to appear before the Council of Ten. At the request of the council, Wilson personally drafts the invitation. Adopted on January 22 and known as the Prinkipo Declaration, it is a moving appeal to the Russian people, accompanied by an explicit assurance that the Allied and Associated governments will refrain from any interference whatsoever in Russian internal affairs.

The above narrative gives the impression that the meetings of the Council of Ten are highly structured and concentrate upon particular questions to the exclusion of others. As the reader will soon discover, these meetings are usually rambling and disorganized, and the council discusses numerous other matters, such as the transport of Polish troops from France to Poland by way of Danzig, the question of the boundaries of the newly created states in Central Europe, Japanese claims in Shantung Province, and so on. Throughout these long and weary discussions, Wilson not only participates actively; he also stands squarely for the principles of the Fourteen Points. At the same time, Wilson is deluged with appeals for support and protection from Jewish leaders and representatives from small and weak states and ethnic groups who look to him to fulfill their aspirations.

Wilson's greatest triumph during the weeks covered by this volume is the adoption by the second Plenary Session on January 25 of a resolution mandating the creation of the League of Nations, which will be, as Wilson states in his address to that meeting, the "keystone of the whole programme which expressed our purposes and our ideal." Wilson, in fact, has already been hard at work with Lord Robert Cecil and others on drafts for a Covenant of the League. The League of Nations Commission, under Wilson's chairmanship, begins its deliberations as this volume ends.

During these same weeks, Wilson, although in Paris, is still President of the United States and is in daily touch with Tumulty, members of the cabinet, and Democratic leaders in Congress. He presses for the adoption of a famine relief bill to provide immediate succor to the peoples of the new states of Europe and to Armenians and other Christian minorities in the former Ottoman Empire. Wilson is also under heavy pressure from Democratic leaders to appoint A. Mitchell Palmer to succeed Gregory as Attorney General, from Daniels to support a new three-year naval building program, and from Tumulty and Redfield to establish an agency for postwar reconstruction. In addition, Wilson continues to bombard reluctant Democratic senators with appeals to vote for the woman suffrage amendment. As the reader will see, these are only samples of the domestic concerns with which Wilson has to deal from day to day.

We call our readers' attention to the Introduction to the Peace Conference Series in Volume 53. They will find therein a description of our editorial method and of the materials that we have selected for the peace conference volumes.

## A SPECIAL NOTE

For the past several years, Wilson scholars have been intensely interested in Wilson's health and its effect on his behavior, and there has been disagreement about the nature of Wilson's illness. In some of the articles listed below, references in *The Papers* to "strokes" in 1896 and 1906 have been called into question. The Editors have taken a stand on what has become a controversial question concerning the two aforementioned episodes, and they wish to call the attention of their readers to the entire body of literature on Wilson's medical history, most of which of course covers the two episodes in which the Editors have said that Wilson suffered strokes.

Walter J. Friedlander, M.D., was the pioneer in the medical diagnosis of cerebral arterial disease, "stroke," and hypertension. See his "Woodrow Wilson's Cerebral Arteriosclerosis and the Failure of the League of Nations," *Stroke*, I (Summer 1966), 11-14, and "About Three Old Men: An Inquiry into How Cerebral Arteriosclerosis Has Altered World Politics: a Neurologist's View," *ibid.*, III (July-August 1972), 467-73. Friedlander's general diagnosis was refined and expanded by Edwin A. Weinstein, M.D., in "Woodrow Wilson's Neurological Illness," *The Journal of American History*, LVII (Sept. 1970), 324-51, and in his book, *Woodrow Wilson: A Medical and Psychological Biography* (Princeton, N.J., 1981)—a Volume Supplementary to The Papers of Woodrow Wilson. The Editors explain their reasons for referring to the incidents of 1896 and 1906 as strokes in a letter to the Editor, *The Journal of American History*, LXX (March 1984), 945-55.

There have been two recent refinements of what some persons have called the "Link-Weinstein thesis." In a paper read to the Section on Medical History of the American Academy of Neurology in 1984, James F. Toole, M.D., stated that Wilson suffered from prolonged hypertension which may have manifested itself most particularly in the small strokes caused by lacunar infarctions (manuscript in A. S. Link's possession). Bert E. Park, M.D., in a chapter on Wilson in *Fit to Lead? The Impact of Illness on World Leaders* (Philadelphia, 1986), affirms this diagnosis in elaborate detail.

For different diagnoses and interpretations (except in the case

of the Weinstein-Anderson-Link article and Weinstein's article in
*Political Psychology*), see Alexander L. George and Juliette L. George,
*Woodrow Wilson and Colonel House: A Personality Study* (New
York, 1956); Weinstein, James W. Anderson, and Arthur S. Link,
"Woodrow Wilson's Political Personality: A Reappraisal," *Political
Science Quarterly*, XCIII (Winter 1978), 585-98; George and George,
"*Woodrow Wilson and Colonel House*: A Reply to Weinstein, An-
derson, and Link," *ibid.*, XCVI (Winter 1981), 641-65; Michael F.
Marmor, M.D., "Wilson, Strokes, and Zebras," *New England Jour-
nal of Medicine*, CCCVII (Aug. 26, 1982), 528-35; Marmor, "A Bad
Case of History," *The Sciences*, XXIII (Jan.-Feb. 1983), 36-38; Jer-
rold M. Post, M.D., "Woodrow Wilson Re-examined: The Mind-
Body Controversy Redux and Other Disputations," *Political Psychology*, IV (June 1983), 289-306; George and George, "Comments
on 'Woodrow Wilson Re-examined . . .'," *ibid.*, pp. 307-12; Weinstein, "Comments on 'Woodrow Wilson Re-examined . . .'," *ibid.*,
pp. 313-24; Marmor, "Comments on 'Woodrow Wilson Re-examined . . .'," *ibid.*, pp. 325-27; Post, "Reply to the Three Comments
. . . ," *ibid.*, pp. 329-31; George, Marmor, and George, "Issues in
Wilson Scholarship: References to Early 'Strokes' in the *Papers of
Woodrow Wilson*," *The Journal of American History*, LXX (March
1984), 845-53; George, Marmor, and George, letter to the Editor,
*ibid.*, LXXI (June 1984), 198-212; and Marmor, "The Eyes of Woodrow Wilson," *Ophthalmology*, XCII (March 1985), 454-65.

For additional comments on Wilson's health, see Patrick Devlin,
*Too Proud to Fight: Woodrow Wilson's Neutrality* (New York, 1974),
pp. 23, 26-27, and 88-89; Dorothy Ross, "Woodrow Wilson and the
Case for Psychohistory," *The Journal of American History*, LXIX
(Dec. 1982), 659-68; John M. Mulder, *Woodrow Wilson: The Years
of Preparation* (Princeton, N. J., 1978), pp. 131, 145-47, and 185-
86; John Milton Cooper, Jr., *The Warrior and the Priest: Woodrow
Wilson and Theodore Roosevelt* (Cambridge, Mass., 1983), pp. 57,
98-99, 105, and 339-43; and Robert H. Ferrell, *Woodrow Wilson
and World War I* (New York, 1985), pp. 158-62. In extensive footnotes on pp. 273-75, Ferrell reviews the efforts to understand Wilson's health problems. Dr. Park, in an appendix in his book cited
above, reviews the differences between Link and Weinstein, on the
one side, and the Georges and Marmor, on the other side.

Any omission of significant literature on this subject is inad-
vertent.

The Woodrow Wilson Foundation, the Editors of *The Papers of
Woodrow Wilson*, and Princeton University Press edit and publish
this series in order to broaden public understanding of the career
of a great statesman and of a complex personality. We hope that

the bibliographic information presented above will promote that objective.

In earlier volumes of this series, we have said the following: "All documents are reproduced *verbatim et literatim*, with typographical and spelling errors corrected in square brackets only when necessary for clarity and ease of reading." The following essay explains our textual methods and review procedures.

We have never printed and do not intend to print critical, or corrected, versions of documents. We print them exactly as they are, with a few exceptions which we always note. We never use the word *sic* except to denote the repetition of words in a document; in fact, we think that a succession of *sics* defaces a page.

We usually repair words in square brackets when letters are missing. As we have said, we also repair words in square brackets for clarity and ease of reading. Our general rule is to do this when we, ourselves, cannot read the word without having to stop to puzzle out its meaning. Jumbled words and names misspelled beyond recognition of course have to be repaired. We correct the misspelling of names in documents in the footnotes identifying those persons.

However, when an old man writes to Wilson saying that he is glad to hear that Wilson is "comming" to Newark, or a semiliterate farmer from Texas writes phonetically, we see no reason to correct spellings in square brackets when the words are perfectly understandable. We do not correct Wilson's misspellings unless they are unreadable, except to supply in square brackets letters missing in words. For example, he consistently spelled "belligerent" as "belligerant." Nothing would be gained by correcting "belligerant" in square brackets.

We think that it is very important for several reasons to follow the rule of *verbatim et literatim*. Most important, a document has its own integrity and power, particularly when it is not written in perfect literary form. There is something very moving in seeing a Texas dirt farmer struggling to express his feelings in words, or a semiliterate former slave doing the same thing. Second, in Wilson's case it is essential to reproduce his errors in letters which he typed himself, since he usually typed badly when he was in an agitated state. Third, since style is the essence of the person, we would never correct grammar or make tenses consistent, as one correspondent has urged us to do. Fourth, we think that it is very important that we print exact transcripts of Charles L. Swem's copies of Wilson's letters. Swem made many mistakes (we correct them in footnotes from a reading of his shorthand books), and Wilson let them pass. We thus have to assume that Wilson did not read his letters before signing them, and this, we think, is a significant fact.

We think that our series would be worthless if we produced unreliable texts, and we go to considerable effort to make certain that the texts are authentic.

Our typists are highly skilled and proofread their transcripts carefully as soon as they have typed them. The Editor sight proofreads documents once he has assembled a volume and is setting its annotation. The Editors who write the notes read through documents several times and are careful to check any anomalies. Then, once the manuscript volume has been completed and all notes checked, the Editor and Senior Associate Editor orally proofread the documents against the copy. They read every comma, dash, and character. They note every absence of punctuation. They study every nearly illegible word in written documents.

Once this process of "establishing the text" is completed, the manuscript volume goes to our editor at Princeton University Press, who checks the volume carefully and sends it to the printing plant. The galley proofs are read against copy in the proofroom at the Press. And we must say that the proofreaders there are extraordinarily skilled. Some years ago, before we found a way to ease their burden, they queried every misspelled word, inconsistencies in punctuation and capitalization, absence of punctuation, or other such anomalies. Now we write "O.K." above such words or spaces on the copy.

We read the galley proofs at least three times. Our copyeditor gives them a sight reading against the manuscript copy to look for remaining typographic errors and to make sure that no line has been dropped. The Editor and Senior Associate Editor sight read them against documents and copy. We then get the page proofs, which have been corrected at the Press. We check all the changes three times. In addition, we get *revised* pages and check them twice.

This is not the end. The Editor, Senior Associate Editor, and an Associate Editor give a final reading to headings, description-location lines, and notes. Finally, our indexer of course reads the pages word by word. Before we return the pages to the Press, she brings in a list of queries, all of which are answered by reference to the documents.

Our rule in the Wilson Papers is that our tolerance of error is zero. No system and no person can be perfect. There may be errors in our volumes. However, we believe that we have done everything humanly possible to avoid error; the chance is remote that what looks at first glance like a typographical error is indeed an error.

We wish to express our deep gratitude to James Gordon Grayson and Cary Travers Grayson, Jr., for giving us the first right of publication of their father's massive diary, a portion of which has already been published in Volume 53. As we said in the Introduction to the Peace Conference Series, Dr. Grayson's diary is the centerpiece of the documents on Wilson in Paris. We continue to be indebted to Elena S. Danielson and her associates at the Hoover Institution Archives, Patricia Bodak Stark of the Yale University Library, and Mary Giunta of the National Historical Publications and Records Commission for their prompt and cheerful responses to our appeals for documents. John Milton Cooper, Jr., William H. Harbaugh, Richard W. Leopold, and Betty Miller Unterberger of our Editorial Advisory Committee have read the manuscript of this volume. We can never express in words our indebtedness to these friends who continue to be our best reviewers and critics. Alice A. Calaprice, our editor at Princeton University Press, has seen this volume through its various stages of production.

The publication of this volume will coincide with the retirement of Herbert S. Bailey, Jr., as Director of Princeton University Press. He has been our staunch friend and supporter since the very inception of *The Papers*. He has been much more than that. On numerous occasions, we have gone to him for advice, and he has always given it wisely and constructively. He has vigilantly maintained the high standards of production of this series, and we thank him for publishing so many handsome volumes. He has taken great pride in this series, and we thank him for that. Our warmest wishes go to him and his wife, Betty, in a retirement which, we are sure, will be active and productive.

Finally, we take note, at this first opportunity, of the death, on January 31, 1986, of Pleasant Jefferson Conkwright. P.J., as he was always called, planned the design of our series with all the consummate skill and love of books that made him world-renowned in his profession as a typographer and book designer. He was also a personal friend of the Editors, and we shall miss him very much.

THE EDITORS

*Princeton, New Jersey*
*February 14, 1986*

# CONTENTS

## General Diplomatic and Military Affairs

.. 

## Domestic Affairs

### Personal Affairs

# ILLUSTRATIONS

Following page 294

*From the collections of the National Archives*

*The opening of the Paris Peace Conference. Paul Mantoux, interpreter, is translating President Poincaré's address of welcome. Wilson is sitting to Mantoux's right, reading.*

*The League of Nations Commission*

*The American Commission to Negotiate Peace*

*Georges Clemenceau*

*David Lloyd George*

*Eleuthérios Vénisélos*

*Vittorio Emanuele Orlando*

*Lord Robert Cecil*

*Arthur James Balfour*

*Emir Faisal with Thomas Edward Lawrence (second from right) and retinue*

*Wilson leaving the American Church in Paris*

*Edith Benham and stenographers: Chief Yeoman Nicholas P. Schindler and Yeoman 1st Class Francis A. Kennedy*

# ABBREVIATIONS

| | |
|---|---|
| ACNP | American Commission to Negotiate Peace |
| ALI | autograph letter initialed |
| ALS | autograph letter signed |
| CC | carbon copy |
| CCL | carbon copy of letter |
| CCLS | carbon copy of letter signed |
| CCS | carbon copy signed |
| CLSsh | Charles Lee Swem shorthand |
| EBW | Edith Bolling Galt Wilson |
| EMH | Edward Mandell House |
| FKL | Franklin Knight Lane |
| FLP | Frank Lyon Polk |
| *FR* | *Papers Relating to the Foreign Relations of the United States* |
| *FR 1918, Russia* | *Papers Relating to the Foreign Relations of the United States, 1918, Russia* |
| *FR Russia, 1919* | *Papers Relating to the Foreign Relations of the United States, 1919, Russia* |
| *FR-WWS 1918* | *Papers Relating to the Foreign Relations of the United States, 1918, Supplement, The World War* |
| GFC | Gilbert Fairchild Close |
| HCH | Herbert Clark Hoover |
| Hw, hw | handwriting, handwritten |
| JD | Josephus Daniels |
| JPT | Joseph Patrick Tumulty |
| MS, MSS | manuscript, manuscripts |
| NDB | Newton Diehl Baker |
| *PPC* | *Papers Relating to the Foreign Relations of the United States: The Paris Peace Conference, 1919* |
| RG | record group |
| RL | Robert Lansing |
| T | typed |
| TC | typed copy |
| TCL | typed copy of letter |
| TLI | typed letter initialed |
| TLS | typed letter signed |
| TS | typed signed |
| WBW | William Bauchop Wilson |
| WCR | William Cox Redfield |
| WJB | William Jennings Bryan |
| WW | Woodrow Wilson |
| WWhw | Woodrow Wilson handwriting |
| WWT | Woodrow Wilson typed |

### ABBREVIATIONS FOR COLLECTIONS
### AND REPOSITORIES

Following the National Union Catalog of the
Library of Congress

| | |
|---|---|
| CaOOA | Canadian Public Archives |
| CSt-H | Hoover Institution on War, Revolution and Peace |
| CtY | Yale University |
| DGU | Georgetown University |
| DLC | Library of Congress |
| DNA | National Archives |
| FO | British Foreign Office |
| NjMD | Drew University |
| PRO | Public Record Office |
| SDR | State Department Records |
| WP, DLC | Woodrow Wilson Papers, Library of Congress |

### SYMBOLS

| | |
|---|---|
| [January 13, 1919] | publication date of published writing; also date of document when date is not part of text |
| *[January 27, 1919]* | composition date when publication date differs |
| [[February 3, 1919]] | delivery date of speech if publication date differs |
| **** *** | text deleted by author of document |

THE PAPERS OF
# WOODROW WILSON
VOLUME 54
JANUARY 11-FEBRUARY 7, 1919

# THE PAPERS OF
# WOODROW WILSON

---

## A Memorandum by Robert Lansing[1]

THE PRESIDENT'S DRAFT OF A
COVENANT FOR A LEAGUE OF NATIONS.
January 11, 1919.

Yesterday the President discussed with the Commissioners his plan for a League of Nations. It is of course a tentative draft and an attempt to harmonize the President's previous ideas with those put forth by General Smuts in his monograph[2] which appealed mightily to the President. The monograph contained the rather novel thought that the League was to be "the heir of the Empires" since Imperialism was no more. This catchy phrase sank deep into the mind of the President and impressed him with the wisdom of Smuts.

Like all trite sayings it is apt to influence one, who rejoices in using catchy phrases, to build around it an entire theory. It reminds the student of those ancient days when the Greek savants expounded with clever adages their philosophic systems to their admiring disciples who valued the substance of the thought by the attractive conciseness of expression.

Whether Smuts expressed in words an idea which had been up to then unformed in the President's mind or whether the thought was wholly new to him I do not know. I only know that the Boer General registers very high in his estimation and will probably have a lot to do with formulating the League.

In our conference yesterday, which was in General Bliss' room, the President astounded us all by his resistance to every form of criticism or suggestion. I do not like to think that he is so vain of his ability as to think that he can produce so perfect a plan that he really believes it cannot be improved, but it is very hard to find any other excuse sufficient to account for his curt, almost insulting, manner of refuting valid objections to the document which he has drawn. House says that he must have been feeling unwell. I wish that I could believe that was the reason. Why he asked us to confer with him I cannot imagine unless it was to have us praise his work. If that was his purpose, he must have been disappointed.

His treatment of the Commissioners, who were all anxious to be helpful, decided us (that is White, Bliss and me) to keep quiet hereafter. This policy we followed today at another conference with him in White's room. I said nothing at all, while White and Bliss, avoiding the merits, offered only some verbal changes.

During yesterday's conference I mentioned that Scott and Miller had prepared a draft treaty, copies of which the Commissioners had. The President in a resentful tone exclaimed, "Who authorized them to do this? I don't want lawyers drafting this treaty." White and Bliss looked at me in amazement. I was deeply incensed at this intemperate remark as he knew I was a lawyer. It shows, however, the general attitude of the President toward the legal profession. After that I shall make no attempt to assist in drafting the articles constituting the League. Let it be drawn by inexperienced and untrained men. Amateurs will certainly muddle the whole business, and in the end some lawyer will have to put the precious "Covenant" in legal form. It will probably be done by someone who never drew a treaty, because the President will consider him unbiased.

The President will find out that this present draft is too loose, too crude and too imperfect to work, at least some of the legal experts of other countries are bound to tell him so. I really am deeply distressed at the situation and would like to help but see no way to do so.

T MS (R. Lansing Papers, DLC).
    [1] Internal evidence strongly indicates that Lansing wrote this memorandum retrospectively. For one thing, as the extract from the House and Grayson diaries printed at January 8, 1919, Vol. 53, reveal, Wilson's meeting with the other commissioners referred to below occurred on January 8, not on January 10, 1919. Second, it is difficult to believe that Wilson resisted "every form of criticism or suggestion" from his colleagues. See, for example, T. H. Bliss to WW, Jan. 15, 1919, in which Bliss said that Wilson, at the meeting of January 8, had said that he would be "glad to have suggestions" regarding the Covenant. Accompanying Bliss' letter is a long list of suggestions. Finally, in spite of what Lansing says in the memorandum printed below about having nothing further to do with the Covenant, he did indeed make suggestions to Wilson in RL to WW, Jan. 31 and Feb. 3, 1919.
    Lansing's memorandum brings up anew the question of whether Lansing did not in fact write *ex post facto* many of the memoranda often collectively but inaccurately referred to as the "Lansing Diary."
    [2] About which, see the memorandum printed at Dec. 26, 1918, Vol. 53.


# From the Diary of Dr. Grayson[1]

Sunday, January 12, 1919.

I persuaded the President to stay at home and rest during the morning as he had been working about ten hours a day since his arrival in Paris. This I had found had been far too great a strain, considering the highly concentrated nature of his application. At 2.30, the President attended the first meeting of the Supreme War Council, at the Quai D'Orsay. It lasted until 6.45. This first gathering of the leaders of the civilized world greatly monopolized the attention of all Paris. They came across the historic Place de la Concorde, under the shadows of the site of Old Mother Guillotine and over the very ground of the bloodiest days in the revolution, to the historic old building on the banks of the Seine, where so much world history had been made in the last hundred years. Lloyd George, Balfour, Poincaré, Clemenceau, Orlando, Sonnino, the Japanese and the Chinese in their native way, looking wise and saying nothing; the Arabians, represented by Prince Hedjez Emil Faisal, in picturesque costume; the Indian princes in their British uniform, but with flowing native turban, all presented a wonderful sight as they drove up in their motor cars and entered the building. The President and Mrs. Wilson drove in their motor to the Quai D'Orsay, where Mrs. Wilson left the President and went for a drive. The leaders gathered in the great conference room, where there was a large table for them and side tables for the secretaries. In the midst of the conference, an amusing incident occurred, which exemplified the exotic atmosphere in which the President was working all the way through. While they were in the midst of discussion on some important point, servants and footmen entered and began clearing away the tables to prepare the room for afternoon tea. The President remarked to me afterward that it was with a little difficulty that he restrained himself from voicing his surprise, that with the great affairs and future of the world under discussion, this conference should be interrupted by what he considered a tea party. He realized, however, that it was a foreign custom, and he was among foreigners so he gracefully accepted and took part in it.

I suppose the Quai D'Orsay had not had a breath of fresh air for a hundred years. The atmosphere was stifling so I opened one of the windows. Lloyd George remarked that it was probably the first fresh air let into the place since the reign of Louis XIV. Clemenceau, Pichon and some of the others however immediately showed their disapproval, waving their hands and making motions to have the window closed. Just at this point, a discussion took place between Clemenceau and Sonnino and Sonnino lost his temper and showed great anger. The two went at it hammer and tongs. They reminded me of a couple of dogs, barking at each other. It was the first display of fireworks in the conference, but it passed off easily. I was hoping the fresh air would help carry off a little of the hot temper. Someone then complained it was getting too cold and we closed the window.

At eight o'clock, we attended the Palais de Glacé, where there was a meeting of the Comrades in Arms,[2] at which the principal speakers were Rabbi Wise, Bishop Brent, Senior Chaplain of the Army, and Chaplain Jones of the Salvation Army.[3] It was a non-sectarian meeting and about five thousand soldiers attended. It was one of the most enthusiastic and delightful meetings I have ever attended. It was also the first gathering of such a great number of soldiers indoors that I ever saw and I was struck by the number of coughs and colds, which I afterward learned seemed to be characteristic of Paris in winter. Bishop Brent's speech was of a serious nature; a straight-forward, patriotic and religious talk. It was soon apparent how popular the Salvation Army was with the soldiers. When Chaplain Jones was introduced, he was greeted with a burst of cheers, which almost raised the roof. Jones has a remarkable personality. He held his audience with a speech which was filled with the humane and material, as well as the religious. It was obvious this was the sort of thing the soldiers enjoyed and very evidently an exemplification of the attitude of the Salvation Army toward the soldiers, which had endeared them so much and, I think, placed them far above all other organizations in the esteem of our troops. Jones told a number of incidents and related stories from his own personal experiences, as well as explaining the work of the Salvation Army lassies at the front. He closed his address with a reference to the President, in which he said:

"Three weeks ago, I was at a convention of the Elks, at Atlantic City and a Republican Congressman, referring to President Wilson, said: 'Woodrow Wilson was not elected by the American people; he was selected by God.'"

Rabbi Wise made a great speech and I recall one of his stories, which made a great hit with the soldiers. He said: "First, I must tell you what a rabbi is, because not everyone knows. I recall a young man, who invited me home to dinner and telephoned his wife, saying: 'My dear, I am bringing a rabbi home for dinner' and his wife replied: 'All right, my dear, I will do anything you say, but you will have to tell me how to cook it.'" The other story he told the boys went this way:

"An Irishman was dying with the smallpox and he said to his wife: 'Bridget, send for a rabbi: I am dying.' The wife said 'No, Mike, you mean you want me to send for a priest.' 'No, Bridget, send for a rabbi; I don't want to give the priest smallpox.'"

T MS (in the possession of James Gordon Grayson and Cary T. Grayson, Jr.).
   [1] About this diary, see n. 1 to the extract from it printed at Dec. 3, 1918, Vol. 53.
   [2] The "Comrades in Service," to give it its correct title, was a newly formed social and religious organization for American servicemen, begun under the auspices of the Y.M.C.A., the Knights of Columbus, the Jewish Welfare Board, the Salvation Army, and Bishop Charles Henry Brent, in his capacity of Senior Chaplain of the A.E.F. See Frederick Harris *et al.*, eds., *Service with Fighting Men: An Account of the Work of the American Young Men's Christian Associations in the World War* (2 vols., New York, 1922), I, 611-12.
   [3] The Rev. Dr. Harry William Jones, a Protestant Episcopal chaplain in the United States Navy, 1896-1907. Although not a member of the Salvation Army, he had entered its program of war work as an "adherent" and had toured the European battlefronts as an evangelistic speaker.

# Hankey's Notes of a Meeting of the Supreme War Council[1]

Quai d'Orsay, January 12, 1919, 2:30 P.M.[2]

IC-103 [BC-A, SWC-1]

[Pichon, who was chairman, called on Foch to report on the progress made in the execution of the Armistice with Germany. Foch said that the terms of the Armistice, which had been renewed on December 13 and would expire on January 17, had been largely satisfied as regards the surrender of guns, machine guns, and aircraft, but not of railway material. Of the French prisoners of war in Germany, 458,355 had been returned, and 28,000 were still in Germany. At Wilson's request, Weygand reported on various incidents of prisoners being killed or mistreated and on various disorders.]

MARSHAL FOCH said that this was the situation in which we had to renew the Armistice.

The question now arose whether we ought to include in the new terms of the Armistice other problems, such as that of Poland. He handed in a Note on Poland (Appendix I).[3]

[1] To record Wilson's participation in the Supreme War Council and the so-called Council of Ten, the Editors have used primarily the British notes prepared by, or under the direction of, Lt. Col. Sir Maurice Pascal Alers Hankey, Secretary-General of the British delegation. These notes are available for all of the sessions which Wilson attended from January 12 through February 14, 1919, when he left Paris for a brief trip to Washington and return. Hankey's notes follow systematically the agenda of the meetings, and they record all substantive statements, all documents cited, and all actions and decisions taken. Copies of these notes were supplied on a current basis to the American Commission to Negotiate Peace and to its secretariat. American notes are lacking for many sessions, and those available are generally less comprehensive than their British counterparts. In several cases, however, they give accounts which differ from them in emphasis, coverage, or detail. Where the variations are significant, the American versions are quoted in footnotes.

The texts of both the Hankey notes and the available American ones, with supporting documents, are mostly in SDR, DNA, with a few in WP, DLC, and in the Tasker H. Bliss Papers, DLC. The Editors have concentrated on Wilson's direct and personal participation in the Paris Peace Conference. Thus they have selected from these collections those records of discussions which are immediately relevant to Wilson's views, acts, and influence, and they have sought to record his work at the conference and his relations with his colleagues in the context of his other activities and concerns. The Editors have accordingly summarized, excerpted, or merely cited the texts of discussions in which Wilson took little or no part. The texts of the British and American notes and of conference papers are printed in full in *PPC*, and are cited hereinafter as appropriate. For a note on the preparation, numbering, and distribution of the minutes in the English language, see *ibid.*, III, 468. The sessions of the Supreme War Council and the Council of Ten were held in Pichon's office in the Ministry of Foreign Affairs at the Quai d'Orsay.

[2] The full text of these notes is printed in *PPC*, III, 469-77.

[3] Foch's note on the situation in Poland stated that hostilities had never altogether ceased on the eastern frontiers of Germany, "owing either to the Bolsheviks or to the Germans," that this situation endangered all of Europe, and that it was "absolutely necessary" to organize the Polish army and transport it from France and Italy to Poland, either by sea or by the land route of Danzig-Thorn. Allied troops were needed to protect the lines of communication, Foch added, and for this he recommended forming an occupation corps under American command and consisting of one American division and one regiment each of French, British, and Italian troops. He also offered the proposed text of a clause for renewal of the Armistice, to put into immediate execution Article 16 of the Armistice Convention of November 11, 1918. Translations of Foch's proposals, which are dated January 11, 1919, are printed in *ibid.*, pp. 477-79.

M. PICHON invited any observations on Marshal Foch's Note.

PRESIDENT WILSON suggested that it might be unwise to discuss a proposal of this sort on its individual merits, since it formed part of the much larger question of checking the advance of Bolshevism to the Westward. There was room for great doubt as to whether this advance could be checked by arms at all. Hence he felt doubtful whether it would be wise to take the kind of action proposed by Marshal Foch until we had agreed on a general policy as to how to meet the social danger of Bolshevism.[4]

MR. LLOYD GEORGE said that he was in general accord with President Wilson. He had serious doubts as to Marshal Foch's proposition. He was certain, however, that we could not support his proposals, having regard to our general policy towards Bolshevism. This was a question we ought to discuss at the earliest possible moment. As yet the Allies had no general policy on the subject, and Marshal Foch's proposals were subsidiary to our general policy.

M. CLEMENCEAU said that, like President Wilson and Mr. Lloyd George, he considered the question had certainly better be postponed until we examined the whole question of Bolshevism. It must be remembered, however, that Marshal Foch was face to face with a renewal of the Armistice. In doing this would it not be wise to reserve the right to use the route from Dantzig to Thorn if we desired it?

MR. LLOYD GEORGE suggested that all the powers required were covered by clause 16 of the Armistice, which was quoted in Marshal Foch's Memorandum.

MARSHAL FOCH agreed that the necessary powers were conveyed by clause 16.

M. PICHON summed up the opinion of those present to be that it would be better to refer to the terms of the Armistice without insisting on additional conditions. The question as to whether we should put the powers in operation was reserved until the Allies had discussed their general policy in Russia.

MARSHAL FOCH handed in a Memorandum on this subject [Russian prisoners detained in Germany] (Appendix II).[5]

---

[4] The corresponding passage in the American notes of this meeting read as follows: "President Wilson pointed out that perhaps it might be unwise to express an opinion on this subject by itself because it would form a part of a much vaster problem; there was great doubt in his mind as to whether Bolshevism could be checked by arms, therefore it seemed to him unwise to take action in a military form before the Powers were agreed upon a course of action for checking Bolshevism as a social and political danger." ACNP notes, Jan. 12, 1919 T MS (WP, DLC). The full text of these notes is printed in PPC, III, 495-507.

[5] This memorandum began as follows:
"The Russian officers and men prisoners of war in Germany are now in true distress.
"The fact is confirmed by all available information.

MR. LLOYD GEORGE suggested that this question formed also part of the general Russian problem. He was informed that there were still 1,200,000 Russian prisoners in Germany who had not been handed over, and that when prisoners crossed the frontier the Bolshevists told them that they might choose between becoming Bolshevists and starving. The question had been put to him whether we ought not to deliver these prisoners in the Ukraine to General Denikin or to Admiral Kolchak in Siberia or in North Russia, instead of sending them across the frontier. This was all part of the larger Russian problem. If we decided to fight Bolshevism, this would be one of the methods available. At any rate, we ought to concert our policy and act together, and act efficiently, which we had not done up to the present.[6]

M. ORLANDO said he was in accord with Mr. Lloyd George.

MARSHAL FOCH said that he simply wished to draw attention to the condition of the Russian prisoners, and all he proposed for the moment was that the Allied Commission dealing with the question in Berlin should utilise all their resources to relieve these prisoners.

PRESIDENT WILSON suggested that the first part of Marshal Foch's memorandum was a question of relief, which might be dealt with by the Relief Commission, and the second part was really a Red Cross matter.

MR. BALFOUR said that everyone would be in agreement in regard to this, and that there was as yet no necessity to decide on the question of repatriation.

PRESIDENT WILSON said that the difficulty was that repatriation

---

"In the camps the situation is appalling. The prisoners are short of clothing, half-starved, and receive no attention of any kind.

"Furthermore, if they are sent back to the East, they incur the risk—

"Either of being shot as suspects,

"Or of being incorporated by force in the Red Army.

"It is for the Entente a duty of humanity to save the lives of soldiers who fought for her.

"It is also her interest to keep them away from Bolshevism, and to prevent the Red Army from being reinforced with their contingents.

"She has two means of realizing this objective:

1. By improving the material and moral situation of Russian prisoners.

2. By sending them back to provinces which are free from the Soviets' regime."

Foch's memorandum then set forth specific measures to carry out this program. It stated, among other things, that the only provinces to which prisoners might be sent were Poland and southern Russia and that "we must be content with forwarding towards these areas cases not suspect of Bolshevism and able there to reinforce parties faithful to our cause." The memorandum ended with the statement that, if the Allied governments approved of the proposed arrangements, appropriate instructions would be forwarded to the Armistice Commission at Spa. A translation of Foch's memorandum, dated, January 11, 1919, is printed in *ibid.*, pp. 479-81.

[6] "Mr. Lloyd George believed that there were 1,200,000 of such prisoners in a state of liberty who were now crossing the frontier; they were asked by Bolshevists either to join their party or to have their throats cut. He thought the treatment of these prisoners was a part of the whole general problem; it was not merely a question of feeding them. The great question was whether the Allies could move them to Ukraine or to any other part of Russia." The ACNP notes cited above.

involved sending the Russians to their own country, which was ruled under conditions that we did not like. There was no question of repatriating Russians to Allied countries as part of the Armistice. Hence we must solve the question of repatriation in some other way.

M. SONNINO said that the terms of the Armistice gave us sufficient power for relieving the prisoners, but they did not give us sufficient power to enable us to send them to some other country.

MARSHAL FOCH said this was not his proposal. All that he asked was that we should allow all the means of transport at Berlin to be operated by the Allied Commission at Spa, for the relief of the Russian prisoners.

M. ORLANDO approved this proposal.

PRESIDENT WILSON also approved.

MR. LLOYD GEORGE approved, while laying stress on no condition being attached, that the Russian prisoners, when released, were to join any particular Russian force.

M. PICHON summed up by saying that Marshal Foch's proposal was agreed to, namely, that all the means of transport in the hands of the Allies at Berlin should be operated by the Allied Commission at Spa, for the relief of Russian prisoners.

MR. BALFOUR reverted to a point which had been mentioned by M. Sonnino, namely, that we ought to put some clause into the Armistice to enable us to send Russian prisoners elsewhere than across the line into Russia. If we did not reserve our rights in the terms of the Armistice we should not be able so to divert them if we wished.

MR. LLOYD GEORGE said he wished to limit any reserves we made to what we could do and to what did not raise controversial questions.

PRESIDENT WILSON suggested that Marshal Foch should be asked to formulate a clause giving to the Allies the right to lay down to which parts of Russia Russians should be sent.

This was agreed to.

[After a short discussion, it was agreed that all four nations present should be entitled to send technical advisers to the discussions at Spa for renewal of the Armistice.]

M. LEYGUES[7] said that the Naval Commission established in London to supervise the execution of the naval clauses of the Armistice had, after an inspection in German ports, extending from the 3rd December to the 20th December, established the presence of—

65 submarines complete in German ports capable of being towed.

[7] Georges Jean Claude Leygues, French Minister of Marine.

125 submarines capable of completion in German yards.

30 submarines were also estimated to be at Dantzig, and in other ports which the Commission had not had time to visit.

The Commission had accordingly made the following proposals for inclusion in the renewed Armistice:

1. All submarines capable of being towed should be sent to England.
2. All submarines in German shipyards and on the stocks should be destroyed.
3. Construction work on all warships in German ports should cease.

PRESIDENT WILSON asked if these were additional to the submarines that had already been handed over.

MR. LLOYD GEORGE explained that the figure of 160 had been chosen because the Germans had insisted that it was all they had. Now it seemed from the investigations of the Naval Commission that there were more. His personal view was that these pests ought to be disposed of.

MARSHAL FOCH read the text of a clause which he proposed to include in the Armistice, stipulating that all submarines were to be handed over.

PRESIDENT WILSON asked why they should demand their delivery in this formal manner. Why should we not demand the execution of the original agreement, namely, that all the submarines should be delivered? He asked what was the text of the original Armistice conditions.

M. PICHON read the text of clause 22, which is as follows:

"Delivery to the Allies and United States of all the submarines (including submarine cruisers and all mine layers) which are at present in existence, with their complete armament and equipment, at the ports specified by the Allies and United States. Those that cannot put to sea will be disarmed and their crews disbanded, and must remain under the supervision of the Allies and the United States. The submarines which are ready to put to sea shall be prepared to leave German ports immediately on receipt of wireless orders to sail to the ports specified for their delivery, the remainder to follow as soon as possible. The terms of this Article shall be carried out within a period of fourteen days after the signature of the Armistice."

PRESIDENT WILSON said that all we had to do was not to add additional conditions to the Armistice, but merely to insist that the terms of the original Armistice should be carried out.

M. SONNINO said he understood the view of the Commission to be that something more was required, since submarines not completed were not specifically included. Thus Germany, by this interpretation of the terms of the Armistice, could undo the intention of the Armistice. By not handing over the submarines remaining in her ports, and by completing those that were building, she would produce a new fleet of submarines.

PRESIDENT WILSON said that the question seemed to come to this: whether a submarine that was not completed was nevertheless a submarine.

MR. LLOYD GEORGE suggested that we should support the Naval Commission by insisting on a proper interpretation of the term "submarine," which should include those building.

PRESIDENT WILSON said he wanted to avoid seeming to add conditions to the Armistice. He wanted a complete fulfilment in the spirit, as well as in the letter, of the terms of the Armistice.

M. PICHON pointed out that the only difference between the original terms of the Armistice and what was now proposed was that, in the original terms, those that could not put to sea would remain under the supervision of the Allies and the United States. This supervision would end with the Armistice, and the enemy would still retain their submarines. He understood now, however, that it was agreed that these should be destroyed.

(The Supreme War Council agreed that clause 22 of the original Armistice with Germany should be so interpreted as to enable the submarines under construction to be destroyed and the remainder to be handed over.)

[Discussion of the status of German naval aircraft was begun but then postponed until a later meeting of the Supreme War Council.]

Printed copy (SDR, RG 256, 180.03101/1, DNA).

## Hankey's Notes of a Meeting of the Council of Ten[1]

Quai d'Orsay, January 12, 1919, 4 P.M.

IC-104 [BC-A, SWC-1]

(Note. This meeting was a continuation of a meeting of the Supreme War Council commenced earlier in the afternoon, procès-verbal of which has been prepared separately.)

M. PICHON said the first question to examine was the general procedure in regard to the Peace discussions. The French Government had circulated a proposal on the subject to the Associated

[1] The complete text of these notes is printed in *PPC*, III, 482-94. The so-called Council of Ten (which was usually attended by more than ten persons) was composed of the heads of government and the Foreign Ministers of the United States, Great Britain, France, Italy, and Japan. About the origin of the name, Council of Ten, see Stephen Roskill, *Hankey: Man of Secrets* (3 vols., London, 1970-74), II, 43.

Governments (Appendix A).[2] If any other document on the same lines had been prepared, a decision would have to be taken as to which proposal should form the basis of discussion.

PRESIDENT WILSON asked whether this was not a question for discussion at the larger Conference to be held to-morrow.

M. PICHON said that there were many questions in regard to procedure which the larger Conference would have to decide itself. But there were certain subjects which must be discussed before the formal Conference, such as the number of Delegates, and how they were to be summoned, etc.

MR. LLOYD GEORGE said that he had studied the French document. He would have some suggestions to make when it was discussed in detail. He considered, however, that the general outlines of the proposal were well arranged, and that it formed a good basis for discussion.

M. PICHON asked whether it was agreed that there should be five Plenipotentiaries of the Great Powers.

MR. LLOYD GEORGE said he agreed to this. But he had something to say as regards the next proposal, that there should be three Representatives of each of the smaller belligerent Powers. If this number was decided on, it would involve an enormous gathering. Two would seem quite enough.

PRESIDENT WILSON suggested that one Representative was sufficient for Siam; two for Belgium, Greece, &c.; while Brazil, as a larger country, should have three.

MR. LLOYD GEORGE said that at previous meetings Belgium had always been satisfied with one Representative. If there were more than one apiece, the Conference would become very unwieldy. There was a second point that he would have to press, namely, in regard to the representation of the British self-governing Dominions and India. They would not be present at all the discussions, but in matters which concerned them they ought to be properly represented.

PRESIDENT WILSON asked whether this could not be effected by making the members of the British Delegation interchangeable.

MR. LLOYD GEORGE said that the British Dominions were entirely autonomous, and that the British Government could not have induced them to send a single unit without their own consent. His proposal would be to reduce the representation of the smaller bel-

[2] The "Plan of the Preliminary Conversations between the Allied Ministers, January 5, 1919," provided for a preparatory meeting of the great powers (Great Britain, United States, France, Italy, and Japan) to decide on: "1. Representation of belligerent and neutral States at the different stages of the negotiations. 2. Leading principles and the order in which questions should be examined. 3. Organisation of the work." A translation of the plan is printed in *PPC*, I, 386-96.

ligerent Powers to two apiece and place the Dominions and India on the same scale, with the sole exception of Newfoundland, which, being a small Dominion, would be content with one Representative.

PRESIDENT WILSON said that this question of representation was largely one of sentiment and psychology. If the Dominions were given this additional representation, the impression amongst those who did not know the full facts would be that they were merely additional British Representatives. This impression would be especially strong among the small Powers. The Great Powers, to put the matter brutally, would appear to be running the Peace Conference.

MR. LLOYD GEORGE pointed out that they had run the war.

PRESIDENT WILSON said he wished to convey a more comfortable impression. If the British Government could form their Delegation, whatever its size, by including as many of their Dominion Representatives as they liked, they would relieve the difficulty.

MR. LLOYD GEORGE said that one reason for which this plan would not meet the case was owing to questions like that of the Colonies. This question of the Colonies was in some cases of less importance to the British Empire as a whole than to particular Dominions, which had a point of view quite apart from the purely British one. If five of the Dominion Representatives were included in the British Delegation, Great Britain would have no representation at all. In his opinion, the smaller Powers ought to be satisfied with one Representative apiece. In this case, he asked for the same representation for the Dominions and India. Take Australia, for example. They had sent more men to the war than Belgium or Serbia or Roumania. They had proved the most magnificent fighters, and had, he believed, actually lost more dead than the United States of America. They said that they were entitled to separate representation. It was no good saying that the British Government represented them, because, in fact, on many questions they could not. He asked, therefore, that they should be on the same footing as the smaller belligerent Powers, that is to say, that they should have the same representation, and should be invited to attend on all questions in which they had a special interest.

PRESIDENT WILSON pointed out that, if the British Delegation did not represent the Dominions, at least they were their friends. Probably they would back them up at the meetings. Consequently, in every question affecting the Dominions which might also affect the rest of the world (and he pointed out that the question of the German colonies was of interest to the rest of the world as well as to the Dominions), Great Britain and the Dominions between them would have 10 or 12 votes.

MR. LLOYD GEORGE pointed out that there would be no votes.

M. CLEMENCEAU agreed.

MR. LLOYD GEORGE said that in his view the British Delegation would ask the Representatives of the Dominions and India to present their own case on many points, particularly where they had a special point of view.

MR. LANSING suggested that there might be five Technical Delegates of the Dominions.

MR. LLOYD GEORGE pointed out that, as President Wilson had said, sentiment was of great importance, and this would rule out this proposal.

PRESIDENT WILSON pointed out that Canada had no special interests. For example, they had no special interest in the German Colonies. When we discussed German South-West Africa, there would be, according to his plan, say, four British and one South African Representative.

MR. LLOYD GEORGE pointed out that in addition to discussions on particular Colonies, there would be general discussions on the disposal of the Colonies. Canada would certainly be interested in these. Canada was also specially interested in President Wilson's third point dealing with economic questions.

PRESIDENT WILSON said that of course their views would be invited, but, according to his idea, this could be done by the adoption of the panel system.

MR. LLOYD GEORGE pointed out that, apart from the Dominions, India had made very great sacrifices and efforts in the war, and should also be fully represented.

M. PICHON said that if Mr. Lloyd George's proposal as to numbers were accepted, there was no doubt that there would be great disappointment amongst such Powers as Greece, Serbia, etc., who had taken a considerable part in the War and sustained great losses. But the great objection of those minor belligerent Allies would be that they were placed on the same footing as countries which had declared war without taking any part in hostilities, or had merely broken off diplomatic negotiations. He suggested, therefore, that if three Representatives were too many, these Powers should, at any rate, have two Delegates.

M. SONNINO wished to know whether Montenegro was to have two Representatives or one.

M. PICHON said that at present the question as to whether certain categories of Powers were to have one or two or three Representatives, was only being discussed as one of principle.

MR. LLOYD GEORGE suggested that there was another method of distinguishing between the status given to the different Powers, namely, the frequency of the occasions on which they would be brought into the discussions. For example, on the question of the League of Nations all the smaller States ought to be consulted, but countries such as Serbia and Belgium, which were concerned in territorial adjustments, would be called in more frequently than others.

MR. LANSING asked whether the Dominions would be brought into the discussions on the European arrangements.

MR. LLOYD GEORGE said that they had as much right to such representation as any American or extra-European nation. They had sacrificed several hundred thousands of their men in Europe, and were entitled to some say in the arrangements for the future peace of the world.

PRESIDENT WILSON said he had a sentimental feeling as regards Roumania and Serbia. He was quite willing that they should be represented out of proportion to any principle.

MR. LLOYD GEORGE suggested that the part which they had taken in the struggle should have some influence on the question. The Dominions and India claimed the same representation as Powers which had made the same contribution as they to the victory. He did not mind whether this representation was by one or two members.

PRESIDENT WILSON said he did not see why Siam should [not] be in the list.[3]

MR. LLOYD GEORGE agreed.

M. PICHON suggested that they should examine the various states one by one.

He suggested—
  2 for Belgium.
  2 for Greece.
  2 for Serbia.
  1 for Portugal.
  1 for Siam.
  2 for Roumania.

MR. BALFOUR pointed out that Portugal had employed troops in Africa as well as in France, and asked that his dissent from the

[3] "Mr. Lansing inquired whether the Dominions would have a voice in discussing the question of the disputed boundaries. Mr. Lloyd George answered that they really have a blood interest in France and Belgium.

"The President interposed by saying that he believed that everything which affected the world's peace was the world's business. He said he had a sentimental feeling for Belgium, Roumania and Serbia which was affecting his thought, and that he would like to give them a greater proportional representation, if possible.

"Mr. Lloyd George thought that the part which they had taken in the struggle should count. The President asked why should Siam have a vote." ACNP notes, Jan. 12, 1919, T MS (WP, DLC). These notes are printed in PPC, III, 495-507.

proposed limitations of Portugal's representation might be recorded.

M. PICHON urged that Roumania should have two Delegates. She had had a Treaty, and after being forced out of the war had again become an Ally.

MR. BALFOUR said he had no objections to Roumania being treated on this footing for purposes of representation, but he did not wish thereby to renew every clause of the treaty which Roumania had broken by going out of the War. He did not wish to put her in exactly the same position as she was before she went out of the War.

M. SONNINO said there were two questions:

1. That of representation. For what Roumania had suffered, and for the part she had taken, she should have proper representation.
2. The question of her Treaty rights. This was a distinct question, which he agreed ought to be reserved.

M. SONNINO's proposal was accepted.

M. PICHON suggested:

2 representatives for China.

2 for Brazil.

These were agreed to.

MR. LLOYD GEORGE said that, as regards the Dominions and India, the only claim which he put in was that they should be called in on questions which affected them, in the same way as Belgium, Serbia, &c. He proposed that each of the Dominions should have two Representatives and Newfoundland one.

PRESIDENT WILSON suggested that other states would have no backers and sponsors like the British Dominions. Great Britain had a full representation as a Great Power. Consequently the Dominions would be supported by five Representatives in the most powerful section of the Conference. It would be open to misconstruction if the British Government insisted, in addition, on two Representatives of each of the Dominions. He himself was quite willing to concede one.

MR. LLOYD GEORGE said that if there was any reluctance to accept his proposal, he would like to suspend the discussion in order to give him an opportunity of discussing the matter with his colleagues in the Imperial War Cabinet.

PRESIDENT WILSON agreed to this procedure, and said that he hoped Mr. Lloyd George would not leave on the minds of the Dominions Representatives the impression that there was the least jealousy.

(The discussion on the representation of the British Dominions was then adjourned.)

M. PICHON's proposal that Poland and the Czecho-Slovak State should each have two Representatives was agreed to, as well as the proposal for one Representative each of the small Powers theoretically belligerent, of those that had broken off diplomatic negotiations, of neutral States, and of States in process of formation.

M. PICHON said that the French Government had received communications from Serbia to the effect that Montenegro had become a part of the State under the rule of the Karageorgivich monarchy. At the same time a message had been received from Podgoritza to the effect that a Constituent Assembly had agreed that Montenegro should be absorbed by Serbia. The King of Montenegro, however, stated that the decision of the Constituent Assembly was invalid and negligible; hence it would seem that a decision could not be taken before the Conference met.[4] This was the point of view of the French Government. The question arose in consequence as to whether Montenegro was to be regarded as a separate State entitled to separate representation at the Conference or as part of the Serbian representation.

PRESIDENT WILSON said that the action of Serbia in regard to Montenegro had gone somewhat towards prejudicing him against the Government of Serbia. To act with force like this was contrary to the principle of self-determination. Although he had no precise knowledge, he would not be surprised to learn that the King of Montenegro was right and that the Constituent Assembly at Podgoritza had not been properly constituted. Serbia had had no right to send her troops into Montenegro. The events of the last few months had almost made him a partisan of Montenegro. Hence he was strongly in favour of taking no notice of the Serbian claims and of giving Montenegro separate representation.

MR. LLOYD GEORGE said he was not sure of the facts, but he felt that Montenegro ought to have the right to state her case before its being determined whether she was entitled to separate representation. He was not anti-Serbian in this matter, but felt that we ought to ascertain the facts.

PRESIDENT WILSON said that he was anti-Serbian in this case, because no country had the right to take the self-determination of another country into her own hands. He asked who was to select the Montenegrin Representatives? The *de facto* Government was clearly under Serbian control, and was not qualified to state the opposite point of view. The King, who was in Paris, could hardly present more than his personal side of the question. Hence, though

    [4] About the confused situation in regard to the status of Montenegro at this time, see T. N. Page to WW, Jan. 7, 1919, n. 1, Vol. 53. The King of Montenegro was Nicholas I.

he was clear that Montenegro ought to be represented, he was not clear how that representation should be settled.[5]

MR. BALFOUR said that he had no clear idea as to when and how the invasion of Montenegro had taken place.

M. SONNINO said that it had occurred immediately after the Armistice. The Serbians had penetrated Montenegro and had opposed any contemporaneous action on Italy's part. In order to avoid fighting between Allies, the Italians had kept away from Cettinje. The movement for inclusion in Serbia was made under Serbian auspices. There was, however, a contrary party which desired to form part of the Yugo-Slav State, but as an autonomous unit in that State. For his part, he could not support a Government which had taken such action. There would always be Representatives of the opposite side in the Serbian delegation, so that if the King of Montenegro nominated Delegates, the other side would nevertheless be fully represented at the Congress. There had been considerable disturbances in Montenegro as a re-action against the Serbian action, and help was being invited. It was a very bad beginning to the new regime to follow the War.

PRESIDENT WILSON suggested that it should be agreed that Montenegro was to have representation, but that no decision should be taken as to how it was to be settled.

M. PICHON asked to whom the invitation to the Conference should be addressed.

MR. LLOYD GEORGE suggested that Montenegro should be treated as a State in process of formation. M. Sonnino had presented the case for Montenegro.

(*M. Sonnino demurred to this.*)

Somebody, Mr. Lloyd George continued, must have presented the case to M. Sonnino. Montenegro ought to be given an opportunity of presenting its case, and it would not be necessary to scrutinise too closely the credentials of the person who represented it.

PRESIDENT WILSON thought it would be important to make sure

[5] "The President said that the action of Serbia toward Montenegro had gone some way toward prejudicing his mind against Serbia. It was absolutely against all principle that the process of self-government should be forced, and 'I consider it likely that the meeting at Poggoritza was an extra constitutional assembly, and called together under conditions which could not be considered legal.' He knew of no reason for the presence of Serbian troops in Montenegro, and the circumstances of the last few months had made him a partisan of the rights of that country.

"Mr. Lloyd George thought that Montenegro ought to have the right to state her own case, and we should hear the case before determining it. He said he was not anti-Serbian.

"The President disclaimed any anti-Serbian feeling, except in this case. He did not very well see who was to select the Montenegrin representative. The de facto government was under Serbian domination and the King was in exile. While he feels that Montenegro ought to be represented, he did not see how the representative should be chosen." ACNP notes cited above.

that the case was represented by somebody who really was entitled to represent Montenegro.

MR. BALFOUR suggested that the question ought not to be decided apart from the question of how the Yugo-Slav State was to be represented. The two cases were on all fours.

PRESIDENT WILSON pointed out that Montenegro was an older State than Serbia. She could therefore be separate from Yugo-Slavia. Some of the other units of Yugo-Slavia were saying the same thing, namely, that Serbia was trying to put them under her own domination rather than to associate them with her. Since the meetings were not going to take place at once, and events were occurring all the time which might influence the ultimate decision, he thought it would be quite unnecessary to do more than decide in principle that Montenegro was to be represented.

MR. LANSING said that America recognised the Government of the King of Montenegro.[6]

M. SONNINO said that no one had stated the case to him. What he had said had been from his own knowledge. He pointed out that Montenegro was a very much older State than Serbia. She alone had resisted for centuries the domination of the Turks. She took part in the War in order to help Serbia and to preserve her own future independence. A good many Montenegrins had continued fighting. They had wanted the Italians to form a separate battalion of them, and some had been sent to Salonika for incorporation in Serbian units. He agreed with President Wilson's view that Montenegro should be represented. He suggested that in the meantime the United States of America should send a representative to discover how things were in that country. No news was allowed to percolate out of Montenegro and no Allied troops were allowed to go there.

M. CLEMENCEAU pointed out that if President Wilson wished to send some one to enquire, he could do so without any authority from the Powers associated with him.

PRESIDENT WILSON said he was quite willing to send someone, but not an official representative on behalf of this Conference.

MR. LLOYD GEORGE entirely agreed with this view. He pointed out that it would be extremely offensive to an Ally that any nation should give expression at this Conference, formally or informally, that there ought to be any inquiry.

*Conclusion*: It was decided in principle that Montenegro should

---

[6] "He [Wilson] remarked that Montenegro was as old a political entity as Serbia, and has handsome political history behind it. Mr. Lansing asked, 'Do you recognize the King of Montenegro?' He answered, 'We do.' Mr. Balfour said, 'We pay for him.'" *Ibid.*

be represented at the Conference, but the decision was left open as to how her Representatives should be chosen.

(*The Conference then had a short adjournment.*)

After the adjournment:

M. CLEMENCEAU raised the question, which had been discussed earlier in the afternoon at the meeting of the Supreme War Council, as to when Marshal Foch was to receive his instructions as to the renewal of the Armistice.

MR. LLOYD GEORGE asked for a list of questions involved in this discussion.

M. CLEMENCEAU said he could not give a complete list, but among the questions was one relating to coke, another relating to the surrender of Germany's merchant fleet, and a third relating to the Reichsbank.

After a short discussion it was agreed that technical Representatives of the various Powers should meet in conference at the Quai d'Orsay at 10 A.M. on Monday, the 13th January, in order to prepare decisions for the consideration of the Supreme War Council, which should meet at the Quai d'Orsay at 2:30 on Monday, the 13th January.

M. CLEMENCEAU undertook to give instructions for a list of the questions for consideration to be circulated on the same evening.

M. SONNINO said that the whole question of Bolshevism was involved.

M. PICHON did not agree. He pointed out that there were various representatives of Russian opinion in Paris—for example, M. Sazonoff,[7] Prince Lvoff and others, including Socialists, who represented every shade of opinion. These asked to be represented. His opinion was that this could not be done. We should first have to acknowledge the Omsk Government,[8] whom they came to represent. At present it seemed impossible to recognise this Government as the Government of Russia. It was not strong enough to be regarded as representative of Russia as a whole. But this was no reason why these personalities should not be allowed to put their views unofficially. His suggestion, then, was that Russia as a State should have no representation, but that the Conference should be allowed to hear such persons as he had mentioned.

MR. LLOYD GEORGE said that this had to be dealt with in one way or another, because at present the Allies had got themselves in a

---

[7] That is, Sergeii Dmitrievich Sazonov, at this time both a representative of Gen. Denikin in Paris and the absentee Foreign Minister of the Kolchak regime in Omsk.

[8] That is, the dictatorship of Adm. Aleksandr Vasil'evich Kolchak. See n. 1 to Enclosure II, printed with RL to WW, Sept. 24, 1918, Vol. 51.

fix for the reason that they had no definite policy in Russia. They ought to decide whether to withdraw their troops or to reinforce them. Unless reinforced, they were of no use whatsoever. He had nothing to say against these people, Prince Lvoff, &c. We were told they represented every shade of opinion. As a matter of fact, they represented every opinion except the prevalent opinion in Russia.

PRESIDENT WILSON pointed out it was prevalent in some respects.

MR. LLOYD GEORGE said he feared the fact that it was prevalent must be accepted. The peasants accepted Bolshevism for the same reason as the peasants had accepted it in the French Revolution, namely, that it gave them land. The Bolshevists were the *de facto* Government. We had formally recognised the Czar's Government, although at the time we knew it to be absolutely rotten. Our reason had been that it was the *de facto* Government. We recognised the Don Government, the Archangel Government and the Omsk Government, although none of them were good, but we refused to recognise the Bolshevists. To say that we ourselves should pick the representatives of a great people was contrary to every principle for which we had fought. It was possible that the Bolshevists did not represent Russia. But certainly Prince Lvoff did not; neither did Savinkoff,[9] although he was a good man. The British Government made exactly the same mistake when they said that the émigrés represented France. This led them into a war which lasted about twenty-five years. The Russian peasants probably felt towards Trotsky much as the French peasants did towards Robespierre. This question must now be settled. He hoped that the Allies would not separate and announce that they had made perpetual peace when Siberia, which formed about half Asia, and Russia, which formed about half Europe, were still at war. He, himself, would make proposals in due course, but, in the meantime, he wished to protest against an attempt to select representatives for some hundred million people.[10]

M. PICHON quite agreed that the persons he had named should not be admitted as representatives of Russia. He only wished to

[9] That is, Boris Viktorovich Savinkov, at this time a representative of Admiral Kolchak in Paris.

[10] "Mr. Lloyd George thought that they should agree upon a policy and should decide whether troops should still be kept there, or whether the existing troops should be reinforced, or whether they should be withdrawn. While he did not greatly admire the Bolshevik Government, it was, nevertheless, a de facto government recognized by about two-thirds of the people. He hoped that the conference would carefully consider what their attitude should be toward the present Russian Government. He added that to pretend to make a permanent, endurable peace when Siberia and Russia were in a state of civil war would be mockery. In the meantime he protested strongly against the conference choosing representatives for one hundred million Russians.

"The President argued that the various Russian leaders in Paris should not be admitted as representatives, but merely be heard." ACNP notes cited above.

take advantage of their presence to hear what they had to bring forward.

MR. LLOYD GEORGE said that to do so would give the public the impression that we considered they represented Russia. The fact that they had been seen by the Conference would be known. If we wished to hear their views, we could obtain a memorandum from them or have a private conversation.

M. PICHON agreed.

*Conclusion*: It was agreed that Russia should not be represented at the Conference, but that the persons named by M. Pichon and others could be interviewed personally or asked to supply memoranda.

M. PICHON then read Section II of the French Memorandum,[11] on which no comments were offered.

M. PICHON then commenced to read section III.[12]

PRESIDENT WILSON said that he did not see how the Allies could work on a programme such as was now proposed. He asked how the Nations could be represented as had been proposed in these discussions. Surely, they must have full representation or none at all. He quoted instances in which Powers which would only be represented part of the time would, in fact, have a great interest in general questions, to the discussion of which they would not normally be invited.

MR. LLOYD GEORGE pointed out that this system had been adopted with success at the Supreme War Council, when Greece, Serbia, Japan, Belgium and other countries had been invited.

PRESIDENT WILSON pointed out that this was only in the War. The present Conference was to settle the world for a long time to come. He did not like to give even the appearance of only consulting Nations when the Great Powers considered that they were concerned.

MR. LLOYD GEORGE asked if this was not reality. Were not the Great Powers, in fact, settling the questions?

PRESIDENT WILSON said this was why he maintained that we ought to have no formal Conferences, but only conversations. The moment the formal Conferences were entered into these difficulties arose. He felt that this would not satisfy the smaller nations, and satisfaction was an essential part of the Peace settlement.[13]

---

[11] That is, the one cited in n. 2 above.

[12] *Ibid.*

[13] "(A remark by the President.) Mr. Lloyd George stated that at the Supreme War Council the smaller nations were only consulted when their intentions [interests?] were involved. The President said he did not like the appearance of [not] consulting nations that we are protecting unless they were interested. Mr. Lansing remarked that if they followed that procedure they would be imitating the Council [Congress] of Vienna. The President was in favor of holding informal conversations amongst the great powers, but

MR. LLOYD GEORGE said he did not see why they should not be satisfied. The questions to be decided in the War were just as difficult as those to be decided in the Peace.

MR. BALFOUR asked why there should not be a number of informal conversations with informal conclusions. These conclusions, labelled as informal and preliminary suggestions, would then be sent to the small Powers for their consideration and returned by them with their remarks, which would be discussed at further informal Conferences.

M. CLEMENCEAU asked whether he was to understand that no decision could be taken without Costa Rica and Honduras being consulted. If so, he could not agree. It was evident that in European questions the danger was not so great for Costa Rica or Nicaragua as for European Powers. But there were many questions of vital importance to the latter. He had always understood that the four Great Powers would meet and settle these questions, admitting the co-operation of the other Powers. They were not bound to decide the question that evening, but there were certain considerations which ought to be taken into account before the decision was taken. There was the great demand for publicity of the proceedings of the Conference, more especially in France. But to solve the questions in private conversation would render any publicity impossible. This would create the utmost disappointment and the belief that things were not right. He insisted that public opinion should be taken into account. He quite agreed in the principle that the small countries were as much concerned as the great, and that nothing ought to be done to wound the susceptibilities of the small countries. But these countries were not in the same position towards the greater problems as the larger Powers. Already Japan had been admitted to the Conference and was to have five delegates, although Japan had not done very much in the War, and what she had done had been mainly in her own interests. He proposed, therefore, that the meeting should adjourn in order to reflect upon the proposals of President Wilson and Mr. Balfour, but that in their reflections all should remember that we must avoid doing anything likely to create distrust in public opinion.[14]

---

believed that they must have an organization of all the nations, otherwise they would run the risk of having a small number of nations regulate the affairs of the world, and the other nations might not be satisfied." ACNP notes cited above.

[14] "Mr. Clemenceau then spoke at some length: 'Am I to understand from the statement of President Wilson that there can be no question however important it may be for France, England, Italy or America upon which the representative of Honduras or of Cuba shall not be called upon to express his opinion? I have hitherto always been of the opinion that it was agreed that the five great Powers should reach their decisions upon important questions before entering the halls of the Congress to Negotiate Peace. If a new war should take place, Germany would not throw all her forces upon Cuba or upon Honduras, but upon France; it would always be upon France. I request then that

MR. BALFOUR asked what were M. Clemenceau's ideas on the question of publicity.

M. CLEMENCEAU replied that in his scheme there would be partial publicity, according as the Allied Governments may think fit.

PRESIDENT WILSON said that, apart from the Armistice, nothing had been discussed to-day but the question of representation at the Conference. He asked what he should say when approached by the Press? What was the Conference to which the discussions on representations related?[15]

M. CLEMENCEAU said they were the preliminary Peace Conferences which all the world was awaiting. He contemplated two Conferences, a preliminary Conference of the Allied Powers, followed by the regular Peace Congress. There were altogether three kinds of Conferences:

1. Informal conversations, about which nothing would be announced;

---

we stand by the proposals which have been made, proposals to the effect that meetings be held in which the representatives of the five countries mentioned shall participate, to reach decisions upon the important questions, and that the study of secondary questions be turned over to the commissions and the committees before the reunion of the conference. We are not convened to reach a decision upon this subject this evening, and I readily concede that we take into consideration all that President Wilson has just stated. But there is a point that must not be lost to view, I refer to the making public of our deliberations. There is a general expectation on the part of the public which desires that everything occurring in the course of our deliberations, all the subjects that are discussed, shall be made known. If we limit ourselves in the publications to conversations invested with an official character, how can we keep the public informed? Would it not be believed that we are concealing something important? On the contrary, in my judgment, it is of the utmost importance for us to show to the public the results of our labor. Unquestionably the smaller Powers are quite as much interested in the conclusion of a peace as are the great Powers. France, England, the United States and Italy have a great past behind them. Upon them devolves the responsibility for the conclusion of peace and in the negotiations their preponderating roles should be recognized. Unquestionably the smaller Powers have the same moral rights as have the great Powers, but it is impossible to permit the small Powers to render decisions on questions which do not directly concern them in any way. We are ready to do everything that is possible to defend their rights and their interests, but it is not possible to say that all the Powers are upon the same footing when they approach the settlement of the controversies raised by the war.

"We have agreed that Japan should have five delegates like the Great Powers. Japan participated in the war in the Far East, but who can say that in the war she played a part that can be compared to that of France? Japan defended its interests in the Far East, but when was requested to intervene in Europe, everyone know[s] what the answer of Japan was. The account that has to be settled is not one alone of money; there is an account for the blood shed that has to be settled also; the blood which France has shed gives to France an indisputable right to raise her voice and to insist upon her point of view in those questions which are exclusively her concern. If this way of looking at the matter is not accepted by all, I could not retain the honor of representing France in the Peace Conference. The question is so important that I propose that we do adjourn its solution until tomorrow, to reflect upon the suggestions which have been made by President Wilson, and upon the remarks which I have just formulated.' This proposal was then adopted by the Assembly." *Ibid.*

[15] "Before those present separated President Wilson raised the question as to what should be stated to the representatives of the press as to what had been done in the course of the deliberations this day. (The President stated that his only suggestion was that they had better not begin the conference until they were in substantial agreement among themselves, otherwise the conference would become a debating society.)" *Ibid.*

2. The formal preliminary Peace Conference; and

3. The Peace Congress.

(After some discussion, it was agreed that the Press should be informed that, after a meeting of the Supreme War Council, which had been concerned with questions relating to the renewal of the Armistice, the Prime Ministers and Foreign Secretaries had had an exchange of views as to the method and procedure at the Conference for formulating in a preliminary way the terms of Peace.)

M. PICHON pointed out that Technical Advisers would be necessary on many questions—for example, on financial questions. He suggested that when required they should take the place of one of the Delegates at the Conference.

PRESIDENT WILSON said he did not require Technical Delegates, but only Technical Advisers.

MR. LLOYD GEORGE suggested that Technical Advisers should sit behind their Delegates without being reckoned as additional Delegates. If it was necessary for them to make an explanation on a technical point, the head of the Delegation would ask the President if this could be permitted.

PRESIDENT WILSON suggested that any formal process which was adopted must not exclude any informal process.

(It was agreed that Technical Advisers should not sit at the table, but should sit behind the Delegates at the Conference.)

(It was agreed that the Japanese Ambassador in Paris[16] be permitted to attend future conversations.)

Printed copy (SDR, RG 256, 180.03101/2, DNA).
[16] Keishiro Matsui, who was in fact a Japanese delegate plenipotentiary.

# Two Telegrams from Frank Lyon Polk to Robert Lansing

Washington, January 12, 1919.

200. For the Secretary of State. The following memorandum was presented to me by the British Chargé d'Affaires on January 3rd:

"His Majesty's Chargé d'Affaires presents his compliments to the Acting Secretary of State and has the honor under instructions from his Majesty's Government to suggest to the United States Government the propriety of transmitting the following message to the Soviet Government at Moscow, to General Kolchak at Omsk, to General Denikin at Ekaterinburg, to Monsieur Tchaikovsky at Archangel, and to the governments of ex-Russian states.

'The great friendly powers are about to assemble in Paris to work for a solution of problems arising out of the war and to bring about a settlement of international and national controversies that still survive it.

One of the first tasks will be an endeavor to bring about peace in Russia, to reconcile the conflicting national parties and territories, and to bring succor to suffering populations pending decisions that will be taken. In this sense the great friendly powers call upon all the governments, parties, and peoples in states and territories in question to abstain from further aggressions, hostilities, and reprisals, and require them to keep the peace both at home and with their neighbors.

If the aforesaid governments and parties will immediately suspend hostilities on all fronts for the duration of the peace negotiations even if they or any of them should desire to send representatives to Paris to discuss with the great powers the conditions of a permanent settlement, the great powers would be prepared to enter on such a discussion with these.'

Some immediate action of this kind would appear to be necessary without awaiting the meeting of the powers at Paris, owing to the urgency of the appeals which are being received by his Majesty's Government from Lithuanians, Estonians, et cetera, and the danger of their extermination within the next few weeks. (Signed) Colville Barclay, dated January 3rd."

This message I regret I did not forward at once, as I expected that the same proposal would be presented to the President or the Commission in Paris, as I understood the whole question was being considered there. See your cable concerning consideration of Bolshevik peace proposals.[1] The newspaper-men asked me Saturday afternoon, January 11th, about Pichon's answer[2] which I had not then seen and did not know of, and whether we had received any proposal regarding Boshevik delegates being sent to Paris. As their question was not clear I did not connect their inquiry with the British memorandum, and accordingly replied we had received no proposal for the Bolsheviki to be allowed to send delegates to Paris. After seeing Mr. Pichon's statement in the morning papers I have now announced that we have the memorandum from the British Embassy, and that it was not sent to Paris, and am assuming full responsibility for the misunderstanding. My announcement is being repeated to you. I told the British Chargé d'Affaires at that time that personally I did not think the statement would have any effect on the Bolsheviki and would only discourage the Omsk government and others, and that I thought it would be better for the Allies and the United States to try first to settle on some policy before making any statement. Confidentially, I would be interested to know how Mr. Pichon's statement was made without apparently discussing question with you. Polk.

[1] RL to FLP, Jan. 4, 1919, *FR 1919, Russia*, p. 3. This telegram reads as follows: "Under date of December 24, 5 p.m., Legation Stockholm informed the Mission [The American Commission to Negotiate Peace] that the British, Italian, French Ministers and himself had received letters dated Stockholm, December 23, from Litvinoff, a plenipotentiary of the Russian Federation of Soviets, expressing a desire to enter upon preliminary peace negotiations. For your information. This matter is receiving consideration." Litvinov's letter is printed at Dec. 24, 1918, Vol. 53.

[2] On January 11, 1919, the French Socialist newspaper *L'Humanité* printed a statement by Pichon in which he flatly rejected the proposal set forth in the British memorandum quoted in the above telegram. After briefly summarizing the British note, Pichon made the following comments:

"While rendering full homage to the generous spirit of universal reconciliation with which the British Government was inspired in making this proposition, the French Government is unable to give its approval to such a suggestion, which fails to take into account the principles which have not failed to dominate its policy and that of the Powers in Russia.

"The criminal regime of the Bolsheviks which does not represent in any degree that of a democratic Government, or furnish any possibility whatever of developing into a Government, since it is supported solely by the lowest passions of anarchical oppression, in negation of all the principles of public and private right, cannot claim to be recognized as a regular Government.

"If the Allies were weak or imprudent enough to act thus, they would give the lie, in the first place, to the principles of justice and right which constitute their force and honor, and would give to the Bolshevik propaganda in the outside world a power and extension to which they would run the risk of being the first victims. The French Government, so far as it is concerned, will make no contract with crime.

"By agreeing to recognize the Bolshevik Government we should give the lie to the policy—which the Allies have not ceased to sustain in agreement—of furnishing at all accessible points of Russia all the aid and succor which it is possible to give to the healthy, faithful, honest elements of Russia, in order to help them escape from the bloody and disorderly tyranny of the Bolsheviks and to reconstitute a regular Government by themselves.

"It may be added that, aside from the Bolsheviks, the Allies can perfectly well admit the different Russian nationalities to present their claims. As regards the dangers which the menace of the Red armies threaten them, we should not cease to supply arms and money and even military support compatible with our aims.

"Method and patience combined, together with the impossibility that any régime can last without a regular organization for maintaining provisioning, transport, order, credit, etc., will in the end overcome Russian internal anarchy. It may be prolonged for a certain time, but it can in no case possibly triumph definitely, and we shall continue resolutely to refuse it any recognition and to treat it as an enemy." C. K. Cumming and Walter W. Pettit, eds., *Russian-American Relations, March, 1917-March, 1920: Documents and Papers* (New York, 1920), pp. 280-81. A slightly variant translation appears in the *New York Times*, Jan. 12, 1919.

Washington Jan. 12th, 1919.

199B. Following statement given press today: "On January third the State Department received from the British Chargé a memorandum proposing that the Allies and the United States call on all the factions in Russia to suspend hostilities pending the Peace Negotiations, and that if the aforesaid governments and parties will immediately suspend hostilities on all fronts for the duration of the Peace Negotiations, even if they or any of them should desire to send representatives to Paris to discuss with the great powers conditions of a permanent settlement, the great powers would be prepared to enter on such a discussion with them. This message was not forwarded to Paris at that time as it was expected that a similar proposal would be presented at Paris in view of the fact that the Russian question was one of the subjects for immediate attention there. It would seem however from the reports in the newspapers that no such proposal was presented to the American Peace Mission in Paris."

The question was asked me as I understood it by a newspaper man yesterday afternoon as to whether a proposal had been made to have delegates from the Bolsheviks attend the Peace Conference and reference was made to Mr. Pichon's statement. Not having seen Mr. Pichon's statement I did not connect the question with the proposal referred to in the memorandum from the British Chargé which had been received by the Department and I therefore replied that no such proposal had been received. I wish to assume full responsibility for the misunderstanding for the Secretary of State.

Polk.

T telegrams (WP, DLC).

## From Herbert Clark Hoover, with Enclosure

Dear Mr. President:          Paris, January 12, 1919.

Please find enclosed herewith extracts from the minutes of the 'Supreme Council for Supply and Relief' which were agreed to today by the representatives of all four Governments. It is of the utmost importance that these minutes should be brought before the Supreme War Council for ratification in order that they may become binding on their Governments and Departments.

Yours faithfully,   Herbert Hoover

TLS (WP, DLC).

## E N C L O S U R E

### I
#### RELIEF OF LIBERATED TERRITORIES.

1. That it is imperative in the interest of humanity and for the maintenance of orderly government that relief should be given to certain European countries. It is provisionally estimated that for the furnishing of this relief till next harvest a minimum sum of 300 million dollars may be necessary apart from the requirements of Germany which will be separately examined.

2. The Council is of the opinion that this sum of 300 million dollars should be placed at its disposal by the four associated Governments.

3. That the financial representatives of the four Governments should consider and make recommendations to meet this expenditure.

4. If these recommendations be accepted by the Council they should then be referred to the respective Governments for their approval.

## II
### GERMAN SHIPPING.

The Supreme Council of General Supply believes that it is indispensable that the Associated Governments recommend to their representatives on the Naval Armistice Commission, which is sitting in London under the chairmanship of Admiral Weymis,[1] that they should insert among the clauses of the new Armistice Treaty which is to be signed with Germany, a provision to the effect that the German passenger and cargo fleet shall be at the disposition of the Associated Governments to be operated through the intermediary of the Allied Maritime Transport Council, for the purpose of augmenting the sum total of the world's tonnage, from which there may be drawn the tonnage necessary for the supply and relief of Europe.

## III
### FOOD SUPPLIES TO GERMANY.

1. The Council has given consideration to the measures already in progress for the relief of the allied, liberated and neutral territories, and is taking steps to provide and expedite such relief.

2. The Council has formed the opinion upon the material already in its possession (which is necessarily incomplete) that additional supply of food will be required in Germany before the next harvest is gathered.

For the purpose of obtaining more precise information the Council is making further investigation.

3. The Council recommends to the Supreme War Council that if the German cargo and passenger fleet is placed at the disposal of the associated Governments, the associated Governments should permit Germany to import a prescribed quantity of food stuffs so limited as not to interfere in any way with the priority of supply which must be assured to Allied, liberated and neutral countries.

4. Under the conditions indicated, the Council would recommend that in the first instance the following supply should be permitted: 200,000 tons of breadstuffs and 70,000 tons of pork products.

5. It must be a condition precedent to any supply that satisfactory

arrangements are made by Germany for providing the necessary payment.

The Council recommend that the representatives of the Treasuries of the Associated Governments be given full discretion to discuss the method of payment with the German representatives and to arrange for the utilization of German credits abroad in preference to other resources; failing these the representatives should make recommendations to the Council and to their respective Treasuries.

6. The Council are of the opinion that the world's position will justify further supplies if the Supreme War Council decide that these should be continued.

IV.

ORGANIZATION OF COMMISSION TO GERMANY.

The Council recommend that the Commanding Generals of the Belgian, French, British, American and Italian Armies should each nominate an Officer of experience who should form a Commission to supervise the distribution of foodstuffs in Germany, acting on behalf of the Armies of the Associated Governments and of this Council and shall take instructions from and report direct to, this Council.

In the assistance of the Commission, this Council will provide it with an expert civilian staff.

T MS (WP, DLC).
    [1] That is, Rosslyn Erskine Wemyss.

## From Joseph Patrick Tumulty

[The White House, 12 January 1919]

No. 15. I take the liberty of suggesting Mitchell Palmer for Attorney General. Selection of a Southern man like Todd or Glasgow[1] will be most hurtful. Palmer has gained respect and confidence of country because of his conduct of his present office, especially in view of his attitude toward investigation which brought out activities of Germans throughout country. Country therefore recognizes his fearlessness and courage. Democrats, both progressives and conservatives, would approve of appointment. It is desirable [essential][2] that a man from East or West or Middle-west should be appointed. This vacancy gives chance to realign independents who have been critical of Southern domination. Issue of Southern domination growing more acute from day to day. Recognition of Palmer, who stands before country as antagonist of Penrose,[3] would be most helpful and cheering to young men of party. Palmer our friend in 1912, and [has been] loyal throughout. Frankly, I thought Palmer at one time rather "chesty." His work here and my close contact with him removed that impression. He is most accessible and democratic. His ability as a lawyer beyond question. You will make no mistake if appointment is made. It will give us all heart and new courage. Party now in need of———[tonic like this.]

Tumulty.

T telegram (WP, DLC).
  [1] That is, George Carroll Todd and William Anderson Glasgow, Jr.
  [2] Corrections and additions in telegrams from Tumulty to Wilson from the "originals" in the J. P. Tumulty Papers, DLC, unless otherwise noted.
  [3] That is, Senator Boies Penrose.


## Ignace Jan Paderewski to Edward Mandell House

Dear Mr House,                          Warsaw. January 12th, 1919.

    I have telegraphed you several times,[1] but evidently not one of my messages has reached you.

    The American Food Commission is going to leave Warsaw to-night. My time is very limited and, to my deepest regret, I shall not be able to fully describe you the situation which is simply tragic. Mr. J. M. Horodyski[2] will give you the details. I wish, however, to add a few remarks to his verbal report, which will be, I am sure, very exact.

    Contrary to the rumors originated by the untiring pro-German propaganda the Poles have been nowhere the aggressive party. Though claiming, most legitimately, the exclusive possession of Dantzig as an indispensable condition for their political, commercial and economic life, they all rely with unshaken confidence on the results of the peace-conference and do not intend to surprise the delegates by any "fait accompli." But could anyone ask them to remain quiet when brutally attacked and not to defend themselves? Surprised by a murderous Ukrainian bolshevik army the women and children of Lemberg[3] took up arms and defended the city. At the present moment a force of about 80000 Ukrainians, armed and equipped by the Germans, led by German and Austrian officers, under the command of the Austrian Archduc, Wilhelm of Habsburg,[4] is at the gates of Lemberg and the number of Polish soldiers, lacking food and munitions, does not exceed 18000 men. In Posen, the day after my arrival, during the procession of 10000 school-children marching through the streets, some Prussian companies, mostly officers, opened fire upon the peaceful and unarmed crowd. Quite a number of shots were fired at my windows, some of them at the window of Colonel Wade.[5] Explosive and dum-dum bullets were used. American and British flags were insulted. Several eye-witnesses, including the officers of the British mission and myself, can testify to these facts.

There is no doubt that the whole affair was organized by the Germans in order to create some new difficulties for the peace-conference. There is also not the slightest doubt that the present Spartacus movement in Germany and the Bolshevik revolution in Russia are most closely connected. They simply intend to meet on our soil.

The Bolshevik army has already taken Vilna. The cities of Grodno and Bialystok are in immediate danger. In a few days the invasion of this part of Poland will be an accomplished fact.

Poland cannot defend itself. We have no food, no uniforms, no arms, no munitions. We have but men, at least 500,000 of them, willing to fight, to defend the country under a strong government. The present government is weak and dangerous;[6] it is almost exclusively radical-socialist. I have been asked to form a new cabinet, but what could I do with the moral support of the country alone, without the material assistance of the Allies and the United States?

If there were any possibility of obtaining immediate help for my country I would suggest:

1) To send a collective note to the Ukrainian Directoriate at Kief, addressed to Messrs Petlura, Winnitchenko and Schwetz,[7] ordering cessation of hostilities in Eastern Galicia and evacuation of the district of Boryslaw, where considerable American, English and French interests are endangered.

2) To send an inter-allied military commission to Warsaw in order to examine the situation and provide the means of assistance.

3) To send as soon as possible some artillery and plenty of German rifle-munitions.

If this action is delayed our entire civilization may cease to exist. The war may only result in the establishment of barbarism all over Europe.

Kindly forgive this chaotic writing.

With very kindest regards I beg to remain most gratefully and sincerely yours                                    I J Paderewski

ALS (E. M. House Papers, CtY).
    [1] I. J. Paderewski to EMH, Jan. 1 and 4, 1919, T telegrams (E. M. House Papers, CtY).
    [2] That is, Count Jan Marie Horodyski, at this time an associate of Paderewski and Roman Dmowski.
    [3] Now known by the Russian name Lvov or the Polish Lwow.

4 Archduke William Francis Joseph Charles, born 1895, a nephew of the former Emperor Charles. He was a colonel in command of the Galician Ukrainian Volunteer Legion of the former imperial army, spoke fluent Ukrainian, and was popularly known among the Ukrainians as Vasil Vishivani, Basil the Embroidered, because of the elaborate blouses that he wore. During 1918, he had been the Austrian contender for Hetman of the Ukraine, the position then held by the German-backed Gen. Pavlo Petrovich Skoropadski. See Oleh S. Fedyshyn, *Germany's Drive to the East and the Ukrainian Revolution, 1917-1918* (New Brunswick, N. J., 1971), pp. 169, 227-30, 300.

5 Lt. Col. Harry Amyas Leigh Herschel Wade, head of the British Mission to Poland.

6 Józef Piłsudski [hereafter Pilsudski] had assumed dictatorial powers in Poland as provisional chief of state in mid-November 1918. Shortly thereafter, he had appointed a largely Socialist cabinet headed by Jędrzej Moraczewski. This government was about to be replaced by a coalition cabinet agreed upon in negotiations between Paderewski and Pilsudski and to be headed by Paderewski himself as Prime Minister and Minister of Foreign Affairs. See Piotr S. Wandycz, *Soviet-Polish Relations, 1917-1921* (Cambridge, Mass., 1969), pp. 72-75, and Kay Lundgreen-Nielsen, *The Polish Problem at the Paris Peace Conference: A Study of the Policies of the Great Powers and the Poles, 1918-1919*, trans. Alison Borch-Johansen (Odense, 1979), pp. 92-119 *passim*.

7 Symon Vasyl'ovich Petliura, Ukrainian nationalist and military leader, former member of the Ukrainian Central Rada, and a member of the five-man Directory which assumed the government of the Ukraine after the fall of Gen. Skoropadski; Volodimir Kirillovich Vinnichenko, Ukrainian nationalist leader and author and a member of the Directory; and Fedir Shvets, geologist and member of the Directory.

# From the Diary of Edith Benham

January 12, 1919

Today was the beginning of the Peace Conference. The President said he arrived promptly and the others came a few minutes later, the English delegates lagging along. Instead of being the Conference, it was a sitting of the interallied High Commission to determine extending the armistice. Finally after two-thirds of the time had been wasted it was agreed to have a meeting of that Commission tomorrow morning and the Conference in the afternoon. I don't wonder in speaking of it that the President said it reminded him of an old ladies tea party for they all talked and when the Peace Conference finally got under way and they were discussing along very well, a tea table was brought in and they all had tea. The President spoke of Bliss in the highest terms, said he had the mind of a statesman and is a man of very clear judgment; also, confidentially, that he was much disappointed not to meet over here a single man whom he considered has a statesman's brain. He said Clemenceau made rather a witty speech. A letter from the Japanese Government was read requesting that the Japanese Ambassador here be allowed to assist at the conferences and C. said the Conference objected because they didn't want him to know the state of Europe at the present time. He, the President, says the work of the Conference is so much complicated because no one knows what is happening in Russia, and no one can believe the men from there for there is no head from which news can be sent.

T MS (Edith B. Helm Papers, DLC).

## From the Diary of Dr. Grayson

Monday, January 13, 1919.

The President spent the morning in his study, writing and preparing for the meeting of the Supreme War Council, at 2:30 in the afternoon. The conference, at this time, began its discussion of dividing its work into committees and determining the representation thereon of the various nations. I noticed that the British and French had called in all their technical advisors. Baruch, Hurley, Hoover and McCormick were with me in the outer room so I went into the conference room and asked the President whether he did not want his technical advisors present. He replied that he did, so all of them went into the meeting. The meeting was prolonged and when Mrs. Wilson returned for the President, he was not ready to leave, so I went for a motor ride with her. After the meeting, I saw Baruch and asked him how things had progressed. He said that the President was complete master of the whole performance and that he entirely dominated the meeting. That night we had a formal dinner at the Murat Palace, the first the President had given since his coming to France. As guests, he had all the technical advisors and members of the Mission.

## Hankey's Notes of a Meeting of the Supreme War Council[1]

Quai d'Orsay, January 13, 1919, 2:30 P.M.

IC-105 [BC-1, SWC-2]

[Discussion continued on the conditions of the renewal of the Armistice. Foch submitted the text of a new clause to be added which required the German government to take the steps necessary to insure the safety of the gold reserve in the Reichsbank and of the machinery required for the issue of bank notes.]

PRESIDENT WILSON pointed out that the question under discussion was not a military one, and, though he had full confidence in Marshal Foch as regards the carrying out of the armistice, he did not think the question under consideration was one which should be left to the military authorities for Marshal Foch to decide.

MR. BONAR LAW agreed that this was not a military question. All he proposed to do was to ask their experts to report on the possibility and desirability of doing what had been suggested. It was even possible that the German Government itself might wish that this should be done, in order to prevent the gold and the presses from falling into the hands of the Spartacus Group.

[1] The complete text of these notes is printed in PPC, III, 508-20.

PRESIDENT WILSON said he wished to avoid the impression that, as an afterthought, they now wished to impound the German gold and the presses used for the emission of paper money. It seemed to him that this procedure would be introducing a novel clause into the armistice. By all means let the envoys look into the facts and form an opinion. They should then submit the matter to the German delegates, and, in co-operation with the Germans, endeavour to arrive at a plan which the Germans themselves might welcome. But they did not wish to introduce new conditions into the armistice.

M. KLOTZ[2] made the following suggestion, which he thought might embody President Wilson's proposals:

He would suggest that, after agreement had been reached by the technical delegates on the lines suggested in the first paragraph of the above text, Marshal Foch should be authorised to add the following clause to the armistice:

"Germany shall forthwith take all necessary measures to ensure the safety of the gold deposits in the Reichsbank and of the machinery required for the issue of bank-notes."

This would mean that the necessary action would be taken in consultation with the German Government, and that it is left to it to take steps to give effect to this decision.

PRESIDENT WILSON enquired whether it would not be sufficient to authorise Marshal Foch, in the event of our own and the German delegates being in accord, to take steps to help the Germans to ensure the safety of the gold.

MR. BONAR LAW thought that if the German Government itself said to our delegates that it would be in a better position to do this if it were made a condition of the armistice, Marshal Foch should not be prevented from doing this.

M. KLOTZ urged that the clause be kept secret. If made public it might lead to serious trouble, and bring about the very danger it was desired to avoid.

PRESIDENT WILSON agreed, but said that that did not prevent their arriving at an agreement with the German Government on this question. Should the German Government prefer that the clause be entered in the armistice, he quite agreed that this should be done.

MR. BONAR LAW suggested that the German Government might, in the future, find itself in difficulties if it were discovered that they had willingly agreed to the removal of the gold without the stimulus of its being a condition of the armistice.

M. KLOTZ thought that the clause, as now amended, met all re-

[2] That is, Louis Lucien Klotz.

quirements. It was first suggested that the Allied and German experts must be agreed that action is necessary. It was then left to Marshal Foch to take action.

PRESIDENT WILSON agreed, provided that it was quite understood that no clause should be inserted in the armistice terms except at the wish of the German Government.

The following text was accepted:

*"Germany must take as soon as possible all measures to ensure the safety of the gold deposits in the Reichsbank, and of the machinery required for the issue of bank-notes. Marshal Foch is therefore authorised to take the necessary measures to give effect to the recommendation of the experts, either by the insertion of a clause in the armistice or otherwise."*

[Amendments were agreed to for Article 22 of the Armistice concerning the surrender or destruction of German submarines, including those under construction. The provisions were in part a penalty for a delay in surrendering submarines.

[Clémentel[3] submitted clauses proposed by the Allied Naval Council for placing the entire German merchant fleet at the disposal of the Allies and the United States with a view to increasing "the tonnage required for supplying foodstuffs to Europe, including Germany."]

MR. BALFOUR said that he had been desired by Lord Reading to put his views before the Conference. He had objected very strongly to any new conditions being added to the armistice, and he considered that the proposals now under discussion made an important addition to the armistice, and that this should be avoided. Lord Reading agreed that it was necessary to obtain the use of these ships, but he thought that this could be done by bargaining, and not by adding new conditions to the armistice. He would say to the Germans: "If you want food you must hand over your ships. If you hand over your ships we would give you sufficient food for a certain number of months." In this way the weapon of food would still be left in our hands. If Germany agreed to these terms the Allies would help to feed them. The inducement to the Germans would be that a certain quantity of food would be handed over to them in return for the use of a certain number of ships. That policy appeared to be different from the policy now set forth in the proposals under consideration.

M. CLÉMENTEL said that Mr. Hoover was, according to his own statement, required to solve the following question: namely, the supply of 200,000 tons of corn and 70,000 tons of meat per month to meet the requirements of Germany, and this implied a total of

[3] That is, Étienne Clémentel.

from 800,000 to 900,000 tons of shipping. Germany had some 2,700,000 tons of shipping lying idle. The Allies were compelled to furnish supplies to the whole of Europe. It was necessary, therefore, to make Germany give up these ships *temporarily* for the good of Europe. Otherwise Germany would say that she would only give up sufficient shipping to transport supplies required by herself. On the other hand, unless they insisted on the setting free of all the available tonnage, it was impossible to furnish supplies to Europe. Negotiations had been carried on for some considerable time without results. They were forced, therefore, to the conclusion that these demands should form part of the armistice conditions, so that the Germans would be bound to reply within a given period of time.

PRESIDENT WILSON enquired whether it would not be sufficient to issue instructions to our delegates forthwith to arrive at an agreement on these lines.

MR. BONAR LAW pointed out that during the last two months endeavours had been made to obtain the use of these ships, but without success: and unless this were made a condition of the armistice the ships would not be obtained. He did not think it would be necessary for the whole of these clauses to be introduced into the armistice, but a clause should be inserted to the effect that an agreement would have to be arrived at in order to set free the German merchant ships. The Germans should be told that, unless these ships are given up, food would not be supplied. The balance of shipping beyond the tonnage required for Germany's food supplies would be used for payment of food supplied.

M. CLEMENCEAU agreed that it was not only a question of feeding Germany; the whole of Europe had to be fed. Over two months had already been wasted in bargaining, and, if further discussion was to take place, more time would be lost. Whatever text was adopted, they must so act as to make Germany yield the shipping required without further delay.

PRESIDENT WILSON then pointed out that the only other means available, except force, was to withhold food, and to that he agreed.

MR. BONAR LAW pointed out that a meeting of the delegates would take place on Wednesday next. The delegates should be given to understand that they would be supported in any steps which they might consider it necessary to take in order to obtain the use of this shipping.

MARSHAL FOCH said that on the 13th December last this question had been considered. At the suggestion of Mr. Hoover, transmitted to him through General Pershing, he had told M. Erzberger that 2,800,000 tons of German shipping should be pooled for the Allies to be used for the supply of food. M. Erzberger had agreed to this proposal, on the condition that the ships and the crews remained German. He had not refused, but had merely made a condition. As that question had not been settled nothing had been done.

MR. BONAR LAW thought they were all agreed that the armistice should be used to bring pressure to bear on the Germans. If the Germans did not agree, they should instruct their delegates to refer the matter back to the Supreme War Council for decision.

M. KLOTZ enquired whether the Council accepted the condition made by M. Erzberger that the ships should remain under the German flag.

MR. BONAR LAW said that the Council had decided that the ships should sail under our own flag. In this connection he would invite attention to Paragraph IV of the clauses under consideration.

M. LEYGUES pointed out that the Council had agreed to make use of German crews under certain conditions.

PRESIDENT WILSON enquired whether any reply had been made to M. Erzberger's condition.

As no reply had been made, they were parties to the delay. He then suggested that the delegates should be authorised to sign without delay an agreement with the Germans on the lines proposed in the clauses under consideration, and he would add that, if the Germans refused to sign such an agreement, Marshal Foch should at once be informed so that it may be made a condition of the renewal of the armistice.

(This proposal was accepted.)

M. CLÉMENTEL said that the next question to be considered related to the supply of food to Germany. Disagreement had arisen between the British, American, and French financial authorities as to the manner in which payment was to be made.

MR. BONAR LAW asked permission to explain the views held by the British authorities. It would be admitted that each of the Allies had got his own debts, but it was now proposed deliberately to add to these debts in order to supply food to Germany. Consequently, this additional debt, in his opinion, ought to be treated as one of the first charges, to be discharged at once. The supply of food was a necessity. It was therefore a necessity that it should be paid for. If payment was not made immediately, the outstanding debts would be proportionately increased.

M. CLÉMENTEL pointed out that the expenditure to be incurred amounted to 4,500,000,000 fr., which was equivalent to 12,000,000*l.* sterling a month.

M. KLOTZ said he fully recognized Mr. Bonar Law's point of view. He also fully recognized the privileged position of the expenditure contemplated. But, in the absence of any Belgian representative, he could not admit that this expenditure should be given priority, that is, the first place above all others. He was, however, quite prepared to give it a privileged position, leaving it to the Peace Conference to decide the order of priority to be given to the various debts incurred by Germany. As a result of the discussion which had taken place that morning, he now wished to submit the following proposal:

"That this question should be referred to a Conference of representatives of the Allied and Associated Powers, who should be required to submit their recommendations within the period of one week."

PRESIDENT WILSON expressed the view that any further delay in this matter might be fatal, as it meant the dissolution of order and government. They were discussing an absolute and immediate necessity. So long as hunger continued to gnaw, the foundations of government would continue to crumble. Therefore, food should be supplied immediately, not only to our friends, but also to those parts of the world where it was to our interest to maintain a stable Government. He thought they were bound to accept the concerted counsel of a number of men who had been devoting the whole of their time and thought to this question. He trusted the French Finance Department would withdraw their objection, as they were faced with the great problems of Bolshevism and the forces of dissolution which now threatened society.

M. KLOTZ said he would gladly meet President Wilson's wishes. But it was not altogether a question of food supplies. They were all fully agreed as to the necessity of feeding the Germans, but he would appeal to President Wilson to consider also the question of justice. He was quite willing to admit that German foreign securities should be earmarked for this purpose. But they were creating a new German debt. There were other German debts which were just as honourable and noble. Therefore, he would ask, as a matter of justice, why Germany should pay for food in preference to paying off debts incurred for the restoration and for the reparation of damage committed elsewhere. Why should exclusive priority be given to such a debt? As a solution of the difficulty he would agree that payment for this food should be made in foreign securities and values. But he would add that *these assets shall be pooled and distribution shall be made by the Allies, taking into account such privileged claims as the Peace Conference would admit.*

He would merely point out that it was not a question of food supply, it was purely a financial question, and no delay need therefore occur in the supply of food.

PRESIDENT WILSON urged that, unless a solution for the immediate situation could be found, none of these debts would be paid. The want of food would lead to a crash in Germany. The great point, however, was this—that the Associated Governments have no money to pay for these supplies; therefore Germany must pay for them. But if they were not paid for and supplied immediately there would be no Germany to pay anything.

MR. BONAR LAW pointed out that, in calculating the sums, they had been going on the assumption that the supply of food would last for one year. He did not think that it would need to last more than a few months, or, say, up to the harvesting of the next crop. The suggestion had also been made that the German merchant ships to be requisitioned would yield funds for the payment of a portion of the sum in question.

M. KLOTZ proposed that they should accept for a period of two months the text as it stood. At the end of that period the Peace Conference would be able to come to a decision on the whole question of policy.

MR. BONAR LAW considered that if sanction for two months' payment only were obtained the food supplies could only last for two months.

M. KLOTZ thought that this showed some confusion of ideas. It was not a question of supplying food for two months. Food supplies could continue. The question to be settled during the course of the two months was merely as to the priority to be given to the payments to be made by Germany. It would be admitted that foreign securities must be considered as gilt-edged securities.

MR. BONAR LAW thought they were arguing in a circle. The first question to be settled was whether a new debt which they had no necessity to incur should be added to previous debts.

M. KLOTZ agreed, but suggested that at the end of the two months a priority list could be prepared.

M. PICHON said he thought that an agreement had now been reached. Everyone was agreed that payment had to be made. The proposal could therefore be accepted. But the Conference could reconsider the question later on should they wish to do so.

(This was agreed to.)

[Loucheur[4] proposed adding a new proviso to Article 19 of the Armistice, to require the Germans to return at once all French and Belgian machinery that had been removed to Germany.]

MR. LLOYD GEORGE enquired which clause of the armistice related to this question.

[4] Louis Loucheur, French Minister of Industrial Reconstruction.

M. PICHON replied that it came under Clause 19, which read: "Reparation for damage done."

MR. LLOYD GEORGE asked whether this was the interpretation of the clause.

PRESIDENT WILSON said he wished to enquire how these things were to be found in the present disordered state of Germany. The authority under which the machinery had been collected and transported no longer existed. How were these things going to be identified? It might be possible to get similar material, but it would be difficult to obtain the same.

M. LOUCHEUR stated that a "pillage corps" had been formed by the Germans, which had worked methodically and systematically. Full records of all machinery stolen, requisitioned, or removed, had been kept, and these papers were available. Everything was known.

MR. LLOYD GEORGE said that at Lille textile machinery had been taken away, and asked if that could be followed up now.

M. LOUCHEUR said that in most cases they knew where the machinery was. For instance, the machinery for the construction of waggons taken from Douai was now at Essen; they knew exactly where to find it.

PRESIDENT WILSON said that the Conference which formulated the terms of the armistice agreed that they should confine themselves to military conditions, and merely affirm other matters, in principle, in general terms, without entering into details.

MR. LLOYD GEORGE said that during the Armistice Conference a question had arisen as to whether Germany should be required to make reparation in kind or in money. The Conference had, for obvious reasons, replied in the negative to the question concerning the supply of machinery. But the question of returning stolen machinery was quite a different one.

M. LOUCHEUR agreed that the French point of view was wholly opposed to payment in kind, but he insisted on the return of stolen goods.

PRESIDENT WILSON said that he accepted the proposals now before the meeting on the understanding that only the things that could be identified were to be asked for.

MARSHAL FOCH enquired whether this clause was to be made a condition of the armistice. Should it not be accepted, was the armistice to be broken?

(It was agreed to accept the text proposed by M. Loucheur.)

Printed copy (SDR, RG 256, 180.03101/3, DNA).

# Hankey's Notes of a Meeting of the Council of Ten[1]

Quai d'Orsay, January 13, 1919, 4 P.M.

IC-106 [BC-1 +]

(This Meeting was a continuation of a Meeting of the Supreme War Council commenced earlier in the afternoon, *procès-verbal* of which has been prepared separately.)

## Procedure of the Peace Discussions.

M. PICHON said that it was proposed to continue the discussion of the Draft (see Appendix (A) of I.C.-104)[2] submitted by the French Government on the general procedure in regard to the Peace Discussions.

MR. LLOYD GEORGE said that he wished in the first place to return to a question which had been postponed the previous evening in order to enable him to discuss it with the Dominion Premiers. The latter were disappointed at the smallness of the representation allotted to them. They had not even received the same representation as had been granted to Belgium and Serbia, though they had supplied a larger number of troops and their losses had been greater. He had explained quite frankly to them the reasons which had guided President Wilson in his desire not to accord a larger representation, as it would have had the appearance of an over-representation of England, regarding her as a unit. He had informed them that they would be treated like the smaller States, and that one Representative would be present whenever any question which affected them came under consideration. He had also agreed to add from time to time one or two of the Dominion Representatives to the British panel of five.

A second question had been raised at the conference of the British Imperial War Cabinet held that morning in connection with the representation of India. The native States of India, which represented a population of 70,000,000 to 80,000,000 men, and had furnished some 180,000 men to the army, had a right, he thought, to be represented. He had promised to put forward their claims.

PRESIDENT WILSON wished to remove any impression that he personally had any objection to the British Dominions being separately represented. He fully admitted that their claims were great. He had merely been guided by the desire to remove any cause of jealousy on the part of the other smaller States. He now understood the proposal to be that from time to time one or two of the Dominion

---

[1] The complete text of these notes is printed in *PPC*, III, 531-38.
[2] That is, the minutes of the Meeting of the Council of Ten printed at Jan. 12, 1919, 4 p.m.

Premiers should be admitted among the five National Representatives, and that, besides these five, there should be one Representative from each of the Dominions whenever any subject of
interest to them came under discussion.

MR. LLOYD GEORGE said that, in connection with this matter, he
wished to quote a remark made to him that day by Sir Robert
Borden. He had pointed out that, if he returned to Canada and
confessed that Canada was getting merely half the number of representatives that had been allotted to Serbia or Roumania or Belgium, there would be a feeling that they were being badly treated,
especially when it was known that the Canadian losses during the
war had been greater than those of Belgium. Nevertheless, if it
were thought that a greater representation of the Dominions would
create a bad feeling outside, he did not wish to press the question.

PRESIDENT WILSON enquired whether Mr. Lloyd George would
feel satisfied to give Canada two Representatives, South Africa two
Representatives, Australia two Representatives, and New Zealand
one Representative. He was trying to find a basis for general application.

MR. LLOYD GEORGE agreed that such an allotment would be fair.
But he would not care himself to make that proposal to the Conference.

PRESIDENT WILSON said that he himself would submit this proposal, and enquired whether Mr. Lloyd George would be satisfied
if one Representative was allotted to British India and one to the
native States of India.

MR. LLOYD GEORGE accepted this number, and explained that,
naturally, these Representatives would only be present when questions affecting them came up for discussion.

(It was agreed that the British Dominions and India should have
the right to be represented by the following number of Delegates:

| | |
|---|---|
| Canada | 2 |
| Australia | 2 |
| South Africa | 2 |
| New Zealand | 1 |
| India, including native States of India | 2 |
| Total | 9 |

(For Newfoundland it was decided that, though it would not be
given separate representation, a Representative from that country could be included in the British Delegation.)

M. PICHON expressed the view that all questions connected with the representation of the great Allied and Associated Powers, the smaller Powers, Russia, and Montenegro, had been settled at yesterday's meeting.

MR. LLOYD GEORGE said that there was some misapprehension as regards Russia. They had decided that representatives of sections in Russia, such as Prince Lvof and M. Savinkof, should not be admitted. But the question of the general representation of Russia had never been discussed.

(It was agreed that the question of the representation of Russia should be postponed until the question of general policy of Russia had been examined.)

PRESIDENT WILSON said that, in connection with the questions settled at yesterday's meetings, he wished again to refer to Brazil. Brazil was the only considerable Latin-American State containing a population of over 30,000,000. She had been more subject to German influence than any other of the South American States. Many of the States which went to constitute Brazil were controlled by the German elements in the population, and in another generation this country might have become wholly Germanised. He was therefore interested in attempting to divorce her from Germany. He thought if she were given an exceptional position—for instance, if three Delegates were allotted to her—she would be attached to our own interests, and so be of use to the Allies as one of the great States of South America.

MR. LLOYD GEORGE felt some doubt in accepting this proposal. He thought that the representation should bear some reference to the sacrifices made by each country. Brazil had certainly sent two or three torpedo-boats, but beyond that she had made no effort at all. He thought it would be invidious if she were to get three Representatives, as compared with the two Representatives allotted to Belgium, Greece, and Serbia.

PRESIDENT WILSON agreed. His heart bled for Belgium and Serbia; but they had not made a voluntary sacrifice.

MR. LLOYD GEORGE suggested that Greece had.

PRESIDENT WILSON pointed out that the argument that he urged concerned the future. It was a political argument. He believed that if they did not carry out his proposal, Germany would at once regain her grip on Brazil.

MR. LLOYD GEORGE said that he did not wish to resist this proposal; he merely wondered what the outside public would think. On the other hand, he did not wish to arrest the progress of the meeting by resisting further.

BARON SONNINO said that he would agree to three Representatives being given to Brazil, provided three were also given to Belgium. He thought it was impossible to give Brazil more Representatives than Belgium.

MR. LLOYD GEORGE thought that if three Representatives were given to Belgium and to each of the other small countries, Brazil would no longer hold a preponderating position, and President Wilson's argument would therefore fall to the ground, as they would all be on the same footing.

(It was agreed to give three Representatives to Brazil, the remaining smaller belligerent Powers retaining the number of Representatives previously agreed upon.)

PRESIDENT WILSON asked permission to raise a purely American question concerning the relations of America and Costa Rica. When he (President Wilson) first became President, revolutions had been fomented in Central America by people desirous of supplying arms and munitions, and anxious to obtain concessions. He had then issued a Note to the effect that the United States of America would not accept any Government formed for the purpose of furthering the ambitions of an individual.[3] An example of this had occurred in Mexico, and for that reason America had refused to recognise Carranza [Huerta?]. Later on, a similar instance had occurred in Costa Rica and the United States of America had refused to recognise the new ruler of that country.[4] Costa Rica had made many attempts, without success, to renew relations with the United States of America. With this object in view, she had first offered to declare war on Germany and, finally, receiving no reply to these overtures, had actually declared war in order to force the United States of America to recognise her. In these circumstances he could not bring himself to sit at the same table as a Representative of Costa Rica. Naturally, if any question directly affecting Costa Rica should come up for discussion he would be prepared to reconsider his decision, but under present conditions he proposed that Costa Rica should not be represented at the Peace Conference.

(This was agreed to.)

[The council agreed to various clauses relating to the representation of neutral states and small states which had broken off relations with the enemy, attendance of delegates, representation of enemy powers, technical advisers, and adoption of the panel system in selecting plenipotentiaries for meetings of the conference.]

M. PICHON then proposed consideration of Part II of the French

---

[3] See the statement on relations with Latin America printed at March 12, 1913, Vol. 27.
[4] That is, Federico Tinoco Granados.

draft note relating to the principles and methods of conducting the Peace Conference. He explained that the proposals therein contained had been drafted on the basis of the principles put forth by President Wilson in his speech of the 8th January, 1918, and in his speech of the 27th September, 1918, and also on the answers which the Allies had drawn up on the 5th November, 1918.

PRESIDENT WILSON proposed, as a practical consideration, that a number of questions should be referred to the Delegates of the five Great Powers, so that they could discover their differences and points of agreement before going into the Conference. For instance, if the League of Nations was to serve as the medium of treatment for any particular question, then they should begin by discussing a League of Nations. Therefore he could not now agree on a sequence or order of discussion. For example, some of the points, such as the publicity to be given to Treaties, could not be decided until they knew what was meant. He did not mean by this that there should not be confidential conversations between countries, but that no Treaty should come into force until it had been published. That was a subject for general discussion. It was proposed that that should be referred to the national Delegates. The same conclusion applied to other questions, such as the treatment of Russia, which called for immediate decision. It was necessary to move quicksands before they could begin to walk. Therefore, the order of discussion should be settled from time to time. A list of subjects to be discussed could be prepared, but not the order of sequence.

MR. LLOYD GEORGE expressed his entire agreement. He thought they must first take Russia and the League of Nations, and there might be other questions which were ripe for immediate settlement, and could be got out of the way.

MR. BALFOUR said that they must not put off too long the discussion of boundaries. The new countries would be in a state of perpetual disturbance until they knew where they were.

MR. LLOYD GEORGE suggested that the question should be discussed from the point of view of its effect on demobilisation.

M. CLEMENCEAU agreed that demobilisation stood in relation to the condition of Russia, Germany, &c.

PRESIDENT WILSON wished to make a suggestion, namely, that each of the following questions be referred to the National Peace Delegates, with a request that they should submit their recommendations as concisely and as soon as possible:

1. The League of Nations.
2. Reparation.

3. New States.

4. Frontiers and territorial changes.

5. Colonies.

These subjects could then be discussed by the present Conference in the order given.

MR. LLOYD GEORGE suggested adding, "The responsibility of the authors of the war."

PRESIDENT WILSON said that this question need not be referred to a Committee, since it could be settled forthwith by themselves.

M. CLEMENCEAU said that President Wilson proposed that certain questions should be referred to the five National Peace Delegates, who would report to this Conference. This Conference was merely a Supreme War Council. As such it had no power to discuss such questions. Nothing could be done until the Peace Conference was brought together. He would therefore propose that an official meeting of the Peace Conference should be called together forthwith. Nothing of importance need be discussed, but the work could be distributed and questions could be referred to the Committees, as suggested by President Wilson. The day afterwards the Delegates of the five Great Powers could meet to examine questions ready for solution, such as Russia, and at the same time the National Delegates could be drawing up their recommendations.

PRESIDENT WILSON explained that his idea was a very simple one. He thought that the five Powers should hold a Conference to find out their own minds before they entered into the process of the Peace Conference.

M. CLEMENCEAU pointed out that President Wilson's proposal came to this: that they intended to arrive at a complete understanding before the Peace Conference could meet. That would take some months, and would be a great disappointment to the public. They had trumpeted abroad that the Conference was going to meet forthwith, and the Delegates had been appointed and had arrived. He fully agreed that the five Powers should first come to a decision amongst themselves; but it was necessary first to hold an initial meeting of the Peace Conference and give the Delegates a mandate to start work. After that the heads of the Associated Powers could meet together.

MR. LLOYD GEORGE pointed out that no great difference existed between the two proposals. He fully agreed with President Wilson that they should exchange views in order to discover their differences and concentrate their efforts on these. But he also agreed with M. Clemenceau that a meeting of the Peace Conference should be called forthwith.

M. PICHON said that President Wilson's proposal was then accepted, with the amendment suggested by M. Clemenceau.

(This was agreed to.)

M. CLEMENCEAU proposed that the meeting of the Peace Conference should be held on Thursday, the 16th January, 1919, at 1430 o'clock.

BARON SONNINO pointed out that the Italian Delegates had not yet been appointed, and that Signor Orlando had left for Italy. The Italian Delegates could be appointed in a day or two, but they would then have to get to Paris. He proposed, therefore, that the Conference should be postponed to a later date.

MR. BALFOUR enquired how many of the important Delegates were now present in Paris.

M. PICHON replied that most of the Delegates had already arrived in Paris.

M. CLEMENCEAU insisted that no further delay should occur in holding the meeting. Two months had passed since the Armistice had been signed, and nothing had been done. He therefore urged that the meeting should be held on Thursday next.

BARON SONNINO said that he would regret the absence of his colleagues, but would withdraw any further objection. On the other hand, he wished to point out that if the object of the Conference was to pass President Wilson's proposal, it would, in his opinion, be found impossible to get twenty States to hand over to five Powers all questions relating to the drawing up of the Peace Treaty.

MR. LLOYD GEORGE thought that the question might be disposed of as follows: The first Peace Conference would be opened by a speech by President Poincaré; then M. Clemenceau would take the chair, and he would invite the small States to put forward their claims, and to submit these to the Great Powers for their consideration.

PRESIDENT WILSON suggested that the small Powers should send the proposals to the Secretary of the Conference, in order to remove the impression that the big Powers were acting independently. M. Clemenceau would impress on these small States that the Great Powers wished to have their views, and, as far as possible, be guided by them.

M. PICHON said that he understood that all the small Powers should be invited to attend the first meeting.

BARON SONNINO proposed that the first meeting should be postponed until Saturday, in order to give time for Signor Orlando and the Italian Delegates to attend.

M. CLEMENCEAU accepted this suggestion, and said that meanwhile other subjects could be brought under discussion. He suggested that a meeting should be held on Wednesday, the 15th instant, to settle the draft regulations of the Conference and to discuss the situation in Russia.

  (It was agreed that the First Allied Peace Conference should be held on Saturday, the 18th January, 1919, at 1430 o'clock, and that a meeting of the Supreme War Council should be held on Wednesday, the 15th January, 1919, at 1030 o'clock.)

  (It was also decided that an announcement should be published in the press to the effect that the formal Conferences would open on the following Saturday, the 18th January, 1919.)

Printed copy (SDR, RG 256, 180.03101/4, DNA).

## To Vittorio Emanuele Orlando

Dear Mr. Prime Minister:                    Paris, 13 January, 1919.

Supplementing the Memorandum which I gave your Excellency yesterday,[1] I venture to call attention to the tremendous advantages which have accrued to Italy under your administration by the successful termination of the war against the Central Empires. These advantages are so great that they could not possibly have been anticipated at the time when Italy joined the Allies. Not only has Italy regained possession of the terra irridenta, the Trentino and Trieste; not only has the German Empire collapsed, but the traditional enemy, the Hapsburg Monarchy, is prostrate and in such a complete state of disintegration that neither to the North, nor in the Adriatic, need the Italian people dread any further menace or reconstitution of it, but will be able to pursue their commercial and economic development without the necessity of maintaining crushing armaments.

It has not, however, been my thought to depend on these general results of war for the safety and the political independence and economic opportunity of Italy. Definite guarantees can be and should be secured. It is for that purpose that I have proposed that, in addition to requiring of the new States that they accept from the League of Nations a limitation of their armaments to a strict peace footing and the requirements of the maintenance of domestic order, a), the Jugo-Slavic State be erected on the understanding that it maintain no navy except the few small craft necessary to maintain a coast police, b) the Austrian fortifications on the islands and eastern coast of the Adriatic be destroyed and the arming of those coasts and islands be forbidden by international mandate, c) that it be one of the fundamental covenants of the Peace that all new

States should enter into solemn obligations, under responsibility to the whole body of nations, to accord to all racial or national minorities within their jurisdiction exactly the same status and treatment, alike in law and in fact, that are accorded the majority of the people, and *d*) that Fiume and Zara be erected into free cities and permanently free ports.

I assume, in all these proposals, that the readjusted boundaries of Italy on the north and northeast will run substantially as indicated by the solid black line on the accompanying map (the dotted black line representing the line proposed, as I understand it, in the "Pact of London").

The "Pact of London," I respectfully submit, cannot wisely be regarded as applying to existing circumstances or carried out consistently with the agreements upon which the present peace conferences are based. The boundaries proposed in that agreement were laid down as a frontier against the Austro-Hungarian Empire; and that Empire no longer exists. It has been broken up into a number of States no one of which will be strong enough seriously to menace Italy. In order to hasten the break-up, Italy, along with all the greater States associated with her in the war, encouraged the Jugo-Slavic peoples to break away from the Empire and assured them of her sympathy with their aspirations for independence and thus herself assisted in radically altering the circumstances which had justified the London agreement. As parts of the Austro-Hungarian Empire the Jugo-Slavic peoples of the Adriatic coast were Italy's enemies. They may now be her friends, and the way of peace and permanent adjustment lies in arrangements of accommodation, not in military preparation. That, at least, the war has demonstrated.

I am seeking, in short, at one and the same time to make the Italian population on the eastern islands and coasts of the Adriatic safe and secure and to assure Italy of neighbors who will henceforth not suspect and jealously watch her but deal with her in every way that is likely to produce mutual trust and confidence. The League of Nations seems now assured; the United States will be a party to that great association—the United States which is made up of and is the friend of all nations—, and the forces of the world are united for the maintenance of all guarantees of right.

I am glad to be able to assure you that the statesmen who represent France and Great Britain unite with the representatives of the United States in entertaining the earnest hope that Italy will accept this just settlement as her contribution to the longed-for peace of the World.

I am, my dear Mr. Prime Minister,
                    Your sincere friend,   [Woodrow Wilson]

CCL (WP, DLC).
    [1] See A. A. Young to WW, Dec. 13, 1918, n. 1, Vol. 53.

## To Robert Somers Brookings

My dear Mr. Brookings:                    Paris, 13 January, 1919.

I warmly appreciate your letter of December 23rd,[1] which was slow in reaching me, and I hereby accept, as you and they request, the resignation of the members of the Price Fixing Committee, as taking effect March first.

May I not say that I do this with a very full and deep appreciation of the laborious and valuable, indeed indispensable, services which the Committee has rendered? I have followed its conclusions with the greatest interest not only, but with an appreciation of the great sobriety and judgment which characterized them, and I shall long remember with the greatest appreciation my association with them.
          Cordially and sincerely yours,   [Woodrow Wilson]

CCL (WP, DLC).
    [1] R. S., Brookings to WW, Dec. 23, 1918, TLS (WP, DLC).

## To Joseph Patrick Tumulty

[Paris, c. Jan. 13, 1919]

My own thought turned to Mitchell Palmer as successor to Gregory but that appointment is much against Gregory's judgment and this disturbs me. It also disturbs me that, beginning at the bottom of the ladder in the Department of Justice, Todd worked his way to the top and earned every step. I wonder if you have any further advice as to this appointment.          [Woodrow Wilson]

T transcript of CLSsh MS (WP, DLC).

## To Lord Rothschild

My dear Lord Rothschild:                  Paris, 13 January 1919.

I ought long ago to have acknowledged your interesting and generous letter of December 29th[1] but I know that you will pardon my delay in the circumstances.

You are right in thinking that I have very much at heart the interests of the Jewish people and am greatly interested in the development of the plans for Palestine. I hope with all my heart that they can be given satisfactory form and permanency.
          With much appreciation,
               Cordially and sincerely yours,   [Woodrow Wilson]

CCL (WP, DLC).
¹ Lord Rothschild to WW, Dec. 29, 1918, Vol. 53.

## To Douglas Fairbanks

My dear Mr. Fairbanks:                    Paris, 13 January, 1919.

I have been a long time thanking you for the motion picture machine which you so generously had installed for me in the White House,¹ but it has not been, I am sure you will believe, because of any lack of appreciation. We were all delighted with the machine, and before leaving Washington I had occasion to realize how much amusement it was going to give us and how useful it was going to be to us.

It was a very generous thought on your part to provide it, and we all appreciate it deeply.

                    Cordially yours,   [Woodrow Wilson]

CCL (WP, DLC).
¹ See WW to JPT, Oct. 29, 1918, and n. 1 thereto, Vol. 51.

## Two Telegrams from Joseph Patrick Tumulty

[The White House, Jan. 13, 1919]

No. 16. In past two weeks the trend of newspaper dispatches from Paris has indicated a misunderstanding of your [general] attitude toward problems pending at peace conference. One newspaper cablegram today says that France, Italy and Great Britain have agreed to subordinate your league of nations programme to the need for counteracting Bolshevism and collecting damages ———[from Germany]. Another a few days ago reported that Clemenceau had made headway with his insistence upon maintenance of balance of power. Still another outlined victory of Great Britain in her opposition to freedom of seas, stating you had abandoned your position in response to arguments of France, supporting Great Britain. Similar stories would give impression that you were yielding, although we are aware that some of the suggestions for compromise are probably your own. Situation could easily be remedied if you would occasionally call in the three press association correspondents who crossed on George Washington with you, merely giving them an understanding of the developments as they occur and asking them not to use information as coming from you but merely for their own guidance. It would show wisdom of various compromises as well as circumstances of such compromises.

Proposal of Lloyd George that the Russian Bolsheviki be invited to send peace delegates to Paris produced very unfavorable impression everywhere. It is denounced as amazing.    Tumulty.

T telegram (WP, DLC).

The White House, January 13, 1919.

Colby in receipt of letter from Franklin, International Mercantile Marine, with reference to sale of ships.[1] Colby wishes to call your attention to following excerpt from this letter quote While we are loath, under the circumstances to press for early action, yet, in view of the time which has elapsed since we were requested to suspend relations with the British syndicate, we must respectfully ask you to move forward to a conclusion of the matter, as the present uncertainty of the situation is most unfavorable and damaging to our business interests. We would appreciate your taking the necessary steps to bring this matter to an early conclusion. unquote. Have you any word for Colby regarding your attitude in this matter?

Tumulty.

T telegram (J. P. Tumulty Papers, DLC).
    [1] About this matter, see JD to WW, Nov. 18, 1918, n. 1, Vol. 53.

## Two Letters from Robert Lansing

My dear Mr. President:                    Paris. 13th January, 1919.

In response to your letter of January 10th[1] I have to report that Buckley [Buckler] is expected to arrive in Stockholm today. (Monday)                    Faithfully yours,   Robert Lansing

    [1] WW to RL, Jan. 10, 1919, Vol. 53.

My dear Mr. President:                    Paris. 13th January, 1919.

Replying your letter of the 11th,[1] regarding an interview for King Nicholas of Montenegro, I believe in view of the attitude of the Allied Governments towards the King it would be unwise at the present time to have an interview with him.

Faithfully yours,   Robert Lansing

TLS (WP, DLC).
    [1] WW to RL, Jan. 11, 1919, PPC, II, 370.

## To Newton Diehl Baker

[Paris] January 14, 1919.

284. For the Secretary of War, from the President.

I believe it to be necessary for the United States representatives at the Peace Conference not only to be furnished with a statement of the claims of the United States for reparation against the Central Empires but also that they should have before them data showing the comparative basis on which the claims of the different Allied Governments are computed. Before I came to Europe Colonel House with my approval requested General Pershing to assign an Officer whose duty it should be to examine into the claims for reparation in process of preparation by France and Belgium. General Pershing assigned General C. H. McKinstry to Colonel House for this work so as to include an examination of the claims to be presented by Great Britain, Italy, Serbia, Greece and Roumania and that he should proceed to investigate carefully certain type cases and to use the law of averages as the basis for his report. General Pershing points out that General McKinstry's work has grown to larger proportions than he had anticipated and that the work will now require a larger number of officers and men, office room and transportation. General Pershing has asked therefore that I explain this situation to you and that I ask you to authorize him to expend such funds as may be necessary in connection with this matter. I regard this work as essential and accordingly I would be grateful to you if you would take such steps as are necessary to authorize General Pershing to expend such funds as are required.   Woodrow Wilson

T telegram (WP, DLC).


## Two Telegrams to Joseph Patrick Tumulty

Paris Received Jan. 14, 1919.

The appropriation about which I cabled to Martin and Sherley[1] is so absolutely necessary that I think we would be justified in publishing my message if it is necessary for its passage.[2] Otherwise I agree with you that it is inadvisable to publish it.

Woodrow Wilson

[1] See WW to JPT, Jan. 10, 1919 (first telegram of that date), Vol. 53.
[2] Wilson was replying to JPT to WW, Jan. 11, 1919 (second telegram of that date), *ibid*. Representative Joseph Swagar Sherley had already read Wilson's message during the debate on the Famine Relief bill in the House on January 13, 1919. *Cong. Record*, 65th Cong., 3d sess., p. 1350.

Paris Received Jan. 14, 1919

I have approved Vance McCormick's resignation at his urgent request.[1] If our friends on the committee desire any advice about his successor, would suggest Cummings as most available candidate.

Please use this confidentially.          Woodrow Wilson

T telegrams (J. P. Tumulty Papers, DLC).
  [1] McCormick had just resigned as chairman of the Democratic National Committee. *New York Times*, Jan. 15, 1919.

## To John Sharp Williams

Paris [Jan. 14, 1919]

May I not refer to my letter to you about the suffrage amendment[1] and express the hope that a new survey of affairs may convince you of the wisdom of its passage.          Woodrow Wilson

T telegram (J. S. Williams Papers, DLC).
  [1] See WW to J. S. Williams, Nov. 29, 1918, Vol. 53.

## To Park Trammell

[Paris] 14 January 1919.

Looking on at a distance, I am more than ever convinced of the necessity for the adoption of the Suffrage Amendment. I therefore take the liberty of appealing to you once more to support it.
                                        Woodrow Wilson

T telegram (WP, DLC).

## To Frank Mason North

My dear Mr. North:                      Paris, 14 January 1919.

I have your letter of January 11th.[1] It grieves me to feel that I cannot receive you at once to hear the message which you bear from the Executive Committee of the Federal Council of the Churches of Christ in America, but I am sure you will understand when I say that no hour of the day is any longer certainly my own and many commissions of the first importance are seeking interviews which I am obliged to decline and therefore I am going to ask if you will not be kind enough to let me have a written memorandum of the message.

I am sure I need not assure you that the message will, in whatever form it reaches me, receive my most careful attention because I know the spirit and purpose of the gentlemen for whom you are speaking.    Cordially and sincerely yours,    Woodrow Wilson

TLS (F. M North Papers, NjMD).
[1] See F. M. North to WW, Jan. 11, 1919, Vol. 53.


## To Grant Squires

My dear Mr. Squires:                              Paris, 14 January 1919.
    I am in receipt of your letter of December 30th[1] which seems to have come direct and without unusual delay and whose enclosures are apparently quite intact.
    I am very much obliged to you for sending me the information and am heartily glad that you are keeping on the watch.
    In unavoidable haste and with the best wishes for the New Year.
        Cordially and sincerely yours,    [Woodrow Wilson]

CCL (WP, DLC).
[1] See G. Squires to WW, Dec. 30, 1918, Vol. 53.


## Three Telegrams from Joseph Patrick Tumulty

Washington 14 Jan 1919
    On strength your cable[1] House passed by big vote appropriation of one hundred million dollars for food relief        Tumulty

[1] That is, WW to JPT, Jan. 10, 1919 (first telegram of that date), Vol. 53.


Washington [Jan. 14, 1919]
    Tonight the Associated Press representative at Washington notified [me] that his correspondent Probert at Paris cabled him that Ambassador Sharp had resigned. This was embarrassing to me because I was told to remain silent. Sharp is at Washington and will think that I leaked on matter. I wished we could have better cooperation on matters on publicity. I told him that the White House refused to discuss it.                              Tumulty.


Washington [Jan. 14, 1919]
    New York World and Springfield Republican in editorials appearing today take issue with Pichon in his denunciation of the British government's attempt to straighten out the Russian problem

by inviting all Russian factions to attend Peace Conference. Spring-
field Republican says Pichon is in the wrong. New York World says
quote This suggestion from London is the only definite and intelligent [intelligible] policy the allied governments have put forth
since the revolution unquote This represents in my opinion the
sober second thought of the country. All well here. Warmest regards.                                                  Tumulty.

T telegrams (WP, DLC).


## From Thomas Watt Gregory

[Washington, Jan. 14, 1919]

No. 18. Following from Attorney General: "Reliably informed that
well organized movement under way in New England in favor of
league of nations. People being [systematically][1] reached by speeches
and lectures. Many Republicans like Lowell and Taft taking part,
and funds available to sustain work. Anderson[2] is actively partici-
pating, and reports situation most promising. Reported that Balfour
has suggested increase in size of commission. In my opinion addition of Taft and Lowell [Eliot] would wonderfully strengthen your
position on this side, cement public opinion, and disorganize opposition. Believe these two men would loyally support league of
nations. Reported Taft has said he would quit Republican party if
it opposed league. Will you not consider landing at Boston on your
return? Believe this would result in wonderful reception (by people
of your way of thinking) from all New England states. If remarkable
impression created in Europe is followed by reception in America,
demonstrating [substantial] unity of our people, opposition would
be unable to maintain a fight. Am satisfied public opinion here is
sound. New England would be a grand place to start demonstration."                                                  Tumulty.

T telegram (WP, DLC).
 [1] Additions from the TS telegram in WP, DLC.
 [2] That is, George Weston Anderson.


## From Herbert Clark Hoover

Dear Mr. President:                    Paris, 14 January 1919.

There appears to be a great deal of discussion in Washington as
to the continuance of the ban on brewing. Owing to the conditions
produced by the armistice, there is now no shortage of feed grains
in the United States and, therefore, the prohibition of brewing

under the Food Act, from a purely conservation point of view, is no longer warranted. It now becomes purely a temperance question and in this sense is, of course, entirely beyond my province to determine, as none of us can weigh the pros and cons of this situation at such a distance. May I suggest to you that you should dispatch the following telegram to the Cabinet in Washington in order that they may make a decision?

"I am informed by the Food, Fuel and War Industries Administrations that there is no longer any necessity from the point of view of conservation in continuing the ban upon brewing. The problem, therefore, becomes purely one of temperance and I would be glad if the Cabinet would advise me whether, from a temperance point of view and from the legal point of view, since the powers of the government in this matter were exerted as a war conservation measure, we are any longer warranted in suppressing brewing. If the Cabinet is of the opinion that we are no longer warranted in using the war powers for this purpose, I would be glad if they would advise me that I may sign the necessary proclamations in the matter."[1]

Faithfully yours,   Herbert Hoover

TLS (WP, DLC).
[1] Wilson sent this message to the members of the cabinet and to Vice-President Marshall as WW to the Cabinet, Jan. 17, 1919, CC telegram (WP, DLC). Marshall was presiding at cabinet meetings during Wilson's absence at the latter's request.

## Ray Stannard Baker to Cary Travers Grayson, with Enclosure

Dear Admiral:                                    [Paris] Jan. 14th [1919]

This is really very serious. Many of the men are sending hot despatches across—quite a number of which I have seen. They feel that a principle is involved. A similar protest is being made by the British correspondents. It is generally reported that there was a vote in the Conference and that the President and Mr. Lloyd-George were voted down by the French, Italian and Japanese. It is felt that no matter what the agreement is the French, each of whom has his newspaper group will pass on the news to his followers. I report this just as I have it: and am anxious that the President shall know just how the correspondents feel.

Sincerely,   Ray Stannard Baker

ALS (WP, DLC).

E N C L O S U R E

## From Herbert Bayard Swope and Others

Mr. President,                                    [Paris, Jan. 14, 1919]

The American Press delegation in Paris has just been officially informed that the Peace Conference has adopted a rule whereby not only is the press barred from the current sessions but is also excluded from personal contact with members of the several missions. We are also advised that all news of the sessions is to be limited to brief daily communiques emanating from the Secretariat which may be followed by second-day statements in the nature of comment upon the minutes.

We direct your attention to the fact that this method, if followed, will limit our information to things accomplished. It will further prevent the publication of those matters not yet closed which the public demand the right to follow through to their consummation. Unless this right be granted the public will be denied the opportunity to be informed of the positions assumed by the various elements within the Conference, and public opinion thus will have no chance to function in the way that you have always advocated and that you defined in the Fourteen Points.

Wherefore, we vigorously protest on behalf of the American press representatives against what we have every reason to regard as gag rule; and, in common with the action of our British colleagues who have laid their case before the Prime Minister, we appeal to you for relief from this intolerable condition.

We stand where you stand: "Open covenants of peace, openly arrived at!"

Respectfully,    Herbert Bayard Swope. N. Y. World
Arthur M Evans Chicago Tribune
Richard V. Oulahan New York Times
Arthur B Krock, *Courier Journal*
John Edwin Nevin
Laurence Hills New York *Sun*
Burr Price—New York Herald.
R Fink—The Day, N.Y.C.
Ed L Keen, United Press
Jay Jerome Williams Universal
    News Service
L C Probert Associated Press.[1]

TLS (WP, DLC).
[1] Full names for those not previously identified in this series are Arthur Maybury Evans, Reuben Fink, and Edward Leggett Keen.

# From the Diary of Vance Criswell McCormick

January 14 (Tuesday) [1919]

A few days after my arrival in Paris I had an interview with President Wilson and Colonel House, by appointment, in Colonel House's room at Crillon to discuss my resignation as Chairman of the Democratic National Committee which I had proposed to President Wilson by cable before I left America and he requested that I withhold definite action until I could talk the matter over with him before giving his approval.[1] After stating my reasons for resigning, I finally secured the President's consent although he said he had hoped that I might continue on for the present.

During the discussion the President asked me who were the prospective candidates for President. I said there was no announced candidate as yet but McAdoo's friends seem to have the most active organization. House suggested Hoover as a possibility for the Democratic nomination and Pershing for Republican. The President then said that he would not consider being a candidate again unless there was some great catastrophe involving the world's affairs as well as our own which might make him the issue, in which event he might be compelled to run.

He asked me who I would suggest as my successor and I suggested Homer Cummings, the present vice-chairman, which he approved and told me to wire Tumulty of his preference which he could use if the President's advice was sought by the National Committee. I at once sent a cable to Hollister,[2] secretary of the National Committee, to release my written resignation which I had left in his hands in America and I also notified Tumulty as directed by the President.

Printed copy (V. C. McCormick Papers, CtY).
[1] V. C. McCormick to WW, Dec. 19, 1918, and WW to V. C. McCormick, Dec. 21, 1918, both T telegrams (WP, DLC).
[2] That is, William R. Hollister, Assistant Secretary of the Democratic National Committee.

# From the Diary of Edith Benham

January 14, 1919

This evening is one of the first times I have had a really long talk with the President about really vital things for conversation is usually more or less general. Tonight Dr. Grayson was out and Mrs. Wilson, he and I were alone. He had been speaking of the Conference, how annoying Pichon, the Minister of Foreign Affairs is, as a presiding officer. He never seems to get any of the proceedings correct and all his summaries are invariably wrong. Yesterday, for instance, there was a question of procedure of the first large general meeting—the number of representatives each nation should have—this for the allies only, and Pichon's summary was that the enemy nations should have no representatives there having been no question of the enemies coming at all. The Conference, too, is very much wrought up over the leakage of news to the press. They have tried to give it out through a central news bureau or committee, but very important things are constantly filtering, with consequent bad feeling with the reporters and very naturally so. The leakage is entirely with the French the President feels, and today he spoke of it and said it could only have come through someone in the room at the sessions.

Mrs. Wilson spoke of what Mr. White had said to her this afternoon at the G.P.[1] in regard to the inadvisability of the President's returning. He said he belonged in the opposite camp but he felt it would be preposterous for anyone to deny that the President is the greatest statesman of the age and *the* man of all the nations, and that his admiration for him was great. He thought from what people told him that it would be in the nature of an anti-climax if he came back again and that it would be better if he could settle most of the great questions before he left, and then leave the others with the fact of his return in case of necessity as a club to hold over the conference. The President said he agreed with the idea in part of an anti-climax and he could see much against it, but he felt Mr. White took his opinion from club men and the newspapers and he couldn't consider them representative of American feeling as they were controlled by large moneyed interests, and not in touch with the people as the small country newspapers, which really don't print much news and are only echos of local life and hence not representative of general thought. He said that he had always found that if you told the people the right and pointed out ideals to be followed, they invariably backed you up. He dwelt on the fact that there is a latent consciousness of world ideals, new ones, which may have come about without the whole body of the people being conscious of them, and yet when they were presented to the American public they were supported and they would say, "Why, yes, that's true," because the consciousness had been latent in them, and when they heard voice given to them they knew they had heard what they had thought. He said he had never spoken at any time to the American people anything which was true, even if a new process of thought was involved, that it had not been enthusiastically supported. In other words, he knew he always had the support of the public for the real and true.

He drew a brilliant parallel of the unconsciousness of thought development from the speeches of Hayne and Webster on the secession question. Hayne's speech was brilliant, he showed the undoubted legal right of the states to secede and that idea found instant response in the Southern states where thought and business were at stagnation point and there had been no change for generations. Then came Webster's great reply. He showed that emigration had gone to the new states in the West, and that for the first time a national spirit was awakened. After the war of 1812 the states began to be a nation, before they were only a confederation, and then when Webster made his great speech the people of the East and Western states recognized that in their latent consciousness had existed the idea of national unity and the impossibility of secession despite the legal right and there must be no division. So he said Webster gave expression to this inarticulate consciousness and men arose to defend this new national ideal.

I asked how he got his impression, if not from the papers, of what the new national ideals are, or what truths are to be presented to the people. He said he would get them from different sources and piece them together as one should a mosaic, that I must remember he had been a student of American political history for years and had saturated himself in it. I said, "But these are deductions only, aren't they,—helpful—but don't you go deeper than that? Don't you feel as though you are dipping into ether which hold[s] all things, getting from some other source than deduction the consciousness of the new ideals of America, and then making them articulate?" He said he thought possibly so, after thinking for a minute, but he felt himself so filled with American thought that the new thoughts came to him and he was able to tell them to his countrymen. All this he said very humbly and very simply as he does everything. I spoke of the way the little people, the poor, look to him as a Messiah to give a new light in the world, possibly because they had not had a practical person to give practical expression to their aspirations. He said the religious teaching hadn't found a practical solution for the troubles of the world and states and they must have some one to give them practical relief for their distress.

He spoke of Mexico and the criticism because he had not intervened and of his belief in the Virginia Bill of Rights and the right of the governed to elect the form of the government under which they should live. He said the Mexicans and the Russians now were groping through infinite bloodshed and in very doubtful ways to evolve their new form of government, and we had no right to tell them what form of government they must have. They must do it themselves. He said that capital which also directly and indirectly controlled the press had criticised this, and had demanded protection for the money they had invested under the unstable Mexican Government, and this had been the outcry we know, but the people of the United States had not been for intervention, recognizing latently the right of the Mexicans to evolve their own form of government.

¹ That is, grand party.


## From the Diary of Dr. Grayson

Wednesday, January 15, 1919.

The Supreme War Council was continuing its sessions endeavoring to deal not only with the matters that affected the German situation but also with a number of problems that had grown out of the Russian problem. The President found it almost impossible to reconcile the views of the French. They were very anxious that whatever modifications were to be made in the coming extension of the Armistice terms provision be made which would render Germany absolutely helpless. Clemenceau was being backed by Foch in the demand that there be created a Rhinish republic which would act in the nature of a buffer state. The President made it very plain in his conferences that the carrying out of such a program would create new animosities that eventually would turn the sympathy of the world generally against France. He was very tired when he returned home tonight and after dinner he and I discussed matters generally.


## Hankey's Notes of Two Meetings of the Council of Ten¹

Quai d'Orsay, January 15, 1919, 10:30 A.M.

BC-2

[The council continued discussion of the draft rules of procedure for the conference. Lloyd George said that there had been unauthorized leaks to the press about protection of the German gold reserve and about the apportionment of delegates. He also thought it important that the press "not give prominence" to views expressed by one power which were "not in complete accord" with those of other powers. The discussions usually ended in agreement, he added, but, if the press "jumped in," the differences might become "stereotyped." He noted that the publication in *L'Humanité*² of Pichon's

¹ The complete text of these notes is printed in PPC, III, 543-56.
² See FLP to RL, Jan. 12, 1919 (first telegram of that date), n. 2.

reply to the British government's views on Russia had had a bad effect. The council agreed that only the secretariat would release information about the meetings and that the press "should be prevented, as far as possible, from discussing controversial matters as between the Great Powers represented."

[After further discussion, it was agreed that the powers would be represented by plenipotentiary delegates as follows: five for the United States, the British Empire, France, Italy, and Japan; three for Brazil; two for Belgium, China, Greece, Poland, Portugal, Rumania, Serbia, and the Czechoslovak Republic; and one for Cuba, Guatemala, Haiti, Honduras, Liberia, Nicaragua, Panama, and Siam. Australia, Canada, South Africa, and India (including the Native States) would have two delegates each, and New Zealand one. The representatives of the Dominions (including Newfoundland) and India might be included in the representation of the British Empire by the panel system. Montenegro would be represented by one delegate, but the rules for this would not be fixed until the political situation there had been cleared up. The "conditions of the representation of Russia" would be fixed by the conference "at the moment when the business concerning Russia" was examined.]

PRESIDENT WILSON thought that some publication should be issued in order to remove any misapprehension. He thought that the Powers might think that each of the Delegates had a vote, and that the number of Delegates would affect the number of votes. That misapprehension should be removed. The newspapers should be put in a position to explain that the number of Delegates did not represent a certain number of votes. Each country was merely put in a position to explain its case and in addition each Power was at liberty to change its Representatives from time to time.

(It was agreed that some publication should be made in newspapers in order to remove any misapprehension which might exist about the functions of the Delegates appointed to the Conference as regards the numbers accredited.)

[It was agreed that the great powers should take precedence in the following order: "Amérique, États-Unis d', Empire Britannique, France, Italie, Japon." Provision was also made for verifying credentials, appointing officers, and establishing a secretariat. An article on providing information to the press through the secretariat concluded: "The Powers here represented and their Delegates expressly renounce all other communications concerning the proceedings of the Conferences."]

MR. LLOYD GEORGE said that this clause dealt with a very important point. Representatives of the Press had enquired from him whether they were entitled to go to any of the delegates and ask for information. He had replied, "Certainly not." This was undoubtedly the view held by his colleagues.

PRESIDENT WILSON enquired whether there was any serious objection in the case of the large Conferences to having members of the Press present. He asked this question because leaks were absolutely certain to occur in such large Conferences, where a number of channels existed. In these large Conferences nothing of an embarrassing nature would be discussed. Important and delicate questions would have been discussed beforehand and only such questions as had been digested in various ways would be placed before these Conferences. Thus, questions such as those of Poland, Russia, etc., would never be discussed in public in the large Conferences. He himself would favour complete publicity rather than the publication of incorrect information through leakage.

MR. BALFOUR thought that President Wilson's proposals were open to the prima facie assumption that all the work of the big Conferences would be formal; that is to say, that merely agreed propositions would come before those Conferences. As a matter of fact, many other questions, such as those relating to the creation of new States, were bound to come under discussion. If Press representatives were admitted at these big Conferences, all questions would have to be thrashed out separately and it would be found necessary to bring into the small Conferences Czecho-Slovaks, Arabs, and others, in order that an agreement might be reached beforehand. It would end in these representatives of small States taking part in the discussions of the Great Powers.

PRESIDENT WILSON replied that his comment on that was, that it would not be possible in a big Conference to discuss such questions. The Representatives of the small States had, as a matter of fact, already stated their case in documents which had been published. They could say no more. It would, however, give them satisfaction to publish their views abroad. But, on the other hand, it would not be necessary for us to state our case in public. Written documents could be issued.

M. PICHON thought if President Wilson's proposals were accepted they would provoke unending discussions. If the Representatives of the smaller States knew that their speeches would be reported in extenso in the newspapers, they would feel bound to enter fully into all discussions.

MR. LLOYD GEORGE hoped that President Wilson would not press the case until it had been further considered. There was a great deal to say in favour of President Wilson's idea as regards the publicity to be given to the large Conferences, but he feared there would be no end to these Conferences if reporters were there. One Delegate would get up and put forward all his case, so that it could be published in his native land and, as there were some twenty native lands, once they began that sort of business there would be no end to it. Again, someone would have to reply and he was not sure whether in the end this might not lead to unpleasant disputes in the Conference Room.

M. PICHON said there was another point of view which should be considered. During the study of the Peace Preliminaries it would be dangerous to let Germany know our difficulties. It was not desired to make a present to her of arguments which might divide the Allies and so enable her to escape the necessity of accepting the conditions of the Preliminary Peace.

M. CLEMENCEAU said there was another point also to be considered. They had agreed that all decisions reached by the five Great Powers should be unanimous. In order to obtain this unanimity he would himself be prepared to give way on some points, and when these questions finally came before the large Conferences he would accept the decision so reached in silence. But if the Press were admitted to these Conferences, and the question came under discussion, he would be bound to take part in the debate. He could not let it be said that he had refused to speak on a question about which he held decided views. It would, however, clearly be seen that if he then expressed his opinion it would raise great confusion at the meetings.

BARON SONNINO expressed his complete agreement with Mr. Balfour. If the Press were admitted, not only would the small Powers put the whole of their case before the Conference, but the Great Powers would be compelled to do the same. Each Power would, therefore, be obliged to put forward the whole of its case—the public would expect that. As a result, the Conferences would never end.

PRESIDENT WILSON enquired whether they could really avoid, in any case, the difficulties mentioned by Baron Sonnino. He did not think they were going to escape a syllable and they would still be obliged to give their answers even if the Conferences were held in private.

BARON SONNINO said a compromise might frequently be arrived at between two small States in private. At a large Conference, if held in private, the grounds upon which this decision had been reached need not be given. But if the Press were admitted, the parties to the compromise would feel compelled to put forward the whole of their case for the benefit of their countrymen.

PRESIDENT WILSON enquired whether, even if the Press were

excluded, any method could be found to prevent the leakage of information regarding the discussions that took place in the Conference.

MR. LLOYD GEORGE thought that the only way to prevent leakage was not to give information. In the case of the Supreme War Council it had been found quite possible to maintain the desired secrecy.

BARON SONNINO held the view that a leakage of information was in many cases preferable to publicity.

PRESIDENT WILSON said he had merely raised the point for discussion and he did not wish to press the question, but there certainly were two big sides to it.

MR. LLOYD GEORGE said that all he wished was to press that for the moment the case should not be decided.

M. CLEMENCEAU thought that, whatever decision was arrived at, it would be necessary to give information to the public of the various countries as a block, giving no advantage to one country over another.

(It was decided that the question should receive further consideration at a later date.)

[The next topic discussed was the provision that French be the official language of the conference. Pichon supported this, but Lloyd George proposed that both French and English be acknowledged as official, and Sonnino said that, if the historic rule was to be changed, the Italian language should also be admitted.]

PRESIDENT WILSON agreed that they all recognised the historic claim of the French language. There were very few languages that excelled it in precision and delicacy of shading. But leaving this question out of consideration, he would invite attention to the fact that English was the diplomatic language of the Pacific. Negotiations, for instance, between Japan and China were conducted in English. All diplomatic transactions on that side of the globe were in English. Further, there was an example of the use of three official languages in Switzerland, where French, Italian and German were used.

MR. LLOYD GEORGE enquired whether this was really the case.

PRESIDENT WILSON continuing, said that the question under consideration was not really a matter for discrimination, but a question of general use. English was comprehended by a larger population than the language of any other of the peoples represented at the Conference. Therefore, it seemed to him that the language which was the official language of the greater part of the world was the most suitable language for a Conference of this nature. But he did not wish to propose that English should be the only official language. His proposal was that both French and English should be accepted as such. He fully recognised the claims of the Italians, both on account of the beauty of their language and on sentimental and other grounds. But it was so plainly the fact that English was now the language used by the great majority of the peoples represented at the Conference that it justified discrimination as against Italian.

BARON SONNINO pointed out that at Versailles, though the procès-verbaux of the Supreme War Council were printed only in English and French, the conclusions reached were printed in three languages. Was there any objection to the resolutions of the Peace Conference being given in three languages.

MR. LLOYD GEORGE suggested that in that case they should also be given in Japanese. He thought the question could only refer to the adoption of two languages or one language.

BARON SONNINO thought that, in the case of disputes, a decision as to the correct interpretation to be given would be easier if three languages were given, especially as it should be remembered that only a slight difference existed between nuances of the French and Italian languages.

PRESIDENT WILSON said he wished to draw attention to the second paragraph of this Article, which apparently entitled Delegates to submit observations in any language they chose, provided a translation in French was provided. It would obviously be a great burden to supply a French translation of every document and this part of the Article should not be retained.

M. CLEMENCEAU said that he was greatly embarrassed. He fully admitted that the English language was a most widely-spread language and had brought with it great activity and liberal institutions. Now, in ancient times, Latin had admittedly been the official language and French had followed it. The French language possessed the great advantage of extreme precision, which was useful in the case of official documents. Mr. Lloyd George had said that in South Africa and Canada the use of two languages had caused no trouble. He had also said that the interpretation of legal documents gave rise to greater troubles than the interpretation of Treaties. As a matter of fact, differences of opinion in the interpretation of Treaties led to the most serious upheavals. This fact had been fully recognised at the Hague and even at the Berlin Conferences, where it had been agreed to accept the French language. Still, he was prepared to admit that other languages (English and Italian) had claims and he was fully prepared to recognise those claims. He proposed, therefore, that they should retain perfect liberty to use the English, Italian, and French languages at the Conferences, without the necessity of supplying French translations. Each of the texts, whether in English, French, or Italian, would be treated as the standard text. But if any difficulties or differences arose as to the correct interpretation, the French text would be recognised as the official text. In other words the three languages received complete recognition, but, in case of dispute, the French text would be accepted as the correct one. To give effect to his views he would make the following proposal:

"The English, French, and Italian languages will be recognised as the official languages of the Conference, the French version holding good in case of dispute."

PRESIDENT WILSON enquired whether the procès-verbaux should be kept in three languages.

M. CLEMENCEAU replied in the affirmative.

MR. BALFOUR thought that in reality there was no difference between the procedure proposed by M. Clemenceau and that given in the original text, since French was still to be the official language, which was to be accepted in case of dispute.

MR. LLOYD GEORGE said he would prefer to leave the case until the afternoon, in order that it might be given further consideration.

(The Meeting then adjourned, to meet again in the afternoon at 2.30 p.m.)

T MS (SDR, RG 256, 180.03101/5, DNA).

Quai d'Orsay, January 15, 1919, 2:30 P.M.[1]

BC-2+

M. PICHON said that the question of languages remained to be settled. He asked whether the text proposed by M. Clemenceau was accepted by the Meeting. This text was to the effect that the English, French, and Italian languages would be recognized as official languages at the Conference, the French version holding good in case of dispute.

PRESIDENT WILSON said that he wished to present one of the aspects of this matter. Undoubtedly, French had been the language of European diplomacy in the past, but we were now dealing with a new case. This case did not affect only Europe: the rest of the world had come into the arena. A new Great Power was now concerned in the business of world diplomacy. He referred to the United States, whose language was English. The precedent in favour of the French language in diplomacy was only a European precedent. The language of diplomacy on the other side of the globe was

[1] The complete text of these notes is printed in *PPC*, III, 557-65.

English. There were, therefore, two precedents. Neither could be followed exclusively, as this was a Congress of the whole world. A very large part of the people affected by the settlements we hope to make use the English language. It was doubtful whether Americans, if they had before them a French document, could ever feel quite sure that it accurately represented their thoughts. The same doubtless was the case with a Frenchman, if confronted with a document in English. He felt, therefore, that there should be two official languages. He made this proposal without intending any disrespect for the Italian language, the literature of which was justly admired throughout the world. The Italian language, however, would be known only to a small part of the representatives constituting the Congress. If the language of a minority were to be given official status, this principle would have to extend to the languages of other minorities. Harmony could be attained as between the languages by the Permanent Secretariat, the creation of which was contemplated. The officials of this Secretariat would, doubtless, have a perfect knowledge both of French and of English. Such knowledge of a greater number of languages would be hard to obtain. He therefore advocated the adoption of a bi-lingual scheme with great earnestness, as what we were about to do was to affect the future of the world, and all needless difficulties should be avoided. He therefore proposed that French and English should be the official languages.

MR. LLOYD GEORGE then suggested that the English and French languages should be recognized as the official languages of the Conferences, and that in any case of dispute the referee should be the League of Nations.

M. PICHON said that he wished to make certain observations. He wished to point out that this was not the first time that the nations of America were represented in an international diplomatic Conference in Europe. He would instance the two Hague Conferences. In both cases French had been adopted unanimously as the official language. At these Conferences, not only had the United States been represented, but also Brazil, Cuba, Mexico, and the Argentine. That very morning President Wilson had recognized that French had an historical privilege in this matter. He therefore appealed to him in order that, at the end of a War in which France had suffered so heavily, she should not find herself by the very first act of the Conference deprived of this ancient prerogative. M. Clemenceau, in a conciliatory spirit, had agreed that there should be two other official languages in addition to French, only reserving for the last the text which might be appealed to in exceptional cases of disputed interpretation.

BARON SONNINO said that he was satisfied with M. Clemenceau's formula, which recognized three languages as equally official, and, as a matter of convenience, reserved one for reference in case of contest. This was a departure from precedent. If a departure from precedent was to be made, he urged most strongly that Italian should not be excluded. Italy had put four to five million soldiers in the field, and that should be taken into account.

PRESIDENT WILSON said that if he listened only to his sentiment he would yield at once to M. Pichon's appeal. He and the people of the United States felt nothing but admiration and affection for France, but he felt obliged in this matter to omit sentiment. The work of this Conference concerned the future and not the past. The documents prepared by it were not merely to be useful to historians, but were to be the basis of the life and of the action of Governments in the future. Amongst the peoples to be affected by these documents were a very considerable number whose speech would be English. He had constantly to remind himself that the task in hand was a practical one and not a sentimental one. He was not concerned with the respective merits of various languages, but only with the case of interpretation in the future furnished by any one of them. He would be greatly distressed if it were thought that he felt any disrespect for any language. He wished the future to think that this Conference had done its best in a practical spirit, and placed in the hands of posterity the most useful instruments that could be devised.

M. PICHON drew attention to the procedure followed by the Joint Secretariat of the Supreme War Council at Versailles. He read the note appended to the procès-verbaux by the Joint Secretariat, which is as follows:

"The French text of the Minutes was prepared in the French Section, and has been approved by the Joint Secretariat. The English text was prepared in advance in the English Section for the benefit of the British Government. It differs in no essential from the French, but the latter is the official text."

MR. LLOYD GEORGE said that when this had been decided the case lay between two European Powers. There was now another Power whose language was English and, moreover, the affairs of the Congress concerned the whole world. He, further, would point out that, when the Supreme War Council met in London, the official language was English. It was only French when the meetings took place in France. In addition to North America, the population of India should be considered. It might safely be said that English was the language of some 500,000,000 or 600,000,000 people. He had no desire to minimise the importance of The Hague Conferences which had been referred to, but there was no doubt that the public had been at that time apathetic, and had taken very little interest in what was debated there. Such was not the case now. Practical considerations, therefore, inclined him to support President Wilson.

M. CLEMENCEAU said there was, perhaps, more agreement than appeared on the surface. He, for one, would never forget that, but for the intervention of English-speaking peoples, not only from America but from the British Empire, France would have been lost. He also, like President Wilson, wished to make a new world and to do new things, but (it was perhaps a trite observation) the future was attached to the past, and had its root in it. The English would remain English and the French French. This war had been a European war. Peoples had come to it from all parts of the world, but it had occurred in France. He agreed that it was indispensable to pay a tribute to the people who had come from so far and in so generous a spirit, but he would point out that in this matter something new was being done. He himself, a French statesman, had proposed that the official documents which an Englishman or an American would get should be in English. That was a novelty, but some care must be taken. If, in the archives at The Hague, for instance, a document in the French language were kept, which in quite exceptional circumstances might be required by a tribunal for the correct interpretation of a text, in what way could this offend any nation? In respect to Italian, he was opposed to its exclusion. Italian was spoken in Italy, in Asia Minor, in the Argentine. We were endeavouring to give a status to small Nations. Why should we therefore limit the official languages of Great Powers? He felt that as each nation matured it would acquire a right to a text in its own language. But, nevertheless, there must at all times be one final text to which to appeal. He therefore held to the proposal he had made that morning.

MR. LLOYD GEORGE said that we need not for the moment decide whether there should be two or three official languages. The point under consideration was whether one should have the position of a final standard, for this language would in effect be the official language. If French were adopted for its purpose, it would be the duty of all concerned to scrutinize the text very carefully. He, for his part, did not feel competent of his ability to detect the shades of meaning in a French text. He would therefore revert to his proposal that when difficulties of interpretation arose the case should be referred to the League of Nations. There was a precedent for this in Canada, where laws and enactments were promulgated in two tongues. When the Court declares that the texts were different the matter was referred to Parliament, which then decided what the meaning should be. He made these observations without prejudice to the question of whether Italian should be an official language or not, though he felt that perhaps one Latin and one Anglo-Saxon language would suffice.

PRESIDENT WILSON pointed out that all Treaties between France and the United States had been drawn up in the two languages; the English version was submitted to the American Senate for confirmation. Should any differences of opinion arise in the interpretation of the agreement between the two countries, the only solution could be a friendly meeting between representatives. Neither language in this case could be the standard.

M. CLEMENCEAU said that if arbitration occurred the arbited [arbiter] would have to decide on the French text. He further pointed out that the Treaty of Versailles,[2] which concerned America, had been drawn up in French.

PRESIDENT WILSON retorted that at the time of that Treaty America had no Constitution requiring reference of Treaties to the Senate. He further pointed out that the Bryan Treaty[3] had been drawn up in two languages, and a special official status had not been granted to either.

M. PICHON said that that was the first time that French had been challenged as the language of diplomacy throughout the world. Even such as related to customs, telegraphs, cables, treaties of commerce, &c., were made in French. Even Bismarck, who was no friend of France, had raised no objection to the use of French in the Treaty of Berlin.

MR. BALFOUR said that Great Britain had always accepted the tradition of French as the diplomatic language. As between France and England, the French text would undoubtedly have been appealed to in any case of dispute; but as in the United States it was the Senate that had authority to conclude treaties, it was clear that that body must ask for an English text.

M. CLEMENCEAU said that he adhered to his proposal, and did not feel that he could make any further concession.

PRESIDENT WILSON suggested that the subject should be postponed and reconsidered at a later date.

[After further discussion and agreement on various procedures to be followed, Pichon noted that the decision that only official communiqués be given to the press required measures to check

---

[2] That is, the Anglo-American Preliminary Treaty of Peace of January 20, 1783.
[3] About which, see the Enclosure printed with WJB to JPT, April 8, 1913, Vol. 27, and the index references under "Bryan, William Jennings, and conciliation ('cooling off') treaties" in Vol. 39.

the dispatch of telegrams to the press in other countries, and he proposed that each power delegate a representative for this purpose.]

PRESIDENT WILSON said that this proposal caused him some embarrassment. Not long before he had left for America the Government had taken over the cables. It had then been suggested that this was done because he was coming to Europe, and meant to prevent the forwarding of any message unfavourable to himself. He had repudiated this insinuation, but if he now agreed to the censorship he would be convicting himself. In effect, he did not believe that anything was sent to America apart from the official communiqués, save what the American journalists obtained from the local Press. There were some eighty American journalists engaged in sending cables. The censorship of all their messages would involve a great deal of work and would entail great delay. He was of opinion that this matter could be set right if great care were taken by all concerned in the Conferences themselves. He also pointed out that France, if she so desired, could refuse any messages returning from America.

MR. LLOYD GEORGE said that he was not certain that if information went to America, it would not on its return find its way into the British Press. It would certainly cause great discontent if the British Press obtained its information in this roundabout fashion. It was not possible to allow one half of the world to obtain news while depriving the other half.

PRESIDENT WILSON said that up to date nothing had been done in America to set the world on fire. He thought we could afford during the initial stage, when nothing of a very inflammatory nature was being discussed, to put the Press on trial. The British Government and the United States Government, and perhaps other Governments, dealt with one man, who acted as liaison between them and the Press. That person could be asked to assemble the pressmen and obtain a pledge from them to do nothing which might hamper the success of the Conference.[4]

M. CLEMENCEAU doubted whether this method would be successful in France.

MR. LLOYD GEORGE was of the same opinion with regard to Great Britain, but was willing to give this method a trial.

[4] "Mr. Wilson thought that what had transpired so far in these private sessions, would not set the world on fire, even if it became public. He suggested that it might be advisable to have the representative of each delegation in charge of the Press, assemble his journalists, and inform them that those present had entered into a gentlemen's agreement not to discuss on the outside what was said during the conversation.

"It was agreed that all those present place themselves under bond not to say to any journalist anything not contained in the official communique." ACNP notes, Jan. 15, 1919. T MS (SDR, RG 256, 180.03101/5, DNA).

MR. LLOYD GEORGE drew attention to Regulation No. 7, which he felt was not practicable. He felt that it would be impossible for the Secretariat to furnish bulletins in the time specified. He therefore suggested the following alternative:

"The Conference to give general directions to the Secretariat as to what should be published, and what should not be published. If the Secretariat were in agreement on the text, publication would follow at once. If not, reference should be made to the heads of Delegations, or to any nominee acting on their behalf."

(This proposal was adopted.)

[There was further discussion of procedures of the conference.]

MR. BALFOUR enquired whether it would be advisable to obtain from the General Conference an endorsement of the regulations now agreed upon.

M. PICHON was of opinion that if all these regulations were submitted to the Conference, there would be a protracted debate, especially on the subject of the numbers of Delegates. The small Powers were well aware that these regulations were being prepared by the Great Powers. No protest had as yet been made.

PRESIDENT WILSON enquired whether there was any objection to the communication to the Press by the Secretariat of all the conclusions reached that day.

MR. LLOYD GEORGE suggested that a short communication should be prepared containing items of such interest as the numbers of Delegates, the panel system, that there was no question of voting by Delegates, but that each Delegation, whatever its size, would be regarded as one.

(It was decided that the next Meeting should take place at 10:30 a.m. on the following day.)

T MS (SDR, RG 256, 180.03101/6, DNA).

## From Raymond Poincaré

Dear Mr President,                                        [Paris] 15.1.19

I thank you very much for the kind invitation Mr Jusserand transmitted to me in your name. My wife and myself, we should be very glad to attend, with Mrs Wilson and with you, the play given to-morrow by the gallant American soldiers. But we have forbidden ourselves to go to the theatre till the treaty of peace, because of the great mourning of the Country I represent and of the still enduring sufferings of the liberated provinces. I am of course obliged to a peculiar reserve. I apologize for that involuntary impediment and I am very grateful to you.

Will you believe me, dear Mr President,

faithfully yours,   R Poincaré

ALS (WP, DLC).

## Joseph Clark Grew to Gilbert Fairchild Close, with Enclosure

Dear Mr. Close:                              Paris, January 15, 1919.

I beg to enclose herewith a copy of a lengthy telegram from Mr. Polk at Washington, embodying the text of a telegram received at the Department of State from the American Legation at Peking, suggesting the inclusion of a permanent settlement of the Chinese question by the Peace Conference, which the American Commission would be pleased to have you bring to the special attention of the President.

I am, my dear Mr. Close,    Sincerely yours,   J. C. Grew

TLS (WP, DLC).

### E  N  C  L  O  S  U  R  E

Washington, January 10, 1919.

168. URGENT.

Following telegram dated January 6th, 8 p.m. received from Legation at Peking.

"I beg to request you present the following to the President while he is in Europe. I feel in duty bound to call your attention to the important necessity of including a thoroughgoing and permanent settlement of the Chinese question among the arrangements to be made for the establishing of a desirable Peace. I appeal to you directly not only because of your determined purpose to create a just foundation for human relations throughout the world but also because you have become to the people of China the embodiment of their best hopes and aspirations. Your championship of the four great principles laid down in your speech of July 4th, has found a deep response throughout China. These people whose rights have been trodden under foot while the War of liberation was going on in Europe, know from their own bitter experience, the vast importance of these principles for protecting free development and justice within the nations and for protecting them from coer[c]ion, plots and conspiracies from without. Never before have the words of a foreign statesman entered so deeply and directly into the hearts of the Chinese people from the President of China[1] who has again and again cited them in his manifestoes down throughout all the ranks of the people. Though with bitterness akin to despair they observed that while the Western Powers were fighting for human rights in Europe the rights of the Chinese people were invaded by one of the Allies[2] with every device of corruption and device of coercion, they now again have raised their hearts with hope and confidence that those who defeated evil in Europe with their leader and spokesman the President of the United States will no longer allow in Asia the unjust practices of military domination, secret trifling with fundamental rights and the corruption of the life of a people. They ask no charity but justice, they ask no succor but the assurance that the constant exertion of evil influences from without and the attempt of Foreign Military Autocrats to seize control of Chinese resources, finance and defenses shall be put an end to so that the Chinese people may continue the arduous work of establishing a representative Government without having every constructive attempt interfered with and every weakness ag[g]ravated by selfish interference from without.

I need not recall to you that the action of China during the war was inspired by the action of America a desire to realize our common ideals of freedom and justice. It was the liberal elements that are working for representative Government which determined the rupture of diplomatic relations in February 1917. Could we at that time have devoted attention to China her entire course in the war could have been guided by America as China sought earnestly of one accord to follow this guidance. The new President though trained in the older school of statesmanship singled out your greeting as the most noteworthy statement upon his accession and has since in words and actions expressed his desire to guide the country after the models of American statesmanship. In their trouble, aggravated by (?) however both sides have repeatedly and fervently expressed the assurance that if you would consent to mediate all China would be happy to accept your judgment and advice. Such has been the attitude of the Chinese people throughout war during the latter part of which unhappily the controlling power in the Government fell into the hands of powerful men who through ignorance, corruption and treachery prostituted their public trust to Japanese desire for power.

[1] That is, Hsü Shih-ch'ang.
[2] Japan.

Nor need I more than summarize the acts of Japan during the fateful years of the war while her Allies were shedding streams of blood for liberty. In 1915 coercion was applied. China was forced by threats to solidify and extend the privileged position of Japan in Manchuria and Mongolia and to agree prospect[ive]ly to a like regime in Shantung together with the beginnings of a special position in Fukien province. After this there was a change of methods although the policy tended to the same end unveiling domination over China. Instead of coercion, used secret and corrupt influence through alliance with purchaseable officials kept in office by Japanese support.

The latter insidious policy is more dangerous because it gives the appearance that rights are duly acquired through grant of the Chinese Government; no demands or ultimatums are necessary because corrupt officials strongly supported by Japanese finance acting absolutely in the secret channels suppressing all discussion with the strong arm of the police, are able to exercise contractual rights regular in form though of corrupt secret origin and evil tendency.

Japanese have used every possible means to demoralize China by creating and sustaining trouble by supporting and financing most objectionable elements, particularly a group of corrupt and vicious military governors or in their methods by employing instigators of trouble by protection given to bandits by the introduction of most favored nation clause and opium, by the corruption of officials through loans, bribes and threats, by the wrecking of native banks and the depreciation of local currency by illegal export of the copper currency of the people, by the local attempts to break down the salt administration monopoly, persistent efforts to prevent China from going into the war and then seeing to it that China was never in a position to render to the common cause such aid as would be in her power, and as she would willingly render if, left to herself, finally by utilizing the war and the preoccupation of the Allies for enmeshing China in the terms of a secret Military Alliance.

As a result of these methods and manipulations, Japan has gained the following: a consolidation of her special position in Manchuria and Eastern Mongolia, and the foundation of the same in Shantung and Fukien; control in the matters of Chinese finance through the control of the Bank of Communication and the Bureau of Public Printing, and the appointment of a high financial adviser together with the adoption of the unsound gold note scheme happily not yet put in force. She has secured extensive railway concession in Manchuria, Shantung, Chihli [Chi-lin?] and Kiangsu, mining rights in various provinces and special monopolistic rights through the KIRIN Forestry Loan, the telephone loan and others. Through the Secret

Military Convention, Japan attempts, not only to control the Military policy of China, but incidently national resources, such as iron deposits. All these arrangements are so secretly made that in most cases, not even the foreign office is in possession of the documents relating thereto. Together with this goes the persistent assertion of special interests, which are interpreted as a position of predominance.

I realize that this is a strong *attaint*, and I feel the fullest responsibility in making these statements to you. Fundamentally friendly to the Japanese as my published expressions show, I have been forced through the experience of five years to the conclusion that the methods applied by the Japanese Military masters can lead only to evil, and destruction, and also that they will not be stopped by any consideration of fairness and justice, but only by the definite knowledge that such action will not be tolerated. As a steady stream of information from every source as well as my own experience have made this conclusion inevitable, I owe the duty to present it to you, and to extend the American government in no uncertain terms, nor is this said in any spirit of bitterness against the Japanese people, but from the conviction that the policy pursued by their military masters can in the end bring only misery and woe to them and the World.

During this period it was not possible for the European Powers or the United States to do anything for China. The United States through assisting all other Allies financially could not contribute one dollar towards maintaining the financial independence of China as undivided attention was necessary to the requirements of the west front. The Lansing Ishii notes[3] undoubtedly intended to express friendly attitude towards any legi[ti]mate aspirations of Japan while safeguarding the rights of China, was pe[r]verted by the Japanese into an acknowledgement of their privileged position in China. Now at last when the pressure has been released America and the European countries must face the issue which has been created which is whether a vast peaceable and industrious population, but not now much above articulate desire, is to be allowed to determine their own life in the exercise of free and just Government, shall become material to be molded by the secrecy and plottings of a foreign military despotism into an instrument of its power. If it is said that the aims of Japan are unfounded but economic and in just response to needs of Japan's expanding population it must be remembered that every advantage is gained and maintained by political and military pressure and that it is exploited by the rights

[3] About which, see the index references under "Ishii, Kikujiro" in Vol. 44 of this series.

of aliens by the same means in a fashion taking no account of the rights of other foreign nations, or of the Chinese themselves. Divested of their political character and military aims, the economic activities of Japan would arouse no opposition. The fact that at present, when it has been announced that Japanese agreement will tolerate only bona fide economic business in China, hushed iron enterprises, loans, mining concessions, etc. are being actively promoted by Japanese with the assistance of subservient members of Northern military clique who desire to use the proceeds for the purpose of increasing their personal forces—gives a clear insight into the method of Japanese economic business in China. * * *

Only the refusal to accept the results of Japanese secret manipulation in China during the last four years, particularly the establishment of Japanese political influence and privileged position in Shantung can avert the only course of either making China a dependence of a (apparent omission) and boundlessly ambitious caste which would destroy the peace of the entire world or bringing on a military struggle inevitable from the estabishment of the rival spheres of interests and privileges in China.

Peace is conditional on the abolition for the present and future, of all localized privileges. China must be freed from all foreign political influence exercised within her borders, railways controlled by foreign nations, and preferential arrang[e]ments supported by political power. If this is done China will readily master her troubles particularly if the military bandits hitherto upheld by Japan shall no longer have the countenance of any foreign power.

The advantages enumerated above were gained by Japan when she was professedly acting as the trustee of the Associated Powers in the Far East and they could not have been obtained at all but for the sacrifices made in Europe. They are therefore not the exclusive concern of any one power. With respect to Shantung the German rights there lapsed together with all Sino-German treaties upon the declaration of war. A succession of treaty rights from Germany to Japan is therefore not possible and the recognition of a special position of Japan in Shantung could only proceed from a new act to which conceivably some weak Chinese officials might be induced but which would be contrary to the frequently declared aim of international policy in China and which would amount to definitive establishment of exclusive spheres of influence in China leading in turn to the more vigorous development of such exclusive spheres by other nations. The present situation of affairs offer[s] the last opportunity by which to avert threatening disaster by removing the root of conflict in China. This can be done only by abolishing localized preference and particularly by commercializing all Chinese railways under unified Chinese control with such foreign non-political expert assistance as may be necessary. Slight sacrifices of special advantages already held by one or two Americans would be justified by the suppression of formidable danger to civilization. Once the opportunity of the infiltration of political influence in the interior of China is precluded the development of stable and fitting government is assured particularly if America should have made some practical indication that we are not indifferent to the need for foundation for Chinese people to develope freely.

Never before was an opportunity for leadership towards the welfare of humanity presented itself equal to that which invites America in China at the present time. The Chinese nation asks for no better fate than to be allowed freedom to follow in the footsteps of America; every device of intrigue and corruption as well as coercion is being employed to force them in a different direction, including constant misrepresentation of American policies and aims which however has not as yet prejudiced the Chinese. Nor is it necessary on this account to exercise any political influence. If it were only known that an agreement in concert with the liberal parties would not tolerate the enfeeblement of China either by foreign or native militarists the natural propensity of the Chinese to follow liberal inclination would guide this vast country towards free government and propitious development of peaceful industrial activities, even though unavoidable in the transition of so vast and ancient a society to new methods of action. The eager attention which has been paid to your words, the trust and confidence which the Chinese feel in your policies and aims, are evidence of a spontaneous desire to follow along the path of American action and aspiration which you have made so clear to the world. If China should be disappointed in her confidence at the present time, the consequences of such disillusionment on her moral and political development would be disastrous, and we instead of looking across the Pacific towards a Chinese Nation sympathetic with our ideals would be confronted with a vast materialistic military organization under ruthless control. Reinsch.                                                    Polk.

T telegram (WP, DLC).


## From Robert Lansing, with Enclosure

Dear Mr. President:                          Paris, January 15, 1919.

The enclosed telegram from the Department of State (No. 188 of January 11th), regarding the question of withdrawing the American troops from Russia, involves a question of such broad policy that I request an expression of your views before replying to it.

I am, my dear Mr. President,

Yours very sincerely,    Robert Lansing.

TLS (WP, DLC).

ENCLOSURE

Washington, January 11, 1919.

188. Strictly confidential. For Secretary of State. There has been considerable discussion in the Senate in regard to the Russian situation. Some senators are demanding that the troops should be withdrawn; others are asking what policy should be pursued in Russia and some are disposed to urge that Russia be allowed to work out its own salvation. In other words that the Bolsheviks be let alone. I think the Hearst papers and the CHICAGO DAILY NEWS and others are going to take the line of procedure last mentioned. Frankly I am disturbed over the situation. It is obvious that great difficulty would be encountered at home by any of the Allied Governments sending troops to Russia. It is also obvious that without support the present expedition at Archangel ought to be withdrawn.

Personally I find that if some arrangement could be made to protect the Russians in the Archangel district this expedition should be withdrawn. In regard to Siberia the situation is difficult. We have for some time been insisting that the railways should be turned over to Stevens.[1] Stevens has now signified his willingness to go ahead immediately with the plan evolved by Mr. Morris with the Japanese Government and as I telegraphed you yesterday Mr. Morris has informed the Japanese Government that we approved the arrangement he has secured.[2] By forcing these negotiations, we have prevented the adoption of any other plan for more than two months and have recently blocked the counter purposes [proposals] made by Colonel Jack.[3] During this period the organization of the railroads have steadily gone from bad to worse. If we withdraw the troops from Siberia it would in my opinion be impossible to keep Stevens and his people there. Moreover the plan upon which we have been working and which is now approved contemplates that at least some American troops shall remain in Siberia. If we withdraw Stevens too, we would be open to the charge that we had blocked the British and Japanese from putting thru some plan for the improvement of railroad communications. I am not arguing in favor of staying in Siberia but merely putting up the questions as I see them.

It has been impossible to get any concerted action in Siberia thus far as the British have felt we have been playing hot and cold. As you know the Japanese are now withdrawing about half their troops leaving apparently from thirty to fifty thousand in Northern Manchuria and Eastern Siberia. Charles Crane who has just returned from Russia said there is no possibility of accomplishing anything through Siberia as the distances are too great. I do not agree with him entirely. There is no free access thru the Black Sea or the Baltic as yet to European Russia consequently the Siberian railway is the only line of communication from European Russia to Siberia. Of course we have an absolute obligation to the Czechs and some obligation to the Russians who have sided with the Czechs. If the decision is to withdraw, it seems to me imperative to have some agreement with the Bolsheviks in order to protect those who have assisted us in these operations, without an agreement there is no question as to the fate of these peoples, even with an agreement which would mean we would have to deal with the Bolsheviks, the result is doubtful.

I am merely putting up these suggestions for your consideration as I am sure careful discussion of Russia must be imminent. In your discussions has it been suggested that one of the solutions of the supply problems in Europe lies with the restoration of normal conditions in Russia especially in regard to the export of grain, sugar, flax, oil, and dairy products.                    Polk.

T telegram (WP, DLC).
    [1] See FLP to RL, Dec. 30, 1918, n. 4, Vol. 53.
    [2] FLP to RL, Jan. 10, 1919, T telegram (WP, DLC).
    [3] Col. Archibald Jack, chief of the British Railway Mission in Siberia, favored a plan which would in effect have eliminated Stevens and his men from the operation of the Trans-Siberian railroad system by placing the lines under the supervision of L. A. Ustrugov, the Minister of Communications in the Kolchak government. See R. S. Morris to RL, Nov. 30, 1918, *FR 1918, Russia*, III, 286-88.

## From Tasker Howard Bliss, with Enclosure

My dear Mr. President:                    Paris, January 15th, 1919.

At the last meeting of the Ameri[can] Peace Commission presided over by you, I understood you to say that you would be glad to have suggestions in regard to the draft of the "Covenant," copies of which you had sent to each of us.

It is in this understanding that I venture to submit to you the attached suggestions for such consideration as you may choose to give them.                    Very respectfully,   Tasker H. Bliss.

TLS (WP, DLC).

ENCLOSURE

Paris, January 14, 1919.

SUGGESTIONS IN REGARD TO THE DRAFT OF THE COVENANT.[1]

1. *Preamble.* There are some people who may be frightened at the use of the words "in order to secure * * * an orderly government." They may regard this as a suggestion of the possible use of the League of Nations to put down internal disorders wherever they occur. As the one essential object of the League of Nations is to prevent international war, and as the prevention of such war will be secured by the doing of the things set forth in the preamble, and as the prevention of such war results in security and will have the greatest tendency to produce orderly government, it is suggested for consideration that the first line of the preamble might read as follows:

"In order to prevent future international wars by the prescription of," etc., etc.

2. The idea in the word "COVENANT" is so good that it is suggested that it be adhered to in the subsequent phraseology, notwithstanding the repetition that will necessarily result. Thus, it is suggested, that the words "Contracting Powers" be made to read "Covenanting Powers"; and that, wherever the word "agreement" (referring to the constitution of the League of Nations) is used, it be replaced by the word "covenant."

3. It is suggested that there should be a positive declaration to provide against secret treaties. In no other way can the League be assured that an alliance may not be formed within itself, with a tendency adverse to the peace of the world. It is suggested that the right of the League to scrutinize individual treaties should be confined to the object of determining whether the treaty is for the purpose of effecting a private alliance.

4. *Article* III. In the second line, after the word "integrity," insert the words "as against external aggression."

Do the words, which appear in Article III, "and also such territorial readjustments as may in the judgment of ¾ths of the Delegates be demanded by the welfare and manifest interest of the peoples concerned," contemplate the possibility of the League of Nations being called upon to consider such questions as the independence of Ireland, of India, etc., etc.?

5. *Article IV.* It does not seem that so important a matter as the reduction of national armaments should be liable to a veto by the action of, possibly, one small power. All hope of disarmament con-

[1] Commentary on Wilson's so-called second draft or first "Paris draft," printed at Jan. 8, 1919, Vol. 53.

sists in the action of the Great Powers. Until they agree to some disarmament there is no use in talking about the matter. When they should agree to disarm, they might well be permitted to exercise such pressure as they, in agreement, should think practicable in order to compel general disarmament.

6. *Article* V. It would seem that some time limit,—say one year,— might well be fixed, within which an award by the arbitrators or a decision by the Executive Council must be rendered.

In clause 4 of Article V, should there not be some limits imposed on the right of appeal?

In the first sentence of clause 6 of Article V appear the words, "the *parties* to the dispute shall apply to the Executive Council," etc., etc. In the second sentence of the same clause appear the words, "the Council shall immediately accept the reference and give notice to the *other* party or parties," etc., etc. It appears that a change in these wordings is necessary.

7. *Article* VI. Is it the intent of this Article to provide two steps, instead of one, in order to bring about the full status of international war? Is it intended that, first of all, there shall be a complete diplomatic, economic and financial pressure exerted, and that only in case this fails in attaining its object there shall be a resort to hostile acts of war as contemplated in the second clause of Article VI.? If the latter be the intent, it is to be noted that the breaching Power, being at war with the League, may immediately use its land and naval force against the League, while the latter must wait for a recommendation from the Executive Council before the several members of the League know what military and naval forces they are to contribute.

In the third clause of Article VI. omit the words, "to perpetual disarmament and"; and change the figure 3 to the figure 4.

8. In regard to Articles VI. and VII., it is again suggested that careful consideration be given to seeing whether a form of words cannot be used that will largely accomplish the object in view, without appearing, in the mind of anyone, to yield (with respect to the United States) to the League of Nations powers which are vested in the American Congress.

9. *Article* X. This Article relates to a dispute between a Contracting Power and a Power which is not a party to this Covenant. The Article provides for action only in the case when the Power not a party to this Covenant "takes hostile action against one of the Contracting Powers before a decision of the dispute by arbitrators or before investigation, report and recommendation by the Executive Council in regard to the dispute, or contrary to such recommendation." There is no assumption that the Contracting Power itself

may be in the wrong, and it is provided that all of the other Contracting Powers shall come to the assistance of the Contracting Power against which hostile action has been taken. How shall we provide for the case where the enlightened sense of the world holds the Contracting Power itself to be in the wrong?

It would seem that careful note should be taken of the possibility of a "Dred Scott" decision being made by the tribunal of the League of Nations.

10. *Article XI.* Under the second clause of Article XI. there is the same possibility of the difficulty which may occur under Article X. Two nations not Covenanting Powers may have a dispute. One of them, which is in the wrong, offers to submit its interests to the decision of the League of Nations. This State immediately becomes, for the purposes of the dispute, one of the Contracting Powers; and as such, the League is bound to support it, right or wrong, as would be the case under Article X.

11. *Article XII.* Change the word "may" at the end of the fourth line of this Article to the word "shall."

SUPPLEMENTARY AGREEMENTS.

1. *Article I.* It would seem desirable to avoid phraseology that would give color to the idea that the proposed League of Nations has for one of its principal objects the control of situations growing out of the present war. If it is possible to avoid the use of the names "Austria-Hungary" and "Turkey" and "the German Empire," it is believed that it would be better.

2. Under the Supplementary Agreements, is it obligatory upon one of the Convenanting Powers to accept the functions of "agent or mandatory" appointed by the League of Nations, or may it decline to exercise this function?

3. What financial obligations are imposed upon a mandatory which accepts its functions as such? It is evident that the mandatory must establish a quasi supervising government of its own. It must appoint someone who will be its local director, and this latter must have a large staff of assistants. If the people of the United States accept this general proposition, they will have an interest in knowing the expense to which they may be subjected. It is easily possible that the representative or agent of the mandatory cannot perform his functions without the support of a powerful military force. Will the United States, for example, be expected to maintain in some foreign country an armed force of their own in order to perform their functions as mandatory?

The sole object of the proposition of General Smuts is to bring the United States into line with Great Britain in exercising supervisory control over certain areas of the earth. The people of the United States will understand that a great burden is contemplated to be thrust upon them by this plan. It is believed that to secure good chance of acceptance by the United States these things should be made clear, or else it should be made clear that no state can be made a mandatory without its own cordial consent.

In the third clause of Article III. it should be made clear that the mandatory state is not to maintain a military force, of *native* troops, in the state of which it is the mandatory, in excess of the standard laid down by the League. This provision in General Smuts' plan is evidently intended to prevent a nation, acting as mandatory over a densely populated area, from there raising a great military force *under the guise of internal police*, which might be used by the mandatory in case of a war outside of this area.

4. In the first clause of Article IV., the provision with respect to conformity to certain standards as to military and naval forces might well be made to apply to all states entering the League after the date of its creation, instead of making them simply apply to territories of the former empires of Austria-Hungary and of Turkey. This will assist in avoiding the giving to the League of Nations the appearance of being a new form of the old Holy Alliance.

It is not improbable that before the League of Nations can become an accomplished fact, it may be quite as desirable "to watch over the relations *inter se* of all new and independent states arising or created out of the" empires of Russia and Germany as it is to do so over the states created out of Austria-Hungary or Turkey. It would seem that this may be an additional reason for omitting, if possible, reference to any existing or formerly existing state *by name*.                                                    Tasker H. Bliss.

TS MS (WP, DLC).


## Two Telegrams from Carter Glass

                                  Washington, January 15, 1919.

244. For the President from Glass.

Your message 252 January 11th 7 p.m.[1] has been received.

First. I am cabling Crosby accompanying direct and instructing Davis to retain if possible the services of Goodhue, Harris and Loree and will endeavor to secure Lamont for service in Europe to aid Davis.

Second: I feel with you the disadvantage of Strauss being opposed to and unable to fulfill his duties as a member of Federal Reserve Board for an extended period. Reluctant to approve his going to

Europe but felt that the opportunity for service as the head of the
commission I suggested would justify the sacrifice. As you do not
consider such commission advisable I entirely agree that Strauss
stay in Europe should be short. In accordance with paragraph five
of your cable, Strauss will leave almost immediately and I hope that
during his short stay in Europe, his wide experience, judgement
and intimate knowledge of treasury, war and post war policies in
the formation of which he has taken an essential part will be availed
of to the fullest extent. I am cabling House approving Davis serving
on the Council.                                    Polk.

[1] WW to C. Glass, Jan. 11, 1919, Vol. 53.


                                    Washington, January 15, 1919.
245. For President from Glass.
First. Your message regarding Roumania[1] was received. Advance
to Roumania will be made when essential requirements imposed
by loan statutes are met. Wired Davis several days ago particulars
and that Treasury would make advance whenever put in position
to do so legally. Understand that State Department has cabled on
subject.
Second. Appreciate importance of food supplies in relation to your
policies and anxious to use powers of treasury to support them.
Treasury has uniformly recognized supplies of foodstuffs to European Allies as a purpose for which loans could be made under
existing law and will continue to do so until conditions change or
you advise to the contrary. In no case has it refused to make such
loans.
Third. Appreciate desirability of marketing our surplus products
and that this is a collateral advantage of the policy of supplying
foods to Europe. The question of Treasury's attitude on prevention
of loss to producers has been raised here. Treasury has taken position that artificial upholding of prices was undesirable because of
burden thereby imposed on commodity in general and the disadvantage at which our industries would be placed in international
markets. Since the armistice many claims for indirect protection of
prices have been put forward in regard to commodities the production of which have been stimulated to meet war needs. Treasury
has maintained that any obligations of our government to producers
of great commodities should be met by direct appropriation and
payment as is proposed by bills now pending. In the case of certain
minerals I am convinced that to meet such obligations indirectly
by using governmental powers granted for other specific purposes
to prevent losses to the producers by artificial maintenance of price

is both economically and politically objectionable. McCormick is familiar with, and I believe fully shares substance my views on these questions which I hope have your approval.      Polk.

T telegrams (WP, DLC).
  [1] WW to C. Glass, Jan. 9, 1919, Vol. 53.

## From Stephen Samuel Wise

My dear Mr. President:                         Paris 15 January 1919.

I write this line at your suggestion, in order to remind you that as soon as it becomes possible for you to do so, you are to send word to Col. T. E. Lawrence, Hotel Continental, Paris, concerning the visit which Prince Feisul of Arabia and Col. Lawrence are to pay you.[1] I have spoken to His Highness and to Col. Lawrence and the latter will have ready for submission to you the memorandum which will cover the case.

I rejoice to think that Prince Feisul and Col. Lawrence are to have the privilege of discussing with you the aspirations for freedom of the Prince's people who have done so much to free the Near East from Ottoman rule.

I am, my dear Mr. President,
                         Very faithfully yours   Stephen S Wise

TLS (WP, DLC).
  [1] About Thomas Edward Lawrence, Prince Faisal, their relationship, and their part in the movement for Arab independence, see Thomas Edward Lawrence, *Seven Pillars of Wisdom: A Triumph* (Garden City, New York, 1935), and John E. Mack, *A Prince of Our Disorder: The Life of T. E. Lawrence* (Boston and Toronto, 1976), pp. 111-273.

## From John Sharp Williams

                                   Washington 15 Jan 1919

Not as long as they keep up their infantile and asinine bonfire performances in Lafayette Park[1]      John Sharp Williams

T telegram (WP, DLC).
  [1] Williams was responding to WW to J. S. Williams, Jan. 14, 1919. Williams referred to an incident during the evening of January 7 in which members of the National Woman's Party first burned a copy of one of Wilson's speeches in Italy before a crowd in front of the White House and then set so-called Liberty bonfires in Lafayette Square. These actions caused a near riot and led to the arrest of three of the demonstrators. On January 9, two members of the executive committee of the party issued a public statement justifying the "Liberty bonfires" as "a symbol of our contempt for words unsupported by deeds." President Wilson, they said, was presenting himself to the people of Europe as "the representative of a free people, when the American people are not free, and he is chiefly responsible for it." They argued that, while Wilson himself had been converted to the suffrage cause, he had failed to exercise his leadership to force the Democratic majority in the Senate to support the suffrage amendment. *New York Times*, Jan. 8 and 10, 1919.

## Gilbert Fairchild Close to William Christian Bullitt

My dear Mr. Bullitt:                          Paris, 15 January 1919.

I took up with the President the desire of Mlle. Thompson[1] to arrange for the President to meet the women workers and he asks me to say that while it is difficult, if not impossible, for him to set any definite date that he can count upon because of the uncertainty of the time of the meetings of the Peace Conference, he hopes to be able to meet the women workers on Saturday, January 25th at three o'clock as you suggest.[2]

Will you not take this matter up with Mlle. Thompson and send me a written statement of just what the plan of the meeting would involve?                          Sincerely yours,   [Gilbert F. Close]

CCL (WP, DLC).
  [1] Valentine Thomson (not Thompson), a French journalist, at this time associated with *La Vie Féminine*.
  [2] Wilson's remarks to this group are printed at Jan. 25, 1919.

## From Sidney Edward Mezes, with Enclosure

Dear Mr. President:                          Paris January 16, 1919

Mr. Leland Harrison has informed us of your request for the accompanying memorandum and map on the Bolsheviki, prepared by Dr. R. H. Lord, specialist on Russia in this Section, to be in your hands by ten this morning.

In accordance with his request seven copies were prepared, of which the remaining six have been delivered to Mr. Harrison.

I am, my dear Mr. President,
                          Sincerely yours,   S. E. Mezes.

TLS (WP, DLC).

### E N C L O S U R E

#### THE PRESENT SITUATION OF THE BOLSHEVISTS IN RUSSIA

I. SUMMARY
*Political* The fear of foreign intervention and of an accompanying counter-revolution is rallying many elements to the Bolshevist government. Otherwise the position of that government seems weaker than formerly, and we have yet no ground for affirming that the majority of the Russian people prefer the Bolshevist rule on its own merits.
*Military* The Bolshevists are transferring their chief efforts to, and

winning successes in, the Baltic Provinces, Lithuania, and the
Ukraine. On the eastern, south-eastern, and northern fronts, recent
operations have gone against them.

*Economic* The situation is now more critical than at any previous
time. The Bolshevist "financial system" can only lead to a catastrophe; the productivity of labor has decreased to less than half of
its pre-revolutionary standard. The transportation system is likely
to be paralyzed completely by the end of the winter; the Bolshevist
system for rationing, as well as their nationalization schemes, seems
to have broken down almost completely.

2. THE POLITICAL SITUATION

Bolshevist political strength depends largely on the success of
their foreign policy which for the time has enabled them to appear
as defenders of Russia against the foreigners. Although otherwise
measurably weaker, as shown by the December Terror proclaimed
in Petrograd and Moscow, which has recently ended; by the conference of the Executive Committee upon Lenin's proposal to surrender to the Allies, which was barely defeated by a majority of
twelve of the 200 votes cast;[1] by the undeniably widening breach
between Lenin and Trotsky;[2] and by the pessimism of Lenin as
expressed in his New Year speech;[3] the government has secured

[1] This statement was apparently based upon "Lenine Reported Ready to Give Up,"
*New York Times*, Dec. 16, 1918. The relevant portion of the text reads as follows:
"Stockholm, Dec. 14.—The Bolshevik leaders in Russia are engaged in heated discussions whether to abandon their entire régime, according to the Swedish Naval Attaché
at Petrograd who has arrived here. Nikolai [*sic*] Lenine, the Premier, and Leo Kameneff
are said to favor abandonment, but they are opposed by War Minister Trotzky, Foreign Minister
Tchitcherin and M. Radek, who urge holding out to the last. The matter was brought before
the Central Council of Workmen's and Soldiers' Delegates and Lenine was defeated by the
slight majority of twelve out of 200 votes." So far as is known, this report had no basis in fact.
[2] This statement had a slight basis in fact. Iosif Stalin and Grigorii Zinov'ev were already
intriguing to create a breach between Lenin and Trotsky. Isaac Deutscher, *The Prophet
Armed; Trotsky: 1879-1921* (Oxford, 1954), p. 425. However, it is highly unlikely that
these intrigues were known in the West at this time. Lord's statement was probably
based upon another erroneous news report, "Trotzky Dictator; Arrests Lenine," *New
York Times*, Jan. 9, 1919. The text of this report reads as follows: "Copenhagen, Jan.
8.—Nikolai Lenine, the Bolshevist Premier of Russia, has been arrested at the command
of Leon Trotzky, Minister of War and Marine, who has made himself Dictator, according
to a Moscow dispatch to the Gothenburg (Sweden) Gazette. Trotzky was prompted to
make the arrest because of a difference of opinion with Lenine concerning the Bolshevist
reforms, the dispatch states. Lenine desired to effect a coalition with the Mensheviki,
or Moderates, while Trotzky wished to continue the reign of red terror."
[3] Lord apparently referred here to a speech on Soviet Russia's international situation
delivered by Lenin on November 8, 1918, on the occasion of the first anniversary of the
Bolshevik revolution. Lenin's thesis was that world proletarian revolution was inevitable
and that the capitalistic, imperialistic nations would ultimately destroy themselves. However, he warned that Soviet Russia might suffer greatly or even be defeated or destroyed
before the final defeat of capitalism. "The main point about the international situation,"
he said, "is . . . that we have never been so close to world proletarian revolution as we
are now. . . . Yet if we have never previously been so close to world revolution, then it
is also true to say that we have never been in such a dangerous situation as we are
now. The imperialists were busy among themselves, but now one group has been wiped
out by the Anglo-French-American group, which considers its main task to be the
extermination of world Bolshevism and the strangulation of its main centre, the Soviet

temporary but real support on the issue that, if it falls, alien invasion will result. Thus in early December the Left Social Revolutionaries and a large group of Mensheviks seem to have accepted the conclusion that rather than aid foreign intervention with a presumably concomitant counter-revolution, they would support the Bolshevist government. Unconfirmed reports relate that the Co-operative Unions tend to share this view, abandoning their neutral policy toward the Lenin régime in face of foreign aggression. Coupled with undoubted increased army efficiency, these elements have enabled the Bolshevists to face the world with some show of a united front.

Further support is derived from the German Revolution, lessened, however, by the failure of the Spartacus *coup d'etat*.[4] Advances into Poland and the Baltic Provinces have been not without political effect at home. The Perm defeat[5] has become known, but its effect on the popular morale cannot yet be gauged. The British note[6] will beyond doubt do much to lend prestige.

It cannot be argued, however, that the Russians support the Bolshevists on their own merits. No reports indicate that the Bolshevists dare venture any elections; the mass of the population appears entirely inert; the occasional "terrors" indicate positive resistance, and the hostile reaction of the Ukrainians seem to show that the general sentiment would not of its own accord establish a Bolshevist regime. The articulate portions of public opinion which have offered support to the present government appear to have

Russian Soviet Republic." Later in his speech, he added: "We must, therefore, face the bitter truth about our international position. The world revolution is not far off, but it cannot develop according to a special time-table. Having survived two revolutions we well appreciate this. We know, however, that although the imperialists cannot contain the world revolution, certain countries are likely to be defeated, and even heavier losses are possible." He concluded the speech by making the point even more specific: "We know the danger is great. It may be that fate has even heavier sacrifices in store for us. Even if they can crush one country, they can never crush the world proletarian revolution, they will only add more fuel to the flames that will consume them all." The full text of the speech appears in Vladimir Il'ich Lenin, *Collected Works* (45 vols., Moscow, 1960-1970), XXVIII, 151-64. The quotations are from pp. 160-61, 163, and 164, respectively.

    [4] As has been noted, the uprising led by members of the German Communist party (formerly the Spartacus League) and other radical socialist groups had begun in Berlin on January 5. The movement was forcibly suppressed between January 10 and 15 by several voluntary paramilitary units made up chiefly of former army officers and enlisted men, known as the *Freikorps*. The greatest blow to the Communists was the murder on January 15 of Rosa Luxemburg and Karl Liebknecht by a unit of the *Freikorps*. See Robert G. L. Waite, *Vanguard of Nazism: The Free Corps Movement in Postwar Germany, 1918-1923* (Cambridge, Mass., 1952), pp. 58-63, and Eric Waldman, *The Spartacist Uprising of 1919 and the Crisis of the German Socialist Movement: A Study of the Relation of Political Theory and Party Practice* (Milwaukee, Wisc., 1958), pp. 161-96.

    [5] Kolchak's Northern Army, under the command of Gen. Rudolf Gajda, had captured Perm on December 14, 1918, taking 31,000 prisoners and a large quantity of war material. See George Stewart, *The White Armies of Russia: A Chronicle of Counter-Revolution and Allied Intervention* (New York, 1933), p. 254.

    [6] That is, A. J. Balfour to Lord Derby, Jan. 2, 1919, Vol. 53.

done so on the theory that the alternative was foreign intervention. Aside from this, the Government rests on Lettish and Mongolian mercenaries, on straightforward terrorism, on the support of a small group of enthusiasts, and on the Red military successes. No "mandate from the people" has yet been shown by Lenin or Trotsky to have been given to the Bolshevist dictatorship.

### 3. THE MILITARY SITUATION

In spite of increased forces and a decided attempt to strengthen the army, the Bolshevists have by no means met with universal success on their several fronts. They have abandoned Petrograd and moved their headquarters to Moscow.

*Ural Front*: During the autumn, Bolshevist forces advanced across the Volga towards the Ural Mountains. The Czechs and loyal Russians, however, have recently been able to retake Perm, and to better their position further South. On this front the Bolshevists have lost considerable ground.

*Caucasus Front*: General Denikin seems to be making rapid progress north of the Caucasus and is now approaching Tsaritzin.

*Ukraine*: The Bolshevists are evidently preparing an offensive against the Ukraine. Troops are being sent South from Petrograd and Moscow. The present objective seems to be Kiev.

*Western Front*: It is in the West that the Bolshevists have met with marked success. They have swept the Baltic provinces and have advanced to the south towards Poland, being now within 160 miles of Warsaw. It should be observed that these advances have been made almost unopposed, following immediately upon the German withdrawal.

*Northern Front*: On the northern front the Bolshevists have met slight reverses near Archangel; their troops, however, are reported to be well fitted out, and to be in good condition.

*Siberia*: The Bolshevists here, by intermittent attempts at an uprising, have succeeded only in somewhat complicating the situation for Admiral Kolchak.

### 4. THE ECONOMIC SITUATION

Economically the Bolshevist situation is now appreciably worse than at any previous time except in the narrow sphere of military equipment. The recent changes in the situation have been the hostilities developing in the Ukraine, the advance of Krasnoff[7] up the Volga river, the Bolshevist defeat at Perm, and the economic barrenness of the conquests in Poland and the Baltic Provinces. As a result:

(1) The raw materials, especially coal and iron secured from the Ukraine and the Urals, have been sharply cut off.

---

[7] That is, Gen. Petr Nikolaevich Krasnov. Actually, he was about to suffer a major military defeat at the hands of the Bolsheviks.

(2) Food conditions have failed to improve. Imported grain fails to penetrate the famine belt outside of Moscow sufficiently to do more than relieve the pressing needs of Moscow itself; (throughout September less than three trains a week reached the city from these provinces). The peasants refuse to sell and the local commissars do not give aid. Food coming into the hands of the central government by agreement with Ukraine has stopped, as have exports from Northern Caucasus. The Petrograd starvation rate is 1000 deaths per day. So far as government rationing is concerned, the old capital and in fact all Northern Russia are practically left to their own resources.

(3) Financial catastrophe must eventually result from the Bolshevist monetary situation. Paper money, substantially without backing, in [is] in circulation to the amount of thirty-two billion rubles. The 1918 budget left a deficit of 48 billion rubles to be met by fu[r]ther paper issues. The gold reserve of about three billion rubles was depleted by payments to Germany in September and October of 93,135 kilogrammes of fine gold. Only foreign speculation gives the paper money a fluctuating and insecure value. The worthlessness of the purchasing medium has led the Bolshevist government to propose payments to laborers in kind, instead of in cash.

(4) Productivity of labor has decreased to less than half its pre-Revolutionary standard. This is the greatest single loss which the Bolshevists have suffered. As a result, factories have closed down and unemployment would be general if it were not for swift mobilisation of the unemployed into the Red Armies.

(5) The transportation system remains physically intact, but the commerce has substantially ceased. The figures for the early summer of 1918 show that water traffic on the Volga had almost stopped. Railroad equipment, according to estimates by observers in September, 1918, was more than 60% out of repair, but much of this could be repaired were spare parts and machine shops available. The railway operatives are the most capable class of Russian labor and the land transportation system seems to be functioning, although inadequately. Lack of fuel will before the winter's end completely stop even the present light traffic.

Summing up, Russia no longer exists as an economic unit and the Bolshevist power over what resources remain is vary [very] small. Their decrees for universal rationing and for nationalizing land, industry, etc., which were to some degree effective last spring, are now enforcible only in the region about Moscow and a few villages where the local commissioners remain loyal and efficient.

T MS (WP, DLC).

# Hankey's Notes of a Meeting of the Council of Ten[1]

Quai d'Orsay, January 16, 1919, 10:30 A.M.

BC-3

M. PICHON, in opening the meeting, said that M. Clemenceau would like to make an observation before the business of the day began.

M. CLEMENCEAU said that he was in doubt whether the question of the Press had been settled in a practical manner. The censorship was being maintained in France. It had been discontinued in America, and was to be discontinued in Great Britain. Hence, news both true and false would be produced freely in some countries and not in others. He gave as an example a despatch produced in the "New York Tribune" attributing to President Wilson a threat of withdrawing all his troops from Europe unless the European Allies agreed to some of his desiderata.[2] The statement was absurd, but it was sure to return to France and Great Britain and no obstacle would be placed to its return in the United States. Hence an absurd situation, certain to cause trouble. He therefore suggested that in

[1] The complete text of these notes is printed in PPC, III, 578-84.
[2] The curious history of this dispatch is related in "Wilson Denied Cable Tribune Did Not Have," New York Tribune, Jan. 18, 1919. The article revealed that Clemenceau had had a copy of the dispatch, presumably obtained from the French censors, on January 16. When he showed the copy to Wilson on January 17, the latter was reported to have called it "an abominable falsehood." On January 16, the New York office of the Committee on Public Information had issued a statement saying that Wilson categorically denied making any such threat as attributed to him in the dispatch printed in the New York Tribune. A few hours later, after it had been pointed out that the Tribune had in fact not printed any such dispatch, the C.P.I. withdrew its first statement and urged the press associations not to print it until the matter could be straightened out. At 11:30 a.m. on January 17, the New York Tribune issued a statement denying that it had ever received, much less printed, any dispatch remotely resembling the one in controversy. At 2:30 p.m. that same day, the long-delayed dispatch finally arrived at the Tribune offices in New York. The editors, justifying their action by the argument that the dispatch had "been made the basis of controversy," printed it on January 18 just as the correspondent (not named) had sent it, as part of the article cited above. The text is as follows:
"Paris.—Among the many sensational rumors habitually afloat in the Chamber of Deputies there has been one to the effect that President Wilson has threatened to withdraw American troops from Europe if certain of his ideas are not followed by the peace conference. How far these things have gone in the three conferences already held it is impossible for me to say, but that the Chamber's report is pretty nearly correct there is no doubt.
"There are numerous indications of this recent attitude on Wilson's part, and that he is now tacitly but definitely, if not actually, threatening other commissioners. He has come here to make a certain kind of peace and intends to do so, his supporters say. And his supporters have frankly said that he will refuse to sign any peace not in accord with what he considers a fair and equitable interpretation of the armistice agreement which accepted his fourteen points with reservations only as to the 'freedom of the seas.'
"Now, his supporters say, some of the Allies are unwilling to abide by the armistice terms and will seek at each renewal to go beyond the armistice terms and impose further penalties on the Germans, who accepted the armistice in good faith.
"Mr. Wilson's supporters feel furthermore that some of the Allies—not including Great Britain—desire to prolong the armistice in order to penalize Germany to the utmost before concluding a peace with her."

addition to the Drafting Committee there should be a political Committee, composed of one representative from the United States, Great Britain, Italy, and France, to correct false news and guide public opinion in the right direction.

BARON SONNINO pointed out that such a Committee would not be able to put a stop to pure inventions like that of the "Tribune."

M. CLEMENCEAU suggested that the Committee could at least correct it.

MR. LLOYD GEORGE thought that it would be quite impossible to put a complete check on inventions of this kind. There were opposition papers in all countries anxious to discredit their Governments by backing the Plenipotentiaries of other countries against their own. It was impossible, nevertheless, to have complete publicity, especially in regard to the proceedings of the small Conference, in which it was public knowledge that the bulk of the business would be transacted.

PRESIDENT WILSON enquired whether the protest from the Press addressed to himself and to the British Government[3] did not refer only to the larger Conference.

MR. LLOYD GEORGE thought that the protest really referred to the proceedings of the smaller Conference. He was of opinion that a general warning issued to the whole of the Press against believing unauthorised communications might serve to guide public belief and to protect the freedom of the Committee's deliberations.

M. CLEMENCEAU thought this warning might have effect if it were signed by President Wilson, Mr. Lloyd George, the Italian representative, and himself.

PRESIDENT WILSON doubted whether anything less than complete publicity would satisfy the American public.

M. CLEMENCEAU pointed out that the French censorship was mainly engaged in preventing such mischief, for instance, as attacks on President Wilson in the "Echo de Paris." The only thing he desired to stop was the pitting of one Allied country against another. This he regarded as extremely dangerous, and he believed that the Press must not be allowed to attribute any given opinion to a particular statesman and a controversial view to another.

BARON SONNINO agreed that it was highly desirable that responsibility for all decisions should appear to be joint, but he did not know how this result could be achieved. If the suggested Committee were to attend meetings the numbers present at these gatherings would be too great. If, on the other hand, the committee did not attend the meetings it would not be in a position to refute false

[3] The Enclosure printed with R. S. Baker to C. T. Grayson, Jan. 14, 1919.

news. There would always be inventions concerning the proceedings of the smaller Conference. False reports would be invented with the deliberate object of obtaining denials. Moreover, if the reports so invented happened to hit the mark, how could they be denied?

MR. LLOYD GEORGE said that he would issue a general caution to the public indicating that these Conferences were held with the object of reaching agreement. The process of reaching agreement necessarily involved debate and a statement of differing views. The differences were transitory, and were eliminated after debate, when the common agreement was reached. It was the agreement that mattered to the public, and not the stages in the discussion.

PRESIDENT WILSON drew attention to another aspect of the case. All the members of the Committee were responsible representatives of their peoples. If it were given out that there was unanimous agreement on any point, their respective Parliaments and peoples would certainly enquire how they had come to consent. They were all responsible to public opinion in their own countries, and the public had a right to know what they had said.

MR. LLOYD GEORGE agreed that in the end each would have to defend himself, but if the defence must be undertaken from day to day as the discussion proceeded, work would be greatly hampered and the Conference would never reach any conclusions at all. He himself believed that the public as a whole meant to allow the Delegates fair play. Some of the newspapers, no doubt, were more concerned with their own tactics. He believed that if the kind of appeal he had suggested were made to the public, newspaper reports unauthorized by the Conference would be largely discredited by them.

PRESIDENT WILSON agreed that this appeared to be the best way. There was a well-known dodge in the American Press by which, after trying falsehood after falsehood and obtaining denial after denial, the seeker after information narrowed down the alternatives to the only possible residuum. He therefore suggested that each Government should through its deputy in liaison with the Press inform the reporters that the purpose of these meetings was to reach agreement, and that temporary disagreement was an ingredient in the process. He suggested that the reporters should be summoned together and asked to suggest their own means of dealing with this situation.[4]

4 "President Wilson stated that the three representatives should call the representatives of the Press and explain the difficulties with which the delegates were faced with regard to the question of giving out information and inform them that the delegates did not think it would facilitate results if the details of the present discussions were outlined in public. The three representatives should also make it clear to the Press that it was

(It was therefore decided that a summons should be issued by each Government to the Pressmen of their own country to assemble that afternoon at 5 p.m. at the Club of the Foreign Press, No. 80 Avenue des Champs Elysees in order to learn from the Press delegates attached to each Government the difficulty experienced in giving information of debates before their conclusion.

The delegates should inform the meeting that the Governments desired to keep the Press fully informed of the results achieved, and should enquire from the representatives of the Press what means suggested themselves as the best to carry out this intention.)

[Pichon read a protest from the Siamese government against its being assigned only one delegate. The note mentioned Siam's actions against Germany and for the Allied cause. The council agreed that Siam should be represented by two delegates.]

MR. LLOYD GEORGE said that the plan put forward by the British Government had been misunderstood in many quarters. It had never been suggested that the Bolshevik Government should be recognized to the extent of offering them a seat at the Peace Conference. It was only proposed that a truce among the various warring factions in Russia should be suggested. When this truce had been made, representatives of the various Governments should be invited to come to Paris to explain their position and receive from the Allies, if possible, some suggestions for the accommodation of their differences. The British Government was in complete accord with the French Government that the Russians could not be put on the same footing as Belgium, for instance, and M. Pichon had been misled if he thought that the British Government meant to offer them membership in the Conference.[5] He made this proposal for the following reasons:

---

the desire of the delegates to tell them as fully and freely as possible of the determination[s] taken at these conferences. In conclusion, the three representatives should ask the Press to express their views as to what they considered the best method for carrying out the desires of the delegates." ACNP notes, Jan. 16, 1919, T MS (SDR, RG 256, 180.03101/7, DNA). These notes are printed in PPC, III, 585-93.

[5] "Mr. Lloyd George commenced his statement setting forth the information in the possession of the British Government regarding the Russian situation, by referring to the matter which had been exposed recently in L'Humanité. He stated that he wished to point out that there had been a serious misconception on the part of the French Government as to the character of the proposal of the British Government. The British proposal did not contemplate in any sense whatsoever, a recognition of the Bolsheviki Government, nor a suggestion that Bolshevik delegates be invited to attend the Conference. The British proposal was to invite all of the different governments now at war within what used to be the Russian Empire, to a truce of God, to stop reprisals and outrages and to send men here to give, so to speak, an account of themselves. The Great Powers would then try to find a way to bring some order out of chaos. These men were not to be delegates to the Peace Conference, and he agreed with the French Government entirely that they should not be made members of the Conference." Ibid.

(a) We did not know the facts about Russia. Differing reports were received from our representatives in Russia, and often reports from the same representative varied from day to day. It was clear that, unless we knew the facts, we should not be in a position to form a correct judgment.

(b) On one subject there could certainly be complete agreement, to wit, that the condition of Russia was extremely bad. There was misgovernment and starvation, and all the suffering resulting from both. It was impossible to know which party was gaining the upper hand, but our hopes that the Bolshevik Government would collapse had certainly been disappointed. Bolshevism appeared to be stronger than ever. Mr. Lloyd George quoted a report from the British Military Authorities in Russia, who could not be suspected of leanings towards Bolshevism, to the effect that the Bolshevik Government was stronger now than it had been some months previously. The peasants feared that all other parties would, if successful, restore the ancient regime and deprive them of the land which the Revolution had put into their hands.

(c) As to the Ukraine, where we had supposed a firm Government had been established, our information was that an adventurer with a few thousand men had overturned it with the greatest ease. This insurrection had a Bolshevik character, and its success made it clear that the Ukraine was not the stronghold against Bolshevism that we had imagined. The same movement was therefore beginning in the Ukraine which had been completed in Great Russia. The former Government of the Ukraine had been a Government of big landlords only maintained in power by German help. Now that the Germans had withdrawn, the peasants had seized their opportunity. Were we going to spend our resources in order to back a minority of big landlords against an immense majority of peasants? There were three policies from which to choose.

(i) We could say that Bolshevism was a movement as dangerous to civilization as German militarism had been, and that we must therefore destroy it. Did anyone seriously put forward this policy? Was anyone prepared to carry it out? He believed that no one could be found to do so. The Germans, at the time when they needed every available man to reinforce their attack on the Western front, had been forced to keep about a million men to garrison a few provinces of Russia which were a mere fringe of the whole country; and, moreover, at that moment Bolshevism was weak and disorganized. Now it was strong and had a formidable army. Was any one of the Western Allies prepared to send a million men into Russia? He doubted whether a thousand would be willing to go. All reports tended to show that the Allied troops in Siberia and in Northern Russia were most unwilling to continue the campaign and determined to return to their homes. To set Russia in order by force was a task which he for one would not undertake on behalf of Great Britain, and he questioned whether any other Power would undertake it.

(ii)  The second policy was a policy of insulation, the policy known as "cordon sanitaire." This policy meant the siege of Bolshevik Russia, that is to say, the Russia that had no corn, but a large famished population. These people were dying by thousands, if not by hundreds of thousands, of famine. Petrograd had been reduced from the proportions of a great city to those of a moderate town. Our blockade of Russia would lead to the killing, not of the ruffians enlisted by the Bolsheviks, but of the ordinary population, with whom we wish to be friends. This was a policy which, if only on grounds of humanity, we could not support. It might be suggested that the continuance of this policy in Russia would lead to the overthrow of the Bolsheviks; but who in Russia was able to overthrow them? General Knox reported that the Czecho-Slovaks were tainted with Bolshevism and could not be trusted neither could the Russian troops of Kolchak. He had just seen a map revealing the area held by Denikin. He occupied with an effective force of perhaps 40,000 men what might be described as a little back-yard near the Black Sea. Denikin was said to have recognized Kolchak, but he was quite unable to get into touch with him, as an immense Bolshevik area intervened between them. Kolchak, moreover, appeared to pursue the revival of the old regime in Russia; hence the lukewarmness of the Czecho-Slovaks in his cause. They were unwilling to fight in order to set up another Tzarist regime. So also were the British. This would not be helping to create a new world.

(iii) The only other way he could think of was the plan he had proposed—that of asking representatives of the various Russian Governments to meet in Paris after a truce among themselves. The name of M. Sazonoff had been mentioned as representing the Government at Omsk. M. Sazonoff had been long out of Great Russia. It was questionable whether he knew anything of the conditions at Omsk. He was a strong partisan, and might as well be consulted on the present temper of Russia as the "New York Tribune" on the opinions of Mr. Wilson. We could not leave Paris at the conclusion of the Peace Conference congratulating ourselves on having made a better world, if at that moment half of Europe and half of Asia were in flames. It had been alleged that if Bolshevik emissaries came to France and England they would proselytise the French and British peoples. It was possible that Bolshevism might gain ground in these countries, but it would not be as a consequence of the visit of a few Russian emissaries. He himself had no fears on this score. Moreover, conditions could be imposed on the delegates, and if they failed to observe them they could be sent back to Russia. With this threat over them it was most likely that they would avoid giving offense as they would be anxious to explain their case.

M. PICHON asked whether the meeting would care to hear M. Noulens, the French Ambassador in Russia, who had just returned from Archangel. If so, M. Noulens could attend the meeting on the following day, and would be able to give very interesting information concerning Bolshevism.

PRESIDENT WILSON said that in his mind there was no possible answer to the view expressed by Mr. Lloyd George. This view corresponded exactly with the information received from Russia by the United States Government. There was certainly a latent force behind Bolshevism which attracted as much sympathy as its more brutal aspects aroused general disgust. There was throughout the world a feeling of revolt against the large vested interests which influenced the world both in the economic and in the political sphere. The way to cure this domination was in his opinion, constant discussion and a slow process of reform; but the world at large had grown impatient of delay. There were men in the United States of the finest temper, if not of the finest judgment, who were in sympathy with Bolshevism, because it appeared to them to offer that regime of opportunity to the individual which they desired to bring about. In America considerable progress had been made in checking the control of capital over the lives of men and over Government; yet, even there, labor and capital were not friends. The vast majority who worked and produced were convinced that the privileged minority would never yield them their rights. Unless some sort of partnership between these two interests could be obtained society would crumble. Bolshevism was therefore vital because of these genuine grievances. The seeds of Bolshevism could not flourish without a soil ready to receive them. If this soil did not exist, Bolshevism could be neglected. British and American troops were unwilling to fight in Russia because they feared their efforts might lead to the restoration of the old order, which was even more disastrous than the present one. He recollected making a casual reference of sympathy to the distressed people in Russia, in a speech mainly dealing with other topics, to a wealthy audience in America.[6] The enthusiasm evinced by this remark had surprised him, especially as coming from such an audience, and this incident remained in his mind as an index of the world's sympathies. These sympathies were against any restoration of the old regime. We should be fighting against the current of the times if we tried to prevent Russia

[6] See the address printed at May 18, 1918, Vol. 48.

from finding her own path in freedom. Part of the strength of the Bolshevik leaders was doubtless the threat of foreign intervention. With the help of this threat they gathered the people round them. The reports of the American representatives in Russia were to this effect. He thought, therefore, that the British proposal contained the only suggestion that led anywhere. If the Bolsheviks refrained from invading Lithuania, Poland, Finland, &c., he thought we should be well advised to allow as many groups as desired to do so to send representatives to Paris. We should then try to reconcile them, both mutually and with the rest of the world.[7]

[7] "President Wilson stated that he did not see how it was possible to controvert the statement of Mr. Lloyd George. He thought that there was a force behind his discussion which was no doubt in his mind, but which it might be desirable to bring out a little more definitely. He did not believe that there would be sympathy anywhere with the brutal aspect of Bolshevism. If it were not for the fact of the domination of large vested interests in the political and economic world, while it might be true that this evil was in process of discussion and slow reform, it must be admitted, that the general body of men have grown impatient at the failure to bring about the necessary reform. He stated that there were many men who represented large vested interests in the United States who saw the necessity for these reforms and desired something which should be worked out at the Peace Conference, namely, the establishment of some machinery to provide for the opportunity of the individuals greater than the world has ever known. Capital and labor in the United States are not friends. Still they are not enemies in the sense that they are thinking of resorting to physical force to settle their differences. But they are distrustful, each of the other. Society cannot go on on that plane. On the one hand, there is a minority possessing capital and brains; on the other, a majority consisting of the great bodies of workers who are essential to the minority, but do not trust the minority, and feel that the minority will never render them their rights. A way must be found to put trust and cooperation between these two.

"President Wilson pointed out that the whole world was disturbed by this question before the Bolsheviki came into power. Seeds need soil, and the Bolsheviki seeds found the soil already prepared for them.

"President Wilson stated that he would not be surprised to find that the reason why British and United States troops would not be ready to enter Russia to fight the Bolsheviki was explained by the fact that the troops were not at all sure that if they put down Bolshevism they would not bring about a re-establishment of the ancient order. For example, in making a speech recently, to a well-dressed audience in New York City who were not to be expected to show such feeling, Mr. Wilson had referred casually to Russia, stating that the United States would do its utmost to aid her suppressed people. The audience exhibited the greatest enthusiasm, and this had remained in the President's mind as an index to where the sympathies of the New World are.

"President Wilson believed that those present would be playing against the principle of free spirit of the world if they did not give Russia a chance to find herself along the lines of utter freedom. He concurred with Mr. Lloyd George's view and supported his recommendations that the third line of procedure be adopted.

"President Wilson stated that he had also, like Mr. Lloyd George, received a memorandum from his experts which agreed substantially with the information which Mr. Lloyd George had received. There was one point which he thought particularly worthy of notice, and that was the report that the strength of the Bolshevik leaders lay in the argument that if they were not supported by the people of Russia, there would be foreign intervention, and the Bolsheviki were the only thing that stood between the Russians and foreign military control. It might well be that if the Bolsheviki were assured that they were safe from foreign aggression, they might lose support of their own movement.

"President Wilson further stated that he understood that the danger of destruction of all hope in the Baltic provinces was immediate, and that it should be made very clear if the British proposal were adopted, that the Bolsheviki would have to withdraw entirely from Lithuania and Poland. If they would agree to this to refrain from reprisals and outrages, he, for his part, would be prepared to receive representatives from as many groups and centers of action, as chose to come, and endeavor to assist them to reach a solution of their problem.

"He thought that the British proposal contained the only suggestions that led anywhere. It might lead nowhere. But this could at least be found out." ACNP notes cited above.

M. PICHON again suggested that before coming to a decision the meeting should hear M. Noulens, whose news from Russia was fresh.

BARON SONNINO suggested that M. de Scavenius,[8] who had been Danish Minister in Petrograd and was now in Paris, could also give very valuable information.

(It was decided that M. Noulens and M. de Scavenius should be invited to attend the meeting on the following day at 10.30 a.m.)[9]

T MS (SDR, RG 256, 180.03101/7, DNA).
  [8] Harald Roger de Scavenius, Danish Minister to Russia, 1912-1918.
  [9] Noulens actually came on January 20, and De Scavenius on the following day.

## To Raymond Poincaré

My dear Mr. President:                    Paris 16 January, 1919.

Mrs. Wilson and I are sincerely sorry that you cannot go with us to the play to be given by the American soldiers, but we perfectly understand, and I beg that you will accept my thanks for your gracious letter.

Cordially and faithfully yours,   [Woodrow Wilson]

CCL (WP, DLC).

## To James Viscount Bryce

My dear Lord Bryce:                    Paris, 16 January, 1919.

I was very much gratified to receive your kind letter written after I left London[1] and am heartily sorry not to have had a glimpse of you, to say what a pleasure it was to see you again and feel the influence of your generous friendship.

I am disturbed to find upon inquiry that the notes which you were kind enough to think of sending me have not reached me. I wonder if you will be kind enough to let me know in what form they were sent—I mean in what external form—so that I may try to trace them if they have been misplaced at this end.

You may be sure that I shall value them very highly and I hope with all my heart that they have not gone hopelessly astray.

I find the prospects for substantial agreement upon a League of Nations much more encouraging than I had dared to hope and I believe that things are moving most favorably in that regard.

In unavoidable haste, with warmest regards,

Cordially and sincerely yours,   [Woodrow Wilson]

CCL (WP, DLC).
¹ Lord Bryce to WW, Jan. 7, 1919, Vol. 53.

## Joseph Patrick Tumulty to Cary Travers Grayson

The White House, 16 January 1919.

American newspapers filled with stories this morning of critical character about rule of secrecy adopted for peace conferences, claiming that the first of the fourteen points has been violated. In my opinion, if President has consented to this, it will be fatal. The matter is so important to the people of the world that he could have afforded to go any length even to leaving the conference than to submit to this ruling. His attitude in this matter will lose a great deal of the confidence and support of the people of the world which he has had up to this time. Tumulty.

T telegram (WP, DLC).

## To Joseph Patrick Tumulty

Paris (Received Jan. 16, 1919 midnight)

Your cable about misunderstandings concerning my attitude toward period[ic] problems created by the newspapers cablegrams concern a matter which I admit I do not know how to handle. Every one of the things you mention is a fable. I have not only yielded nothing but have been asked to yield nothing. These maneuvers which the cablegram speak of are purely imaginary. I cannot check them from this end because the men who sent them insist on having something to talk about whether they know what the facts are or not. I will do my best with the three press associations.

Woodrow Wilson

T telegram (J. P. Tumulty Papers, DLC).

## From Newton Diehl Baker

Washington, January 16, 1919.

268. For the President from the Secretary of War.

"Situation with regard to pork products described in your 216¹ has been fully presented by Mr. Whitmarsh of Food Administration here. We have effected arrangements whereby pork products are served as part of the ration in the country and have asked the Chief Quartermaster in France to do likewise. I have directed that army purchases for January and February be increased as far as storage facilities and possible use will permit.

Have serious doubts as to the legality of purchases from War Department funds for distribution through Poland Food Commission. Senate Committee is now investigating pork packers and showing enormous profits and generally the public mind is greatly excited on the subject and an order now for purchases of such products in great volume would be immediately scrutinized and any doubt as to its legality emphasized. I realize that the purpose in view is not to help the packers, but to keep faith with the farmers and yet the rightfulness of such expenditure by the War Department being doubtful and the public mind excited on the whole question, serious misunderstanding would arise. However, if in your judgment the situation is serious I will direct that it be done. Possibility of taking up of the whole surplus of food products here producing stimulus of war conditions does not seem great. In the meantime the House of Representatives has passed the Hundred Million Dollar Relief Bill and the Senate is now considering the subject. If this bill is passed there will be a very much better source of funds to make these purchases than specific War Department funds."                                                    Polk.

T telegram (WP, DLC).
[1] WW to NDB, Jan. 9, 1919, Vol. 53.


## Joseph Patrick Tumulty to Cary Travers Grayson

The White House, 16 January 1919.

Swope story this morning fine human interest one.[1] Seibold[2] treating us fine. There is no truer friend. Know you will not forget him. President must show appreciation. Brainerd[3] of Brooklyn Eagle fine also. Roosevelt's death left great gap here. We must from now on make the people not only admire but love the President. Your interview with French reporter about President's personal traits fine.[4] Could you have Dave Lawrence write story of opinions and impressions men in streets of England, France and Italy have of the President? Life magazine in editorial says of Mr. Roosevelt quote He had power of embracing and capturing the spirits of his associates. Mr. Wilson has little of that. He loves his fellow man but has always found it hard to make him feel it. He has shown more signs of gaining that power since he went to Europe than he has ever shown before unquote.[5] All the friends who have returned have told me of your kind references to me. I will not forget this.

I am sending this message from my bed where I am down with the influenza.                                            Tumulty.

T telegram (J. P. Tumulty Papers, DLC).

[1] He referred to Herbert Bayard Swope, "Personal Cordiality Wins Colleagues to President," New York *World*, Jan. 15, 1919. Swope stated that he had "surreptitiously" received details of the first two meetings of the Council of Ten from an informant who was not a member of the American delegation. The significant portion of Swope's dispatch reads as follows: "He [Swope's informant] said that after the first formality, where President Wilson became the central figure in the room, the others paying him marked deference, he talked freely and to the point, never directing, but always suggesting. His famous 'May I not?' was called frequently into use. Seemingly he had set for himself the task of impressing his personal charm upon his associates, succeeding to such an extent that even those who were cold at first thawed under his influence. Without undertaking individual comparisons as to individual influence, my informant summarized the Wilsonian impression by saying that the president impressed himself deeply upon his colleagues by his courtesy, by his clarity of purpose, by his honesty of expression, by his vision and by his reason. *President Wilson's influence is purely personal, scarcely including the rest of the commission. There is a grave question as to what will happen after he returns to the United States, unless the basic work is completed then.*"

[2] That is, Louis Seibold.

[3] Chauncey Corey Brainerd, Washington correspondent of the *Brooklyn Daily Eagle*.

[4] See the translation of a news report of a press conference held by Dr. Grayson printed at Dec. 19, 1918, Vol. 53.

[5] A paraphrase from an untitled editorial in New York *Life*, LXXIII (Jan. 16, 1919), 88-89.

## From Jessie Woodrow Wilson Sayre

Darling Father,              Acorn Club [Philadelphia] Jan. 16, 1919

Here I am in Philadelphia[1] and very happy and comfortable. I have spent a week here at this pleasant sunny little club with Aunty Blanche,[2] and very cheery and pleasant it has been. Now Frank has come and we are moving to the Aldine Hotel because men are not allowed inside these doors on any pretext whatever. He can be here about ten days before his job at Harvard begins and we are having the very jolliest time. Of course he has to work hard on his preparation but on off hours we are to have walks and spins of one sort or another.

His book[3] is out and we are planning to send you one, of course, but are in doubt as to whether to send it across the ocean or to await your arrival here. The papers say you are coming back Feb. 15. Is it so, I wonder.

Frank moved the family up to Cambridge—22 Berkeley St is our new address—and the children are well established. Sarah Scott[4] is presiding over the household and Frank says I could not have chosen a better person, that she is a perfect trump. *Her* letters, too, seem cheery and as if she were really enjoying herself. So peace of mind reigns.

We are reading all about you in the papers, but I wonder most greedily at times what is going on underneath all the Peace-pipe smoking and love-feasting. Are the powers arrayed against us showing their claws? My questions are purely rhetorical; I should be ashamed of myself if I expected letters at such a time as this! I *am* ashamed that *I* haven't written since my wedding-anniversary letter Dec. 18th.[5] Hours of proof reading, Christmas celebrations and the double moving of me here and the children to Cambridge absolutely precluded letters for a while.

This is really just a little note of love from your adoring daughter
                                                                    Jessie.

ALS (WP, DLC).
   [1] She was in Philadelphia to be under the care of Dr. Edward Parker Davis for the birth of her third child.
   [2] That is, Blanche Nevin, about whom see n. 5 to the news report printed at Nov. 10, 1916, Vol. 38.
   [3] Francis Bowes Sayre, *Experiments in International Administration* (New York and London, 1919).
   [4] Sarah Post Scott, daughter of Professor William Berryman Scott of Princeton University.
   [5] Jessie W. W. Sayre to WW and EBW, Dec. 18, 1918, Vol. 53.


# Hankey's Notes of Two Meetings of the Council of Ten[1]

Quai d'Orsay, January 17, 1919, 10:30 A.M.

BC-4

M. CLEMENCEAU said that before beginning the business of the meeting, he wished to inform the Conference that Marshal Foch had obtained the signature of the Germans to the Armistice clauses drawn up on the previous Monday, concerning finance, Russian prisoners, the occupation of a bridgehead east of Strasburg, the delivery of the German commercial fleet, and, in fact, of all the clauses which had been proposed.

MR. LLOYD GEORGE, referring to the anxiety of the Press to attend the meetings of the Peace Conference, said that two classes of general conference might be distinguished. Firstly, there was the kind of conference to which all were admitted. Such conferences would be of a formal nature and little business would be transacted in them. Secondly, there would be conferences of the Great Powers with two or three of the smaller Powers, or young nations, such as Yugo-Slavs, the Poles, and Czecho-Slovaks associated with them. If publicity could safely be given to the first class, he asked whether it should be held to extend to the second. The second class of conference would be dealing with highly contentious questions,

   [1] The full text of these notes is printed in *PPC*, III, 594-600.

and he felt that their business would be much hampered by publicity.

PRESIDENT WILSON suggested that the reporters could be told that admission would be confined to conferences held in the large room at Quai d'Orsay. Conferences of the second class mentioned by Mr. Lloyd George could be held in the small room, and the Press could be thereby excluded from hearing the discussion.

M. CLEMENCEAU said that, apart from this question, it must be clearly stated that no publicity would be granted to the kind of conference now sitting. He suggested that the Press should be definitely informed of this, and that there should be a unanimous vote to that effect.

MR. LLOYD GEORGE suggested that what took place on these occasions could correctly be termed conversations, but not conferences. He pointed out that all the Delegates of the Powers represented were not present, but only two. These meetings, therefore, were in no sense conferences.

M. CLEMENCEAU said he wished to issue a communique to the Press telling them clearly in what cases publicity would be allowed, and in what cases it would be refused.

PRESIDENT WILSON, quoting the resolutions of the Special Committee appointed by the delegates of the Allied and American Press, observed that they asked for "full publicity for the peace negotiations." The proceedings now going on were not peace negotiations. The peace negotiations would, doubtless, be undertaken only in the big conferences. The second point asked for was that the official communique should be as complete as possible. The third was that, in addition to communiques, full summaries of the day's proceedings should be issued for the guidance of the members of the Press, "who would maintain full freedom of comment." The fourth was that free intercourse should be allowed between Delegates and responsible journalists.

M. MANTOUX,[2] who attended the meeting of the Press, stated that their demands related to the small as well as the big conferences.

MR. LLOYD GEORGE asked whether the full summaries requested by the Press, in addition to communiques, meant an account of the speeches made in the conferences. If this was so, he was opposed to the granting of such summaries. The procès-verbaux of the meetings could not be made public, otherwise business would become impossible. The Conference would tend to resemble the Council of

[2] Paul Joseph Mantoux, formerly Professor of Modern French History and Institutions at the University of London and interpreter for the inter-Allied conferences of the Supreme War Council; at this time the official interpreter for the peace conference.

Trent, whose labours were terminated in forty-three years after the death of all the original members.

PRESIDENT WILSON suggested that the matter should be approached from the other end. He suggested that representatives of the Press be admitted to conferences held in the large room.

M. CLEMENCEAU enquired how the representatives were to be selected.

PRESIDENT WILSON said that it would be enough to fix a number and leave it to the pressmen to elect their own delegates.

M. CLEMENCEAU said that if the decision was that the pressmen should not enter the smaller conferences, it was necessary to state this clearly.

BARON SONNINO suggested that their attendance should be limited to plenary conferences. He did not think a discrimination could be based upon the size of the room. Summaries of the smaller conferences would be furnished. He quite agreed that no pressmen could be allowed to attend the private conversations of the Great Powers.

MR. BALFOUR observed that the only plenary conferences would be those dealing with subjects in which all nations were concerned. It had been laid down that the small nations should only be present to watch their special interests. Hence, the range of subjects for plenary conferences was very limited. The question of the League of Nations might be instanced as one, and possibly there were financial questions concerning all nations. In any case, the subjects requiring plenary conferences would be very few. Hence, though the privilege granted to the Press might appear great, in practice it would be found insignificant.

PRESIDENT WILSON asked whether a plenary conference could not be held to mean a conference attended by all those interested in any given question. If, for instance, there were a question in which only the Great Powers were concerned, there would be a plenary conference when their entire Delegations were present.

MR. BALFOUR said that on this definition a subject like the territorial adjustment of Poland, Czecho-Slovakia or Yugo-Slavia, which required the presence of the Delegates of these peoples together with those of the Great Powers, would give rise to a plenary conference. Even if such a conference were held in the smaller room, we should be bound to admit the Press. He considered this very alarming.

PRESIDENT WILSON said it was, then, perhaps wiser to mention the room instead of defining the nature of the conference.

BARON SONNINO said that in his view a plenary conference was not one held to decide a particular interest even should all those concerned in it be present. A plenary conference would be one dealing with a group of questions, or one held to give final sanction to a group of decisions. For instance, reparation due to a damaged country would not be a question for a plenary conference, but the whole principle of reparation and its distribution over the whole of the damaged countries would be a subject for a plenary conference. Further, if general rules were laid down, it would be necessary to obtain sanction to them from a plenary conference.

M. PICHON said that he wished to make an observation which, in his opinion, had an important bearing on this subject. We were only considering Allied and Associated Nations, but there were also enemy nations, and this should not be overlooked. It had been decided that those nations should not be admitted to the Conference until the Allies had agreed among themselves. Were the Allies then to inform them in advance of their decisions and of all the discussions undertaken in the process of reaching these decisions? This would be in effect admitting them to the Conference, from which it had been decided to exclude them. He could not but regard this as extremely dangerous.

PRESIDENT WILSON said that the question under discussion was not so much a question of publicity or no publicity, as one of useful as opposed to perverted publicity. Publicity as such could not be avoided. It had not been avoided in reference to the meetings held hitherto. The only problem, therefore, was to obtain correct publicity.

MR. LLOYD GEORGE said that he did not feel quite sure that this was so. There was a great difference between conjectural reports and official summaries. The authority of the latter was infinitely greater than that of the former. If questions were put in Parliament regarding the former, it was always possible to reply that they were incorrect or incomplete. This answer was not possible in regard to the latter. If at every state of the discussion public and parliamentary agitation had to be pacified the discussion might be prolonged ad infinitum. What he wished to avoid was a Peace settled by public clamour. He had just had the experience of an election in England, during which the public was beginning to ask embarrassing questions concerning peace. Had the election lasted longer he might have come to the Conference with his hands tied by pledges, and deprived of his freedom of action. He wished to remain free to be convinced. If there were daily reports of the discussions as soon as the representative of any country yielded on a point that he had maintained on the previous day there would be headlines in the Press: "Great Britain is betrayed," or "France is betrayed." He therefore, on the whole, agreed with M. Pichon. He felt great misgiving concerning the view taken by Baron Sonnino that all final decisions on big questions should go to the plenary conference. There were numerous subjects concerning which premature publicity would render it impossible for any statesman to sign any treaty at all. He instanced the question of Syria and of indemnities. At a later stage it would be possible to show to the public that, if this or that had been conceded, other advantages had been obtained. He was not afraid of facing the Press, as he did not believe their demands were backed by the public. The Press was well aware that it was excluded from proceedings of Cabinets. This was a Cabinet of the nations. Furthermore, the enemy must not know beforehand what our decisions were, and still less what our differences were. Dangerous agitations might be aroused even in our own countries by premature publication of news, and he pointed out that in France and Italy the elections had not yet taken place.

PRESIDENT WILSON said that he might agree with all Mr. Lloyd George had said and yet feel that the difficulty had not been met. He gave as an instance certain conversations which had occurred in the house in which he lived, and had been reported shortly after in the Press with a considerable degree of accuracy. The subject discussed was one of great concern to a large group of nations.[3] Leakages, he felt sure, could not be prevented. The Press would

[3] "President Wilson thought that he might agree with what Mr. Lloyd George had just said, if it were not for the fact that he still thought that leaks were bound to occur of what transpired in the small conversations, because recently a private conversation which he had held in his own house regarding the solution of the Adriatic question was reported a day or so thereafter with a considerable degree of accuracy in The Daily Mail. He was afraid that the Press would be able to find out or divine what transpired at the private conversations.

"Mr. Lloyd George did not think that the publication of information of that kind had the same effect as if it had been an accurate statement from an official source." ACNP notes, Jan. 17, 1919, T MS (SDR, RG 256, 180.03101/8, DNA). These notes are printed in PPC, III, 612-22.

The article, in the London Daily Mail, Jan. 15, 1919, follows:

"Persons in touch with the Italian mission commenting on Signor Orlando's conference with President Wilson last Friday declare that the Italian Premier was surprised at the President's attitude. It is also reported that Mr. Wilson was firm not to recognise the Italian claims beyond Trieste and Trente. It is known that Baron Sonnino insisted on demanding also an important part of the Dalmatian coast and Fiume. On the other hand, Signor Orlando would cede the Dalmatian coast if he were sure of Fiume, but it is reported that even on this point Mr. Wilson is unwilling to give way.

"The majority of the population of the Dalmatian coast are Slav, although, in some towns like Zara, the majority is Italian. 'But the majority in Fiume is Italian,' Signor Orlando is reported as saying. Mr. Wilson announced that principles ought to guide the Peace Conference, construing this as principles of nationality and the commercial needs of the nation. The natural outlet of the Austrian Slavs was Fiume on the Adriatic, therefore the claims of the few thousands of Italians in Fiume were not to be balanced against the needs of a sea outlet for the millions of Slavs, that in fact the commercial necessity of the Slav confederation of the Austrian Balkans demanded the Adriatic outlet, and that if Italy ignored this necessity, she would incur the enmity of those populations and create a new danger to the peace of Europe.

"It is supposed that the President does not consider that Fiume as a free port in Italian hands would meet the needs of the Slav hinterland. The Italians in Fiume form a small

always either find out what had happened or make very accurate guesses.

MR. LLOYD GEORGE gave as an instance of a well-kept secret the debate on the language of the Conference, which had lasted some hours in that room, and had not been divulged in any newspaper, as far as he was aware. He thought that we should stand in the main on the line we had already taken up. What occurred in M. Pichon's room should be treated as conversations held with a purpose of reaching agreement. The Press should be given the result of each day's work. No summary should be given, as he wished to be able to say on one day what he thought, but on the morrow, if he had changed his mind after hearing his colleagues, to be free to do so. As to the Conference on Saturday, he proposed that the Press should be informed that 15 of their number should be admitted, and this without prejudice to the question of their admission at other conferences hereafter.

M. CLEMENCEAU suggested a text in the following sense: "The widest publicity will be given to accurate reports of both plenary and partial sittings."

MR. BALFOUR suggested that the word "general" should be substituted for the word "plenary." He deprecated the offer of any information concerning partial conferences.

PRESIDENT WILSON said that in the communication to the Press there should be a full and considerate explanation of the reasons for refusing the admission of reporters to the conversations. It might be added that those reasons did not apply with the same force to sessions of the general Conference.

MR. LLOYD GEORGE said he would not like to pledge himself to admitting the Press constantly to the general Conference. He saw difficulties ahead. Extreme views might be uttered in open meetings which it might not be convenient to refute there and then. He would prefer to offer the Press an invitation for Saturday only, without reference to the future.

PRESIDENT WILSON suggested that in addition to an explanation concerning the conversations, it might be said that even the general

---

pocket in the midst of the Slav population and to limit the ports of the Jugo-Slav States to the Dalmatian coast, would handicap Slav commerce by necessitating a long railroad transport in difficult country.

"The Italians argue that it is evident that Mr. Wilson in taking this position does not place importance on the so-called strategic needs of the countries as a principle of the Peace Conference. They say that if the Jugo-Slavs hold the coast and Fiume, they will have strategic control of the Adriatic. Pola, between Trieste and Fiume, is the only strong naval base of the Italians, and if a virile young Slav federation develops from the Austro-Balkan situation it would, through the possession of the Dalmatian coast, have the means of creating a powerful navy controlling the Adriatic. So, according to Italian opinion, it must be supposed that Mr. Wilson intends to substitute for the strategic needs of nations a League of Nations sufficiently strong to guarantee peace."

Conferences might find it necessary to enter into what was called in America "Executive Session." He suggested that Mr. Lloyd George should draft the message to the Press on the lines explained by him so persuasively in the Meeting.

MR. LLOYD GEORGE undertook to do so and present the draft at the afternoon's Meeting.

M. CLEMENCEAU said that he felt bound regretfully to draw attention again to certain mischievous statements in the American Press. He drew special attention to a despatch published in the "New York Tribune."[4]

PRESIDENT WILSON undertook to send a protest to the editor of the newspaper.

M. CLEMENCEAU also pointed out that it was stated in the American Press that the French censorship prevented telegrams from going to America.

(It was agreed that M. Clemenceau should deny this.)

[Balfour asked for representation for the Kingdom of the Hedjaz, which had taken an effective part in "one of the most successful of the subsidiary campaigns of the war." It was decided that the Hedjaz should be represented by two delegates.]

PRESIDENT WILSON drew attention to the representation of States, such as Ecuador, Peru, Bolivia, and Uruguay. He had understood that these States attended the Conference as of right when they were concerned in the subjects under discussion. In the Regulations, however, they were placed on the same footing as neutral Powers, attending meetings only when summoned. He, therefore suggested that the Regulations should be amended.

The Regulations were accordingly amended as follows:

"Article I, paragraph 3. The Powers in a state of diplomatic rupture with the enemy Powers (Bolivia, Ecuador, Peru, Uruguay) shall take part in the sessions at which questions concerning them are discussed."

The last paragraph of Article I will read:

"Neutral Powers and States in process of formation shall be heard either orally or in writing, when summoned by the Powers with

---

4 "M. Clemenceau called President Wilson's attention to an article carried in the New York Tribune, which, like many others, had been very severe to France. In this article it was claimed that the President did not deny certain things.

"President Wilson agreed that this was the most abominable form of lying, and pointed out that of course he had not denied things which they claimed he would not deny, as he had never been asked about them. The President assured M. Clemenceau that he would telegraph to the editor of the New York Tribune about the matter.

"Mr. Balfour inquired whether anything would be gained by asking American newspaper owners to come over here.

"President Wilson replied that there were usually quite a number of owners of American papers, and in many cases the owners' control was occasional and indirect." ACNP notes cited above.

general interests, at sessions devoted especially to the examination of questions directly concerning them, but only in so far as those questions are concerned."

The last clause of the first paragraph of Article II will read:

"One for Bolivia, Cuba, Ecuador, Guatemala, Hayti, Honduras, Liberia, Nicaragua, Panama, Peru, and Uruguay."

M. CLEMENCEAU proposed that, at the afternoon meeting, an agenda should be fixed for the opening session of the Peace Conference on Saturday. He thought it was most important that discussions at the big conferences should not stray beyond the agenda. This agenda should, in all cases, be prepared in the small committee. This was specially necessary for the first occasion. He did not wish the gathering to be of a merely formal nature. Certain points should be laid down as questions for study. These would be referred, according to President Wilson's suggestion, to the various Delegations, and the public would infer that the Congress meant to work. The public would further understand that another sitting could not follow at once, as time would be required for the completion of the study of the various points enumerated.

(It was agreed that proposals should be made for this agenda in the afternoon.)

T MS (SDR, RG 59, PPC 180.03101/8, DNA).


Quai d'Orsay, January 17, 1919, 3 P.M.[1]

BC-4A

[Pichon said that he had received formal protests from Belgium and Serbia at being allotted only two delegates each. After discussion, it was agreed to allot three to each, and it was also agreed that the question of the number of delegates to be apportioned to each country "must now be regarded as finally closed."]

M. PICHON said that the next question to consider would be the drafting of the Agenda for the first Preliminary Conference. As regards the subjects to be entered on the Agenda, he suggested the list of questions proposed by President Wilson at a previous meeting, namely:

1. League of Nations.
2. Reparations.
3. New States.
4. Frontiers and territorial changes.
5. Colonies.

These subjects to be discussed in the order given.

[1] The complete text of these notes is printed in PPC, III, 601-11.

PRESIDENT WILSON said that that list had really been put forward to form the basis of discussion at the small meetings and not for the large Conference.

MR. BALFOUR wished respectfully to put the following point to the meeting. He agreed that questions such as the League of Nations and Reparations were eminently suitable for discussion at a full Conference, but when it came to discussing the creation of New States, frontiers and territorial changes, and Colonial possessions, he dreaded the position in which they might find themselves. If these questions were to be put to the Delegates sitting at the full Conference, they would also have to be debated in full Conference. He asked his colleagues to imagine what would be the state of the full Conference if all these explosive subjects, full of difficulties and likely to lead to violent disputes, came up for discussion in this manner.

PRESIDENT WILSON enquired whether the following proposal would be preferable. The presiding officer at the Conference would appoint Committees on such and such subjects (large and small Committees), each consisting of a chosen number of Delegates who would be required to report to the Great Powers. The Great Powers would then decide on each question whether it should be sent back to the full Conference or not.

MR. LLOYD GEORGE said that a suggestion had occurred to him. No regular resolution should be proposed to the Conference, but a statement should be made by M. Clemenceau, as Chairman of the Conference, giving the general headings under which they would be prepared to study the various questions to be taken up by the Conference and he would invite each of the Delegations to submit to the Secretariat their views on such questions as might concern them. It would not be necessary to ask each of the Delegations to submit their views on every question. For instance, the Hedjaz need not be asked to give its views on Poland. But each of the Delegations should be invited to send their views to the Secretariat on subjects which concerned them. This would meet the wishes of people such as M. Veniselos, who were anxious to present their case to the Great Powers before any decision was reached by these. As soon as these reports were received, the Great Powers could direct their advisers to examine these documents and to extract irrelevant matter. It was very important that each country should have an opportunity of presenting its case, particularly as regards boundaries which it might covet. This would give the Delegation something to do—a very important matter. It would also give a reality to the Conference on the next day. It would not make the Conference formal and it would give the Delegates an opportunity of putting questions affecting themselves.

PRESIDENT WILSON thought that if Mr. Lloyd George's proposals were accepted, the large Conference, having nothing to discuss, would die of inanition. M. Clemenceau had said that his proposal would set the machinery working and he agreed that the Great Powers might be able to draw therefrom the work required by them. What they wanted was to give the members something real to do connected with the work of the Conference and not merely the appearance of work.

MR. LLOYD GEORGE thought that if a large number of committees was set up, a machinery would be created which it would be impossible for them to control, especially if the small Powers were represented on each of these small committees. Dozens of subjects would have to be considered and it would be impossible for the small States to be adequately represented on all. On the other hand, each Delegation could prepare reports which would assure their interests being duly considered. The resolution which Mr. Clemenceau had proposed was intended as a guide for the meeting of the Great Powers. When extended to a large Conference of thirty Powers, it was, in his opinion, quite inapplicable, whereas, if the Chairman made a speech asking the Delegations to put forward their views on any subjects included in the approved list which might concern them, the best results would be obtained. The Delegations themselves could decide what were the subjects of interest to them.

M. PICHON said that the Secretariat would receive all the reports and would make a digest of them.

M. CLEMENCEAU enquired what would happen to these reports after they had been dealt with by the Secretariat.

MR. BALFOUR thought that if these reports were then transmitted to the Great Powers, that would be a satisfactory arrangement, but if they were referred back to the big Conference, it would be extremely dangerous.

PRESIDENT WILSON proposed that the reports so received by the Secretariat should be submitted "for such reference as the Chairman may determine."

MR. BALFOUR suggested as an amendment that the reports should be forwarded to the Secretariat, "who will transmit the same to the Great Powers."

MR. LLOYD GEORGE agreed that that was exactly what the small Powers wanted. The small Powers all wished that the Great Powers should receive and give due consideration to their views.

M. CLEMENCEAU said they would adopt Mr. Lloyd George's proposal, but he wished to add to it something of his own which would to some extent include the proposal originally made by President Wilson. Mr. Balfour had admitted that certain questions, such as the League of Nations and Reparations, could at once be referred to the big Conference. If they agreed to take these two subjects only, that alone would give enormous work to do. On the other hand, President Wilson had asked that the consideration of the League of Nations should be deferred till the second meeting of the Conference. There remained the question of Reparations—a most important one. Why should not that be placed before the Conference on the next day? Why should not a large committee, with financial experts, be appointed to consider that question?

MR. LLOYD GEORGE said that he was altogether in favour of that suggestion, but he hoped it would not be discussed on the next day. He hoped that the question of Reparations would first be discussed here and that, after discussion, a commission would be appointed to deal with the whole question. With this reservation, he would support M. Clemenceau's proposal. He was of the opinion that each of the Delegations should be asked to send their views on all subjects of interest to them, including the question of a League of Nations.

M. CLEMENCEAU agreed.

MR. LLOYD GEORGE wished to suggest one more subject to be entered on the list, if the list was to be complete, namely, "Punishment of those guilty of offences against the Law of Nations."

M. PICHON wished to invite attention to the list included in the Note of Procedure,[2] which would be found to be more complete than President Wilson's. This list included the following:

1. League of Nations.
2. Polish affairs.
3. Russian affairs.
4. Baltic Nationalities.
5. States formed from the late Austro-Hungarian Monarchy.
6. Balkan affairs.
7. Eastern affairs.
8. Affairs of the Far East and of the Pacific.
9. Jewish affairs.
10. International river navigation (Rhine, Danube, Elbe, Scheldt and Vistula).
11. International railways (45th parallel, Adriatic to Baltic, Bagdad railways, African railways, Cape to Cairo and Cape to Algiers).
12. Public legislation ensuring to the peoples their self-determination, combined with the right of ethnical and religious minorities.

[2] It is printed in *PPC*, I, 386-96.

13. International legislation on labour.
14. International legislation, patents and trade marks.
15. Penalties against crimes committed during the war.
16. Economic system.
17. Reparation.
18. Financial questions.

It would be noticed that Mr. Lloyd George's proposal regarding penalties against crimes committed during the war was included.

PRESIDENT WILSON held that subjects such as those included in items 10 and 13 could not be brought under discussion at the Conference. Special technical committees would have to be appointed to draft the necessary regulations.

M. CLEMENCEAU thought that two or three questions only might be suggested for submission to the first Conference.

M. PICHON suggested that in submitting the list to the Delegations special attention should be drawn to the question of the "Responsibility of the authors of the war."

MR. LLOYD GEORGE asked that they should add to that, "International legislation on labour."

MR. BALFOUR enquired what elasticity was given to the Great Powers to add subjects to the list. He thought the Chairman should be authorised to add any subjects which might at some future date require consideration.

M. CLEMENCEAU said that the five Great Powers should decide what subjects were to be placed on the list. As Chairman he could not take upon himself the responsibility of deciding this question.

BARON SONNINO agreed that the Chairman should be the mandatory of the five Powers, but any Delegate could present an additional subject, which the Chairman would refer to the five Powers, who would give their decision as to its inclusion in the approved list.

MR. BALFOUR wished to raise one point of great importance. President Wilson, the Prime Minister and M. Clemenceau had pointed out how important it was to settle as soon as possible all questions which would facilitate demobilisation. Therefore it would be necessary to indicate the order in which the Delegates should settle the various questions entered on the list. This order would not be settled tomorrow, but they would reserve to themselves later on the right of settling the order of precedence.

BARON SONNINO thought that if they put off fixing the order of precedence the Delegates would not know what subjects to study and would do nothing.

PRESIDENT WILSON thought that demobilisation could not take place before their work had been completed. Demobilisation up to a certain point was taking place at present and could go on as at present. But could they hasten the final demobilisation except by making peace?

BARON SONNINO thought that if all questions which would facilitate demobilisation were to be considered first, the territorial questions should take precedence of all others.

M. CLEMENCEAU said that he agreed with President Wilson that peace alone could settle the question of demobilisation.

To sum up, he understood that the Delegations would be invited to submit reports on all questions which might interest them. These reports would be sent to the Secretariat for transmission to the five Great Powers.

The attention of the Delegations would be specially invited to two of these questions namely:

1. Responsibility of the authors of the war and penalties for crimes committed during the war.

2. International legislation on labour.

[Agreement was reached on procedures for proposing additional subjects for discussion.]

MR. LLOYD GEORGE distributed a draft note to be issued to the Press for publication, drawn up in accordance with a resolution adopted at that morning's meeting.

PRESIDENT WILSON wished to preface what he was going to say by the statement that he did not know how it would be possible for him to defend privacy for the meetings of the full Conference except on unusual occasions. The argument for privacy in these conversations between the Great Powers was conclusive. He wished to draw a distinction between the two. He would therefore suggest certain amendments in order to allow full publicity for the full Conference proceedings. He could not defend entire secrecy for the big Conferences. He felt compelled to draw a distinction between the two.

(President Wilson then read the text as amended by him[3] in order to give effect to his proposals. Mr. Lloyd George and Mr. Balfour proposed minor amendments in the wording of certain sentences.)

The following text was then unanimously accepted: . . .

(With regard to the full Conferences, the following rule was adopted: "Representatives of the Press shall be admitted to the meetings of the full Conference, but upon necessary occasions the deliberations of the Conference may be held in camera.")

M. CLEMENCEAU communicated to the meeting the substance of

---

[3] It is printed as the following document.

a telephone message received from Marshal Foch, to the effect that the German Delegates had agreed to sign an agreement relating to the German mercantile fleet in accordance with the conclusion reached by the Supreme War Council at the meeting held in Paris on Monday, 13th January, 1919. (See I.C.-105.)

T MS (SDR, RG 256, 180.03101/9, DNA).

## A Memorandum on Publicity[1]

[Jan. 17, 1919]

The Representatives of the Allied and Associated Powers have given earnest consideration to the question of publicity for the proceedings of the Peace Conference. They are anxious that the public through the Press should have the fullest information compatible with safeguarding the supreme interest of all, which is that a just and honourable settlement should be arrived at with the minimum of delay. It is, however, obvious that ⟨the⟩ publicity ⟨for the Conference proceedings⟩ with regard to the preliminary conversations now proceeding must be subject to the limitations necessarily imposed by the difficult and delicate nature of their ⟨task⟩ object.

The ⟨proceedings of a Peace Conference⟩ conversations of the Great Powers are far more analagous to ⟨those⟩ the meetings of a Cabinet than to those of a ⟨Parliament⟩ legislature. Nobody has ever suggested that Cabinet Meetings should be held in public, and if they were so held, the work of government would become impossible. One reason why Cabinets are held in private is in order that differences may be reconciled and agreement reached before the stage of publicity is begun. The essence of democratic method is not that deliberations of a Government should be conducted in public, but that its conclusions should be subject to the ⟨revision⟩ consideration of a popular Chamber and to free and open discussion on the platform and in the Press ⟨before they are binding upon the people⟩.

The representatives of the ⟨Allied and⟩ Associated Powers ⟨have met⟩ are holding conversations in order to solve questions which affect the vital interests of many nations, and upon which at present they may hold ⟨the most⟩ many diverse views. ⟨The Conference⟩ These deliberations cannot proceed by the method of a majority vote. No nation can be committed except by the free vote of its own delegates. The conclusions arrived at ⟨the Conference⟩ at these consultations therefore can only be formed by the difficult process of reaching agreement among all. This vital process would only be hindered if the discussion of every disputed question were to open by a public declaration by each Delegation of its own national point of view. Such a declaration would in many cases be followed by a ⟨violent⟩ *premature* public controversy. This would be serious enough if it were confined to controversy between parties within each State. It might be extremely dangerous if, as would often be inevitable, it resulted in controversy between nations. Moreover such public declarations would ⟨make⟩ *render* that give and take on the part of the delegates themselves, which is essential to a successful negotiation, a matter of infinitely greater difficulty.

It is also extremely important that the settlement should be not only just but speedy. Every belligerent Power is anxious for the early conclusion of peace, in order that its armies may be demobilised and that it may return once more to the ways of peace. If premature publicity is given to the negotiations, the proceedings of the Peace Conference would be interminably protracted, and the delegates would be forced ⟨not only⟩ to speak not only to the business before the Conference, but to ⟨deal⟩ *concern themselves* with the controversies which had been raised by the account of their proceedings outside.

Finally, there will often be very strong reasons against announcing the conclusions of the ⟨Conference⟩ *conversations* as they are arrived at. Representatives of a nation may be willing to give their assent on one point only provided they receive a concession on another point which has not yet been discussed. It will not be possible to judge of the wisdom and justice of the Peace settlement *until it can be viewed* as a whole, and premature announcements might lead to misapprehensions *and anxiety* as to the ultimate results for which there was no real foundation.

In calling attention to these necessary limitations on publicity the representatives of the Powers do not underrate the importance of carrying public opinion with them in the vast task by which they are confronted. They recognise that unless public opinion approves of the result of their labours they will be nugatory. ⟨They cannot forget that the conclusions at which they arrive can only become operative after they have received the free and unfettered assent of the representatives of the people. Communiques as full as is compatible with the public interest will be issued regularly, and representatives of the Press will be invited to attend the proceedings *of the full Conference* whenever possible.⟩ This reasoning applies with great force to the present conversations between representatives of the Great Powers.

T MS (WP, DLC).
    ¹ Words in angle brackets in the following document deleted by Wilson; words in italics added by him; words underlined our transcripts of WWsh. There are a few minor differences in the above version and the one printed in *PPC*, III, 610-11.

## To Tasker Howard Bliss

My dear General Bliss:                    Paris, 17 January, 1919.

It was kind of you to send me the suggestions about the draft of the Covenant for the League of Nations. I have gone over the draft with your suggestions by me and they have been of great service. I think all the points are covered.

In haste,
Cordially and sincerely yours,   Woodrow Wilson

TLS (T. H. Bliss Papers, DLC).

## From Arthur James Balfour

My dear Mr. President,                    Paris. 17th January 1919.

I listened with the deepest concern to what passed at this morning's conference relative to the article in the "Daily Mail" which professed to give your views upon the question of the Adriatic. The idea seemed to prevail that the foundation of this article must have been obtained from some unintentional indiscretion on the part of those who discussed this subject with you at the Hotel Murat and as nobody was present at this conversation but yourself and three English Cabinet Ministers I was a good deal perturbed.

I have now, however, seen the article, of which I enclose a copy, and I am inclined to believe from the internal evidence that its source is not what *you* supposed and *I* feared. It refers, as you will observe, not to any conversation held with us but to a Conference you were supposed to have held with Signor Orlando.

Now it was common gossip in the British and other Foreign Offices that in a conversation which you are alleged to have had with Signor Orlando, *not* last Friday but some time during a brief visit paid some time ago by Signor Orlando to Paris, that the results had not been satisfactory (on the Dalmatian question) to the Italian Minister.[1] I have not the slightest idea as to what passed at this conversation or as to whether it ever took place, but I heard the gossip to which I refer some time before I came to Paris myself last Sunday at the meetings of the International Conference, and I have not the slightest doubt in my own mind that the gossip which the "Daily Mail" got held [hold] of was based upon these old rumours and not upon anything which passed in the course of the present week.

I think when you have looked at the article you will probably come to the same opinion.

Pray do not take the trouble to answer this and believe me
Yours most sincerely,   Arthur James Balfour

P.S. The Prime Minister to whom I have shown this letter asks me to add that neither he nor Mr. Bonar Law have mentioned to anyone the matters which were discussed at the Hotel Murat. A.J.B.

TLS (WP, DLC).
  [1] About this conversation, see the extracts from the diaries of Dr. Grayson and Col. House printed at Dec. 21, 1918, Vol. 53.


# A Memorandum by the French Delegation

French Suggestion A plan of organization for the discussion of economic questions.[1]

January 17, 1919

If an era of permanent peace is to be inaugurated, it is essential that certain economic principles be adopted, such for instance, as are embraced in the phrase: "elimination of economic barriers." It may be equally important, before attempting to fix the permanent economic principles which should govern the world, that consideration be given the question of ensuring the several nations of the world an opportunity to start under these new conditions on a basis approaching normal. Due to war conditions, involving dislocation and destruction of industrial areas, several nations—notably Belgium, France, Serbia, and the territory which may comprise the Czecho-Slovak and Jugo-Slav nations—are economically at an abnormal disadvantage, which may be indefinitely perpetuated unless certain emergency economic measures are adopted to permit these nations to overcome the economic handicap under which the war has placed them. For instance, certain important industries of Belgium and France may never revive unless certain emergency measures are adopted by the world as a whole to assist them to a basis where it will then be practicable to remove artificial controls of trade.

It is, therefore, suggested that the economic work of the Commission naturally falls into three subdivisions:

(1) The determination of what measures, if any, may be desirable to bring the world economically to a condition so that the permanent principles which are to govern the world economically may equitably be applied;

(2) The determination of what part the enemy shall play in solving the preceding problem through making restoration and reparation;

(3) The determination of the economic principles which should permanently govern the trade relations of the world.

It is believed that these economic problems should be worked out under the direction of an economic committee, of not more than three, from the four great Powers. The limitation in number is suggested in order that the representatives of the four nations dealing with these economic problems may sit frequently in council and work out the problems together. Under the chief economic representatives of each Government should be special commissions, which also should work in an inter-allied manner.

CC MS (WP, DLC).
[1] WWhw and transcript of WWsh.


## To Joseph Patrick Tumulty

Paris (Received Jan. 17, 1919, 315pm)

Distressed to hear of your illness. Beg that you will make it your chief duty to take care of yourself and get well. All unite in most affectionate message. Everything going well here. Very few of the troubles spoken of by the newspapers are visible to me on the spot.

Woodrow Wilson.

T telegram (J. P. Tumulty Papers, DLC).


## From Thomas Watt Gregory

Dear Mr. President:                    Washington Jan. 17/19.

I will be leaving in a few moments for Chicago & St. Louis on some important Government business. Will you not excuse me for thus hurriedly adding something to my reply to your question as to my successor. Since you sailed I have found out some additional favorable things about Whipple. Papers have suggested Palmer, Ham Lewis Frank Polk & Wallace.[1] If you conclude to go outside of the present Departmental force it would be to strengthen your administration politically & otherwise. In that event Whipple offers the best solution as between those mentioned, & indeed as between all who have occurred to me. He is no better than Polk, who would make an ideal appointment, but I assume you could not spare him from his present work. Wallace is a good man but would be of no political value. Besides he is not near so forceful a man as Whipple or Polk.

In my judgment the selection of Palmer would be most unfortunate & cause you much trouble & regret. If you are considering him seriously I urge you not to reach a conclusion until I can write or talk to you fully. If you wish me to write in detail on this point cable me.                    Devotedly yours   T. W. Gregory.

ALS (WP, DLC).
[1] That is, Hugh Campbell Wallace.

## Frank Lyon Polk to the American Commissioners

Washington January 17, 1919.

7011. Very Confidential.

Department is receiving applications from negroes from various parts of the United States desiring to proceed to Paris to take part in a proposed Pan African Congress through which it is their intention, so they say, to solidify the sentiment of the negro race into a statement and petition which will be presented to the President regarding the right of self government, self determination and future status of the negro race of the world.[1] The Department assumes that the French Government are receiving similar requests from negroes from their possessions and would like to know what attitude they propose to take. On its part this Government questions whether any solid benefits would result in the proposed Congress at Paris. Cable reply.                                        Polk.

T telegram (WP, DLC).
   [1] William Edward Burghardt Du Bois was the driving force behind the proposed Pan African Congress. He secured the somewhat reluctant support of the National Association for the Advancement of Colored People for the project. Blaise Diagne, a Senegalese representative in the French Chamber of Deputies, persuaded Clemenceau to allow the congress to meet in Paris. The group which met in that city from February 19 to 21, 1919, consisted of fifty-seven "representatives of the Negro race": sixteen from the United States, twenty-one from the West Indies, twelve from Africa, and eight from Europe. Diagne was elected president of the congress and Du Bois executive secretary. For the background of, and the resolutions passed by, the congress, see Elliott M. Rudwick, *W. E. B. Du Bois: Propagandist of the Negro Protest* (New York, 1968), pp. 208-15.

## From the Diary of Dr. Grayson

Saturday, January 18, 1919.

This was the history making day of the conference. It marked the first plenary session. Early in the day it appeared as though the President might be unable to be present. He awakened suffering from a very bad cold. However, by keeping him in bed until noon and giving him heroic treatment he was sufficiently rested and his cold enough under control, to allow him to proceed to the Quai D'Orsay for the session. It was remarked that this was the 48th Anniversary of the day the French and Germans signed the shameful peace at Versailles, in the Hall of Mirrors, where William I was proclaimed King of Prussia and Emperor of Germany. The President was accompanied to the Quai D'Orsay by Mrs. Wilson and myself. Mrs. Wilson left us at the entrance to the foreign office. Weather conditions could hardly have been worse and rain fell in torrents, but it did not seem to dampen the spirits of the crowd gathered at

the entrance to the building to view the advent of the various no-
tables. The President reached the famous clock room at exactly one
minute to three. Most of the other delegates had already put in an
appearance. The President was greeted at the entrance by Foreign
Minister Pichon, who escorted him to his seat on the right of the
chair reserved for Premier Clemenceau and directly in front of the
big clock with the winged victory figure. At the left of Clemenceau
sat Lloyd George heading the British delegation. The American
delegates were seated in the following order: The President, Secretary of State Robert Lansing, a vacant chair for Colonel E. M.
House, Henry White and General T. H. Bliss. To their right were
seated the technical advisers of the American delegation, including
Admiral Benson, B. M. Baruch, Vance McCormick and E. N. Hurley. I had a seat to the right of Admiral Benson, in close touch with
the President, where he could reach me whenever he desired. At
exactly three o'clock Clemenceau took his chair and called the
assembly to order. He then introduced President Poincaré, who
delivered an address of welcome opening the conference. Poincaré
spoke in French and at the conclusion of his remarks it was translated into English by the official interpreter. The first real order of
business after Poincaré had concluded and withdrawn from the
room was the selection of the permanent chairman of the conference. Under diplomatic precedent the selection was confined to
the country in which the conference was held so it had been agreed
upon that Clemenceau should be chosen. President Wilson made
the nominating speech, placing the French Premier's name before
the conference. The hall was crowded, every seat being filled with
the exception of the three set aside for the Japanese delegates who
had not yet arrived. Gathered in the ante-chamber, watching the
proceeding through curtained arches, were some five hundred
newspaper men, representing nearly every country in the world
excepting the enemy ones. The President's speech was well received. At the conclusion of the President's speech Clemenceau
took him by the hand and said:

"You are much too good, Mr. President, you cover me with confusion."

Seconding speeches were made by Lloyd George and Baron Sonnino. During his speech Lloyd George referred to Clemenceau as
"The grand young man of France," but the interpreter confused
the term and translated it as "The grand old man," whereupon
Clemenceau got up and waved his hand in protest. Clemenceau
put the motion for his own selection which was of course carried
unanimously. The organization was then perfected by the selection
of the secretariat. Adjournment was taken at 5:30. According to

French custom when the presiding officer puts on his hat the meeting is adjourned, disregarding whether the members desire to adjourn or not. The President returned immediately to the Murat Palace and retired very early.

## From Edward Mandell House

Dear Governor:                                         Paris, January 18, 1919.

Poincare will open the session this morning by an address of welcome and you as ranking delegate will be expected to reply. You doubtless know this but here are some suggestions that have occurred to me.

I would speak of the privilege it is to be here at Paris in the center of French Civilization under such circumstances and for such purposes. I would say something regarding Paris as an ancient city, and speak of this event as the crowning glory of her history.

I would say that the eyes of the world are upon us watching anxiously. We are trusted, elese [else] we would not be here, but the people have been tricked in the past so many times that they cannot feel secure in this instance. They will be impatient at delay after nearly five years of the agony of war, and they are looking eagerly towards the day when the world shall be again released and under conditions which it is hoped will bring about a better and more enduring international society.

I would suggest that the windows be left open so that they [the] people may hear, not indeed all our deliberations, but, at least, before those deliberations have become fixed conclusions and have assumed concrete form.

Affectionately yours,   E. M. House

TLS (WP, DLC).

## Protocol of a Plenary Session of the Inter-Allied Conference for the Preliminaries of Peace[1]

Quai d'Orsay, January 18, 1919.

Protocol No. 1

[Poincaré opened the session at 3 p.m. In welcoming the delegates, Poincaré said that "not only Governments, but free peoples" were represented at the conference, and there was great need for unity. He then continued:]

---

[1] The complete text of this document, including Annex I, Bureau of the Conference, and Annex II, Rules of the Conference, is printed in *PPC*, III, 157-75.

"Even before the armistice, you placed that necessary unity under the aegis of the lofty moral and political truths of which President Wilson has nobly made himself the interpreter, and in the light of these truths you intend to accomplish your mission.

"You will therefore seek nothing but justice: 'justice that has no favourites,' justice in territorial problems, justice in financial problems, justice in economic problems.

"But justice is not inert, it does not submit to injustice. What it first demands, when it has been violated, are restitution and reparation for the peoples and individuals who have been despoiled or maltreated. In formulating this lawful claim, it obeys neither hatred nor an instinctive or thoughtless desire for reprisals; it pursues a two-fold object: to render to each his due and not to encourage crime through leaving it unpunished.

"What justice also demands, inspired by the same feeling, is the punishment of the guilty and effective guarantees against an active return of the spirit by which they were tempted. And it is logical to demand that these guarantees should be given above all to the nations that have been, and might again be, most exposed to aggressions or threats, to those who have many times stood in danger of being submerged by the periodic tide of the same invasions. . . ."

[After his address, Poincaré withdrew, and Clemenceau asked for the nomination of a permanent president of the conference. Wilson then spoke as follows:]

Mr. Chairman, It gives me great pleasure to propose, as permanent Chairman of the Conference, M. Clemenceau, the President of the Council. I would do this as a matter of custom. I would do it as a tribute to the French Republic; but I wish to do it as something more than that. I wish to do it as a tribute to the man, and you will certainly join with me in wishing it. France deserves the precedence, not only because we are meeting in her capital and because she has undergone some of the most tragic sufferings of the war, but also because her capital—her ancient and beautiful capital—has so often been the centre of conferences of this sort, upon which the fortunes of large parts of the world turned. It is a very delightful thought that the history of the world, which has so often centred here, will now be crowned by the achievements of this Conference, because there is a sense in which this is the supreme conference in the history of mankind. More nations are represented here than were ever represented at such a Conference before; the fortunes of all peoples are involved. A great war is ended which seemed about to bring a universal cataclysm. The danger is past. A victory has been won for mankind and it is delightful that we should be able to record these great results in this place. But it is the more delightful to honour France, because we can honour her in the person of so distinguished a servant. We have all felt in our participation in the struggles of this war the fine steadfastness which characterized the leadership of the French people in the hands of M. Clemenceau. We have learnt to admire him and those of us who have been associated with him have acquired a genuine affection for him. Moreover, those of us who have been in these recent days in constant consultation with him know how warmly his purpose is set towards the goal of achievement to which all our faces are turned. He feels, as we feel, as I have no doubt everybody in this room feels, that we are trusted to do a great thing; to do it in the highest spirit of friendship and accommodation and to do it as promptly as possible in order that the hearts of men may have fear lifted from them and that they may return to those pursuits of life which will bring them happiness, contentment and prosperity. Knowing his brotherhood of heart in these great matters, it affords me a personal pleasure to propose, not only that the President of the Council of Ministers, but M. Clemenceau shall be the permanent Chairman of this Conference.

[Wilson's motion, seconded by Lloyd George and Sonnino, was adopted unanimously, and Dutasta[2] was chosen as Secretary-General. Clemenceau then expressed gratitude for his election, and continued:]

"Gentlemen, I must nevertheless say that my election is necessarily due to the high international tradition of time-honoured courtesy towards the country which has the honour of greeting the Peace Conference in its capital. The proof of friendship (they will permit me to use the English word 'friendship' employed by Mr. Wilson and Mr. Lloyd George) has deeply touched me, because I see in it a new strength for all three of us, which will allow us to carry through, with the help of the whole Conference, the arduous work entrusted to us. I derive from it new confidence in the success of our efforts. President Wilson has special authority for saying that this is the first occasion on which a delegation of all civilised peoples of the world has been seen assembled. The greater the bloody catastrophe which has devastated and ruined one of the richest parts of France, the ampler and more complete should be the reparation— not only the reparation for acts committed—material reparation, if I may say so, which is due to all of us—but the nobler and higher reparation which we shall try to make, so that the peoples may be able at last to escape from this fatal embrace, which, piling up ruin and grief, terrorises populations, and prevents them from devoting

[2] That is, Paul Eugène Dutasta.

themselves freely to their work for fear of enemies who may arise against them at any moment. Ours is a great and noble ambition. We must hope that success will crown our efforts. This can only be if we have clear and well-defined ideas. A few days ago I spoke in the Chamber of Deputies, and I wish to repeat here, that 'success is only possible if we all remain firmly united.' We have come here as friends; we must leave this room as brothers. That is the first thought which I wish to express. Everything must yield to the necessity of a closer and closer union among the peoples who have taken part in this great war. The League of Nations is here. It is in yourselves; it is for you to make it live; and for that it must be in our hearts. As I have said to President Wilson, there must be no sacrifice which we are not ready to accept.

"I doubt not that you are ready for it.

"We shall arrive at this result only if we try impartially to reconcile interests apparently opposite, by looking above them at a greater and happier humanity. That, gentlemen, is what I have to say to you.

"I am touched beyond expression at the mark of confidence and friendship which you are good enough to give me. The programme of this Conference has been laid down by President Wilson; we have no longer to make peace for territories more or less large; we have no longer to make peace for continents; we have to make it for peoples. This programme is self-sufficing. There is no word to be added to it. Gentlemen, let us try to act quickly and well.

"I lay on the table the rules of the Conference, which will be distributed to you."

[Clemenceau then invited the delegates of all the powers to hand in memoranda on the responsibility of the authors of the war, the penalty for the crimes committed during the war, and international legislation on labor, as well as memoranda of a more general character. He drew the attention of the conference to the urgency of the first question, concerning the responsibility of the authors of the war, and said that, if the conferees wished "to establish law in the world, penalties for the breach thereof" could be applied at once, since the Allied and Associated Powers were victorious. A memorandum on this subject would be distributed to all the delegations. The protocol concludes as follows:]

This programme of work having met with general approval, the President informs the Conference that at the head of the order of the day of the next session stands the question of the League of Nations.

Finally, the President thinks right to add that as the different Delegations are to work in complete agreement, each member of the Conference is invited to present such observations as he may consider necessary. The Bureau will welcome the expression of any opinion which may be manifested, and will reply to all questions asked of it.

As nobody wishes to speak, the sitting adjourns at 16.35 o'clock (4.35 p.m.).

Printed text (SDR, RG 256, 180.0201/1, DNA).

## From Joseph Patrick Tumulty

Washington, 18 Jan. 1919

Ralph Pulitzer in striking article this morning[1] uses the following quote If he allows precedent to keep him closeted with those leaders and to keep their peoples and our own locked out his task seems hopeless of accomplishment stop. If he boldly breaks out through precedent and takes the issue between liberalism and reaction to the peoples of the nations as he has so often taken the issues of less world-wide importance to our own people I believe he will win his victory for humanity and peace end quote.

I thought you would be interested in it stop. Am feeling better and keeping touch with things here. Thank you sincerely for your telegram it helped a lot.                    Tumulty.

T telegram (WP, DLC).
   [1] He referred to Charles H. Grasty, "Forces at War in Peace Conclave," *New York Times*, Jan. 18, 1919. This article consisted of a lengthy statement given to Grasty by Ralph Pulitzer just prior to his departure from Paris for New York. The passage quoted by Tumulty was the final paragraph of the article. Pulitzer had begun by declaring that the Entente powers were "suffering all the vicissitudes of victory." "The solidarity of a common danger," he wrote, "has departed. The joint instinct of self-preservation has given place to conflicting aims of self-aggrandizement." Pulitzer saw three forces making for a bad peace settlement: the "bourbonism of politicians . . . playing for advancement on the chauvinism of the people"; the "materialism of industrial and commercial circles appealing to the business classes"; and the "militarism of professional soldiers appealing to pride or fear of imperialism and Jingoes." However, Pulitzer also discerned three forces making for a just and lasting peace: the "inarticulate masses of the nations whose hearts' desire is the perpetuation of peace"; the leaders of liberal thought in all nations; and President Wilson, who had made himself the spokesman of both the masses and the liberal leaders. Pulitzer praised the presence of Wilson at the peace conference: "It seems safe to assert that lacking the potentiality of President Wilson's physical presence here his fourteen points, which with one qualification were the bases of the armistice, accepted by the Allies, would not have the remotest chance of surviving obliteration or at least mutilation at the hands of the elder statesmen of the conference." Pulitzer pointed out that Wilson, in his quest for a good peace settlement, had an "uncongenial but powerful ally in the menace of Bolshevism." This menace to some degree had replaced Germany as a unifying factor among the Allies. Pulitzer believed that two things had to be accomplished quickly to secure a just and lasting peace: a viable league of nations had to be agreed upon in the early stages of the peace conference, and the blockade of Germany had to be relaxed in order to permit the feeding of her people. These two things offered both the best defense against Bolshevism and the only real hope for a lasting peace.

# From Marguerite de Witt Schlumberger

Mr. President:                          Paris, le 18the January 1919

I have the honor of soliciting from you an audience for a few members of the officers of the *Union francaise pour le Suffrage des Femmes*, which has called for 10th February, next, an Inter-Allied Conference of Women in Paris. This federation counted before the war 100 groups of suffragists and 12,000 or 13,000 members. It is affiliated with the International Woman Suffrage Alliance, its President Mrs. Chapman-Catt of New York.

We wish, Mr. President, to thank you personally for answering favorably on 7th June 1918, through Mrs. Catt and the Reverend Anna Shaw, to a memorandum about your opinion on Woman Suffrage which the *Union francaise* communicated to you in February 1918,[1] and to tell you about the preliminary understandings which we hope to arrive at with the peace envoys before the sitting of our conference.

We desire, also, to express the deep admiration of French women for the policies which you inaugurated so nobly and with so lofty a view, and we wish to ask you how we may help to vindicate those policies during the Peace Conference as concerning the Society of Nations.

We would beg of you to use your immense influence for introducing Woman Suffrage together with the other world questions necessary to discuss at the Peace Congress, and we petition that you affirm on the score of the organization and maintenance of peace the importance you attach to giving vocal expression to more than half of humanity represented by women who in many countries have been condemned to an unjust and cruel silence by the denial of the vote.

Therefore we beg of you, Mr. President, to be so good as to assign to us a rendezvous as soon as possible before your departure to America, and we express beforehand our deep thankfulness.

For the Executive Committee of the
*Union francaise pour le Suffrage des Femmes*
Marguerite de Witt Schlumberger   The President
Vice President of the International Alliance for Woman Suffrage

TLS (WP, DLC).
[1] See WW to Carrie C. L. C. Catt, June 13, 1918, and the Enclosure printed with WW to JPT, May 16, 1918, both in Vol. 48.

## A Translation of a letter from Vittorio Emanuele III

Mr. President,                                    Rome, 18 January 1919

The courteous letter which you were pleased to send to me on the 9th. inst.[1] was most gratifying. I thank you most sincerely for it, and I wish to repeat with what great pleasure the Queen and I received your kind visit and that of Mme. Wilson and Miss Wilson. Your stay in Rome was all too short for us—it will always remain a most precious souvenir for the Queen and myself.

Be so kind as to receive, with these sentiments, the renewed expression of my cordial and most friendly greetings, with the best wishes of the Queen for Mrs. Wilson and for Miss Wilson.

Your affectionate,   Vittorio Emanuele

T MS (WP, DLC).
[1] See WW to Vittorio Emanuele III, Jan. 9, 1919, Vol. 53.

## Thomas Nelson Page to the American Commissioners

Rome, January 18th, 1919.

84. Confidential. Have seen Orlando who expressed himself in terms of much politeness. Greatly troubled to find the President's views regarding Istria and the Dalmatian coast such that the Italian people would not be satisfied with their acceptance. He specified among these the divisions of Istria peninsula about half and the leaving in the hands of the Jugo-Slavs of the Italian cities from Zara south. I suggested that the present press campaign has excited the people and caused them to make much more extended claims than before. He admitted that the press has had exciting effect, but says that the action of the Jugo-Slavs is the chief cause of Italians' excitement over the possibility of leaving their brothers unredeemed under the heel of a foreign oppression which will destroy them sooner or later. This is undoubtedly one of the causes. I urged him to get into accord with the President as Italy will have at the Peace Table no better or more disinterested friend. He said that any peace treaty which he and the President will sign Sonnino will accept, but it would be destructive for him to sign a treaty which the people will refuse to accept. He says Salandra[1] will act with him. Both the British and French Ambassadors[2] were seeing him this evening before his departure for Paris.

Undoubtedly the people are becoming more and more assertive of their determination not to sacrifice Italians to Jugo-Slavs. Orlando knows that Sonnino must yield some of his contentions and hear he admits that even should England and France hold to the treaty of London this will not serve unless the United States does also, but hopes he may be strong enough to claim a victory over Bissolati and the Moderates. Meantime, the press campaign which, it is believed, is supported by the Foreign Office has excited the people so that it will be difficult to appease them without satisfying them that all Italians are secured against oppression.

The new note in the press is that England and France are grabbing territory, and therefore Italy should have equal freedom. The Colonial Congress[3] already reported took this stand and I hear it has caused their representatives considerable anxiety as it is widening the division against Italy and them. One of them I heard has taken the matter up here.

On the other hand the press campaign has stirred up strong opposition in Milan where a serious riot has occurred and excitement still continues.                                   Nelson Page.

T telegram (WP, DLC).
[1] That is, Antonio Salandra, at this time one of the Italian plenipotentiary delegates to the peace conference.
[2] Sir James Rennell Rodd and (Pierre Eugène) Camille Barrère, respectively.
[3] Apparently a reference to the Congress of Oppressed Nationalities of Austria-Hungary, which had met in Rome April 9-11, 1918. This congress had included numerous prominent Italian delegates, and the unofficial but influential "Pact of Rome" which resulted from its deliberations discussed Italian territorial aims in general terms. See Victor S. Mamatey, *The United States and East Central Europe, 1914-1918: A Study in Wilsonian Diplomacy and Propaganda* (Princeton, N. J., 1957), pp. 239-46, and René Albrecht-Carrié, *Italy at the Paris Peace Conference* (New York, 1938), pp. 44-48. A partial text of the Pact of Rome is printed in *ibid.*, pp. 347-48.


# William Hepburn Buckler to Robert Lansing

Copenhagen, January 18, 1919.

116. Strictly confidential and secret. From Buckler for Secretary Lansing, to be decoded by or under the supervision of Grew or Harrison: As (group omitted) to day for Paris via Basle, and as my journey across Germany may be delayed, the following summary is submitted pending full report:

I saw Litvinoff on January 14th, 15th and 16th, explaining I was merely a private telephone without authority to make proposals of any kind. He agreed that our talk should be confidential.

The Soviet Government, he declared, is anxious for permanent peace and fully indorses his telegram to the President of December 24.[1] They detest the military preparations and costly campaigns now forced upon Russia after four years of exhausting war and wish to ascertain whether the Allies and the United States desire peace. If they do, it can easily be negotiated for the Soviet Government is prepared to compromise on all points, including the Russian

Foreign Debt, protection to existing foreign enterprises and the granting of new concessions in Russia. Details as to possible compromises cannot now be given because Litvinoff has no idea of what claims the Allies will present nor of what resources Russia will have wherewith to satisfy those claims. As stated, [when] these data are available the particulars can be worked out by experts and on all points. The conciliatory attitude of the Soviet Government is unquestionable.

He showed me an open wireless telegram just received from Tchitcherine[2] affirming the willingness of the government to conciliate on the question of the foreign debt. Litvinoff and his associates fully realize that for a long time Russia will need expert assistance and advice especially in technical and financial matters and that she cannot get on without foreign machinery and manufactured imports. If peace were once made Russian Bolshevist propaganda in foreign countries would cease at once. The war declared on Russia by the Allies called forth that revolutionary propaganda as a measure of retaliation just as it has produced violence and terror in other (apparent omission) these will all cease as soon as the war stops. Against Germany propaganda has been freely used but militarist Germany was till recently Russia's most dangerous enemy and was really at war with her notwithstanding the nominal peace of Brest Litovsk. During the eight months in which Litvinoff was Russian Representative he conducted [no] political propaganda except defense of his government against attack and everything issued by him was printed in England. This the Foreign Office which seized all his papers can confirm. Russians realize that in certain western countries conditions are not favorable for a revolution of the Russian type. No amount of propaganda can produce such conditions. If Russia could make peace with the Allies these results would immediately follow:

1st. An amnesty would be extended to Russians who have been hostile to the Soviet government and bitterness against them would soon disappear. Such persons being few in number would be allowed to leave Russia if they chose.

2nd. The intrinsic weakness of the forces opposed to the Soviet government south Russia Siberia and Archangel would at once be revealed. These represent only a minority in each district and have owed their local successes solely to Allied support.

3rd. The present hostility toward Russia of Finland and other countries needing Russian products would speedily vanish. Russians have no imperialistic designs on Finland, Poland or Ukraine and wish only to give them full rights of self-determination but so long as foreign powers support the capitalist classes there Russia feels justified in supporting the working classes in those countries.

Litvinoff does not deny the many Soviet blunders but says that the system has worked well considering the enormous difficulties faced during the past year and that its efficiency is constantly improving. The peasant cooperatives now working with the Soviet are managing well the distribution of food. If this new system were now overthrown by force more anarchy and starvation must ensue. Insofar as the League of Nations can prevent war without encouraging reaction, it can count on the support of the Soviet Government.

So much for Litvinoff. The following information was given to me by Arthur Ransome Daily News Correspondent who left Moscow last August but has kept constant contact with Bolshevists in Stockholm and knows their views intimately. He believes they would compromise as to the Ural and other frontiers a point on which I pressed L. but got no definite answer beyond a claim that all Siberia must be Russian. Ransome also believes that continued intervention by the Entente can in time smash the Soviet power. When however this has been accomplished intervention on a still larger scale must continue in an indefinite period in order to cure the inevitable anarchy. The Soviet Government is the only one showing capacity to hold the Russian people and no successor to it could exist without military support. This fact and the discontent certain to be caused in Entente countries by such prolonged military effort are fully appreciated by a large class of Bolshevists, who oppose Tchitcherin's and Litvinoff's plans for compromise and hope for more active Allied intervention. The continuance of such intervention plays into the hands of these extremists whereas a policy of agreement with the Soviet Government will counteract their influence, will strengthen the Moderates and by reviving trade and industry will procure prosperity the best of all antidotes to Bolshevism.

If you care to bring Ransome to Paris he could inform you almost as well as Litvinoff respecting the Soviet Government attitude on any question.

Since L. has for a month been deprived of mail and of wireless cipher no effective negotiation can begin until the Allies arrange with Sweden and Finland so that he may communicate confidentially with his government; and since he fears expulsion at any moment from Sweden this can be arranged without delay if negotiation is contemplated. As Litvinoff is the only possible channel for such negotiation as The Legation at Stockholm may not appear to you a suitable intermediary and as the journey from here to Paris takes three and a half days I await your instructions here in case you should wish me to return to Stockholm. If you wish me to come to Paris please instruct me as promptly as possible.

T telegram (WP, DLC).
  [1] See M. M. Litvinov to WW, Dec. 24, 1918, Vol. 53.
  [2] See I. N. Morris to EMH, Jan. 19, 1919.


## William Christian Bullitt to Gilbert Fairchild Close

My dear Mr. Close:                              [Paris] 18 January 1919.

In accordance with your letter of January 15th, I have taken up with Mlle. Thomson the details of the manifestation which the groups of French working women wish to make in honor of the President on Saturday, January 25th at 3 o'clock.

Mlle. Thomson has prepared the program which I append.[1] I hope that you will be able to reply to Mlle. Thomson in the very near future; for January 25th is but a week away and this is a very short time in which to arrange a meeting of so many thousands of women.          Very respectfully yours,   William C. Bullitt

TLS (WP, DLC).
  [1] Valentine Thomson to GFC, Jan. 18, 1919, TLS (WP, DLC). She described the proposed ceremonial presentation to Wilson by French women workers of a bas relief by the sculptor, Paul Landowski, depicting a woman holding a child. She also indicated the subjects of the brief speeches to be made on the occasion.


## Wilson's Second "Paris Draft" of the Covenant

[Jan. 18, 1919]

### PREAMBLE

In order to secure international peace and security by the prescription of open, just, and honorable relations between nations, by the firm establishment of the understandings of international law as the actual rule of conduct among governments, and by the maintenance of justice and a scrupulous respect for all treaty obligations in the dealings of organized peoples with one another, and in order to promote international cooperation, the Powers signatory to this covenant and agreement jointly and severally adopt this constitution of the League of Nations.

### ARTICLE I.

The action of the Signatory Powers under the terms of this covenant shall be effected through the instrumentality of a Body of Delegates which shall consist of the ambassadors and ministers of the contracting Powers accredited to H[olland]. and the Minister for Foreign Affairs of H. The meetings of the Body of Delegates shall be held at the seat of government of H. and the Minister for Foreign affairs of H. shall be the presiding officer of the Body.

Whenever the Delegates deem it necessary or advisable, they may meet temporarily at the seat of government of B[elgium]. or of S[witzerland]., in which case the Ambassador or Minister to H. of the country in which the meeting is held shall be the presiding officer *pro tempore.*

It shall be the privilege of any of the contracting Powers to assist its representative in the Body of Delegates by any method of conference, counsel, or advice that may seem best to it, and also to substitute upon occasion a special representative for its regular diplomatic representative accredited to H.

### ARTICLE II.

The Body of Delegates shall regulate their own procedure and shall have power to appoint such committees as they may deem necessary to inquire into and report upon any matters that lie within the field of their action.

It shall be the right of the Body of Delegates, upon the initiative of any member, to discuss, either publicly or privately as it may deem best, any matter lying within the jurisdiction of the League of Nations as defined in this covenant, or any matter likely to affect the peace of the world; but all actions of the Body of Delegates taken in the exercises of the functions and powers granted to them under this Covenant shall be formulated and agreed upon by an Executive Council, which shall act either by reference or upon its own initiative and which shall consist of the representatives of the Great Powers, together with representatives drawn in annual rotation from two panels, one of which shall be made up of the representatives of the States ranking next after the Great Powers and the other of the representatives of the minor States (a classification which the Body of Delegates shall itself establish and may from time to time alter), such a number being drawn from these panels as will be but one less than the representatives of the Great Powers; and three or more negative votes in the Council shall operate as a veto upon any action or resolution proposed.

All resolutions passed or actions taken by the Executive Council, except those adopted in execution of any direct powers herein granted to the Body of Delegates themselves, shall have the effect of recommendations to the several governments of the League.

The Executive Council shall appoint a permanent Secretariat and staff and may appoint joint committees, chosen from the Body of Delegates or consisting of specially qualified persons outside of that Body, for the study and systematic consideration of the international questions with which the Council may have to deal, or of questions likely to lead to international complications or disputes. It shall also take the necessary steps to establish and maintain proper liaison both with the foreign offices of the signatory powers and with any governments or agencies which may be acting as mandatories of the League of Nations in any part of the world.

### ARTICLE III.

The Contracting Powers unite in guaranteeing to each other political independence and territorial integrity as against external aggression; but it is understood between them that such territorial readjustments, if any, as may in the future become necessary by reason of changes in present racial conditions and aspirations or present social and political relationships, pursuant to the principle of self-determination, and also such territorial readjustments as may in the judgment of three-fourths of the Delegates be demanded by the welfare and manifest interest of the peoples concerned, may be effected if agreeable to those peoples and to the States from which the territory is separated or to which it is added; and that territorial changes may in equity involve material compensation. The Contracting Powers accept without reservation the principle that the peace of the world is superior in importance to every question of Political jurisdiction or boundary.

### ARTICLE IV.

The Contracting Powers recognize the principle that the establishment and maintenance of peace will require the reduction of national armaments to the lowest point consistent with domestic safety and the enforcement by common action of international obligations; and the Executive Council is directed to formulate at once plans by which such a reduction may be brought about. The plan so formulated shall be binding when, and only when, unanimously approved by the Governments signatory to this Covenant.

As the basis for such a reduction of armaments, all the Powers subscribing to the Treaty of Peace of which this Covenant constitutes a part hereby agree to abolish conscription and all other forms of compulsory military service, and also agree that their future forces of defense and of international action shall consist of militia or volunteers, whose numbers and methods of training shall be fixed, after expert inquiry, by the agreements with regard to the reduction of armaments referred to in the last preceding paragraph.

The Executive Council shall also determine for the consideration and action of the several governments what direct military equipment and armament is fair and reasonable in proportion to the scale of forces laid down in the programme of disarmament; and these limits, when adopted, shall not be exceeded without the permission of the Body of Delegates.

The Contracting Powers further agree that munitions and implements of war shall not be manufactured by private enterprise or for private profit, and that there shall be full and frank publicity as to all national armaments and military or naval programmes.

ARTICLE V.

The Contracting Powers jointly and severally agree that should disputes or difficulties arise between or among them which cannot be satisfactorily settled or adjusted by the ordinary processes of diplomacy, they will in no case resort to armed force without previously submitting the questions and matters involved either to arbitration or to inquiry by the Executive Council of the Body of Delegates or until there has been an award by the arbitrators or a decision by the Executive Council; and that they will not even then resort to armed force as against a member of the League of Nations who complies with the award of the arbitrators or the decision of the Executive Council.

The Powers signatory to this Covenant undertake and agree that whenever any dispute or difficulty shall arise between or among them with regard to any question of the law of nations, with regard to the interpretation of a treaty, as to any fact which would, if established, constitute a breach of international obligation, or as to any alleged damage and the nature and measure of the reparation to be made therefor, if such dispute or difficulty cannot be satisfactorily settled by the ordinary processes of negotiation, to submit the whole subject-matter to arbitration and to carry out in full good faith any award or decision that may be rendered.

In case of arbitration, the matter or matters at issue shall be referred to three arbitrators, one of the three to be selected by each of the parties to the dispute, from outside their own nations, when there are but two such parties, and the third by the two thus selected. When there are more than two parties to the dispute, one arbitrator shall be named by each of the several parties and the arbitrators thus named shall add to their number others of their own choice, the number thus added to be limited to the number which will suffice to give a deciding voice to the arbitrators thus added in case of a tie vote among the arbitrators chosen by the contending parties. In case the arbitrators chosen by the contending parties cannot agree upon an additional arbitrator or arbitrators, the additional arbitrator or arbitrators shall be chosen by the Executive Council.

On the appeal of a party to the dispute the decision of the arbitrators may be set aside by a vote of three-fourths of the Delegates, in case the decision of the arbitrators was unanimous, or by a vote of two-thirds of the Delegates in case the decision of the arbitrators was not unanimous, but unless thus set aside shall be finally binding and conclusive.

When any decision of arbitrators shall have been thus set aside, the dispute shall again be submitted to arbitrators chosen as heretofore provided, none of whom shall, however, have previously acted as arbitrators in the dispute in question, and the decision of the arbitrators rendered in this second arbitration shall be finally binding and conclusive without right of appeal.

If for any reason it should prove impracticable to refer any matter in dispute to arbitration, the parties to the dispute shall apply to the Executive Council to take the matter under consideration for such mediatory action or recommendation as it may deem wise in the circumstances. The Council shall immediately accept the reference and give notice to the parties, and shall make the necessary arrangements for a full hearing, investigation, and consideration. It shall ascertain and as soon as possible make public all the facts involved in the dispute and shall make such recommendations as it may deem wise and practicable based on the merits of the controversy and calculated to secure a just and lasting settlement. Other members of the League shall place at the disposal of the Executive Council any and all information that may be in their possession which in any way bears upon the facts or merits of the controversy; and the Executive Council shall do everything in its power by way of mediation or conciliation to bring about a peaceful settlement. The decisions of the Executive Council shall be addressed to the disputants, and shall not have the force of a binding verdict. Should the Executive Council fail to arrive at any conclusion, it shall be the privilege of the members of the Executive Council to publish their several conclusions or recommendations; and such publications shall not be regarded as an unfriendly act by either or any of the disputants.

Every award by arbitrators and every decision by the Executive Council upon a matter in dispute between States must be rendered within twelve months after formal reference.

### ARTICLE VI.

Should any contracting power break or disregard its covenants under ARTICLE V, it shall thereby *ipso facto* be deemed to have committed an act of war against all the members of the League, which shall immediately subject it to a complete economic and financial boycott, including the severance of all trade or financial relations, the prohibition of all intercourse between their subjects and the subjects of the covenant-breaking State, and the prevention, so far as possible, of all financial, commercial, or personal intercourse between the subjects of the covenant-breaking State and the subjects of any other State, whether a member of the League of Nations or not.

It shall be the privilege and duty of the executive Council of the

Body of Delegates in such a case to recommend what effective military or naval force the members of the League of Nations shall severally contribute, and to advise, if it should think best, that the smaller members of the League be excused from making any contribution to the armed forces to be used against the covenant-breaking State.

The covenant-breaking State shall, after the restoration of peace, be subject to the regulations with regard to a peace establishment provided for new States under the terms SUPPLEMENTARY ARTICLE IV.

### ARTICLE VII.

If any Power shall declare war or begin hostilities, or take any hostile step short of war, against another Power before submitting the dispute involved to arbitrators or consideration by the Executive Council as herein provided, or shall declare war or begin hostilities, or take any hostile step short of war, in regard to any dispute which has been decided adversely to it by arbitrators chosen and empowered as herein provided, the Contracting Powers hereby engage not only to cease all commerce and intercourse with that Power but also to unite in blockading and closing the frontiers of that Power to commerce or intercourse with any part of the world and to use any force that may be necessary to accomplish that object.

### ARTICLE VIII.

Any war or threat of war, whether immediately affecting any of the Contracting Powers or not, is hereby declared a matter of concern to the League of Nations and to all the Powers signatory hereto, and those Powers hereby reserve the right to take any action that may be deemed wise and effectual to safeguard the peace of nations.

It is hereby also declared and agreed to be the friendly right of each of the nations signatory or adherent to this Covenant to draw the attention of the Body of Delegates or of the Executive Council to any circumstances anywhere which threaten to disturb international peace or the good understanding between nations upon which peace depends.

The Delegates and the Executive Council shall meet in the interest of peace whether war is rumored or threatened, and also whether [whenever] the Delegates of any Power shall inform the Delegates that a meeting and conference in the interest of peace is advisable.

The Delegates may also meet at such other times and upon such other occasions as they shall from time to time deem best and determine.

### ARTICLE IX.

In the event of a dispute arising between one of the Contracting Powers and a Power not a party to this Covenant, the Contracting

Power involved hereby binds itself to endeavor to obtain the submission of the dispute to judicial decision or to arbitration. If the other Power will not agree to submit the dispute to judicial decision or to arbitration, the Contracting Power shall bring the matter to the attention of the Executive Council. The Delegates shall in such a case, in the name of the League of Nations, invite the Power not a party to this Covenant to become *ad hoc* a party and to submit its case to judicial decision or to arbitration, and if that Power consents it is hereby agreed that the provisions hereinbefore contained and applicable to the submission of disputes to arbitration or discussion shall be in all respects applicable to the dispute both in favor of and against such Power as if it were [a party] to this Covenant.

In case the Power not a party to this Covenant shall not accept the invitation of the Executive Council to become *ad hoc* a party, it shall be the duty of the Executive Council immediately to institute an inquiry into the circumstances and merits of the dispute involved and to recommend such joint action by the Contracting Powers as may seem best and most effectual in the circumstances disclosed.

### ARTICLE X.

If hostilities should be begun or any hostile action taken against the Contracting Power by the Power not a party to this Covenant before a decision of the dispute by arbitrators or before investigation, report and recommendation by the Executive Council in regard to the dispute, or contrary to such recommendation, the Contracting Powers engage thereupon to cease all commerce and communication with that Power and also to unite in blockading and closing the frontiers of that Power to all commerce or intercourse with any part of the world, and to employ jointly any force that may be necessary to accomplish that object. The Contracting Powers also undertake to unite in coming to the assistance of the Contracting Power against which hostile action has been taken, and to combine their armed forces in its behalf.

### ARTICLE XI.

In case of a dispute between states not parties to this Covenant, any Contracting Power may bring the matter to the attention of the Delegates or the Executive Council, who shall thereupon tender the good offices of the League of Nations with a view to the peaceable settlement of the dispute.

If one of the states, a party to the dispute, shall offer and agree to submit its interests and cause [course] of action wholly to the control and decision of the League of Nations, that state shall *ad hoc* be deemed a Contracting Power. If no one of the states, parties to the dispute, shall so offer and agree, the Delegates shall, through the Executive Council, of their own motion take such action and make such recommendation to their governments as will prevent hostilities and result in the settlement of the dispute.

### ARTICLE XII.

Any Power not a party to this Covenant, whose government is based upon the principle of popular self-government, may apply to the Body of Delegates for leave to become a party. If the Delegates shall regard the granting thereof as likely to promote the peace, order, and security of the World, they shall act favorably on the application, and their favorable action shall operate to constitute the Power so applying in all respects a full signatory party to this Covenant. This action shall require the affirmative vote of two-thirds of the Delegates.

### ARTICLE XIII.

The Contracting Powers severally agree that the present Covenant and Convention is accepted as abrogating all treaty obligations *inter se* which are inconsistent with the terms hereof, and solemnly engage that they will not enter into any engagements inconsistent with the terms hereof.

In case any of the Powers signatory hereto or subsequently admitted to the League of Nations shall, before becoming a party to this Covenant, have undertaken any treaty obligations which are inconsistent with the terms of this Covenant, it shall be the duty of such Power to take immediate steps to procure its release from such obligations.

### SUPPLEMENTARY AGREEMENTS.

### I.

In respect of the peoples and territories which formerly belonged to Austria-Hungary, and to Turkey, and in respect of the colonies formerly under the dominion of the German Empire, the League of Nations shall be regarded as the residuary trustee with the right of oversight or administration in accordance with certain fundamental principles hereinafter set forth; and this reversion and control shall exclude all rights or privileges of annexation on the part of any Power.

These principles are, that there shall in no case be any annexation of any of these territories by any State either within the League or outside of it, and that in the future government of these peoples and territories the rule of self-determination, or the consent of the governed to their form of government, shall be fairly and reasonably applied, and all policies of administration or economic development be based primarily upon the well-considered interests of the people themselves.

### II.

Any authority, control, or administration which may be necessary in respect of these peoples or territories other than their own self-determined and self-organized autonomy shall be the exclusive function of and shall be vested in the League of Nations and exercised or undertaken by or on behalf of it.

It shall be lawful for the League of Nations to delegate its authority, control, or administration of any such people or territory to some single State or organized agency which it may designate and appoint as its agent or mandatory; but whenever or wherever possible or feasible the agent or mandatory so appointed shall be nominated or approved by the autonomous people or territory.

### III.

The degree of authority, control, or administration to be exercised by the mandatory State or agency shall in each case be explicitly defined by the Executive Council in a special Act or Charter which shall reserve to the League complete power of supervision, and which shall also reserve to the people of any such territory or governmental unit the right to appeal to the League for the redress or correction of any breach of the mandate by the mandatory State or agency or for the substitution of some other State or agency, as mandatory.

The mandatory State or agency shall in all cases be bound and required to maintain the policy of the open door, or equal opportunity for all the signatories to this Covenant, in respect of the use and development of the economic resources of such people or territory.

The mandatory State or agency shall in no case form or maintain any military or naval force, native or other, in excess of definite standards laid down by the League itself for the purposes of internal police.

Any expense the mandatory State or agency may be put to in the exercise of its functions under the mandate, so far as they cannot be borne by the resources of the people or territory under its charge upon a fair basis of assessment and charge, shall be borne by the several signatory Powers, their several contributions being assessed and determined by the Executive Council in proportion to their several national budgets, unless the mandatory State or agency is willing itself to bear the excess costs; and in all cases the expenditures of the mandatory Power or agency in the exercise of the mandate shall be subject to the audit and authorization of the League.

The object of all such tutelary oversight and administration on the part of the League of Nations shall be to build up in as short a time as possible out of the people or territory under its guardianship a political unit which can take charge of its own affairs, determine its own connections, and choose its own policies. The

League may at any time release such a people or territory from tutelage and consent to its being set up as an independent unit. It shall also be the right and privilege of any people or territory to petition the League to take such action, and upon such petition being made it shall be the duty of the League to take the petition under full and friendly consideration with a view to determining the best interests of the people or territory in question in view of all the circumstances of their si[t]uation and development.

### IV.

No new State shall be recognized by the League or admitted into its membership except on condition that its military and naval forces and armaments shall conform to standards prescribed by the League in respect of it from time to time.

The League of Nations is empowered, directly and without right of delegation, to watch over the relations *inter se* of all new independent States arising or created and shall assume and fulfil the duty of conciliating and composing differences between them with a view to the maintenance of settled order and the general peace.

### V.

The Powers signatory or adherent to this Covenant agree that they will themselves seek to establish and maintain fair hours and humane conditions of labor for all those within their several jurisdictions who are engaged in manual labor and that they will exert their influence in favor of the adoption and maintenance of a similar policy and like safeguards wherever their industrial and commercial relations extend.

### VI.

The League of Nations shall require all new States to bind themselves as a condition precedent to their recognition as independent or autonomous States and the Executive Council shall exact of all States seeking admission to the League of Nations the promise, to accord to all racial or national minorities within their several jurisdictions exactly the same treatment and security, both in law and in fact, that is accorded the racial or national majority of their people.

### VII.

Recognizing religious persecution and intolerance as fertile sources of war, the Powers signatory hereto agree, and the League of Nations shall exact from all new States and all States seeking admission to it the promise, that they will make no law prohibiting or interfering with the free exercise of religion, and that they will in no way discriminate, either in law or in fact, against those who practice any particular creed, religion, or belief whose practices are not inconsistent with public order or public morals.

### VIII.

The rights of belligerents on the high seas outside territorial
waters having been defined by international convention, it is hereby
agreed and declared as a fundamental covenant that no Power or
combination of Powers shall have a right to overstep in any particular the clear meaning of the definitions thus established; but that
it shall be the right of the League of Nations from time to time and
on special occasion to close the seas in whole or in part against a
particular Power or particular Powers for the purpose of enforcing
the international covenants here entered into.

### IX.

It is hereby covenanted and agreed by the Powers signatory hereto
that no treaty entered into by them, either singly or jointly, shall
be regarded as valid, binding, or operative until it shall have been
published and made known to all the other signatories.

### X.

It is further covenanted and agreed by the signatory Powers that
in their fiscal and economic regulations and policy no discrimination shall be made between one nation and another among those
with which they have commercial and financial dealings.[1]

Printed copy (W. Wilson Miscellaneous Coll., CtY).
  [1] Wilson sent a copy of this draft, probably on January 19, 1919, to General Smuts,
with the following comment:
  "It is with real pleasure that I send you the enclosed draft, and look forward to co-
operating with you in perfecting it.
  "Since drafting it I have made some emendations and additions which I shall hope
to discuss with you, but they do not affect the larger features of the plan."
  Printed in W. K. Hancock and Jean van der Poel, *Selections from the Smuts Papers*
(4 vols., Cambridge, Eng., 1964-66), IV, 48. The curator of the Smuts Papers in the
State Library, Pretoria, South Africa, has been unable to find this letter in the Smuts
Papers.

## From the Diary of Edith Benham

January 18, 1919

Today at luncheon the President described the way the United
States was first in the Peace Conference. The French suggested
that they use the French nomenclature "Etats Unis d'Amerique,"
then Lloyd George said jokingly, if that were so they should give
Great Britain her title, "Empire de la Grande Britayne," but Mr.
Lansing capped it all by saying that the United States was designated, "L'Amerique, les Etats Unis de," and so we finally came
first. He spoke of the difficulties with the newspaper men and told
Dr. Grayson, who gives the interviews to the newspaper men and
is the general goat to whom all people come with their complaints,
that he hoped they would not put much stress in Jugo Slavia having

a navy. It will be a turbulent nation as they are a turbulent people, and they ought not to have a navy to run amuck with. Someone asked about Foch, and the President said he considered him very able but narrow and given to prejudices. He had been imposing very severe restrictions on the part of Luxumburg, who are a perfectly friendly people, more Belgian than anything else, and had been overrun by the Germans. General Pershing had objected to these conditions on order from the President who said that the Americans would not hold their part if the French insisted on making life so intolerable for the inhabitants. Foch consented to remit the conditions, but grudgingly, and said it was difficult to command an army when the generals under his command differed in this way with his orders.

At dinner the President asked Dr. Grayson to carry down to General Smuts a copy of his draft of the Constitution of the League of Nations. It was, of course, such an important document and still so secret that Grayson had to deliver it into the hands of Smuts himself. Smuts, as you may remember I wrote, had written what the President considers one of the best expositions of the aims of the League of Nations and its practical application and constitution.[1] Someone asked the President if he hadn't written most of this present draft himself, and he said no, that the original was made by an English Society. He had made certain additions and changes to that, then Smuts had presented certain other features and a very statesmanlike addition and he (the President) had made another draft of his own which he had sent down to Smuts for criticism and change. The reporters, I imagine, would have given a great deal to have waylaid the little doctor and gotten the document from him. (I think a copy went to Lloyd George, too.)

The President in describing the seating of the members of the Peace Conference spoke of the fact of Botha and Smuts both being there at this Conference, and a few years ago they were fighting Great Britain. He spoke of Smuts and the English who were friendly to the League of Nations and mentioned particularly the Canadians—notably Borden. They were particularly eager for it was through his efforts he said that the Colonials had been admitted there at the Peace Table.

[1] About which see the memorandum, and the notes thereto, printed at December 26, 1918, Vol. 53.

## From the Diary of Dr. Grayson

Sunday, January 19, 1919.

I persuaded the President to remain in bed during the morning in order to combat his cold. In the afternoon he and I took a long ride with Mrs. Wilson into the country. We passed a very quiet day and the rest did the President a great deal of good.

## From Edward Mandell House

My dear Governor:                    [Paris] 19 January 1919.

I suggest that at your conference with Lord Robert Cecil this evening you take the opportunity of ascertaining from him his views as to the form and substance of the resolution to be adopted by the Conference upon referring to a committee the preparation of the covenant dealing with the League of Nations.

I regard this resolution as of great importance. It should be drawn so as to secure the acceptance with the least possible discussion of what we deem vital. Points which may give rise to controversy should be left to the Committee to discuss.

The resolution when adopted should be made public as the solemn declaration of the Conference. The world is waiting for an announcement on this subject and we should not wish the matter to be referred except under a resolution containing substantially the following declarations. Committments should be secured in advance of submitting the resolution. This should not be difficult and I will undertake to secure these if you so desire.

(1) It is essential to the maintenance of the world peace which the Associated Nations are now met to establish, that a League of Nations be created at the Conference with a permanent organization and regular meetings of the members.

(2) The League of Nations should promote the firm establishment of the understandings of international law as the actual rule of conduct among governments and the maintenance of justice and the scrupulous respect for all international obligations in dealings of organized peoples with one another.

(3) The League of Nations should provide for open diplomacy by the prompt and complete publication of all International Agreements.

I am sending you herewith *confidentially* a copy of draft of treaty prepared by Lord Robert Cecil,[1] which was handed me by Sir William Wiseman. I have marked the clauses which I think are of special interest.[2]                    Faithfully yours,   E. M. House

TLS (WP, DLC).
¹ A slightly different copy is printed as an Enclosure with R. Cecil to WW, Jan. 20, 1919.
² Chapter I, iii, 5; Chapter II, 1, 2, 9, 12; and Chapter III, 3.

## From the Peace Conference Diary of Sir William Wiseman

January 19, 1919. (Sunday).

I intended to discuss INDEMNITIES, but, on learning from HOUSE that the PRESIDENT was going to see CECIL and SMUTS that night, we turned on to the LEAGUE OF NATIONS. Cecil had that morning given me the draft of his treaty, which I showed to HOUSE, who showed me the PRESIDENT's Convention.¹ House thinks the President has the idea that SMUTS is working more on his lines than CECIL, and he particularly asked that SMUTS should go there with CECIL. The President was to see LEON BOURGEOIS at 6. House thinks that both the President and Cecil have failed in their draft scheme by not insisting upon compulsory arbitration, or, at any rate, making some provision binding the League that there shall be no more world-wars.

MILLER came over, and he and I and G.A.² drafted a letter for House to sign, addressed to the President, suggesting that as soon as possible the Peace Conference should pass certain resolutions committing them to the broad principles of the LEAGUE OF NATIONS. House suggested that someone ought to spring on the Conference a proposal that they should bind themselves not to engage again in a world-war. It would be interesting to see the man who would first dare to oppose that.

We discussed INDEMNITIES, and House quite approves of the proposal for a fixed sum, dependent upon Germany's position, which would be distributed among the Allies according to their claims, and which they could either label "indemnity" or "reparation."

At House's request, I marked the parts of CECIL's treaty which I thought most important, and it was sent on to the President to give him a chance of reading it before he saw Cecil and Smuts. House gave me a copy of the President's draft Convention, which I was to give to Cecil in confidence. I went back to the Majestic, and discussed the matter with Cecil and gave him the draft Convention.

T MS (W. Wiseman Papers, CtY).
¹ That is, the second "Paris draft" just printed.
² That is, Gordon Auchincloss.

## From the Diary of Lord Robert Cecil

Jan. 19 [1919]

Sunday: church, then lunch at Versailles, where we met two Frenchwomen dressed in the newest fashion, which must be rather cold in this weather. When I got back I found the President had sent for me that evening, so I had a scramble dinner with Moucher, Mima[1] and one or two others, and went off with Smuts to see him at 8.30. I was rather amused by the great state which he keeps—policemen watching his street and soldiers watching his door, and an army of private secretaries waiting for you in the hall. He received us very cordially, and immediately produced his scheme for the League of Nations,[2] which we went through clause by clause. It is almost entirely Smuts and Phillimore combined, with practically no new ideas in it. He is anxious, as far as I could make out, for he was not very definite, that there should be an informal committee of the French, Americans and ourselves to thresh this out, and that when threshed out it should be submitted to a large conference attended by neutrals as well as Allies. He hoped that the whole thing might be done in a fortnight, which I am afraid is fantastic, though I did not say so. On the whole he was not difficult to deal with, and readily accepted minor amendments. I began by treating him with the utmost deference, and got very little out of him. Then I began to press rather more strongly, and found that answered much better. He is, if one may say so, a trifle of a bully, and must be dealt with firmly, though with the utmost courtesy and respect—not a very easy combination to hit off. He is also evidently a vain man, and still with an eye all the time on the American elections. He was very anxious therefore that the scheme which we should work on should be, nominally at any rate, his scheme, and did not mind that in actual fact it was very largely the production of others. He has a quick businesslike mind, and undoubtedly a broad outlook. He referred many times to the importance of working with us, and the difficulty he found in dealing with the French and the Italians. He is evidently very disillusioned about both of those nations. Altogether we were very nearly three hours there, the last twenty minutes being spent in the inevitable American stories.

T MS (R. Cecil Papers, Add. MSS, 51071-51157, PRO).
　[1] Not identified.
　[2] That is, the so-called second "Paris draft."

# Ira Nelson Morris to Edward Mandell House

Stockholm, January 19, 1919

32, 14th Urgent. For Colonel House.

Personally, have just received following telegram from Petrograd dated January 13th, signed by Schitcherin Commissary for Foreign Affairs:

"Radio-telegram received from Lyon on January 12th communicates declaration made by Senator Hitchcock, Chairman of Foreign Relations Committee, concerning reasons of American Troops being sent to Russia.[1]

1st reason given is that American troops were to prevent establishment of German submarine (apparent omission) in Bay of Archangel. Previously justified or not at any rate at present this reason exists no more.

As to 2nd reason, guarding all feed stores. Already in spring of last year we entered into negotiations with view to guarantee interests of Entente Governments in this respect and we are ready now to give every reasonable satisfaction upon this question. As to alleged danger of these stores falling into hands of Germany previously justified or not question is now without object.

3rd reason given is to maintaining way for departure of diplomats and others. We think best way to attain that end is to enter into agreement with our government. American Ambassador, Mr. Francis at time when he left our country could fully unprevented depart or arrive. We had asked him not to remain in Volodga for sole reason that this residence there was accompanied with great danger for his personal safety and we offered him as most appropriate residence some villa in Moscow or in its suburbs.

4th reason. Guaranteeing of safety of Tchecoslovaks; there is nothing to prevent this being attained in full by agreement with our own government. We have officially proposed to Tchecoslovaks their passage home through Russia under conditions securing their safety and ours, and having come to complete agreement with President of Tchecoslovak National Council in Russia, Professor Maxa,[2] he has now gone to Bohemia to communicate our proposals to Tchecoslovak Government.

Last reason given by Senator Hitchcock is preventing of formation of army composed of German and Austrian prisoners. At present, only thing preventing all German and Austrian prisoners from returning home is presence of Entente troops or of White Guards, barring way to prisoners. We are, therefore, at loss to understand how further maintenance of American troops in Russia can be justified.

As we can see from this same Radio-telegram received from Lyon [per]plexity is shared by some of most prominent leaders of principal political parties of America. They expressed desire that American troops should be withdrawn from Russia as soon as possible. We share their desire of normal relations between our two countries being reconstituted, and we are ready to remove all that can be of hindrance to such normal relations. It is not first time that we make such declaration. On October 24th, we sent communication to that effect through Norwegian Minister in Russia.[3] When week later Norwegian Attache, Mr. Christensen,[4] left Moscow, we made through him verbal overtures in order to put end to bloodshed. On November 3rd we invited all neutral representatives then in Moscow and communicated through their medium written proposals to powers of Entente in order to open negotiations for putting end to struggle between our armies.[5] On November 8th, 6th Congress of Soviets of Russia declared before face of world to powers of Entente that it proposes to them opening of peace negotiations and this declaration may appear by stations. On December 23rd, our representative, Litvinoff, informed Entente Minister in Stockholm of desire of Russian Government to settle all outstanding questions.[6]

In addition to his circular letter, he wired to President Wilson in London suggesting again peaceful issue.[7] It lies therefore not with us if such settlement has not yet been reached. Perplexity about presence of American troops in Russia has also been raised by American Officers and soldiers themselves and we have even had opportunities of hearing from some of them directly expressions of this perplexity. When we pointed out to them that in fact their presence aimed at attempt to put Russian people under yoke of oppressors whom it had cast away result of this disclosure was not unfavorable personal relations of these American citizens to ourselves. We hope that peaceful views of above mentioned senators will be shared by American Government and we request American Government to kindly make known place and date for opening peace negotiations with our representatives."          Morris.

T telegram (WP, DLC).
    [1] In the Senate on January 9. See *Cong. Record*, 65th Cong., 3d sess., pp. 1161-66.
    [2] That is, Prokop Maxa.
    [3] See G. V. Chicherin to WW, Oct. 29 and Nov. 2, 1918, Vol. 51.
    [4] He cannot be further identified.
    [5] Chicherin had told the neutral representatives that the Soviet government "was prepared to make far more concessions to the Entente Powers, in order to arrive at an understanding" and that it "particularly desired that an opportunity be afforded it to enter into negotiations with the United States." A. G. Schmedeman to RL, Nov. 5, 1918, *FR-WWS 1918*, 1, I 471.
    [6] M. M. Litvinov to WW, Dec. 24, 1918, Vol. 53.
    [7] M. M. Litvinov to L. Meyer, Jan. 10, 1919, *ibid.*

## From the Diary of Dr. Grayson

Monday, January 20, 1919.

The President attended the conference at the Quai D'Orsay in the morning. At noon he and I went to the French chamber for luncheon. This was an elaborate affair of two hundred guests. The President's speech pleased the French more than any of his speeches since his arrival in France. The President of the French Senate following the President's speech, when asked how he liked it said,

"It was simple, sincere and grand."

Much to the President's disappointment the Peace Conference had adjourned business for the afternoon on account of the luncheon, thereby wasting time which he had expected to put in dealing with the great problems under discussion. As a result the President lost the afternoon. The other delegates have a tendency to procrastinate; he, alone, seems anxious to push the business thru.

## Hankey's Notes of a Meeting of the Council of Ten[1]

Quai d'Orsay, January 20, 1919, 10:30 A.M.

BC-5

[The session was given over to a discussion by Noulens on Bolshevism in Russia. Wilson's only comment was to ask "whether it must be understood that all but the intellectual minority were with the Bolsheviks." Noulens replied "that what he wished to convey was that all the well-to-do classes, including the richer peasants and working men, were against the Bolsheviks." Noulens said that the Bolshevik government had set up inequality as a principle. The discussion ended as follows:]

Finally, he [Noulens] wished to point out that the Bolshevik Government was definitely imperialist. It meant to conquer the world, and to make peace with no Governments save Governments representing only the labouring classes. It stated openly that the only legitimate war was civil war. It would respect no League of Nations. Should we even be weak enough to undertake any agreements with such a Government, they would, on the very next day, send among us propagandists, money, and explosives. According to their open professions they intended to spread revolution by every means.

MR. LLOYD GEORGE asked M. Noulens whether it was Lenin or Trotsky who really ran the Government.

M. NOULENS replied that Lenin was the more popular of the two. He was the pontiff of the creed and Trotsky was the man of action.[2]

(The meeting adjourned at mid-day.)

(It was agreed that the next meeting should take place on the following day at 10:30 a.m.)

T MS (SDR, RG 256, 180.03101/10, DNA).
    [1] The complete text of these notes is printed in *PPC*, III, 623-28.
    [2] "M. NOULENS explained that Lenin was more popular than Trotsky, but that Trotsky was the more energetic character, and had not hesitated to use force to achieve his ends.
    "After it was agreed to meet the following morning at 10:30, the meeting came to an end, to enable some of those present to attend the luncheon given by the French Senate to President Wilson." ACNP notes, Jan. 20, 1919, 10:30 a.m., T MS (SDR, RG 256, 180.03101/10, DNA).

## An Address to the French Senate

January 20, 1919.

Mr. President of the Senate,[1] Mr. President of the Republic: You have made me feel your welcome in words as generous as they are delightful, and I feel that you have paid me today a very unusual and distinguished honor. You have graciously called me your friend. May not I in turn call this company a company of my friends? For everything that you have so finely said today, Sir, has been corroborated in every circumstance of our visit to this country. Everywhere we have been welcomed not only, but welcomed in the same spirit and with the same thought, until it has seemed as if the spirits of the two countries came together in an unusual and beautiful accord.

We know the long breeding of peril through which France has gone. France thought us remote in comprehension and sympathy, and I dare say there were times when we did not comprehend, as you comprehended, the danger in the presence of which the world stood. There was no time when we did not know of its existence, but there were times when we did not know how near it was. And I fully understand, Sir, that throughout these trying years, when mankind has waited for the catastrophe, the anxiety of France must have been the deepest and most constant of all. For she did stand at the frontier of freedom. She had carved out her own fortunes through a long period of eager struggle. She had done great things in building up a great new France; and just across the border, separated from her only by a few fortifications and a little country whose neutrality it has turned out the enemy did not respect, lay the shadow cast by the cloud which enveloped Germany, the cloud of intrigue, the cloud of dark purpose, the cloud of sinister design. This shadow lay at the very borders of France. And yet it is fine to remember, Sir, that for France this was not only a peril but a challenge. France did not tremble. France waited and got ready, and it is a fine thing that, though France quietly and in her own way prepared her sons for the struggle that was coming, she never took the initiative or did a single thing that was aggressive. She had prepared herself for defense, not in order to impose her will upon other peoples. She had prepared herself that no other people might impose its will upon her.

As I stand with you and as I mix with the delightful people of this country, I see this in their thoughts: "America always was our friend. Now she understands. Now she comprehends; and now she has come to bring us this message, that understanding she will always be ready to help." And, while, as you say, Sir, this danger may prove to be a continuing danger, while it is true that France will always be nearest this threat, if we cannot turn it from a threat into a promise, there are many elements that ought to reassure France. There is a new world, not ahead of us, but around us. The whole world is awake, and it is awake to its community of interest. It knows that its dearest interests are involved in its standing together for a common purpose. It knows that the peril of France, if it continues, will be the peril of the world. It knows that not only France must organize against this peril, but that the world must organize against it.

So I see in these welcomes not only hospitality, not only kindness, not only hope, but purpose, a definite, clearly defined purpose that men, understanding one another, must now support one another, and that all the sons of freedom are under a common oath to see that freedom never suffers this danger again. That to my mind is the impressive element of this welcome. I know how much of it, Sir, and I know how little of it, to appropriate to myself. I know that I have the very distinguished honor to represent a nation whose heart is in this business, and I am proud to speak for the people whom I represent. But I know that you honor me in a representative capacity, and that my words have validity only in proportion as they are the words of the people of the United States. I delight in this welcome, therefore, as if I had brought the people of the United States with me and they could see in your faces what I see—the tokens of welcome and affection.

The sum of the whole matter is that France has earned and has won the brotherhood of the world. She has stood at the chief post of danger, and the thoughts of mankind and her brothers everywhere, her brothers in freedom, turn to her and center upon her. If this be true, as I believe it to be, France is fortunate to have suffered. She is fortunate to have proved her mettle as one of the champions of liberty, and she has tied to herself once and for all all those who love freedom and truly believe in the progress and rights of man.

Printed in *Addresses of President Wilson on First Trip to Europe December 3, 1918 to February 24, 1919* (Washington, 1919).
    [1] Henri Antoine Dubost, usually known as Antonin Dubost.

## To Joseph Patrick Tumulty

Paris, 20 January, 1919.

The issue of publicity is being obscured, not cleared, by the newspaper men and we have won for the press all that is possible or wise to win namely complete publicity for the real conferences. Publicity for the conversations I am holding with the small group of the great powers would invariably break up the whole thing whereas the prospects for agreement are now I should say very good indeed. Delighted that you are up and beg that you will not expose yourself or exert yourself too soon. Affectionate messages from us all.                                    Woodrow Wilson.

T telegram (WP, DLC).

## To Robert Lansing

My dear Mr. Secretary:                    Paris, 20 January, 1919.

I should have answered this letter[1] sooner. I willingly concur in this plan as the best that can be obtained and hope that you will apprise the War Department of my concurrence and my willingness that General Graves should be instructed accordingly.

Faithfully yours,   [Woodrow Wilson]

CCL (WP, DLC).
    [1] RL to WW, Jan. 17, 1919, TLS (SDR, RG 256, 861.77/35A, DNA). It enclosed a telegram from Polk of January 16, 1919, which said that the Japanese government had accepted, with one change, the so-called Japanese plan for the supervision of the Trans-Siberian and Chinese Eastern railways, about which see FLP to RL, Dec. 30, 1918, n. 4, Vol. 53. Polk also asked for explicit approval of the plan. Polk's telegram is FLP to RL, No. 265, Jan. 16, 1919, T telegram (SDR, RG 59, 861.77/621a, DNA). Lansing, in a telegram to Polk on January 21, conveyed Wilson's approval of the plan "as the best that can be obtained." RL to FLP, Jan. 21, 1919, No. 376, T telegram (SDR, RG 59, 861.77/634, DNA).

## Robert Lansing to Frank Lyon Polk

Paris, January 20th, 1919.

349. Your 272, January 16th, 7:00 P.M.[1] I am awaiting the President's decision as to acceptance of the plan approved by Ambassador Morris and concerning the authorization asked for cooperation of General Graves. In the meantime please cable text of the President's memorandum to which War Department refers as lim-

iting the use of American troops in Siberia.[2] The War Department of course means no more than an intention to adhere to that policy so long as it is not modified. Since the Japanese after withdrawal of forty-seven thousand troops as intimated will have according to their statement but twenty-five thousand left the proportion furnished by the United States if as much as you state will not be inconsiderable and is apparently regarded by Morris and Stevens as sufficient for the purpose.                     Lansing.

T telegram (WP, DLC).
    [1] FLP to RL, Jan. 16, 1919, T telegram (SDR, RG 256, 861.77/31, DNA).
    [2] That is, Wilson's aide-mémoire of July 17, 1918, printed as an Enclosure with WW to FLP, July 17, 1918, Vol. 48.


## To Henry Wilson Harris[1]

My dear Mr. Harris:                     Paris, 20 January, 1919.

I ought long ago to have acknowledged your kind letter of January 10th[2] but I am sure you will pardon me in the unusual circumstances which engross me here. I have been reading the book[3] you so kindly undertook about me and my problems and am greatly gratified to find how entirely you have understood the different matters which I had to address myself to as President of Princeton and as Governor of New Jersey. That is as far as I have gotten yet but I have got far enough to feel that I owe you a debt of sincere gratitude.

Cordially and sincerely yours,   [Woodrow Wilson]

CCL (WP, DLC).
    [1] Diplomatic correspondent of the London *Daily News.*
    [2] H. W. Harris to WW, Jan. 10, 1919, TLS (WP, DLC).
    [3] Henry Wilson Harris, *President Wilson, His Problems and His Policy,* 2d edn. (London, 1918). A copy of this book is in the Wilson Library, DLC.


## To Edward Price Bell

My dear Mr. Bell:                     Paris, 20 January, 1919.

You were certainly most kind to send me your letter of December 27th[1] with its enclosure and you may be assured I greatly appreciate the efforts you have been making rightly to interpret to the English people my real attitude and sentiments.

Cordially and sincerely yours,   [Woodrow Wilson]

CCL (WP, DLC).
    [1] E. P. Bell to WW, Dec. 27, 1918, TLS (WP, DLC). Bell enclosed, and asked Wilson's opinion of, his article "Britain's Fleet a Shield of World's Liberties," London *Daily Sketch,* Dec. 27, 1918. The thesis of the article was that Wilson, far from being an enemy of

British seapower, had in fact a proper appreciation of the vital role of the British navy in world affairs. The British had nothing to fear from the rapidly growing American navy, Bell believed. The United States only wished in the future to do her fair share in the defense of liberty at sea.


## From Lord Robert Cecil, with Enclosure

*Confidential*

Dear Mr President                                    Paris. 20 Jan: 1919.

I send you in accordance with my promise a copy of the Draft Convention prepared by the British League of Nations Section. It has not yet been considered by the Cabinet though in its general lines it has been approved by them. It would have reached you some days ago but for difficulties in printing

Yours very sincerely   Robert Cecil

ALS (WP, DLC).


ENCLOSURE

SECRET.                                              January 20, 1919.

## LEAGUE OF NATIONS.

### DRAFT CONVENTION.

#### CHAPTER I.

*Functions and Organisation of the League.*

1. IMPRESSED by the horrors of the late War, and convinced that another war of the same kind would be productive of still greater disasters to humanity and civilization, the High Contracting Parties* unite in constituting a League of Nations.

The primary object of the League is the promotion of peace among the nations of the world. With this intent the H.C.P. solemnly pledge themselves to co-operate in the League for the prevention of war by eliminating, so far as possible, the causes of international disputes, by providing for the pacific settlement of such disputes should they arise, and by encouraging a general system of international co-operation for promoting the peaceful progress of mankind.

For achieving these ends the H.C.P. adopt the following measures:

(i.)  They enter into the obligations intended to secure the avoidance of war which are contained in Chapter II. of this Convention.

*Hereinafter referred to as "H.C.P."

(ii.) They undertake to respect the territorial integrity of all States members of the League, and to protect them from foreign aggression, and they agree to prevent any attempts by other States forcibly to alter the territorial settlement existing at the date of, or established by, the present treaties of peace.

(iii.) They recognise the duty incumbent upon the more advanced members of the family of nations to render help and guidance, under the sanction of the League, in the development of the administration of States and territories which have not yet attained to stable government.

(iv.) They entrust to the League the general supervision of the trade in arms and ammunition with the countries in which the control of this traffic is necessary in the common interest.

(v.) They will endeavour to secure and maintain freedom of transit and just treatment for the commerce of all States members of the League.

(vi.) They appoint commissions to study and report to the League on economic, sanitary, and other similar problems of international concern, and they authorise the League to recommend such action as these reports may show to be necessary.

(vii.) They appoint a commission to study conditions of industry and labour in their international aspects, and to make recommendations thereon, including the extension and improvement of existing conventions.

Stipulations for securing the above objects are embodied in separate Conventions annexed hereto or in the general treaties of peace.

(2.) The H.C.P. place under the control of the League all international bureaux established by general treaties and now located elsewhere if the parties to such treaties consent. Furthermore, they agree that all such international bureaux to be constituted in future shall be placed under the supervision of the League and shall be located at the capital of the League.

2. If at any time it should appear that the boundaries of any State guaranteed by Article 1 (i), (ii) do not conform to the requirements of the situation, the League shall take the matter under consideration and may recommend to the parties affected any modification which it may think necessary. If such recommendation is rejected by the parties affected, the States members of the League shall, so far as the territory in question is concerned, cease to be under the obligation to protect the territory in question from forcible aggression by other States, imposed upon them by the above provision.

3. The H.C.P. agree to accept as the basis of the organisation of the League the provisions contained in the following articles.

4. A General Conference of the League shall be held within six months of the date when the present Convention comes into force, and similar conferences shall be held from time to time as occasion may require, and in any case at intervals of not more than four years.

A General Conference of the League shall be composed of responsible representatives of the States members of the League.

The meetings of the General Conference of the League are referred to in the present Convention as the Conference of the League.

5. The H.C.P. appoint the following States members of the League to constitute the Council of the League: France, Great Britain, Italy, Japan, and the United States of America. The Council may at any time co-opt additional members. Except as provided hereafter, no State shall be represented at any meeting of the Council by more than two members.

Meetings of the Council shall be held from time to time as occasion may require, and in any case at intervals of not more than one year.

6. The Council of the League will be responsible for ensuring the successful working of the League of Nations, and for seeing that it secures the harmonious co-operation of all the States members of the League.

In particular, it is charged with the duty of watching over the development of the new States which may be recognised by the general treaties of peace, and of settling all differences which may arise between them connected with the arrangements effected by those treaties.

7. The Council shall invite any State member of the League to send representatives to any meeting of the Council at which matters affecting that State will be under discussion.

No decision on any matter directly affecting the interests of a State member of the League which is not represented on the Council will be binding upon any such State unless its representatives have been invited to the meeting when the decisions in question were taken.

8. The Conference of the League shall regulate its own procedure, and may appoint committees for any purpose it may deem convenient. In all matters covered by this Article the Conference may decide by a majority of the representatives present at any meeting. The provisions of this Article apply also to the Council of the League.

9. There shall be established a permanent international secre-

tariat of the League. The secretariat shall be under the general control and direction of the Chancellor of the League, who shall hold office during the pleasure of the Council. The first Chancellor of the League shall be the person named in the Protocol hereto. Any successor shall be appointed by the Council.

10. The Chancellor of the League shall be assisted by such number of assistant secretaries as he may find it necessary to appoint and such further staff as he may think necessary within the limits of the expenditure which may be authorised.

11. The Chancellor shall act as the Secretary of the Conference of the League and of the Council of the League, and will be responsible to them for such duties as may be entrusted to him.

12. Representatives of the States members of the League attending meetings of the League, the representatives of the H.C.P. at the capital of the League, the Chancellor and the members of the permanent secretariat of the League, and the members of any judicial or administrative organ or of any commission of enquiry working under the sanction of the League, shall enjoy diplomatic privileges and immunities while they are engaged in the business of the League.

All buildings occupied by the League, or by any organisation placed under the control of the League, or by any of its officials, or by the representatives of the H.C.P. at the capital of the League shall enjoy the benefits of extra-territoriality.

13. The Secretariat of the League shall be established at [blank]. This City shall constitute the capital of the League.

The meetings of the Conference of the League and of the Council of the League shall be held at the capital of the League, or in such other place as may be determined.

14. Each of the H.C.P. may maintain a representative at the capital of the League.

15. The expenses of the League, other than those occasioned by meetings of the Council of the League, shall be borne by the States members of the League, in accordance with the distribution among the members of the Postal Union of the expenses of the International Postal Bureau. The expenses occasioned by meetings of the Council of the League shall be divided equally among the States represented on the Council.

16. The H.C.P. recognise the right of the British Empire to separate representation in respect of the Dominions of the British Empire, including India, at meetings of the Conference of the League, and also at meetings of the Council, at which matters affecting any particular Dominion are under discussion.

CHAPTER II.

*Avoidance of War.*

1. Each of the States members of the League agrees that it will not, except in accordance with Article 12, go to war with another State member of the League:

(*a.*) without submitting the matter in dispute to a Court of International Law or to the Conference or the Council of the League; and

(*b.*) until the Court or the Conference or the Council of the League has had reasonable time to render its decision or report on the matter, provided that in the case of the Conference or of the Council the time shall not exceed [blank] months; and

(*c.*) within a period of three months after the rendering of the decision or the report, including for this purpose a majority report, or after the expiration of the reasonable period referred to in (*b*);

and also that it will not go to war with another State member of the League which complies with the decision of the Court or, subject to Article 9, with the recommendations of the Conference or of the Council.

2. If there should arise between States members of the League any dispute likely to lead to a rupture, which both parties agree to refer to the decision of a court of international law, or which under some convention between them either party is entitled to claim as of right should be referred to the decision of a court of international law, the parties or party as the case may be shall inform the Chancellor of the League, who shall forthwith make all necessary arrangements for bringing the dispute before the Court accordingly. All questions of procedure shall, if not settled by agreement between the parties, be decided by the Court, and, pending the assembly of the Court, may be decided by the Chancellor.

3. Pending the creation of a permanent court of international justice, the court of international law to which the case is referred under the preceding article shall be the court agreed on by the parties or stipulated in the convention existing between them.

4. If there should arise between two States members of the League any dispute likely to lead to a rupture which is not submitted to a court of international law under Article 2, it shall be open to either of them to demand the reference of the matter to the League. The object of the League in dealing with the matter shall be to effect a just and lasting settlement of the difference. The Chancellor of the League shall in that case convoke a meeting of the Council of the League at such place as may be deemed most convenient under

the circumstances, and the Council shall forthwith proceed with the investigation of the dispute.

5. In the event of any State represented on the Council or of any party to the dispute notifying the Chancellor within a period of 14 days after the demand for reference to the League that in its opinion the dispute is one which should be referred to the Conference, the Chancellor shall convoke a meeting of the Conference. Pending the assembly of the Conference, the investigation of the dispute by the Council shall continue.

6. The party upon whose demand the matter has been referred to the League shall file with the Chancellor of the League a statement of its case with all the facts and papers relevant to the dispute. The party against whom the complaint is made shall be invited by the Chancellor to file a statement of its case with all relevant facts and papers.

The Chancellor shall forthwith publish the statements of the parties.

The H.C.P. agree that, in the case of the reference of any dispute to the League under Article 4, they will each, whether parties to the dispute or not, place at the disposal of the Conference or the Council to the fullest possible extent compatible with their interests all the information in their possession which bears upon the questions under discussion.

7. Where the Conference or the Council finds that the dispute can with advantage be submitted to a court of international law, or that any particular question involved in the dispute can with advantage be referred to a court of international law, it may submit the dispute or the particular question accordingly, and may formulate the questions for decision, and may give such directions as to procedure as it may think desirable. In such case, the decision of the Court shall have no force or effect unless it is confirmed by the Report of the Conference or Council.

Pending the creation of a permanent court of international justice, the court of international law referred to in this article shall be a tribunal of arbitration nominated by the Conference or the Council from among the members of the Permanent Court created by the Convention for the Pacific Settlement of International Disputes.

8. Where the dispute is under investigation by the Council, the Council shall, after considering the merits of the dispute, and the decision of a Court under Article 7, make a report to the H.C.P.

9. Where the efforts of the Conference or of the Council have led to the settlement of the dispute, a statement shall be prepared for publication indicating the nature of the dispute and the terms

of settlement, together with such explanations as may be appropriate.

If the dispute has not been settled, the report of the Council to the H.C.P., or a similar report by the Conference, shall be published. This report shall set forth, with all necessary facts and explanations, the recommendations which the Council or Conference think just and proper for the settlement of the dispute. If the Report is unanimously agreed to by the members of the Conference or Council, other than the parties to the dispute, the H.C.P. hereby agree that none of them will go to war with any party which complies with its provisions, and that they will take all the measures described in Articles 12 and 13 to prevent any other Power going to war with such party. If no unanimous report can be made it shall be the duty of the majority to issue a report indicating what they believe to be the facts and containing the recommendations which they consider just and proper.

10. The Council may at any time in the course of its investigation of a dispute, or within the period of three months after the making of its report, convoke a meeting of the Conference and transfer to it the consideration of the dispute.

11. Where any dispute arises between any States, whether members of the League or not, which, in the opinion of the Council, may lead to a rupture, the Council may take the dispute into consideration, and may deal with it as though it had been referred to the League under Article 4, or in such other way as will in their opinion best conduce to the peace of the world.

12. The H.C.P. agree that, in the event of any State member of the League committing a breach of Article 1, it will become, *ipso facto*, at war with all the other States members of the League; they will all regard each other as co-belligerents, and will take and support each other in taking all such naval, military, or economic measures as will best avail for restraining the breach of covenant.

In particular, they shall each forthwith take all measures necessary to suspend financial, commercial, postal, and telegraphic relations with such State, and, as far as possible, shall prevent that State from having any such relations with any other Power.

13. For the above purposes, each of the H.C.P. agrees that it will detain all ships and goods within its jurisdiction belonging to any person resident in that State; it will prohibit all vessels flying the flag of its mercantile marine from entering the ports of that State; it will prohibit all exports to or imports from, and all financial transactions direct or indirect, with any person in the territory of such State; and it will also take such further economic and commercial measures as the League may deem necessary.

Furthermore, each of the H.C.P. agrees that, if it cannot make an effective contribution of naval, military, or aerial force, it will co-operate to the utmost of its power in the naval and military measures which may be taken.

The naval, military, and economic operations undertaken in pursuance of this article and of the immediately preceding article shall be carried out without regard to any limitations hitherto imposed on belligerent States by any convention or rule of international law.

14. The H.C.P. agree, further, that they will mutually support one another in the financial and economic measures which they are bound to take under the preceding article in order to minimise the loss and inconvenience resulting therefrom, and that they will mutually support one another in resisting any special measures aimed at one of their number by the State with which relations have been broken off, and that they will afford passage through their territory to the armed forces of any of the H.C.P. who are co-operating to resist the breach of Article 1.

15. The H.C.P. agree that, as part of the terms of peace imposed upon the State which has violated the provisions of Article 1, it shall be called upon to restore all contracts existing at the date of the outbreak of hostilities between their nationals and the nationals of the enemy State which their nationals wish to maintain, and also to provide without reciprocity security for the payment of all debts owing at that date to nationals of the co-operating States members of the League.

16. In the event of disputes between one State member of the League and another State which is not a member of the League, or between two States neither of which is a member of the League, the H.C.P. agree that the State or States not members of the League shall be invited to become members of the League *ad hoc*, and the above provisions shall be applied with such modifications as may be necessary.

CHAPTER III.
*General.*

1. The H.C.P. agree that the provisions of this Convention shall override any previously existing treaty stipulations which may be inconsistent by which they may be bound to any other members of the League. Furthermore, they agree that they will not enter into treaty engagements in future which are inconsistent with it.

2. Powers not represented at the present Conference may be invited to become parties to the present Convention. These invitations will be conveyed by the Chancellor of the League.

Powers not invited to become parties to the present Convention may apply for leave to become parties. The League shall in such case decide whether the Power so applying can be relied on to observe the terms of the Conventions, and, if not, the League may refuse the application, or, alternatively, may impose upon such Power such further conditions as it may deem necessary.

4. The provisions of this Convention shall come into effect so soon as it has been ratified by Great Britain, the United States of America, France, Italy, and Japan.

NOTES ON THE LEAGUE OF NATIONS DRAFT CONVENTION.

*Note to Chapter I.*

The Conventions to be annexed to the Covenant will be, roughly, the following:

(*a.*)   Conventions defining territorial settlements;

(*b.*)   Conventions defining the responsibilities of mandatory States;

(*c.*)   Conventions dealing with arms traffic, liquor traffic, and other tutelage of backward races;

(*d.*)   Conventions defining general economic policy (*e.g.*, transit, air, trade conditions);

(*e.*)   Conventions dealing with international labour conditions;

(*f.*)   Conventions establishing the legal machinery of the League;

(*g.*)   Conventions dealing with standard international activities of a more scientific or technical character (*e.g.*, health);

and establishing in each case the international organs, whether Commissions of Enquiry or Administrative or semi-Administrative Commissions, required to carry out the terms of each Convention.

These Conventions will probably include not only new Conventions signed at Paris, but a number of existing agreements which the League will take over (*e.g.*, existing agreements under (*g*), such as the Postal Union.

*Note to Chapter I, Article 10.*

The duties of the Chancellor should be somewhat as follows, and directions to that effect might be given to him by the States composing the Council in a protocol:

(*a.*)   He should convene the meetings of the Conference and the Council, prepare the work of these meetings, and record the business transacted at them.

(*b.*)   He should facilitate and register the results of the work of the various international organs indicated in the Note to Chapter I, and, in this connection, he should carry out the provisions of Chapter I, article 1 (2) of the Convention.

(c.) He should take the action required of him in connection with international disputes, as provided in Chapter II.

(d.) He should register all international treaties brought to the cognisance of the League.

(e.) In general, he should collect, for the information of the Council and the Conference, all facts affecting the purposes and obligations of the League.

(f.) The Conference and Council of the League should correspond through him, as the sole responsible channel, with the member States, with the international bodies indicated under (b), and with any court of international law or conciliation operating in pursuance of this Convention.

(g.) He should maintain current relations at the capital of the League with any official representatives whom the member States may accredit to the League.

(h.) He should, at the request of two or more member States, make arrangements for any official inter-State meetings which it may be desired to hold.

(i.) He should make similar arrangements for any unofficial meetings of an international character which he, as the representative of the Council, may consider it advisable to invite to the capital of the League.

*Note to Chapter I, Article 11.*

It might be well to agree in a protocol that the Council shall, in the first instance, direct the Chancellor to select the secretariat in a particular way. Such a protocol, signed by the States composing the Council, might stipulate that the Chancellor shall appoint ten permanent secretaries at his discretion, subject to the following provisions:

He shall choose one national of each of the States members of the Council, two nationals of two European States not members of the Council, one national of one of the States of America other than the United States, and two nationals of any States members of the League at his discretion. Before appointing a national of any State, the Chancellor ought, however, to secure the approval of the Government of such State, and the Council should have the right to veto any given appointment by unanimous vote.

*Note to Chapter III, Articles 1 and 2.*

1. On the assumption, as a matter of procedure, that the Convention will in the first instance be negotiated and initialled by the States forming the Council of the League, and that it will then be offered for signature, during the Conference of Peace, to all the other States represented at that Conference (except the enemy

Powers), it is suggested that a protocol should be annexed to the Convention, as originally initialled, naming the States to whom invitations should be issued as soon as the Convention is finally signed by the States represented at the Conference. It is suggested that invitations should be issued as follows:

(a.)   to any States at war with Germany, or having broken off diplomatic relations with her, which may not be represented at the Conference;

(N.B. It is possible that the United States may advise against the inclusion of some Latin-American State coming within this category, e.g., Costa Rica.)

(b.)   to European neutrals, i.e., Sweden, Norway, Denmark, Holland, Switzerland, and Spain;

(c.)   to Latin-American States not represented at the present Peace Conference, except Mexico, Hayti, San Domingo, and any other State which, in the opinion of the United States, may be considered unready for membership (without prejudice to the right of such State to apply for membership under Article 17).

(d.)   to Persia.

2. The protocol should further set out that invitations should be issued to new States recognised as sovereign and independent by the Peace Conference. Jugo-Slavia would be included in this class of States, unless it were organically united to Serbia.

3. The policy with regard to the admission to the League of enemy Powers, i.e., Germany, Austria, Hungary, Bulgaria, and Turkey, remains to be decided. On the whole, it might be well to state in a protocol that they will be invited to apply, under Article 17, "when they have given proof of their genuine acceptance of the present Convention, of the treaties and agreements annexed thereto, and of the present general treaties of peace, and of their determination to abide by those obligations."

Russia cannot probably be invited to adhere, but it may be advisable to state in a protocol the reasons for this omission.

Printed copy (WP, DLC).


# From George V

Sandringham [Jan. 20, 1919]

The Queen and I are deeply touched by your kind telegram[1] and we thank you and Mrs Wilson for all your sympathy in our sorrow.[2]

George R I

T telegram (WP, DLC).
    [1] It is missing in all collections.
    [2] Prince John Charles Francis, the youngest of the five sons of King George and Queen Mary, had died at age thirteen after a severe epileptic seizure in the late afternoon on January 18, 1919.

## Two Letters from Edward Nash Hurley

My dear Mr. President:                              Paris, January 20, 1919.

I have your letter of January 17, 1919, with cablegram No. 17 from Mr. Tumulty[1] relative to the International Mercantile Marine.

About two weeks ago in London, Sir Joseph Maclay, the British Minister of Shipping, gave me a copy of an agreement between the British Admiralty and the International Mercantile Marine, dated August 1, 1903, which provides that the British Admiralty may, in its discretion, take over any of the British ships of the various British companies included under the International Mercantile Marine stock-ownership. This agreement refers to another agreement between the White Star line and the British Admiralty which sets forth the terms of any such purchase by the British Admiralty. My files here did not contain either of these agreements and your Secretary, Mr. Close, advises me they were not in the papers sent to you from Washington. I therefore cabled to Washington for these papers and am advised by Mr. Colby that the International Mercantile Marine has cabled to London requesting the British Admiralty to send them to me.

Inasmuch as Sir Joseph Maclay has notified me that the British Admiralty would exercise its option to purchase these ships if the Shipping Board should purchase the stock of the International Navigation Company, it seems essential to me that we await the arrival of these underlying agreements and certain subsequent agreements embodying modifications of the original ones, before we arrive at a definite conclusion in the matter of this stock purchase.

In view of the International Mercantile Marine cable to London to forward these papers to us here, I believe the matter can rest at least until such time, without grave prejudice to the interests of the International Mercantile Marine.

I assure you that this matter is receiving my earnest consideration.                    Very faithfully yours,    Edward N. Hurley

    [1] G. F. Close to E. N. Hurley, Jan. 17, 1919, CCL (WP, DLC), enclosing JPT to WW, Jan. 13, 1919 (second letter of that date).

My dear Mr. President:                    Paris, January 20, 1919

As instructed by the Supreme War Council at its meeting Monday afternoon, January 13, 1919, I accompanied the Allied and United States representatives of shipping of food and of finance to Treves.

After several conferences with the German delegates an agreement was reached to the satisfaction of all concerned whereby certain amounts of food were to be shipped to Germany in exchange for German passenger and cargo tonnage. Payment is to be made for food in accordance with a reasonable price schedule and the German Government will be reimbursed for the use of its tonnage at reasonable rates to be determined later.[1]

I attach a copy of the Civilian Agreement[2] signed jointly by Allied and United States representatives on the one hand, and by the Chairman of the German delegation on the other. I also include a copy of the clauses concerning German tonnage which were inserted by Marshal Foch in the agreement extending the Armistice.[3]

The German delegates have agreed to meet the Allied and United States delegates as soon as practicable, and submit a complete list of all ships, their material condition, and indicate the time at which they can be delivered ready for operation.

                              Yours sincerely,   Edward N Hurley

TLS (WP, DLC).
[1] About this agreement and the subsequent solution of the problem of food for Germany, see EMH to WW, March 7, 1919, n. 1.
[2] "ARRANGEMENT OF 17TH JANUARY, 1919 IN RESPECT OF RELIEF ARRANGEMENTS AND THE EMPLOYMENT OF GERMAN TONNAGE," TC MS (WP, DLC).
[3] "CLAUSES INSERTED IN THE ARMISTICE Jan. 16, 1919," TC MS (WP, DLC).


# A Memorandum by Bernard Mannes Baruch

MEMORANDUM FOR THE PRESIDENT—1/20/19.

## From Mr. Baruch.

In the drawing up of any memorandum regarding International Labor, Mr. Samuel Gompers should be considered. He is here, and it would be an unfortunate circumstance in case he should be overlooked. Mr. Gompers and other American Labor leaders are very much irritated, owing to the fact that they have not been considered heretofore, but I explained to them that when these matters come up the President would discuss the subject with them or see that they would be consulted, as I knew the President appreciated the work of Mr. Gompers and his associates. I understand Mr. Gompers is now in London and will soon arrive in Paris. A friend of mine who returned only yesterday from Poland 'phoned me that the working men there have great confidence in two people, President Wilson and Samuel Gompers.

T MS (WP, DLC).

## From Arthur James Balfour

My dear Mr. President,                    Versailles. 20 January 1919.

The Prime Minister asks me to send you a memorandum which has been compiled by our War Office on the situation in Russia.[1] He very much hopes that you may find time to glance through it before the meeting tomorrow

Yours most sincerely,    Arthur James Balfour

ALS (WP, DLC).

[1] General Staff, War Office, *Appreciation of the Internal Situation in Russia. 12th January, 1919*, printed copy (WP, DLC). In this thirty-six-page analysis, the British General Staff stated that, according to all available evidence, the internal political position of the Bolsheviks was stronger than ever. Although a "great, though incalculable number" of Russians would "gladly be freed from Bolshevik domination," the prospects of renewed fighting, fears of the return of an even more repressive regime, and control by the Bolshevik government of all food supplies kept the Russian workers and peasants in a state of "general inaction and submissiveness." The few peasant revolts which had occurred had been easily put down, and the Bolshevik reign of terror had successfully crushed any opposition. Thus, the General Staff found, there was at present little chance of a counterrevolution in Soviet Russia, and even the various non-Bolshevik socialist parties were gravitating toward the Bolsheviks rather than toward the anti-Bolshevik governments supported by the Allies. The memorandum then described at length the composition, character, and policies of the anti-Bolshevik governments which had sprung up all over Russia, in the Baltic states, and in Poland, and it singled out the Omsk government of Admiral Kolchak as particularly worthy of Allied assistance.

While the Bolshevik prospects in Soviet Russia itself were thus undoubtedly "good," the General Staff maintained that, in their external policies and in their attempts to foment "world revolution," the Bolsheviks had suffered serious setbacks. Their opportunities in neutral countries were already "very seriously curtailed," and even their unsparing efforts to hasten the "Bolshevising" of the German revolution had so far been unsuccessful. Moreover, the memorandum continued, the overwhelming victory of the Allies had taken the Bolshevik leaders by surprise and had confuted their premise that world peace would be brought about by a series of successive revolutions. Faced with the failure of revolutions outside Russia and with the possibility of a large-scale Allied intervention, the Bolshevik leaders, on several occasions, had thus indicated their willingness to negotiate with the Allies in order to gain a "breathing space" for the consolidation of their regime and the creation of a great Soviet army.

The memorandum then proceeded to discuss the economic and financial policies of the Bolsheviks. It observed that, throughout the area controlled by the "Bolshevik Autocracy," the industrial and commercial system based on models of western civilization had been destroyed. As a result of the nationalization of all Russian banks, the banking system had completely broken down, and "trade and industry in the accepted sense," if not at a total standstill, were not conducted on an economically sound basis. The measures inaugurated by the Bolsheviks and the means by which they were applied, the General Staff believed, could have but one effect—"the bankruptcy of Government and the country."

The remainder of the memorandum analyzed and assessed the strength and the composition of the Bolshevik and anti-Bolshevik military forces; commented in great detail on the situation on the various Russian fronts; and estimated that, by the spring of 1919, the Bolsheviks would be able to put into the field approximately half a million men on a front extending from the Baltic to the Black Sea. With regard to the over-all political prospects of Bolshevism, the General Staff concluded: "The political results of the continuation of the struggle as at present will depend primarily on the military success of the Bolsheviks and upon their economic and financial position. The pressure of a vigorous blockade would put a check to the military conquests of the Bolsheviks, and would turn the economic and financial factors still more against them than at present."

## From George Davis Herron

Dear Mr. President:                    Paris, le Jany 20 1919.

Our Peace Commissioners have summoned me here for an informal conference—not for long, I presume.

It is an impert[in]ence to suggest taking any of your supremely valuable time. But if you if [*sic*] could find a moment wherein I could speak to you a word about the European situation, I should be glad.            Most faithfully Yours,   George D. Herron

ALS (WP, DLC).

## Frank Lyon Polk to Robert Lansing

Washington. Jan. 20, 1919.

322. For the Secretary of State.

Martin and Lodge say there is no chance of the Food Bill[1] passing unless Lodge amendment preventing feeding of Germans[2] was allowed to stand. I tried to explain that there was no intention of giving food to the Central Powers but they say there is so much opposition to the bill;[3] if the amendment were stricken out the bill surely would not pass. The amendment, I am informed, is so drawn that Armenians and other friendly people in Turkey can be taken care of.                                         Polk.

T Telegram (WP, DLC).
  [1] That is, the Famine Relief bill (H.R. 13708), about which see WW to C. Glass, Jan. 1, 1919, and C. Glass to WW, Jan. 7, 1919, Vol. 53. After its passage in the House on January 13, the bill had been referred to the Senate on the following day and had been debated on January 18 and 20. *Cong. Record*, 65th Cong., 3d sess., pp. 1383, 1653-66, 1743-60.
  [2] In fact, the provision which prohibited the donation of foodstuffs and supplies to Germany had been part of the bill as originally drafted and had never raised any controversy. The admendment which Henry Cabot Lodge introduced on January 18 and which the Senate adopted without much debate stipulated that, in addition to Germany, "German Austria, Hungary, Bulgaria, and Turkey" were excluded from the benefits of the relief bill. However, the amendment also provided explicitly for the furnishing of relief to "the Armenians, Syrians, Greeks, and other Christian and Jewish populations of Asia Minor, now subject to Turkey." *Ibid.*, p. 1662.
  [3] While some of the criticism of the bill was based on the alleged lack of sufficient information about the exact purpose of the appropriation and on the question of the constitutionality of the measure, the most vociferous opposition was due to the fact that Herbert Hoover would be in charge of the disposition of the fund. In particular, Senators William Edgar Borah, Thomas Pryor Gore, and Boies Penrose sharply attacked Hoover for allegedly favoring the meat-packing interests and for allowing them to direct and control the policies of the Food Administration. Passage of the bill, Borah and Gore argued, would permit the packers to unload their surplus stocks upon Europe and to increase further their already exorbitant profits. *Ibid.*, pp. 1653-66, 1743-60.

## From the Diary of Edith Benham

January 20, 1919

The French are making rather a mistake in making a concerted effort to induce him [Wilson] to go at once to the devastated regions. He is obstinate and they have started sort of a propaganda to ask him on all and every occasion and by all sorts of different persons, to go to the old Front, with the idea to make him realize more fully the horrors France has had to suffer. He intended to go in the natural course of events and had they left him alone it probably would have accomplished the desired result. The French are getting quite mad because he doesn't drop the Conference and go and he may be hounded into it, but he will go irritated and they will have defeated their own objects. He said today apropos of the luncheon that he was really getting seriously annoyed about it, as so many people had spoken to him about it, and he said that even if France had been entirely made a shell hole it would not change the ultimate settlement (the settlement he had in mind for the peace terms). The question was agitated before he went away for Colonel House said he was afraid he (the President) would have to start off immediately on his return from Italy as there was such strong sentiment about visiting these devastated parts. The French have a feeling he is unsympathetic because he doesn't go at once, and they are very fearful he may give too good terms to Germany if he doesn't see the horror of the war and is prejudiced in their favor. I had a little interview here the other day with Jusserand about some lists. He brought the matter up and I told him quite plainly as a friend of France that the people who were carrying on the crusade were simply prejudicing him and he agreed with me, though he has done it constantly himself.

## From the Diary of Dr. Grayson

Tuesday, January 21, 1919.

The President attended meeting at Quai D'Orsay in the morning and afternoon. That evening the President had, as a guest for dinner and for some hours afterward, A. G. Gard[i]ner, the noted English publicist and editor of the London News. They discussed public men, past and present. At the table the President and Mr. Gardner discussed the lives of General Robert E. Lee and Abraham Lincoln, the President emphasizing the similarity of character of the two men. He expressed the belief that the spirits of the two men had long since met in the better world and that there they had come into perfect harmony of soul and purpose. It struck me as very remarkable the wonderful grasp which Mr. Gardner had on American affairs, particularly those of a political nature and his intimate knowledge of men who are figuring in the political history of America. The conversation varied from Andrew Jackson, Grant, Roosevelt and Booker T. Washington to Crum, the notorious appointee of Roosevelt as collector of customs at Charleston, South Carolina.[1] Gardner thought Roosevelt should have known better, because his mother was born in the South, and he, Roosevelt was acquainted with Southern traditions. Mr. Gardner said to the President that it was too bad Grant had been elected President, because the World had gained the impression that he was a great general, but had proven an utter failure as a President. Gardner had the impression of him as having been very stern, sober and lacking both animation or humor. The President said he could recall one humorous incident about Grant which however might have been accidental. A friend asked Grant to come out and witness a game of golf. Grant, never having seen a golf game, went with this friend, who explained the details of the game. Then after placing his ball he drew back his club but missed it. Upon a second stroke he topped it and the ball went about six inches from the tee. Becoming very much embarrassed he made another attempt. Again he missed it, whereupon Grant remarked. "It seems to be good exercise, but may I ask what is the ball for?" They agreed that the poorest President probably that America ever produced was Benjamin Harrison of Indiana.

Discussing Colonel Roosevelt the President told Mr. Gardner of an incident that took place some years ago when agitation over the drawing of the color line was at its height in the United States. President Wilson said he had asked a noted educator who he considered the two men in America whose achievements were most striking. The educator replied, in his opinion, they were Booker T. Washington and Theodore Roosevelt. He said, however, that while he admired the achievements of both, he would hardly consider it any honor to have shaken hands with Roosevelt after he had invited Washington to the White House for luncheon.

Discussing Gladstone, of Great Britain, the great Liberal Leader, Mr. Gardner related an incident which he did not attempt to explain. It seems that Gladstone had an absent minded habit whereby during his speeches he would throw his hand back and scratch his head, sometimes continuing in that attitude until he finished his remarks. Some of Gladstone's closest friends disapproved of the habit, so they selected James Bryce, now Lord Bryce, the noted British author and former Ambassador to the United States, to call

[1] About whom see n. 1 to the news report printed at Feb. 14, 1903, Vol. 14.

upon Gladstone, direct his attention to the habit and explain that the force of his remarks sometimes were lost by the performance. Gladstone was stern and did not relish rebukes, with the result that when Bryce reached him he found him rather bad tempered. Bryce discreetfully came away without delivering his message. Singularly enough, however, the next night Gladstone delivered an address and did not scratch his head, neither did he do so on any subsequent occasion. Earl Bryce took credit for having secured the desired reform, although he never explained how he accomplished it. The theory of thought transferrence by mental telepathy seems the only explanation suggested.

Gardner, commenting on the recent British elections, spoke of Mr. Asquith's defeat, saying that he made no political effort or campaign, remaining at home, while on the contrary his opponent made numerous speeches and won out at the polls. The President said that this explains the difference between the British method of "standing for office" and the American method of "running for office."

President Wilson explained the real reason why he had been unable to disclose all of his plans to Congress and the American people before he left for France. In the first place he said that had he announced a concrete program in the United States he would have incurred the resentment of the European powers, and might encounter difficulty in their acceptance of anything that had been completely arranged for them and simply presented for their approval and signature. He explained that he had allowed everyone to suggest plans along all lines, so that when the agreement was reached all would feel that they had equally participated. In explaining his exact position the President told this story. A drummer upon alighting from a train in Richmond, Virginia, got into a cab drawn by a horse, driven by an old time negro. The drummer said, "Drive me to the nearest haberdasher." The negro said, "Yassir, gid up." After going about a block he pulled up his horse and opened the door of the cab and said, "Scuse me boss, but where is it you said you wanted to go?" The drummer answered, "Nearest haberdasher," and the negro responded, "Yassir, gid up." After going another block he repeated his inquiry and said, "Scuse me boss, but this nigger been drivin white folks for twenty years and he ain't never give one away yet, so jus' tell this nigger exactly where you do want to go."

They then discussed the conditions which developed following the armistice, especially the frame of mind of the French people following the campaign of personal propaganda that has been carried on by the present governmental leaders. Both Mr. Gardner and the President agreed that the French public opinion had become so hysterical, as a result of the suggestions that at least an army of 3,000,000 should be kept to protect France against the Germans, or Germany would renew the war, that it failed utterly to take into consideration what had been accomplished through the armistice terms, and the fact that Germany's fangs had been drawn through the surrender of her fleet, her U-Boats and her rolling stock and munitions. The French still suffer from militarism and still are fearful of being overwhelmed. It was their opinion that the creation of the league of nations and the making of it a virile force was the one remedy for this condition. The President said that the French people were very impatient and disappointed because he had not gone to the front to see the battlefields. "I regret that they want to make me see red, thinking it will affect me in my deliberations at the Peace Conference," he said. "I have followed the war closely and realized what they have suffered, but they seem to insist that I must see red before I can render a decision just to France on the peace terms."

Mr. Gardner remained with us until eleven o'clock. I recalled that I had introduced Mr. Gardner to the President about four years ago by finding in a book store in Washington a little book entitled "Prophets, Priests and Kings" by A.G.G., and also another volume called "Pillars of Society." The President would very often read aloud from these books a chapter or two on some character like Lloyd George, Balfour or the King of Italy, and pronounced Gardner one of the best writers he had ever read. I was anxious for Gardner to meet the President and discuss matters of common interest. The meeting between them was a real love feast.

## From Edward Mandell House

Dear Governor:                              Paris, 21 January 1919.

I enclose a copy of a letter that has just been brought me by hand from Paderewski in Warsaw.[1] I think that his requests are moderate and I believe that you should urge the Allied Governments to accede to his wishes.

Now that Paderewski has formed a Government in Poland which is apparently being supported by Pilsudski and the other more prominent leaders, I suggest that you, on behalf of the United States, immediately recognize this Government as a de facto government.[2] I believe that we should take the lead in this matter. The British are certain to follow us inasmuch as they sent Paderewski to Dantzig on a British Warship.

If the Allied Governments and the United States agree to the sending of arms and ammunition and military supplies to Poland, I suggest that you request General Pershing to put this matter, so far as the United States is concerned, in the hands of one of his most competent officers.

Affectionately yours,   E. M. House

TLS (WP, DLC).
  [1] I. J. Paderewski to EMH, Jan. 12, 1919.
  [2] See G. F. Close to RL, Jan. 25, 1919.


## Hankey's Notes of Two Meetings of the Council of Ten[1]

Quai d'Orsay, January 21, 1919, 10:30 A.M.

BC-6

[Most of this meeting was given over to a statement on Bolshevism by De Scavenius, who favored immediate intervention in Russia, and to comments and questions by Lloyd George, Balfour, and Clemenceau. Wilson did not take part in this discussion. De Scavenius then withdrew.]

PRESIDENT WILSON said that he wished to draw attention to the request made to him by the King of Montenegro. The King of Montenegro wished to send by telegraph a message to his people. The message was in the following terms:

"To my people,

I implore you to return quietly to your homes and not to combat with arms the forces which are seeking to obtain control of our country. I have received the highest assurances that early and ample opportunity will be given to the people of Montenegro to decide upon the political form of their future government.

And by this decision, so far as it concerns me, I will gladly abide.                                           Nicholas."

PRESIDENT WILSON enquired whether there was any sufficient reason for stopping this message.

It was generally agreed that there was none, and that the message should be forwarded. The French Government undertook to do this.

PRESIDENT WILSON read a letter addressed to him by M. Paderewski. The letter concluded by suggesting that the Allies should send a collective Note to the Ukrainian Directorate at Kieff ordering them to withdraw from Galicia and to cease interference in Polish territory. He further suggested that an Allied Commission be sent to Warsaw to gauge the situation, and that the Polish Government be supplied with artillery and German rifle ammunition.

  [1] The full text of these notes is printed in PPC, III, 634-46.

MR. LLOYD GEORGE questioned whether it was safe to admit that Galicia was Polish territory. Any summons to Kieff should be accompanied by a similar summons to the Poles to abstain from entering disputed territory such as Eastern Galicia.

(It was agreed that a French translation of this letter should be made, and that it should be discussed at the afternoon meeting.)[2]

PRESIDENT WILSON read to the meeting the telegraphic report annexed (Annex "A") from Mr. Butler [Buckler], who had interviewed Litvinoff in Stockholm.

(It was agreed that this letter should also be translated and discussed at the afternoon meeting.)

MR. LLOYD GEORGE said that there was a small matter which he wished to bring to the notice of the meeting. The British Government had at their disposal a number of German submarines. It had been suggested that these submarines should be sunk, but the Controller of the Ministry of Shipping and the Director of Contracts had been consulted, and all agreed that the ex-German submarines had considerable commercial value. The Director of Contracts considered he could dispose of forty or fifth [fifty] within a month, the condition of sale being that they would be broken up and the proceeds of the sale divided amongst the Allies on a scale to be subsequently settled. It was, therefore, suggested that all surrendered submarines in excess of eighty be disposed of by sale on these conditions.

(It was agreed that this course should be followed.)

ANNEX "A" to I.C. 113.
AMERICAN COMMISSION TO NEGOTIATE PEACE.
I.

Report, Dated January 18, 1919, of Agent Who Held Confidential Conversations with Litvinoff on January 14, 15, and 16.[3] . . .

II

The Agent[4] in question submits the following estimate of the situation based on information obtained by him.

Military intervention and occupation of Russia, even if ultimately

[2] "President Wilson read a letter which had been addressed by Mr. Paderewski to Colonel House, in which the former, among other things, stated that the Poles were nowhere the aggressive party, asked for certain assistance in the way of artillery, rifles and ammunition, and requested the Allies to insist on the withdrawal of the Yugo-Slavs [Ukrainians] from Western Galicia.
"It was agreed that the whole Polish question should be taken up, and some line of action decided upon, after some decision had been reached with regard to the Bolshevik question." ACNP notes, Jan. 21, 1919, T MS (SDR, RG 256, 180.03101/11, DNA). These notes are printed in PPC, III, 655-69.
[3] Here follows a brief paraphrase of W. H. Buckler to RL, Jan. 18, 1919.
[4] That is, Buckler.

successful, can only succeed at an indefinite date in the future, meanwhile war conditions following Bolshevism there and elsewhere will continue.

It is possible for an agreement with Russia to be made at once, thus obviating conquest and policing, and reviving normal conditions as a counteracting agency against Bolshevism.

In spite of the guarded language used by Litvinoff, I feel convinced that we can make a fair bargain regarding foreign interests and the foreign debt if we do not greatly curtail Russian territory. If Siberia and the coal and oil fields should be lost to Russia the terms granted relative to the debt will be proportionately less good.

If the Allies boldly say, "We are now convinced that the Soviet Government has firm hold on the Russian people, and will recognize it upon conditions, but we shall not drive a Brest-Litovsk bargain, we contemplate generous treatment and expect the same in return:" such an attitude will be of value both in the course of events and immediately, by strengthening the Moderates, such as Tchitcherine and Litvinoff; moreover, it will drag the Soviet Government to the right, and keep in power men who see that foreign capital and industry must be fairly treated.

To embitter Russia by a repetition of German territorial rapacity would mean less advantageous terms for Allied interests here.

The account in the "Times," January 10, page 9, of the increasing strength and efficiency of the Soviet Government is fully confirmed by Dr. Davidsohn,[5] Major Wardwell's[6] former assistant, who left Moscow only last November.

T MS (SDR, RG 256, 180.03101/11, DNA).
[5] The Editors have been unable further to identify Dr. M. Davidson.
[6] That is, Allen Wardwell, head of the American Red Cross Commission to Russia from May to October 17, 1918.

Quai d'Orsay, January 21, 1919, 3 P.M.[1]

BC-6A

M. CLEMENCEAU said they had met together to decide what could be done in Russia under present circumstances.

PRESIDENT WILSON said that in order to have something definite to discuss, he wished to take advantage of a suggestion made by Mr. Lloyd George and to propose a modification of the British proposal. He wished to suggest that the various organised groups in Russia should be asked to send representatives, not to Paris, but to some other place, such as Salonica, convenient of approach, there to meet such representatives as might be appointed by the Allies,

[1] The complete text of these notes is printed in PPC, III, 647-54.

in order to see whether they could draw up a programme upon which agreement could be reached.

MR. LLOYD GEORGE pointed out that the advantage of this would be that they could be brought straight there from Russia through the Black Sea without passing through other countries.

M. SONNINO said that some of the representatives of the various Governments were already here in Paris, for example, M. Sazonoff. Why should these not be heard?

PRESIDENT WILSON expressed the view that the various parties should not be heard separately. It would be very desirable to get all these representatives in one place, and still better, all in one room, in order to obtain a close comparison of views.

MR. BALFOUR said that a further objection to M. Sonnino's plan was that if M. Sazonoff was heard in Paris, it would be difficult to refuse to hear the others in Paris also, and M. Clemenceau objected strongly to having some of these representatives in Paris.

M. SONNINO explained that all the Russian parties had some representatives here, except the Soviets, whom they did not wish to hear.

MR. LLOYD GEORGE remarked that the Bolsheviks were the very people some of them wished to hear.

M. SONNINO continuing, said that they had heard M. Litvinoff's statements that morning. The Allies were now fighting against the Bolsheviks, who were their enemies, and therefore they were not obliged to hear them with the others.

MR. BALFOUR remarked that the essence of President Wilson's proposal was that the parties must all be heard at one and the same time.

MR. LLOYD GEORGE expressed the view that the acceptance of M. Sonnino's proposals would amount to their hearing a string of people, all of whom held the same opinion, and all of whom would strike the same note. But they would not hear the people who at the present moment were actually controlling European Russia. In deference to M. Clemenceau's views, they had put forward this new proposal. He thought it would be quite safe to bring the Bolshevik representatives to Salonica, or perhaps to Lemnos. It was absolutely necessary to endeavour to make peace. The report read by President Wilson that morning went to show that the Bolsheviks were not convinced of the error of their ways, but they apparently realised the folly of their present methods. Therefore they were endeavouring to come to terms.[2]

---

[2] "Mr. Lloyd George thought that the document which President Wilson had read in the morning session from Litvinoff was remarkable, not that it showed that the Bolsheviki were converted to a realization of the error of their ways, but that it showed that they had at last seen that their plan would not do, and that they were in the mood to come

PRESIDENT WILSON asked to be permitted to urge one aspect of the case. As M. Sonnino had implied, they were all repelled by Bolshevism, and for that reason they had placed armed men in opposition to them. One of the things that was clear in the Russian situation was that by opposing Bolshevism with arms they were in reality serving the cause of Bolshevism. The Allies were making it possible for Bolsheviks to argue that Imperialistic and Capitalistic Governments were endeavouring to exploit the country and to give the land back to the landlords, and so bring about a reaction. If it could be shown that this was not true and that the Allies were prepared to deal with the rulers of Russia, much of the moral force of this argument would disappear. The allegation that the Allies were against the people and wanted to control their affairs provided the argument which enabled them to raise armies. If, on the other hand, the Allies could swallow their pride and the natural repulsion which they felt for the Bolsheviks, and see the representatives of all organised groups in one place, he thought it would bring about a marked reaction against Bolshevism.[3]

M. CLEMENCEAU said that, in principle, he did not favour conversation with the Bolsheviks; not because they were criminals, but because we would be raising them to our level by saying that they were worthy of entering into conversation with us. The Bolshevik danger was very great at the present moment. Bolshevism was spreading.[4] It had invaded the Baltic Provinces and Poland, and that very morning they had received very bad news regarding

---

to terms. He pointed out that in hearing Sazonov and others like him, the same side of the arguments would always be heard. He thought it most necessary to hear from the representatives of the different governments in Russia, including the Bolsheviki. If Saloniki did not serve, why then another place might do, such as the island of Lemnos." ACNP notes, Jan. 21, 1919, 10:30 a.m., T MS (SDR, RG 256, 180.03101/11, DNA). These notes are printed in *PPC*, III, 655-69.

[3] "President Wilson ventured to think that what was back of Baron Sonnino's suggestion was an antipathy to the Bolsheviki, and a natural repulsion against their acts. He would observe, however, that by opposing the Bolsheviki by armies, the cause of the Bolsheviki was being served by the Allies. They were being given a case. They could say to their followers that the imperialistic and capitalistic governments were desirous of destroying Russia. They would represent the Allies as the advocates and supporters of reaction. If the Allies could make it appear that this was not true, most of the moral influence of the Bolsheviki would break down, as their case would be gone. They could no longer allege that it was the purpose of the Allies and the United States to enslave the Russian people and to take charge of their affairs. It was therefore desirable that the Allies show that they are ready to hear the representatives of any organized group in Russia, provided they are willing and ready to come to one place, to put all their cards on the table, and see if they could not come to an understanding. He ventured to think that such a line of action, if adopted, would bring about more reaction against the cause of the Bolsheviki than anything else the Allies could do." *Ibid.*

[4] "M. Clemenceau stated that in principle he was not favorable to holding conversations with the Bolsheviki, as he considered them to be criminals. He objected principally for the reason that it would raise them to the level of the Allies and give them prestige. But sometimes in politics it is necessary to hold conversations with criminals. Moreover, things were going from bad to worse." *Ibid.*

its spread to Budapest and Vienna. Italy, also, was in danger. The danger was probably greater there than in France. If Bolshevism, after spreading in Germany, were to traverse Austria and Hungary and so reach Italy, Europe would be faced with a very great danger. Therefore, something must be done against Bolshevism. When listening to the document presented by President Wilson that morning, he had been struck by the cleverness with which the Bolsheviks were attempting to lay a trap for the Allies. When the Bolsheviks first came into power, a breach was made with the Capitalist Government on questions of principle, but now they offered funds and concessions as a basis for treating with them. He need not say how valueless their promises were, but if they were listened to, the Bolsheviks would go back to their people and say: "We offered them great principles of justice, and the Allies would have nothing to do with us. Now we offer money, and they are ready to make peace."

He admitted his remarks did not offer a solution. The great misfortune was that the Allies were in need of a speedy solution. After four years of war, and the losses and sufferings they had incurred, their populations could stand no more. Russia also was in need of immediate peace. But its necessary evolution must take time. The signing of the world peace could not await Russia's final avatar. Had time been available, he would suggest waiting, for eventually sound men representing common sense would come to the top. But when would that be? He would make no forecast. Therefore they must press for an early solution.

To sum up, had he been acting by himself, he would temporise and erect barriers to prevent Bolshevism from spreading. But he was not alone, and in the presence of his colleagues he felt compelled to make some concessions, as it was essential that there should not be even the appearance of disagreement amongst them. The concession came easier after having heard President Wilson's suggestion. He thought that they should make a clear and convincing appeal to all reasonable peoples, emphatically stating that they did not wish to interfere in the internal affairs of Russia, and especially that they had no intention of restoring Czardom. The object of the Allies being to hasten the creation of a strong Government, they proposed to call together representatives of all parties to a conference. He would beg President Wilson to draft a paper, fully explaining the position of the Allies to the whole world, including the Russians and the Germans.

MR. LLOYD GEORGE agreed, and gave notice that he wished to withdraw his own motion in favour of President Wilson's.

MR. BALFOUR said that he understood that all these people were to be asked on an equality. On these terms he thought the Bolsheviks would refuse, and by their refusal they would put themselves in a very bad position.

M. SONNINO said that he did not agree that the Bolsheviks would not come. He thought they would be the first to come, because they would be eager to put themselves on an equality with the others. He would remind his colleagues that, before the Peace of Brest-Litovsk was signed, the Bolsheviks promised all sorts of things, such as to refrain from propaganda, but since that peace had been concluded they had broken all their promises, their one idea being to spread revolution in all other countries. His idea was to collect together all the anti-Bolshevik parties and help them to make a strong Government, provided they pledged themselves not to serve the forces of reaction and especially not to touch the land question thereby depriving the Bolsheviks of their strongest argument. Should they take these pledges he would be prepared to help them.

MR. LLOYD GEORGE enquired how this help would be given.

M. SONNINO replied that help would be given with soldiers to a reasonable degree or by supplying arms, food, and money. For instance, Poland asked for weapons and munitions; the Ukraine asked for weapons. All the Allies wanted was to establish a strong Government. The reason that no strong Government at present existed was that no party could risk taking the offensive against Bolshevism without the assistance of the Allies. He would enquire how the parties of order could possibly succeed without the help of the Allies. President Wilson had said that they should put aside all pride in the matter. He would point out that, for Italy, and probably for France also, as M. Clemenceau had stated, it was in reality a question of self-defence. He thought that even a partial recognition of the Bolsheviks would strengthen their position, and, speaking for himself, he thought that Bolshevism was already a serious danger in his country.

MR. LLOYD GEORGE said he wished to put one or two practical questions to M. Sonnino. The British Empire now had some 15,000 to 20,000 men in Russia. M. de Scavenius had estimated that some 150,000 additional men would be required, in order to keep the anti-Bolshevik Governments from dissolution. And General Franchet d'Esperey also insisted on the necessity of Allied assistance. Now Canada had decided to withdraw her troops, because the Canadian soldiers would not agree to stay and fight against the Russians. Similar trouble had also occurred amongst the other Allied troops. And he felt certain that, if the British tried to send any more troops there, there would be mutiny.

M. SONNINO suggested that volunteers might be called for.

MR. LLOYD GEORGE, continuing, said that it would be impossible to raise 150,000 men in that way. He asked, however, what contributions America, Italy and France would make towards the raising of this army.

PRESIDENT WILSON and M. CLEMENCEAU each said none.

M. ORLANDO agreed that Italy could make no further contributions.

MR. LLOYD GEORGE said that the Bolsheviks had an army of 300,000 men and would, before long, be good soldiers, and to fight them at least 400,000 Russian soldiers would be required. Who would feed, equip and pay them? Would Italy, or America, or France, do so? If they were unable to do that, what would be the good of fighting Bolshevism? It could not be crushed by speeches. He sincerely trusted that they would accept President Wilson's proposal as it now stood.

M. ORLANDO agreed that the question was a very difficult one for the reasons that had been fully given. He agreed that Bolshevism constituted a grave danger to all Europe. To prevent a contagious epidemic from spreading the sanitarians set up a *cordon sanitaire*. If similar measures could be taken against Bolshevism, in order to prevent its spreading, it might be overcome, since to isolate it meant vanquishing it. Italy was now passing through a period of depression, due to war weariness. But Bolsheviks could never triumph there, unless they found a favourable medium, such as might be produced either by profound patriotic disappointment in their expectations as to the rewards of the war, or by an economic crisis. Either might lead to revolution, which was equivalent to Bolshevism. Therefore, he would insist that all possible measures should be taken to set up this cordon. Next, he suggested the consideration of repressive measures. He thought two methods were possible— either the use of physical force or the use of moral force. He thought Mr. Lloyd George's objection to the use of physical force unanswerable. The occupation of Russia meant the employment of large numbers of troops for an indefinite period of time. This meant an apparent prolongation of the war. There remained the use of moral force. He agreed with M. Clemenceau that no country could continue in anarchy, and that an end must eventually come; but they could not wait; they could not proceed to make peace and ignore Russia. Therefore, Mr. Lloyd George's proposal, with the modifications introduced after careful consideration by President Wilson and M. Clemenceau, gave a possible solution. It did not involve entering into negotiations with the Bolsheviks; the proposal was merely an attempt to bring together all the parties in Russia with a view of finding a way out of the present difficulty. He was prepared, therefore, to support it.

PRESIDENT WILSON asked for the views of his Japanese colleagues.

BARON MAKINO said that, after carefully considering the various points of view put forward, he had no objections to make regarding the conclusion reached. He thought that was the best solution under the circumstances. He wished, however, to enquire what attitude would be taken by the representatives of the Allied Powers if the Bolsheviks accepted the invitation to the meeting and there insisted upon their principles. He thought they should under no circumstances countenance Bolshevik ideas. The conditions in Siberia east of the Baikal had greatly improved. The objects which had necessitated the despatch of troops to that region had been attained. Bolshevism was no longer aggressive, though it might still persist in a latent form. In conclusion, he wished to support the proposal before the meeting.

PRESIDENT WILSON expressed the view that the emissaries of the Allied Powers should not be authorised to adopt any definite attitude towards Bolshevism. They should merely report back to their Governments the conditions found.

MR. LLOYD GEORGE asked that that question be further considered. He thought the emissaries of the Allied Powers should be able to establish an agreement if they were able to find a solution. For instance, if they succeeded in reaching an agreement on the subject of the organisation of a Constituent Assembly, they should be authorised to accept such a compromise without the delay of a reference to the Governments.

PRESIDENT WILSON suggested that the emissaries might be furnished with a body of instructions.

MR. BALFOUR expressed the view that abstention from hostile action against their neighbours should be made a condition of their sending representatives to this meeting.

PRESIDENT WILSON agreed.

M. CLEMENCEAU suggested that the manifesto to the Russian parties should be based solely on humanitarian grounds. They should say to the Russians: "You are threatened by famine. We are prompted by humanitarian feelings; we are making peace; we do not want people to die. We are prepared to see what can be done to remove the menace of starvation." He thought the Russians would at once prick up their ears and be prepared to hear what the Allies had to say. They would add that food cannot be sent unless peace and order were established. It should, in fact, be made quite clear that the representatives of all parties would merely be brought together for purely humane reasons.

MR. LLOYD GEORGE said that in this connection he wished to invite attention to a doubt expressed by certain of the delegates of the British Dominions, namely, whether there would be enough food and credit to go round should an attempt be made to feed all Allied countries, and enemy countries, and Russia also. The export of so much food would inevitably have the effect of raising food prices in Allied countries and so create discontent and Bolshevism. As regards grain, Russia had always been an exporting country, and there was evidence to show that plenty of food at present existed in the Ukraine.

PRESIDENT WILSON said that his information was that enough food existed in Russia, but, either on account of its being ho[a]rded or on account of difficulties of transportation, it could not be made available.

(It was agreed that President Wilson should draft a proclamation, for consideration at the next meeting, inviting all organised parties in Russia to attend a meeting to be held at some selected place, such as Salonica or Lemnos, in order to discuss with the representatives of the Allied and Associated Great Powers the means of restoring order and peace in Russia. Participation in the meeting should be conditional on a cessation of hostilities.)

M. CLEMENCEAU considered it to be most urgent that the delegates should be set to work. He understood that President Wilson would be ready to put on the table at the next full Conference proposals relating to the creation of a League of Nations. He was anxious to add a second question, which would be studied immediately, namely reparation of damages. He thought the meeting should consider how the work should be organised in order to give effect to this suggestion.

MR. LLOYD GEORGE said that he agreed that these questions should be studied forthwith. He would suggest that, in the first place, the League of Nations should be considered, and that, after the framing of the principles, an international committee of experts be set to work out its constitution in detail. The same remark applied also to the question of indemnities and reparation. He thought that a Committee should also be appointed as soon as possible to consider International Labour Legislation.

PRESIDENT WILSON observed that he had himself drawn up a constitution of a League of Nations. He could not claim that it was wholly his own creation. Its generation was as follows: He had received the Phillimore Report, which had been amended by Colonel House and re-written by himself. He had again revised it after having received General Smuts' and Lord Robert Cecil's reports. It was therefore a compound of the various suggestions. During the week he had seen M. Bourgeois, with whom he found himself to

be in substantial accord on principles. A few days ago he had discussed his draft with Lord Robert Cecil and General Smuts, and
they had found themselves very near together.

MR. BALFOUR suggested that President Wilson's draft should be
submitted to the Committee as a basis for discussion.

PRESIDENT WILSON further suggested that the question should
be referred as far as possible to the men who had been studying it.

MR. LLOYD GEORGE expressed his complete agreement. He thought
they themselves should, in the first place, agree on the fundamental
principles, and then refer the matter to the Committee. When that
Committee met they could take President Wilson's proposals as the
basis of discussion.

(It was agreed that the question of appointing an International
    Committee, consisting of two members from each of the five
    Great Powers, to whom would be referred President Wilson's
    draft, with certain basic principles to guide them, should be
    considered at the next meeting.)

M. PICHON called attention to the necessity for replying to the
demand addressed by M. Paderewski to Colonel House, which had
been read by President Wilson that morning, and asked that Marshal Foch should be present.

(It was agreed that this question should be discussed at the next
    meeting.)

Mr. Balfour called attention to the urgency of the question of
disarmament, and said that he would shortly propose that a committee should be appointed to consider this question.[5]

T MS (SDR, RG 256, 180.03101/12, DNA).
    [5] "He [Balfour] pointed out that if the League of Nations is to be practical, the delegates
must make up their minds as soon as possible regarding the question of disarmament.
It was most important in this connection, to come to some agreement as to what arms
Germany was to be allowed to have. It is evident that a League of Nations would be a
sham if there be no disarmament.
    "President Wilson suggested that those present compare their views on this matter
before referring it to a committee." *Ibid.*

# From Ray Stannard Baker

My dear Mr. President:                         [Paris] January 21, 1919.

I have been studying the "Covenant" of the League of Nations
with reference to securing the greatest possible publicity for it, and
for all the ideas in it—in the event that you decide to make it public.

1. We should know, if it is a possible thing, three or four days in
advance, in order to build up and intensify the interest beforehand.

2. The document itself should not be given out until we have
prepared the way with two or three preliminary "intimations" of

what your plan is to be. I would suggest at least two such preparatory articles, the first giving a general outline of the plan with the assurance that it comes from authentic sources, and the second dealing more intimately with the specific territorial suggestions contained in the supplementary articles. I can also see a possible third article.

3. All this would prepare the way and sharpen men's minds for the document itself when it is actually laid on the table.

In order to get this plan more definitely before you, I enclose the rough draft of a proposed first article[1] which, it seems to me, should be put out to our newspaper correspondents at the earliest possible moment.

I do hope, Mr. President, that you will put out your own plan. This document seems to me a very wonderful one, and the more I read it, the more comprehensive and far reaching its provisions seem to me to be. If it can be even nearly approached in the agreement at the Conference the world will be a better and a happier place to live in.

In just one respect, in studying the "Covenant," did I feel a certain something lacking. I speak of it with much hesitation, knowing how much more thought you have given it than I have, but remembering that once, long ago, in your quiet study at Princeton— the first time I ever talked with you—you spoke of the value of the letter-writing of our founders, the Adams' and Madisons, and the friendly discussion of difficult problems before a policy had been definitely announced, so I am venturing frankly to give my reaction.

As you know, I have been traveling for the past eleven months in England, France, and Italy, seeing all the liberal and radical leaders and trying to understand the deep under-currents of working class opinion. Within the last week I have had long talks with Mr. Arthur Henderson, the leader of the British Labor Party, M. Huysmans,[2] one of the chief socialist leaders of Belgium, and with several of the chief labor leaders of France. All of these men and the great masses of their followers, are your nearest, most sincere, and most dependable supporters. They will go with you to the last ditch.

I think I may confidently affirm, as a result of this association and understanding, that my reaction in reading the "Covenant" was very nearly what theirs would be. The certain lack I felt, then, was the absence of all reference to economic problems, except the very satisfactory article dealing with labor—which will be welcomed by all of these under-groups. If there could be some recognition of the problems now involved in food and financial control, tariffs, shipping, and the distribution of raw materials—even though this recognition merely suggested the organization of future conferences to deal with them—it would ease off the deep-seated feeling among millions of workers that economic problems lie at the bottom of most of our political problems. Such a recognition would round out and make more appealing this magnificent document. Even a glimpse at the economic side of international relationships in your "Convenant" will convince the under-groups that you are in touch with their thoughts. In a time like this, and with your unexampled prestige, you can scarcely ask too much of the faith and idealism of the world.

Very sincerely yours,    Ray Stannard Baker

TLS (WP, DLC).
    ¹ T MS (R. S. Baker Papers, DLC). This "proposed first article" was a fairly detailed summary of the main provisions of Wilson's second "Paris Draft."
    ² Camille Huysmans.

## From Ray Stannard Baker, with Enclosure

[Paris] January 21, 1919.

MEMORANDUM FOR: THE PRESIDENT.

Subject: Resolutions of the Newspaper Correspondents.

1. At the request of the officers of the Newspaper Correspondents' Association, I am enclosing herewith a copy of the resolutions adopted at the recent meeting relative to publicity of the Peace Conference. It is a response to the statement of the Peace Conference on the same subject, issued last Thursday.

Ray Stannard Baker

TS MS (WP, DLC).

E N C L O S U R E

The American press delegation acknowledges receipt of the reply of the Peace Conference to the resolutions addressed to them.

The delegation notes that the decision that "representatives of the press shall be admitted to the meetings of the full Conference" is an acceptance of the principle of direct press representation for which the press of America, Great Britain, Italy and the smaller nations contended.

The value of this principle, however, turns upon the extent and frequency of its limitations in practice. The Peace Conference announces its intention to limit it to the extent that "upon necessary occasions the deliberations of the Conference may be held in camera." Without assent on our part to this limitation, we trust that if ever it is applied the public will be advised through the press at the outset of each session in camera of the subject to be discussed and the name of the delegate or delegation making the motion to go into camera; and at the close of the session the conclusions or agreements reached.

In view of the fact that we have not been advised to the contrary, we necessarily assume that any rule designed to prohibit communication between individual delegates and the press on the subjects of the Conference has now been abrogated; and that the press is to have access to verbatim records of the proceedings.

We call the attention of the Peace Conference to our request for not fewer than five direct press representatives at each session of the Conference and we submit that, because of the manner in which the several press associations serve the newspapers of America and because of the attendance upon the Conference of numerous individual press representatives, American newspapers cannot carry on their business of informing their vast public with fewer than five.

> Committee:
> Mark Sullivan, Chairman.
> Arthur B. Krock, Secretary.
> R. V. Oulahan,
> Herbert Bayard Swope,
> John Edwin Nevin,
> Paul Scott Mowrer,
> David Lawrence.

T MS (WP, DLC).


## From Vance Criswell McCormick

My dear Mr. President:                    [Paris] January 21, 1919.

I am in receipt of your note of January 20th[1] requesting my advice on two communications received by you relative to removing export control from cotton and permitting cotton shipments to Germany and Austria.

These communications raise very important questions of policy which should, I feel, be worked out with our associates. There is the question of what, if any, raw materials should be exported to the Central Powers as a relief measure to afford employment to the idle sections of their population. In determining what, if any, exports of raw materials should be made, the Allies will also desire to consider the financial aspect of the question and to reduce to a minimum imports from Germany, payment for which would require the use of foreign credits, which otherwise could be applied in the making of reparation. The Allies will also desire to consider the affect upon their own industries of imports of raw materials into the Central Powers and will, I anticipate, raise rather serious objection to imports of cotton to any appreciable extent, which cotton will be manufactured on spindles in part pillaged from Belgium and France, thus permitting Germany to repossess herself of markets for cotton manufacturers while the cotton mills of Belgium and France are still unrestored.

There is also to be considered the economic and political effect at home of an early resumption of trade with the enemy in cotton. While the cotton growers desire this, we have protests from many others for economic and sentimental reasons.

Irrespective of what may be our judgment on these matters, I feel that we cannot but give a friendly hearing to the views of the Allies, particularly as under the terms of the Armistice the blockade is to be maintained.

Exports of cotton to all neutral countries are now allowed to the extent adequate to meet the needs of these neutrals, and, in view of the large problems of policy involved in permitting exports on a larger scale, I suggest the following reply to the two communications which you referred to me and which are returned herewith:

"Cotton may now be exported to all neutral countries in amounts adequate for their needs. Further exports to or for account of enemy countries raise important questions of policy which are the subject of attentive consideration by associated governments."        Faithfully yours,    Vance C McCormick

TLS (WP, DLC).
¹ WW to V. C. McCormick, Jan. 20, 1919, CCL (WP, DLC).

# From Joseph Patrick Tumulty

[The White House, Jan. 21, 1919]

Following sent at request of cabinet quote

The cabinet believes that your proclamation in the matter of use of cereals for manufacturing beverages should be modified to permit resumption of production of non-alcoholic drinks stop. Further relaxation is not recommended as the act authorizing proclamation bases the discretion both on food conservation and national security and defense stop. During demobilization of army and re-adjustment of industry national security would seem better protected by not changing existing situation stop.

Attorney General will cable form of proclamation to carry this out if acceptable to you unquote.　　　　　　　　Tumulty.

T telegram (WP, DLC).


# Frank Lyon Polk to Joseph Patrick Tumulty, with Enclosure

Dear Mr. Tumulty:　　　　　　Washington January 21, 1919.

I enclose herewith a copy of a despatch from the American Minister at Peking[1] transmitting a free translation of the text of an inscription written by the President of the Republic of China for presentation to the President. The Minister states that the autographed inscription was being forwarded by the hands of Dr. W. W. Willoughby.[2]

The Department has not received the inscription.

I am, my dear Mr. Tumulty,

Sincerely yours,　Frank L Polk

TLS (WP, DLC).
　[1] P. S. Reinsch to RL, Nov. 29, 1918, CCL (WP, DLC).
　[2] That is, Westel Woodbury Willoughby, Professor of Political Science at The Johns Hopkins University since 1897 and a former student of Wilson's at that institution; constitutional adviser to the Chinese government, 1916-1917.


## E N C L O S U R E

# A Translation of a Letter from Hsü Shih-ch'ang

[Peking] November 20th, 1918.

Messages coming from the pacific horizon afford me genuine pleasure to learn of the highest leadership which you take in laying down lofty rules of conduct to guide all peoples. Assiduous study of Confucianism has enabled me to come to the conclusion that be it in the east or the west, there is only one right standard for political action. Though we are separated by a great distance, yet I feel your influence as if we were face to face. It is my sincere hope to labor with you hand-in-hand to achieve further human progress so that peace may reign throughout the world. May our ideals be exchanged by constant communications and our happy accord suffer no interruption. In availing myself of this auspicious moment to send to you this souvenir, I can but fully disclose what is in my bosom, and, I have the honor to send to you my best wishes for your personal welfare.　　　　　　Hsü Shih-Chang

T MS (WP, DLC).

## Gilbert Fairchild Close to Thomas Edward Lawrence

My dear Colonel Lawrence:                    Paris—21 January, 1919.

I am writing on behalf of the President to say that in accordance with a memorandum sent him by Rabbi Stephen F. Wise, he would be very glad to meet Prince Feisul of Arabia, and yourself, on Thursday afternoon, January 23rd, at 5:45 p.m., at his residence, 28 rue Monceau.                    Sincerely yours,    [Gilbert F. Close]

CCL (WP, DLC).

## Thomas Edward Lawrence to Gilbert Fairchild Close

Dear Sir                                        Paris 21.1.19.

Will you please tell President Wilson that Prince Feisal will be very glad indeed to meet him at 5.45 P.M. on Thursday next (Jan. 23) as arranged by you.    Yours sincerely   T E Lawrence

ALS (WP, DLC).

## Ignace Jan Paderewski to Robert Lansing

Warsovie. January 21, 1919.

At the request of Generalissimo Pilsudski, Chief of the Polish State, I have assumed today the duties of Prime Minister and Secretary for Foreign Affairs, of the Provisional Polish Government, which I have formed with the consent of all the parts of the former Polish Republic with the approval of almost all the Polish political parties. While hastening to notify your excellency of this fact, I wish to express on behalf of Poland and of the Polish Government the deep felt gratitude of my country for the United States. Your great President has been the first to proclaim the resurrection of Poland as a free Independent and united state, and by the glorious victories of the American and Allied armies our liberation has been attained. Free at last thanks to the generous efforts of the United States and the Entente Powers, Poland aspires to cooperate as one of the Allied nations in the great task of all civilized democracies in the suppression of anarchy the greatest enemy of civilization. I cherish the hope that the United States will recognize Poland as a free sovereign state as well as the Polish Government. I am confident that having so generously assisted in bringing about the regeneration of the Polish Republic the great American Republic will grant us her precious support and lend us a helping hand in

this difficult hour when the dangerous wave of anarchy threatens
the Polish eastern borders.                    I. J. Paderewski

T telegram (WP, DLC).


## From the Diary of Vance Criswell McCormick

January 21 (Tuesday) [1919]

Worked in office until 5.30, when I had an appointment with the
President at the Hotel Murat. Suggested the importance of his
having weekly conferences with his advisers similar to War Cabinet
meetings in Washington. He agreed to start them this week. It will
help us all, I feel sure. Discussed organization plans for closer Allied
co-operation. He has heard from reliable sources the Allies want to
pool the total expense of the war and have us pay our proportionate
share of the whole. This, of course, is not to be considered, and the
President was considerably exercised over this proposal and wanted
me to tell the other advisers not to get mixed up in any of their
committees by discussing this subject at this time; but we were to
confine ourselves only to our own Allied financial or other problems
in which the enemy countries are involved, thereby keeping clear
of embarrassing discussions which have nothing to do with Germany. Colonel House has been getting about for the first time in
ten days, but very weak.


## From the Diary of Edith Benham

January 21, 1919

This has been a most interesting evening. Mr. A. G. Gardiner, of
the London News, a man who has written some very remarkable
essays and character studies, came to dinner. He was a steadfast
supporter of the President when the latter's popularity was at low
ebb in England and the President had been very eager to meet
him. So Gardiner made this trip to Paris to see him. The great and
central interest came late—the discussion of the League of Nations—and I am going to begin backward, recapitulating somewhat
what I wrote the other night and did not get exactly straight. The
President said he had the Fillamore resolution[1] that he revised and
sent to Colonel House who made some changes and returned to
him. After reading Botha's paper[2] he (the President) made again
criticisms and revisions and sent to Botha, as you know the other
night, then Lloyd George and Sir Robert Cecil came Sunday night
and they all went over it working until midnight. Now tonight the

President has given it to Gardiner to look over and make any suggestions which occur. In speaking of the session with Lloyd George and Sir Robert Cecil, the President said it was astonishing how much alike they thought and their differences were more the approach of the same subject from a different angle. Gardiner would ask different questions and the President would enlarge on them. He said there had been criticism of the President not taking the public into his confidence, telling them of the League of Nations and what he expected to do here. That, he replied, would have been impossible for he would have defeated his own object. If he had laid down a set of principles dictatorily he would have antagonized the governments as he would have seemed to be dictating or suggesting terms to them in advance of the conference; that he would have liked to take the country into his confidence, but he realized though he had a tentative plan and scheme drawn up, he knew it would be changed as he got into contact with the minds over here and familiarized himself with the European state of mind. He discussed with Mr. Gardiner the constitution of the League of Nations and said that he had found in the conference even among those who had not accepted it definitely, an unspoken adherence in the fact that they put off certain questions which came up in the Peace discussion to be settled later by the League of Nations. . . .

Gardiner advanced the subject of the mandatory nations which I take it means that to every nation is assigned the care of a small one, and to that the President said come[s] the principal objection from America. Ingrained in us was our national dislike to acquiring new territory that is outlying and he instanced the Philippines as a case of which [the] American national thought. That we were impatient of the time when we could give them autonomy. He was greatly doubtful if the American people would consent to be a mandatory power save for the German colonies in Africa for instance, or Constantinople which Mr. Gardiner said we should very properly take. He seems to think that as a people we have misinterpreted George Washington's idea about alliances, but [a] misinterpretation it [which] is deeply ingrained in our national conscienciousness [consciousness]. He said America entered the war with the highest ideals of no territorial gain, and though the administration of these new states born of the war was a very important duty, we should assume he doubted if the American people would see it in that light and would consider it a subterfuge to obtain territory.

He spoke again of the Italian question of the very just claim of the Italians that if the new Jugo Slavia state was given what it claimed they would have a bold rocky shore with harbors commanding the opposite low sandy shore, and for that reason as one the League of Nations should allow the Jugo Slavs no navy, for in fact, the state of Jugo Slavia was only a name, for there are several states and it might be years before they decided to unite as one large one.

The freedom of the seas he only touched on because he said if the League was united against one rebellious nation there could be no freedom of the seas. He had only recently arrived at that because out of the welter of confusion into which international law had fallen since the war, he had expected to make certain changes in regard to international law and then he had seen this.

I forgot to say he had also seen Leon Bourgeois and consulted with him over the League of Nations and he went even further than the President holding there should be unified command by the League of Nations over the military forces of the nations constituting the League. This he characterized as impossible for the question of who should command them would present insuperable difficulty.

At table there was some little talk of the personalities of the Conference and the President said that Sonnino always irritated Lloyd George so much, and that Clemenceau showed the peculiar French trait of standing still mentally. He said of Clemenceau laughingly that in '70 he was nearly hung for being a radical, and that now he was considered a conservative—all going to show he had not kept up with his world.

Gardiner is a wonderfully well informed man on all things pertaining to the United States, though he has never been there, and took up the subject of Lincoln showing an intimate and sympathetic insight into his character, and that is always a favorite subject with the President. Coming to later figures in American politics, the President spoke of Mr. Roosevelt and of his unreliability for the reporters said when he would tell them certain things, he would add that he would deny if they published it. He spoke of the famous interview he had with T.R. and that he was amazed to find that T.R. wanted to go in command of the First Army,[3] just as a spectacular feat to put himself before the public, and said quite frankly that he did not consider he had the necessary qualifications, but he wanted to take along a certain number of officers who would advise him and cover up his mistakes! The President said these were the best men of the Army, invaluable for building up the new Army, and added had he published this conversation T.R. would have denied saying any of it.

[1] That is, the Phillimore Report, about which see Lord Reading to WW, July 3, 1918 (second letter of that date), n. 1, Vol. 48.
[2] That is, in fact, General Smuts' report, the proposals of which are printed at Dec. 26, 1918, Vol. 53.

³ See EMH to WW, April 10, 1917, n. 1, and the extract from the Brahany Diary, printed at April 10, 1917, both in Vol. 42.

## From the Diary of Dr. Grayson

Wednesday, January 22, 1919.

The President prepared the outline of what was later adopted by the Peace Conference as the Prince's Island Invitation. It was an invitation to all of the factions in Russia to declare a truce, and to send delegates to meet in February to determine whether they could reconcile their views and thus secure representation at the Peace Conference. The President's suggestion was that there should be no interference with internal affairs of Russia, but that the Allies would do everything possible they could to help the Russian people from the outside. In this connection the French position again was entirely the opposite to that of the American and British, the French advocating armed intervention by allied forces sufficiently strong to overwhelm Bolshevism. The President's suggestion was adopted and sent broadcast despite the French position. The remainder of the day was devoted to committee conferences. In the evening at eight o'clock the President attended a dinner at the Hotel Crillon, given by Secretary and Mrs. Lansing in honor of the United States Ambassador to Great Britain and Mrs. John W. Davis. The President was very tired and excused himself at ten o'clock.

## Hankey's Notes of a Meeting of the Supreme War Council[1]

Quai d'Orsay, January 22, 1919, 11 A.M.

BC-7

M. CLEMENCEAU, in opening the meeting proposed that the plan suggested by Marshal Foch of sending Polish troops from France to Poland via Dantzig and Thorn should be discussed. He had received a telegram that morning stating that the British Government had agreed to this operation.

PRESIDENT WILSON said that he was without advice from his military counselors. The proposal, as he understood it, was that the Polish troops now under French command should be shipped to Dantzig, and that to facilitate their arrival in Poland an Allied control of the railway from that port to Thorn should be established. He asked by whom this control would be exercised, and whether the object of the expedition was exclusively to protect the Poles against external enemies.

[1] The complete text of the following minutes is printed in PPC, III, 670-75.

M. CLEMENCEAU said that Marshal Foch would give the requisite explanation.

MARSHAL FOCH said that there were in France a number of Polish troops ready to start. One division was quite ready; another was forming; and a third was in an early stage of formation, but could count on 20,000 men. He thought they would be ready to embark as soon as transport could be assembled to convey them to Dantzig.

M. ORLANDO asked whether Marshal Foch was taking into account the Poles in Italy.

MARSHAL FOCH replied that, taking these into account, there was a fourth possible division.

M. CLEMENCEAU enquired whether Italy agreed to the incorporation of the Poles in that country.

M. ORLANDO said he agreed.

MARSHAL FOCH (resuming) said that the troops therefore existed. The next question was ships to take them to Dantzig. Thenceforward these troops must use the Dantzig-Thorn railway line. This line, according to the terms of the Armistice, was at our disposal. But the Poles said that the Germans would not allow them to land at Dantzig or to use the railway to Thorn. They therefore suggested that the line should be held by Allied troops.

M. CLEMENCEAU asked Marshal Foch to state his own opinion as to whether the Germans would resist the passage of Polish forces, and to give an estimate of the strength of the resistance, should it take place.

MARSHAL FOCH said that, in his view, as long as the Polish programme remained as indeterminate as it now was, there would undoubtedly be German resistance. The Germans certainly intended to dispute the possession of Posen, and still more, of Dantzig. Possibly German consent to the passage of Polish troops might be obtained if the Poles agreed to a restricted programme. For instance, that these troops should only go to Russian Poland to defend it against the Bolsheviks, and that the Polish authorities should undertake not to occupy any debatable ground. The Germans had eighteen divisions near their eastern frontier. He therefore thought that the Polish army could only be safely sent to Poland under cover either of a definite policy which obtained consent of the Germans or of Allied troops in occupation of the railway. To occupy this line effectually two Allied divisions would be required.

In order to give a firmer basis to the contemplated operation, it would be necessary that all the Allied Missions in Poland should be reorganised. There was at present a British Military Mission under Colonel Wade attached to M. Paderewski at Posen; there was a French Mission under General Barthelemy[2] at Lemberg; there were other Missions elsewhere. Their information and views varied. It was desirable to have a unified Mission to study in particular the means of landing forces and of conveying them to Poland.

MR. BALFOUR pointed out that the policy of uniting all the Missions in order to obtain their collective advice would involve delay. If it were true that Poland was threatened by an imminent Bolshevik attack, this delay might be disastrous. He would like to know whether, in Marshal Foch's opinion, a Bolshevik attack was really to be feared.

MARSHAL FOCH said that he thought it was important to gather the scattered Missions into one, and to get the Poles to have a definite policy. Their actions at present were divergent and eccentric. They were facing the Bolsheviks on the east, invading Posen on the west, and Galicia in the south. Some of these actions were not in any way forced upon them. The result was that they were wasting their energies and would not be able to succeed anywhere.

M. CLEMENCEAU enquired how much time would elapse, according to the Marshal's programme, before the Poles from the west landed in Poland.

MARSHAL FOCH pointed out that all his proposals could be carried out concurrently. The Missions could be unified; the Poles could be prevailed on to amend their policy; and the despatch of the troops could be prepared at the same time. If all these problems were tackled at once he thought the troops might begin to arrive in three weeks or a month.

MR. BALFOUR expressed the opinion that among the many difficulties the greatest would be to get the Poles to accept a restricted programme. He felt that this would have to be imposed upon them. The Poles were using the interval between the cessation of war and the decisions of the Peace Congress to make good their claims to districts outside Russian Poland, to which in many cases they had little right, although in others their claims were amply justified. To Posen, no doubt, they were entitled. The case of Dantzig was of peculiar difficulty. Eastern Galicia, according to all the information at his disposal, did not desire to be Polish. He suggested that the Polish representatives should be gathered here and told that they must limit their actions to the protection of indisputable Polish territory against invasion from without. The ultimate frontiers of Poland should be left to the Peace Congress. He proposed that M. Clemenceau, President Wilson, Mr. Lloyd George and M. Orlando

---

[2] Gen. Marie Joseph Raoul Léon Barthélemy.

should tell them, in the name of the Powers exactly what their line of conduct should be before the final decision. Meanwhile, the Polish forces in France could be organised, transport could be made ready in Great Britain, and the missions in Poland could be unified.

PRESIDENT WILSON said that this policy raised many grave doubts in his mind. It would involve the Allies in very complicated matters. It was proposed not only to send Polish contingents from France, but also two Allied divisions to hold the railway against five German divisions. These Allied troops would be employed for a purpose that might be highly offensive to the German Government, which would undoubtedly raise objections. These objections might have to be admitted. Dantzig must remain an open question, yet its occupation was suggested. With the object of sending Polish troops into Poland we were going to prejudge the whole Polish question. This question, moreover, should not, he thought, be isolated from all others. Many other questions resembled it. The Roumanians, for instance, were taking action of a similar kind. The Serbians also were behaving towards Montenegro in what appeared to him to be a questionable manner. The Hungarians also were trying to bring about a *fait accompli* before the termination of the Peace Congress. If we were to say to the Poles, "You must hold your hand," the same must be said to the rest. They must all be told that they prejudiced their case by premature action. If you had to take a thing by force, the inference was that it did not belong to you. It would not, therefore, be fair to segregate this case entirely. Further, it had previously been agreed upon in the case of Russia that, on condition all parties held their hand, the Allies would meet them. This alone would put an end to the threatened Bolshevik attack on Poland. M. Paderewski, in his letter, only suggested that the Allies should supply him with weapons. He said that he had at his disposal from 600,000 to 800,000 men ready to fight if they could obtain ammunition. If this were the case, why should the Allies do what the Poles could do for themselves? The question was whether, since the Armistice, the Allies had enough German rifles and ammunition to equip the Poles. These stores could be sent to them via the Dantzig-Thorn railway, the use of which was guaranteed by the Armistice.

MARSHAL FOCH said that he had no objection to this proposal. He was unable to check M. Paderewski's estimate of his forces, but he thought it was fair to assume that they had not a high military value. The supplies for these troops must go by the Dantzig-Thorn route, the free use of which could not be guaranteed. We must be able to explain the purpose of these arms. Failing that, the Germans might stop them. Paderewski's programme was a vague one. He therefore suggested that the Allied Missions should get into touch with the Poles and arrange an agreement ensuring the passage of the supplies.

PRESIDENT WILSON pointed out that M. Paderewski, in his letter, had undertaken not to surprise the Powers by a *fait accompli*, or attempt to obtain one in Dantzig.

MR. LLOYD GEORGE said that he had come to the meeting with certain views, but admitted that he was much shaken by the opinions expressed by President Wilson. His impression was that we did not know enough about the facts of the situation in Poland. Action undertaken without further knowledge might lead to a mess. What Marshal Foch had said had great force, and was not inconsistent with the President's remarks. He could not see any great difference between conveying armed men and conveying arms over the Dantzig-Thorn railway. We could not expect the Germans to allow arms to go through if they were to equip a Polish army to attack them. This would be asking more than was laid down in the Armistice. Fairness was due even to the enemy. He was not prepared at the present moment to make any declaration concerning the rights to Posen, which the Poles were attempting to conquer by force, and thereby to prejudge what the Congress was assembled to do. He pointed out that, although the Roumanians were doing the same thing, they were not asking the Allies to assist them. The Poles, on the other hand, were asking for all kinds of help—transport, supplies, rifles, ammunition.

PRESIDENT WILSON observed that M. Paderewski asked for this help specifically for defence against the Bolsheviks.

MR. LLOYD GEORGE replied that he had no doubt of the honourable character of M. Paderewski. But the Poles were not all united, and M. Paderewski was unlikely to maintain complete control of the situation. The arms might pass into other hands. He felt that the representatives of the Powers should see the Poles, or appoint a Committee to meet them in Paris.

PRESIDENT WILSON pointed out that in sending Polish troops to Poland we should not only be sending armed men, but strong partisans on Polish questions. These were burning questions, and great caution should be exercised in dealing with them.

MARSHAL FOCH said that he wished again to draw attention to the danger that Poland might be suffocated before its birth. It had no bases, no outlets, no communications, no supplies, no army. The Poles were fighting the Bolsheviks who might be attacking them, the Ukrainians whom they chose to attack, and the Germans from whom they wished to wrest Posen. From a military point of view, the policy they were pursuing was likely to be fatal to them.

M. CLEMENCEAU pointed out that the British Government could

not settle the question of sea transport without reference to London. He wished, however, to draw attention to the suggestions made by M. Paderewski that an International Commission should be sent to Warsaw to report to the Congress on conditions in Poland. The Military Missions already in Poland might be utilised as a nucleus, and additional representatives might be deputed by the Supreme War Council.

MR. LLOYD GEORGE said that he supported this proposal. He would suggest, however, that the Commission should not be entirely military, but that it should be fortified by a political element. There was an ancient quarrel in Poland between the feudal elements and the peasants. We should not take sides in this contest blindly. Men of political experience should therefore be sent with the Commission to enquire into the matter.

BARON SONNINO said that the Commission should try and induce the Poles to confine their activities to resisting the Bolsheviks.

MR. LLOYD GEORGE agreed, provided that under this pretence they did not attempt to push their conquest eastwards and face the Congress with the capture of Kovno[3] or Grodno.

M. CLEMENCEAU suggested that the names of the delegates should be brought forward at the meeting on the following day. He asked the Japanese Representatives whether they desired to send delegates to this Commission.

BARON MAKINO replied that the Japanese Government did not desire to do so.

> (It was decided that two Commissions should be appointed by the United States of America, the British Empire, France and Italy.)
>
> (It was further decided that the question of furnishing sea transport should be investigated in London, in case Marshal Foch's scheme were adopted.)

T MS (SDR, RG 256, 180.03101/13, DNA).
[3] Now Kaunas, in Lithuania.


## Hankey's Notes of a Meeting of the Council of Ten[1]

Quai d'Orsay, January 22, 1919, 3:15 p.m.

BC-7+

PRESIDENT WILSON read a draft proclamation which he had prepared for the consideration of his colleagues, in accordance with the decision reached at yesterday's meeting.

[1] The complete text of these notes is printed in PPC, III, 676-83; the corresponding American notes are printed in ibid., pp. 686-90.

After a discussion the following text was adopted, to be publicly transmitted to parties invited:

The single object the representatives of the Associated Powers have had in mind in their discussions of the course they should pursue with regard to Russia has been to help the Russian people, not to hinder them, or to interfere in any manner with their right to settle their own affairs in their own way. They regard the Russian people as their friends not their enemies, and are willing to help them in any way they are willing to be helped. It is clear to them that the troubles and distresses of the Russian people will steadily increase, hunger and privation of every kind become more and more acute, more and more widespread, and more and more impossible to relieve, unless order is restored, and normal conditions of labour, trade and transportation once more created, and they are seeking some way in which to assist the Russian people to establish order.

They recognise the absolute right of the Russian people to direct their own affairs without dictation or direction of any kind from outside. They do not wish to exploit or make use of Russia in any way. They recognise the revolution without reservation, and will in no way, and in no circumstances, aid or give countenance to any attempt at a counter-revolution. It is not their wish or purpose to favour or assist any one of those organized groups now contending for the leadership and guidance of Russia as against the others. Their sole and sincere purpose is to do what they can to bring Russia peace and an opportunity to find her way out of her present troubles.

The Associated Powers are now engaged in the solemn and responsible work of establishing the peace of Europe and of the world, and they are keenly alive to the fact that Europe and the world cannot be at peace if Russia is not. They recognise and accept it as their duty, therefore, to serve Russia in this matter as generously, as unselfishly, as thoughtfully, as ungrudgingly as they would serve every other friend and ally. And they are ready to render this service in the way that is most acceptable to the Russian people.

In this spirit and with this purpose, they have taken the following action: They invite every organised group that is now exercising, or attempting to exercise, political authority or military control anywhere in Siberia, or within the boundaries of European Russia as they stood before the war just concluded (except in Finland) to send representatives, not exceeding three representatives for each group, to the Princes Islands, Sea of Marmora, where they will be met by representatives of the Associated Powers, provided, in the meantime, there is a truce of arms amongst the parties invited, and that all armed forces anywhere sent or directed against any people or territory outside the boundaries of European Russia as they stood before the war, or against Finland, or against any people or territory whose autonomous action is in contemplation in the fourteen articles upon which the present negotiations are based, shall be meanwhile withdrawn, and aggressive military action cease. These representatives are invited to confer with the representatives of the Associated Powers in the freest and frankest way, with a view to ascertaining the wishes of all sections of the Russian people, and bringing about, if possible, some understanding and agreement by which Russia may work out her own purposes and happy co-operative relations be established between her people and the other peoples of the world.

A prompt reply to this invitation is requested. Every facility for the journey of the representatives, including transport across the Black Sea, will be given by the Allies, and all the parties concerned are expected to give the same facilities. The representative[s] will be expected at the place appointed by the 15th February, 1919.

MR. LLOYD GEORGE read a draft of preliminary resolutions for a League of Nations. This document was intended primarily for the guidance of a special Committee to be appointed to draw up the constitution of the League of Nations.

After a discussion, the following text was adopted:

The Conference having considered the proposals for the creation of a League of Nations, resolves that:

(a) It is essential to the maintenance of the world settlement, which the associated nations are now met to establish, that a League of Nations be created to promote international co-operation, *to ensure the fulfillment of accepted international obligations*,[2] and to provide safeguards against war.

(b) This League should be created as *an integral* part of the *general treaty of* peace, and should be open to every civilised nation which can be relied on to promote its objects.

(c) The members of the League should periodically meet in international Conference, and should have a permanent organisation and secretariat to carry on the business of the League in the intervals between the Conferences.

The Conference therefore appoints a Committee representative of the associated Governments to work out the details of the constitution and functions of the League.

BARON MAKINO wished to explain the position of Japan in connection with the subject of the League of Nations. In the first place, his country was sincerely desirous of co-operating with the Great Powers in this work of great importance, which had for its object

[2] Words in italics added by Wilson to a British draft of this resolution dated Jan. 15, 1919. The emended copy is in WP, DLC.

the future welfare of mankind, but on account of the great distance and the lack of sufficient preparation, he was not prepared to bind his Government to the above resolutions or to any other definite action until he had received the instructions of his Government. As the work was of such very great importance his Government expected to have the opportunity of studying and understanding the duties and obligations of the new organisation before accepting it. If the work of the Committee was to be preparatory, and opportunity for further scrutiny was to be accorded to his Government, his work would be greatly facilitated. He did not wish to introduce any discordant note, but he simply desired to make matters quite clear. As regards the principles of the League of Nations, he noticed that in clause (b) of the preliminary resolutions, the stipulation was made that the League was to be treated as an integral part of the general treaty of peace. He wished to make it quite clear that his observations applied to that point as well.

M. CLEMENCEAU enquired whether Baron Makino had any objection to his observations being published.

BARON MAKINO replied that he would ask that his observations be kept confidential.

PRESIDENT WILSON invited attention to the fact that these preliminary resolutions contained nothing new. The League of Nations had been accepted by the Supreme War Council as a basis for the armistice and for the peace treaty. He wished therefore to enquire whether Japan had not been represented on that Council.

M. MATSUI stated that he had participated in the meetings of the Supreme War Council: but the fourteen points had not then been discussed.

PRESIDENT WILSON, continuing, said that at any rate the Supreme War Council had accepted the League of Nations as a basis for the armistice. Therefore he would like to enquire from Baron Makino whether he wished it to be understood that his Government reserved its decision with regard to the basis already accepted by the other Governments.

BARON MAKINO replied that his Government had given a general assent to the agreements reached up to the time of the signing of the armistice, but they made reservations as to future detailed developments.

MR. LLOYD GEORGE enquired whether the interpretation to be given to Baron Makino's statement was that Japan did not wish to be represented, even without prejudice, on the Committee to be appointed.

BARON MAKINO replied that, on the contrary, he wished to be represented on that Committee.

(It was agreed to adopt the text of preliminary resolutions for a

League of Nations given above, the reservations made by Japan being duly noted.)

MR. LLOYD GEORGE proposed that each of the Great Powers should appoint two representatives to form a drafting committee, and that the Great Powers should in addition nominate two or more delegates to represent the whole of the small Powers. A plenary Conference should be summoned, so that these proposals could be laid before it. The names of the representatives of the small Powers nominated by the Great Powers would also be communicated.

PRESIDENT WILSON said he had an amendment to propose. He thought the initial draft should first be drawn up by the delegates of the Great Powers alone. On completion of their report it would be submitted to a larger Committee, on which all the small Powers would be represented. That is to say, the small Powers would not form part of the drafting Committee, but of a criticising Committee, which would follow.

MR. LLOYD GEORGE thought that the League of Nations, however important it might be to the Great Powers, must be even more important to the small Powers, since, if efficacious, it would constitute their shield and protection. For this reason he thought the latter should be represented on the drafting Committee. Still, he saw the force of the objection made by President Wilson. He would therefore propose that the Great Powers should nominate their representatives to form a Committee, which would be authorised to add to their numbers representatives of the small Powers.

PRESIDENT WILSON said that he would rather see a more elastic arrangement. He thought the opinion of the most thoughtful and experienced men of the small Powers should be sought. He had expected that their Committee of ten would call in men like M. Veniselos from time to time, and put to them those features of the scheme that were most likely to affect the small Powers. In this way a considerable number of the representatives of the small Powers would from time to time be consulted as friends and advisers. Advice drawn from men who did not form part of the drafting Committee would be better than that given by men who could put in a caveat. In this way he thought they would avoid the difficulty of seeming to pick out representatives among people who were anxious to appoint their own representatives.

M. CLEMENCEAU said it was his most earnest desire that the work of the small Powers should, as far as possible, be linked up with that of the Great Powers. In his opinion it was very important that this should be done to please the public; otherwise it would be said that they had agreed to publicity and yet worked in private. He agreed to the proposal that the Great Powers should nominate ten

representatives, but he would leave it to the small Powers to nominate their five representatives. He was firmly convinced that on
these Committees the small Powers would merely follow the lead
of the Great Powers, but it was necessary to give them the idea that
they were being consulted. He was anxious to call them together
and to ask them to select five representatives to act on this Committee.

M. SONNINO enquired whether both neutrals and belligerents
were included amongst the small Powers.

M. CLEMENCEAU replied that at present the belligerent Powers
alone should be summoned.

MR. BALFOUR thought that if an attempt were made to hold an
election at a full Conference, serious trouble might arise. They had
no apparatus for voting.

M. CLEMENCEAU said that he did not think it would be necessary
for the small Powers to vote. They should merely be asked to meet
anywhere they liked and select five representatives.

M. SONNINO thought that if they gave the small belligerent Powers
five delegates, they would find themselves in a great difficulty,
because each of the more important small Powers—Belgium, Serbia, Roumania, Greece, Portugal—would want to be represented.
He thought it would be more practicable if the delegates appointed
by the Great Powers received a mandate to make proposals, a large
number of the representatives of the small Powers being called in
subsequently to consider the same.

PRESIDENT WILSON thought that it would be impossible for so
large [a] Committee to draft any instrument. But, as soon as some
sort of a draft had been prepared, it should be shown to as many
of the representatives of the small Powers as possible, and their
impressions and opinions taken. This procedure would greatly shorten
the process of drafting. A public man, who had not previously made
a careful study of the question, would necessarily require to see
the proposals in a concrete form before expressing an opinion.

MR. LLOYD GEORGE said that the procedure now suggested would
not bring in the small Powers, who were beginning to complain
bitterly at their exclusion. They were here in Paris, and they were
doing nothing. They felt they were locked out, and they ought to
be brought into the making of the peace. He thought there would
be no difficulty in including a certain number of the representatives
of the small Powers on the Committee to be formed, because there
was a draft ready. This draft had been thought out very carefully.
He favoured a process of a select Committee, without reporters, to
go through the draft, and to make the necessary amendments. On
such a Committee a large number of representatives could be in-

cluded. He thought that was very important. It was immaterial whether they asked the smaller Powers themselves to select their five representatives or whether the representatives were nominated by the Great Powers. He would propose, therefore, that they should in the first place meet all the Powers at a full Conference in order to ask them to accept the principles set forth in the resolutions for a League of Nations. The Conference would then be informed that the Great Powers had selected their delegates, and the small Powers would be asked to meet together and select their delegates.

PRESIDENT WILSON pointed out that at a previous meeting it had been agreed that there should be no voting. Was an exception to be made in this case? This would be setting a precedent which should be seriously considered.

MR. LLOYD GEORGE replied that the delegations would not be asked to vote. The small Powers would only be entitled to record their dissent. The Great Powers need merely say that they would take note of any suggestions or dissent and consider it later. The Great Powers must reserve the great decisions to themselves.

M. CLEMENCEAU, summing up, said that he understood the sense of the meeting to be that the above resolutions should be submitted for discussion to a full Peace Conference to meet on Saturday. The small Powers would then be invited to meet separately and to select five delegates to be added to the ten representatives of the Great Powers. The text of the preliminary resolutions for a League of Nations would not be communicated to the Press before the meeting on Saturday next, but it would be circulated forthwith to the various delegations.

As regards the selection of the delegates to be nominated by the small Powers, it was understood that the principle of one nation, one vote, would apply.

(It was agreed that the above resolutions should be submitted for discussion to a full Peace Conference to meet on Saturday afternoon, the 25th January, 1919. The small Powers would then be invited to meet separately and to select five delegates to be added to the ten representatives of the Great Powers. The text of the preliminary resolutions for a League of Nations would not be communicated to the Press before the meeting on Saturday next; but it would be circulated forthwith to the various delegations.)

MR. LLOYD GEORGE proposed the following resolution:

"That a Commission composed of two representatives apiece from the five Great Powers, and five representatives to be elected by the smaller Powers, be appointed to consider the establishment of a permanent organisation for concerting joint legislation in regard to industrial and labour questions between the States."

PRESIDENT WILSON enquired whether it was contemplated that the acceptance of the recommendations of that Committee would involve something being put in the peace treaty. He thought that a proposal of this kind was pertinent to the League of Nations, and the agreement reached should not be included in the peace treaty. He enquired whether it would not be better to redraft the resolution in order to make this point quite clear.

(This suggestion was accepted, and Mr. Lloyd George agreed to prepare a fresh draft, embodying this point, for discussion at the next meeting.)

MR. LLOYD GEORGE proposed that a Commission be appointed, with three representatives apiece for each of the five Great Powers and Belgium and Serbia, to examine and report on the question of the amount of the sum for reparation and indemnity which the enemy countries should pay or are capable of paying, and the form in which payment should be made.

PRESIDENT WILSON proposed that the word "indemnity" should be omitted. He thought the word "reparation" would meet the case. Bodies of working people all over the world had protested against indemnities, and he thought the expression "reparations" would be sufficiently inclusive.

MR. LLOYD GEORGE accepted the proposal, provided the word "reparations" was taken in its widest terms.

(This proposal was accepted.)

M. PICHON drew attention to the fact that Greece had been given no representation.

MR. BALFOUR said that Russian Poland had suffered more than any country, and almost as badly as Belgium.

M. SONNINO also mentioned Roumania.

MR. LLOYD GEORGE suggested that the small Powers should be invited to select five delegates.

PRESIDENT WILSON thought that Belgium, Serbia, Greece and Roumania might be given two representatives apiece.

M. PICHON said that Poland had two representatives at the Peace Conference, and should also be included.

(It was agreed that a new draft should be prepared by Mr. Lloyd George and submitted for consideration at the next meeting.)

(The meeting then adjourned, to meet again at 10 hours 30 the next day.)

T MS (SDR, RG 256, 180.03101/14, DNA).

# From Norman Hezekiah Davis

Dear Mr. President:                    Paris, January 22, 1919.

I have the honor to submit the following report regarding the financial questions involved in the recent negotiations at Treves incident to the renewal of the Armistice.

### Re Safety of gold and note issuing plant.

The first matter discussed with the German Financial Delegates was relative to the safety of the gold in Berlin and the advisability of moving this gold and the note issuing plant to some safer place in Germany, nearer the Armies of occupation and further away from the centre of the activities of the Spartacus Party.

The German Delegates explained that they were equally concerned about the safety of their gold reserve and note issuing plant, but pointed out that only about one-third of the total gold reserve was in Berlin, and that the balance was distributed in the other German cities. They also enumerated the various elaborate safeguards which had been placed over the gold and the note issuing plant and emphasized the great danger of any attempt to move this gold or note issuing plant at the present time. They admitted that by the failure of the guards to offer resistance the Spartacus group got control of the government printing offices for a time, but said they did no damage and that the Government has placed guards in control whom they think are dependable. The German Delegates further stated that if it seemed advisable or if a favorable opportunity offered in the future for the movement of this gold and printing plant, they would do so, and advise the Associated Governments. They stated that for reasons which were obvious it was most important that the discussions regarding the movement of the gold and bank note issuing plant be kept entirely secret, and this was agreed to by the representatives of the Associated Governments.

### Re Payment for food shipments to Germany.

The German Delegates first explained their financial and economic position and stated it would be impossible to pay cash for food without creating a situation which would make it impossible for them to resume their industrial life if their liquid assets were further used up.

They evidently expected us to give them credit, but after explaining to them that we could only furnish limited quantities of food for cash upon certain conditions to meet an emergency situation in Germany, and that this was not the appropriate time to discuss the restoration of their industrial life, the German Delegates then enumerated the following possible means of payment:

1. Gold in possession of the Reichsbank;
2. Balances, credits or securities, in neutral countries, and foreign stocks and bonds in the hands of German citizens;
3. Credit balances in enemy countries and proceeds of German property seized or liquidated in those countries.

The Germans stated that these were only theoretical means, because their gold reserve was already most dangerously low; that they had practically exhausted all balances and resources for obtaining credits in neutral countries, and that their nationals now held an insignificant amount of foreign securities. As to the use of German private assets in enemy countries, principally the United States, many complicated questions were involved, and they would have to consult their Government about the possible use of same, provided the Associated Governments would permit same.

We then informed them that upon the conclusion of the proposed arrangement for operating the German mercantile marine, we were disposed to recommend that the net freight receipts be applied in payment of food, but it would take some time to derive any appreciable amount from this source.

They then stated that as we must know the situation in Germany, they felt no hesitancy in stating frankly that their condition is almost desperate; that the mortality rate is increasing rapidly from underfeeding and that with the people in such a nervous condition caused by continued underfeeding and present lack of employment, the Government could not cope with the situation without food and work for the masses. They further stated that for certain supplies desperately needed immediately, they would be compelled to make payment almost entirely with gold, which placed them in a dilemma, because of the difficulty of deciding between the lesser of two evils, namely, to allow starvation, mortality and disorder to increase, or to use their gold supply, which could only last a short time and which is already insufficient to maintain credit stability. They stated that if any appreciable amount of their gold is used it would make it impossible for them to resume trade and give employment to their people.

The German Delegates, after having communicated with Berlin, where a meeting was held of the various Ministers concerned, stated that the position taken by the Associated Governments necessarily precluded Germany from securing all the food she needed, but that the situation was so grave they had decided they must secure enough food and supplies, at least for the hospitals, aged persons, babies and women who have just had children, and that for this purpose they were willing to place at the disposal of the

Associated Governments one hundred million marks in gold, twenty-five million marks in neutral currency or credits (which is all they have), and to apply when available the proceeds from the freight earnings, and fifty thousand tons of potash (which they could deliver immediately), and to give any further commodities in payment for food which might be available and required.

We explained to them we were under the impression that they could and should obtain neutral credit either publicly or privately without the necessity of using their gold; that the gold and currency offered would only pay for about half of their emergency requirements, and that before agreeing to accept gold in payment, we would have to report the matter to our respective Governments.

The list of the emergency requirements, in the order of priority and necessity consisted of 75,000 tons of fats (pork products),

10,500 tons of condensed milk,
10,000 tons of oatmeal,
4,000 tons of rice,
3,500 tons of meat extract,
Rubber nipples, and
Rubber gloves for surgeons.

It was then agreed that the Germans would communicate with us through the Armistice Commission at Spa, their proposals for making payment for the balance of this order, and that we would accordingly advise them of our decision.

*Remarks.*

The Germans may be exaggerating their inability to obtain neutral credits and apparently are reluctant to take German private property, possibly in order to be in a position to resume their commercial life, but I am inclined to think that they are in much worse condition than we thought. As commercial credits can often be obtained when impossible to secure banking credits, the British Treasury representative and I still think Germany might thus obtain considerable food from northern neutrals and Swiss merchants if given the opportunity. With this in view and also because it is thought advisable under present circumstances for Germany to purchase food by credit rather than by use of liquid assets, the Supreme Council of Supply and Relief has passed a resolution at our suggestion recommending that above neutrals be permitted to reexport to Germany the amounts of specified foods approved by the Council.

In my opinion it is almost as essential for the German people to have employment as to have food, and I think we will soon be confronted with the necessity of deciding whether or not Germany shall be permitted to import certain raw materials in order to start her industries and give work to her people, and thus be enabled to assist materially in paying for her food requirements until the next harvest.

A memorandum[1] has been prepared embodying the measures which, in the opinion of the representative of the British Treasury and myself would be the most practicable and expedient way to enable Germany to purchase and pay for food. In substance, we are recommending that the German proposal to pay for her immediate requirements in gold and neutral exchange should be accepted, but that the German representatives should be advised that in the future they must devise other means of payment than that of gold. Our recommendation has been presented informally to the French Treasury, which, as yet, has not accepted same, but promises a definite answer tomorrow. In the discussions with the French Treasury, they have taken the same position which Mr. Klotz took at the meeting of the Supreme War Council, and even went so far as to argue that the freights on German ships should not be applied to the payment for this food, but should be held for future determination at the Peace Conference. We were under the impression that this was disposed of at the meeting of the Supreme War Council, but as it may come up there again, I am enclosing herewith for your information a copy of the memorandum.

The Germans claim that even their present neutral balances which they propose to apply towards the payment for food, are part of loans obtained which have not been expended, which creates for them a difficult situation, because they have obligations maturing very shortly with certain neutral countries, especially Switzerland. Under the Armistice the Germans are not permitted to dispose of bullion, currency, securities, or assets at home or abroad, without the consent of the Associated Governments, and I have just received a cable from the Treasury to the effect that the Swiss Minister[2] has applied to the Acting Secretary of State for our consent to the German Government selling to Switzerland ten to fifteen thousand bales of cotton from stocks held in Switzerland for German account, to be applied on Germany's debt to Switzerland, and requesting that favorable consideration be given to this and any other request of the German representatives tending to facilitate the meeting of German obligations to Switzerland. This and other similar questions will undoubtedly arise at once for determination by the Supreme War Council, as to whether or not Germany should be permitted under present circumstances to pay loans contracted in neutral countries during the war and maturing before the signing of peace, thus giving a preference to certain creditors, provided Germany is now in a bankrupt condition.

I am, my dear Mr. President,

Most respectfully yours,   Norman H. Davis

TLS (WP, DLC).
[1] Untitled memorandum, c. Jan. 16, 1919, CC MS (WP, DLC).
[2] That is, Hans Sulzer.


## From Herbert Clark Hoover

Dear Mr. President:                          Paris, 22 January 1919.

I understand the brewing question is referred back to you by the Cabinet, with what recommendations I do not know. It appears to me that one portion of the problem could be settled at once, that is, the brewing of non-alcoholic beers which are also closed for conservation reasons. There would appear to be no temperance question involved in this and I would like to suggest to you that the limitations on this portion of the industry at least should be lifted. I enclose herewith the necessary proclamation to effect this end, if you conclude that it is desirable to do so.[1]

Yours faithfully,   Herbert Hoover

TLS (WP, DLC).
[1] See GFC to HCH, Jan. 24, 1919.


## From Scott Ferris[1]

Washington, January 22, 1919.

366. For the President from the Secretary of the Interior.

"Conferees have reached tentative agreement on salient features of oil leasing bill.[2] Senator Shafroth and I have been specially delegated to present same to executive branch of Government. Conferees agree exact ⅛ royalty prior claim passage of legislation and a minimum ⅛ and maximum of ¼ for subsequent production. Full claim to be leased to O'Farrel [bona fide] claimant outside naval reserves when claimant is free from all fraud.[3] Inside naval reserves your proposition as to wells drilled and the President given authority to make additional leases when public interest requires. It is thought important this legislation should pass this session for we feel certain a better solution of this troublesome problem can be made by those who have had matter in hand all along."          Polk.

T telegram (WP, DLC).
[1] About the authorship of this telegram, see FLP to WW, Jan. 30, 1919.
[2] That is, the General Leasing bill.

3 The relevant section of the conference report reads as follows: "That any person who, at the time of any withdrawal order, or on January first, nineteen hundred and eighteen, was a bona fide occupant or claimant of oil or gas lands not withdrawn from entry, . . . shall be entitled to a lease thereon under such terms as the Secretary of the Interior may prescribe unless otherwise provided for in section eighteen hereof: Provided, That such lands are not reserved for the use of the Navy: Provided, however, That no claimant who has been guilty of any fraud or who had knowledge or reasonable grounds to know of any fraud or who has not acted honestly and in good faith shall be entitled to any of the benefits of this section." *Oil and Gas Lands Bill. Conference Report on the Bill (S. 2812) to Encourage and Promote the Mining of Coal, Phosphate, Oil, Gas, and Sodium on the Public Domain,* 65th Cong., 3d sess., Sen. Doc. No. 392, p. 9.

## Robert Lansing to Ignace Jan Paderewski

[Paris] January 22, 1919.

The President of the United States directs me to extend to you, as Prime Minister and Secretary for Foreign Affairs of the Provisional Polish Government, his sincere wishes for your success in the high office which you have assumed and his earnest hope that the Government of which you are a part will bring prosperity to the Republic of Poland.

It is my privilege to extend to you at this time my personal greetings and officially to assure you that it will be a source of gratification to enter into official relations with your Government at the earliest opportunity. To render to your country such aid as is possible at this time as it enters upon a new cycle of independent life will be in full accord with that spirit of friendliness which has in the past animated the American people in their relations with your countrymen.                                                        Lansing.

T telegram (WP, DLC).

## From the Diary of Edith Benham

January 22, 1919

This day, Mrs. Wilson and I have devoted to shopping and done great execution. Now that the conferences are on she is much more alone. The President hates to walk and is like a bad child in trying to find excuses not to walk to the Quai d'Orsay where the Conferences are held, or to walk at other times. She insisted he had the newspaper men trained to stop him at a certain point on the deck of the George Washington and stop his walk. Usually he is too busy for he is seeing people nearly all day when he isn't at the Foreign Office. She always drives or walks over with him, and sometimes I go, but usually go there to pick her up and go on some shopping excursion.

I didn't think two people ever loved each other as they do. In all the weeks with them I have never heard one cross word, seen them look at each other in any way than the most devoted lovers. They are two very unusual people and don't have the flare-ups ordinary people have. She is unusually self-contained, admits scarcely anyone to her friendship, though always wonderfully gracious. Her smile and charm are proverbial. I do not believe there has been any woman who has occupied the position she has who has her beauty and charm and is so good. The first two qualities fit a number of sovereigns, but the last usually seem to have been left out and given to the stodgy and amiable Victorias. She is very quiet about her dislikes, but a very intense and very loyal friend. There never was anyone with a keener sense of humor. He has the same, but she is a born mimic. I have never seen anyone enjoy anything more than he does one of her stories or experiences after she has been somewhere without him, for she always sees something funny. I was amused the other night when he was talking to A. G. Gardiner to hear him say he would like to kill the man who had invented the myth that he couldn't smile and was a Puritan thinking machine. With all the adulation both have had over here, neither is the least bit spoiled.

## Hankey's Notes of a Meeting of the Council of Ten

Quai d'Orsay, January 23, 1919, 10:30 A.M.[1]

BC-8

[The names were announced of some of the members of the Commission for Poland and the Commission for the Russian Conference.

[The following names were given for the Commission for the League of Nations:
France: Bourgeois, Larnaude.
United States: Wilson, House.
Great Britain: Cecil, Smuts.
Italy: Scialoja, Ricci-Busatti.
Japan: Chinda, Otchiai.[2]]

M. CLEMENCEAU said the next subject to be dealt with was that of the reduction of armaments, concerning which a draft had been proposed by Mr. Lloyd George. (See Appendix "A.")

---

[1] The complete text of these notes is printed in *PPC*, III, 693-703.
[2] Persons not heretofore identified in this series were Fernand Larnaude, Dean of the Faculty of Law of the University of Paris; Vittorio Scialoja, a senator and former Italian Minister of Justice (1909-1910); Arturo Ricci-Busatti, chief of the claims section in the Italian Foreign Ministry; and Kentaro Otchiai, the Japanese Minister at The Hague.

MR. LLOYD GEORGE pointed out that the draft contained two distinct proposals. The first dealt with the immediate situation. A decision on this point was, for Great Britain, a matter of very grave moment. Unless the enemy's forces were immediately reduced, the British Government might be forced to maintain compulsory service. He did not know what might be the political result of such a decision. In another month's time, the renewal of the Armistice would be considered. He felt that at that time we should demand a drastic reduction of the armed forces of Germany to a fixed quotum, such as might suffice to maintain internal order. It would also be necessary to place a limit on the armaments and munitions available for these forces; the surplus could be placed under Allied guard. If the Germans maintained armaments and munitions sufficient for an army of two or three million men, their demobilization would be nugatory. He was informed by the British War Office that to fulfil Marshal Foch's requirements, a British Army of 1,700,000 men must be kept with the colours. This was a very serious demand which would not be readily accepted by the country. He would, therefore, urge that the first clause in the draft be proceeded with at once. The second could be reserved for a future date.

PRESIDENT WILSON, commenting on the terms of the draft, suggested the elimination of the words "and drastic," as conveying the impression of a threat.

M. SONNINO suggested, as an alternative, the words "prompt reduction."

MR. LLOYD GEORGE pointed out that the text was not intended for communication to the enemy but only as a guidance to the Allied Commission that was to be set up to consider it. What he wished to convey to the Committee was that the enemy's forces should be reduced to the minimum necessary for the maintenance of internal order.

PRESIDENT WILSON asked whether this could be done without consultation with the Germans and whether it ought not to be taken up by the Armistice Commission, so as to give the Germans a chance to state the numbers they actually needed.

M. CLEMENCEAU said that, if there was no objection, he would propose to summon Marshal Foch.

MR. LLOYD GEORGE said that he would not be able to accept Marshal Foch's opinion unsupported by British military experts on [a] subject of such political moment to Great Britain. Marshal Foch had forwarded a demand for British troops which it would be extremely difficult for the country to honour. It was for this reason that he had suggested as an alternative to increasing the Allied forces the reduction of the enemy's troops. It would be necessary for British members to be present on the Committee when dealing with this subject.

M. CLEMENCEAU said that he had no objection whatever to the presence of British, American or other representatives on the Commission. He fully understood the reasons which prompted Mr. Lloyd George's remarks. The question, however, was more difficult to solve than might appear. He, himself, had been asked in the Chamber of Deputies why Marshal Foch had not included in the Armistice an article requiring the demobilization of the German Army. Marshal Foch had explained that he had made no provision for this, as he did not wish to put any clause in the Armistice, the execution of which he would be unable to control.

The situation in Germany had grown worse during the last few days. He had brought telegrams with him which he proposed to show to the Meeting. It appeared that, since the defeat of the Spartacus party, German officers were resuming their arrogant attitude and were considerably harder to deal with than before. Moreover, German troops were being massed against the Poles. The "Frankfurt Gazette" made mention of a large concentration on the Eastern frontier. He was very much afraid that the Poles might be so imprudent as to attack the Germans, and, in connection with the Allied Mission that was going to Poland, he had intended to suggest that it be instructed to forbid the Poles from engaging in any such adventure. The Allies would always be considered the supporters of Poland and they could not at the same time support the Poles in attacking Germany and ask the Germans to disarm.

MR. LLOYD GEORGE said that he had felt bound to give notice to the Allied and Associated Governments that he was not able to undertake to maintain the forces demanded by Marshal Foch.

M. ORLANDO said that he would like to raise a point of procedure. He fully understood Mr. Lloyd George's reasons. He also understood M. Clemenceau's anxiety. He wished to suggest that the question of immediate reduction of the enemy's forces was not a Peace Conference but an Armistice matter. The question of form often had a close relation to substance. He thought that we could obtain prompt demobilisation of the German armies more effectually by dealing with it as a condition of the renewal of the Armistice through the agency of Marshal Foch and the Allied Military Advisers, than by treating it as a question for the Peace Conference. He thought it would be a mistake to consult on a question of this kind all the Small Powers collected at the Peace Conference, which had no concern with the military commitments on the Western Front.

M. CLEMENCEAU said that he also fully understood Mr. Lloyd George's point. Mr. Lloyd George had been bound to make it, but the military front must be maintained. He was not aware of the demands addressed by Marshal Foch to the British Government. He would therefore suggest that a British, a French, an American and an Italian General should meet and report to the meeting what military forces it was necessary for the Allies to maintain.

PRESIDENT WILSON said that he had thought the question was still under discussion. He also was deeply interested in the question of maintaining American troops in Europe. What [When] he had last met Marshal Foch, final figures had not been given him, but only approximations. He had therefore concluded that the matter was still being considered. He thought that this was a question for the Supreme War Council and suggested that the Military Advisors should be heard on the subject.

MR. LLOYD GEORGE said that on the following day the British Secretary of State for War would be in Paris and could be present at the Meeting.

M. ORLANDO said that General Diaz would also be present.

M. CLEMENCEAU said that a Meeting of the Supreme War Council would take place at 10 hrs. 30 in M. Pichon's room on the following day.

(It was agreed that Marshal Foch and the Military Experts of the Governments of the United States of America, the British Empire, France and Italy be invited to advise the Supreme War Council on the following day as to the size of the armies to be maintained by the Allied and Associated Powers on the Western Front, and more particularly as to the possibility of an immediate and drastic reduction in the armed forces of the enemy.)

[Clemenceau read a draft resolution proposed by Lloyd George regarding international legislation on industrial and labor questions. After discussion and amendment, the following text was adopted:]

That a Commission composed of two representatives apiece from the five Great Powers, and five representatives to be elected by the other Powers represented at the Peace Conference be appointed to enquire into the conditions of employment from the international aspect, and to consider the international means necessary to secure common action on matters affecting conditions of employment and to recommend the form of a permanent agency to continue such enquiry in co-operation with and under the direction of the League of Nations.

MR. LLOYD GEORGE said that he would like to have the opinion of the Conference concerning the kind of delegates that should be appointed to this Commission. As there were to be only two, he asked whether it would not be desirable that one should be an employer, and the other a representative of the working classes. In the alternative, one could be an official. He thought it desirable that the representatives of all the Powers should have the same character.

PRESIDENT WILSON pointed out that uniformity might not be feasible. For instance, American officials might not be easy to obtain.

M. SONNINO pointed out that as the smaller Powers among them only found 5 delegates, the same composition could not apply to their membership.

PRESIDENT WILSON pointed out that an American employer might be hard to get.

MR. BALFOUR said that the countries in which conditions of employment were bad were the only countries that need feel much anxiety about their representation on this Commission. America, for instance, where conditions of employment were exceptionally good, need feel no anxiety on this score. There might be countries, however, in which the impression would be formed that they could only compete with such favoured countries as the United States or Canada by keeping down wages. Those countries must have an employer among their representatives, otherwise the employers of labour in those countries would think that wages were being raised in order to render competition with their rivals in other countries impossible. It is therefore, in his opinion, unnecessary to insist on an identical form of representation for all.

BARON MAKINO said that he entirely agreed with Mr. Balfour, and the case last cited was that of Japan.

M. SONNINO thought that this discussion somewhat anticipated the probable course of events. The means of procuring full and adequate representation could be dealt with at a later stage. The question was for the time being in the stage of study. This study could be adequately undertaken by officials, such, for instance, as the Italian officials serving on the Emigration Committee. After receiving their advice, further decisons could be taken. He thought it would be unfortunate to establish a precedent for a permanent organization not yet formed by insisting on one delegate from the employers and one from the workmen.

M. CLEMENCEAU said that he agreed with M. Sonnino. The Governments were now asked to nominate two delegates each. He for himself proposed to nominate two officials. The Commission was to report on the best means of getting all the interests concerned represented. The delegates would doubtless for their own work consult the various interests in their own countries.

(It was therefore decided that each of the Great Powers should appoint two delegates.)

[Clemenceau read a draft resolution proposed by Lloyd George regarding reparations. After discussion and amendment, the following text was adopted:]

That a Commission be appointed with not more than three representatives apiece from each of the five Great Powers, and not more than two representatives apiece from Belgium, Greece, Poland, Roumania, and Serbia, to examine and report first on the amount for reparation which the enemy countries ought to pay, secondly on what they are capable of paying, and thirdly on the method, form and time in which payment should be made.

[Clemenceau read a draft resolution proposed by Lloyd George regarding breaches of the laws of war. After discussion and amendment, the following text was adopted:]

That a Commission, composed of two representatives apiece from the five Great Powers, and five representatives to be elected by the other Powers, be appointed to inquire and report upon the following:

(1) The responsibility of the authors of the war.

(2) The facts as to breaches of the laws and customs of war committed by the forces of the German Empire and their allies on land, on sea, and in the air during the present war;

(3) The degree of responsibility for these offences attaching to particular members of the enemy forces, including members of the General Staffs, or other individuals, however highly placed:

(4) The Constitution and procedure of a tribunal appropriate to the trial of these offences;

(5) Any other matters cognate or ancillary to the above which may arise in the course of the inquiry, and which the Commission finds it useful and relevant to take into consideration.

M. CLEMENCEAU said that the Agenda for Saturday would be composed of the resolutions accepted at this Meeting and on the previous day.

(This was agreed to)

MR. LANSING pointed out that according to the rules, they should be in the hands of the delegates 24 hours before the meeting.

(The Secretary-General undertook to fulfill this regulation).

M. CLEMENCEAU said that a number of territorial and colonial questions remained to be discussed. Of these the territorial were the most delicate problems.

Doubtless each power would feel inclined to put off their discussion, but it must be undertaken. Before discussion these questions required classification. He would therefore beg the Governments to think of this, and at a later meeting to bring with them a classification.

M. SONNINO asked whether the most practical means would not be to fix a time by which each Delegation should present their wishes. The meeting would then have a notion of the ground to be covered. This applied to the Great Powers and to the smaller countries alike. A complete picture of the whole problem would then be available.

MR. LLOYD GEORGE said that considerable delay might be involved in waiting for the completion of all this work. European questions were so complicated that it would take a long time for such peoples as the Czecho-Slovaks and Poles to set forth a reasoned case. On the other hand Oriental questions and Colonial questions were less involved and to economize time he suggested that these matters might be tackled at once.

M. SONNINO pointed out that Mr. Lloyd George's proposal was not in contradiction with his. It was a question of the order in which problems were examined. Mr. Lloyd George proposed one subject to be discussed first. He agreed with him but before long questions would arise which concerned a great number of interests and then it would be necessary before settling them to have a statement from all the Delegations concerned.

M. CLEMENCEAU said that he would agree then to begin with the Colonial questions.

PRESIDENT WILSON observed that the world's unrest arose from the unsettled condition of Europe, not from the state of affairs in the East, or in the Colonies, and that the postponement of these questions would only increase the pressure on the Delegates of the Peace Conference. He would therefore prefer to set in process immediately all that was required to hasten a solution of European questions. He entirely approved of utilizing intervals for the discussion of less important matters.

M. CLEMENCEAU summing up, said that he understood Mr. Lloyd George to propose giving precedence to Oriental and Colonial questions, while President Wilson preferred to begin with European ones.

MR. LLOYD GEORGE said that he entirely agreed with the President in his estimate of the relative importance of these matters, and that he had only suggested dealing with the East and with the Colonies in order to save time while the various delegations were preparing their case.

[It was then decided that the Secretary General should ask all delegations representing powers with territorial claims to send to the Secretariat their written statements within ten days.

[Clemenceau read a resolution proposed by Lloyd George concerning the international regulation of ports, waterways, and railways. After discussion the following resolution was adopted:]

That a Commission composed of two representatives apiece from the five Great Powers and five representatives to be elected by the other Powers represented at the Peace Conference, be appointed to inquire into the Question of the international regime of Ports, Water-ways and Railways.

M. CLEMENCEAU pointed out that many complicated financial questions required settlement.

M. SONNINO said that the questions of Public Debts and paper money were especially difficult.

PRESIDENT WILSON questioned whether these problems could be isolated from territorial problems.

MR. BALFOUR thought that even in so complex a case as that of the previous Austro-Hungarian Monarchy, some general principles of financial obligation should be laid down.

PRESIDENT WILSON thought that these questions varied so much that their settlement should not be subjected to any general rule.

M. SONNINO said that on certain definite questions a common principle could be found, for instance, to what extent were new States responsible for the debts of the older States they replaced? At what date did the State in process of dissolution cease to be responsible for the paper money it issued? Who was responsible for the money now circulating throughout the former Dual Monarchy? These questions related to phenomena of common occurrence and some principle could be laid down to deal with them.

MR. LLOYD GEORGE added the instance of the Turkish Empire, a large part of which would be parceled out. What part, if any, of the Ottoman debt must be taken over with each portion? Who the Mandatories would be was not yet settled, but what their relations would be to the monetary obligations of the Turkish Empire was a difficult problem. Would they, for instance, be compelled to take over the debt at par or at the present value? Was Palestine to bear a share of the burden, and Syria, the Armenians and the peoples of the Caucasus?

PRESIDENT WILSON suggested that these problems be drafted in the form of resolutions on which the representatives could take action.

M. SONNINO said that an expert committee would be [needed?] to frame these questions in appropriate terms.

(It was therefore decided that the Great Powers should appoint a Committee of five, composed of one member from each, to frame and set in order the financial questions requiring solution)

MR. LLOYD GEORGE said that one of the problems requiring solution was whether claims for reparation should take precedence of the national debt in enemy countries.

(It was agreed that this was one of the problems that should be referred to the Committee above mentioned)

(The meeting then adjourned)

APPENDIX "A"

DRAFT RESOLUTION IN REGARD TO THE REDUCTION
OF FORCES AND ARMAMENTS
for presentation to the Peace Conference.

That a Commission be appointed with two representatives apiece from each of the five Great Powers, and five representatives to be elected by the other Powers represented at the Conference:

1.  to advise on an immediate and drastic reduction in the armed forces of the enemy:
2.  to prepare a plan in connection with the League of Nations for a permanent reduction in the burden of military, naval and aerial forces and armaments.

T MS (SDR, RG 256, 180.03101/15, DNA).

## To Boghos Nubar[1]

My dear Mr. Nubar:                    Paris, 23 January, 1919.

I have received your very moving letter of the 20th of January[2] and in reply beg to assure you that on every hand among the delegates to the Peace Conference I find the most sincere and outspoken sympathy with the Armenians. It is very difficult indeed, as you will realize, to assign representatives to political units which have not yet been received into the family of nations. That is the only reason, I am sure, why no representation was assigned to the Armenians but I feel confident in the assurance that this will not mean the slightest neglect of the interests of Armenia and that you may count upon the views of the Armenians being as fully considered as if they were represented in form.

Very sincerely yours,   [Woodrow Wilson]

CCL (WP, DLC).
[1] Head of the Armenian National Delegation in Paris.

² Boghos Nubar to WW, Jan. 20, 1919, TLS (WP, DLC). He stated that the Armenians had been "profoundly moved" by the fact that Armenia, despite its unquestioned loyalty to the Allied cause from the very first day of the war, had not been permitted to be represented at the peace conference. Not only had Armenians willingly shed their blood on all fronts on behalf of the great aims of the Allies, but, by losing one quarter of its population on the battlefields and through massacres and deportations, Armenia had paid a price heavier than that of any other nation. This martyrdom, the most outrageous ever known in history, placed Armenia, together with Belgium and Serbia, in the same rank of nations for whose liberation and restoration the Allies had proclaimed their battle cry. "All Armenians," Nubar concluded, "hereby appeal to you, Mr. President, who have proclaimed the sacred principles of justice and humanity towards oppressed Nations, ... that the Armenian Nation be admitted into the Conference, by the side of the Representatives of the Powers to whom she has ever remained faithful and loyal to the end."

## To Newton Diehl Baker

My dear Baker:                                    Paris, 23 January, 1919.

May I not thank you very warmly for your letter of January 1st?[1] It was just the sort of letter I have been wanting from home, though I do not know anybody but yourself who could have written it. It is full of meat and also full of evidences of a generous friendship which I value more and more as the days go by. I dare say you know as much about what is going on over here as we do who are on the ground. It is very interesting but in a way tedious, and the difficulty of weaving all the threads into a single pattern sometimes bewilders me.

Mrs. Wilson joins in the warmest regards to you and your dear ones, and I am,     Your grateful friend,   Woodrow Wilson

TLS (N. D. Baker Papers, DLC).
[1] NDB to WW, Jan. 1, 1919, Vol. 53.

## To Joseph Patrick Tumulty

Paris, 23 January, 1919.

I am entirely willing to make the modifications suggested by the Cabinet with regard to the use of cereals for the manufacturing of beverages[1] and hope the Attorney General will be kind enough to send me the proper form of proclamation. Please say to Mr. Ziegfeld and the other theatre people interested that it seems to me impossible to form any judgement about individual items in the revenue bill[2] and that I must depend upon them to put their cases in the fullest way before the committees of the House and Senate. I might make a sad mess of it by interfering with so little knowledge.
                                        Woodrow Wilson.

CC telegram (WP, DLC).

¹ See JPT to WW, Jan. 21, 1919.
² Wilson's message was prompted by appeals from the well-known theatrical producer, Florenz Ziegfeld, Jr., and other theater managers, who had protested against the proposed increase of the tax on theater tickets from 10 per cent to 20 per cent in the revenue bill of 1918. Ziegfeld maintained that this "appalling plan" was a "crying injustice" to the theaters as well as to the American people. It would be the "death blow" for the theaters, would ruin theater companies, and would throw thousands of people out of work. F. Ziegfeld, Jr., to WW, Jan. 18, 1919, T telegram (WP, DLC).

## To Joseph Eugene Ransdell

Paris, 23 January, 1919.

Cotton may now be exported to all neutral countries in amounts adequate for their needs.¹ Further exports to or for account of enemy countries raise important questions of policy which are the subject of attentive consideration by associated governments.

Woodrow Wilson.

CC telegram (WP, DLC).
¹ Wilson was replying to J. E. Ransdell to WW, Jan. 17, 1919, T telegram (WP, DLC). Wilson sent the same telegram, on the same day, *mutatis mutandis*, to Senator Ellison DuRant Smith; I. H. Barnell, president of the Memphis Cotton Exchange; James Henry Claffy, president of the South Carolina Farmers' Union; A. J. Rich, president of the Savannah Cotton Exchange; John A. Simpson, president of the Oklahoma Farmers' Union and president of the Association of State Farmers' Unions Presidents; and the Columbus, Ga., Clearing House Association, all CC telegrams (WP, DLC).

## From Edward Mandell House

Dear Governor:                          Paris, January 23, 1919.

It occurred to me after you left this afternoon that it would be a good move to get Orlando to appoint himself one of the two to represent Italy on the Committee for the League of Nations. He has agreed to do this and with much enthusiasm.

Lord Robert Cecil and General Smuts will undertake to do some missionary work not only with the Italians but with the Japs. In a few days I think we will have the situation sufficiently well in hand to call a meeting of the Committee as a whole.

Affectionately yours,   E. M. House

TLS (WP, DLC).

## From Joseph Patrick Tumulty

Washington, 23 Jan. 1919.

Number twenty-one. Suffrage still requires one democrat stop. Sallsbury [Saulsbury] could not now be charged with to returning

[turning] to Suffrage Amendment for personal political purposes stop. Wolcott might sacrifice personal views for you and party stop. Telegrams from you and [to] them and [to] Williams might get results stop. Some action must be taken soon or it will be too late stop. Have consulted with suffrage leaders.        Tumulty.

T telegram (WP, DLC)


## From Herbert Clark Hoover

Dear Mr. President:                                    Paris, 23 January 1919.

As a measure of obstruction to the passage of the hundred million dollar relief appropriation, I have been subjected to a general mud bath from Penrose, Reed, Gore and Borah, in which my principal crime seems to be in connection with the Chicago packers.[1] The matter only interests me as a measure of obstruction and my friends in Washington think it extremely desirable that you should authorize the publication of the written opinion which I gave to you on the necessity of the legal control of the packing industry, some six or seven months ago.[2] I would be glad to know if you can see your way to give such permission.[3]

In reply to press inquiries, I have given the press representatives the following statement this morning:

"When asked for a statement in reply to the reported criticisms of certain Senators, Mr. Hoover said:

" 'I apparently emerge in a new light, as the friend of the Chicago packer. The same mail brings a report from Swift & Company blaming the Food Administration for reducing their profits by ten million dollars during the last year. I don't imagine the packers would appreciate a wide circle of such friends. I notice also I committed a crime for holding joint conferences of farmers, representatives of the forty small packers, as well as the big packers together with representatives of the Allied Governments, for the purpose of settling on a price for exports that would give the American farmer a square deal, and a distribution of orders that would protect the small packer.

" 'If the American farmer and the small packer feel that these arrangements are wrong it would be the greatest burden off my shoulders if I could know it quickly for the British Government particularly is anxious to be relieved from these arrangements.' "

All this makes it very difficult for me to secure settlement of the pressing relations with Allied Governments on our outstanding food matters. I have just yesterday proposed the enclosed contract to the British Government for the equitable winding up of their moral

obligations in the matter of relations with our farmers in pork products,[4] and already I hear that their representatives feel that this
opposition in the Senate gives them some justification for delay in
settling this matter. This has nothing to do with the above matter,
except as it shows how difficult a path these people can provide
for us.                     Yours faithfully,   Herbert Hoover

TLS (WP, DLC).
    [1] See FLP to RL, Jan. 20, 1919, n. 3.
    [2] HCH to WW, Sept. 11, 1918, Vol. 49.
    [3] "Answered 'Yes,' by Phone 1/24/19." Hw note on CC of this letter in WP, DLC.
Hoover's "written opinion" was published, e.g., in the *New York Times*, Feb. 19, 1919.
    [4] HCH to Sir John Field Beale, British representative on the Allied Supreme Council
of Supply and Relief, Jan. 22, 1919, TCL (WP, DLC), enclosing draft of a contract
(T MS [WP, DLC]) for the purchase by the British government of 100,000 tons of pork
products in the United States before January 25, 1919.


## From Peter Goelet Gerry

My dear Mr. President:     [Washington] January 23, 1918 [1919].

I am taking the liberty of bringing to your notice a situation in
the National Committee in which Senator Pittman and I believe
the advice of Mr. Baruch might be of some assistance if you cared
to consult him. Not knowing whether he is to return home with
you I thought it advisable to write this letter.

A new chairman is to be chosen on February 26th, and it is
almost essential to have a man of executive and organizing ability,
and one not only willing to give practically his entire time to the
office, but also ready to visit all the doubtful states, as the Republican chairman, Mr. Hays, has done. Such personal contact would
rejuvenate many semi-moribund state Democratic organizations,
and would keep the National Headquarters in closer touch with
the different localities. The success of the Republican party last fall
was in no small way, in my judgment, due to the adoption of this
plan. If, for any reason, the Committee does not see fit to choose
such a chairman would it not be the part of wisdom to leave vacant
the office of vice-chairman until such a man could be found. Here
is where we feel Mr. Baruch could offer very valuable recommendations.

The Republican leaders in the Senate are trying to iron out the
controversies between the different factions of their party which
would prevent their organizing the next Senate. They seem to have
met with some success, and the party has been extraordinarily
united in their attacks on the administration, due, I believe, to
continual caucusing and fully laying out their plans previous to any
remarks on the floor of the Senate. My feeling is, that we should

have adopted the same policy of caucusing to meet these attacks, and by so doing would have kept a better front in our own membership, but older heads thought differently. I understand, however, that as soon as we go into the minority our policy is to be reversed. Undoubtedly there is an ever increasing desire among Democratic Senators towards better organization and team work, and when the body is organized I believe if Senator Pittman is chosen as deputy floor leader he will be able to render valuable assistance to Senator Martin, and help the party take the offensive. I do not apprehend any opposition to this choice, as Senators from the South are beginning to realize the bad effect on the party nationally that the cry of Southern domination is having. There is no doubt that in New England and the Western States it is militating strongly against us and is reviving sectional feeling. A western man in such a prominent position would have a good effect, and the Democracy can be aided further by still more recognition of the North and West.

During the past month I have been North, and the feeling, as I found it, was distinctly in favor of your cause and policies, even among Republicans, and in opposition to the nagging and criticising attacks of the spokesmen of their own party.

With best wishes for a pleasant homeward voyage,

Very sincerely yours,   Peter G. Gerry

TLS (WP, DLC).


## From Chaim Weizmann, with Enclosure

Sir,                                          London 23rd January 1919.

I have the honour to communicate to you the enclosed message which has reached us from the Zionist Organisations for Poland.

I take this opportunity of thanking you on behalf of the Zionist Organisation for the support which you have shown to the justice of our Cause on recent occasions, and confidently depend upon the continuance of your support when the question of the reconstitution of Palestine is dealt with at the Peace Conference.

I have the honour to be,

Yours obediently,   Ch. Weizmann

TLS (WP, DLC).

E N C L O S U R E

Copy Telegram from Copenhagen received 21st January 1919:

"Zionist Organisations for Poland, Warsaw, request you forward following telegram to President Wilson:

["]'The First Jewish Preliminary Conference in Poland consisting of 498 delegates of Jewish communities in Jewish Advocate Professional Cultural and Women Unions assembled in the Capital of Poland to create a Jewish National Representation which together with the National Representatives of the Jewish nation in all other countries is to present the Jewish demands to the Peace Congress considers it its most sacred duty as citizens of the country they are living in which thanks to your great human ideas gains its liberty and as a nation since two thousand years the most oppressed and persecuted on the whole globe to express to you the most Venerable President the profoundest gratitude for your great and generous ideas in your Peace Programme and which are giving to all oppressed nations the possibility to live and develop freely for the happiness of the country in which reigns equal treatment of all the citizens without difference of nationality or religion stop Your country has always been an asylum for all our persecuted brothers that were compelled to leave their homes because of ill-treatment and torments stop With full confidence the Jewish people turns to you and is sure you will defend with your authority the accomplishment of your sublime programme.' "

T MS (WP, DLC).


## Gilbert Fairchild Close to George Davis Herron

My dear Mr. Herron:                    Paris, 23 January, 1919.

In reply to your note of January 20th the President has asked me to say that he will be very glad to see you if you will call at the Hotel Murat, 23 rue Monceau, at 6:15 o'clock this afternoon, Thursday.                    Sincerely yours,   [Gilbert F. Close]

CCL (WP, DLC).

## A Translation of a Memorandum

[Jan. 23, 1919]

Conversation between Mr. Gustave Ador,
President of the Confederation,
and Mr. Wilson,
President of the United States of America.

Mr. Ador was received January 23 at 5:30 p.m. by President Wilson at his residence in the Rue de Monceau. He was accompanied by his personal secretary, Mr. Lucien Cramer, and by Mr. de Weck,[1] First Secretary of the legation.

The conversation, in English, was most cordial.

Mr. Ador began by thanking Mr. Wilson for all that the United States had done for Switzerland in the course of the war and, in particular, for the generosity with which the great American republic had worked for the provisioning of our country. "All that we have done," replied Mr. Wilson, "we have done from the bottom of the heart. We would have desired to do more, but we could not do it. I know that you have passed through extremely difficult times and, in those moments, I thought of your country with an uneasy sympathy while deploring not having the power to assist it more completely."

The two Presidents spoke of the role, during the war, of the International Committee of the Red Cross and found themselves in perfect agreement to affirm that this association, considered up to this point as a work destined to alleviate the miseries of the war, could and should become a powerful permanent organization, capable of struggling against all the scourges which, even in times of peace, can afflict humanity. Their thought meets in the affirmation that the International Red Cross is destined to become one of the essential and permanent organs of the League of Nations.

Mr. Wilson repeated the expression of his absolute faith in the future of the League of Nations. He is convinced that the proposals, almost identical, which will be submitted to the peace conference by the American and British governments, will be adopted as the basis of the future organization of the world. He did not hide from view, however, that only the essential lines could be immediately traced and that the rest will be the fruit of long labor and repeated experiences. Certain nations, he says, are coming into being and will need to find in older and better organized nations tutors and guides (for example, Yugoslavia). But, according to Mr. Wilson, the value of the League of Nations is already proved by the fact alone that the great empires, founded on force, have been dissolved by the war, while the British Empire which, with its autonomous dominions, constitutes for him only a league of nations, affirms the proof [of the value of the league].

President Ador did not fail to emphasize that Switzerland, herself also, was a model, reduced but consolidated by the experience of centuries, of the future League of Nations. Without mentioning the word "neutrality," he thanked America for having, in the course of the war, explicitly recognized and respected the territorial integrity, the independence, and the sovereignty of Switzerland.[2]

Mr. Wilson then observed that the period which is opening is one of a total reconstruction of the world and that Belgium, for example, no longer wanted a neutrality which was imposed upon her and which did not protect her against invasion. Mr. Ador did not fail to reply that the neutrality of Switzerland was the expression of the unanimous will of its peoples, a will acknowledged by Europe at the Congress of Vienna. He wished it understood that Switzerland desired today, even though the League of Nations could offer it certain guarantees of its independence, to preserve the status which she has possessed for a century. The President of the United States did not see any objections to seeing this desire respected and which he will, at an opportune time, call to the attention of the peace conference.

Mr. Wilson gave to Mr. Ador the assurance that all the statesmen of the Associated Powers, with whom he has talked about the European situation, have manifested, regarding Switzerland, the most friendly feelings. The complete independence of our country, with or without a League of Nations, is for Mr. Wilson a question so resolved in advance that it is not even necessary to ask it.

In order to bring the meeting to a close, the American President declared himself completely disposed to receive all communications which we might wish to make to him concerning the wishes and needs of Switzerland and to plead with his best efforts our cause at the conference. He repeated that the League of Nations was for him, above all, a protection for the small countries, for, without the League of Nations, the great nations can live to themselves and conduct all their own affairs, while the little ones are constantly menaced and even constitute a permanent danger on account of the appetites that their weakness evokes among the great powers.

T MS (J. I. 149, Mission Paris 1919 [I-III], Swiss Federal Archives).
[1] René de Weck.
[2] See the memorandum by W. E. Rappard, printed at Nov. 1, 1917, and n. 5 thereto, Vol. 44.

# Lord Curzon to Lord Derby

CONFIDENTIAL.
(No. 165.)

My Lord, *Foreign Office, January 23, 1919.*

The French Ambassador,[1] who had just returned from France, called upon me this afternoon. Although he explained that the observations which he addressed to me at considerable length about the position in Paris were delivered in a personal rather than in an official capacity, it seemed to me that, as they in all probability reflected the state of opinion in the highest political circles in Paris when he left that city, they might be worthy of record.

M. Cambon expressed great disappointment and irritation at the slow progress that was being made with the business of the Conference, and he attributed this in the main to the unfortunate lead which had been given to the proceedings by President Wilson. Of the latter he spoke in very critical terms. He regarded him as an academic lecturer with considerable literary gifts, but out of touch with the world, giving his confidence to no one, unversed in European politics, and devoted to the pursuit of theories which had little relation to the emergencies of the hour. The business of the Peace Conference was to bring to a close the war with Germany, to settle the frontiers of Germany, to decide upon the terms which should be exacted from her, and as soon as possible to conclude a just peace. All such questions as the Freedom of the Seas and the League of Nations, though they might find a place in the discussions later on and might eventuate in some form of agreement for the betterment of the world, had nothing whatever to do either with the war or with the immediate task of concluding peace. They could very well be postponed to a subsequent stage. The Conference was committing a great mistake in allowing its time to be taken up in these initial stages by the pursuit of these matters at the instance of President Wilson, instead of dealing with the far more urgent problems of the moment.

The Ambassador said that much irritation was already felt in France at the delay which these tactics involved, that he felt sure that this feeling would grow with great rapidity, and that later on, when at the end of a number of weeks the Conference was found to have done little or nothing, there would be such a demand for more expeditious procedure that questions would be hurried through without due examination, and settlements arrived at which could not last.

The tone of the Ambassador throughout reflected the feelings, which I understand exist in France, of profound annoyance at the line adopted and the influence exercised by the American President.

When I said that I was myself somewhat surprised at the predominant part that President Wilson appeared to play in the proceedings, of which I had seen the reports, the Ambassador replied that this was due to his position as the Head of a State, which rendered it difficult for any sort of control to be imposed upon his conduct.

I told M. Cambon that I was rather astonished that M. Clemenceau had not, if my memory was correct, taken an even more active part in the proceedings, and that I thought his prestige and authority were sufficient to guide them in whatever direction he pleased.

The Ambassador concurred with me in recognising that the object of President Wilson, in pushing forward his scheme for the League of Nations at the present stage, was probably to a large extent political, and sprang from the desire to have something in his hand when he returned, as he would presently have to do, to his own country. If he could say in the United States that he had persuaded the Conference to accept the principle, and even to define the outline, of a League of Nations, he might safely leave the matter to be discussed in Paris in his absence, and he could more easily obtain permission to return to Europe later on in order to see the matter through its final stages.

This did not, however, in M. Cambon's view constitute any justification for the line at present being pursued, and he felt that, when President Wilson sailed for America on or about the 10th February, and Mr. Lloyd George was compelled to return to England for the opening of Parliament at about the same time, there would be a serious danger of the business of the Conference being suspended at a critical stage, and of a wide-spread feeling of disappointment, even dismay, being aroused.

The Ambassador was not much more complimentary in his allusion to the decision which had just been arrived at with regard to the summoning of representatives of the various Governments or organisations in Russia to an island in the Sea of Marmora. He attributed this equally to the Utopian and idealistic promptings of President Wilson's mind.

I pointed out that this was not quite fair, either to the President or to our own representatives, since the decision which had been arrived at, although not exactly identical with that for which Mr. Lloyd George had pressed, was in principle the same, and the credit or the blame, whichever it might be, for originating and pressing the idea, rested therefore with the British and American representatives jointly, rather than with any individual.

The Ambassador thought that there was something ridiculous in the idea of the various Russian political or fighting leaders, each exceedingly insecure in his own immediate surroundings, being invited to meet one another in the Sea of Marmora, and he did not anticipate for the experiment any possible success.

These observations will in all probability cause no surprise to those who are acquainted with what is passing in Paris, but they may not be without interest if they confirm an impression, no doubt already existing, of the effect that has been produced upon the French mind by the temperament and tactics of President Wilson.

The Ambassador did not add, nor did I remind him, that while the French were thus disappointed in President Wilson, the latter was in all probability equally disappointed with them, having discovered in their present temper and attitude characteristics so much out of harmony with some of the ideals that have figured so prominently in his public harangues.

I am, &c.                              Curzon of Kedleston.

Printed copy (FO 115/2542, p. 196, PRO).
[1] That is, Paul Cambon.


## From the Diary of Dr. Grayson

Friday, January 24, 1919.

I accompanied the President to the usual morning conference at the Quai D'Orsay. This evening before dinner I asked him what sort of a day he had. He replied, "Not very satisfactory; the French consumed most of the time talking without result."

At six o'clock the President and Mrs. Wilson gave a tea at the Murat Palace for the three hundred American and French soldiers detailed as guards, chauffeurs, telegraph operators and orderlies about the premises. After refreshments the men gathered around the President and he told them a number of interesting anecdotes which produced loud laughter and took all of the stiffness out of the atmosphere. I was the only officer present. Before the gathering broke up the President and Mrs. Wilson posed for a flash light picture with the soldiers. The President had a French soldier on his right hand and an American on his left. The comment of the soldiers after this personal contact with their Commander-in-Chief was that he was the "grandest man in the world."

## Hankey's Notes of a Meeting of the Supreme War Council[1]

Quai d'Orsay, January 24, 1919, 10:30 A.M.

I. No. 118. S.W.C. 364 [BC/A9-1]

1. M. CLEMENCEAU having declared the meeting open, said they were met together to consider Mr. Lloyd George's proposal to fix the strength of the forces to be maintained by the Allied and Associated Powers on the Western Front during the period of the Armistice.

MARSHAL FOCH then read the following memorandum:

"From the demobilization or re-embarkment schedules, which the various Allied Governments seem to have settled, each for their own account, it appears that the following forces will be available on March 31st in the Franco-Belgian zone:

| | | | |
|---|---|---|---|
| French Armies | : | 46 Inf. Div. | and 6 Cav. Div. |
| British Armies | : | 18 Inf. Div. | and 2 Cav. Div. |
| American Armies | : | 15 Inf. Div. | (and 5 in base ports) |
| Belgian Armies | : | 6 Inf. Div. | |
| TOTAL | | 85 to 90 Inf. Div. | and 8 Cav. Div. |

"In his memorandum No. 52.P.C.L., dated December 24th the Marshal Commanding in Chief the Allied Armies stated that it was necessary to keep in arms, opposite Germany, until the signature of the Preliminaries of Peace, a total of 120 to 140 Allied Infantry Divisions.

"Since that date, the German demobilisation has followed its course. From the information given on January 13th by General von Winterfeldt[2] at SPA, and on January 15th by M. Erzberger at TREVES, the German forces still included, during the first fortnight of January, the following organized great units:

37 Divisions on the Western Front;

Between 15 and 18 Divisions on the Eastern Front; that is a total of 52 to 55 Divisions.

"The same information stated that the German figures included at the same time, as under the colours, the two classes of 1898 and 1899—200,000 men by class, that is * * * 400,000 men: and "several" hundred thousand men, kept in active service, either as volunteers, either as out of work. Therefore it follows that the actual number of the German army may be estimated at 600 to 700,000 men.

"As the correctness of this information cannot be confirmed, we

---

[1] A highly edited version of these notes is printed in PPC, III, 704-14.

[2] That is, Maj. Gen. Hans Karl Detlof von Winterfeldt, the head of the German Armistice Commission.

must, in consideration of their source, look upon the figures above given as a minimum.

"Taking into account these remarks, the number of 120 to 140 Allied Divisions given on December 24th as necessary to be maintained in front of Germany, may be reduced to 100.

"Therefore, the figure of 80 to 90 Allied Divisions mentioned in the first lines of this memorandum appears as an extreme minimum, under which it would be dangerous to fall, as long as the Preliminaries of Peace are not signed. And yet this figure can only be agreed to at the express condition that these units, the number of their men, the degree of their efficiency, will be kept up, so that they may go back in action without any delay.

"As long as the Preliminaries of Peace are not signed, it is therefore impossible to proceed farther with the carrying out of the schedules of demobilization, and to let the number of divisions which are being kept up fall under the above mentioned figures.

"Or else, it shan't be victorious Armies, which will confront the defeated German forces—Armies able to renew the fight,—if Peace is not signed—but Armies which are in process of demobilization or being moved will appear on our side, both being powerless for military action. To sum up, the debate will start on the base of an equal military situation, and then how shall we be able to speak of compensation, important indemnities? How shall we be able to impose any terms on the enemy?"

M. CLEMENCEAU enquired whether the number of men could be given corresponding to the number of divisions quoted.

GENERAL WEYGAND replied that taking an average of 20,000 men per division, there would be a total of 1,800,000 men; the following would be very approximate totals for each country[:]

| | |
|---|---|
| France | 900,000 |
| Great Britain | 350,000 |
| America | 450,000 |
| Belgium | 120,000 |
| Approximate total | 1,820,000 |

This figure included Cavalry divisions.

MARSHAL FOCH laid stress on the fact that the above figures included combatants only. This total was in accordance with the programme at present accepted by the Allied Governments and he pressed that no alterations should be made before the 31st March next.

MR. LLOYD GEORGE said that he had nothing to say regarding the figures given by Marshal Foch. His first comment, however, would relate to the number of German divisions, as obviously the number of troops to be kept under arms by the Allies would have to bear a direct reference to the number of German troops. Marshal Foch made no proposals for the reduction of the number of German divisions. The Germans were supposed to have 37 divisions on the Western Front, in addition to two classes with a total of 400,000 men, plus 15 to 18 divisions on the Eastern Front. Why should the Germans keep all these troops under arms? There was nothing in Marshal Foch's document about calling on the Germans further to demobilise. He would like to propose that when the Armistic[e] should be renewed in three weeks' time, the Germans should be asked to explain why they wished to keep all these troops. They could offer no real resistance; therefore we should refuse to renew the Armistice unless further demobilisation were carried out. The Allies should fix a definite number for the Germans, adequate for the maintenance of internal order. They must have a sufficient number of troops to police, in order to put down Spartacists and other revolutionary parties. Naturally, the Germans should not be permitted to maintain any forces to carry on warfare against the Poles; though on the other hand the Allies must undertake to keep the Poles within their frontiers. The Allies should refuse to give the Poles arms or assistance in order to take the law into their own hands and so attempt to settle their own frontiers. That would obviously be a question for the Peace Conference. He (Mr. Lloyd George) firmly believed that the Germans would like us to put forward proposals of this kind. The German soldiers were not under control, and were merely hanging around the Depots in order to get food and housing.

It must be clearly understood that the figures given in Marshal Foch's memorandum did not represent the total number of men which would have to be maintained under arms. Together with the British quota of 350,000 divisional troops prescribed, hundreds of thousands additional men would have to be kept for other purposes, which would probably represent a total of 7 to 800,000 men in France alone. He proposed, therefore, that they should consider the question of imposing, as a condition of the renewal of the armistice, a reduction of the German forces. This would permit of a corresponding reduction of our own. In addition, he would insist on the delivery of arms and of the machinery for the construction of arms, e.g. at Essen, Minden and elsewhere, until Peace would be signed.

MARSHAL FOCH said that if he correctly understood Mr. Lloyd George's proposal, it meant that an effective demobilisation should be imposed on Germany. There would be no difficulty in adding such a clause to the Armistice. The Germans would no doubt accept it, but it would be extremely difficult to ensure its execution. In a country like Germany it would be very easy for the people to take up arms again. Should a real leader arise, it would not be difficult for him to reconstruct the armies—trained men, officers, staff and a skeleton organisation existed. In a short time it would be possible to have a good army, in splendid fighting trim. In his opinion, therefore, such a clause could no doubt be included in the Armistice, but it would be ineffective.

M. CLEMENCEAU suggested that a control could be exercised.

MARSHAL FOCH replied that the controlling parties would only be allowed to see what the Germans wished them to see. Undoubtedly, guarantees could be taken by seizing arms, but it was doubtful whether they would give them all up. In addition, munition factories could be taken over, but it would be quite impossible to occupy them all. Our own line of action could not be based on the estimate of the military situation existing in Germany at any given time, because it would be impossible to say what the actual military strength of Germany at the time really was. Therefore, conditions might be made but in reality there was no gurantee that they would be adhered to. He would not take up time in referring to the clauses entered by Napoleon in the Treaty of Tilsit, limiting the Prussian Forces to 40,000 men. It was well known how Prussia, notwithstanding these conditions, had been able to prepare for a levy en masse in 1813. Herr Erzberger on the 14th January last at Treves had said, "The German army has ceased to exist." Nevertheless, over 70 divisions still existed. Von Winterfeldt maintained at the same meeting that it was not encumbent on the Germans to supply figures relating to their demobilisation, but since false and exaggerated statements had appeared in the British Press, he had supplied the figures which had been quoted in his (Marshal Foch's) memorandum. To sum up, he maintained that clauses relating to demobilisation, including the surrender of areas and the seizure of munition factories, could be entered in the Armistice, but it would be very dangerous to base our policy on the assumption that these conditions would be fulfilled. He urged, therefore, that the Allied Governments should ask no reductions in the agreed strengths of the Armies of Occupation, at all events before the 31st March next.

PRESIDENT WILSON asked that the following aspect of this matter be considered before coming to a conclusion. It had been stated that the officers of the German army had no control over their men; consequently, even if demobilisations were ordered, it could probably not be carried out. They had also been told that the men were merely hanging round the Depots in order to be fed. It was admitted that it would be very difficult for Germany to establish any credit until she could resume her economic life, obviously this was dif-

ficult under present conditions—meanwhile, the number of unemployed must increase and would still further increase if demobilisation were hastened. The increase of unemployment would
widen the soil for the seeds of Bolshevism and so create a Germany
with which it would be impossible to deal at all. Moreover, looking
ahead, sooner or later, the Allies would be compelled to trust Germany to keep her promises. When Peace would be signed, should
we still be compelled to maintain a great Army of Occupation to
make sure that she would keep her promises? In the Peace Treaty,
Germany might agree to maintain a smaller army. Should we be
compelled to keep an army on her border to ensure the fulfilment
of this promise? The real solution of the question lay in an early
Peace, this would bring with it a settlement of the many questions
which were troubling Europe which now consisted of a seething
body of an uncertain and fearful people who did not know what
fate awaited them. He put forward these considerations though he
realised they did not lead to a definite conclusion.

MR. LLOYD GEORGE agreed with President Wilson that the only
satisfactory solution of the difficulty would be the making of Peace.
But they in Great Britain were compelled to face the problem of
demobilisation at once. It was a very serious problem. Great Britain
was not a military nation like France and the people were not
disciplined, therefore he felt compelled at once to say that he was
doubtful whether Great Britain could contribute the troops asked
for. At any rate, he could give no undertaking. He would without
further delay have to discuss the question with his advisers in order
to arrive at an immediate conclusion. He admitted it might be best
to put off the decision until the signing of the Peace Treaty, but
they could not do that in Great Britain. Some means must therefore
be devised for reducing their effort.

Marshal Foch's argument really meant that Germany could never
be trusted and therefore that the Armies of Occupation could never
be materially reduced. On the other hand, he thought they had in
food, raw material, and the seizure of arms better means of controlling the situation in Germany. As long as it was a question of
fighting, they had had no difficulty with the British troops, but now
that they were standing to their arms whilst many of their comrades
were being demobilised and were able to obtain good employment
at high rates of pay, the feelings of discontent were bound to arise
which made matters extremely difficult. Therefore, he would still
press that they should make an effort to reduce the German armies,
using food, raw material, and the surrender of arms as levers. The
Germans had already surrendered most of their cannon and, without cannon men alone constituted a small danger.

GENERAL BLISS expressed the view that the problem that confronted the United States of America was different to that which
Great Britain had to solve. The two, however, were the same in this
respect—that behind the Government were the people who might
at any moment take matters into their own hands. Consequently,
in drawing up their plans that fact had to be taken into consideration. As regards the United States, taking the rate at which troops
could be shipped to America, it did not appear that the numbers
could be reduced to the figures required by Marshal Foch before
next summer. As peace would doubtless be concluded before that
time, the problem became one of little moment as far as America
was concerned.

Looking at the question from a broader point of view, he wished
to support Mr. Lloyd George's proposal that they should do all they
could to reduce the armies and to reduce the output of armament
and munitions in Germany. While complete disarmament might
be impossible to attain, much could be done along those lines to
improve the situation. On the other hand, he was of the opinion
that these limiting conditions should be included in the Treaty of
Peace and not in the Armistice. In the Treaty of Peace it would be
possible to lay down any conditions they liked relating to the reduction of the armies, the dismantling of factories, the output of
munitions, etc. Therefore, he urged his colleagues to hasten the
conclusion of peace.

GENERAL PERSHING said that in his opinion the position of Germany today was such that it would be impossible for her to resume
offensive operations with any possible chance of holding her own.
Demobilisation had proceeded so far that possibly not more than
1,000,000 men were under arms and these were not in a state of
discipline or efficiency such as to cause alarm. They were at rest
or scattered about and not in any sense an organized body of troops
well in hand. Food conditions were such that she could be prevented from carrying on military operations. Her ports were all open
to the British navy and her rivers could be ascended with facility.
The Allies controlled the Rhine and its commerce. They occupied
a large part of her territory. As regards armaments, she had surrendered such an amount that what was left would not permit her
resuming hostilities. Therefore the situation did not require the
Allies to fix the numbers of troops they should retain and with the
prospects of early Peace he could see an early settlement of these
questions. Under these conditions he thought that the demobilisation of all the Armies might proceed without bothering much
about it. The demobilisation of the American troops, however, depended on the quantity of shipping available, but if their calcula-

tions held good, they would be able to reduce their troops by April next to the numbers prescribed by Marshal Foch.

SIR DOUGLAS HAIG said that he could add no fresh arguments but he could state his opinion. General Pershing had stated that Germany would be unable to offer any marked resistance, in which view he differed somewhat from the opinion expressed by Marshal Foch. In his opinion, Germany was still in a position to cause a great deal of trouble. Therefore until Peace was signed, the Governments ought to maintain their forces up to the strength prescribed by Marshal Foch. Unless they could obtain guarantees that arms would be surrendered and munition factories destroyed, they must maintain the forces laid down by Marshal Foch. These forces were not excessive in his opinion.

GENERAL SIR HENRY WILSON agreed that they ought to do what Mr. Lloyd George had said to get the German army reduced, but until they saw that this had been done, they could not reduce their own forces. Until they had sufficient guarantees, they ought to be careful what they did. The Germans were a martial people, magnificent soldiers and a proud people, and if the opportunity came, they would certainly be able to do as well as the Bolsheviks. The Prime Minister, Mr. Lloyd George, wished to discuss with Marshal Haig, Mr. Winston Churchill and himself, the question of the strength of the Army of Occupation to be maintained by Great Britain, so that he was obliged to reserve his decision. But he would point out that Great Britain had large commitments elsewhere, including maintenance of the Navy, which might militate against her keeping in France the forces asked for.

MR. LLOYD GEORGE enquired whether the destruction of the machinery at Krupps and Minden would not be sufficient guarantee.

MARSHAL FOCH replied that the Germans had had another factory at Mayence [Mainz], which the Allies had now seized, but there might be many other factories and a full list of these was not in their possession.

MR. LLOYD GEORGE said that he had had considerable experience of munitions. In every country two or three factories alone were absolutely essential, and when these went the others would prove inadequate. Guns, for instance, could only be manufactured in one or two places.

GENERAL PERSHING remarked that it was largely a question of the supply of material and a large percentage of the necessary material was already controlled by the Allies.

GENERAL DIAZ said that they were discussing a question which greatly affected Italy. They had so far demobilized 13 divisions and the balance of 38 divisions were kept under arms, merely to satisfy the requirements of the Alliance. For instance, one division was kept at Innsbruck merely with the object of acting with the Allies against Germany if necessary. In many parts of the old Austro-Hungarian Empire there was a tendency to increase the number of troops using these as a nuclei to form large armies. In a word, they were carrying out the principle adopted by Prussia in 1806. This, he thought, constituted a great danger. On the other hand, he agreed that they could not indefinitely remain mobilised on a war footing and a way out of the difficulty must be found. In his opinion, they should take action against Germany and Austria by removing all the artillery, by destroying munition factories and by regulating the output of mines. In other words, the Allies should hold in their hands all the sources from which engines of destruction were produced. Without artillery the Central Powers would have no means of carrying out a successful war. Therefore he would insist that the Allied should take essential guarantees, otherwise the difficulty would never be solved.

GENERAL PERSHING said that he would aprove of any steps being taken to reduce Germany's means of producing war material.

PRESIDENT WILSON said that he did not think that the German people would be willing to take up arms again, nor that Germany could in her present condition possibly carry out an organized war against organized Governments. He would ask that a draft resolution be drawn up embodying in explicit terms the proposals made by Mr. Lloyd George. This resolution could then be submitted to the meeting and brought under discussion. He thought they should at the same time study a scheme to relieve unemployment in Germany. In his opinion, Bolshevism was the greatest danger and the only real protection against it was food and industry. Consequently, whilst demobilising the German Army, they should take steps to protect themselves against the great danger of Bolshevism.

MR. LLOYD GEORGE said that following what President Wilson had said, the question of immediate disarmament was important, because it was understood that the German troops were selling their machine-guns, rifles, etc. and it was possible that these were being sold to Bolshevist agents. In his opinion, that danger added to the argument in favour of disarmament. Again, whatever figures were put down on paper, it was evident that the Allied Armies would become less efficient as time went on. Germany would then be more formidable in proportion to ourselves unless she were disarmed. He quite agreed with President Wilson's suggestion that they should have a definite proposal placed before them. He would suggest, therefore, a small Committee, including some member with a knowledge of manufactures, should be appointed to consider and put forward proposals as to the best manner of disarming Germany.

(This proposal was agreed to.)

M. LOUCHEUR, who at this stage entered the Council Chamber, said, in reply to a question put to him by M. Clemenceau, that all the production of Germany depended on the basin of Westphalia, and if Essen and its neighbourhood were seized, Germany could under no circumstances go on fighting. As regards the surrender of artillery, if this included machine guns, he felt convinced that Germany would be effectually disarmed.

M. CLEMENCEAU said that Mr. Lloyd George's proposal had been accepted: it remained to nominate the members of this Committee. He himself would nominate M. Loucheur.

MR. LLOYD GEORGE nominated Mr. Winston Churchill.

PRESIDENT WILSON nominated General Bliss.

M. ORLANDO nominated General Diaz.

(It was agreed that a Special Committee, composed of Mr. Churchill, M. Loucheur, Marshal Foch, General Bliss and General Diaz should be appointed to consider and report on:

(1) The strength of the Armies to be maintained by the Allies and Associated Powers on the Western Front during the period of the Armistice:

(2) The demobilization of the German Army and the guarantees (e.g. surrender of arms, seizure of munition factories, etc.,) to be necessary to ensure the fulfilment of the conditions imposed.[)]

MARSHAL FOCH asked permission to take this opportunity of suggesting that the Chiefs of the Allied Armies should meet together to devise a means of keeping each other informed regarding the process of demobilisation. In his opinion it was very necessary for them to have advance information regarding the number of troops under arms at given dates.

M. ORLANDO proposed that these plans of demobilisation should also include data relating to the small powers. He thought that was most important. In the old Austro-Hungarian Empire it would be found that some of the States, instead of demobilising, were calling men under arms. He thought that the scheme prepared should include both maximum and minimum figures.

(As this matter did not require action by the Supreme War Council, it was decided that Marshal Foch should assemble the Allied Commanders-in-Chief, and arrange to obtain from them required data relating to the programme of demobilization.)

MARSHAL FOCH then read the following proposal:

"I have the honour to propose to the Supreme War Council of the Allies that those who have fought in the great war, of all the Allied nations alike, should receive one identical commemorative medal. This glorious emblem worn by them in all parts of the world, would help to maintain among them the feeling of close fellowship which, after fortifying our Armies on the battlefield, will assure during Peace, by the bond of common memories, the greatness of the Associated Nations."

PRESIDENT WILSON, in approving the idea, enquired whether the intention was that each individual Government should strike a medal of the same design.

MARSHAL FOCH explained that this applied for each Government to agree to issue to their troops the same medal and the same ribbon.

(The Supreme War Council agreed to recommend for the approval of the Governments concerned, the issue of an identical medal and ribbon to all the troops of the Allied and Associated Powers who have fought in the war.)

CC MS (T. H. Bliss Papers, DLC).

## Hankey's Notes of Two Meetings of the Council of Ten

Quai d'Orsay, January 24, 1919, 12:15 P.M.[1]

BC-9

President Wilson read the following communication, which he suggested should be published and transmitted by wireless telegraphy to all parts of the world:

"The Governments now associated in conference to effect a lasting peace among the nations are deeply disturbed by the news which comes to them of the many instances in which armed force is being made use of, in many parts of Europe and the East, to gain possession of territory, the rightful claim to which the Peace Conference is to be asked to determine. They deem it their duty to utter a solemn warning that possession gained by force will seriously prejudice the claims of those who use such means. It will create the presumption that those who employ force doubt the justice and validity of their claim and purpose to substitute possession for proof of right and set up sovereignty by coercion rather than by racial or national preference and natural historical association. They thus put a cloud upon every evidence of title they may afterwards allege and indicate their distrust of the Conference itself. Nothing but the most unfortunate results can en-

[1] The complete text of these minutes is printed in PPC, III, 715.

sue. If they expect justice, they must refrain from force and place their claims in unclouded good faith in the hands of the Conference of Peace."

(This was agreed to.)

The meeting adjourned until 3 o'clock in the afternoon.

T MS (SDR, RG 256, 180.03101/16, DNA).

Quai d'Orsay, January 24, 1919, 3 P.M.[1]

BC-10

[The council agreed that Pichon should draft instructions for the commission that was to go to Poland.]

MR. LLOYD GEORGE said that he heard through Sir George Riddell[2] that the Press were very anxious to send two pressmen from each nation to accompany the Commission to Poland.

M. SONNINO expressed the opinion that this would not assist the labours of the Commission.

M. CLEMENCEAU was of the same opinion.

PRESIDENT WILSON pointed out that the Press were clearly entitled to send a Mission independently.

MR. LLOYD GEORGE agreed, but thought that the pressmen would not be able to reach their destination save under the aegis of the official Mission. Dantzig was in enemy country and the railway from that port was in German hands.

M. SONNINO thought that the introduction of irresponsible politics into the labours of the Mission would be highly embarrassing.

PRESIDENT WILSON expressed the view that English and American pressmen had no special views on Polish politics. They would merely report events as they saw them.

M. CLEMENCEAU was of the opinion that they would undoubtedly send telegrams and attempt to exercise a control over the Delegates.

M. PICHON strongly supported this view.

PRESIDENT WILSON said that, as far as the American Press was concerned, the pressmen would not represent individual papers but News Associations without any particular bias. They would send bare news without any colouring. Unfortunately, there were in America three such News Associations and the choice of two delegates might be difficult.

M. PICHON pointed out that the same was the case in France, where there were three News Agencies.

[1] The complete text of these notes is printed in PPC, III, 716-28.
[2] Sir George (Allardice) Riddell, newspaper publisher and representative of the British press at the peace conference.

MR. LLOYD GEORGE then proposed that there should be only one press delegate from each nation, and that the choice of the delegate should be left to the Press.

M. CLEMENCEAU agreed, provided that it be well understood that the delegates sent only news and not views.

(It was accordingly agreed upon that one Press delegate from each of the five Powers, chosen by the Press, should be allowed to proceed to Poland with the Commission on the express understanding that he should only transmit news and not expressions of opinion.)

[Discussions of a proposal to establish a commission to classify and formulate financial and economic questions for the council was postponed, at Wilson's suggestion, until the following day.]

At this stage the Dominion Prime Ministers entered the room.

M. CLEMENCEAU welcomed the Prime Ministers of the British Dominions.

MR. LLOYD GEORGE said that he thought it best that each of the Dominions should present its case separately. As far as the British Empire was concerned, most of the Colonies captured had been taken by Dominion troops. This even applied to German East Africa, where a considerable contingent of home troops had been employed. All he would like to say on behalf of the British Empire as a whole was that he would be very much opposed to the return to Germany of any of these Colonies. His reasons for saying so had been put in writing, and he was prepared, if necessary, to circulate the document to the Council. In many cases the Germans had treated the native populations very badly. For instance, in South-West Africa, they had deliberately pursued a policy of extermination. In other parts of Africa they had been very harsh, and they had raised native troops and encouraged these troops to behave in a manner that would even disgrace the Bolsheviks. The French and British, doubtless, had also raised native troops, but they had controlled them better.

PRESIDENT WILSON said that he thought all were agreed to oppose the restoration of the German Colonies.

M. ORLANDO, on behalf of Italy, and Baron Makino, on behalf of Japan, agreed.

(There was no dissentient and this principle was adopted. It was agreed that no public announcement of this policy should at present be made.)

MR. LLOYD GEORGE said that the second question, therefore, was to decide in what manner these territories should be dealt with. There were two or three methods proposed. The first was internationalisation or control by the League of Nations. It was generally agreed that these territories could not be directly administered internationally. Therefore, it was suggested that some one nation should undertake the trusteeship on behalf of the League as mandatory. The conditions of the trust would doubtless include a stipulation that the territory should be administered, not in the interests of the mandatory, but in the interests of all the nations in the League. There must be equal economic opportunity for all, and, further, there must be a guarantee that the natives would not be exploited either commercially or militarily for the benefit of the mandatory. There would also, no doubt, be a right of appeal to the League of Nations if any of the conditions of the trust were broken. For instance, if the missionaries or concessionaires of any nation complained of unfair treatment. He did not suggest that this was an exhaustive account of the conditions, and if his account were in any way inaccurate, it would, no doubt, be set right hereafter.

He would like to state at once that the definition he had just attempted to give did not differ materially from the method in which the British Empire dealt with its Colonies. In all British Colonies there was free trade. He did not think there was such a thing as a preferential tariff in any. Germans or Americans could trade throughout the British Colonies on the same terms as British subjects. In fact, in British East Africa, most of the commerce was done by a German firm and Germany subsidised a shipping line which carried the bulk of the trade. No troops, save for police purposes, were raised in the British Colonies. British coaling stations were as free to foreign as to British ships, and German battleships coaled in them as freely as British battleships. As far as Great Britain was concerned, therefore, he saw no objection to the mandatory system.

The next alternative was frank annexation. The German Colonies conquered by Australia, New Zealand and South Africa would be dealt with in detail by the Ministers representing these Dominions.

German South West Africa was contiguous to the territories of the Union. There was no real natural boundary and unless the Dutch and British populations of South Africa undertook the colonisation of this area it would remain a wilderness. If the Union were given charge of German South West Africa in the capacity of a Mandatory there would be in a territory, geographically one, two forms of administration. It was questionable whether any advantage would be derived from this division capable of outweighing its practical difficulties.

In the case of New Guinea, one-third of the island was already under direct Australian administration, another third had now been conquered from Germany. It was manifest that to draw a customs barrier between one portion of the island and the other presented disadvantages. Yet, if Australia were the Mandatory of the League of Nations for the administration of what had been German New Guinea, it might have to administer this portion of the island on different lines to those followed in its previous possessions.

Samoa also would be best administered directly by New Zealand. He pointed out that the task of administering Colonies was an expensive one. The British Colonial Budget was steadily increasing. Unless money were to be spent upon them colonies should be dropped. The Dominion of New Zealand had a population of little more than one million souls. It had put 100,000 men into the field, had incurred a war debt of £100,000,000 sterling, had suffered 60,000 casualties and lost 16,000 killed. New Zealand had taken Samoa and fully realized that money would have to be spent upon it if the island was to be retained. It might not think it worth while to undertake the task of administration only as a Mandatory.

To sum up, he would like the Conference to treat the territories enumerated as part of the Dominions which had captured them rather than as areas to be administered under the control of an organisation established in Europe which might find it difficult to contribute even the smallest financial assistance to their administration.

[Hughes then presented the case for Australia's claim to the German portion of New Guinea, which Australia had captured in 1914. He pointed out the strategic importance of New Guinea and other islands to the region, and continued:]

As to internationalisation, he would endeavor to show why this principle should not be applied in this particular case. As Mr. Lloyd George had pointed out, part of the country was under Australian administration and Australian laws were current there. Control by the League of Nations would lead to confusion of authority, which could only be harmful. If the Mandatory were to exercise real authority, its policy would have to be directed presumably by the League of Nations. In this case the Mandatory would be so overwhelmingly superior in power to Australia that Australian authority would be completely overshadowed. The Mandatory, as it were, would be living in a mansion and Australia in a cottage. Any strong power controlling New Guinea controlled Australia. He questioned whether any country represented at the meeting would consent to be overshadowed in such a way, even by an international authority. The policies of nations were liable to change, and history showed that friends in one war were not always friends in the next. From this point of view he was prepared to say that in the Mandatory Power established in New Guinea under international control, Australia would see a potential enemy. It was reasonable and fair that the rights of the natives should be insisted upon. Australia was ready to agree to such requirements, but Australia also had a right to claim freedom from the menace of any enemy such as had weighed upon her before this war. The security of Australia would threaten no one. No state would suffer if Australia were safe, Australia alone would suffer if she were not. Australia had suffered 90,000 casualties in this war and lost 60,000 killed. Her troops everywhere had fought well. Her war debt alone amounted to £300,000,000 sterling exclusive of another £100,000,000 for the repatriation and pensioning of her troops. Australia did not wish to be left to stagger under this load and not to feel safe.

GENERAL SMUTS said that the Union of South Africa was putting forward a claim to the German territory in South-West Africa. The map would show the two countries were geographically one. The reason why South-West Africa had not been annexed to the Union was the dilatoriness of the Imperial Government. The Imperial Government had regarded the country as a desert and had taken no action. In 1884 any possible action on their part had been suddenly forestalled by Bismarck. As to the subsequent history of the country its administration under the Germans had been a failure. The country was only fit for ranching. The Germans had not colonised it. They had done little else than exterminate the natives. It must be remembered that, at the outbreak of this war, there had been a rebellion in the Union, very largely fomented by the Germans in South-West Africa.[3] Some of the officers of the Defence Force had been seduced, and General Botha, after his victory had found German telegrams offering to recognize the independence of South Africa if the rebellion succeeded. The rebellion had been very formidable, and its suppression had employed 40,000 troops. It was only after this that the Union had been able to conquer German South-West Africa.

[3] In August 1914, Gen. Louis Botha, the first Prime Minister of the Union of South Africa, had agreed to a British request that the Union take an active part in the war and send an expeditionary force into German South-West Africa to destroy several wireless stations and the powerful long-range radio transmitter at Windhoek. The prospect of having to take up arms for the British Empire generated a serious revolt by discontented Afrikaners in the Transvaal and the Orange Free State against what they perceived as oppression by the British. Led by several prominent Afrikaner generals of Anglo-Boer war fame, including the then commander in chief of the Defence Force, the Union's army, they hoped to rid themselves of British domination and to reestablish the independence of their former republics. Although the Governor of German South-West Africa had promised that, if the revolt should succeed, he would recognize the new Afrikaner state and was willing to lend material aid to the insurgents, there is no evidence that the rebellion was part of a conspiracy inspired by Germany. For detailed accounts, see D. W. Krüger, *The Making of a Nation: A History of the Union of South Africa, 1910-1961* (Johannesburg and London, 1969), pp. 79-96, and Johannes Meintjes, *General Louis Botha: A Biography* (London, 1970), pp. 232-53.

The question to be decided was whether the Union of South Africa should absorb this country, or should be appointed mandatory for its administration. He would point out that this territory was not in the same category as other German possessions in Africa. The Cameroons, Togo-Land and East Africa were all tropical and valuable possessions; South-West Africa was a desert country without any product of great value and only suitable for pastoralists. It could, therefore, only be developed from within the Union itself. He thought, therefore, that, although there might be a good case for the administration of the other German possessions in Africa by a mandatory, there was not, in this instance, a strong case. It was on this ground that South Africa claimed the country. A white community in South Africa had been established there for two or three centuries. It had done its best to give a form of self-government to three million natives, and its policy had been tested and found good. It was suited as much to the whites as to the natives, and this policy should be applied to the natives in South-West Africa. The fiscal system, he also thought, should be the same. It would be impossible to set up police posts along many hundred miles of desert frontier.

Another very serious ground for the claim as made was that in the rebellion General Botha had gone a very long way to do his duty to the British Empire in fighting his own people. There was at that time a great issue at stake in South Africa. The Dutch people, to whom General Botha and he himself belonged together with many who were of German descent, wished to be neutral in this war. Their position, however, was such that they could not legally or constitutionally remain neutral. If the territory in question were not ceded to the Union, the result would be the overthrow of General Botha and of all his policy. Apart from the interest of the British Empire, it was to the interest of South Africa that the two white peoples inhabiting it should live in harmony. He would greatly deprecate that this Conference should adopt any form of settlement that would justify the rebellion of 1914. This would render the position in South Africa most deplorable. On these grounds he would press very strongly that, whatever might be decided in respect to the valuable African Colonies in other parts of the Continent, this desert country, so closely connected with South Africa, should be included in the Union. The community to which he belonged had been in South Africa since 1650. They had established a white civilization in a savage continent and had become a great cultural agency all over South Africa. Their wish was that one of the effects of the great settlement now to be made should be to strengthen their position and to consolidate the union of the white races in South Africa. The Boer pastoralists were always looking for uninhabited country in which to settle. He was quite sure that if German South West Africa were given by the Conference to the Union, its work in this respect would be good.

In conclusion, he would like to add that the Union had made great sacrifices. He did not wish to stress them particularly as all had made great sacrifices; but he believed that the effort made by South Africa, sometimes with a divided heart, would prove on examination to be second to none among the small States that had partaken in the war.

[Massey[4] presented the case for annexation of Samoa by New Zealand, on strategic and humanitarian grounds, and he added:]

With regard to the League of Nations, which had not yet been established, he hoped that it would be established and that it would be very successful. He would like to remind those present that we had had experiences in the past, which had sometimes been sad experiences, of joint control of native races. Mr. Mass[e]y mentioned the case of the New Hebrides. We were the best of friends today with the citizens of France and the Government of France, and he hoped and believed that that very satisfactory state of things would continue for all time. But he thought it would be admitted, not only by the people of France, but by others, that our joint control of the New Hebrides had been an ignominious failure. Egypt, too, had not been a success under joint control, neither had Samoa. He was very sceptical in regard to the success of any joint arrangement in regard to the German Colonies.

[Sir Robert Borden said that Canada had no territorial claims to advance.] There was one thought, however, that he would like to present to the Council on behalf of the claims put forward by the other Dominions. Those Dominions were autonomous nations within an Empire which might more properly be called itself a League of Nations. He realised that the British Empire occupied a large part of the world, but the prejudice raised by the word Empire might be dispelled by considerinig the matter from the angle he had just suggested. All the cases advanced rested upon the plea of security, and he considered that the arguments put forward deserved the closest attention of the Council.

M. Clemenceau thanked the Dominion Ministers for the statements they had made. The Council had listened to them with the greatest attention, and he begged to assure them that no decisions would be taken without full consideration of all they had said, with regard both to the interests of each and to the interests of all.

T MS (SDR, RG 256, 180.03101/17, DNA).
   [4] William Ferguson Massey, Prime Minister of New Zealand.

## To Tasker Howard Bliss, with Enclosure

My dear General Bliss:　　　　　　　　Paris, 24 January, 1919.

I dare say from what I have heard in different quarters that there is a good deal in what the writer of the enclosed letter says, and I would like very much to know from you whether you think there is anything that can be wisely done, or suggested to the Commander in Chief in this connection.

　　　　　Cordially and sincerely yours,　　Woodrow Wilson

TLS (T. H. Bliss Papers, DLC).

## E N C L O S U R E

## From Francis Call Woodman

　　　　　　　　　　Montrichard, (Loir-et-Cher) *France.*
My dear Sir:　　　　　　　　　　　18 January 1919

The President will perhaps remember the writer—as Headmaster of the Morristown School in New Jersey—who is now serving as an educational secretary of the Y.M.C.A., at present stationed at Montrichard (Loir-et-Cher)

After a month of work, and rich experience, here, I have arrived at some conclusions one or two of which I feel it my duty to try to bring before the attention of the President.

A large majority of the "enlisted men" whom I have met are suffering from a condition or attitude of mind which both impairs their efficiency as soldiers, and renders them almost wholly unfit for educational work. I refer to their being subjected to live in wet, and otherwise uncomfortable, Camps, and to being constantly moved from one Camp to another after having been given pretty definite promises of going home. As a matter of psychology this disagreeable & unsettled life effects [affects] the "men" unfavorably, and of course reacts upon their physical condition. As a result I believe we are losing many men in this region from unnecessary exposure.*

Another fact, worth emphasizing perhaps, is that many men are returning home without any knowlege of, or interest in, the fine things of France, or its people. Their memories are largely of monotonous drills, rain, mud, 'frogs,' and general discomfort & suffering. From an educational point of view it seems highly desirable to give as many men as possible a chance to see Paris, or some other beautiful & interesting part of France, or, where impossible,

* The Camp at St. Aignan (Loir-et-Cher), which I recently visited, is literally "a sea of mud."

a change [chance] to attend lectures & talks so that the "men" may at least hear about what they cannot see with their own eyes.

Being a teacher of boys, and having a lively interest in the youth of America, I venture to send these lines to the President.

I am, dear Sir,

Respectfully & faithfully yours,   Francis Call Woodman

ALS (T. H. Bliss Papers, DLC).

## Two Letters to Robert Lansing

My dear Mr. Secretary:                    Paris, 24 January, 1919.

I have to be very cautious indeed about this oil legislation and some of the men of best intentions are far from being the best advisors. I would be very much obliged if you would ascertain through Mr. Polk whether this suggestion[1] has the approval of the Attorney General and the Secretary of the Navy.

Cordially and sincerely yours,   Woodrow Wilson

[1] See S. Ferris to WW, Jan. 22, 1919.

My dear Mr. Secretary:                    Paris, 24 January, 1919.

As these two communications show,[1] both the City of Dublin and the City of Cork are offering me the freedom of the City. Is there any diplomatic way in which we could ascertain whether the British would be embarrassed in any way by my accepting these compliments. I hardly know upon what grounds to decline them.

Cordially and faithfully yours,   Woodrow Wilson

TLS (WP, DLC).
[1] Henry Campbell, Town Clerk of the City of Dublin, to GFC, Jan. 4, 1919, and Florence W. McCarthy, Town Clerk of the City of Cork, to WW, Jan. 11, 1919, both TLS (WP, DLC).

## To Edward Nash Hurley

My dear Mr. Chairman:                    Paris, 24 January, 1919.

I have given a great deal of thought to the question of the purchase of the shares of the Mercantile Marine but still find myself in doubt as to what is the right and just conclusion. There are some serious international aspects in the matter. Personally I seriously doubt whether it would be feasible for the British Government to exercise the right to condemnation which they claim, if the shares become the property of the Government of the United States but that is a matter which has many angles. I would be very much obliged if you would lay the case in all its particulars before the Department of State in order to obtain from them such light upon it and such advice as they may be able to give us.

Cordially and sincerely yours,   [Woodrow Wilson]

CCL (WP, DLC).


## To Baron d'Estournelles de Constant[1]

Paris, 24 January, 1919.

My dear Baron d'Estournelles de Constant:

Thank you for you letter of January 20th.[2] You may be sure I will bear in mind the two remaining duties which you so eloquently pressed upon me.

Cordially and sincerely yours,   [Woodrow Wilson]

CCL (WP, DLC).
[1] Baron Paul Henri Benjamin Balluat d'Estournelles de Constant de Rebecque, former diplomat and senator for Sarthe since 1904. The author of numerous books and articles on international peace, he was an ardent advocate of disarmament and international conciliation and arbitration. He was a French delegate at The Hague Conference of 1907 and a corecipient, in 1909, of the Nobel Peace Prize.
[2] Baron d'Estournelles de Constant to WW, Jan. 20, 1919, ALS (WP, DLC). He wrote that the French people were "more than grateful" to the United States and to Wilson, but that they expected two more "great services" from him: a visit to the devastated regions of France and "a word of gratitude & justice" to the women who had done so much to finish the war by a just and durable peace but who were now excluded from the deliberations of the peace conference.


## To Arthur Henderson

My dear Mr. Henderson:                    Paris, 24 January, 1919.

The beautifully engrossed resolutions of the British Trades Union Congress and the British Labour Party[1] reached me through the mails and I want to tell you with what interest and with what deep gratification at the generous confidence expressed in me, I have received them. It increases my consciousness of responsibility to be so depended on to speak for Justice and I hope with all my heart that I shall never prove unworthy of it. I beg that you will express to your associates my deep sense of the honor they have done me and of the cheer their message has given me.

Cordially and sincerely yours,   [Woodrow Wilson][2]

CCL (WP, DLC).
[1] Printed at Dec. 28, 1918, Vol. 53.
[2] Wilson sent this letter, *mutatis mutandis*, as WW to Charles William Bowerman, Jan. 24, 1919, CCL (WP, DLC). Bowerman was secretary of the Parliamentary Committee of the Trades Union Congress.

## From Joseph Patrick Tumulty

[The White House, Jan. 24, 1919]

Number twenty-four One hundred million dollar food relief bill passed Senate today fifty three to eighteen.     Tumulty

T telegram (WP, DLC).


## From Chaim Weizmann

Sir,                                    London 24th January 1919.

I have the honour to communicate to you the Resolutions adopted by Jewish Organisations in various parts of the world[1] in view of the coming Peace Conference.

The Jewries of nearly every country have assembled in Council to consider their attitude towards the question of the reconstitution of Palestine as a Jewish National Home. It is with the greatest satisfaction that we are able to transmit to you at the request of the several Jewish Organisations of the world (both Zionist and non-Zionist) the enclosed Resolutions showing that the whole of the Jews of the world are united in favour of a Jewish Commonwealth in Palestine and that a large majority of them have already definitely pronounced themselves in favour of a British Trusteeship of Palestine.

I have the honour to be, Sir,

Your obedient Servant,   Ch. Weizmann

TLS (WP, DLC).
[1] Nine resolutions adopted in December 1918 and January 1919 by the American Jewish Congress, the Czecho-Slovakian Jewish Congress, the Jewish National Council for Bukowina and Eastern Galicia, the Provisional Jewish National Council of Ukrainia, the Provisional Jewish Council of Poland, the Jewish National Council of Russia, the General Conference of Palestinian Jews, the German Zionist Organisation, and the Jewish National Council of German Austria, all T MSS (WP, DLC).


## From Vance Thompson[1]

Dear Mr. President:                     Rome January 24, 1919.

With this letter, I take the liberty of sending you a report of a conversation I had with a high authority of the Vatican regarding your Excellency's recent visit to the Pope.[2]

(I may state that five or six weeks ago, in Washington, it was thought my knowledge of Europe might be of service to our Government, at this time; and I was asked to go to Rome and, acting under Colonel M. C. Buckey,[3] our Military Attaché, procure what political information might be had regarding the troubled situation in South Eastern Europe; and, naturally, I have been in touch with the Vatican.)

The statements, embodied in the accompanying report, were made by one in authority. Of course, I do not know whether they are true or false; but they have been made to me and it is a fair assumption that they will be stated to other persons—if it is thought a purpose can be served.

As, Sir, these statements had to do with a private conversation you had with the Pope, I felt they should not be submitted to anyone save to yourself; and in this Colonel Buckey concurred.

I have the honor to be, Sir,

Very respectfully,   Vance Thompson

TLS (WP, DLC).
[1] Vance (Charles) Thompson, Princeton, 1883, prolific author and playwright, at this time an attaché at the American embassy in Rome.
[2] It is missing in WP, DLC, and there is no copy in the files of the State Department.
[3] That is, Mervyn Chandos Buckey.

# Two Telegrams from Frank Lyon Polk to Robert Lansing

Washington, January 24th, 1919.

391. Very Confidential. For the Secretary of State. Referring to my answer to 376, January 21st regarding Siberian railway plan, I take the liberty of calling your attention to the political situation here. Critical spirit to-day is being clearly manifested in regard to Russia:

1. By attacks on War Trade Board Russian bureau.[1]

2. By attacks on personal conduct of Ambassador Francis. La Guardia apparently got his information from Consul Winship now at Welland and Lieutenant Commander Crolley formerly at Saint Petersburg now Naval Attaché at Madrid.[2]

3. By Senator Johnson's continually attacking Administration for keeping troops in Russia and Siberia.[3]

There is no question but that the Republicans are trying to force an extra session and leading Democrats seem to feel that the extra session should be considered inevitable. If successful Republicans resenting control of various committees will make attacks on every phase of policy of Administration in Russia. We are committed now to a plan for operation of Railways in Siberia and the need is as urgent as ever but I wish to lay stress on the fact that money must be supplied in large sums in order to carry through the plan. In view of the attitude of Congress on the food bill, I should give up the possibility of securing money for this purpose by an appropriation. The Russian Ambassador has no funds for any real railway reorganization and has already exhausted sums set aside for maintaining railway service corps.

I am taking the liberty of stating the case baldly so the President and yourself may have all the facts before you before he commits himself to supply the money for the purpose from his private fund. I have asked Woolley to express his views on the situation and as soon as I hear from him will cable you again.

I have not communicated with the Japanese Government our formal acceptance and for this reason would like to have your views as soon as possible.                                    Polk.

T telegram (WP, DLC).
¹ James William Good, a Republican congressman from Iowa, had attacked the legality, objectives, and funding of the Russian Bureau in a highly sarcastic speech in the House of Representatives on January 13. He charged Wilson with illegally appropriating $5,000,000 out of his emergency fund to create a commercial enterprise. He read aloud the lengthy certificate of incorporation of the bureau in the State of Connecticut, doing so in such a fashion as to cause repeated laughter in the House over its detailed provisions allowing the bureau to conduct many kinds of business in all parts of the world, except in Connecticut. He even brought into question the wisdom of feeding the hungry in Russia or anywhere else. *Cong. Record*, 65th Cong., 3d sess., pp. 1341-44. About the Russian Bureau (Inc.) of the War Trade Board, see n. 4 to the extract from the House Diary printed at Sept. 24, 1918, Vol. 51.
² In a debate in the House on January 22 about the Diplomatic and Consular Appropriation bill, Fiorello Henry LaGuardia, then a Republican congressman from New York, had attacked David R. Francis as "absolutely hopelessly incompetent." "If there is one man in the United States," LaGuardia declared, "who does not understand, and never did understand, the Russian conditions, it is Mr. Francis." LaGuardia was joined in his criticism of Francis by Clarence Benjamin Miller, a Republican congressman from Minnesota. When Champ Clark came to the Ambassador's defense and asked Francis' critics to specify their accusations, LaGuardia charged that Francis had not worked in accord and in sympathy with the diplomatic representatives of France and Great Britain and had not cooperated with them. Moreover, LaGuardia continued, Francis had not been in sympathy with the Russian Revolution, had not familiarized himself with the Russian situation, and had sent misleading reports to the State Department. He had allowed himself to be influenced by Kerensky and had advised the State Department to support the Provisional Government when the British and French Ambassadors had clearly understood that Kerensky was weak and was bound to fall. In the struggle between Kerensky and Kornilov, the State Department, upon Francis' recommendation, had backed Kerensky and, as it turned out, had backed the wrong horse. Other American representatives—particularly North Winship, the Consul General at Petrograd from April 1914 to July 1917, and Capt. Walter Selwyn Crosley, the Naval Attaché in Russia from March 1917 to March 1918—had judged the situation correctly, but Francis had refused to listen to their advice. When asked to reveal the sources of his information, LaGuardia stated that he had personally interviewed both Winship and Crosley. He had seen Winship in Milan, where Winship had been the American Consul since July 1917, and had talked to Crosley in Madrid. *Cong. Record*, 65th Cong. 3d sess., pp. 18876-81.
³ The attacks by Senator Hiram W. Johnson were the opening salvos of what was to become a continued sharp criticism by Congress of the presence of American soldiers in Russia. As early as December 12, 1918, Johnson had introduced an interrogatory resolution, about which see NDB to WW, Jan. 1, 1919, n. 5, Vol. 53. In the face of continued criticism by Johnson, La Follette, Kenyon, and other Republican senators, Senator Hitchcock, on January 9, attempted to explain the administration's policy. In the ensuing debate, Johnson, Borah, and some of their Republican colleagues again questioned the purpose of keeping American troops in Russia. *Cong. Record*, 65th Cong., 3d sess., pp. 1101-1105, 1161-71. Not satisfied with Hitchcock's explanation, Johnson, on January 13, introduced another resolution (S. Res. 411) to the effect that "in the opinion of the Senate, the soldiers of the United States, as soon as practical, should be withdrawn from Russia." He claimed that the administration had been unable to answer his previous queries because it had no policy in Russia. He concluded: "We are neither one nor the other; we are neither intervening in sufficient force to be of consequence,

nor are we getting out of Russia. We are to-day simply inviting disaster in Russia, and interfering here and there, without knowing why, and in matters, too, in which we have no concern." *Ibid.*, p. 1313. For the fate of the Johnson resolution, see EMH to WW, Feb. 19, 1919 (first letter of that date), n. 1.

Washington, January 24, 1919

392 IMMEDIATE for the Secretary of State:

Your 376, January 21, 6 pm. greatly appreciated.

*First*: does announcement of policy towards Russia printed in yesterday's papers[1] modify approval of railway plan in any way. I am withholding formal approval until I hear from you.

*Second*: Am I to assume that President's authorization to General Graves is along lines suggested in my 113, January 6, 6 pm[2] QUOTE To make the plan effective will require the cooperation of General Graves with Mr. Stevens to assist in providing military protection to the different stations in order to maintain the free movement of trains in cooperation with the powers having military forces in Siberia. UNQUOTE. May I inform Secretary of War that the President's authorization is in these terms, and to cooperate with Inter-Allied Committees.

*Third*: In view of attitude of Congress since my 234 January 14, 1 pm. I believe you and McCormick may wish to consider whether it is advisable to advance any money to Stevens from the War Trade Board Fund. If not, what other fund would then be available. Have informed Woolley.

*Four*: How soon will President set aside fund for maintenance of Russian Railway Service Corps.

*Fifth*: Am I correct in understanding that, in expressing this Government's willingness to join in some scheme to be worked out for financing railways, you see means to do so effectively?

I have asked these questions because I think situation here requires we should look ahead. Please consider them against background of telegram I am sending you today giving situation as I see it.                    Polk   Acting

TS telegram (SDR, RG 59, 861.77/634, DNA).

[1] That is, the so-called Prinkipo Declaration, embodied in the minutes of the Council of Ten printed at Jan. 22, 1919, 3:15 p.m. The declaration was printed, e.g., on the front page of the *New York Times*, Jan. 23, 1919.

[2] It is printed at this date in Vol. 53.

## Gilbert Fairchild Close to Francis Call Woodman

My dear Mr. Woodman:                    Paris, 24 January, 1919.

The President asks me to acknowledge receipt of your letter of January 18th and to thank you for the very valuable suggestions which you have made. The President is looking into the matter to see whether these suggestions can be followed up.

Sincerely yours,   [Gilbert F. Close]

CCL (WP, DLC).

## Gilbert Fairchild Close to Marguerite de Witt Schlumberger

My dear Madame Schlumberger:          Paris, 24 January 1919.

I am writing on behalf of the President to acknowledge receipt of your letter of January 18th, and to say that the President will be glad to meet the delegation representing the Union Francaise Pour le Suffrage des Femmes on Monday, January 27th, at 6 o'clock in the afternoon, at 23 Rue de Monceau.

Sincerely yours,   [Gilbert F. Close]

CCL (WP, DLC).

## Gilbert Fairchild Close to Herbert Clark Hoover

My dear Mr. Hoover:                    Paris, 24 January, 1919.

The President has asked me to return to you the proclamation with reference to the brewing of non-alcoholic beers which you enclosed with your letter of January 22nd and which the President has signed.[1]          Sincerely yours,   [Gilbert F. Close]

CCL (WP, DLC).
[1] It is printed in the *Official Bulletin*, III (Feb. 21, 1919), 3.

## From the Diary of Dr. Grayson

Saturday, January 25, 1919.

We attended the second plenary session of the Peace Conference. It was again presided over by Premier Clemenceau and the general program for the conference was adopted. The first business was the creation of a committee to take over the framing of the constitution of the League of Nations. President Wilson made a very strong speech, emphasizing the necessity for the creation of the League. His speech was declared by many of those who had heard it, to have been the best since his arrival in France. Only one of his hearers defied the rule of no demonstration of approval and applauded vigorously. This was Jesse H. Jones, a tall Texan, who recognizes no foreign formalities. The President moved that the committee be made up of two representatives from each of the five great powers and three representatives to be selected from the smaller nations. Following translation of the President's speech into French, Premier Hughes of Australia demanded to know whether debate would be allowed on the constitution when it was finally framed. He was assured it would be. The Belgian representatives then protested against the limitations which fixed the representation of the smaller nations at only three members. The protest was backed up by Brazil, Greece, Serbia and several of the other smaller nations, they taking the position that the small nations had been overrun by Germany and the central powers and had large problems that would be affected by the League of Nations program. Lloyd George and Orlando seconded the President's original motion and the feeling was running rather high, indicating the imminence of the first open break when Clemenceau took the floor and made an impartial plea for the original plan. He said it had been his experience in his many years of political life, that the larger the committee, the less work accomplished. He assured the smaller nations that their rights would be amply and completely protected and upon that assurance, the demand for increased representation was withdrawn and the original plan adopted by unanimous vote.

Committees were appointed to pass upon the personal guilt and responsibility of the authors of the war; on the internationalization of waterways; on the question of reparation and damages and on the League of Nations. President Wilson was made chairman of the League of Nations Committee and the conference adjourned, having set all this machinery in motion.

## From Edward Mandell House

Dear Governor:                              Paris 25 January 1919.

Clemenceau will ask you this afternoon to make a speech respecting the League of Nations.

I suggest that during your remarks you bring out the following points:

(1) Perhaps, of all nations, the United States has the least selfish interest in the formation of a League of Nations. This is

on account of our isolation and of the fact that a blockade of our ports would probably never be effective.

(2) If the League of Nations is to be formed at all, it must be formed at this Conference. If it is put off, the peoples of the world will soon be lulled into a sense of false security.

(3) The amazing development of science bids fair eventually to destroy the civilization which has created it. The League of Nations is essential to control this development in the interest of peace instead of war.

(4) Unless the League of Nations can be established in such a way as to make safe the reduction of military and naval armaments, the burden of taxation on the people of the world will become unbearable.

Affectionately yours,   E. M. House

TLS (WP, DLC).


## Protocol of a Plenary Session of the Inter-Allied Conference for the Preliminaries of Peace[1]

Quai d'Orsay, January 25, 1919.

Protocol No. 2

[Clemenceau, as president, opened the session at 3 p.m. Representatives were present from the United States (Wilson, Lansing, White, House, Bliss), the British Empire, France, Italy, Japan, Belgium, Bolivia, Brazil, China, Cuba, Ecuador, Greece, the Hedjaz, Peru, Poland, Portugal, Rumania, Serbia, Siam, the Czechoslovak Republic, and Uruguay. Cecil, Bourgeois, and Scialoja represented their respective countries as technical delegates for the League of Nations.]

The President informs the Conference that, at the request of the Delegation of the United States, the approval of the Protocol of the first Session is postponed to the next Session, as that Delegation has not yet received the English text of Protocol No. 1, which it reserves the right to present to the Conference.

The order of the day calls for the appointment of five Commissions charged with the duty of examining the following questions:
1. League of Nations.
2. Responsibility of the authors of the War and enforcement of penalties.
3. Reparation for damage.
4. International Legislation on Labour.
5. International Control of Ports, Waterways and Railways.

[1] The complete text of these minutes is printed in PPC, III, 176-207.

The first Commission to be nominated concerns the League of Nations, on the subject of which the Bureau presents a draft resolution which has been distributed, in English and French, to all the members of the Conference.

The discussion is opened on the question of the League of Nations.

The President of the United States delivers the following speech:

"I consider it a distinguished privilege to open the discussion in this Conference on the League of Nations. We have assembled for two purposes—to make the present settlements which have been rendered necessary by this war, and also to secure the peace of the world, not only by the present settlements but by the arrangements we shall make in this Conference for its maintenance. The League of Nations seems to me to be necessary for both of these purposes. There are many complicated questions connected with the present settlements which, perhaps, cannot be successfully worked out to an ultimate issue by the decisions we shall arrive at here. I can easily conceive that many of these settlements will need subsequent reconsideration; that many of the decisions we shall make will need subsequent alteration in some degree, for if I may judge by my own study of some of these questions they are not susceptible of confident judgments at present.

"It is, therefore, necessary that we should set up some machinery by which the work of this Conference should be rendered complete. We have assembled here for the purpose of doing very much more than making the present settlement. We are assembled under very peculiar conditions of world opinion. I may say without straining the point that we are not representatives of governments, but representatives of peoples. It will not suffice to satisfy governmental circles anywhere. It is necessary that we should satisfy the opinion of mankind. The burdens of this war have fallen in an unusual degree upon the whole population of the countries involved. I do not need to draw for you the picture of how the burden has been thrown back from the front upon the older men, upon the women, upon the children, upon the homes of the civilized world, and how the real strain of the war has come where the eye of government could not reach, but where the heart of humanity beats. We are bidden by these people to make a peace which will make them secure. We are bidden by these people to see to it that this strain does not come upon them again, and I venture to say that it has been possible for them to bear this strain because they hope that those who represented them could get together after this war, and make such another sacrifice unnecessary.

"It is a solemn obligation on our part, therefore, to make permanent arrangements that justice shall be rendered and peace maintained. This is the central object of our meeting. Settlements may be temporary, but the actions of the nations in the interests of peace and justice must be permanent. We can set up permanent processes. We may not be able to set up permanent decisions, and therefore, it seems to me that we must take, so far as we can, a picture of the world into our minds. Is it not a startling circumstance for one thing that the great discoveries of science, that the quiet study of men in laboratories, that the thoughtful developments which have taken place in quiet lecture-rooms, have now been turned to the destruction of civilisation? The powers of destruction have not so much multiplied as gained facility. The enemy whom we have just overcome had at its seats of learning some of the principal centres of scientific study and discovery, and used them in order to make destruction sudden and complete; and only the watchful, continuous co-operation of men can see to it that science, as well as armed men, is kept within the harness of civilisation.

"In a sense, the United States is less interested in this subject than the other nations here assembled. With her great territory and her extensive sea borders, it is less likely that the United States should suffer from the attack of enemies than that many of the other nations here should suffer; and the ardour of the United States—for it is a very deep and genuine ardour—for the Society of Nations is not an ardour springing out of fear and apprehension, but an ardour springing out of the ideals which have come to consciousness in the war. In coming into this war the United States never thought for a moment that she was intervening in the politics of Europe, or the politics of Asia, or the politics of any part of the world. Her thought was that all the world had now become conscious that there was a single cause which turned upon the issues of this war. That was the cause of justice and liberty for men of every kind and place. Therefore, the United States would feel that her part in this war had been played in vain if there ensued upon it merely a body of European settlements. She would feel that she could not take part in guaranteeing those European settlements unless that guarantee involved the continuous superintendence of the peace of the world by the associated nations of the world.

"Therefore, it seems to me that we must concert our best judgment in order to make this League of Nations a vital thing—not merely a formal thing, not an occasional thing, not a thing sometimes called into life to meet an exigency, but always functioning in watchful attendance upon the interests of the nations, and that its continuity should be a vital continuity; that it should have functions that are continuing functions and that do not permit an intermission of its watchfulness and of its labour; that it should be the eye of the nations to keep watch upon the common interest, an eye that does not slumber, an eye that is everywhere watchful and attentive.

"And if we do not make it vital, what shall we do? We shall disappoint the expectations of the peoples. This is what their thought centres upon. I have had the very delightful experience of visiting several nations since I came to this side of the water, and every time the voice of the body of the people reached me through any representative, at the front of its plea stood the hope for the League of Nations. Gentlemen, select classes of mankind are no longer the governors of mankind. The fortunes of mankind are now in the hands of the plain people of the whole world. Satisfy them, and you have justified their confidence not only, but established peace. Fail to satisfy them, and no arrangement that you can make would either set up or steady the peace of the world.

"You can imagine, gentlemen, I dare say, the sentiments and the purpose with which representatives of the United States support this great project for a League of Nations. We regard it as the keystone of the whole programme which expressed our purpose and our ideal in this war and which the Associated Nations have accepted as the basis of the settlement. If we return to the United States without having made every effort in our power to realise this programme, we should return to meet the merited scorn of our fellow-citizens. For they are a body that constitutes a great democracy. They expect their leaders to speak their thoughts and no private purpose of their own. They expect their representatives to be their servants. We have no choice but to obey their mandate. But it is with the greatest enthusiasm and pleasure that we accept that mandate; and because this is the keystone of the whole fabric, we have pledged our every purpose to it, as we have to every item of the fabric. We would not dare abate a single part of the programme which constitutes our instructions. We would not dare compromise upon any matter as the champion of this thing—this peace of the world, this attitude of justice, this principle that we are masters of no people but are here to see that every people in the world shall choose its own master and govern its own destinies, not as we wish but as it wishes. We are here to see, in short, that the very foundations of this war are swept away. Those foundations were the private choice of small coteries of civil rulers and military staffs. Those foundations were the aggression of great Powers upon small. Those foundations were the holding together of empires of unwilling subjects by the duress of arms. Those foundations were the power of small bodies of men to work their will upon mankind and use them as pawns in a game. And nothing less than the emancipation of the world from these things will accomplish peace. You can see that the representatives of the United States are, therefore, never put to the embarrassment of choosing a way of expediency, because they have laid down for them their unalterable lines of principle. And, thank God, those lines have been accepted as the lines of settlement by all the high-minded men who have had to do with the beginnings of this great business.

"I hope, Mr. Chairman, that when it is known, as I feel confident that it will be known, that we have adopted the principle of the League of Nations and mean to work out that principle in effective action, we shall by that single thing have lifted a great part of the load of anxiety from the hearts of men everywhere. We stand in a peculiar case. As I go about the streets here I see everywhere the American uniform. Those men came into the war after we had uttered our purposes. They came as crusaders, not merely to win the war, but to win a cause; and I am responsible to them, for it fell to me to formulate the purposes for which I asked them to fight, and I, like them, must be a crusader for these things whatever it costs and whatever it may be necessary to do, in honour, to accomplish the objects for which they fought. I have been glad to find from day to day that there is no question of our standing alone in this matter, for there are champions of this cause upon every hand. I am merely avowing this in order that you may understand why, perhaps, it fell to us, who are disengaged from the politics of this great Continent and of the Orient, to suggest that this was the keystone of the arch and why it occurs to the generous mind of our President to call upon me to open this debate. It is not because we alone represent this idea, but, because it is our privilege to associate ourselves with you in representing it.

"I have only tried in what I have said to give you the fountains of the enthusiasm which is within us for this thing, for those fountains spring, it seems to me, from all the ancient wrongs and sympathies of mankind, and the very pulse of the world seems to beat."[2]

MR. LLOYD GEORGE (Great Britain) delivers the following speech:

"I arise to second this resolution. After the noble speech of the President of the United States I feel that no observations are needed in order to commend this resolution to the Conference, and I should not have intervened at all had it not been that I wished to state how emphatically the people of the British Empire are behind this proposal. And if the national leaders have not been able during the last five years to devote as much time as they would like to its

---

[2] There is a two-page WWT outline of this address in WP, DLC.

advocacy, it is because their time and their energies have been absorbed in the exigencies of a terrible struggle."

[Lloyd George then spoke of the devastation and "the acres of graves of the fallen" that he had seen in France, which were the results of] "the only organised method that civilised nations have ever attempted or established to settle disputes amongst each other. And my feeling was: surely it is time that a saner plane for settling disputes between peoples should be established than this organised savagery.

"I do not know whether this will succeed. But if we attempt it, the attempt will be a success, and for that reason I second the proposal."

MR. ORLANDO (Italy), having asked leave to speak, delivers the speech of which the following is a translation:

"Allow me to express my warmest adhesion to the great principle which we are called upon to proclaim to-day. I think that we are thus accomplishing the first and the most solemn of the pledges which we gave to our people when we asked them to make immense efforts in this immense war; pledges of which the counterpart was death, nameless sacrifices and boundless grief. We are therefore fulfilling our duty in honouring this sacred pledge. That is much, but it is not all. We must bring to the task a spontaneous spirit and, if I may be allowed the mystic expression, purity of intention. It is not in any spirit of petty national vanity that I allow myself to recall the great juridical traditions of my people and its aptitude for law. I only do so the better to prove to you that the mind of the Italian people is well fitted to accept this principle spontaneously and wholly. . . ."

MR. LÉON BOURGEOIS (France) speaks in French in these terms:

"I am deeply grateful to the President of the French Council of Ministers for having done me the distinguished honour of entrusting to me the task of speaking in the name of France. Recollections of the Conference of the Hague have probably led him to this choice; the honor therefore belongs to the very numerous colleagues present here with whom I collaborated in 1899 and 1907.

"President Wilson has just eloquently and finally said that we do not, that you, Gentlemen, do not represent governments alone, but peoples. What do the peoples wish to-day, and what, therefore, do the governments wish who are really free, really representative, really democratic, that is to say, those whose wishes are necessarily in agreement with those of their peoples? They wish that what we have seen during these four horrible years shall never be repeated in this world. Their wishes are the wishes of all the victims of this war, of all those who have breathed their last for liberty and for right. Those men fought not only to defend their country, but came together from all parts of the world for this crusade of which President Wilson so rightly spoke, and they know that they died not only for France, but for universal freedom and universal peace. For universal peace: the Premier of England has just described with striking eloquence the picture of ruin and desolation which he has seen. That ruin, that desolation we ourselves have witnessed, and you have seen them very far from the spot where hostilities began. For, in fact, henceforth no local conflict can be confined to some one part of the world; whatever may be the State where the difficulty arose, believe me, it is the whole world that is in danger. There is such an interdependence in all the relations between nations in the economic, financial, moral and intellectual spheres that, I repeat, every wound inflicted at some point threatens to poison the whole organs.

"There is another reason why it is impossible that humanity should again witness such spectacles. President Wilson has just alluded to the alarming progress of science, turned from its proper object, which is continually to give to mankind greater well-being, a surer moral, more hope for the future, and which was used for the most terrible and miserable of purposes—the purpose of destruction. Now science daily makes fresh progress and fresh conquest; daily it perfects its means of action and, in the light of what we have seen during these last five years in the way of terrible and destructive improvements in machinery and gunnery, think of the fresh destruction with which we might be threatened in a few years.

"We have, then, the right to face a problem of conscience which thrills us all, that is what we are to do to reconcile the special interests of our peoples, which we cannot forget, with those of our common country—all humanity. . . .

"I think that, even without any further statement, I have thus correctly interpreted the general feeling. It is enough for me to have shown with what deep enthusiasm France joins those who but lately proposed the creation of the League of Nations. President Wilson said that this question was at the very heart of mankind. That is true. He said we must constantly have an eye open on humanity, a watchful eye that never shuts. Well, I will end by recalling another memory of the Hague. It has been said that we heard there the first heart-beats of Humanity. Now it lives indeed, thanks to you. May it live for ever!"

MR. HUGHES (Australia) having asked whether it will be possible to discuss the scheme when it is complete, the President replies that the members of the Conference would be quite at liberty to do so.

The President calls successively on the Delegates of various Powers, who, speaking in French, support the draft resolution in these terms. . . .

Printed text (SDR, RG 256, 180.0201/2, DNA).

## To Edward Mandell House

[Paris, Jan. 25, 1919]

Herron said that an immediate assurance was necessary that we meant to see our whole programme through and the latter part of what I said was a response to his suggestion. Do you think it met the purpose?[1]                                    W.W.

ALI (E. M. House Papers, CtY).
[1] This and the following note exchanged during the plenary session.

## From Edward Mandell House

Dear Governor,                          [Paris, Jan. 25, 1919]
That is the very best speech you ever made.      E.M.H.

ALI (E. M. House Papers, CtY).

## Remarks to Working Women in Paris[1]

January 25, 1919.

Miss Thomson and ladies: You have not only done me a great honor, but you have touched me very much by this unexpected tribute. And may I add that you have frightened me? Because, realizing the great confidence you place in me, I am led to question my own ability to justify that confidence. You have not placed your confidence wrongly in my hopes and purposes, but perhaps not all of those hopes and purposes can be realized in the great matter that you have so much at heart, the right of women to take their full share in the political life of the nations to which they belong. That is necessarily a domestic question for the several nations. A conference of peace, settling the relations of nations with each other, would be regarded as going very much outside its province if it undertook to dictate to the several states what their internal policy should be.

At the same time, those considerations apply also to conditions of labor, and it does seem to be likely that the conference will take some action by way of expressing its sentiments, at any rate with regard to the international aspects at least of labor, and I should hope that some occasion might be offered for the case, not only of the women of France, but of their sisters all over the world, to be presented to the consideration of the conference. The conference is turning out to be a rather unwieldy body, a very large body, representing a great many nations, large and small, old and new, and the method of organizing its work successfully, I am afraid, will have to be worked out stage by stage. Therefore, I have no confident prediction to make as to the way in which it can take up questions of this sort.

But what I have most at heart today is to avail myself of this opportunity to express my admiration for the women of France, and my admiration for the women of all the nations that have been engaged in the war. By the fortunes of this war, the chief burden has fallen upon the women of France, and they have borne it with a spirit and a devotion which has commanded the admiration of the world. I do not think that the people of France fully realize, perhaps, the intensity of sympathy that other nations have felt for them. They think of us in America, for example, as a long way off, and we are in space, but we are not in thought. You must remember that the United States is made up of the nations of Europe; that French sympathies run straight across the seas, not merely by historic association but by blood connection; and that these nerves of sympathy are quick to transmit the impulses of the one nation to the other. We have followed your sufferings with a feeling that we were witnessing one of the most heroic and, may I add at the same time, satisfactory things in the world—satisfactory because it showed the strength of the human spirit, the indomitable power of women and men alike to sustain any burden if the cause was great enough. In an ordinary war there might have been some shrinking, some sinking of effort, but this was not an ordinary war. This was a war not only to redeem France from an enemy but to redeem the world from an enemy, and France, therefore, and the women of France strained their heart to sustain the world.

I hope that the strain has not been in vain. I know that it has not been in vain. This war has been peculiar and unlike other wars, in that it seemed sometimes as if the chief strain was behind the lines and not at the lines. It took so many men to conduct the war that the older men and the women at home had to carry the nation. Not only so, but the industries of the nation were almost as much part of the fighting as what actually took place at the fronts. So it is for that reason that I have said to those with whom I am at present associated that this must be a people's peace, because this was a people's war. The people won this war, not the governments, and the people must reap the benefits of the war. At every turn we must see to it that it is not an adjustment between governments merely, but an arrangement for the peace and security of men and women everywhere. The little, obscure sufferings and the daily unknown privations, the unspoken sufferings of the heart, are the tragical things of this war. They have been borne at home, and the center of the home is the woman. My heart goes out to you, therefore, ladies, in a very unusual degree, and I welcome this opportunity to bring you this message, not from myself merely, but from the great people whom I represent.

Printed in *Addresses of President Wilson on First Trip . . .*
  [1] For a description of this affair, see the extract from the diary of Edith Benham printed at Jan. 27, 1919.


## To William Shepherd Benson

My dear Admiral:                    Paris, 25 January, 1919.

I am ashamed not to have scrutinized the submarine proposal more carefully and you may be assured will consult with you hereafter when questions of this sort arise.[1] I am going to try, if it is not too late, to straighten the submarine matter out.

Cordially and sincerely yours,   [Woodrow Wilson]

CCL (WP, DLC).
  [1] Wilson was responding to W. S. Benson to WW [c. Jan. 24, 1919], ALS, enclosing W. S. Benson, memorandum, Jan. 24, 1919, TS MS, both in WP, DLC. Benson was concerned about Lloyd George's brief comment on the disposal of German submarines, for which see the final paragraph of the notes of the meeting of the Council of Ten held on January 21, 1919, 10:30 a.m. Benson believed that the United States could have no objection to the breakup and sale of surrendered German submarines in the possession of the Allies and the United States, provided that the breakup was complete and that no part of those submarines should enter into the construction, alteration, or repair of other submarines. If such use of the submarine parts was permitted, Benson pointed out, it would allow a great increase of the submarine flotillas of "Foreign Powers," and especially of Great Britain, at very little expense. Benson also believed that the United States should not participate in the distribution of the proceeds of the sale of the submarine parts, as Lloyd George had proposed. Benson said that not doing so would place the United States in a good position to oppose strongly any later proposal to distribute other German submarines and surface vessels among the victorious powers.


## To David Lloyd George

My dear Mr. Prime Minister:            Paris, 25 January, 1919.

The other day, when the proposal to break up the German submarines and sell the material out of which they were made came up, I had of course given no thought to the matter. I have been thinking it over since, and write to suggest the importance of the following:

First. Ought it not to be understood that the break-up must be complete and that no part of these submarines shall enter into the construction, alteration or repair of other submarines? Such use might easily be made not only of the parts but of the machinery, and at comparatively small expense some power might be able to construct a considerable submarine fleet.

Second. Ought it not also be more clearly defined what is meant by division of the proceeds of sale, and what disposition is contemplated of the eighty submarines which it is not proposed to break up?

I would be very much obliged to you for your views of these matters.

Cordially and sincerely yours,    [Woodrow Wilson]

CCL (WP, DLC).


## To Joseph Patrick Tumulty

Paris, 25 January, 1919.

Have tried both Trammell and Williams by cable with no results as far as I know and must admit that I am quite hopeless of Wolcott.

Allotment 150,000 dollars for Employees Compensation Commission has been approved.                Woodrow Wilson.

T telegram (WP, DLC).


## To Robert Lansing

My dear Mr. Secretary:              [Paris] 25 January, 1919.

I am sorry to send you this letter,[1] because it means that Nelson Page wishes to retire from his work after the Peace has been signed. And I do not like to answer the letter before letting you see it and getting from you any comments or suggestions you may care to make.    Cordially and faithfully yours,    [Woodrow Wilson]

CCL (WP, DLC).
[1] The Editors have been unable to find this letter.

## From John Joseph Pershing

My dear Mr. President:                    Paris, January 25, 1919.

In the note submitted by Marshal Foch to the Supreme War Council on January 24, the following appears: "According to the information given January 13th by General von Winterfeldt at Spa, and 15th of January by Mr. Erzberger at Treves, the German forces still include in the first two weeks of January the following organized large units:

37 Divisions on the Western Front."

I think that this statement might perhaps convey an erroneous impression.

The actual wording of the note presented at Spa on January 13th by General von Winterfeldt is as follows:

"In the West * * * On the 6th of January, 5 complete divisions— In addition 32 were on the march for home."

The latest information appears to make it certain that *all* German Divisions which formerly faced the Allies in the Region of the Rhine have now reached or started for their home stations.

Telegraphic information received from Coblenz to-day indicates that the German Authorities have ordered the demobilization of the class of 1898; one of the two German classes mentioned in Marshal Foch's note as being still under arms.

With great Respect   John J. Pershing.

TLS (WP, DLC).

## From Edward Price Bell

My dear Mr. President,                    [London] January 25, 1919.

Please accept my very great thanks for your cordial letter of January 20. It is intensely gratifying to me to know that I do not appear to have gone far wrong in my effort during the past two years to make yourself and our country somewhat better understood by the British people. As you know, we here have witnessed several disquieting phases of public opinion during the war: I acted only when it seemed clear that action by someone was urgently required.

Wishing you every success in the unspeakably grave and weighty tasks that confront you in Paris, I am,

Yours sincerely,   Edward Price Bell.

TLS (WP, DLC).

# From Herbert Clark Hoover

Dear Mr. President:                    Paris, 25 January 1919.

The Relief Bill having passed Congress, I desire to place for your approval the form of administration which I believe is necessary in order to comply with the law and with the American instinct in the matter.

First, I propose to set up a new organization, to be called the United States Relief Administration, and to transfer to this administration not only the $100,000,000 appropriation but also the accounting for the $5,000,000 which I have already received from your Presidential fund. I propose to establish offices for this Administration in Washington, New York, London, Paris, and the other capitals of Europe where we actually engage in work. I propose to enter into a contract between the Relief Administration and the United States Grain Corporation by which the Grain Corporation undertakes to deliver foodstuffs into various ports in Europe and to sell it at these ports to the Relief Administration.

The object of this latter matter is two-fold. First, the Grain Corporation has a large and skilled staff and working capital, out of which it can conduct these operations, thus making available the whole hundred million dollars for relief purposes and without necessary reserves of a large amount of money for working capital. Second, under the activities of the various Allied buying agencies there is a tendency to control the market in American foodstuffs abroad, and I have established agencies of the Grain Corporation in various countries in order to secure a market free from interference for our great food surpluses so that the Grain Corporation would not only be selling foodstuffs to the Relief Administration but would also be engaged in normal commercial transactions. The paralleling of the administrations to this point has the further advantage that a great deal of the feeding of Europe will be accomplished through normal commercial transaction which can be carried on by the Grain Corporation without trespassing on the capital and operations of the Relief Administration.

I also propose that the advances made by the United States Treasury to some of the minor governments in Europe under the old legislation, which advances are made primarily for the purchase of foodstuffs, such as the Belgians, Czecho-Slovacs, Roumanians, Servians, and so forth, should be handled by the new Relief Administration.

In the matter of personnel, I propose to appoint a commission, comprising some of the leading men of the Food Administration as the managers in the United States and I am endeavoring to secure

the services of Mr. Swager Shirley, not only to join this administrative body in the United States but also to join the Sugar Equal-
ization Board, the Belgian Relief and the Grain Corporation. The
activities of the Food Administration will quickly resolve themselves
into practically the administration of these four bodies and it is my
view that the Food Administration should be rapidly retired and all
of these organizations will naturally dissolve some time next July.

There is one matter in connection with this proposal upon which
we require some clarity of understanding. The Allies have proposed
to us that our hundred million dollar appropriation should be practically placed in the Treasury of the Allied Supreme Council of
Supply and Relief together with such moneys as they may contribute and the whole should be dealt with by this Council. I am
legally advised that it is doubtful whether we have any right to do
this and I feel strongly that from a moral and a business point of
view it would be a mistake; that we should pursue the policy that
we have insisted upon from the beginning, that we are prepared
and will co-ordinate our American activities in relief with the activities of the European Governments but that we cannot allow
them by majority to administer funds and supplies of the United
States.

Under the plan that I propose we will co-ordinate the programme
of foodstuffs required for any given country and the programme of
finance required for this food with the programmes of the Allies.
We will take our allotted share of these programmes and give execution to it through our own appointed officials.

If you approve of this general plan of organization and of my
appointment as Director General of the United States Relief Administration, I will have the necessary executive orders drawn to carry
the Act into practical operation upon the above lines.

Faithfully yours,   Herbert Hoover.

Approved Woodrow Wilson[1]

TLS (Hoover Archives, CSt-H).
 [1] WWhw.

## From Frederick Henry Lynch

My Dear Mr President:                    Paris Jany 25, 1919.
   Dr Frank Mason North, President of the Federal Council of the
Churches of Christ in America; President Henry Churchill King of
Oberlin College; Mr. Hamilton Holt and myself were deputed to
convey to you and through you to the Peace Conference a state-

ment, with resolutions, passed at the recent annual meeting of the Federal Council at Atlantic City, endorsing the League of Nations.[1] They are *strong* and they have behind them the whole Protestant body of America. They represent 33,000,000 people.

We are in Paris and if you could see us for a moment, we would of course highly appreciate the honor

Mr Holt and I heard your address at the Peace Conference this afternoon and we never were so proud before that we were Americans. We both feel that it ushered in a new era in the history of the world.

Yours Most Respectfully and Cordially   Frederick Lynch

ALS (WP, DLC).
[1] Frank Mason North *et al.* to the Peace Conference of the Allied and Associated Nations, Dec. 20, 1918, TLS (WP, DLC).


## Gilbert Fairchild Close to Robert Lansing

My dear Mr. Secretary:                Paris, 25 January, 1919.

The President asks if you will not be kind enough to send the following reply, if you approve it, to the enclosed telegram from the Prime Minister of the Government of Poland.[1]

"The Government of the United States takes pleasure in recognizing the new Government of Poland and will take every opportunity to render Poland any service which it is in its power to render."                Sincerely yours,   [Gilbert F. Close]

CCL (WP, DLC).
[1] I. J. Paderewski to RL, Jan. 21, 1919.


## From the Diary of Dr. Grayson

Sunday, January 26, 1919.

The President left Paris at 8:00 A.M., to visit Chateau Thierry, Belleau Woods and the devastated districts between there and Rheims. We left the Murat Palace in seven motor cars, headed by a French pilot car, while a special train was dispatched on the railroad to bring us back. The first stop was made on the highway overlooking Belleau Woods, where the Second Division held the line. The President and his party got out of the car and the positions during the battle were explained by Lieutenant Colonel Edward Watson,[1] who had commanded the battery of regular artillery that supported the Fifth and Sixth Regiments of Marines. The President

[1] Actually, Lt. Col. Edwin Martin Watson, military aide to President Wilson, 1915-1917; at this time again a military aide to Wilson in Paris.

climbed the hill and visited a trench which the Marines occupied before advancing on the Germans. To the right of the spot where the President stood, was the first graveyard of Americans that he had seen since arriving in France. The President uncovered his head as he gazed over the row of crosses with the identification discs marking the name of the dead Marines. We then proceeded by motor to Chateau Thierry and crossed the bridge to the railroad station. The bridge we passed had been blown up by the French retreating from Chateau Thierry killing many Germans, who were crossing at the time of the explosion. Entering the train, which was in waiting, the President and party had luncheon. It was now commencing to snow quite hard, giving promise of a nasty after-noon.

Luncheon consumed an hour, after which a start toward Rheims was made. The road wound through small villages, some of which had been completely, others partially, destroyed by either the German or American artillery. One singular feature, upon which most of the party commented, was the great tall chimneys of the factories, which, although the factories to which they belonged had been crushed into dust by the hammering of heavy guns, remained in their original state. Passing through one of the villages, a small boy tried to run across the road in front of one of the cars. Only the quick work of the chauffeur saved him from being killed. As it was, he was knocked down by the fender. We carried him into a house, where I examined him and found no injuries.

At Rheims, we visited the Hotel De Ville, where we were greeted by the Mayor[2] and Members of the City Government. The Mayor, who had remained in the City during the entire siege, expressed his deep thanks for the thoughtfulness of the party in visiting the ruined city. In reply, the President made a touching little address, paying tribute to the good work of the French Garrison, which by the way, was made up almost entirely of Colonials and to the manner in which they had held out against successive heavy assaults. A number of Red Cross workers, who had given aid and assistance to the inhabitants, were on hand to see the President. Following the speech-making, the Mayor produced some excellent refreshments. Leaving the Hotel De Ville, we went direct to the Cathedral. Here the Cardinal of Rheims[3] was waiting for us and a large crowd of sightseeing soldiers made it necessary literally to fight our way to get through and enter the Cathedral. The Cardinal personally escorted the party through the building, stopping at each point to show where the German shells had landed during the bombardment. He laid a special stress on the demolished windows.

[2] Dr. Jean Baptiste Nicolas Langlet, physician as well as Mayor of Rheims.
[3] Louis Henri Joseph Cardinal Luçon, Archbishop of Rheims.

After inspecting the Cathedral from the inside, we were escorted around the outside, so that we could see the effect of the German shells and also had pointed out where a shell had shifted the base of the statue of Joan of Arc almost five inches. The Cardinal assured the President that he had been in the town during the entire bombardment and that the tower of the Cathedral had never been used for military purposes. The President listened attentively to all the Cardinal said on this subject but made no comment. Leaving the Cathedral, we were driven up and down through the various streets, along past the municipal gas works and then to the Red Cross Canteen, where American women had been doing most excellent work in feeding and caring for the homeless inhabitants of the city. Their work was described to the President by Miss Porter,[4] an American woman in charge and an old friend and acquaintance of Mrs. Grayson. There was hardly a house that had not suffered somewhat from the bombardment, but many of them can be repaired. Explaining the systematic manner in which the Germans bombarded the town, it was stated that their plan was to shell it block by block daily. So methodical was their work, that it was stated to us that the inhabitants moved back each day as the bombardment progressed, until finally they were driven to the outskirts. After inspecting the City, we drove to the station, where the special train was in waiting. It was then snowing very hard. This was the first real snow we had seen this winter. Before the war, Rheims had a population of approximately 250,000, but today it had been reduced to less than 3,000 who burrowed in the cellars, in a vain effort to keep warm. We were told that stored in the cellars under the City, were over 70,000,000 bottles of champagne. Ten millions were taken by the soldiers, French and Germans. The German soldiers in the original invasion stole the wine and drank it, becoming drunk and thus their capture was facilitated. A Frenchman said to me that it was a good thing that the American and French soldiers had not arrived first or the same thing might have happened to them. A Frenchman told me that when the Germans went through Rheims in 1914, they paid for all the wine they drank, but when the French reoccupied the town, they drank much but paid for none. One reason may have been that Baron Mumm,[5] one of the

[4] She cannot be further identified.

[5] Baron Walter de Mumm (or Walther von Mumm), who was of German birth. Dr. Grayson was misinformed. Mumm left France at the beginning of the war to join the German cavalry and air force. (He fought on the Russian front, but "declined" to fight against the French.) His estate was, of course, forfeited. His American wife took their child back to the United States, where she died in 1920. Mumm came to New York after the war and rebuilt his fortune on the stock market. He committed suicide in 1931 after a series of financial disasters. *New York Times*, Dec. 27, 1921, and Oct. 22, 1931.

big champagne producers in this region, was arrested as a German spy at the beginning of the war. While it was claimed that his guilt was conclusive, he was confined, but had never been punished. I asked a Frenchman why this was and he said it was due to the combination of politics in France and to the great wealth of the accused. It was accepted that he, Mumm, probably would be released as soon as peace is declared. His property in France has been confiscated, but he is reported to have enormous resources elsewhere. We left Rheims for Paris by special train, at five o'clock, reaching Paris at 9:20; the President going direct to the Murat Palace. Enroute to Paris, when the President was asked for an expression of his feelings over what he had witnessed during the day, he said:

"No one can put into words the impressions received amid such scenes of desolation and ruin."

## Two Telegrams from Josephus Daniels

[Washington, Jan. 26, 1919]

Have had long talk with Senator Trammell and urged him to save the day for submitting of Suffrage Amendment. A cable at this time from you would have great weight.

Washington. January 26, 1919.

There is a division of opinion among our friends in the House on the Naval Three Year Program. Sherley, Oliver[1] and others feel inclined to oppose unless you earnestly desire its passage. They have view that you have succeeded in securing league of peace, and authorization of large new building is not now justified. Padget[t] can get favorable majority report from Committe[e]. Has anything occur[r]ed since you went to Europe that will justify change in your recommendation made to Congress in December? In view of big destroyer construction during the war, I have withdrawn recommendation for small craft.

Necessity for rushing work on Navy small craft and merchant vessels made it impossible for us to make much progress on dreadnoughts and cruisers authorized by last Congress. Work not begun on some of them, which fact causes some to say new program should be delayed until next Congress.

Unless conditions abroad change, my own view is that Three Year Program should be adopted with proviso that if Peace Mission orders reduction of armament, the President be authorized not to make contracts. Will you please cable your suggestion? If our friends in Congress are told that you feel this program will be helpful, there is no doubt of success. If it is purely a domestic policy looking toward a bigger American Navy now, there is strong sentiment to postpone authorization.

T telegrams (WP, DLC).
 ¹ William Bacon Oliver, Democratic congressman from Alabama.

## Robert Lansing to Frank Lyon Polk

Paris, January 26, 1919.

454 Department's 366, January 22, 7 p.m. CONFIDENTIAL FOR POLK:

The President asks that you ascertain whether this suggestion has the approval of the Attorney General and the Secretary of the Navy.                                    Lansing

TS telegram (SDR, RG 59, 811.001/127, DNA).

## From the Diary of Dr. Grayson

Monday, January 27, 1919.

The President again attended the conference of the Council of Ten in the morning and afternoon. He worked in his study all the evening. Most of his work today was devoted to the perfection of the terms upon which the armistice is to be renewed and he had the able assistance of General Bliss in combatting execessive French claims.

## Remarks to French Protestants¹

[Jan. 27, 1919]

Gentlemen: I thank you for your visit; you have spoken words which have deeply touched me. I am moved and overcome by the confidence shown in me for the work of reconstruction which is the task of humanity. I do not hide from myself its difficulties, for the road leading to the goal is ⟨strewn⟩ *beset*² with old difficulties and ⟨much greed⟩ *new desires*.

Happily I believe in God's providence. Simple human intelligence is incapable of taking in all the immense problems before it at one time throughout the whole world. At such a juncture if I did not believe in God I should ⟨lose my head.⟩ *feel utterly at a loss.*

⟨True, i⟩ *It* is impossible for me to prophesy what will be the precise success of our efforts; but I have the personal conviction that the final result will be good. Under these difficult circumstances, when complex questions crowd upon us, the surest [way] is always to apply without hesitation first Principles in their purity.

Gentlemen, I thank you. You have comforted me. Count upon me to bring to the defense of our common ideal all the perseverance of the spirit of the Puritans.

T MS (WP, DLC).

¹ A delegation from the Federation of Protestant Churches of France. The Rev. Wilfred Monod, pastor of the Reformed Church at the Oratoire du Louvre and professor of the Faculty of Protestant Theology in Paris, and Cornélis Henri Wilhelm de Witt, of the Protestant Committee to Aid the Invaded Regions, gave brief addresses. English translations of their remarks are in the enclosure (Hw MS) with W. Monod to WW, Jan. 28, 1919, and in C. H. W. de Witt to WW, Jan. 27, 1919, both ALS (WP, DLC).

² Words in angle brackets deleted by Wilson; those in italics added by him.

# Hankey's Notes of Two Meetings of the Council of Ten¹

Quai d'Orsay, January 27, 1919, 10:30 A.M.

BC-11

[The council agreed to Clemenceau's suggestion that Jules Cambon be chairman of a meeting of the small powers that afternoon to elect their delegates to the commissions.

[Clemenceau said that so far he had received only two formal protests against the arrangements made for the conference, from Belgium and Portugal, and the council agreed that he should delay his reply for some days.

[The council agreed to accept Klotz's proposal that the word "guarantees" be included in the terms of reference of the Commission on Reparation, so as to read, as amended:]

That a Commission be appointed with not more than three representatives apiece from each of the five Great Powers, and not more than two representatives apiece from Belgium, Greece, Poland, Roumania and Serbia, to examine and report, first on the amount for reparation which the enemy countries ought to pay, secondly on what they are capable of paying, thirdly on the method, form and time in which payment should be made, and fourthly on the guarantees that should be obtained for payment.

[Clemenceau said that Klotz also proposed that there be a financial section of the League of Nations. The council approved Wilson's suggestion to refer this proposal to the Drafting Committee on Financial Questions. The names of four members of this committee

¹ The complete text of these notes is printed in *PPC*, III, 729-37.

were announced, and the American nominee would be appointed shortly.]

6. M. CLEMENCEAU said that he proposed to nominate a similar Commission to deal with Economic Questions. This Commission should frame in appropriate language questions arising under the following suggested headings:

Revictualling.

Raw Materials.

Industrial Re-constitution.

Privileges that should be granted to the devastated regions for their revictualling in raw materials and for the sale of their manufactured products. (President Wilson's suggestion.)

Customs Regulations.

PRESIDENT WILSON said that he thought a distinction should be maintained between the questions of immediate moment to the Allied and Associated Powers and those which should form a part of the peace settlement proper. Certain questions related merely to co-operation between ourselves; others required consideration from the point of view of conferring with the enemy and with neutral Powers. These two categories should not be confused.

M. PICHON suggested that the Committee might be charged with the task of discriminating between those two classes of problems.

PRESIDENT WILSON gave, as an illustration of his meaning, the revictualling and re-starting of industries in devastated regions. This would call for co-operation between the Allied and Associated Powers in respect to shipping, priority of supply, etc. This question was one strictly confined to the Allies and not one connected with making peace with the enemy.

MR. BALFOUR observed that the question of preferential dealing in the matter of raw material appeared to involve both kinds of interest. The re-constitution of Belgian and French manufacturing industries was hard to separate from the re-construction of German industries. Germany could not pay for the re-building of the former unless herself assisted to re-start manufacturing. Priority of supplies, therefore, had a direct bearing on the Peace Treaty as well as on the arrangements to be made between the Allies.

PRESIDENT WILSON pointed out that it was quite true that Germany could not make reparation unless she had the means therefor. Unless German industries were reconstituted, it was clear that Germany could not pay. The means of obtaining reparation from Germany was obviously a question to be considered by the Commission on Reparation. He could see ahead certain difficulties in connection with this matter. If he were to carry back to America a treaty in which economic arrangements with America's friends were included in the settlement made with her enemies, the Senate might raise objections. Congress was jealous of being forestalled in commitments on economic matters. He could see no objection to the proposal under consideration provided it were not tied up with other matters in which the constraint of making peace was involved.

MR. LLOYD GEORGE said that he also anticipated considerable difficulty in dealing with matters of this sort. Much of the raw material that would be required by Germany could only be found in the British Empire. France also, by the acquisition of Alsace-Lorraine would dispose of more raw material than she did before. This would be still more the case were she to acquire the Saar Valley. Germany, therefore, could not start her industrial life again save at the good pleasure of the Allies. There would be in England parliamentary difficulties similar to those alluded to by President Wilson in the United States. It was clear that Germany would be entitled to ask what her economic future was going to be. It would be very difficult to obtain her consent to a Peace Treaty which took from her all her colonies and left the victorious Powers in exclusive possession of a number of raw materials which she required. Unless we were prepared beforehand, we should be met by a series of questions on these subjects to confront our territorial demands and we might be at a loss to answer them. He felt that we ought to be prepared to meet this situation, and, therefore, supported the proposal that a Committee be set up to investigate these questions without, in any way, committing the Allied Powers.

PRESIDENT WILSON asked whether the questions enumerated above by M. Clemenceau were the only questions the Committee was to deal with.

M. CLEMENCEAU replied that other questions might be added if occasion arose.

M. ORLANDO stipulated that the Committee should only be asked to frame the questions and not to offer solutions.

PRESIDENT WILSON remarked that every time a report was received on any question, territorial or otherwise, problems of this nature were bound to arise. The Committee, therefore, would be dealing with conjectures. It could not know exactly what questions would arise. It might be preferable to deal with them only as they came up for solution in conjunction with other problems.

MR. LLOYD GEORGE remarked that the investigations of the Committee might influence the judgment of the Council on territorial questions.

MR. BALFOUR wished it to be recorded that the Committee should be entitled to add questions not included in the list given above.

(It was, therefore, agreed that each of the five Powers should nominate one member to form a Committee to investigate and to formulate economic questions having a direct bearing on the peace negotiations, and requiring solution by the Allied and Associated Powers before conferring with the enemy.)

7. M. CLEMENCEAU proposed that a Commission should be established to consider the following subjects:

Reestablishment of the conventional regime of the treaties.

Settlement of private claims.

Enemy ships seized at the beginning of the War in Allied Ports (Hague Convention 1907).

Goods on enemy ships that have taken shelter and remained in neutral ports.

Restoration of illegal prizes.

Goods which have been stopped without being captured. (O.C. March 11th, 1915.)[2]

MR. LLOYD GEORGE was of the opinion that a very big issue was raised by this proposal, but he did not think that all these questions could be settled in the Peace Treaty with the enemy. The whole subject appeared to him to be more suitable for the League of Nations. These matters, moreover, could be discussed in a more favourable atmosphere in the League of Nations than in debate with Germany. It would be far more difficult for himself to make concessions in dealing with the enemy than in treating on behalf of Great Britain with the League of Nations.

M. SONNINO agreed with Mr. Lloyd George that four-fifths of these subjects would be better dealt with by the League of Nations. They referred not so much to the consequences of this war, as to the future conditions of the world. There were, however, among the subjects proposed, some such as the disposal of enemy ships and the restoration of illegal prizes, which were strictly suitable for inclusion in the Peace Treaty with the enemy.

M. CLEMENCEAU agreed on this point with Baron Sonnino.

PRESIDENT WILSON also expressed the view that the cases cited were matters for immediate disposal, but felt with Mr. Lloyd George that questions of principle should be referred to the League of Nations.

M. CLEMENCEAU proposed that the list should be divided into two.

PRESIDENT WILSON suggested that the special cases alluded to in the list should be referred to the Commission on Reparation,

---

[2] That is, the British Order in Council of that date, about which see WW to WJB, March 19, 1915, n. 1, Vol. 32.

while the question of general principles should be reserved for the League of Nations.

(This proposal was adopted).

8. M. CLEMENCEAU said that he had received a despatch from M. Bratiano, who wished it to be laid down that Bessarabia was not to send delegates to Prinkipo.

M. PICHON explained that according to M. Bratiano, Poland and Finland had been expressly excepted, whereas Bessarabia had not been mentioned. Bessarabia had willingly joined Roumania, and should therefore not be affected by the invitation to the various Governments of Russia.

M. PICHON was of opinion that it should be left to the Bessarabians themselves to decide whether or not they wished to go to Prinkipo. He himself felt convinced that they would not go.

(It was decided that no reply was immediately necessary, and that the question should stand over until the question of the meeting at Prinkipo came up for discussion.)

9. MR. BALFOUR said that he wished to raise a point which he thought had been settled, but of which he could find no record in the Minutes. He wished to know whether those elements of Old Russia which, we hoped, would succeed in forming se[parate states?], such as Esthonia, Georgia, possibly Russian Armenia and Daghestan, were invited to the meeting on Prince's Island.

(It was decided (See I.C. 116 (1)),[3] that all such elements, unless expressly excluded, were invited to attend.)

10. MR. BALFOUR said that the British Government had been asked by the French Government to recognize Finland. The British Government hitherto had been friendly to Finland, but had stopped short of official recognition. At the present moment the Finns were behaving well, and he was inclined to agree. But as recognition of the Finnish Government would add one or possibly two delegates to the Peace Conference, he felt that the matter was not one which could be settled simply between the French and British Foreign Offices.

M. PICHON agreed that it was necessary to consult the Conference, but he had made the communication in question to the British Government, because both France and Great Britain had been concerned in dealings with General Mannerheim;[4] he also pointed out

[3] That is, BC-7+, Jan. 22, 1919, 3:15 p.m.

[4] Carl Gustav Emil, Baron Mannerheim, scion of an aristocratic Swedish-Finnish family, served as a general in the Russian army until the Bolshevik revolution and returned to Finland just as that former Russian grand duchy declared its independence in December 1917. When civil war broke out in Finland in 1918 between Bolshevik and anti-Bolshevik elements, Mannerheim organized the White army and led it to victory over the Reds. The Finnish Diet had elected him Regent of Finland in December 1918.

that Finland figures not as a belligerent in the Conference, but as a neutral.

MR. LLOYD GEORGE said he saw no objection to recognizing Finland. Even Mr. Sazonoff did not propose its incorporation in Russia. Poland had been recognized, and Finland had far clearer boundaries than Poland.

M. PICHON said that France was all the more disposed to agree, as she had previously recognized Finland, and had only withdrawn her recognition when the Finns had displayed obvious pro-German leanings. This had now been amended.

BARON SONNINO thought that the Finnish question was too closely bound up with the Russian question as a whole to be prejudged at the present time. Any decision concerning the frontiers of Finland might be regarded as a settlement hostile to Russia, if made without hearing the Russians.

Finland was pro-Ally now, but a short time ago she had chosen for herself a German Prince. These alternations of conduct seemed to recommend caution and delay on the part of the Powers.

M. PICHON said that there was one advantage in avoiding delay, which was that General Mannerheim's Government might be overthrown if it failed to obtain recognition. He would, however, ask that, if a decision were not taken there and then, it should not be too long delayed.

PRESIDENT WILSON said that he agreed with Baron Sonnino.

M. SONNINO proposed that the Finnish question should be taken up again when the question of the meeting on Prince's Island came up for discussion.

M. PICHON pointed out that the Powers had given a mark of confidence to the Finns by excluding them from the invitation.

(It was, therefore, decided that the question of recognizing Finland should be taken up in connection with the general problem of Russia.)

11. (It was decided that the instructions drafted by M. Pichon for the Commission to proceed to Poland should be discussed on the following day.)

12. MR. BALFOUR said that he wished to draw attention to a matter which was rather of form than of substance. On the previous Friday the representatives of the British Dominions had been here. No discussions had followed on the statements they had made. Their position might appear somewhat ambiguous. According to the regulations, smaller belligerent powers with particular interests were entitled to participate in the Conference, while matters concerning them were discussed. It had originally been intended to deal with Colonial questions at this meeting, but other urgent matters came

up for discussion. He would therefore suggest that in all such cases the meeting should be devoted primarily to the discussion of matters in which representatives of the Smaller States were interested, and at which they should be present throughout. At such meetings no other questions should be given precedence.

PRESIDENT WILSON expressed the opinion that this proposal was fair, but he would like to ask that the representatives of powers with special interests be required by the Chairman to confine their attention to the subject for which their attendance had been requested.

(The Chairman undertook to do this.)

13. PRESIDENT WILSON, referring to the discussion on the previous Friday (I.C. 120),[5] asked whether it was wise to deal with the Pacific piecemeal. He asked whether the Japanese case should not be heard before any partial decision was taken. If ready, he suggested that it should be heard first.

M. CLEMENCEAU agreed.

MR. LLOYD GEORGE suggested that, as Australia and New Zealand held views on these subjects which in some respects might not be the views of the British Government, these Dominions be present at the statement of the Japanese case.

M. CLEMENCEAU said, that as the Dominions had been heard it appeared to him reasonable to hear Japan and then, after the statement had been heard, to open the discussion with the representatives of the Dominions in the room.

MR. LLOYD GEORGE pointed out that Japan had been represented when Australia and New Zealand had been heard.

M. CLEMENCEAU pointed out that Japan had a seat among the five Powers.

MR. LLOYD GEORGE was of the opinion that Chinese as well as Australian and New Zealand Delegates should be present at the Japanese statement.

14. MR. BALFOUR thought that if his Japanese colleagues would agree, the case of the Japanese acquisitions in this war would fall into two categories—first, the Pacific Islands, second, those parts of China conquered from the Germans. In the first Australia and New Zealand were concerned. In the latter they were not at all concerned. He hoped, therefore, that the two cases would be dealt with separately.

BARON MAKINO said that he had no objection to the presence of the Dominion representatives, but he had prepared a statement including both Kiaochow and the Pacific Islands, as the capture of

---

[5] That is, BC-10, Jan. 24, 1919, 3 p.m.

both had been the result of one campaign. He would therefore not be able, in his statement, to follow the distinction laid down by Mr. Balfour. He again stated that he had no objection to the presence of any interested Power.

MR. BALFOUR thought that great difficulties would be encountered if the discussion on China and the Pacific Islands was treated as one.

PRESIDENT WILSON suggested that even if the case for both were presented at one time and in one document the discussion might afterwards be held separately on each question.

BARON MAKINO asked whether the question would be discussed at once after his presentation of the Japanese case, or whether all statements of Colonial claims would be awaited.

M. CLEMENCEAU said that France had no claim to advance in the Pacific. He was therefore prepared to deal with this question first in isolation.

MR. LLOYD GEORGE pointed out that South Africa had raised a question which had no connection with the Pacific, namely, that of German South West Africa. Were we going to discuss the whole question of the Colonies or only some portion?

PRESIDENT WILSON pointed out that the case as a whole interested many Powers. The effect of dealing with each portion of the subject in the presence of the Powers specially interested in it would be kaleidoscopic. There would be a number of partial discussions followed by a general discussion with all parties previously heard present. This would be both a lengthy and unwieldy procedure.

MR. BALFOUR said that underlying the whole discussion was the question of the mandatory principle. He asked when this was to be discussed.

PRESIDENT WILSON then suggested that the question of the Pacific should first be taken up and a decision reached as to whether the mandatory principle should, or should not, apply in that area. The discussion might then move to another quarter and investigate whether or not the principle was applicable there. This would avoid very large conferences and very long discussions. He therefore proposed that the Japanese case should be heard in the presence of the Chinese delegates and that after the statement, that part of the case concerning the Pacific should be discussed in the presence of the Dominion delegates. At a later meeting the other portion might be taken up in the presence of the Chinese delegates.

BARON MAKINO said that the mandatory system mentioned by Mr. Balfour was not the only principle underlying the Colonial question. There were others. He therefore urged that the discussions to be undertaken should, for the time being, only have a provisional character.

BARON MAKINO said that he had another point to make. The presentation of the Japanese case concerning Kiaochow would be made with reference to Germany only. Japanese relations with China on these questions were on a different footing. The claim he would put forward was addressed to Germany alone, not to China. He did not wish to discuss in the presence of the Chinese delegates Japanese relations with Germany.

PRESIDENT WILSON said that he did not understand Baron Makino to contend that the disposition of Kiaochow did not affect China.

BARON MAKINO said that he was not very well versed in the procedure of the Conference. He asked whether he was to conclude that third Powers interested were to join in the discussion.

(It was pointed out by the Chairman that this had been so decided in the regulations.)

(It was therefore decided that the Japanese statement should be heard both by the Chinese and the Dominions delegates:

and

That in the discussion to follow, the Dominions delegates should participate with regard to the Pacific Islands, and the Chinese delegates with regard to Kiaochow.)

T MS (SDR, RG 256, 180.03101/18, DNA).

Quai d'Orsay, January 27, 1919, 3 P.M.[1]

BC-12

M. CLEMENCEAU having declared the meeting opened, said that he would call on the Japanese representative, Baron Makino, to put forward the views of the Japanese Government on the question of the Pacific, with special reference to the German Pacific Islands. It has been decided to take into consideration the question of Kiaochow at a subsequent meeting.

BARON MAKINO then read the following statements:

"The Japanese Government feels justified in claiming from the German Government the unconditional cession of:

(a) The leased territory of Kiaochow together with the railways, and other rights possessed by Germany in respect of Shantung province.

(b) All of the Islands in German possession in the Pacific Ocean

---

[1] The complete text of these notes is printed in PPC, III, 738-48.

North of the Equator together with the rights and properties in connection therewith.

At the outbreak of the war, the German military and naval base at Kiaochow constituted a serious menace to the international trade and shipping, jeopardising the peace in the Extreme Orient. The Japanese Government in consultation with the British Government conformably with the agreement of 1911,[2] gave notice to the German Government to surrender the leased territory of Kiaochow with a view to its restoration to China. The German Government failing to make reply within the specified time limit, no other course was left to Japan but to proceed to reduce the German base by recourse to arms. The Japanese forces have, in conjunction with the British contingents, succeeded in taking the leased territory as well as the railway line connecting Tsingtao with Chinanfu, which the Germans used for military purposes. Japan has since continued in possession of the rights then enjoyed by Germany. By the reduction of the German stronghold, the base of her military as well as political offensive in the Extreme Orient has been completely destroyed, thereby re-establishing the uninterrupted course of trade, commerce, and communication in these regions.

Now that the primary object for which Japan entered the war and which was clearly set forth in her Declaration of war against Germany, has been successfully achieved, Japan cannot view with equanimity anything that may tend to revive German activities in the Far East to the undoing of all that has been achieved at no small sacrifice, and is compelled to advance the claims under item A.

Subsequently to the fall of Kiaochow it became a matter of urgent necessity to clear the Indian and Pacific Oceans, including the Australian routes, of the enemy ships and to keep these waters free and secure from enemy raids; and for carrying out this object, the Japanese navy extended its sphere of activities in co-ordination with those of the British navy. The enemy ships had been planning to escape from the superior Japanese and British naval forces, and the Japanese squadron, upon arrival at Ponape, of the East Carolina group, found that they had just left. From the objects and materials left behind, it was abundantly clear that a full preparation for further raids was being made, using the harbour as their naval base. The circumstances demanded that the German South Sea Islands should forthwith be taken possession of in order to defeat the enemy's object, and the German possessions North of the Equator have

---

[2] "Agreement between Great Britain and Japan, revising the Agreement of 1905, for the Maintenance of Peace, Interests, and Territorial Rights in China, Eastern Asia, and India. Signed at London, July 13, 1911." Printed in Great Britain, Foreign Office, *British and Foreign State Papers. 1911*, CIV (London, 1915), 173-74.

since remained under Japanese occupation and control. The inhabitants of these Islands are being given employment so as to ensure livelihood for them, besides being provided with schools for their instructions, and they are fully contented under the present Regime. The total area of these Islands is about two thousand five hundred square kilometres with the population of some fifty thousand in all, composed of many different tribes. These tribes have each its own peculiar language, unable to understand one another without resorting to the medium of interpretation; and being on the whole still in a primitive state, they are not in a position to organize themselves politically, economically, or socially, in the modern sense. Japan being in actual possession and having regard to the circumstances which led to such occupation and to the present conditions above alluded to, and further, in view of the public opinion of Japan which is unanimous in this connection, she claims the definite possession of these Islands where she may continue to protect the inhabitants and to endeavour to better their conditions.

In conclusion, it may be stated that, in view of the extent of their efforts and achievements in destroying German bases in the Extreme Orient and the South Seas, and in safeguarding the important routes on the Pacific and Indian Oceans and the Mediterranean waters, to say nothing of their contribution in other respects, the Japanese Government feels confident that the claims above advanced would be regarded as only just and fair."

BARON MAKINO added that a documentary statement setting forth the Japanese claims in full would be handed in by him at a later date.

DR. C. THOMAS WANG[3] said that the question was of such vital interest to China that he hoped the Great Powers would reserve decision until the views of China had been heard.

(This was agreed to)

PRESIDENT WILSON said that in order that the field of discussion should be defined as clearly as possible perhaps it would be better to begin with a clear statement of what was the mind of those who proposed a trusteeship by the League of Nations through the appointment of mandatories. The basis of this idea was the feeling which had sprung up all over the world against further annexation. Yet, if the Colonies were not to be returned to Germany (as all were agreed), some other basis must be found to develop them and to take care of the inhabitants of these backward territories. It was with this object that the idea of administration through mandatories acting on behalf of the League of Nations arose. This idea would

[3] Wang Cheng-t'ing, usually known in the West as C. T. Wang, a plenipotentiary delegate of China to the peace conference.

be most distinctly illustrated by an example. The case of South West Africa would be found a most favourable instance to make a clear picture. South West Africa had very few inhabitants, and those had been so maltreated, and their numbers had been so reduced under German administration, that the whole area was open to development that could not yet be determined. Therefore, either it must be attached to its nearest neighbour and so establish what would seem a natural union with South Africa, or some institution must be found to carry out the ideas all had in mind, namely, the development of the country for the benefit of those already in it, and for the advantage of those who would live there later.

This he assumed to be the principle: it was not intended to exploit any people; it was not intended to exercise arbitrary sovereignty over any people.

The purpose was to serve the people in undeveloped parts, to safeguard them against abuses such as had occurred under German administration and such as might be found under other administrations. Further, where people and territories were undeveloped, to assure their development so that, when the time came, their own interests, as they saw them might qualify them to express a wish as to their ultimate relations—perhaps lead them to desire their union with the mandatory power.

Should the Union of South Africa be the mandatory of the League of Nations for South West Africa, the mandate would operate as follows: In the first place, the League of Nations would lay down certain general principles in the mandate, namely, that districts be administered primarily with a view to the betterment of the conditions of the inhabitants. Secondly, that there should be no discrimination against the members of the League of Nations, so as to restrict economic access to the resources of the district. With this limitation, the Union of South Africa would extend such of its laws as were applicable to South West Africa and administer it as an annex to the Union so far as consistent with the interest of the inhabitants. The expense of its administration would be met by fiscal arrangements, which, if they involved customs duties, would be the same for all nations trading with South West Africa; all countries would pay the same duties, all would have the same right of access.

MR. LLOYD GEORGE stated that South Africa under present arrangements gave a preference to Great Britain of 3 per cent. He enquired whether that preference would extend to South West Africa under the scheme proposed by President Wilson.

PRESIDENT WILSON replied in the negative. Preference, as far as South-West Africa was concerned, would be excluded under the

The opening of the Paris Peace Conference. Paul Mantoux, interpreter, is translating President Poincaré's address of welcome. Wilson is sitting to Mantoux's right, reading

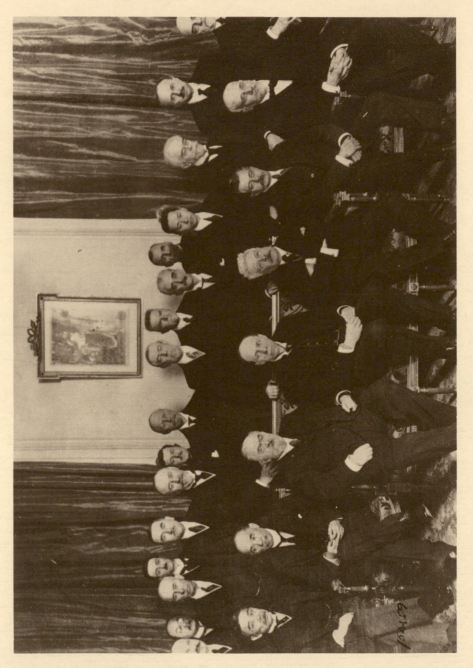

The League of Nations Commission

The American Commission to Negotiate Peace

Georges Clemenceau

David Lloyd George

Eleuthérios Vénisélos

Vittorio Emanuele Orlando

Lord Robert Cecil

Arthur James Balfour

Emir Faisal with Thomas Edward Lawrence (second from right) and retinue

Wilson leaving the American Church in Paris

Edith Benham and stenographers: Chief Yeoman Nicholas P. Schindler and Yeoman 1st Class Francis A. Kennedy

circumstances, but, with the elimination of that exception, there would be no administrative difference between his scheme and annexation.

It was in the mind of many people that the mandatory power might be subject to constant irritation and constant interference by the League of Nations. In his opinion, that would not be so, as long as the mandatory performed his duties satisfactorily. In so far as the administration by the mandatory power became a financial burden, it was clearly proper that the League of Nations should bear a proportion of the expense. The fundamental idea would be that the world was acting as trustee through a mandatory, and would be in charge of the whole administration until the day when the true wishes of the inhabitants could be ascertained. It was up to the Union of South Africa to make it so attractive that South West Africa would come into the Union of their own free will. Should that not be the case, the fault would lie with the mandatory.

He would ask: Was this merely camouflage: a means of bringing about the willingness of the people to be united with the Union, to which the Great Powers were not now willing to consent? He would answer, No, as under the Mandatory the administration would be so much in the view of the world that unfair processes could not be successfully attempted. If successful administration by a mandatory should lead to union with the mandatory, he would be the last to object. Therefore, the only difficulty which might arise would be that associated with the dangers of aggression. In this connection he was reminded of a story he had recently heard: In the United States a man bought an inordinate amount of real estate. When asked by a friend when this process would stop, he replied that he would never be satisfied so long as anyone owned any land adjoining his own.

With all respect, it seemed to him that this was the difficulty in the mind of the representative of Australia. If the present conditions in regard to annexation were permanently to continue, he would himself feel inclined to agree with the representative of Australia. But this position was based on a fundamental lack of faith in the League of Nations.

If any nation could annex territory which was previously a German Colony, it would be challenging the whole idea of the League of Nations. Under the League of Nations they were seeking to lay down a law which would rally the whole world against an outlaw, as it had rallied against Germany during the last war. Should a nation attempt to take from a mandatory the country entrusted to it, such nation would become an outlaw. When any nation became an outlaw, all nations should rise up against it, and treat it as such.

If they had any confidence in the League of Nations there was not the slightest danger that anyone else except the mandatory power could take possession of any colony entrusted to it, such as New Guinea, because all the other nations would be pledged, with the United States in the lead, to take up arms for the mandatory.

Therefore, all danger of bad neighbours was past, and the only question remaining was whether administration by a mandatory would not be as useful as direct Australian administration. If the League of Nations did not prove adequate to its task, general chaos and confusion would arise in all parts of the world. Therefore, the League of Nations must succeed, and if all the delegates in this room decided that it must succeed, it would succeed.

As regards who should be the mandatory in New Guinea, his mind was absolutely open. It was perhaps so near to Australia that no other alternative was possible. This reminded him of a story he had read in regard to the annexation of Mexico by the United States of America. Someone had asked whether America would annex that country. The reply was that the country was so contagious that America might be forced to take it whether it wanted to do so or not. Now, New Guinea might be so contagious that Australia would be obliged to take it whether it desired to do so or not. But this was in the lap of the gods.

If the process of annexation went on, the League of Nations would be discredited from the beginning. Many false rumours had been set about regarding the Peace Conference. Those who were hostile to it said that its purpose was merely to divide up the spoils. If they justified that statement in any degree, that would discredit the Conference. The attitude of the people on this point had been quite clearly expressed. Therefore he would say, "Let us have a frank interchange of views on this question," and he would put two questions:

Assuming the League of Nations existed (and it was born on Saturday), was it necessary, from the point of view of protection to have annexation? If not, what was there in the principle of a mandatory that would make its adoption objectionable?

GENERAL BOTHA said that he did not wish to go over the ground which had been traversed by his colleagues last week. German South West Africa, as everybody knew, was part and parcel of South Africa. It was a piece of land cut out of the Union. The Eastern and Southern frontiers of German South West Africa were merely lines drawn on a map. The only good port on the West Coast was Walfish Bay, which belonged to the Union of South Africa. Walfish Bay had always been under the administration of the Union of South Africa. German South West Africa was a desert. It had been occupied by Germany for 30 or 40 years; but it had never been used for colonising purposes. There were no white people, with the exception of a few pensioned soldiers, who had been given grants of land as an inducement to remain. The only real settlements consisted of immigrants from the Union of South Africa. But these settlers were extremely few in numbers on account of the disabilities to which they had been subjected by the Germans. The Germans used the country only as a military station. The natives were utterly miserable; they were merely slaves of the Germans. On the other hand, these people must be given protection because the country was still full of wild bushmen, and for this purpose a big force would have to be maintained. The country had been very peaceful since its occupation by the Union of South Africa, and the people were quite happy. As already stated, the Germans never had any idea of settling the country. It was merely used as a military station. A large wireless station had been set up in direct communication with Berlin and it was also connected with other wireless installations 50 miles to the North. At present, under its constitution, the Union of South Africa enjoyed certain free rights. If a mandatory were now appointed to administer German South-West Africa, the trade relations of that territory with the Union would necessarily undergo a great change, and the Union would be compelled to protect itself economically, and to place customs houses round the frontiers. That naturally implied a large expenditure.

The Union of South Africa had suffered greatly from animal diseases, which invariably came from the North. Nothing was being done in the North of Africa to stop these diseases, and the South was compelled to take the necessary measures. If a mandatory were placed there, and if it did not spend money to stop these diseases, the Union would be obliged to do so. In his opinion, there was therefore only one solution, namely, complete union between the two territories.

The few German colonies still remaining in German South-West Africa had recently passed a resolution proclaiming a republic. Should a mandatory be appointed, would it be obliged to respect that decision? This demand for a republic had been merely put forward in order to favour the Germans, and, should it be granted, the Union would be the only sufferers. The League of Nations was a long way off, and could not possibly know the true requirements of the country. Had there been a large population in German South-West Africa, he would have concurred in President Wilson's proposal. He would ask that the point of view of the Union should not be lost sight of. For the sake of peace, in order to satisfy the peoples of South Africa, German South-West Africa must be incorporated in the Union. Should this not be done, then there would be constant agitation. The small German population would continue to foment trouble in order to get back to Germany, and those troubles might extend to the Union. It must be recollected that in South Africa there had been two republics (Transvaal and Orange Free State) and two British Colonies (The Cape and Natal). In the past there had been a great struggle between the two. It was no use to talk about the past, but the struggle still existed, and the danger of an uncertain frontier might re-open the sore. The Union consisted of two peoples—the English and the Dutch. He had spent his life in an endeavour to get those two races to understand each other. It was necessary that they should co-operate for their own good and for their own future and, unless their requirements were fully understood, grave trouble might at any moment arise.

He himself was a great enthusiast for the League of Nations, and realized that all must be ready to make great sacrifices to attain that high ideal. But they must not be too hasty in settling these questions, lest the burden prove to be too heavy in the beginning. Therefore, they should settle each case on its merits, and let the League of Nations start with a clean sheet.

SIR ROBERT BORDEN enquired whether both races—the Dutch and British—in South Africa were agreed on this question.

GENERAL BOTHA replied in the affirmative.

MR. HUGHES said he would, in the first place, direct himself to the general principle of mandatories before applying the principle to Australia. The mandatory principle, although generally applied to the management of estates and private affairs, but [had] never been applied to countries. He would, to begin with, ask the question: Was the mandatory principle *per se* desirable? If contrasted with the direct control, which every country exercised over its own territories, the answer must be in the negative. Consequently, the mandatory principle was merely a compromise suggested by the circumstances in which the Allies now found themselves. It was not suggested that either the United States of America or Great Britain, or France should be governed through a Mandatory State. It was only suggested that the mandatory system should be applied to the territories previously under German Dominion. He was not personally, in principle, opposed to the idea of a mandatory, but he thought it would be necessary to prove the necessity for making use of this machinery in each case separately. If it were asked what was the best form of Government: clearly the most direct form would be the best, and the most indirect form the worst. Therefore, as a general principle, the mandatory system would have to give way, and direct Government would be given the preference. This being the case, he would ask: Why have a mandatory? The President replied: Because the world was against annexations. To that, he would reply: Was it proposed then, to adopt that principle to all questions to be dealt with by the Peace Conference? Was it proposed to appoint mandatories to the New States to be created in Europe? It was proposed to take away the Pacific Islands from Germany because she had not governed them well. But why should the mandatory principle be applied to any of the territories taken by the Dominions? It was for those who wished to apply the principle to prove their case. They all desired to do what was right; but what advantage was to be gained by the appointment of a mandatory for New Guinea in preference to handing it over to Australia? Geographically, and by virtue of its action during the war, Australia had a just claim. President Wilson had said that Australia should accept the mandatory system as she would thereby obtain greater security. Australia owned, at present, governed, and had for many years governed, parts of New Guinea. Australia possessed a good Government; the people were very critical and censorious, and had shown that they were capable of taking over responsibilities. Consequently, that Government which had been governing adjoining territories for centuries had the best claims. To sum up: Australia had governed New Guinea; New Guinea was essential to the safety of Australia; Australia was a democracy; the Australians were on the spot; Australia knew what New Guinea wanted far better than any League of Nations. Australia actually at the present moment represented the Nations, and if the claims of Australia were not now accepted, what more attention would it in future receive from the League of Nations? Were this mandatory principle applied to Great Britain, to America, to France, it would not work. As Ireland is to the United Kingdom, as Mexico is to the United States of America, as Alsace-Lorraine is to France, so was New Guinea to Australia; but it was said that the taking over of Alsace-Lorraine by France merely meant a restoration. The mandatory system could never be as satisfactory for New Guinea as the direct system. It is said that the World favours the mandatory system because it is against annexations; but annexation was only bad when it made for Imperialism. The Australians had fought to govern themselves in their own way, and New Guinea was the outward and visible sign of the World's recognition that they were worthy to be entrusted with the Government of that country. Next, it would be asked, what assurances could Australia give for its good behaviour? Australia would be a member of the League of Nations. The League would control their members, and if necessary outlaw them. He would point out, however, that progress had not been made by the

World in general, but by peoples in particular. France and England and America were examples of this. They had now reached their present stage not because the World had put them there, but because they had worked out their own salvation. Australia was a democracy, not unworthy of comparison with any other. The people of Australia would never tolerate the ill-treatment of other peoples. They had fought against militarism and for the liberty of the people. The choice between annexation and the mandatory system was a narrow one. There was nothing to be gained by the mandatory system that could not be got by direct Government, except that the World was said to dread annexations. But he was positive that no one dreaded the annexation of New Guinea by Australia. The world only dreaded annexation for Imperialistic purposes or for the purpose of exploiting other peoples. But Australia was a democracy and responsible for its actions to its people. He would readily admit that the mandatory system would be applicable to other parts; but it could never apply to New Guinea.

MR. LLOYD GEORGE said that before examining particular cases he thought the meeting should have an opportunity of considering the practical application of the mandatory system. This was the first time they had heard an exposition of the principle. As far as the principle was concerned, apart from certain particular cases, he had no objections to make; but its practical application required careful consideration and he would like to consult his experts and discuss with them the proposals put forward in President Wilson's speech. He saw a practical difficulty, for instance, as regards the expenditure of money. Colonies, as far as Great Britain was concerned, did not mean a division of spoils, but rather the incurring of expenditure. Great Britain had no Colony from which a contribution towards the national expenditure was obtained. He thought the same consideration would present itself were the mandatory system applied to Mesopotamia, Syria, and other parts of the Turkish Empire. Whoever took Mesopotamia would have to spend enormous sums of money for works which would only be of profit to future generations. It might pay in the future, but who was to pay at present? Was the League of Nations to pay? How would it be possible to raise sufficient money to carry out all the necessary works for the development of these countries from which no returns could be expected for many decades. Consequently, if a country was to be merely a mandatory, it would be necessary to have a levy from all members of the League of Nations in order to make good the annual deficit. But would countries be able to raise money by taxation in order to enable, say, France to develop the Cameroons? Take again the protection of the shores. Where would the League of Nations come in with reference to all these questions? Therefore, he thought each of those present at this meeting should consult their advisers purely on the practical application of the principles of the mandatory power, as laid down by President Wilson in his speech.

MR. MASSEY enquired whether, if the meeting were adjourned, he would have an opportunity of putting forward his case when debate was resumed.

M. CLEMENCEAU replied in the affirmative.

PRESIDENT WILSON said that experts could give opinions only on subjects in which they were experienced. Undoubtedly, their training was such that they had experience only in what they had been accustomed to; but a new regime was now about to be established. It had been said that the British Colonies had cost Great Britain a large amount. But he preferred to say that Great Britain had carried the burden of their development up to the point where they were prepared for independence and self-Government. They were then admitted to a little family of nations. It was just this burden which he wanted the League of Nations to take up, and it was not inconceivable that an assessment might be made against the members. General Smuts, in his pamphlet,[4] had rightly compared the British Empire to a League of Nations. Undoubtedly, the obligation of defending the territory would rest upon the mandatory but part of the expense of the defence, if too heavy, would be borne by the League of Nations.

MR. LLOYD GEORGE repeated that a new principle had been put before them and he would like to have it examined, before its application to particular cases came under consideration. He was not afraid of the principle, because in the British Crown Colonies they did not differentiate between nationals as regards the grant of concessions; but he would like to have time carefully to examine the scheme proposed.

(Mr. Lloyd George's proposal was accepted, and the Meeting adjourned until 11 o'clock next morning.)

T MS (SDR, RG 256, 180.03101/19, DNA).

[4] About which, see n. 1 to the memorandum on a league of nations printed at Dec. 26, 1918, Vol. 53.

## To David Lloyd George

My dear Mr. Prime Minister:                Paris, 27 January, 1919.

I am taking pleasure in sending you a copy of the letter I showed you this afternoon.[1] Of course, you are free to use the information, but I would be very much obliged if you would guard the disclosure of the source as far as possible.

Cordially and faithfully yours,   [Woodrow Wilson]

CCL (WP, DLC).
¹ A copy of J. J. Pershing to WW, Jan. 25, 1919. See WW to J. J. Pershing, Jan. 28, 1919.

## To Park Trammell

[Paris] 27 January 1919.

Permit me to say that I think you would be doing the country and the World a great service if you would cooperate in bringing about the submission of the Suffrage Amendement. I hope that you will pardon my repeated suggestions and believe that I would not venture upon them if I did not think the matter of the greatest gravity.                                     Woodrow Wilson.

T telegram (WP, DLC).

## From Edward Mandell House

Dear Governor:                        Paris, January 27, 1919.

President Ador of Switzerland called yesterday. He was much concerned about the neutral governments not being represented upon the League of Nations. He is in favor of it but believes that his people will not approve an organization in the formation of which they have had no part.

I suggested that the Great Powers might be willing to confer with neutral representatives unofficially and ask them to make any suggestions or criticisms as the formation of the League progressed. He was entirely satisfied with this.

If this is agreeable, I would be willing personally to keep in touch with the representatives of Switzerland, Poland and Spain. Each delegate representing the Great Powers on the League of Nations might also keep in touch with three other neutral governments. In this way there would be no hurt sensibilities and the cause would be very much strengthened.

Affectionately yours,   E. M. House

TLS (WP, DLC).

# From Herbert Clark Hoover

Dear Mr. President:                    Paris, 27 January 1919.

The Senate amended our $100,000,000. Relief Bill excluding Bulgaria, German Austria-Hungary and the Mahomedan population of Turkey from the provinces of the Bill. These populations have to be fed if the prime objective of the action is to be secured. The Bill goes into conference and I am wondering if you could send a cablegram to Mr. Glass asking him to represent you in requesting that these exceptions should be taken out. Germany is of course excepted from the whole sense of the Bill and we do not wish to withdraw this exception.

The fact is that three of these countries have established democratic governments and are really making an honest struggle towards respectability. The men in charge of each country are men who have been against the war, and it must be desirable from a political and a humane point of view that they should be supported. The Turkish situation is one of complexity as it will be almost impossible to sort out the Christian population from the rest, and in any event we do not look for a very large expenditure of money in this direction as they have commodities ready to export and it becomes a matter of trade rather than international finance.

The Bill as passed by the House was in the form that we hoped the Senate would accede to. The large majority by which it passed the Senate and the House would seem to indicate some hope of getting it reviewed in conference without too much of a struggle.

Yours faithfully,   Herbert Hoover

TLS (WP, DLC).

# Gilbert Fairchild Close to William Shepherd Benson

My dear Admiral Benson:                    Paris, 27 January 1919.

The President asks if you will not be kind enough to send the following message to Secretary Daniels in reply to the message forwarded with your note of January 26th:

"I can say with very deliberate conviction that it is necessary for the accomplishment of our objects here that the Three-year Building Program should be adopted as recommended. I am quite willing that the proviso should be included that if by international agreement a reduction of armaments is arranged, that I will be authorized to withhold further contracts until Congress is consulted, but it would be fatal to go beyond that at this juncture. Woodrow Wilson."

Sincerely yours,   [Gilbert F. Close]

CCL (WP, DLC).

## From the Diary of Colonel House

January 27, 1919.

My early morning visitor was Wickham Steed of the Northcliffe Press. He asked who I thought would be the best man for the British to send as Ambassador to the United States. I told him they would not send the best man who was Sir William Wiseman. He thought he could force them to do it. It will be interesting to see him try. Northcliffe himself has invited me to visit him at Cannes. His influence is a potent weapon for one to have at this time, particularly when Northcliffe seems to want to use it for the public rather than for private good.

Samuel Gompers and his confreres came to see the American Delegates at 12.15. I had hardly seated myself before the President was announced. The President and I went to my private study and had a half hour's talk. He told of the happenings at the Quai d'Orsay and asked my advice upon several matters. In speaking of his speech on the League of Nations at Saturday's session, he said he had forgotten to use the economic argument which I had given him. He spoke with regret because he said he could have made it clear to the minds of those present how necessary it was that the world should not become involved in another war from an economic as well as from a humane viewpoint.

Although I wrote and gave the President the substance for his speech,[1] yet in a note he wrote me at the Peace Table he attributed it largely to the instigation of Prof. Herron. What Herron told him was that he ought to state that the American Delegation intended to insist upon the principles for which America had fought in the war.

We talked of the German Colonies and came to a conclusion as to the position that should be taken. When we had finished, I took him in to see Gompers and his fellow delegates.

T MS (E. M. House Papers, CtY).
   [1] That is, EMH to WW, Jan. 25, 1919.


## Edith Bolling Galt Wilson to John Randolph Bolling

Dearest Randolph:                                    [Paris] Jan. 27, 1919

Your letter of Jan. 5th came on Friday (the 24) & was much appreciated & enjoyed. Thank you for the information in regard to our Bank accounts. I had asked you in my other letter about these & our letters crossed.

I also had letters from J.F.V.[1] which I will answer soon—but, of course, each letter is meant for you all. I am so glad Viola[2] is okeh again—give them & all the others love for me.

I suppose you will read in the Post this morning of our journey yesterday to Chateau Thierry & Rheims for you seem to follow all we do in 24 hours time. We left by motor at 8 A.M. reaching Chateau Thierry at 11—after seeing all of the remains of the awful fighting around there. You will remember Watson,[3] one of the Aides—he was with us & as he was in the fighting there for 37 days, he told us all of the situation of troops. He is now Major & has the Choix de Gare. [Croix de Guerre]. From there, we went through town after town which is now just a mass of ruins, & desolation until we reached Rheims. Here the pathetic old Cardinal who had stayed nearly the entire 4 years in the City, watching over his people & beloved Cathedral met us & showed us all over the latter.

There is no use describing the details. You all have read & seen it pictured until you would have had the same feeling I did that you had seen it all before—lived through the awful years when fresh destruction came every day until at last—it was finished! We took the train there at 4.30 & reached Paris at 9.20 having dinner on the train. We took Wilmer[4] Dr. G. Miss Benham, Gen. Harts, Watson, Hoover, Swem & Close, & had a very comfortable trip.

Here I stopped to go to the conference with Woodrow; I mean just to drive down with him—they meet at 10.30 A.M. & 2.30 or 3 P.M. & I always drive or walk with him. Bless his heart, he never has one minute to himself, for there are people from every country & Station begging him to see them, & it often requires until 10 or 11 at night to keep up with such appointments.

Saturday he felt encouraged over the "League of Nations" general acceptance at the big Conference. Of course it was only the fact & not the detail which was decided but that much, at least is gained.

We had such an interesting evening the night we had Mr. A. G. Gard[i]ner dine with us. He is most delightful. Then on Saturday we had Mrs. Humphry Ward[5] to Tea, & found her charming.

Friday night the Director of the Opera[6] asked us as his guest to see "Castor & Pollux."[7] The box was decorated with white & crimson roses & an American flag & the house was crowded. As an opera it was disappointing but the Ballet was beautiful, & one interesting thing we were taken behind the curtain, where there is a beautiful room for the ladies of the Ballet to rest & receive their friends. They were all assembled & in their costumes & paint & brief skirts—it was very amusing.

On Thursday I had an "At home" for the many French people who have called & on Friday we had 310 American boys who act as a guard round the house, & 35 French guard to tea. W. came home from the Conference & they all requested to have a picture taken with us, which was done by flash light, & which I am sure will be terrible.

The only girls we had were 3 American telephone girls who take care of our Switch Board, but they all seemed to have a good time & we enjoyed them.

By the way will you ask Bert.[8] to call up Annie Fendall[9] & say that at last I have heard from Sterling Jr.[10] I wrote him 3 days after we got here, but did not hear until 4 days ago that my letter reached him after he got back from his 10 days leave which he had to take while we were in England & Italy.

He had to return & leave Paris the day we got back.

He wrote in good spirits & the letter had been on its way nearly 2 weeks.

Mail is awful here, & the telephone is impossible.

Today I go to the Y.W.C.A. for a Reception at 4.30 & tomorrow with Jus[s]erand to the Gobelin Tapestry to meet the artist who designed my tapestry[11] & see the Factory.

I am delighted you are replenishing your wardrobe & hope things are less expensive there than here. I wrote Mother the other day of the prices here. I don't see how poor people live at all.

Woodrow would have messages if he knew I was writing. He always enjoys the home letters. Now I must stop & see Benham about my mail.

Lots of love to each one & a big kiss to Mother.

Fondly,   Edith.

I got the Commercial Dec. Statement, & everything checked up okeh.

ALS (EBW Papers, DLC).
[1] Unidentified.
[2] Unidentified.
[3] That is, Lt. Col. Edwin Martin Watson.
[4] That is, Richard Wilmer Bolling.
[5] Mary Augusta Arnold (Mrs. Thomas Humphry) Ward, British novelist, social worker, and opponent of woman suffrage.
[6] Jacques Rouché.
[7] An opera by Jean Philippe Rameau (1683-1764).
[8] That is, Bertha Bolling.
[9] Annie (Mrs. Reginald) Fendall of Washington, sister-in-law of Mrs. Wilson.
[10] Capt. Sterling Galt, Jr., U.S.A., Princeton 1915, nephew-in-law of Mrs. Wilson, at this time stationed with the 310th Infantry Regiment, A.E.F.
[11] About which, see J. J. Jusserand to S. Pichon, Aug. 1, 1918, Vol. 49.

# From the Diary of Edith Benham

January 27, 1919

The President read us today from a memorandum marked confidential which had been sent him and which throws a curious light on the double dealing of the French. Some time ago he had been told that the working women of France had said he had received all the men and everything else but had not met the women. He said he would be glad to if they had arranged it with the Government. He was duly invited to go last Saturday to the Trocadero palace and accepted, and then was informed that the whole thing in which 10,000 women were to be represented had been called off. Certain delegates, however, came here on Saturday, some sixty in all and brought their little gifts and speeches of welcome. It was downstairs and quite informal and I didn't go down, but Mrs. Wilson said it was quite a touching ceremony for they represented women from the humbler walks of life, some working women, suffragists and literary societies. They were bitterly disappointed they couldn't have their large meeting.

Today he received, from whom I don't know, the explanation. Before they came over they went to the proper government officials and received from them assurances that they could have their meeting and went ahead. After the President arrived they went to arrange the date and arrange finally about the Trocadero. Then they were told that Clemenceau objected to any more demonstrations in favor of the President, that they could have the meeting but were to make no laudatory remarks about him or about America's part in the war. They were not to speak of the League of Nations or to endorse it in any way, nor to bring up the matter of women's receiving equal rights and justice after the peace settlement. That seemed quite an extraordinary piece of duplicity for the French delegates to the Commission have all endorsed the League of Nations and I am beginning to believe more and more truly that France and England were ready to quit when our men came in in June. I didn't hear the other side, but Harts and the President were talking the other day and Harts said the British were telling Pershing the morale of their men was gone and for God's sake to hurry. I think the President's meeting at Buckingham with Winston Churchill must have been amusing. The President said Churchill had been saying we owed all to the British Navy and had sneered publicly at the President, so he said: "Well, Mr. Churchill, and how is the Navy?" Churchill flushed and never said a word. The officials all over are afraid of the President for they know the people of all the allied countries will follow him. This stopping of the meeting is the second one of the same thing. A few days after he came the labor people wanted to have a meeting and the Government would not allow it, but would only let in a few representatives from each group. The President seems to think we are living over an economic abyss and if certain concessions are not made to the working men, a great social and economic upheaval will come and society as we have it now will go, and there won't be any gradual readjustment unless capital meets labor half way. Labor will take what it should be given.

## From the Diary of Dr. Grayson

Tuesday, January 28, 1919.

The President attended the morning conference. After luncheon he talked to me. Another real fight—the sharpest to date—had taken place in the morning session. The question of the disposition of the captured German colonies was under consideration. Japan and Australia wanted the Pacific Islands, Australia to get New Guinea and Japan, control of the Shantung Peninsula Railways. At the conference, Wellington Koo, the Chinese Minister to the United States, took sharp exception to the Japanese contention regarding Shantung and he made one of the best speeches yet delivered. Koo pointed out that the Japanese control the railroads that run north from Port Arthur to Manchuria. He said that when they landed at Tsing-Tau, they landed on the Peninsula, directly across from Port Arthur and worked in behind the then German town. When the Germans capitulated, the Japanese laid a railroad from their original landing place to Tsing-Tau and also took over the railroad lines running north toward Peking. It was China's contention that the Japanese domination of this railroad gave them absolute control over all of China's natural resources and he demanded that the railroads be turned back to China with compensation, to be fixed in a manner satisfactory to both sides. The President found himself in an absolute minority during the early proceedings, because the representatives of the colonies, seated with the British, favored the distribution of the captured colonies and the majority of the delegates wanted to "divide the swag," and then have the League of Nations created to perpetuate their title. The President made it plain that he would not stand for any such arrangement; that he believed it was absolutely essential that the captured colonies should be controlled by the League of Nations and administered under the mandatory system, whereby the nations best fitted to do so would have control of the colonies, but would have its rule always subject to a direct appeal to the League to remedy any injustice. In connection with the Chinese argument, it had been pointed out that the Japanese had taken over some of China's most sacred soil, including the Tomb of Confucius. Naturally, the President sympathized with the Chinese viewpoint. The entire matter was still open when the President left today's session. In the afternoon, he saw Mr. Samuel Gompers, President of the American Federation of Labor, for two and one-half hours. They discussed, at great length, the plans dealing with the international labor problem and especially to what extent it would be possible for the League of Nations to devise and control a labor plan that would prevent world wide economic unrest and trade disturbances. Gompers told the President that the American Federation of Labor would not be represented at the coming Berne Conference,[1] which he described as designed "to play the German game." He told the President what had transpired at his conferences earlier in the day with the Belgian and British labor leaders and expressed the hope that the general labor program would be agreed upon by the international labor organizations of the world. After dinner, the President relaxed by reading aloud to Mrs. Wilson and me, the poem "The Future," by Matthew Arnold and further diverted himself by playing canfield[2] before retiring.

[1] About which, see FLP to RL, Dec. 6, 1918, n. 1, Vol. 53. The organizers of the conference had finally decided in early January that it would be held in Bern. See Arno J. Mayer, *Politics and Diplomacy of Peacemaking: Containment and Counterrevolution at Versailles, 1918-1919* (New York, 1967), pp. 380-82.
[2] That is, Canfield, a form of the card game, solitaire, named for its inventor, Richard A. Canfield, gambling-house proprietor of New York.

## Remarks in Paris to the League for the Rights of Man[1]

January 28, 1919.

Gentlemen: I particularly appreciate your courtesy in coming in person to convey these admirable sentiments to me. The phrase "the rights of man" is somehow associated more intimately with the history of France than with the history of any other country, and I think that the whole world has regarded France as a sort of pioneer in the ideal interpretation of that phrase. It was not an accident which drew France and the United States into close association. The Marquis Lafayette did not come to the United States because he alone entertained the sentiment of sympathy. He came, and we recognized that he came as a representative—shall I say, knight errant?—of the sympathy of France. And when this opportunity came, not to repay our debt to France, for such debts are not repaid, but to show the similar sentiment that moved us and the equal willingness on our part to help France in her time of need, it was with genuine satisfaction that we came to help. It is true, Sir, I believe, that our coming prevented a catastrophe that might have overwhelmed the world. That adds to our delight; that adds to our gratification that we could have served France in so exigent an hour.

Therefore, when you, who have through many difficulties represented an ideal principle, bring me these assurances of your friendship, it causes me an unusual emotion. I am grateful to you. I appreciate your homage and feel that it brings a message not only of friendly feeling but a message of comprehension and sympathy which is peculiarly delightful and acceptable.

Printed in *Addresses of President Wilson on First Trip* . . .
[1] The Ligue des Droits de L'Homme. See Mayer, *Politics and Diplomacy of Peacemaking*, p. 173, *passim*.

## Hankey's Notes of Two Meetings of the Council of Ten[1]

Quai d'Orsay, January 28, 1919, 11 A.M.

BC-13

MR. LLOYD GEORGE said that on the previous evening he had had an opportunity to consult his Colonial experts. All that he was, for the moment, prepared to say was that in so far as the territories conquered by troops from the United Kingdom (in distinction from those conquered by Dominion troops) were concerned, he saw no insuperable difficulty in reconciling the views of Great Britain with those expressed by President Wilson. There certainly were practical difficulties, but there were always practical difficulties in attempting to realize any ideal. He was trying to formulate a plan which would overcome those difficulties, and he had good hope of success. The Dominions case, however, was a special case, and he hoped that President Wilson would look into it again. He did not think that a special exception in favor of the Dominions would spoil the whole case, possibly the reverse might be true. A scheme might more readily be wrecked by courting resistance than by avoiding difficulties. The contiguity of the territories in question to the Dominions claiming them suggested that they should form an integral part of those countries, more especially as it would be from them that emigration would take place. Another point he would like to put to the Allied Powers, including France, was that there was no large difference between the mandatory principle and the principles

[1] The complete text of these notes is printed in *PPC*, III, 749-57.

laid down by the Berlin Conference, under which Great Britain, France, and Germany held many of their colonies.[2] This Conference had framed conditions about the open door, the prohibition of the arms and liquor traffic, which resembled those President Wilson had in view in many respects, except that no external machinery had been provided for their enforcement. It followed, therefore, that by adopting the mandatory principle wherever possible Great Britain would not be altering her Colonial regime to any appreciable extent. He would be very glad to hear the French view, as France was as much concerned in the question as Great Britain.

M. CLEMENCEAU said that the French Minister for the Colonies[3] would be ready to make a statement on the following day.

M. PICHON said that on the points raised by Mr. Lloyd George he thought there would be no differences between France and Great Britain.

M. CLEMENCEAU pointed out that there were certain Franco-British conventions relating to the German colonies; for instance Togoland. He asked whether these conventions should be produced before the Council.

MR. LLOYD GEORGE was of the opinion that any arrangements made during the war should be placed before the meeting.

M. CLEMENCEAU undertook to produce them, and asked whether the Japanese delegates would do likewise.

BARON MAKINO said that he had no objection to doing so, and would send all such agreements to the Chairman. He would point out, however, that the Japanese conventions were in the form of an exchange of ideas rather than formal conventions.

MR. BALFOUR asked whether Baron Makino alluded to the agreement reached in 1917.

BARON MAKINO replied that this was the agreement to which he referred.

M. ORLANDO said that Italy also had a convention with France and Great Britain concerning German colonies.

M. PICHON asked if M. Orlando referred to the Pact of London.

M. ORLANDO replied in the affirmative.

PRESIDENT WILSON asked that if drafts were submitted to the Council, no sense of finality should be attached to them.

MR. LLOYD GEORGE entirely agreed. He was much influenced by what the President had said on former occasions, and quite agreed that any proposal submitted should be provisional.

[2] That is, the conference of fourteen nations on African affairs, held in Berlin, November 15, 1884-February 26, 1885, the result of which was the so-called Berlin Act of 1885. See Wm. Roger Louis, "African Origins of the Mandates Idea," *International Organization*, XIX (Winter 1965), 20-36, and Arthur Berriedale Keith, *The Belgian Congo and the Berlin Act* (Oxford, 1919), pp. 57-65.

[3] That is, Henry Simon.

MR. MASSEY said that he had not much to add to the two speeches made on the previous day. He wished, however, to assure President Wilson that though he did not quite take his point of view, he would speak in no spirit of opposition to the idea of the League of Nations. He could not, however, help recalling the precedents of history. Similar attempts had been made before. The most notable instance was that of the Congress of Vienna, where all the nations of Europe had been gathered in order to frame universal peace. The results of its labors had been a failure. He hoped that this Congress would not end in the same way, but it was well to remember that history repeated itself.

He wished to point out that New Zealand and Australia were, so to speak, in the same boat. If Australia were invaded by an enemy power, New Zealand must fall, as her communications would be cut. The converse applied with equal force. The danger to both would doubtless grow less in course of time as the populations of these countries increased.

Samoa was of vital importance to New Zealand. It was situated on the main water route to the South Pacific from the Panama Canal. If, by any chance, Samoa were in hostile hands, New Zealand would be strangled. This eventuality, therefore, was a cause of anxiety to the country he represented, and on this point, despite other differences, all its inhabitants were of one mind. He hoped that he would be able to induce President Wilson to see the question from their standpoint.

One of the main purposes laid down by President Wilson for the mandatory system was the betterment of the inhabitants. He felt he could claim that New Zealand had done in this respect as well as any mandatory power was ever likely to do. New Zealand was not only composed of the two islands generally attributed to her. She also governed the Cook Archipelago, which had been assigned to New Zealand twenty years ago. The experiment made by New Zealand in administering this territory had been highly successful. Schools had been instituted in all the larger islands; agricultural experts had been sent to train the populations, which had now become industrious and productive; hospitals had been set up at Rarotonga, which was the seat of the New Zealand Commissioner and of his staff. The same system had been applied to the natives there as since the treaty of 1840 had been applied to the Maoris. The Maoris of New Zealand were highly respected by the whites, and every trade and profession was open to them. One of his own colleagues in the government, Dr. Pomare,[4] was a Maori. His great

---

[4] Maui Wiremu Piti Naera Pomare, M.D., Minister of the Cook Islands in Massey's cabinet.

knowledge of the Polynesian races had suggested that he should come to the Peace Conference, and, but for the expense of sending an additional minister from New Zealand, he thought that he would have been a most suitable delegate.

When Samoa was taken over at the beginning of the war, the same policy of education and improvement was started there, and had been satisfactory. The Cook Islanders and Samoans were related, and spoke dialects of the same language. If a change were to be made, the inhabitants of Samoa would be dissatisfied.

The difference between the mandatory principle and that instituted by New Zealand was that between leasehold and freehold tenure. No individual would put the same energy into a leasehold as into a freehold. It would be the same with governments.

President Wilson had suggested improvements. He agreed it was necessary to increase production, but certain financing would have to be done. On the credit of a government like Australia, loans could be raised for the development of New Guinea, which, before it could support a civilised population, would require docks, roads, telegraphs, and a number of other improvements. The country itself, when developed, would afford ample security for further loans. Could this process be as successfully set in motion by a mandatory power? Though it might not be the time to discuss what should be done with the German Empire, he held that Germany was an outlaw among nations, and should be treated as such. Unless broken up, it would become a danger again, and future generations must be safeguarded against its pernicious activities.

Unless these territories were annexed to some strong state, the Germans would attempt to get them back. All knew what German intrigue and peaceful penetration meant. It had occurred even in New Zealand.

The phrase "division of spoils" had been used. He begged to point out that New Zealand would not obtain much spoil. Her financial burdens incurred during this war were very heavy. At a time when New Zealand was not half developed, it had been called upon to send volunteers immense distances to take the field in Europe. It had done so willingly, and not only lost a valuable portion of its population, but had also incurred 100 millions of debt. There was little prospect of any recoupment of such losses. The financial value of Samoa was a mere trifle in comparison. He appealed to the President to look at the whole question from the New Zealand point of view. He would ask him to recall the period immediately after the American War of Independence. What would Washington have done had it been suggested to him that a mandatory power, or even the colonists themselves as mandatories of a League of Nations, should be given charge of the vast territories in North America not at that time colonised? There was little doubt that the American settlers would have protested at this offer, and rightly so, for, had this taken place, the United States would not have grown into one of the greatest Powers of the World. New Zealand had only fought to protect the citizens of the South Pacific and all decent citizens of the world from future wars.

PRESIDENT WILSON said that for the sake of keeping history straight, he would make a passing comment on one of the remarks just heard. He would not admit that there was any historical precedent for the work now in hand; least of all should the Congress of Vienna be cited as such. The Holy Alliance of that time existed professedly to extend the system of monarchical and arbitrary government in the World. Such, he hoped, was not the purpose of the present conference. It was the Holy Alliance which had provoked in the Western Hemisphere the Monroe Doctrine, which was a protest against the system brought about by the Congress of Vienna. Great Britain had soon dissociated herself from the Holy Alliance and supported the Monroe Doctrine.

The present enterprise was very different from that undertaken at Vienna a century ago, and he hoped that even by reference no odor of Vienna would again be brought into its proceedings.

As to Samoa, he had one remark to make. There was another Power present in the Samoan Islands which was not unfriendly either to Great Britain or to New Zealand. This power had not played the same part as New Zealand in the war in the Southern Pacific, because it was not then at war with Germany. The Power in question was the United States of America. He dared assert, however, that under the regime of the League of Nations there was little chance that any Power would be able to play in Samoa the part played by Germany without attracting the attention of the United States.

M. CLEMENCEAU said that this part of the discussion was now adjourned. The Council would proceed to discuss the question of the German possessions in the Far East, together with the Chinese delegates.

As the question of restitution of the fortress had been raised, he thought it useful to read the words of the Japanese ultimatum to Germany, because it had a bearing on the purpose in hand:

"Considering it highly important and necessary in the present situation to take measures to remove all causes of disturbance to the peace of the Far East, and to safeguard the general interests contemplated by the agreement of the Alliance between Japan and Great Britain in order to secure a firm and enduring peace in Eastern Asia, the establishment of which is the aim of the said agreement—the Imperial Japanese Government sincerely believe it their duty to give advice to the Imperial German Government to carry out the following two propositions:

(1) To withdraw immediately from Japanese and Chinese waters German men-of-war and armed vessels of all kinds, and to disarm, at once, those which cannot be withdrawn.

(2) To deliver on a date not later than the 15th September, 1914, to the Imperial Japanese authorities, without condition and compensation, the entire leased territory of Kiaochow, with a view to eventual restoration of the same to China."

Since the occupation of Kiaochow, Japan has been in actual possession. In view of all that had passed between the Governments of China and Japan, Baron Makino thought that China fully realized the import of Japanese occupation. The friendly interchange of views on this subject had been entered into, and Japan had agreed to restore Kiaochow as soon as Japan had free disposal of the place. Agreements had also been reached with regard to the (leased) railway.

As notes had been exchanged, he thought that a statement of these engagements might be worth the consideration of the members of the Council.

PRESIDENT WILSON asked Baron Makino whether he proposed to lay these notes before the Council.

BARON MAKINO said that he did not think the Japanese Government would raise any objection, but as the request was an unexpected one he would be compelled to ask its permission.

PRESIDENT WILSON asked on behalf of China if Mr. Koo would do likewise.

MR. KOO said that the Chinese Government has no objection to raise.

M. CLEMENCEAU asked both the Japanese and Chinese Delegates to state whether they would make known to the Council the conditions of the restoration agreed between them.

BARON MAKINO said that he would do so, provided his Government would make no objection. He did not think it would. If it were within his own power, he would produce these documents as soon as possible. There was, however, one point he wished to make clear. Japan was in actual possession of the territory under consideration. It had taken it by conquest from Germany. Before disposing of it to a third party it was necessary that Japan should obtain the right of free disposal from Germany.

PRESIDENT WILSON pointed out that the Council was dealing with territories and cessions previously German without consulting Germany at all.

BARON MAKINO said that the work now in hand was one of preparation for the presentment of the case to Germany. It followed therefore that the cession of Kiaochow would have to be agreed upon by Germany before it was carried out. What should take place thereafter had already been the subject of an interchange of views with China.

MR. KOO said that he was very glad, on behalf of China, to have the opportunity of putting the case of his country. He had heard with interest the Dominion speakers, who spoke on behalf of a few million people. He felt his own responsibility was enhanced by the fact that he was the spokesman of 400 millions, one quarter of the human race. The Chinese delegation would ask the Peace Conference for the restoration to China of the Leased Territory of Kiaochow, the railway in Shantung, and all other rights Germany possessed in that province before the war. He would confine himself to broad principles in order not to employ too much of the Council's time. Technical details would be explained in full in a memorandum which he proposed to submit. The territories in question were an integral part of China. They were part of a province containing 3 million inhabitants, of Chinese in race, language and religion. The history of the lease to Germany was doubtless familiar. The lease had been extorted by force. The German fleet had occupied the coast of Shantung and landing parties had penetrated into the interior. The lease had been extorted as a price for the withdrawal of the expedition. The pretext of this proceeding was the accidental killing of two missionaries in the interior of the country in a manner quite beyond the control of the Chinese Government. On the principles of nationality and of territorial integrity, principles accepted by this Conference, China had a right to the restoration of these territories. The Chinese delegation would feel that this was one of the conditions of a just peace. If, on the other hand, the Congress were to take a different view and were to transfer these territories to any other Power, it would, in the eyes of the Chinese Delegation, be adding one wrong to another. The Shantung province, in which Kiaochow and the railway to Chinanfu were situated, was the cradle of Chinese civilisation, the birthplace of Confucius and Mencius, and a Holy Land for the Chinese. This province had always played a very important part in the development of China. Economically, it was a densely populated country, with 36 million people in an area of only 35,000 square miles. The density of the population produced an intense competition and rendered the country quite unsuitable for colonisation. The introduction of a Foreign Power could only lead to the exploitation of the inhabitants, and not to genuine colonisation. Strategically, Kiaochow commanded one of the main gateways of North China. It controlled one of the shortest approaches from the sea to Pekin, namely, the railway to Chinanfu which, at its junction with the railway from Tientsing, led straight to the capital. In the interest of Chinese national defence which in time would be organised, the Chinese Delegation would be unable to admit that any Foreign Power had claims to so vital a point. China was fully cognisant of the services rendered to her by the heroic Army and Navy of Japan in rooting out German power from Shantung. China was also deeply indebted to Great Britain for helping in this task at a time of great peril to herself in Europe. China also was not forgetful of the services rendered her by the troops of the other Allies in Europe, which had held in check an enemy who might otherwise have easily sent reinforcements to the Far East and thereby prolonged hostilities there. China appreciated these services all the more because the people in Shantung had also suffered and sacrificed in connection with the military operations for the capture of Kiaochow, especially in regard to requisitions for labour and supplies of all kinds. But, grateful as they were, the Chinese Delegation felt that they would be false to their duty to China and to the world if they did not object to paying their debts of gratitude by selling the birthright of their countrymen, and thereby sowing the seeds of discord for the future. The Chinese Delegation therefore trusted that the Conference, in considering the disposal of the leased territory and other rights held by Germany in Shantung, would give full weight to the fundamental and transcendent rights of China, the rights of political sovereignty and territorial integrity.

BARON MAKINO said that he had listened with great attention to what had fallen from his Chinese colleague concerning the direct restitution of Kiaochow to China. In the statement put forward on the previous day, he had explained the reasons for which the Japanese Government had undertaken the reduction of this German stronghold.

MR. KOO said that the Chinese Delegation did not adopt quite the same view as Baron Makino. He was well aware that Japan after her undertaking in 1914—which he was glad to note had just been renewed by Baron Makino—would not retain the territory.

But there was a choice between direct and indirect restitution. Of the two China would prefer the first. It was always easier to take one step than two if it led to the same place. They had always considered all the Conventions made with Japan as provisional and subject to revision by the Peace Conference. Before becoming a belligerent China had agreed to accept all the conditions made to Germany by Japan.

China's entry into the war, however, had completely altered her status. None of the previous arrangements precluded China either from declaring war on Germany, or from being represented at the Peace Conference. Nor could they preclude her now from demanding from Germany direct restitution of her rights. China's belligerency had in itself put an end to the leases obtained by Germany in Chinese territory. Furthermore, there was a clause in the lease to the effect that Germany could not transfer her rights to another power.

(The meeting then adjourned.)

T MS (SDR, RG 256, 180.03101/20, DNA).

Quai d'Orsay, January 28, 1919, 4 P.M.[1]

BC-14

M. Clemenceau, after declaring the meeting opened, said he would ask M. Simon, the French Minister for the Colonies, to submit the French case on the African question.

M. SIMON said that as it had been decided that the German Colonies should not be given back to Germany, the two questions to be decided were: To whom should these Colonies be given, and what should their form of government be? He would place before them the French point of view. In the first place he would read two letters exchanged between M. Cambon[2] and Sir Edward Grey during the war, dealing with the provisional division of Togoland and the Cameroons.

MR. LLOYD GEORGE said he did not think it would serve any useful purpose to read these documents just then. Other agreements would have to be put before the meeting also, and the delegates could take a note of the complete file. They were only concerned that afternoon with the French point of view.

M. SIMON said these agreements were merely temporary. They were to be submitted to the Peace Conference, who would decide whether they should be considered as definite agreements or not. There was also a similar agreement in Article XIII of the Pact of London, under which possible rectifications of frontiers in Africa, in favour of Italy, France and Great Britain, subject to certain territorial compensations, were considered.

France at once had declared that she was not concerned in the German East and West African Colonies, but on the other hand she wished to state her claims to the Cameroons and Togoland.

[1] The complete text of these notes is printed in *PPC*, III, 758-71.
[2] That is, Paul Cambon, French Ambassador to Great Britain.

For what reasons did France claim those territories? She claimed them for the same reasons that had been used by the Dominions in putting forward their claims. They had had to take account of the sacrifices which they had been forced to make to conquer these territories from Germany, who, in spite of her undertakings, had violated the acknowledged neutrality of these regions.

Historically, the French also had certain claims. They had been the first to explore those territories; they had also been the first to sign agreements or treaties with the native races. There had been a signed agreement with Togoland since 1892, and some years later they had signed one also with the Cameroons. The treaty with Malemba, which gave Duala to France, would also be recalled. He would lay stress upon this point, because allusion to this treaty had been made when difficulties occurred with England about the possession of Duala.

They would consider the treaties signed with Germany as abrogated. Furthermore, certain of these treaties had been signed under the pressure of political events. He would refer in particular to the Treaties of 1895 and 1897 in regard to Togoland, and to that of 1911 in regard to the Cameroons.

They would now have to consider certain political considerations. Ever since they had occupied these territories the tribes had been happy, and they had asked to remain under French control. He would refer in particular to the requests made by Garna and Marna, in the name of the inhabitants, that the Cameroons should be united to France.

Then there were also the questions of economic and geographical contiguity, as had been set forth by Mr. Hughes in respect to New Guinea.

Geographically, Togoland was an integral part of Dahomey, which was rather closely wedged in between Nigeria and the Gold Coast. Togoland and Dahomey were inhabited by the same tribes, possessing the same traditions.

The same reasons of contiguity existed between the French Congo and the Cameroons. The policy of Germany, which ended in the agreement of 1911, had been to cut the French possessions off from the sea, so as to smother the French economically later on. The large sea coast of the Cameroons, and the port of Duala were required for the development of French Equatorial Africa.

It now remained for them to consider the question of the Government to be given to these territories, which had become ownerless.

There were three possible solutions:

1. Internationalisation, pure and simple.
2. A mandate given to one of the Powers by the League of Nations.
3. Annexation, pure and simple, by a sovereign Power.

Mr. Lloyd George had frankly condemned the first system in the course of the conversation of 24th January, when he had said that it could not be adopted in regard to backward countries—that it would lead to disorder, and that the high ideals for which such a system would be established could not be reached.

He would agree with this view for humanitarian reasons. Similar experiments tried in the past had failed ignominiously. He would only mention the dual control over Samoa, against which the American President himself had spoken, and that of the New Hebrides, which, he hoped, would not be allowed to continue, where, under British control, a tribunal composed of a Spanish judge and a Dutchman, etc. existed.

What was not possible for small territories, was all the less possible for large regions.

The second system consisted in the appointment of a mandatory by the League of Nations. The Dominions had made very strong objections to this system, and these objections were supported by France also. When, in two territories inhabited by the same population, two different systems of government were created, difficulties would ensue and the very opposite of what was desired would result.

The mandatory system consisted of empowering one nation to act on behalf of another. Every mandate was revocable, and there would therefore be no guarantee for its continuance. There would thus be little inducement for the investment of capital and for colonisation in a country whose future was unknown. The mandatory would be content to live quietly without trying to develop the colony, or to improve the conditions of life of the natives, and the desired ideal would not be attained by this means.

Another question occurs. Who would be the mandatory? Would it be a little nation, without colonising traditions, capital, or men? Or, would the mandatory be a large nation whose presence would be a danger and compel the adjoining nations to organize for defence, as Mr. Hughes said in regard to New Guinea? This same remark applied to the Cameroons and to the Congo. It would also be necessary to take into account the uncertainty of alliances, which were always liable to be changed.

He (M. Simon) could not, therefore, favour the system of a mandate to be given to one Power by the League of Nations.

The third system still remained to be considered—that of annexation, pure and simple, which he had come to support that day. It was the only one which would accomplish the double object of every colonial government worthy of the name, namely, the development of the country and the effective protection of the natives during the period required for their development towards a higher plane of civilization.

He would ask his hearers to consider the objections that could be raised against a policy of annexation. Annexation might be said to lead to the exploitation of the country for the benefit of the individual; it might be said to lead to the ill-treatment of the natives; it might permit of the setting up of the economic policy of the "closed door."

All these points were part of a theory which was today quite obsolete and condemned by all. France had higher aspirations, and the Colonies were no longer considered as a kind of close preserve, for the exploitation and benefit of the individual.

Higher moral principles now guided the nations. All the great Powers worthy of the name, considered their colonies as wards entrusted to them by the world. They accepted this guardianship and the duties connected therewith, duly appreciating their duties in regard to the maintenance of peace, their duties in regard to the protection of the people either by the limitation of the sale of alcohol, the prevention of gun-running, etc., and their duties in regard to the provision of social education. Only a great nation, in possession of trained administrative services, and with men and money at its disposal could undertake and carry through such an enterprise. The work of civilization could only be carried out under the auspices of the sovereignty of a country.

If France were to receive the territories under consideration, she would be prepared to give assurances to those who might still harbour fears. The French formally announced that day that their policy in regard to the territories formerly German would entail the application of a liberal system, practically open to everybody, the "Open Door" system, without differential tariffs. Everybody would be able to enter and to trade in Togoland and the Cameroons without let or hindrance. France henceforth renounced all economic protective measures. She accepted what she had always done for the protection of the natives, the limitation of alcohol, the stoppage of traffic in arms, etc. She would not attempt to enforce any policy which might appear to be directed against the natives, for she had always co-operated with them. The French had always desired that the natives should take part in the management of their own territory. He had enunciated the general principles which guided the French. These principles were such that they were bound to satisfy all those interested in the moral development and liberties of the population.

President Wilson's fifth point in his message of the 8th January read as follows:

"A free, open-minded, and absolutely impartial adjustment of all colonial claims based upon a strict observance of the principle that in determining all such questions of sovereignty, the interests of the populations concerned have equal weight with the equitable claims of the Government whose title is to be determined."

As regards this clause, he had already stated how, in his opinion, the interests of the population in question would be protected. He had also explained the just claims of France. As to the claims of France, these were based on sacrifices made by them in the course of past centuries in Northern Africa. And now that work would appear to be concluded, for their old Colonies formed part of the old country. The inhabitants had equal rights, they had their representatives in the French Chamber, their system of local government was exactly the same as that of the French, and the natives enjoyed the same rights as French citizens.

For centuries past France had used all her strength for the purpose of exploring and developing the territories of Northern Africa; and the whole world had been able to enjoy the benefits to be derived therefrom.

France had spent 9 milliards of francs on the Mediterranean coast, 626 millions on West Africa, and 272 millions on equatorial Africa. When the efforts made by France for the civilization of Northern Africa were considered they would feel fully confident that she would be able to carry out the same programme in Equatorial Africa. That was his reply to President Wilson's third condition.

France relied on these facts that day, in asking to be allowed to continue her work of civilization in tropical Africa, and he hoped the delegates would give her the means of doing so by recognizing her right to sovereignty in those regions, subject to the assurances he had outlined.

(M. Simon then withdrew.)

M. CLEMENCEAU said that after having heard M. Simon's statement, he proposed that they should now return to the question of the claims put forward by the British Dominions to certain German Colonies. He trusted the discussion would be completed that day.

MR. LLOYD GEORGE expressed the view that it would be better in the first place to come to a decision on the general principle without reference to particular cases. Were annexations to be permitted? Or was some other method to be adopted?

PRESIDENT WILSON observed that the discussion so far had been, in essence, a negation in detail—one case at a time—of the whole principle of mandatories. The discussion had been brought to a point where it looked as if their roads diverged. He thought it would be wise to discontinue this discussion for a few hours, say until the next day, as he feared it might lead to a point where it would otherwise appear as though they had reached a serious disagreement, and this he particularly wished to avoid.

MR. BALFOUR enquired whether it was not true that whilst a good deal of thought had been given to the League of Nations, very little thought had been given to the position of a Mandatory Power. The British Delegates did not reject the idea of a Mandatory Power. On the contrary, broadly speaking, as far as the greater part of the areas conquered by British arms and managed from London were concerned, they regarded that idea with favour.

The objections so far raised had been made, not as regards areas under the direct control of the Capital of the Empire, but as regards the areas conquered by the self-governing Dominions within that empire. Therefore, it might be said that the Delegates of the British Empire were not antagonistic to the principle of the Mandatory.

He (Mr. Balfour) was strongly in favour of the principle. But he was convinced that it had not been worked out. He knew of no paper or speech in which the practical difficulties which they had to face had been worked out in detail. For instance, with reference to the financial question, it had been stated yesterday that should the Mandatory require funds, it would be for the League of Nations to supply the same. That might be a good plan, but he was faced with insuperable difficulties. He agreed that these were not essential to the application of the principle, though they were undoubtedly important points for consideration.

No conclusion had been reached, and no authoritative statement had been made regarding another point, namely, should the tenure of the Mandatory be made temporarily or not? If the tenure were merely temporary, difficulties would arise and there would be perpetual intrigues and agitation. For instance, if a German population were left in one of the German Colonies who could hamper the mandatory and promote a sense of grievance in the minds of the natives by raising expectations of some elysium to come, that might lead to a change in the Mandatory by the League of Nations. In his opinion, the thing could only work, firstly, by the appointment of an honest and competent mandatory, and secondly, by securing his tenure of office. He would like to think these questions over. Further, it appeared to him that exactly the same conditions of trusteeship would not be applicable everywhere, and there were several other similar questions which deserved critical attention. Should not, therefore, those interested carefully consider together what the difficulties were? Any decision come to now would be premature. As regards the general principle, however, the British Empire Delegates favoured it. Moreover the Delegates of the United Kingdom were prepared to go further, and for the areas which fell to them they were prepared to accept the idea. In conclusion he said that he only spoke for himself. He had not consulted the Prime Minister.

MR. LLOYD GEORGE said that he had some discussion about mandatories with the representatives of the British Colonial Department, who raised no difficulties. They thought the difficulties were more imaginary than real. He had been greatly struck by the fact that M. Simon, in his speech, had in the beginning appeared to be bitterly opposed to the whole idea, but in the end he had detailed as acceptable to France the whole list of conditions proposed for a mandatory, except the name. As far as the British Empire was concerned, most of the conquests had been accomplished by British troops, and as far as those territories were concerned Great Britain would be prepared to administer them under such conditions as might be laid down by the League of Nations. He could see no difficulties except perhaps difficulties of definition. Exceptions might have to be made; but then every rule had an exception. He could see no reason why any difficulties should arise in laying down general principles. He was afraid the delegates might, when confronted by a difficulty, get into the habit of putting it off. He himself could not stay here indefinitely, therefore he would ask his colleagues to face the difficulty and to come to a decision. There would be special applications to be thrashed out, but until the principle had been adopted no conclusion on the details could be come to.

PRESIDENT WILSON agreed with Mr. Balfour that there were many points to be cleared up. He admitted that the idea was a new one, and it was not to be expected that it would be found developed in any records or statements. He agreed with what Mr. Lloyd George said were the views of his Colonial Department, viz., that the difficulties were more imaginary than real. In the first place, the composition of the League of Nations, whenever spoken of heretofore, had left the lead to the Great Powers.

Taking the case mentioned by Mr. Balfour where an area contained a German population inclined to intrigue, the mandatory would certainly not be a friend of Germany's; and even if the latter should eventually qualify and be admitted to the League of Nations, at least during a generation her disposition and efforts would be so well known that no responsible man would be misled by them.

He wished that he could agree with Mr. Lloyd George that there was no great difference between the mandatory system and M. Simon's plan. The former assumed trusteeship on the part of the League of Nations; the latter implied definite sovereignty, exercised in the same spirit and under the same conditions as might be imposed upon a mandatory. The two ideas were radically different, and he was bound to assume that the French Colonial Office could not see its way to accept the idea of the mandatory.

He pointed out that Australia claimed sovereignty over German New Guinea; the Union of South Africa over German South West Africa, and Japan over the leased territory of Shantung and the Carolina Islands; while France claimed a modified sovereignty over the Cameroons and Togoland under certain terms. Here they were at this stage when the only acceptance had been on the part of the Imperial British Government with respect to the area taken from Germany by troops under the direct authority of the Government in London. This was an important exception in which he rejoiced, but it appeared to be the only exception to the rejection of the idea of trusteeship on the part of the League of Nations.

They must consider how this treaty would look to the world, for as it looked to the world it would be, since the world would not wait for explanations. The world would say that the Great Powers first portioned out the helpless parts of the world, and then formed a League of Nations. The crude fact would be that each of these parts of the world had been assigned to one of the Great Powers.

He wished to point out, in all frankness, that the world would not accept such action; it would make the League of Nations impossible, and they would have to return to the system of competitive armaments with accumulating debts and the burden of great armies. There must be a League of Nations, and they could not return to the *Status quo ante*. The League of Nations would be a laughing stock if it were not invested with this quality of trusteeship. He felt this so intensely that he hoped that those present would not think that he had any personal antagonism. To secure it no sacrifice would be too great. It was unfortunate that the United States could not make any sacrifice in this particular case as she held none of the territories in dispute. But her people would feel that their sacrifice in coming into the war had been in vain, if the men returning home only came back to be trained in arms and to bear the increased burden of competitive armaments. In that case the United States would have to have a greatly increased navy and maintain a large standing army. This would be so intolerable to the thought of Europe, that they would see this great wave from the East, which would involve the very existence of society, gather fresh volume, because the people of the world would not permit the parcelling out among the Great Powers of the helpless countries conquered from Germany. He felt this so solemnly that he urged them to give it careful thought.

He desired the acceptance of the genuine idea of trusteeship. He regarded this as a test of their labours, and he thought the world would so consider it. He thought it would be most unfortunate if they were, in the instance, to give the world its initial cold bath of disappointment. Sacrifices which seemed critical would have to be made, but if they were not made, they would have to face constant intolerable burdens. He believed that it was from this point of view that the question should be approached and examined. He appreciated the difficulties mentioned by Mr. Balfour, but he believed they were soluble. However, they could not be solved by discussion until they arose in concrete form. They must agree on the principle and leave its application to the League of Nations.

SIR ROBERT BORDEN enquired from President Wilson, purely for his information, with a view to the removal of the difficulty in case it became acute, whether the nomination of a mandatory need be postponed until the League of Nations was constituted. Under the scheme for the creation of a League of Nations, he understood that the five Great Powers would form a Council controlling the work of the League. Therefore the difference between making the decision now or leaving it to the Council of the League of Nations was not great. He would, therefore, ask whether President Wilson would take that suggestion into consideration.

PRESIDENT WILSON replied that he had himself, informally, made that suggestion.

M. ORLANDO said that as regards Colonial questions, the Italian point of view was extremely simple. Italy would readily accept whatever principles might be adopted, provided they were equitably applied and also provided that she could participate in the work of civilization. He did not wish to make the slightest allusion to article 13 of the Pact of London[3] because, even if that agreement had not existed, its principles were so just that they would be applied as a

---

[3] Article XIII of the agreement of Italy with France, Great Britain, and Russia, signed at London on April 26, 1915, provided that, if France or Great Britain were to augment their colonial domains in Africa at Germany's expense, these two powers would recognize in principle that Italy could claim equitable compensations, notably settlement in her favor of the questions concerning the boundaries of the Italian colonies of Eritrea, Somaliland, and Libya and the neighboring British and French colonies. Clive Parry, ed., *The Consolidated Treaty Series*, Vol. 221 (Dobbs Ferry, N. Y., 1981), pp. 56-61.

matter of course. The question they were considering was one of extreme gravity, and the consequences of their decision might be even more serious. Therefore, he thought that perhaps a short adjournment might be advisable. He fully understood Mr. Lloyd George's contention that an adjournment would not of itself lead to a solution of the difficulty, whilst an indefinite adjournment would naturally be a confession of impotence. But President Wilson had proposed that a short adjournment should take place in order that the delegates might have time to reflect and, perhaps, to consider and understand the practical aspect of the question. Under those circumstances he felt inclined to ask one or two questions. Was it the intention of President Wilson that all questions relating to the disposal of conquered territories should, without discussion, be referred to the League of Nations? The consequences of such a procedure would be extremely grave, because the world would think that this Conference had done nothing, and a confession of impotence would be even more serious than disagreement amongst the delegates. He thought that the Conference should lay down general principles, whilst leaving to the League of Nations the practical application of these principles to special cases. There were a number of questions that might well be considered during a short period of adjournment. For instance, should all the German Colonies, without exception, be confided to the League of Nations? In other words, was the rule to admit of no exceptions? As was well known, exceptions proved the rule. He agreed that no exceptions could be made for purely private reasons. But if exceptions were made, based on concrete reasons, then such exceptions would not weaken the rule, but strengthen it. Again, if adjoining territories craved for union on the same grounds that union had been fought for by peoples in Europe, should no exception be made? For instance, if part of a Colony lately under German sovereignty could be joined to an existing colony of which, ethnographically, it formed a part, he thought that an exception should be made and such a decision would be in accordance with President Wilson's ideas on the subject, the rights of peoples to self-determination.

Another point he wished to raise was, how far should the power of a mandatory extend? He thought this trusteeship need not be purely transitory. The difference in the powers accorded to trustees were extreme. In some cases, the trusteeship meant nothing, whereas in other cases it practically meant ownership.

The attributes of the mandatory might well be camouflaged by hypocrisy. Therefore he thought that the powers of the mandatory should be properly graduated to meet the requirements of each case, and in his opinion it was necessary from the very commencement to define the powers to be attributed to mandatories. For instance, South Africa had claimed the right to extend its laws to German South West Africa; but such action would obviously mean the exercise of the powers of sovereignty by a mandatory.

In conclusion he thought the whole question required very careful consideration. He himself was disposed to make every sacrifice to avoid disagreement; but the various issues of the question should be very clearly defined. Personally, he hoped that the general principles would be accepted.

M. CLEMENCEAU wished, in the first place, to say that Mr. Lloyd George had interpreted M. Simon's speech better than President Wilson. The French Colonial Office had expressed its views, but that did not mean that he himself was not ready to make concessions if reasonable proposals were put forward. All his sentiments were in agreement with those of President Wilson. He agreed with him as to the gravity of the decision to be taken, and the seriousness of the situation that would result therefrom. There was danger in refusing a means of salvation; but there was greater danger in adopting the wrong means of salvation. The League of Nations, he thought, was to be a League of Defence to ensure the peace of the world. But it appeared they had now gone beyond that limit when they proposed to create a League of Nations with governmental functions to interfere in internal affairs, with trustees in various places sending reports to—he did not know whom. Throughout the world, even in Europe, and perhaps in the Adriatic, a control would be set up. President Wilson himself had said so, and, as a result, appeals would be heard from all parts of the world. Who would deal with those appeals? It had been said that an International Legislature and some sort of executive power, about which he knew nothing, would have to be created, without any power to administer penalties, since this question had never been raised. The idea of an unknown mandatory acting through an undetermined tribunal gave him some anxiety. He did not regret the discussions which had taken place on the subject, since these discussions had impressed him with the justness of the claims of the Dominions. However, since Mr. Lloyd George was prepared to accept the mandate of a League of Nations he would not dissent from the general agreement, merely for the sake of the Cameroons and Togoland. But, when President Wilson asked that every question should be referred to the League of Nations, he felt a little nervous, and feared that the remedy might be worse than the disease. President Wilson had said that the opinion of the world would rise up against them and that savagery was ready to flow over the world from the East to the West. That might be, but he was not in full agreement with

President Wilson when the latter said that they had to choose between a League of Nations with legislative initiative, as he had already dealt with that question. He would at once take up the question of a League for the preservation of Peace. He greatly favoured such a League, and he was prepared to make all sacrifices to attain that object. If insisted upon, he would assent to a League with full powers to initiate laws, but he would ask that his objections be recorded, as he had no confidence in such a scheme. He might be too conservative—that being a fault of age. In a speech which he had made to the Chamber of Deputies a few days ago he had stated that if, before the war, the Great Powers had made an alliance pledging themselves to take up arms in defence of any one of them who might be attacked, there would have been no war. Today they had not only five nations in agreement but practically the whole world. If the nations pledged themselves not to attack any one without the consent of the members of the League, and to defend any one of them who might be attacked, the peace of the world would be assured. Such an alliance might well be termed a League of Nations. Such procedures, and tribunals, as might be thought necessary could be added. He would accept all these. If Mr. Lloyd George were to promise that he would accept these two conditions, the League of Nations would be created in less than three days.

MR. LLOYD GEORGE said that he agreed with M. Clemenceau that if the League of Nations were made an executive for purposes of governing, and charged with functions which it would be unable to perform, it would be destroyed from the beginning. But he had not so interpreted the mandatory principle when he had accepted it.

PRESIDENT WILSON said he too had not so interpreted it.

MR. LLOYD GEORGE, continuing, said that he regarded the system merely as a general trusteeship upon defined conditions. Only when those conditions were scandalously abused would the League of Nations have the right to interfere and to call on the mandatory for an explanation. For instance, should a mandatory allow foul liquor to swamp the territories entrusted to it, the League of Nations would have the right to insist on a remedy of the abuse. The Powers now exercised this right by diplomatic correspondence, resulting in the giving of assurances, but frequently nothing was done. He would, however, make an appeal to President Wilson to consider the following point of view. He trusted the President would not insist on postponing the selection of mandatories until after the League of Nations had been established. That was a serious matter, for, as long as all these questions were unsettled, everything would be unsettled. People were unsettled all over the world, not only the labourers and the soldiers, but also the employers. Great Britain now occupied territories where they had no intention of remaining even if the League of Nations asked them to stay. For instance, British troops occupied Russian Armenia and Serbia. They did not wish to be there, but some one had got to be there. Was Great Britain to be compelled to keep its troops there until the League of Nations was a going concern? Again, as regards German East Africa, if Great Britain was not to be the mandatory, it had a big force there now which it would not wish to keep there. Therefore, they must know what their position was to be, and they would not settle down to their own business until these questions were decided. During the past week, the question of the renewal of the Military Service Act in the United Kingdom had come under consideration. It appeared they were now maintaining large forces—over 170,000 British troops alone in Syria, Caucasus, East Africa, and other out-of-the-way places. These troops must sooner or later be withdrawn, but they could not do that without knowing who would take their place. They could not withdraw and leave the people to massacre each other. They would be compelled to hand the country to some one. Therefore, he would leave the settlement to this tribunal, and an early solution was urgently needed. As Sir Robert Borden had stated, this Council was practically the League of Nations, which was born on Saturday. In conclusion, he asked whether he had correctly interpreted M. Clemenceau's views to the effect that he was prepared to accept trusteeship.

M. CLEMENCEAU replied that although he did not approve of it, he would be guided by the judgment of his colleagues.

MR. LLOYD GEORGE enquired whether this meeting would, under those conditions, be prepared to accept the principle of trusteeship.

PRESIDENT WILSON observed that the difficulty about troops mentioned by Mr. Lloyd George applied equally well to the 371,000 troops on the Western front. He also observed that the question of deciding the disposition of the German Colonies was not vital to the life of the world in any respect. It was the determination of the pressing European questions which was all-important. They could address themselves to the solution of those European questions while waiting for a solution of the Colonial questions.

As to what Mr. Lloyd George was so kind as to call an appeal, of course he appreciated its weight; but his difficulty was to prevent the assignment of mandatories, if they were to be the Great Powers, from appearing to the world as a mere distribution of the spoils.

MR. HUGHES expressed the view that "trustee" was a better word to employ than "mandatory."

MR. MASSEY agreed that the public did not know what was meant by the word "mandatory."

BARON MAKINO enquired whether the principle of a mandatory had been accepted.

M. CLEMENCEAU replied in the negative, and added that the question had merely been adjourned.

(The Meeting adjourned until 11 a.m. on the following day.)

T MS (SDR, RG 256, 180.03101/21, DNA).

## To Hsü Shih-ch'ang

My dear Mr. President:          Paris, 28 January, 1919.

Your letter[1] so kindly handed me yesterday by Mr. Lou Tseng-Tsiang,[2] Minister of Foreign Affairs, has given me the greatest gratification.

I share with you the hope that in the years to come the friendly relations between China and the United States will be rendered even more intimate and cordial than in the past. I am sure that in all circumstances you can count upon the good will of the United States and the interests of her Government in the independence, safety, and prosperity of China.

It gives me pleasure to send you my warm personal greetings.

I am finding pleasure in being associated with the representatives of China in the Peace Conference.

With the best wishes,

        Cordially and sincerely yours,    [Woodrow Wilson]

CCL (WP, DLC).
   [1] Hsü Shih-ch'ang to WW, Nov. 20, 1918, printed as an Enclosure with FLP to JPT, Jan. 21, 1919.
   [2] That is, Lu Cheng-hsiang.

## To John Joseph Pershing

My dear General:          Paris, 28 January, 1919.

I very much appreciated your note of the twenty-fifth correcting the wrong impression which might have been conveyed by the form of the information which General Foch gave us concerning the German forces at the Western front. It is very serviceable indeed to have that erroneous impression corrected.

Knowing that the British were basing their conferences as to the number of men they should maintain at the Western front upon the memorandum of General Foch, I took the liberty of sending

Mr. Lloyd George a copy of your letter, requesting that he regard it as confidential.

          Cordially and faithfully yours,   [Woodrow Wilson]

CCL (WP, DLC).

## To Carter Glass

Paris, 28 January, 1919.

I sincerely hope that you will represent to the conferees on the Food Relief Bill in my name how important it is that the Bill should pass in the form in which the House has passed it. There is no purpose or possibility of our using the money for credits to Germany but some very complicated questions are connected with the relief of the Christian people mixed in with the Mohammedan people in the southeast.          Woodrow Wilson.

T telegram (WP, DLC).

## To Thomas Staples Martin

Paris, 28 January, 1919.

May I not express my very deep gratification at the passage of the Food Relief Bill and congratulate you upon the public service you have rendered in its advocacy. I sincerely hope that it will be possible to bring the bill out of conference in the form in which it left the House. There is no purpose or possibility of our using the money for credits to Germany but some very complicated questions are connected with the relief of the Christian people mixed in with the Mohammedan people in the southeast.

          Woodrow Wilson.

T telegram (WP, DLC).

## From Joseph Patrick Tumulty

The White House, 28 January 1919.

I am afraid if I convey your message about home rule to Flood[1] of whose friendship I am not assured, that improper use will be made of it. Your message might be construed as opposition. If Flood was in our confidence, I would not be afraid. Is it not well understood on the other side that you cannot control action of House of Representatives? There is deep sentiment here for home rule and

I do not wish you to be put in position of seeming to oppose it. That is what would result if it appeared that upon your request no action was taken by House Committee.                    Tumulty.

T telegram (J. P. Tumulty Papers, DLC).

¹ It is missing in both the Wilson and Tumulty Papers. However, it concerned House Joint Resolution 357, which had been introduced by Thomas Gallagher, Democratic congressman from Illinois, on December 3, 1918. The resolution requested the American commissioners to the peace conference to present to, and urge upon, the conference "the right to freedom, independence, and self-determination of Ireland." About the fate of the Gallagher resolution, see E. F. Kinkead to WW, March 8, 1919, n. 4.

## From Edward Mandell House

Dear Governor:                    Paris, January 28th, 1919.

I believe the entire British Delegation, including the other dominion representatives, are opposed to Hughes in his claim for annexation as opposed to the mandatory system. Either Hughes claims the Pacific Islands by right of conquest and as a reward for Australia's services in the war or he must accept the mandatory of the League of Nations for the better government of the backward people of the Pacific Islands. It is doubtful if public opinion in Australia is really behind Hughes and if he persists in his claim the best solution would be to tell him that the whole arguments on both sides must be published in order that the world may judge Australia's claims, but so far as the Conference is concerned his proposal strikes at the whole idea of the League of Nations and cannot be accepted.    Affectionately yours,   E. M. House

I have written this with a full knowledge of the case.

TLS (WP, DLC).

## From the Diary of Colonel House

January 28, 1919.

The President called me over the private wire at 9.30 and I have just had a twenty minute talk with him. He is much disturbed at the turn of things this afternoon. The French and British are demanding that if the "Mandatory" is used by the League of Nations as to the German Colonies, it shall be used immediately and the different powers designated now rather than later. The President asked my advice as to procedure. He had in mind to tell them that if they maintained their attitude, he intended to give both sides to the public. In lieu of this I suggested that he tell them that he did not believe they voiced the opinion of the Conference as a whole, and that it was his purpose at the next general meeting to bring the matter before the Conference and ask for an opinion. My purpose in this is that since proceedings of the General Conference are public, he will get exactly the same publicity as he would by the method he suggested, and there could be no criticism by the powers. He thought well of this and said he would keep it "up his sleeve" and if he could not bring them to terms tomorrow, he would use it.

I told him these secret meetings smacked largely of "star chamber methods" and were creating criticism and dissatisfaction. I was certain if the meeting had been open, Lloyd George and Clemenceau would never have dared express the views they expressed this afternoon. He agreed to this and yet I cannot get him to break away and demand open sessions.

## From the Diary of Dr. Grayson

Wednesday, January 29, 1919.

Another day was spent fighting over the mandatory question at the conference. When I asked the President at dinner what had been accomplished, he replied with one word: "Neutral." As a matter of fact the President was gaining ground but only by constant fighting and at a very severe tax upon his mental resources.

## Hankey's Notes of Two Meetings of the Council of Ten[1]

Quai d'Orsay, January 29, 1919, 11 A.M.

BC-15

[The council adopted the following draft of instruction for the delegates of the Allied governments in Poland:]

It will be the business of the Delegates of the Allied Governments to convey as early as possible information to their Governments on the present situation in Poland. The Military question and the Food question are the most urgent, but reports on the political and social conditions of the country should be sent without unnecessary delay.

The Polish Government should be warned against adopting a policy of an aggressive character. Any appearance of attempting to prejudge the decisions of the Conference will have the worst possible effect. The Delegates should invite the most earnest consideration of the Polish Government to the declaration recently made on this subject by the representatives of the Powers at Paris.[2]

[1] The complete text of these minutes is printed in PPC, III, 772-79.
[2] See the minutes of the Council of Ten printed at Jan. 24, 1919, 12:15 p.m.

Every effort should be made to bring to an end the hostilities which are now taking place between the Poles and neighbouring peoples. Armistices should be arranged wherever possible and the Delegates should use their good offices to bring them about.

In this connection it should be noted that the invasion by the Poles of German territory tends to restore the German military spirit and to delay the breakup of the German army; and it has the further disadvantage of complicating the arrangements for German disarmament which the Allies desire to carry out with the least possible delay.

The Delegates should enquire how far the Polish Government possess the means to maintain order within their existing territory and of preserving it from external aggression whether carried out by Bolshevists or any other forces and they should study and report on the measures necessary to supply any deficiencies which may be found to exist.

The food question will require their earnest attention and they should co-operate with the Mission about to be despatched to Poland by the Supreme Council of Supply and Relief. In order to secure this co-operation the principal Delegates of the Supreme Council of Supply and Relief should be attached to the Delegation whenever questions of food supply have to be dealt with.

[Clemenceau, responding to a question by Sonnino, said that a decision as to whether some Polish prisoners in Italy should be sent to Poland should be delayed until a decision was reached as to the Polish soldiers in France.]

2. Thereupon M. Dmowski, accompanied by M. Erasme Piltz[3] were called in in order to enlighten the meeting as to the position in Poland.

M. DMOWSKI wished to know on what particular point he should first attempt to speak, or what points the meeting specially desired information upon.

M. CLEMENCEAU replied that it would perhaps be best that he should say whatever he might have to say so as to place the meeting in a position to consider the question as a whole. It would be possible later on to take the various points in rotation.

PRESIDENT WILSON stated that he was anxious to know the whole case, but that the present object of the Allies was to assist Poland, as far as the Allies could, and they were certain that his views on that subject would be most interesting.

M. DMOWSKI then proceeded to state that the Poles had not been protected to any large extent by the Armistice, but two things did have reference to the situation in Poland. By Article 12 of the Ar-

[3] Member of the Polish National Committee in Paris.

mistice the Germans were obliged to occupy the Eastern Frontier until such time as the Allies should request them to withdraw their troops. And secondly, Article 16 provided that access should be given the Allies to Poland via the Dantzig-Thorn railway. If the German troops had remained, under the terms of the Armistice, in the Eastern Provinces, their presence would have protected the Poles against the Bolsheviks; and if the route through Dantzig had remained open Poland would have been able to have obtained all the arms and ammunition and supplies that she might require. The revolution in Germany had prevented the carrying out of the terms of the Armistice, and the German troops withdrew in a disorderly manner before the Allies had requested them to do so. On their way they were guilty of committing crimes, and they carried away supplies and railway material with them as they went. Dantzig was situated within German territory and was in German possession after the signing of the Armistice. The railway from Dantzig to the Frontier of Poland (a distance of some 100 miles) ran through German territory, and since the conclusion of the Armistice the Germans have shown more and more hostility towards the Poles. Secondly, Article 16 was altogether a dead-letter. In order to make it effective it was absolutely necessary to occupy Dantzig and the railway line running to the Polish frontier so as to allow of arms, ammunition and supplies being forwarded to Poland. Unless this was done, both Articles would remain a dead-letter.

3. M. DMOWSKI next turned to the situation in German Poland specifically. He stated that, according to German statistics, there were four million Poles in Eastern Posen, Eastern Prussia, Western Prussia and Upper Silesia; but, according to the Polish estimate, this number was five million. These Poles were some of the most educated and highly cultured of the nation, with a strong sense of nationality and men of progressive ideas. Even according to the German statement, in these Provinces it was admitted that the Polish farmers and merchants were of a higher standing than the German ones. As soon as the opportunity offered itself to organise themselves, these Poles established a Government by pacific means and then waited until the Peace Conference should have decided upon the status of Poland. All they desired was that Germany should not put anything in the way of their joining up with the other Polish Provinces. But this movement, as showing the aim of the Poles, rather frightened the Germans who immediately proceeded to take steps to suppress it and organised a special corps, known as the "Heimatschutz Ost," consisting largely of officers, with the idea of crushing this political movement. Troops had been concentrated in the Eastern Provinces waiting for the opportunity to attack. When

M. Paderewski came to Posen, he was most enthusiastically received by the population, which remained quite pacific. But the Germans attacked them with machine guns. In consequence an armed conflict arose and fighting took place in the streets of Posen. The Poles were victorious and occupied the city and the fortress. Once that conflict had begun it was bound to spread, and it spread throughout the whole of the Province until the Germans were practically pushed out of the district. The Poles established a civic government which kept order without doing harm to the inhabitants: conduct very different from that of the Germans, possibly because the Poles were at home, or the Germans were in a foreign territory to them. Further, he reminded the meeting that the Conference had issued a declaration with regard to disputable territory. (see I.C. 119).[4] The Poles in Posen would understand that this declaration and this warning was addressed to them as well, and as it is their desire to stand well with the Allies, they will certainly respect it and it will make a great impression on them. But the Germans certainly will not respect it, but are continuing their organisation against Poland. The result will be that unless the Allies stop both sides (the Germans as well as the Poles), Poland inevitably must be crushed. The Germans have a great respect for the power of the Allies, and M. Dmowski felt that if they received a similar order to cease fighting the possibility was they would accept the same.

M. DMOWSKI added that German Poland had as much in the way of supplies as she wanted, in fact more than she required, as the German soldiers, on their return, had requisitioned food along the way to carry themselves on. But the other Polish provinces were starving for want of food. He compared Germany to the god Janus. Germany had one face towards the West, where she had made peace, and the other face towards the East, where she was organising for war. Her troops there were concentrated and out for war. She might have given up the West, but she had not given up her plan for extending her Empire to the East. As regards German Poland, he made one proposition only, and that was that both sides should discontinue fighting, and should be ordered to stay where they were. The Poles were extremely anxious to keep the rolling stock at present at Posen which the Germans were threatening to take away as they themselves were short of rolling stock.

4. Russian Poland found itself, after the Armistice, in a most difficult position. The nucleus of the Government, which the Germans had established in 1916, continued until the Armistice, but once the Armistice was concluded it could not stand, on the one hand be-

4 That is, the declaration cited in n. 2 above.

cause it had been established by the Germans, and on the other hand, because it was too conservative. The Government was then handed over to General Pilsudski, a member of the Socialist Party, who had become very popular as he had fought against Russia in the beginning of the war and afterwards had been imprisoned by the Germans. It was perhaps the safest thing for Poland that she now had a Socialist Government, because she had no arms or army to protect herself. On the one side there was a Socialistic Revolutionary Government, and on the other, a Democratic Government, which had established a revolution in Germany. Had this not been the case, the Socialistic Government of Pilsudski could not have lasted. As it was, his Government was in great difficulties, as there was a majority against them even in Russian Poland, but more particularly in German Poland and also in Austrian Poland, the two latter provinces being much better organised and more advanced than Russian Poland. But the greatest weakness of all was that the Pilsudski Government had no money. Inevitably, therefore, attempts were made to overthrow his Government, and even the National Council of the Poles in Paris was approached to aid in this object. The National Council refused because it felt that a Socialistic Government, situated between two extreme Socialistic Governments, was necessary for the safety of Poland at the time, and it concentrated its efforts on arranging a compromise with the Socialists. Consequently, the National Council sent M. Paderewski to Poland in order to establish a Government by compromise, his strong point being that he had so far taken no part in party politics. He was successful and formed a Government representing all portions of the provinces of Poland and also the main parties. We had, perhaps, taken too long to come to this compromise, but the reason was that Socialistic Governments were, from their very nature, not given much to compromise.

5. As already mentioned the German soldiers on returning from the Eastern front committed many crimes, but their worst crime of all was the fact that they assisted the Bolsheviks by leaving them their arms and ammunition, and also by allowing them to follow the Germans up in close succession. At the same time the German General at Vilna refused passage to the Polish troops. In this way the Germans were advancing the aim of Bolshevism to get into touch with German territory and so to join hands and make common cause with the Spartacist group inside Germany. Today the Bolshevik troops were threatening Poland and were about 150 miles from Warsaw. The difficulty of Poland was not the lack of men; she had enough to defend herself, but her difficulty was that she had no arms to arm them with or ammunition with which to fight.

As evidence of the shortage of ammunition, he stated that the inhabitants of Poland had sent 8 million rounds of cartridges to Warsaw in order to assist in defending the country.

6. The Austrian troops on their return from Eastern Galicia distributed their arms amongst the people, and, at the same time, were guilty of atrocious massacres, particularly of landowners. It was estimated that some 2,000 landowners with their families were murdered in this fashion. In Eastern Galicia, Ukrainian bands actually took Lemberg and held it for a few days, and even though they had been driven out, they were not far from the town.

M. DMOWSKI summed up the position by stating that Poland was threatened on three sides; first by the Bolsheviks on the East, second by the Ukrainian bands on the South-East and by the Germans on the North-West. The problem to settle was not the question of supplying Poland with men, but with arms and ammunition and assistance to organise their army. This object could only be attained by using the railway running from Dantzig to the Polish frontier. It was impossible to use the Austro-Hungarian railway system, as that system was not extensive enough and it would take too long, and the question of assistance was extremely urgent. He suggested the temporary occupation by Allied troops of Dantzig and of the railway line between Dantzig and Poland. He further suggested that some agreement should be made with the Germans whereby arms, ammunition and troops could be sent along this railway line and the railway line be occupied by Polish troops. In his opinion it would be much better for the Allies to occupy this line in agreement with the Germans, as if the Poles were to do so the Germans might regard this as an aggressive act by Poland. If Poland could not be assisted and assisted quickly, she must be crushed and submerged by Bolshevism. The only way was to open a means of rapid and sure communication and the only sure and rapid route was that between Dantzig and Thorn. He expressed the opinion that there was not much fear of Bolshevism extending to German and Austrian Poland because those provinces were well organised and politically sound. In his opinion Bolshevism really was the rule of a despotic organisation representing a well organised class in a country where all other classes were passive and disorganised. In a country where the various classes were politically organised and enlightened, Bolshevism in the true sense of the word was not a serious danger. It was only possible where a country was passive and disorganised.

7. The province of Teschen in Silesia is occupied partly by Czechs and partly by Poles, the latter of whom are in a great majority. It was accordingly agreed in November, 1918, that that portion of the country where the majority of the inhabitants are Poles should be

regarded as the Polish sphere, and that portion which is inhabited by the Czechs as the majority, should be the Czech sphere. This agreement, which had been concluded by the local organisations, was approved by the Polish Government, but not by the Czecho-Slovak Government and recently Czech troops had entered this disputed territory. This act was not only one of violence but it was a dangerous act because if the Czech troops continue to remain there bloodshed inevitably must follow and much more harm might be done to the ultimate settlement of this dispute. M. Dmowski urged that the only settlement was that these Czech troops should be withdrawn to the territory as arranged in the terms of the agreement of the 5th November, pending a settlement by the Peace Conference.

8. M. DMOWSKI proceeded to direct attention to the anti-Polish policy of the Germans and referred to their anti-Polish laws; their prohibition of the use of the Polish language in the schools and their confiscation of the property of Poles. He quoted the special and powerful company which had been erected for the special purpose of colonising portions of Poland with German settlers and in that connection quoted von Bülow's[5] remarks that the whole of Poland is an enemy and pointed out that Germany had employed means to influence both Austria and Russia to adopt the same line of policy. During the war there were two policies, one of annexation of Poland, but this plan was given up because there had been so much difficulty with the five million Poles in the German Eastern provinces, that it was felt to increase the number of recalcitrant subjects would only make matters more difficult. So the other programme was adopted of establishing a small kingdom consisting of some twelve million inhabitants and round it to place two other small states, Lithuania and Ukrainia. The latter two, in case of a German victory, would be completely under German domination, as neither Lithuania nor Ukrainia could, strictly speaking, be said to have reached the stage of nationhood. The national movement in Lithuania was not older than 40 years, and, although the movement had shown great activity, the Lithuanians had not advanced so far yet as to entitle themselves to be called a nation fit to protect themselves and to accept the responsibilities and duties of the state. The same remarks applied to Ukrainia. The aim of this arrangement of establishing two small states was to split up Russia and Poland, both of whom were enemies. The whole idea dominating this programme was that by this means Poland would ultimately be strangled and submerged.

5 That is, Bernhard Heinrich Martin Karl, Prince von Bülow.

M. DMOWSKI suggested that in reaching the settlement of the territory to belong to Poland, we should start from the date 1772, before the first partition. This did not mean that she must be reconstituted on the same boundaries as then existed, but this must be the point of departure and the boundaries should be rectified according to present conditions. France, Italy, Great Britain and similar countries, owing to the statistics they kept, and to their well-defined boundaries, were able to state immediately what their territory was, and what their people were. But not so with Poland. In settling the boundaries of Poland, the principle of including within those boundaries those territories where the Poles were in a large majority, must not be accepted altogether. In the West, Poland could not be satisfied with the historical boundaries of 1772. For instance, Silesia was lost in the 14th Century, but today 90% of the population, owing to the national revival, had kept its language and was strongly Polish. For instance, 15 years ago, Silesia sent a Polish representative to the Austrian Reichsrat. Furthermore, geographically speaking, Silesia falls within the whole territory of Poland.

(The Meeting adjourned until 3.30 p.m. in the afternoon.)

T MS (SDR, RG 256, 180.03101/22, DNA).

Quai d'Orsay, January 29, 1919, 3:30 P.M.[1]

BC-16

1. M. DMOWSKI, resuming his statement, stated furthermore that the whole territory of Eastern Germany was not naturally German but was Germanised, and quoted Von Bülow as saying what Germany had lost in the West as a result of the break up of the Empire of Charlemagne, she had gained in the East. He quoted Dantzig as an illustration, saying that though, according to the German statistics, only 3 percent of the inhabitants were Poles, he felt certain that at least 40 percent belonged to that nationality. As the Poles were mostly employees, they would be afraid of stating that their nationality was Polish for fear of being dismissed, and he referred to the fact that soon after the Armistice a protest meeting had been held by the Germans against Dantzig being incorporated in Poland. When the petition which had been drawn up at that meeting was circulated for signature, only 16 signatories were to be found, and of those 14 were those of officials. Ethnographically, the limits of Poland were irregular, and pointed to the fact that some wrong would have to be done East Prussia. Either a small

[1] The complete text of these notes is printed in PPC, III, 780-84.

island of Germans must be left in the midst of Polish territory, or
the large Polish population must remain under Germany. His suggestion was that the small island of German people should be made
a republic with its capital at Königsberg. He maintained that it
would be more just to expose a small Germanised country to infiltration by Poles, than to deprive all Poland of economic independence and to expose it to German aggression. Summing up the
question of what is, or what is not, Polish territory, he said that a
rough definition would be that such territory as had been oppressed
by anti-Polish laws was Polish territory. From the point of view of
the preservation of peace, it was evident that if the coast belonged
to one nation and the land to another, there would be mutual tendency to conquest. This had been fully appreciated by the Germans
with the result that was apparent in their policy, which had aimed
at the gradual absorption of Polish lands, and pointed out the colonisation schemes not only in German Poland but also in Russian
Poland, and in this connection he quoted Herr Bebel, the Socialist
Democrat, in his work "*Die Frau*: Our task is not to colonise Africa,
but to colonise the Vistula."[2] It could not be expected that this idea
of absorbing Poland would die amongst the Germans. Therefore,
he urged that the frontiers should be so arranged that Poland should
no longer be exposed to this danger.

2. Polish land reached to the Dnieper and the Dwina when the
union of the colonies of Poland and Lithuania took place in the
13th and 14th centuries, but to-day the bulk of the population of
Lithuania was not Polish, though the Lithuanians were closely
allied, so he conceded that the Eastern Frontiers of Poland should
be curtailed and a large portion remain under Russia. Both Lithuania and Ukrainia he excluded, and did not lay claim to these
countries as part of Poland.

Finally, he suggested that the subject of Poland should be viewed
from the standpoint of a League of Nations and he defined a nation
as a race of men capable of so organising itself as to be able to
express collective will and of organising its affairs both externally
and internally. In a word, it must be able to govern itself and to
oppose oppression. Tested by this test Russia, strictly speaking, was
not fit for admission to a League of Nations, nor were the Lithuanians advanced far enough in national unity or ideals to be included amongst the nations. The Ukrainian State at present was
really organised anarchy and the Ukrainians were not so far ad-

---

[2] The book mentioned is presumably August Bebel, *Die Frau unter dem Sozialismus*,
which appeared under at least two titles and in many editions from c. 1870 until well into
the twentieth century. However, the Editors have not found any such statement in the editions
in German and English.

vanced as the Lithuanians on the road to nationality. The great need in Eastern Europe was to have established Governments, able to assure order and to express their will in foreign and in internal policy. It was too early to think of Lithuania or Ukrainia as independent States. Therefore, it would be best that, if organized as separate states they should be united in some other state, and as the Lithuanians were closely allied to the Poles, he suggested Poland as the best state to which they should be united. All that remained East of Poland, he feared, would remain for a long time subject to anarchy. He expressed the opinion that in Russia there would be a despotism for some time to come, because the masses were too indolent and passive. They were able to be ruled but not fit to rule. The red despotism of Bolshevism would last for some time but the reaction would come and a possible return to Czardom with all its vices. In Poland they were afraid of the anarchy prevalent in the Eastern districts of old historical Poland and, therefore, they were satisfied to renounce these districts for the sake of preserving peace and order within their own borders.

3. Eastern Galicia was, he admitted, a disputed territory, but he claimed that they were unable to organize a Government and pointed to the fact that in the intellectual professions, excluding small farmers and clergy, there were 400,000 Poles and only 16,000 Ruthenes. They might be entitled to home rule but they were unable to create a separate state.

M. ERASME PILTZ wished to associate himself with M. Dmowski as to the danger threatened from the Bolsheviks, and expressed the fear that if troops were sent they would arrive too late. The point he wished to express most forcibly was the urgency of sending help to Poland as soon as possible.

MR. BALFOUR remarked that the first portion of M. Dmowski's statement dealt with the immediate and pressing question of the Polish situation. The latter part dealt with territorial questions which would have to be discussed later on by the Conference. To-day they were only concerned with the first question.

M. CLEMENCEAU said that the Czecho-Slovak representatives were there to deal with the Teschen question, which is disputed territory.

(It was decided that the Czecho-Slovak representatives should be admitted.)

4. DR. BENES, on behalf of Czecho-Slovakia, proceeded to make a statement as to the position of Bohemia, Moravia, and Eastern Silesia.

MR. LLOYD GEORGE said that he was sorry to intervene to point out that the meeting was not dealing with the whole question of Czecho-Slovakia to-day, but would have to enter into that whole question at a later date. They were dealing to-day with one narrow point, and that was the territory in dispute between the Czecho-Slovaks and the Poles.

M. CLEMENCEAU said he thought it was necessary to have the whole case of the Czechs as the meeting had had the whole case of Poland.

PRESIDENT WILSON suggested that the only question which was the business of the day was information as to the position in Eastern Silesia between the Poles and the Czecho-Slovaks, and suggested that the statement should be confined to that point only.

M. CLEMENCEAU then requested Dr. Benes to confine himself to the dispute between the Czecho-Slovaks and the Poles.

DR. BENES proceeded to deal with this question at length on statistical, ethnological, historical and economic grounds.

(Full details are available in the Pamphlet entitled "The Problem of Teschen Silesia" submitted by the Czecho-Slovak delegation.[3] Copies of this pamphlet are obtainable at the office of the Sec-retary-General.)

DR. BENES added, as regards the ethnological question, that his government disputed the correctness of Austrian statistics. For in-stance in the case of the town of Richvaldt the Austrian statistics gave as the population in 1900: 4,500 Poles against 11 Czechs; and in 1910, 2,900 Czechs against 3,000 Poles. This gives a clear idea of the manner in which Austrian statistics are compiled.

DR. KRAMARTZ[4] asked to be allowed to emphasise certain points made by Dr. Benes and stated that he had always thought that the points of difference between the Poles and the Czecho-Slovaks would be settled by mutual agreement. To his surprise, the Poles invaded this territory, mobilized the male population, and even went so far as to fix an election day, and settled that the Courts should fall under the Court of Cracow. On representations being made to him by the population of that quarter, his reply was that the Peace Conference must decide the question of disputed territory, and that he had been informed by France and Great Britain that the Czecho-Slovaks were entitled to occupy the historical boundaries of the old Czech Kingdom. He had protested to the Polish Government, and has sent a second protest; but no reply was forthcoming. He was told that if this present condition continued, it was very likely the Bolshevist activity would follow, and therefore he had acted care-fully so as to avoid bloodshed.

The second point he emphasised was the fact that the Czecho-

---

[3] Not found.
[4] Karel Kramář (Karl Kramartz in German), Prime Minister of Czechoslovakia from Novem-ber 1918 to July 1919; at this time he and Edvard Beneš, the Czechoslovakian Foreign Minister, were the official delegates of Czechoslovakia at the Paris Peace Conference.

Slovak Republic could not exist without the large coal area which was within the disputed area.

In conclusion, he stated that they had always endeavored to arrive at a private agreement with Poland, but this had failed. Therefore, they now desired to place themselves entirely in the hands of the Peace Conference, in the full confidence that the Great Powers would not forget the great sacrifices which they had made in their cause during the war, and that they would not lose sight of the economic requirements of the country upon which the whole prosperity of the Czecho-Slovak Republic depended.

MR. BALFOUR suggested that the representatives of Poland and of the Czecho-Slovaks should meet the members of the Commission appointed by the Peace Conference to investigate Polish questions the following morning at 10 o'clock, so that they could commence that work of pacification and arrangements could be made in Paris immediately.

(This was agreed to.)

M. CLEMENCEAU expressed the wish to hear what M. Dmowski had to say on this subject.

M. DMOWSKI in a short reply, regretted that apparently the Czecho-Slovak Government had not been fully informed as to what was taking place in Silesia, and stated that it was not the Poles that had invaded Teschen, but the inhabitants had organised themselves militarily; not a single soldier had been sent from Poland. He suggested that any further movement of the Czecho-Slovak Army should be stopped, pending the decision of the Conference.

5. MR. BALFOUR suggested that the Commission which would meet on the morrow should also consider the question of supplying arms and munitions to Poland.

M. CLEMENCEAU, in summing up, stated that the delegates would meet the representatives of Poland and of Czecho-Slovakia the following morning, Thursday, the 30th January, at 10 o'clock, at the Quai d'Orsay, and would report on the Teschen dispute as well as on the supply of arms and munitions to Poland.

(This was agreed to, and the meeting adjourned until 11 o'clock on Thursday, January 30th.)

T MS (SDR, RG 256, 180.03101/23, DNA).


# From Georgii Vasil'evich Chicherin

Moscow, 29th January 1919.

A radio-telegram of Carnavon date of Jan. 23rd, containing press review states that according to your proposition the Allied Powers sent per radio the previous night an invitation to the various Governments existing in fact in Russia to the conference on the sea of Marmara stop. The Government of the Russian Soviet Republic has not received their invitation stop. We see ourselves compelled to draw your attention to this fact in order that the absence of an answer from our side should not be a cause *nof* Minster presentation [of misrepresentation] stop. Peoples commissary for foreign affairs Tchitcherine

T telegram (WP, DLC).

## From Boghos Nubar

Mr. President,                                   Paris, le January 29th 1919

I feel deeply grateful for your sincere and sympathetic expressions wherewith you have been kind enough to acquaint me the reason for the non-admittance of Armenia's representative into the Peace Conference.

Your letter, testifying as it does to your solicitude for the Armenian cause, is the first comforting word, officially expressed, that we have received in these fateful hours when Armenians anxiously await the decisions of the Conference upon the destiny of their Mother Country.

In the name of the National Delegation and in that of all Armenians, I beg to tender to you our heartfelt gratitude.

We felt confident that our cause, that of a martyred christian nation, would have within the Conference its champion in your person, who as the incarnation of the ideals of the United States, consistently proclaimed the sacred principles of Right & Justice, whereon shall dwell the future Peace.

But your kind disposition encourages me to request the honor of a short audience which will enable me to put before you certain aspects of the Armenian question, which it is well and important that you should know before the Conference tackles the question.

I am well aware, Mr. President, how completely your time is taken up with your most important work, but the solution of the Armenian problem will have such an important bearing on the future peace of the Near-East that I hope you will be good enough to grant me a short audience before you return to America.

I have the honour to be, Mr. President,

Most Respectfully yours,    Boghos Nubar

TLS (WP, DLC).

## Gilbert Fairchild Close to Chaim Weizmann

My dear Doctor Weizmann:                    Paris, 29 January, 1919.

The President asks me to acknowledge receipt of your letter of January 24th conveying to him the resolutions adopted by Jewish Organizations in various parts of the world and to say that he has read it with the greatest interest. The whole subject is very much in his thoughts.          Sincerely yours,   [Gilbert F. Close]

CCL (WP, DLC).

## From the Diary of Colonel House

January 29, 1919.

General Smuts came to see me at 10.30 in order to see whether we could not get together on the colonies question. He had drafted a paper which he said Lloyd George and some of them approved, but which they had not offered Hughes and Massey.[1] They did not want to present the paper unless they knew it was satisfactory to the President and to me. When I read it I saw they had made great concessions from the position they took yesterday, and I told him, with a few slight verbal changes, I was ready to accept it.

Lloyd George "cut" the meeting at the Quai d'Orsay and waited for Smuts' return. They had their meeting with the Prime Ministers of the Colonies and succeeded in putting the resolution through. In the meantime, I had sent it to the Quai d'Orsay with a memorandum on the margin stating that I approved. The President's memorandum back to me is also attached.[2] In talking to him about it later, he thought it was a basis for an agreement.

The President came tonight and had a meeting with the Commissioners; and among other subjects discussed was this memorandum. He was not ready to accept it as a whole or at once.

[1] The Appendix printed with the minutes of the Council of Ten, Jan. 30, 1919, 11 a.m.

[2] A typed copy of House's note, dated January 29, 1919, appears on a copy of the resolutions cited in n. 1 above, T MS (E. M. House Papers, CtY). House's note reads as follows: "L.G. and the colonials are meeting at 11:30 and this is a draft of a resolution that Smuts hopes to get passed. He wants to know whether it is satisfactory to you. It seems to me a fair compromise. E.M.H." Wilson's reply follows: "I could agree to this if the interpretation in practice were to come from Gen'l Smuts (and on the understanding that the conditions—slave trade &c—are illustrations). My difficulty is with the demands of men like Hughes and the *certain* difficulties with Japan. The latter loom large. A line of islands in her possession would be very dangerous to the U. S. W.W." WWhw MS (E. M. House Papers, CtY).

## From the Diary of Dr. Grayson

Thursday, January 30, 1919.

The morning session of the Peace Conference was devoted to further consideration of the mandatory question. The President clashed with Premier Hughes of Australia, who bitterly opposed any agreement that did not transfer New Guinea to Australia. At luncheon, when I asked the President what the situation was, he replied:

"Australia and New Zealand are trying to block the world."

At the afternoon session, the President continued to force the issue and the British representatives, headed by Lloyd George, supported him in the face of opposition from their own Colonial representation. Japan and Italy swung over to the President's side; Italy, however, making the reservation that the application of the mandatory system should be only to the Pacific Islands and the captured German possessions, leaving the European disposition open to further debate. When the conference adjourned that night, the President had won a complete victory; the minority had swung the majority and the mandatory system had been approved and adopted so far as it applied to African and Pacific Islands.

## William Christian Bullitt to Edward Mandell House

This is worth considering—you may wish to take it up with L.G. this morning   E.M.H.

MEMORANDUM FOR COLONEL HOUSE:

Subject: Withdrawal of American Troops from Archangel.

Dear Colonel House:                    [Paris] 30 January 1919.

The twelve thousand American, British and French troops at Archangel are no longer serving any useful purpose. Only three thousand Russians have rallied around this force. It is the attacked, not the attacker, and serves merely to create cynicism in regard to all our proposals and to stimulate recruiting for the Red Army.

Furthermore, the four thousand Americans, six thousand British, two thousand French and three thousand Russian troops in this region are in considerable danger of destruction by the Bolsheviki. General Ironside has just appealed for reenforcements and the British War Office has directed the Commanding General at Murmansk to be prepared to despatch a battalion of infantry to Archangel.

Instead of transferring troops from Murmansk to Archangel, it seems to me that we should at once transfer to Murmansk, and bring home, the troops which are now at Archangel. Aside from the needless suffering which these men are enduring, aside from the demands of the public in the United States and England for the return of these men, it seems to me that the withdrawal of these troops would be of great value as a proof that we have made the Prinkipos proposal in full good faith.

I have asked General Churchill to obtain the most expert opinion available on the practicability of moving the twelve thousand American, British and French troops, and such Russians as may wish to accompany them, from Archangel to Murmansk. The appended memorandum and map, which he has prepared, show that unless the ice in the White Sea suddenly becomes thicker, it is at present possible with the aid of six ice breakers which are now at Archangel to move these troops by water to Kem on the Murmansk Railroad, whence they may be carried by train to Murmansk.

Buckler discussed the matter of the withdrawal of these troops with Litvinoff, who said that unquestionably the Bolsheviki would agree to an armistice on the Archangel front at any time and, furthermore, would pledge themselves not to injure in any way those Russians in and about Archangel who have been cooperating with the Allies. He furthermore suggested that such Russians as did not care to trust their lives to such a promise should be taken out with the troops.

The Provisional Government at Archangel has just notified us that it will not except [accept] the proposal for a Conference at Prinkipos. It seems dignified and honorable at this moment to inform the Archangel Government that since it can not agree to the Allied proposal, presented after the most serious consideration, we shall decline to support it further with arms, but will make provision for the safety of all Russians who are unwilling to remain at Archangel.

I have discussed this Archangel business at some length with Philip Kerr, Lloyd George's Secretary who says that L.G. intends to bring the British troops out on the first day of May, which he believes to be the first practicable moment. The first practicable moment, however, seems to be now.

The situation at Archangel is most serious for the soldiers who are stationed there, but it is also serious for the Governments which sent them out and seem to have abandoned them. Unless they are saved by prompt action, we shall have another Gallipoli.

Very respectfully yours,   William C. Bullitt.

TS MS (WP, DLC).

Hankey's Notes of Two Meetings of the Council of Ten

Quai d'Orsay, January 30, 1919, 11 A.M.[1]

BC-17

1. M. CLEMENCEAU said that it was intended that morning to continue the exchange of views on the question of the disposal of the German Colonies.

MR. LLOYD GEORGE said that he had circulated a document (see Annexure A)[2] to each of the representatives of the Great Powers. That document did not represent the real views of the Colonies; but it had been accepted by them as an attempt at a compromise. Great Britain had deliberately decided to accept the principle of a mandatory; but that decision had not been wholly accepted by the Dominions. The Dominions, however, were prepared to accept the conclusions reached in the document as a compromise, because they fully realized that there could be no greater catastrophe than for the delegates to separate without having come to a definite decision. It had been decided to accept the doctrine of a mandatory for all conquests in the late Turkish Empire and in the German Colonies. But three classes of mandates would have to be recognized, namely:

*Firstly*: Mandates applicable to countries where the population was civilized but not yet organized—where a century might elapse before the people could be properly organized. For example, Arabia. In such cases it would be impossible to give full self-government and at the same time prevent the various tribes or units from fighting each other. It was obvious that the system to be applied to these territories must be different from that which would have to be applied to cannibal colonies, where people were eating each other.

*Secondly*: Mandates applicable to tropical Colonies situated a long way from the country of the possible mandatory. In other words, territories which did not form an integral part of any particular mandatory country. For example, New Guinea. In these Colonies the full principle of a mandatory would be applied, including the "open door."

*Thirdly*: Mandates applicable to countries which formed almost a part of the organization of an adjoining power, who would have to be appointed the mandatory.

Finally, he wished to emphasize the fact that the memorandum was intended to deal only with those parts of the Turkish Empire and of the German Empire, which had actually been conquered. Districts such as Smyrna, Adalia, the North of Anatolia were pur-

[1] The complete text of these notes is printed in *PPC*, III, 785-96.
[2] That is, the Appendix.

posely excluded. Such territories would have to be considered separately on their merits.

MR. HUGHES said that the Prime Minister of Great Britain had accurately set out the position taken up by the Dominions. The members of the Conference had already heard his own views and they knew that Australia desired direct control. But, Australia fully recognized that grave interests, involving the fate of humanity were at stake, and, therefore, he did not feel justified in opposing the views of President Wilson and those of Mr. Lloyd George, beyond the point which would reasonably safeguard the interests of Australia. He had indicated to the Conference substantially the position as it stood, because his Government had desired him to emphasize its position and its attitude towards it, and it had asked him to press for direct control. As soon as his Government had heard that the mandatory principle was to be imposed, it had asked for full details and for an opportunity of considering those details. His colleagues were to meet for this purpose that afternoon and he felt compelled, therefore, to withhold his assent until they had communicated their decision.

2. PRESIDENT WILSON said that, first of all, in unaffected good humor, he wished to refer to a question of privilege. Each morning in the Paris press, printed in English, appeared a great deal more information regarding the meetings than was given in the official communiqués. He referred especially to the comments on President Wilson's idealistic views. It was stated, for instance, that, as regards President Wilson's ideals, he (President Wilson) did not know how his ideals would work. If those articles continued to appear, he would find himself compelled to publish his own views. So far he had only spoken to people in that room and to the members of the American Delegation, so that nothing had been communicated to the Press regarding President Wilson's views, either by himself or by his associates. He and his colleagues had been extremely scrupulous that nothing should come from them that implied that there were divergences of view. For example, the Press had disclosed that morning that there was, apparently, a Dominion point of view, and that the United States of America was in some way or another standing out against that view.[3] If these articles continued to appear

[3] Wilson referred to an article which had appeared that morning in the Paris edition of the London *Daily Mail.* It asserted, with quotations from the meeting of the Council of Ten at 4 p.m. on January 28, that Great Britain, by taking the part of the United States in the controversy over German former possessions in the Pacific area, was threatening the breakup of the British Empire. L. F. Fitzhardinge, *William Morris Hughes, A Political Biography* (2 vols., Sydney and London, 1964-79), II, 393.

All scholars, including Fitzhardinge, and contemporaries agree that Hughes was the source of the article. For example: "It should be added that during the Conference of Thursday, the action of Mr. Hughes in giving confidential information to the Daily Mail was strongly de-a public discussion would become inevitable, and such a public discussion would be fatal at this juncture. He himself was greatly distressed at these occurrences, but he did not know how they could be prevented. Nevertheless the time might come when he would be compelled against his own wishes to make a full public exposé of his views.

3. Next, to take the document circulated by the Prime Minister of Great Britain, he considered it to be a very gratifying paper. It made a long stride towards the composition of their differences, bringing them to within an easy stage of final agreement. On the other hand he did not think they could have a final decision immediately. Mr. Hughes, for instance, wished to discuss the question with his colleagues, who were anxious to know just what it all would mean. Mr. Hughes was not in a position to answer that question, neither could anyone else answer it. He could say that President Wilson said that a mandatory would work in a certain manner, but President Wilson's views had not been adopted. There were obviously other views but he could not say what they were. He (President Wilson) had in his possession a separate paper showing how the scheme would work in connection with the League of Nations,[4] but that scheme had not yet been accepted. He had discussed it with Lord Robert Cecil and Mr. Balfour, and that day he would discuss it with M. Orlando. So far these were merely the exchange of general views in an attempt to arrive at a decision.

Furthermore, the difficulty with which they were faced was not to satisfy the Powers in that Room (France, the United Kingdom, Italy and America), but to satisfy the disturbed communities of the world, mostly on the other side of the Rhine. It would be difficult to harness these communities to any kind of arrangement. It would be impossible to drive them tandem; they must be driven abreast. Mr. Lloyd George was disturbed with regard to the number of troops which had to be maintained in different parts of the world—troops which could not be withdrawn until Peace was signed. Even if an understanding could be reached with another country to replace these troops, the world would ask "Are you exchanging territories before peace is made?" For instance, it had been suggested that America should act as a mandatory. The people of America would be most disinclined to do so. He himself had succeeded in getting the people of America to do many things, and he might succeed in getting them to accept this burden also. But even if it was suggested

---

nounced by President Wilson, General Botha and others. Mr. Hughes was not named, but the members of the Conference perfectly understood from whom the Daily Mail had received its inspiration." R. L. Borden to W. T. White, Feb. 1, 1919, TLS with T memorandum (R. L. Borden Papers, CaOOA).

[4] The plan embodied in the Appendix.

that American troops should occupy Constantinople, or Mesopotamia, it was evident that they could not do so as they were not at war with Turkey. Therefore, it would, in his opinion, be extremely unwise to accept any form of mandate until they knew how it was intended to work.

To return to the immediate subject, could they take a clean sheet, and say that Australia, for example, would accept a mandate about New Guinea? How would that mandate be exercised? What would it involve? No one could give an answer to Australia. He could say that he himself had proposed various forms of mandate. He surmised that the character of the mandate would be left in the hands of an Executive of the League of Nations, consisting of the Great Powers with a minority representation of the Smaller Powers. He imagined, also, that no action could be taken by that Council in the face of three negative votes. Should that system be adopted it would be impossible for any harmful conditions to be imposed upon the mandatory state. But that arrangement had not yet been adopted; no agreement had as yet been reached. He had been accused of being a hopeless Idealist, but as a matter of fact he never accepted an ideal until he could see its practical application. The practical application was always the more difficult. Mandatories might work unsatisfactorily under one programme, whilst they might work well under another. Therefore no-one should accept the scheme unless it was shown how it was going to work. The mandatory system was not intended to satisfy merely the interests of the mandatory Power but to care for, protect and develop the people for whom it was intended. Consequently to hand over distinguishable people to a mandatory in perpetuity and to say: "You never shall have a voice in your future; you are finally disposed of," would be contrary to the principles of that Conference and contrary to the principles of self-determination accepted by it. For instance, if South Africa managed South-West Africa as well as she had managed her own country, then she would be married to South West Africa. Further, it would be necessary to define the methods of self-expression of the ward or people under tutelage. There must be a responsible body which would be in a position to hear that self-expression and not be carried away by its sympathies. As had already been stated, in many parts of the world hitherto German, strong German influences might remain; but they were familiar with German methods and the body proposed would be most familiar with the German nature. However, his was merely a personal proposal and he could give no assurances that it would be accepted. But, whilst accepting the paper of Mr. Lloyd George as a precursor of agreement, it did not constitute a rock foundation, as the League of Nations had not yet been fixed, on which this superstructure would rest.

Therefore, he thought that the whole idea on which this principle depended should be put forward and then the Nations would know where they stood. Meanwhile, he would accelerate discussion of all these disturbing questions of the world which prevented Europe from settling down to normal life. The Great Powers had agreed that the League of Nations should form an integral part of the Peace Treaty. Therefore, it could not be accepted by itself, and to make the document presented by Mr. Lloyd George valid, they were bound to complete a preliminary peace. He thought that could be done in a few weeks. Disinterested students had been studying territorial questions on documentary evidence of every kind, working like scholars and basing their conclusions on acknowledged facts as far as they were ascertainable. If a map of Europe were produced showing the limits of the territories to be created, based on historical, racial and economic facts, the Great Powers could then sit down to consider these suggestions and give weight to these points of view, such as expediency, natural antagonisms, etc., which played no part in scholarly wisdom. They could then arrive at a conclusion quickly and be able to conclude the preliminary peace, and the League of Nations would thereby be established without the haunting element of conjecture. In every instance the mandate should fit the case as the glove fits the hand. In conclusion, accepting the document presented by Mr. Lloyd George as practically clearing away all prospects of serious differences he thought they should build upon this agreement the solid foundations which would carry this superstructure.

MR. LLOYD GEORGE remarked that, with all due deference to President Wilson, he could not help saying that the statement to which they had just listened filled him with despair. Should that attitude be taken about each question, no agreement would ever be reached. If the delegates said that they could not agree to problem (a) until agreement had been reached regarding questions (b), (c), (d), (e) and (f), the result would be disastrous. Each of them had his questions (b), (c), (d) and (e) which he considered more important than any other. Further, he would point out that it was only with the greatest difficulty that the representatives of the Dominions had been prevailed upon to accept the draft submitted, even provisionally. These gentlemen were not enamoured of the mandatory system: they represented real democracies and the people were solid behind them on this question. He had reminded them that they were not only members of a particular democracy but also members of a Conference which had met to settle the peace of the world. Consequently, they had accepted his proposals, but only as a compromise. Now, President Wilson had expressed the view that the mandatory business should not be trusted until more was known about it, that was to say, until the League of Nations was definitely set forth on paper. To this, the representatives of the Dominions would obviously reply that they wished to see it working and not on paper. President Wilson had suggested that they should leave the Colonial questions for the moment and take up those relating to Europe. There, again, they would be met with difficulties which would have to be settled by the League of Nations, so that the proposal really meant a 15 days' adjournment until a paper League of Nations was produced. He felt confident that what had been done last Saturday in giving birth to a League of Nations was a reality. It had really been born. That he treated as a fact. Therefore, he begged them to accept it as such and to get to business. The suggestion that the constitution of the League of Nations would be completed by the end of next week, he considered rather sanguine, as it meant formulating the constitution of the whole world. How long did it take to lay the foundations of the 13 original states of the United States of America? How long did it take to produce the constitution of the Federation of the states of Australia? To think that a federation of the whole world could be produced in 9 or 10 days would be ideal. However, he was only pleading for immediate peace. It was not across the Rhine that his Government had to keep their eyes, but at home. At the present moment, the British Empire was maintaining 1,084,000 troops, including 300,000 British troops, in the Turkish Empire alone, and the settlement of that part of the world was, therefore, important. In conclusion he felt that if the delegates continued to adjourn questions, because they were not as important as others, no final decision would ever be reached. He sincerely hoped, therefore, that his colleagues would provisionally adopt the resolutions he had submitted (see appendix "A"), subject to such reconsideration as might be required when the complete scheme of the League of Nations was formulated.

PRESIDENT WILSON expressed the view that he had said nothing which need justify discouragement. He was willing to accept Mr. Lloyd George's proposals, subject to reconsideration when the full scheme of the League of Nations was drawn up. He suggested that the resolutions be accepted as an immediate settlement, and, if the previse added by Mr. Lloyd George were added, it would prevent any misunderstanding. Mr. Lloyd George said that the League of Nations had already been accepted, and that it would [be] necessary to turn to it for the settlement of various questions. In his opinion, that view emphasised the necessity to know the instrumentality which was to deal with these questions. It would be impossible to refer to an undefined instrument. He did not wish to delay any decision and he was ready to accept any provisional arrangement.

Yesterday they had listened to a discussion between the Czecho-

Slovaks and the Poles, but it was inconclusive because there was nothing on the table saying what was to be discussed. M. Dmowski had said that Poland must be a barrier between Russia and Germany. Did that mean a barrier based on armaments? Obviously not, because Germany would be disarmed and if Germany was disarmed Poland could not be allowed to arm except for police purposes. To carry out such disarmament the necessary instrumentality for superintendence would have to be set up. That was the gist of the question. Therefore, he would urge his colleagues to press on the drafting of the League of Nations in a definite form.

MR. LLOYD GEORGE enquired whether the actual constitution itself of the League of Nations would have to be settled before the meeting of the delegates could discuss the Italian, French or Polish question.

PRESIDENT WILSON replied in the negative and added that in future only definite propositions should be discussed and meanwhile the drafting of the constitution of the League of Nations should be pressed forward. Yesterday, they had been unable to confine the discussion within the proper limits because they did not discuss anything in particular, therefore he would urge that they should formulate the League of Nations as a final court of appeal. In conclusion he expressed his readiness to accept as a provisional arrangement the resolutions proposed by Mr. Lloyd George.

4. M. ORLANDO expressed his pleasure at the agreement reached. He fully understood the difficulties of the question and he raised no objection provided everyone was willing to accept the proposals, but he would like to clearly understand the situation. If Mr. Lloyd George's resolutions were accepted it would mean that all territories of Austria, Turkey, and the late German territories of Africa and in the Pacific, would be reserved to the League of Nations. He thought that was agreed. The League of Nations would administer these territories through mandatories which would reserve to themselves the choice of the mandatories, as well as the terms of the mandate, which would differ in each case until the League of Nations was constituted and able to give its decision. These countries would remain under a provisional *status quo* which was equivalent to saying that during the period between the decision reached on that day and the final decision to be given by the League of Nations, temporary mandatories would be established, subject to future changes, if so desired by the League of Nations. Was that agreed or was the *status quo* to be maintained, namely, a military occupation in virtue of the armistice, by troops (chiefly British), occupying the territories in the name of the Allied and associated powers in accordance with the terms of the Armistice. In that case he had only one observation to make from the point of view of the particular

interests of Italy. As he had already stated on previous occasions, Italy had only one simple and perfectly just desire, namely, that a proper proportion between the Allies should be maintained in respect of the occupation of these territories. Consequently whether a temporary mandatory were appointed or the *status quo* maintained, he would ask, and he trusted this would not be considered excessive, that Italy obtain its share of mandates or territories to be militarily occupied.

M. CLEMENCEAU enquired what subject should next be placed on the agenda now that Mr. Lloyd George's resolutions had been accepted. From what had been said it would appear that everything depended on a decision being reached regarding the constitution of the League of Nations, consequently, the meeting would be bound to wait until the League of Nations had been established, and it would be obviously useless to discuss the claims of the Roumanians, Yugo-Slavs and others. If he had correctly interpreted what had been said that morning he felt compelled to make serious formal reservations. In his opinion it would be impossible to establish a League of Nations which was not to be a common organism of defence, but an organism to deal with all the world. Furthermore, if this new constitution for the whole world was to be produced in eight days he was bound to feel some anxiety.

5. BARON MAKINO expressed his satisfaction that a provisional agreement had been reached on the question of mandatories. As regards the League of Nations, he wished to state that as the matter was so important his Government was quite ready to associate itself with the work of this very important organization. Frankly there were difficulties, and his Government was not quite certain how it would work. But, seeing that it was a matter which was being very earnestly considered by the Great Powers it was quite ready to associate itself with this great work. Although so far his Government was not in possession of any official plan of the organization, he had had the privilege a few days ago of receiving President Wilson's exposition, and yesterday he had received the more concrete plans of Mr. Lloyd George. Yesterday he had telegraphed both documents to Tokio, and he had added that it was desirable that his Government should favorably consider the proposition suggested by Mr. Lloyd George. Naturally no reply could yet have been received; but since he had already asked for instructions his duty was to wait for the receipt of his Government's reply before giving his definite adherence. Meanwhile all he could do was to adhere to the resolutions *ad referendum*.

6. MR. HUGHES asked to be permitted to say one word on the matter as the question had now taken a new aspect, since hearing President Wilson's statement. When the British Empire Delegates

had discussed the question yesterday, they had agreed to the proposals of Mr. Lloyd George as a compromise. But the basis of the proposals had now been disturbed by what President Wilson had said that morning. He thought President Wilson had set out the case for Australia better than he himself could do. President Wilson had said things which he (Mr. Hughes) had been afraid to say; they were things which agitated the minds of the Colonies. It was proposed really to govern the fate of people by declaring that a certain principle should apply, but to what extent that principle should apply, or by whom that principle should be applied, or when it should be applied, no one knew. For that reason President Wilson had pointed out that the acceptance of Mr. Lloyd George's resolutions would not settle anything until the League of Nations had been created and clothed with authority and with certain powers, duties and functions. Meanwhile he was faced with a great difficulty, for he would have to say to the people of Australia not what he thought, but what he was permitted to say. For Australia the War had been a question of life and death, and still remained so. Now he would have to tell the people of Australia how the whole matter was to be settled, and they would ask, how? His reply would be that the mandatory principle was to apply but he did not know how except that the arrangements would be such that the scheme would fit like a glove to the hand. Having lived all his life in Australia and knowing the Australian temperament, he thought it would be impossible to expect them to accept a principle the nature of which was not known. A definite decision could only be expressed when they knew what it all meant. In conclusion, he enquired whether they should wait the acceptance of the League of Nations by the Conference and by the world whilst they were waiting for a decision. Was not the *de facto* League of Nations already in existence in that room? He suggested that they as a League of Nations should act as the executive of the future League of Nations and settle the various problems which awaited settlement. This League should say who were to be the mandates outside the Polish question and impose their will on Germany. No League of Nations could be superior to the members of that Conference. Those that came after could only have one-tenth of the power. The world looked to them for decisions, and the world would breathe more freely if those decisions were made.

7. SIR ROBERT BORDEN expressed his pleasure at the fact that an agreement, if only provisional, had been reached. He was one of those who most earnestly desired the establishment of the League of Nations. He agreed that the future destinies of the world depended largely on it because there were forces in Russia which would manifest themselves unless some proposal of that kind could

be accepted. The success of the League of Nations would not depend upon the machinery that might be created, but on something behind it, namely, public opinion, which would give it the power; the same power which steam or electricity gave to the machinery of a factory. He would beg them to be careful not to impose too heavy a burden on it in the first instance. Born as an infant it might develop as a giant, but whilst an infant too much should not be imposed on it. He had carefully studied the organisation of the British Empire, which was not unlike the proposed organization of the League of Nations, and he knew that the British Empire depended only on public opinion. Not one of the Dominions could have been forced to send a single man to the war; they joined in the war because of the cause involved, and because of public opinion. The League of Nations would have to depend on the same considerations. Therefore as far as possible, he hoped that the Conference would come to a conclusion on all proper matters with as little delay as possible. It would be for the representatives to decide forthwith whether they would themselves settle this question or whether they would constitute themselves into machinery to settle such questions at some future date. At any rate it was essential that the organisation of the League of Nations should be determined without imposing too much on it at once. It was well known that no democratic country attempted to enforce every law to its fullest extent as that would be impossible. Government by convention and goodwill founded on public opinion was the only Government possible; and the working of the League of Nations would depend on similar foundations. Therefore he hoped the matter under consideration would be determined as speedily as might be possible because the world was looking to the proceedings of the Conference and might become tired in face of any delay.

PRESIDENT WILSON pointed out that M. Orlando had raised a very important question that would have to be discussed later on. He suggested that further discussion of the question should be postponed until the afternoon meeting.

(This was agreed to.)

The Meeting then adjourned until 3.30 p.m. in the afternoon.


### APPENDIX.

#### DRAFT RESOLUTIONS IN REFERENCE TO MANDATORIES

January 29, 1919.

1. Having regard to the record of the German administration in the colonies formerly part of the German Empire, and to the menace which the possession by Germany of submarine bases in many

parts of the world would necessarily constitute to the freedom and security of all nations, the Allied and Associated Powers are agreed that in no circumstances should any of the German Colonies be restored to Germany.

2. For similar reasons, and more particularly because of the historical mis-government by the Turks of subject peoples and the terrible massacres of Armenians and others in recent years, the Allied and Associated Powers are agreed that Armenia, Syria, Mesopotamia, Palestine and Arabia must be completely severed from the Turkish Empire. This is without prejudice to the settlement of other parts of the Turkish Empire.

3. The Allied and Associated Powers are agreed that advantage should be taken of the opportunity afforded by the necessity of disposing of these colonies and territories formerly belonging to Germany and Turkey which are inhabited by peoples not yet able to stand by themselves under the strenuous conditions of the modern world, to apply to those territories the principle that the well-being and development of such peoples form a sacred trust of civilisation and that securities for the performance of this trust should be embodied in the constitution of the League of Nations.

4. After careful study they are satisfied that the best method of giving practical effect to this principle is that the tutelage of peoples should be entrusted to advanced nations who by reason of their resources, their experience or their geographical position, can best undertake this responsibility, and that this tutelage should be exercised by them as mandatories on behalf of the League of Nations.

5. The Allied and Associated Powers are of opinion that the character of the mandate must differ according to the stage of development of the people, the geographical situation of the territory, its economic conditions and other similar circumstances.

6. They consider that certain communities formerly belonging to the Turkish Empire have reached a stage of development where their existence as independent nations can be provisionally recognised subject to the rendering of administrative advice and assistance by a mandatory power until such time as they are able to stand alone. The wishes of these communities must be a principal consideration in the selection of the mandatory power.

7. They further consider that other peoples, especially those of Central Africa, are at such a stage that the mandatory must be responsible for the administration of the territory subject to conditions which will guarantee the prohibition of abuses such as the slave trade, the arms traffic and the liquor traffic, and the prevention of the military training of the natives for other than police purposes, and the establishment of fortifications or military and naval bases,

and will also secure equal opportunities for the trade and commerce of other members of the League of Nations.

8. Finally they consider that there are territories, such as South-West Africa and certain of the Islands in the South Pacific, which, owing to the sparseness of their population, or their small size, or their remoteness from the centres of civilization, or their geographical contiguity to the mandatory state, and other circumstances, can be best administered under the laws of the mandatory state as integral portions thereof, subject to the safeguards above-mentioned in the interests of the indigenous population.

In every case of mandate, the mandatory state shall render to the League of Nations an annual report in reference to the territory committed to its charge.

T MS (SDR, RG 256, 180.03101/24, DNA).

Quai d'Orsay, January 30, 1919, 3:30 P.M.[1]

BC-18, IC-128

1. M. CLEMENCEAU, having declared the meeting open, called on Mr. Massey to address the meeting.

MR. MASSEY said that he found it necessary to say just a few words, because he had expected some fairly clear and definite statement from President Wilson with regard to the proposals contained in Clause 8[2] of the document which they had been discussing. In that expectation he had been disappointed, and he need hardly tell the members of the Council, or remind his colleagues from the Dominions, that the matters referred to in Clause 8 were matters of the utmost importance to the people whom they represented there. They had repeatedly expressed to him that it was a matter of life and death to many of them. He would like to say that he had not gone back in the very slightest on the opinions that he had expressed on the first occasion when he addressed the Council. He knew the very serious, important and urgent matters that were waiting to be dealt with as soon as that Council and Conference could find it convenient to do so, and on that account he did not want to waste any more time than he could possibly help, or place any more difficulties in the way of a settlement. He was still prepared, as far as the Dominions were concerned, to accept the suggestions contained in Clause 8, which had been inserted there to meet the cases of Australia, South Africa and New Zealand. He would like to quote the last three lines of the Clause, which were

[1] The complete text of these notes is printed in PPC, III, 797-817.
[2] That is, of the Appendix to the minutes of the meeting of Jan. 30, 1919, 11 a.m.

intended to meet the cases of the Dominions, whose—"geographical contiguity to the mandatory state, and other circumstances, can be best administered under the laws of the mandatory State as integral portions thereof, subject to the safeguards above-mentioned in the interests of the indigenous population." The safeguards were as follows: The prohibition of abuses such as the slave trade, the arms traffic, the liquor traffic, and the prevention of the military training of the natives for other than police purposes. Those were the conditions, and, so far as he was concerned—and he thought he could speak for his colleagues in these respects—they were prepared to accept them. They were prepared to accept them right away, but they had not yet had any definite opinion or statement from President Wilson that he was willing to accept them. If President Wilson would say he was willing to accept them, he thought it would clear the ground sufficiently to enable them to proceed, and in saying that he was not suggesting in the very slightest degree any delay so far as he was concerned. The sooner they came to a conclusion on these matters the better for all concerned. He believed, as he had already indicated, in the principle of direct annexation, because direct annexation would enable them to proceed very much more quickly with the development of the territories concerned. He believed it would be better for the European races, and also better for the native races. They would be able to proceed with the education of the native races, not only in secular matters, but also in the principles of Christianity, which he believed were necessary for the welfare of all nations.

There was just one other point to which he would like to make some reference. It had been said by some of the previous speakers that the Dominions entered into this war because they knew it was right to do so—because it was a good cause. That was only one reason. They went into this war because the Empire, of which they were a part, was fighting for a great cause—fighting for its honour—for humanity—for civilisation, and in order to keep faith with its Allies, and fighting for the defence of the smaller nations. There was also another reason why the Dominions entered this war—because they had confidence in the leaders of the Empire and their judgment—in their discretion—and, in saying that, he hoped that if it ever became necessary for Great Britain again to go to war, the Dominions would be officially represented as never before in the Council of the Empire. He would like to say that he supported the proposal of a League of Nations. He hoped and believed it would be a good thing; he believed it would do much to prevent war in the future. Members of that Conference had a tremendous responsibility so far as the prevention of war in the future was concerned.

He believed that if war was not to be renewed in the near future—
he meant from 25 to 50 years hence, which was a very short period
in the life of a nation—they had not only to see that justice was
given on the one hand to those who had suffered in this war—and
there were many—but to those who had broken the laws of civilisation during the last 4½ years. He believed that would do more
to prevent war than anything else. So far as he was concerned, he
was responsible to his constituents, and he was prepared to shoulder
the responsibility.

PRESIDENT WILSON asked if he was to understand that New Zealand and Australia had presented an ultimatum to the Conference.
They had come there and presented their cases for annexation of
New Guinea and Samoa. After discussion among themselves, themselves, they agreed to present to the Conference that proposal. Was
he now to understand that that was the minimum of their concession? That their agreement upon a plan depended upon that concession? And that if they could not get that definitely now, they proposed to do what they could to stop the whole agreement?

MR. MASSEY said: "No"—but he thought he had made himself
perfectly clear. Of course he could not speak for his colleague from
Australia.

MR. HUGHES said he did not know how he could put it better than
he had done that morning. He would like to say that Clause 8 of
that proposal—

PRESIDENT WILSON enquired if Mr. Hughes had heard his question.

MR. HUGHES replied in the negative.

PRESIDENT WILSON then said he wanted to know if they were to
understand that Australia and New Zealand were presenting an
ultimatum to that Conference, and that finding the Conference
probably disinclined to agree upon the annexation of New Guinea
by Australia and Samoa by New Zealand, they had reluctantly agreed
to the modification of Clause 8; and that was the minimum of what
they would concede, and if that was not conceded definitely now,
they could not take part in the agreement at all.

MR. HUGHES replied that President Wilson had put it fairly well,[3]
that that was their attitude subject to the reservation which he had
stated that morning. Like his colleagues from New Zealand and
South Africa they were in favour of direct control. They found the
Conference (as President Wilson had remarked) not in accord with

---

[3] Hughes is reported elsewhere as having said at this point: "That's about the size of
it, President Wilson." L. F. Fitzhardinge, "W. M. Hughes and the Treaty of Versailles,
1919," as cited in Wm. Roger Louis, *Great Britain and Germany's Lost Colonies, 1914-
1919* (Oxford, 1967), pp. 136-37.

their views. The Dominions had fallen in with the suggestion put forward by the Prime Minister of Great Britain. For the present that represented the maximum of their concession in that direction, but he would like to say: that he had put the position, as he understood it, for his colleagues, and if they were prepared to go further he would offer no objection. He thought it would be agreed that because they were unable to put any definite concrete proposal before the Conference, at least they should be asked to be clothed with those plenary powers giving them discretion to accept whatever that Conference was able to accord to them. Speaking for himself, with great reluctance, he agreed to the proposal in Clause 8. Beyond that he felt that he ought not to go.

GENERAL BOTHA asked that he might be allowed to address a few words to the conference. As everybody knew he was not a British subject of very long-standing and therefore his English was not so good as it might be. He would like to say that he heartily supported President Wilson with regard to what was in the papers that morning. When he saw the paper he had thrown it away. What had appeared in those papers was being sent by cable all over the world. It would upset the people of South Africa, as they did not understand the position. That afternoon he hoped to have a peaceful lunch, but in the middle of it he received a cable to return at once. They were there as gentlemen and they must keep those things out of the newspapers or it would be impossible for other people to remain there. He was of opinion that such an article ought to be investigated to see whence it came, and have a stop put to it. It would create a great deal of mischief.

He would like to tell President Wilson that he had understood that in the speeches which had been delivered that morning there was no threat. He observed that the Prime Minister of Great Britain had met the Dominion representatives and had discussed the question with them and he (General Botha) could assure President Wilson that it was only after very serious discussion, worry and trouble and through the influence of Mr. Lloyd George, that the resolution had been handed in that morning. He was one of those who would give up everything to reach the highest ideal. Therefore he supported Mr. Lloyd George but he sincerely trusted that President Wilson would also agree. Do not let them stop at small things. If they could gain that bigger and higher ideal, then smaller versions of it ought not to stand in the way. He remembered that after the war in his own country, which was on a smaller scale than the present, but which was just as bloody and miserable, they got self-government; but he saw at once that four different self-governing bodies in that country must lead to war. He was one of the original promoters of the Union of South Africa. He had his ideals and they were very high indeed. When he assembled all the leading statesmen he found then that the other people held views from which it would be impossible to persuade them. He had then personally investigated these and had come to the conclusion that these were smaller things. On that occasion he asked his colleagues to stick to one thing, to aspire to the higher ideal and that was the Union of South Africa. They must give way on the smaller things. He would like to say the same on this occasion. They must give way now and get their higher ideal, get a better understanding and bring the people together, and through that they would gain eventually all the things that they wanted to get. It was a small thing on which he had given way after the war in his own country, but unless they had done so they would have been in a very miserable condition to-day.

He appreciated the ideals of President Wilson. They were the ideals of the people of the world, and they would succeed if they all accepted them in the same spirit and supported them in the manner in which they were intended. If they departed in an indifferent spirit it would not have the success that they would all wish it should have. Therefore, to his own mind, if they differed it was not a threat because at the back of everybody's heart there was only one idea,—that of attaining a better world understanding. Mankind looked upon them for support to do away with all future wars. He felt that by conceding smaller things they made the higher ideal more acceptable, and it would have the hearty support of the whole world. They must remember that their various peoples did not understand everything from the same point. In that light therefore they must guide them to the bigger ideal. Personally he felt very strongly about the question of German South-West Africa. He thought that it differed entirely from any question that they had to decide in this conference, but he would be prepared to say that he was a supporter of the document handed in that morning, because he knew that, if the idea fructified, the League of Nations would consist mostly of the same people who were present there that day, who understood the position and who would not make it impossible for any mandatory to govern the country. That was why he said he would accept it. He hoped that the second document[4] there was entirely unnecessary because the first document that was handed in that morning was an entirely provisional one. They could not

[4] A slight revision of the British draft resolutions just cited. It used the word "oppression" instead of "misgovernment" in Resolution 2 and the "Pacific Islands" instead of "certain of the Islands in South Pacific" in Resolution 8. See David Hunter Miller, *My Diary at the Conference of Paris, with Documents* (21 vols., New York, 1924), I, 96.

accept anything by resolution now on hard and fast lines; everything depended on the ultimate resolution. That was how he understood the matter, and he hoped that they would try in a spirit of
co-operation, and by giving way on smaller things, to meet the
difficulties and make the bigger ideal more possible.

MR. MASSEY said that the representatives of Australia and New
Zealand had been asked a direct question by President Wilson. Mr.
Hughes had answered for Australia and he (Mr. Massey) would
answer for New Zealand. The position of Mr. Hughes and himself
was practically on all fours up to a certain point. It was on all fours
so far as the desire of their people was concerned for what they
considered direct control—"annexation" to put it bluntly; but perhaps it was not on all fours after that, because Mr. Hughes had
been communicated with by the acting Prime Minister of Australia.[5]
He (Mr. Massey) had not been communicated with by his Government and he had not communicated with it. Therefore he was
prepared to take the responsibility of supporting the proposals contained in Clause 8. He wanted to emphasise that again. He wanted
to assure President Wilson that if he (President Wilson) imagined
that any threat was intended he had quite misunderstood the matter
so far as both he and Mr. Hughes were concerned. As a public man
he never used threats and he did not accept threats from any one
if he could possibly meet them. However, he had made that point
perfectly clear and he might go so far as the proposals of Clause 8
without consulting his own Government. He was prepared to go so
far because he could not get what his Government wanted and in
that case he was prepared to accept the next best proposal. If he
found it necessary he would communicate with his Government
and explain the position; but he was prepared to accept and support
the provisional proposal put forward by Mr. Lloyd George.

MR. LLOYD GEORGE said that he would like to suggest, after everybody had made his position quite clear and when nobody was under
any illusions as to Mr. Hughes' position, or General Botha's position,
or Mr. Massey's or anybody else's, that they take that as a provisional
decision subject to revision when either they found the League of
Nations unsatisfactory, or that there was some other reason for
revising it.

SIR R. BORDEN proposed some slight alteration in one of the clauses
in order to prevent misunderstanding. Was the proposal in clause
7 to encourage the establishment of military or naval fortifications?

PRESIDENT WILSON said it was intended to prevent them.

SIR ROBERT BORDEN observed that at present it might mean other-

---

[5] William Alexander Watt, Federal Treasurer of Australia.

wise. Therefore he would read the clause as he proposed it should read, subject to the opinion of the conference, as follows:

"They further consider that other peoples, especially those of Central Africa, are at such a stage that the mandatory must be responsible for the administration of the territory subject to conditions which will guarantee the prohibition of abuses such as the slave trade, the arms traffic and the liquor traffic, and the prevention of the establishment of fortifications or military and naval bases and of the military training of the natives for other than police purposes and the defence of territory, and will also secure equal opportunities for the trade and commerce of other members of the League of Nations."

PRESIDENT WILSON said that made it clearer.

(This was agreed to.)

M. PICHON said that France could not renounce the right of raising volunteers in the countries under her administration, whatever they might be. The Germans had recognised the importance of the support France had received from her Colonies. Before powerful American troops came to her aid, they had resisted with their own forces for a long time, together with the British Armies, and it was certain, but for the help they had received from their Colonial Possessions, the situation would have been very critical. It was necessary for them to be able to recruit not conscripts but volunteers from all colonial territories under French control. This was absolutely necessary for the future security of the French territory.

PRESIDENT WILSON enquired if this referred to the territories controlled as mandatory states as well as the present.

M. CLEMENCEAU said that the French were the nearest neighbours of Germany, and could be at all times, and had been in the past, suddenly attacked. He did not know whether it was possible to disarm Germany, but they would try. They knew Great Britain had responsibilities in all parts of the world, and could not have the whole of her strength concentrated at one point at a moment's time. America was far away, and could not come at once to the assistance of France. If the League of Nations and the peace of the world were to be established, it must not begin by putting France in a position of peril which would be much more dangerous for them than for any other Power. America was protected by the whole breadth of the ocean, and Great Britain by her fleet. If the French could not find any territories for which they would have to take the responsibility, and on which they would have to spend money in improving;—if they could not raise volunteers without compulsion—then they felt that the people of France would resent this very much, and would have a grievance against the Government.

MR. LLOYD GEORGE said he was thinking of what the position was in the French and British Colonies at the beginning of this war. Great Britain had native forces in Uganda and Nigeria and other places, and the French also had forces in Senegal and other territories.

Algeria and Morocco were in a different position. He was thinking of the tropical colonies. The only forces Great Britain had there were forces for the defence of those territories. That was equally true of France. France had not raised and armed and equipped great forces for any offensive purposes outside.

M. CLEMENCEAU observed that they were free to do it.

MR. LLOYD GEORGE said that there was nothing in the clause under review to prevent that. The words used there were: "for other than police purposes and the defence of territory." He really thought that those words would cover the case of France. There was nothing in the document which would prevent their doing exactly the same thing as they had done before. What it did prevent was the kind of thing the Germans were likely to do, namely, organise great black armies in Africa, which they could use for the purpose of clearing everybody else out of that country. That was their proclaimed policy, and if that was encouraged amongst the other nations even though they might not have wars in Europe, they would have the sort of thing that happened in the 17th and 18th century in India when France and Great Britain were at war in India, whilst being fairly good friends in Europe. Then they were always raising great native armies against each other. That must now be stopped. There was nothing in this document which prevented France doing what she did before. The defence of the territory was provided for.

M. CLEMENCEAU said that if he could raise troops, that was all he wanted.

MR. LLOYD GEORGE replied that he had exactly the same power as previously. It only prevented any country drilling the natives and raising great armies.

M. CLEMENCEAU said that he did not want to do that. All that he wished was that the matter should be made quite plain, and he did not want anybody to come and tell him afterwards that he had broken away from the agreement. If this clause meant that he had a right of raising troops in case of general war, he was satisfied.

MR. LLOYD GEORGE said that so long as M. Clemenceau did not train big nigger armies for the purposes of aggression, that was all the clause was intended to guard against.

M. CLEMENCEAU said that he did not want to do that. He therefore understood that Mr. Lloyd George's interpretation was adopted.

PRESIDENT WILSON said that Mr. Lloyd George's interpretation was consistent with the phraseology.

M. CLEMENCEAU said that he was quite satisfied.

MR. LLOYD GEORGE said that he would like to move an amendment to his own document. He said that he was sorry that he had left out one country in Turkey which ought to have been inserted. He did not realise that it was separate. He thought Mesopotamia or Armenia would cover it, but he was now informed that it did not. He referred to Kurdestan, which was between Mesopotamia and Armenia. Therefore, if there was no objection, he proposed to insert the words: "and Kurdestan."

(This was agreed to.)

M. ORLANDO said that the question he put was: With regard to the situation concerning the German Colonies, was it to be considered as the continuation of occupation *de facto*, or was it to be, after they had passed that resolution, a system of provisional mandate—German or Turkish? After having heard the discussion, M. Orlando said that he had come to the conclusion that the solution was to give provisional mandates. If that were so, he asked whether those mandates would be distributed by a further resolution of the conference.

MR. LLOYD GEORGE replied that the resolution did not deal with the distribution of mandates at all, but only laid down the general principles.

M. CLEMENCEAU said that was accepted. The question put by M. Orlando was then discussed.

PRESIDENT WILSON said that he had a suggestion to offer. The maintenance of the *status quo* involved the difficulties which the Prime Minister of Great Britain had pointed out about the maintenance of large forces of troops. It ought to be possible by agreement among the Allies. He said that, because the United States could not participate at present, as they had not declared war against Turkey. By agreement with the Allies, the military control of those several parts of the Turkish Empire could be arranged as they pleased by substitution. Would not that be better than going through the difficult form of provisional mandate?

M. CLEMENCEAU thought that they were to discuss M. Orlando's proposal. His proposal was that as France, England and her Dominions had had their share, Italy wanted to have her own share. That was what he understood.

MR. LLOYD GEORGE thought the problem put by M. Orlando was one that they would have to face. M. Orlando said, either they could leave things as they were—leave the mandatories to be settled by the League of Nations and the occupation go on exactly as at the present moment—or they could have a provisional mandate, leaving the definite final thing to be settled by the League of Nations; or they could now say they were the League of Nations and settle the business finally. Those were the three points and he would say quite frankly that he would rather face them at once, as he could not see that there would be any greater light thrown on the subject when the League of Nations came to deal with it or that there would even be a different tribunal—they would be exactly the same people; as a matter of fact, there would be this difference, perhaps— they might not then be able to have the advantage of the presence of the President of the United States at the League of Nations.

MR. LLOYD GEORGE said that they could not accept the *status quo*. He wanted to put the British position again. The German colonies did not matter very much, although the maintenance of troops in German East Africa was a very considerable burden. He could not say exactly how many troops they had in that theatre, but he knew it was a very considerable number. Coming to the Turkish Empire, he had handed some figures to the President of the United States and to M. Clemenceau, and he had also told M. Orlando that they had 1,084,000 men there. It was true that only between 250,000 and 300,000 were British troops, but they had to maintain the lot, and it was an enormous expense. The difficulty was to keep all these various tribes in some sort of peace with each other. If they kept them there until they had made peace with Turkey, and until the League of Nations had been constituted and had started business, and until it was able to dispose of this ques- tion, the expense would be something enormous, and they really could not face it, especially as they had not the slightest intention of being mandatories of a considerable number of territories they now occupied, such as Syria and parts of Armenia. He thought the same thing applied to Kurdestan and the Caucasus, although they had rich oil-wells. He did not think that they had the slightest intention of being mandatories even for the oil-wells of Baku, but somebody had to be there to protect the Armenians and to keep the tribes and sects in Lebanon from cutting each other's throats and attacking the French or Turks, or whoever also might be there. Therefore, he was afraid that they must insist (he was not using that word in a military sense but from the point of view of those who had to pay taxes in the United Kingdom, and to propose it to Parliament). He was afraid however that Parliament would want to know: Why should they keep 1,084,000 men there? Did they really mean to occupy the country? Why should they do so when they had no intention of having a permanent garrison there? This question specially affected them, and unless the Conference was prepared to relieve them of that responsibility, he would really have to press very hard for a definite appointment of the mandatories, which he should have thought was the most satisfactory way of dealing with it. Then they could clear out, and leave the mandatory to undertake the job.

As to the remark made by President Wilson in regard to Turkey, Mr. Lloyd George said that he did not think that was a conclusive reason. Matters could easily be arranged with Turkey. It would not be regarded as a hostile act by the Turk. He knew he was not going to Armenia and Syria, and he also knew that that was going to be taken away from him, and the Turk would not object to the United States going there instead of the British; in fact, he might object much less, for the reason that the United States had not been fighting him for the last four or five years, whereas the British had.

PRESIDENT WILSON stated what seemed to him to stand in the way of a permanent designation.

Many of these mandates would constitute a burden—by no means a privilege—and a very serious burden, but while he should not[6] be disinclined to see the United States get any advantage out of this war, he should be equally disinclined to see her shirk any burden or duty. But he could think of nothing the people of the United States would be less inclined to accept than military responsibility in Asia. If the United States of America, therefore, was to be asked to share a burden of mandates, the request would have to be postponed until he could explain the whole matter to them, and try to bring them to the point of view which he desired them to assume. That, if the United States was to be included in the request, would lead to permanent assignments. He would therefore like to make a suggestion. The question in the meantime was chiefly a military question, and he wished to suggest that the military advisers of the Supreme War Council should have this question of the military occupation and control of these various regions referred to them for recommendation to that Council as to the distribution of the burden, so that they should have something definite for the military authorities to consider.

(There was no objection to this.)

MR. LLOYD GEORGE said that this would clarify the question. The Secretary of State for War would be there the following day, so that he, Mr. Lloyd George, would be quite prepared to have it examined, say, on Saturday.

PRESIDENT WILSON said that his advisers were already there.

M. CLEMENCEAU said everything depended on the situation in Russia. The French had troops in the East, the British had troops

---

[6] *Sic* in both the manuscript and printed versions. Wilson undoubtedly said "but while he should not be inclined. . . ."

in the Caucasus, the French had troops in Odessa,[7] as also had the British and the Italians. As long as they did not know exactly what they would do with Russia, he doubted if they could do anything at all. It was very difficult to recall troops.

PRESIDENT WILSON observed that it was a question of redistribution and substitution.

MR. LLOYD GEORGE said that supposing the British agreed to withdraw from Syria altogether, he would like to know the attitude of the military authorities. This was a point put to him by Mr. Balfour.

PRESIDENT WILSON said "Or from Mesopotamia."

MR. LLOYD GEORGE added "Or Kurdestan."

He also said that they had troops in Persia.

MR. LLOYD GEORGE, in answer to M. Clemenceau, said that he was prepared, so far as the British delegates were concerned, to examine the matter on Saturday with his military experts and that they would have them there.

PRESIDENT WILSON enquired whether it would not be better for someone to formulate the question in writing for the military men to discuss, and present a memorandum to that meeting. If they brought their military experts there it would probably lead to a long discussion.

MR. HUGHES said there was one small point to which he would like to call the attention of the President. He did not like the wording "principle afforded by the necessity of disposing of these Colonies and territories." He did not think that that was the best way of expressing it. It seemed to be opposed to the principle. Therefore he suggested that it should be made to read "apply to" or "dealing with." It was a small thing, but it seemed to be against the general spirit of the clause, which did not mean the disposing of people at all. Perhaps, therefore, this alteration might be made.

PRESIDENT WILSON said that the meaning would be the same.

Continuing, President Wilson said they had not yet adopted the instructions to the Polish delegates.

M. CLEMENCEAU thought that they were going to have the reports of the people who were now considering the question.

In regard to the Czecho-Slovaks, there would be a paragraph to introduce into the instructions.

[7] A British force under the command of Maj. Gen. William Montgomerie Thomson had occupied the Caspian Sea port of Baku on November 16-17, 1918. In December, the British occupied the Black Sea port of Batum and stationed a small garrison at Tiflis, the capital of the province of Georgia. Meanwhile, the French 156th Division, consisting of Moroccan and French troops, had occupied Odessa on December 17. For the complicated political and diplomatic maneuvers that preceded and followed these actions, see George A. Brinkley, *The Volunteer Army and Allied Intervention in South Russia, 1917-1921* (Notre Dame, Ind., 1966), pp. 73-112.

M. CLEMENCEAU asked if those present were willing to hear the Belgian representatives in regard to the Congo.

MR. LLOYD GEORGE said that the Congo was not a German conquest. He did not know on what point the Belgians wished to make themselves heard. No doubt there were many other Powers who would like to be heard. There was the question of the Portuguese Colonies, about which General Botha would probably like to say a good deal. There was a good deal that he himself would like to say about the Congo which would be very useful, but not at that Conference.

PRESIDENT WILSON said that they had got a big enough job already, and that if they went into history by mending the actions of previous Conferences, they would have a very difficult business.

M. CLEMENCEAU thought that it was a little harsh to say they would not hear them.

M. PICHON observed that the Belgians had some claims to certain parts of the German Colonies.

(At this point the Belgian representatives entered.)

M. Orst[8] said that the participation of Belgium in the discussion on the fate of the German colonies in Africa was justified by the importance of the political and economic interests of Belgium in that part of the world, and by the fact that the Belgian Colonies in Africa were neighbours both of the Cameroons and of German East Africa. Also it should be mentioned that the Belgian troops took a considerable part in the fighting that took place in those districts. . . .

The claims of Belgium might be summarised as follows: They wished that the former conquests made by the Germans and the points of the Cameroons towards the Congo should disappear and the same on the Eastern side. They had no desire for conquest, but they thought it would be only fair in view of all the losses they had sustained, and it would complete the Congo Colony in many respects, if they could be allowed to retain permanently under their administration the territories of East Africa which they now provisionally occupied.[9] Belgium accepted the 14 points as laid down

---

[8] Pierre Charles Auguste Raphaël Orts, Acting Secretary General of the Belgian Ministry of Foreign Affairs.

[9] "In conclusion, the claims of Belgium could be summarised as follows: In order to protect herself from future German aggression, Belgium desired that Germany should henceforth cease to occupy any territory adjoining the Belgian Congo. The Cameroons, which would have to be confiscated from Germany, should be ceded to France, with whom good and friendly relations had always existed. On the other hand, Belguim claimed as compensation for the sacrifices she had made during the war, to retain permanently under her administration the territories of East Africa which she now provisionally occupied." Revised text in Miller, XIV, 118.

by President Wilson, and especially point number 5 dealing with colonial claims and with the legitimate interests of those concerned in that question, which was the title upon which they had based their present claim.

M. PICHON said that Portugal had asked to be heard during the last few days. The Portuguese Minister[10] had been to see him at the beginning of the Conferences and said that Portugal would have something to say about the settlement of all those regions when the time came.

MR. LLOYD GEORGE said that Belgium asked for something that they had not yet started to discuss, namely, who should be the mandatory. They were making out a case that they should be the mandatory in respect of those territories, a question which had not yet been reached.

PRESIDENT WILSON added: "to divide up East Africa."

MR. LLOYD GEORGE said Belgium asked for the most fertile portion of East Africa whereas they had not made good use of what they had on the Western side.

MR. BALFOUR stated that Portugal wanted to say the same thing. The Portuguese Ambassador[11] had often been to see him in London, and among other grievances he had tried to bring before his notice, was the question that Portugal would like to have some part of German East Africa, and would also like to have a large British loan in order to enable them to exploit and develop the side they have had for centuries. He did not know whether all those points should be discussed there. He thought not.

(The question was reserved.)

M. CLEMENCEAU said that the Roumanians wished to be present the next day.

MR. LLOYD GEORGE said that raised the question of the agenda and he thought it was very important that some sort of agenda should be formulated. He was not complaining. But he did not know that the Belgians were coming there that afternoon and they were putting up a claim which very specially affected the British and he found himself without experts on this question and without maps, etc.

In regard to Roumania, Mr. Lloyd George enquired if that meant that they were beginning the following day with the discussion of the territorial questions in Europe. He thought the discussion on Czecho-Slovakia and Poland the other day was absolutely wrong. He would not use the term "a waste of time" because that was a very provocative one, and he could already see the glare in the

---

[10] João Pinheiro Chagas.          [11] Augusto Cezar de Vasconcellos.

President's eye! At the same time he thought it was not quite the best method of dealing with the business. If they were going to begin to hear them in part, let them each make their statements before the matter had been broached at that Conference. Unless they began business with Roumania and considered her claims the next day, he did not think the Roumanian representatives ought to be present. If they came without intending to do business, it would be a waste of time.

M. SONNINO thought that the question of the Czechs and the Poles could not be considered as a waste of time. They knew that the Poles and Czechs were fighting and they wanted to stop that, consequently they had decided to send a Mission to Warsaw. It was their duty to hear the Czechs and the Poles with the least possible delay, instead of sending a Mission which would take a fortnight. If the Poles put out all their aspirations, that was another question.

MR. BALFOUR said that was their fault.

M. SONNINO thought that the talk with the Czechs and the Poles was very useful and if, as a consequence of that conversation, they could decide how to put a stop to the fighting, they would have gained and not lost time.

M. CLEMENCEAU said that those present did not always share the same views. President Wilson had proposed that they should begin to deal with territorial questions. They began with the Pacific, then passed to Africa. Now they had come to Europe, beginning with Poland, because there was a pressing necessity and fighting was taking place there. If it were decided not to hear the Roumanian case the following day, well, let it be so; but they must have courage to begin with those questions one day or other. If Mr. Lloyd George wished to have another agenda, of course he (M. Clemenceau) was ready to accept his suggestion, but he only wished that suggestions should be other than negative ones. If it was suggested that they should leave out the Colonial question, that they should not deal further with Poland, that they should not hear the Roumanian case, then that would lead them to a *cul de sac*. President Wilson had given very important reasons why the discussion of the Colonial questions should be postponed for the moment. They had reached an agreement on the proposal made by Mr. Lloyd George that morning, and President Wilson had said he wished to stop at that stage for the present. Now, if they did not courageously deal with the European questions, what else was there for them to do? M. Clemenceau said that he expected to receive a report from the Committee on the Czecho-Polish dispute the following day, and it would be ready for issue the same afternoon.

MR. LLOYD GEORGE said that he was afraid he had not made

himself very clear but did not object to Roumania being taken. What he said was that if they took Roumania they must examine the territorial question. That was what he meant. If Roumania was to be taken as a serious examination of the problem, he had not a word to say. If the Roumanian and Serbian delegates had come there for the conference to hear what they had to say, then he had not the slightest objection to Roumania being taken the following day, so long as it was with a view to serious discussion.

PRESIDENT WILSON said that he had a suggestion to make, which at least looked practical. Discussions such as they had heard on the previous day he admitted were most instructive. His only objection was that they did not bear upon a single point that was in doubt in their minds. Now he wanted to hear the full Roumanian case and it was probable that an opportunity could not be found the next day. His suggestion was that the British students of the subject, and the Americans, French, Italians, and Japanese if they had a body of students conversant with those things, should take up any one of those questions and find how near they were in agreement upon it, and then submit to the conference for discussion their conclusions as to what, for example, the territory of Roumania should be. Then they should submit their conclusions to the Roumanians for their opinion. By this means they would eliminate from the discussion everything in which they were in agreement.

Continuing, President Wilson said that he had on his desk the recommendations of the American students on all those questions, in a digested form,[12] so that he would not be laying them before the conference as American proposals, but as a basis of discussion.

MR. BALFOUR said that the only observation he had to make was that he was quite sure that the President was right in thinking that a discussion among the experts who had studied those questions would be most valuable, and that it would tend to eliminate a great many agreed points, and therefore enable them to concentrate their attention on points upon which agreements had not been reached. He was not sure that it would not be wise to allow those people to have their day to explain their case. He thought they would be much happier, although he admitted it took up a great deal of time. He thought it would make a great difference to them if they came

[12] Wilson might have referred to S. E. Mezes, D. H. Miller, and W. Lippmann, "*Memorandum, January 2, 1917 [1918]*. A SUGGESTED STATEMENT OF PEACE TERMS," T MS (WP, DLC). This sixty-seven-page memorandum went into territorial questions in some detail. More likely, Wilson referred to "Outline of Tentative Report and Recommendations Prepared by the Intelligence Section, in accordance with instructions, for the President and the Plenipotentiaries January 21, 1919," T MS (WP, DLC). This report, ninety-eight pages in length, surveyed in detail, with maps, charts, etc., the territorial, economic, and labor questions which might come before the conference.

there and said that they would put their whole case before the conference.

The second part of his suggestion was that they should have representative experts there.

MR. BALFOUR, continuing, said that with regard to the suggestion for allowing each of these groups to have it out before the conference with their experts, he thought that the discussions would be more fruitful, and they would know exactly what these people were thinking in their own minds. The Americans had done most of their work in America. The British had done their work in England and France. They had had books but more than that they had seen the representatives of these countries. If they could come face to face with the actual living feelings of the people concerned, he thought it would be beneficial. That is why he suggested they should have the Roumanians there the following day.

M. CLEMENCEAU said that he agreed.

MR. LLOYD GEORGE added that Serbia must also be present.

MR. LLOYD GEORGE then drew attention to a paragraph which had appeared in the "Daily Mail" published that morning. He said that it was really a very monstrous report, and one might have thought that there was a battle going on between them. President Wilson had called his attention to it that morning. In the afternoon he had obtained a copy, and he thought the language of the President had been very restrained and very moderate, and he was not at all sure that it was adequate having regard to the seriousness of the article.

PRESIDENT WILSON replied that he had left his profane vocabulary at home.

MR. LLOYD GEORGE said that this article gave the impression of a royal row between America, Japan, Great Britain and her Dominions, France, and everybody else, with quotations from the speeches of some of the delegates which appeared in inverted commas, and which were correct. General Botha had already told them that he had received a number of telegrams of a serious nature from South Africa. They would get some in from Great Britain, and would have to give an explanation. It was a grossly inaccurate account, and yet one could see that it was accurate enough to have been supplied by somebody who either directly or indirectly had inside knowledge. That must be stopped.

MR. LLOYD GEORGE said that he did not see how that Conference could be conducted at all if such statements were allowed to continue. In that case they would have to have public séances with speeches, which meant that they would never settle the Peace of Europe or of the Pacific either, because there would be no Pacific.

What he wanted was a clear understanding that whatever communiqué was issued, it should be the only communiqué. The next thing that he wanted to know was what the communiqué should be. He hoped for the moment that it would give the impression of an agreement being arrived at so as not to excite further the disturbed state of the people in all those countries, because that was the way to Bolshevism, if the peoples thought that they in that Conference were wrangling and tearing each others' eyes out. They could say what was absolutely true, that they had arrived at a satisfactory provisional agreement and were examining the question later on.

MR. HUGHES enquired if they were going to put their decisions into the communiqué.

MR. LLOYD GEORGE replied in the negative.

PRESIDENT WILSON suggested that they should say that they had arrived at a satisfactory provisional arrangement with regard to dealing with the German and Turkish territory outside Europe. Then they should say that they had heard the Belgians with regard to the Congo, and that the military advisers of the Supreme War Council should make a report to the Conference as to the best and most advisable disposition of troops to take care of the Turkish territories that are now outside Europe and were now being occupied.

(This was agreed to.)

MR. LLOYD GEORGE then read the draft terms of reference to the Supreme War Council on the Turkish question:

"The Military Representatives of the Allied and Associated Powers at Versailles are directed to meet at once and to present a report as to the most equitable and economical distribution among these Powers of the burden of supplying military forces for the purpose of maintaining order in the Turkish Empire,[13] pending the decisions of the Peace Conference concerning the Government of Turkish territory."

T MS (SDR, RG 256, 180.03101/25, DNA).
[13] A correction, added to the minutes on February 1, 1919, reads as follows:
"*Page 29, last paragraph, line 8.*
"After Turkish Empire" insert 'Trans-Caucasia.'
"NOTE: This addition has been agreed to between President Wilson, Mr. Lloyd George, M. Clemenceau and M. Orlando."

# From the Diary of David Hunter Miller

Thursday, January 30th [1919]

After the meeting the President came up to me and talked for fifteen or twenty minutes. He first spoke of the English of certain definitions but then went on to serious subjects, and he said that he spoke of the ultimatum so as to clear up the situation; that Australia and New Zealand with 6,000,000 people between them could not hold up a conference in which, including China, some twelve hundred million people were represented.

He then spoke of the resolution as not going as far as he had hoped, to which I replied that it was in my opinion a great achievement and pointed out how far it went in respect of Turkish territories and in Central Africa. To this the President assented, saying that he had not thought of it as going quite that far.

He then spoke of the limitation in the resolution to the islands in the South Pacific and asked me to consider this question in respect of the islands in the North Pacific which Japan held. He said that these islands lie athwart the path from Hawaii to the Philippines and that they were nearer to Hawaii than the Pacific coast was, and that they could be fortified and made naval bases by Japan; that indeed they were of little use for anything else and that we had no naval base except at Guam.

The President said that he did not trust the Japanese; that he had trusted them before,—in fact they had broken their agreement about Siberia. We had sent 7,000 troops to Siberia and they promised to send about the same number but had sent 70,000 and had occupied all the strategic points as far as Irkutsk, and that he would not trust them again.

Miller, *My Diary at the Conference of Paris*, I, 99-100.

# To Robert Lansing

My dear Mr. Secretary: Paris, 30 January, 1919.

Will you not be kind enough to have the following message conveyed to the King of Roumania?

By some unexplained mistake Your Majesty's generous message of the 7th of January[1] was not placed before me until today. It has given me the most genuine satisfaction. You are right in assuming that America's friendship for Roumania is genuine and lively and that those who represent America will always be ready to do anything that they can to manifest that friendship. Our best wishes go out towards the stout kingdom over which you preside and it is our universal hope that the new year may bring a new happiness and prosperity.

I wish that it were possible for me to hope that I might respond to the gracious invitation to visit Roumania which has been conveyed to me through Mr. Horton.[2] Apparently my duties here will render it impossible but my thoughts are constantly visiting the countries which, like Roumania, have suffered so much and whose interests deserve the most careful and studious attention of the Conference of Peace.

Cordially and faithfully yours,   [Woodrow Wilson]

CCL (WP, DLC).
    [1] Ferdinand I to WW, Jan. 7, 1919, T telegram (WP, DLC).
    [2] George Horton, Consul General at Saloniki.


## To Robert Woods Bliss

My dear Mr. Bliss:                          Paris, 30 January, 1919.

I have your letter of the 29th[1] about Bishop de Wolf Perry of Rhode Island[2] and his desire, shared by his associates,[3] to hold a public meeting at which Mr. Lloyd George, Lord Robert Cecil and I should call upon the nations of the associated Governments to unite on a given day in prayer to invoke Divine intercession and help in the councils of the Peace Conference. My sympathy for the kind of thing he proposes is so great that it goes hard with me to suggest difficulties, but I believe we ought in candor to tell him that I doubt if it would be feasible to get up such a meeting for the reason that it is our conscientious duty, all of us, to devote our time to the business of the Peace Conference which we all feel to be lagging and are all desirous of pushing forward.

Sincerely yours,   [Woodrow Wilson]

CCL (WP, DLC).
    [1] R. W. Bliss to WW, Jan. 29, 1919, TLS (WP, DLC).
    [2] The Rt. Rev. James De Wolf Perry, Jr., Protestant Episcopal Bishop of Rhode Island; at this time a chaplain in the A.E.F.
    [3] Three of these "associates" were the Rev. Dr. Arthur Stanley Vaughan Blunt, rector of the British Embassy Church in Paris; the Rev. Dr. Frederic Anstruther Cardew, chaplain of St. George's Episcopal Church, Paris; and the Rev. Dr. William G. Allen, pastor of the Methodist Church in Paris. Bliss also mentioned one "Captain MacDonald, a Canadian and a Minister of the Scotch Presbyterian Church." MacDonald cannot be further identified. According to the *Scottish Church and University Almanac, 1919* (Edinburgh, 1919), p. 78, the pastor of the Scottish Presbyterian Church in Paris was the Rev. T. H. Wright.

## To Joseph Patrick Tumulty

[Paris, Jan. 30, 1919]

I frankly dread the effect on British public opinion with which I am daily dealing here of a Home Rule resolution by the House of Representatives[1] and I am afraid that it would be impossible to explain such a resolution here, but I willingly trust your discretion in handling the matter at Washington. It is not a question of sympathy but of international tactics at a very critical period.

Your messages are exceedingly serviceable and it is delightful to have your thought following affairs here so watchfully. Hope you are entirely well.

T transcript of CLSsh (WP, DLC).
  [1] Wilson was replying to JPT to WW, Jan. 28, 1919.

## From Walter Stowell Rogers

Dear Mr. President:                      Paris, 30 January, 1919.

Permit me to call your attention to the strategic importance, from a communication point of view, of the Island of Yap, a former German possession now held by the Japanese. The ultimate ownership of the Island of Yap will no doubt determine the ultimate ownership of the German cable system in that part of the Pacific. The German cable runs from Yap direct to Shanghai and from Yap to the Dutch East Indies, where it connects with a cable system owned by the Dutch Government, which system, in turn, connects with cable systems running westward to India and Europe and southward to Australia.

There is also a cable connection between Yap and Guam. The latter point is a relay station for the cable from the United States to the Orient. With Yap in control of the Japanese, American messages passing over the Yap route for the East Indies and adjacent places would have to pass through Japanese hands.

No doubt were the Island of Yap left in possession of Japan, the Japanese would promptly lay a cable direct from Japanese territory to Yap, thus obtaining a most effective commercial and political line, over which the Japanese would exercise a close scrutiny and give themselves preferential rates and service.

A rearrangement of the whole cable system of the Pacific is a necessary incident to any world development of cable communication. Certainly the destiny of Yap and the German cable in the Pacific should not be finally decided without reference to the communications problem as a whole.

I might add that there is a low-power radio station now on Yap, and that Yap is ideally located for radio purposes.

Respectfully,    Walter S. Rogers

TCL (received from Mrs. William S. Bellamy).


## From George Davis Herron

Dear Mr. President,                        Paris, le Jany 30th, 1919

May I take the liberty of telling you I shall be returning to Geneva on Sunday, and of thanking you for hearing my report of the present crisis so graciously.

I have presented the same view to Mr. Balfour, Signor Orlando, Baron Sonnino, and many others. I have laid something of the "burden of the Lord" upon them.

Your noble and enthralling address introducing the Society of Nations went far toward renewing the faith of the peoples.

May I say to you, in concluding, that I am always at your command for any service I may render, and beg you to remember, for whatever it may be worth to you, that I am always daily upholding you with the prayer of intimate and undoubting faith.

Yours most faithfully,    George D Herron

ALS (WP, DLC).


## Charles Seymour to His Family

Dear people:                        [Paris] January 30, 1919.

I have had a very busy and a very interesting two days. Much of the work involves what we call "T N T stuff" which I hardly dare put on paper but I can talk about the associations involved which I shall be glad to remember.

Yesterday morning I was just getting ready for a peaceful day in the hope of clearing my desk of a mass of accumulated papers and was cheered by the thought of no luncheon engagement, when a call came from Bowman to pack up my available stuff on the Czechs and come right over to the Quai d'Orsay. As you will have seen by the papers the Prime Ministers and Foreign Ministers of the big five Powers, the "Council of Ten" they are beginning to call them, was to consider Polish affairs and it was expected that relations with the Czechs would come up. We had very short notice, which was regrettable, for I had no chance to get into "diplomatic clothes"; fo[r]tunately my fur coat was on my back, but when I got inside I felt that my trousers should have been pressed. We felt quite as though we were arbiters of the nations as we whirled into the entrance of the Quai d'Orsay through the crowd which waits to see the big men come in. Inside I found myself giving up my coat and hat to the French orderly, side by side with Mr. Balfour and General Botha. The secret conferences are held in the small room, Pichon's private office, which opens to the right off the main waiting room. I suppose there were about twenty of us in all, including the commissioners. As we came into the room Wilson came up to us and shook hands very cordially. He is brisk and genial as ever. Lansing looks very tired; he walks very slowly and told Young yesterday that he is bothered by his heart.

Everything reminded me of a faculty committee meeting, rather than a gathering of statesmen. Proceedings opened very informally when Clemenceau suggested that the doors be closed and that they begin work. The room is about double the size of our library in the Hillhouse Avenue house (imagine two libraries running side by side). It is oak with a few good carvings (cupids over the main door) with two empire commodes, a very simple fireplace, and Rubens tapestries, copied from the Marie de Medicis pictures in the Louvre; one side has two big windows looking out on the garden. There is a plain empire table in the centre, at which Clemenceau sits. Almost immediately behind him is Paul Mantoux, interpreter; to the latter's right, by the side of the fireplace, Pichon, who is the living image of that good-natured Wallingford doctor, Doctor Atwater,[1] wasn't it? He is rounder, more bunched up, and sloppier, but his image. On Clemenceau's right is Wilson, and then Lansing. Then Balfour and Botha; Lloyd George came only to the afternoon session. Then a chair for whoever is being heard by the commissioners, in this case the Pole, Dmowski. Then the two Japs.[2] Facing Clemenceau Sonnino and Orlando and two or three secretaries. Bowman and I faced Clemenceau immediately behind the Italians. Everything was very informal, each of the men speaking when they felt like it and with very little direction from Clemenceau. The latter wore his grey gloves every moment of the session even when writing. Most of the time his face was expressionless, even rather bored, with his long moustache covering his mouth and his eyebrows his eyes, which were generally half closed. When particularly interested, which is rare, he opens his eyes very wide and leans forward. His English is perfectly grammatically, but has a decided accent. Sonnino, on the other hand, has a perfect Oxford accent; to hear him one would swear that he was pure English. He has an attractive manner and

[1] Caleb Huntington Atwater, M.D.
[2] That is, Baron Nobuaki Makino and Viscount Sutemi Chinda.

shows the force which we know him to possess; Orlando, on the other hand, appears rather weak. In talking, Dmowski was at as much pains to impress Sonnino as Wilson, but rather ignored Orlando. Botha looked his part perfectly, rather hard-headed and business-like. He took little part in the discussion. He was there as the British commissioner to Poland I suppose. Balfour rested his head on the back of his chair and stretched his enormously long, crossed legs out in front of him, and looked the image of "Spy" 's[3] caricature of him in the House of Commons. He never looked bored, however. Wilson is absolutely at home and seems to get on very well with the Europeans, speaking naturally, almost colloquially, and without affectation or any trace of didactiveness. He likes to make a humorous allusion and Balfour, Lloyd George, and Clemenceau are evidently glad of some excuse for a smile. Dmowski spoke of the qualifications of Paderewski, and particularly that he had never joined in party struggles: "Fortunate man," said Clemenceau with an indescribable gesture. The session is carried on in English and French. Mantoux translates everything, very well indeed, rarely using a literal rendering but putting the idea into perfect idiom. Dmowski asked that he be allowed to translate for himself, so that Mantoux was out of a job all morning, and went to sleep for most of the time. The poor man has been translating for over a year in the allied war council. Wilson and Balfour appear to be in close understanding, and in the afternoon Wilson and Lloyd George frequently whispered together. It is generally understood that so far as the League of Nations and the disposition of German colonies go, we and the British are in close accord. I suppose that Hughes may put up objections and I know that Simone,[4] the French minister of colonies is opposed, but Clemenceau has practically agreed to come with Lloyd George in supporting Wilson. The only trouble is that they dont know what they mean about mandatory powers.

The morning session lasted until after one, when Wilson said he had a luncheon engagement and suggested adjournment; all right, said Clemenceau shall we meet at three? Half-past three said Sonnino, and everybody got up. In the afternoon session the Czechs came in, when it was half way over and for the first time I had to get down to business and stop watching proceedings as a witness. I went in late and was glad I did, for while I was outside I had a very interesting talk with Lloyd George's secretary.[5] Then Mr. Wilson came out for a minute, and seeing me there came up to discuss the way things were going. Both he and the British are tried in

[3] Sir Leslie Ward, who published numerous cartoons of Balfour in *Vanity Fair* during his many years as a cartoonist for that magazine.
[4] That is, Henry Simon.
[5] That is, Philip (Henry) Kerr.

their patience by the difficulty of getting down to brass tacks and are very anxious to get things started towards a preliminary settlement. He said he had made a suggestion to Mr. Lloyd George, who had approved it, told me what it was, and asked me to take steps to put it into effect, at least in principle. I was glad that I happened to be there, for he is impulsive, had evidently spoken as a result of the long session, which was accomplishing nothing and he might have said nothing if someone has not happened to meet him. But I think his idea is an excellent one, and can be used to expedite matters. I have been working on it much of today.

The discouraging part of the conference is that it seems so difficult to get an orderly program. Much matter, which should be put before subordinates,—details, technical disputes, etc., comes before the Council of Ten, takes up their time, and perplexes them. They dont know any details, of course. Yesterday Orlando didnt know what Austrian Silesia was. The claimants, who are putting their case, cannot be restrained from going into a thousand minor points, which the Commissioners are wholly unqualified to consider. What we are working for is to have questions at issue brought first before sub-committees, appointed by the Powers, and composed of the various experts, so-called. These are the only men who are capable of deciding the details and of presenting the matter fairly to the commissioners. These sub-committees can be working all at the same time, make reports to the Council of Ten, which can then pass on the large question. It is the easiest and quickest way or [of] disposing of all territorial questions and will leave the Commissioners free during the next weeks to decide on the League of Nations and international control of transportation, of labor, etc, etc. Of course the Conference is working under difficulties far greater than those of the Congress of Vienna, for conditions in central Europe are in such a state of flux, to say nothing of Russia, that it is impossible to know what the latest developments are. The conference has to determine not merely the articles of general peace, but the details of current policy towards the Bolsheviks, Poland, the Ukrainians, the Lithuanians, the Jugoslavs, as well as how to save Hungary, Austria, Bohemia, etc. from anarchy and labor upheavals. For example half of my work, which ought to be devoted purely to the consideration of the claims of Danubian peoples and planning for a future long ahead, is devoted to the study of measures to be taken day after tomorrow to meet an immediate and temporary crisis. Of course this cant be avoided. . . .

Lots of love,   Good-night, C.

TLI (C. Seymour Papers, CtY).

## From the Diary of Colonel House

January 30, 1919.

Lord Robert Cecil was my most important visitor. We went over the Covenant for the League of Nations and there was but little disagreement between us. He agrees with our views more than he dares admit because he sees that his people will not follow him. I am to get Orlando in line and he is to get the French, and when this is done we will have a general meeting.

We discussed the colonial question and agreed absolutely. Strangely enough, at the same time that Cecil and I were discussing it here, the President was having "a first class row" with Lloyd George, Clemenceau, Hughes and Massey. It looked as if the whole thing had "gone to pot." However, the row may do good. It will teach them all a lesson. The President was angry. Lloyd George was angry and so was Clemenceau. It is the first time the President has shown any temper in his dealings with them and it was a mistake I think to show it at this time. The British had come a long way, and if I had been in his place, I should have congratulated them over their willingness to meet us more than half way.

Vance McCormick came and we arranged to have a meeting of the Economic Committee at five o'clock tomorrow. They wanted the President to make the call but in lieu of that, I did it myself.

I sent for Sir William Tyrrell in accordance with the understanding I had with the President last night regarding the united report which I desire the British and American Technical Advisers to make concerning boundary questions. I put Tyrrell in touch with Mezes and urged them to facilitate the matter as much as possible.

Frazier told the President yesterday that he thought he was making a mistake in not insisting that I be present at the Quai d'Orsay meetings. The President did not know how it could be managed since tentatively only the Prime Ministers and Foreign Secretaries were supposed to be there. Frazier thought I could attend as a "technican [technical] adviser" and that my "moral influence would have a good effect." Lloyd George also told Wiseman that he wished I would attend. Wiseman replied that I was too busy doing things worth while to waste my time in the manner in which they were doing at these meetings. He said this humorously, but really meant it in earnest.

We had a meeting of the Economic Specialists and decided many matters of passing importance. I have been trying to get the President to call this meeting for sometime, but failing to do so, I called it myself. There were present, Benson, Bliss, Hoover, Baruch, McCormick and Robinson,[1] representing Hurley. Davis was sick and could not come. I outlined a program and they are to set to work tomorrow.

The President, Orlando and I met at the Hotel Murat tonight in order to compare our Covenant for the League of Nations with that which the Italians have drawn.[2] The meeting was very successful. We came to near agreement and without much difficulty. The exceptions that Orlando made to our draft were rather pertinent and some of them we agreed to accept. Frazier, who was present, is to write an account of the meeting which will be attached.

I suggested to the President that we meet with the British tomorrow night in my rooms at the Crillon, and that the following night we bring and [the] British and Italians together, leaving the French for another day.

Lord Robert Cecil said the President would naturally become Chairman of the League of Nations Committee, but after the President left, he would like very much for me to assume the Chairmanship in order that there might be no possibility of Bourgeois being chosen. His objection to Bourgeois is the objection we all have to him and that is his verbosity and utter inability to conduct meetings expeditiously. I declined the offer for myself and suggested that he, Cecil, be made Vice Chairman so when the President left, he would preside. I shall try to see that this goes through.

[1] That is, Henry M. Robinson.
[2] It is printed in David Hunter Miller, *The Drafting of the Covenant* (2 vols., New York, 1928), II, 246-55.


## Notes of a Conversation by Arthur Hugh Frazier

[Jan. 30, 1919]

The President asked for Signor Orlando's views on the covenant which had been submitted to him the day before.

Signor Orlando replied that he was in the main in entire agreement with President Wilson, but he had a few technical suggestions to make. He drew especial attention to Article I of the supplementary agreements[1] which, he thought, was open to misconstruction. If the Trentino and Trieste were to be handed over to a mandatory by the League of Nations, it would seriously compromise Italy's dignity.

The President pointed out that this was far from his mind. In fact, he intended that this question should be settled before the creation of the League of Nations. In other words, the Trentino and Trieste had, as far as he was concerned, already been ceded to Italy. He said that the reason why he had drafted the paragraph in this form, was because Yugo-Slavia might be divided into one, two or three States. He was prepared to admit two Yugo-Slav States to the League of Nations but, if it were found advisable to separate them into three parts, he would prefer to place the more unformed and less developed of the new States under the mandatory of the League of Nations.

Signor Orlando thanked the President warmly for this explanation but he nevertheless recommended that the language of Article I be altered.

This, the President promised to do.

Signor Orlando drew attention to another reason for not postponing too many of the settlements until the creation of the League of Nations. He said the Czecho-Slovaks and the Poles might decline to compose their differences in Silesia if hope were held out that the controversy could later be referred to the League of Nations.

The President then explained why he proposed that the General Court should be composed of the resident diplomats in one of the smaller capitals rather than of special delegates; if special delegates were appointed, there would surely be jealousy between them and the resident diplomats. In a small capital, a resident diplomat would have leisure to devote a portion of his time to the work of the League of Nations. This might not be the case in a large capital.

Signor Orlando said that these remarks had convinced him absolutely. In fact, he added that the experience of the last few days had satisfied him that a large capital was not a good place in which to hold a Peace Conference.

Signor Orlando did not find the idea of giving three votes the power of veto upon any action of the Council practical. To illustrate his meaning he gave the case of an internationalized railway: supposing that a State, through which this railway passed, imposed exorbitant tariffs and refused to alter them at the request of its neighbours, all action could be paralyzed if three adverse votes prevented the Council from reaching a decision.

The President admitted that this might take place but he said that, as there could be no resort to arms before a delay of one year, public opinion would have time to reflect upon the gravity of the step.

Signor Orlando then hastily went over the remaining part of the covenant and said that his comments were very trifling, except on the subject of the abolition of conscription. He thought that this would work hardship upon the poorer Powers. In other words, rich Powers could afford to pay their standing army well. This would place the poorer Powers at a disadvantage. He did not think the voluntary system would work in Italy. They were already having trouble with their paid carabinieri which demanded higher wages. He suggested that a minimum conscription be allowed to be modelled out after the Swiss system. He also thought that the presence of a large body of trained officers in a country might militate against the President's system as, with trained officers, it would be easy to drill new men rapidly.

The President thought that if the number of officers were limited to the number of troops they could legitimately be called upon to command, this objection would disappear.

Signor Orlando asked what would be the result if all the Allied Powers abolished conscription and the Germany army remained intact.

The President replied that Germany would be forced to disarm before she could be admitted as a member of the League.

Signor Orlando promised to send an English translation of the Italian text to the President as soon as possible.

From Miller, *My Diary at the Conference of Paris,* IV, 341-43.
[1] He referred to the second "Paris draft" printed at Jan. 18, 1919.


## To Arthur Bernard Krock

My dear Krock:                                    Paris, 30 January, 1919.

Thank you for your note of the 28th.[1] As a matter of fact I have a very soft place in my heart for old Colonel Watterson but I am sure that if I were to make any public contribution to the introduction which Judge Bingham is planning to the Colonel's memoirs,[2] it would be considered insincere. I hope therefore that you will beg Judge Bingham to excuse me, and you may assign as a reason either what I have just said or what is equally true, that my duties here so hurry me from one thing to another as to render such things practically impossible.

Cordially and faithfully yours,   [Woodrow Wilson]

CCL (WP, DLC).
[1] A. B. Krock to WW, Jan. 28, 1919, TLS (WP, DLC).
[2] Actually, Robert W. Bingham had requested, through Krock, that Wilson supply "some expression . . . concerning Mr. Watterson" which could be included in a special supplement on Watterson's life work to be published in the Louisville *Courier-Journal* on March 2, 1919, the date on which the serial publication of Henry Watterson's memoirs was to begin in the *Saturday Evening Post.* The memoirs were later published in book form, without an introduction, as *"Marse Henry": An Autobiography* (2 vols., New York, 1919).

## From Joseph Patrick Tumulty

Dear Governor:                    The White House 30 January 1919.

I am sending these thoughts on to you for your consideration.

Many urgent matters await your return. They should be tackled with the same vigor and enterprise that you rushed the war work. Necessary readjustments brought about lessened production and reduction of business in many lines. Business conditions are strange and there is some uncertainty. There are a great many idle men in places and a natural anxiety as to the immediate future. It is feared by many that bad conditions cannot be avoided in the early spring and naturally there is a disposition in certain quarters to hold the Administration responsible.

It will meet the approval of the people if profitless discussion of reasons be cut out and an aggressive programme of remedial action be immediately put into effect. You should have prepared and considered plans so that you can begin issuing orders as soon as you land. It will be half the battle to act promptly and powerfully. The country will be imspired [inspired], individuals will be incited to strenuous endeavors, the newspapers will extoll your practical and robust enterprise, and results will be gained quickly and generally. In fact it would be my idea that you should discuss as soon as you arrive the future of American business, European needs, and the basic elements of prosperity that are present in our own situation.

To aid you, brief reports should be prepared by heads of departments. These should mainly deal with plans for the employment of men and should include definite recommendations as to means of putting them into immediate effect.

1)[1]    For instance, Secretary Lane may report that he has plans for the reclamation of swamp lands by drainage and levee construction. He has plenty of such projects which he has been talking about for a number of years but little or no land has been reclaimed. By co-operating with the War Department, the Engineer Corps can be put on the job. There are twenty-five or thirty million acres of these lands ready to be turned into farms and seventy-five or a hundred thousand soldiers can be given work. An appropriation of fifty or a hundred million dollars should be made and a provision included which would give soldiers first call for the lands. This would be very popular in the Mississippi Valley. If the idea is adopted, you should cable Secretary Lane and Secretary Baker to prepare plans, draft legislation and be ready to rush it through. Lane has written and spoken reams on this and should know how to turn his words into action.

[1] Numbers WWhw.

Secretary Lane should have a number of projects in hand in his Department which, if adopted and funds furnished for carrying them out, would result in the employment of many men, especially soliders, and do much towards the development of the country.

Secretary Houston should have some schemes which will furnish work and help the farmers.

2)     In the Department of Agriculture is Logan Page[2] with his Good Roads Bureau. It is not likely that the Government wants to undertake the construction of roads on a large scale, but Page could call the heads of the roads departments of different states to Washington and urge them to get as large appropriations in their state legislatures as possible and begin spending the money and giving employment at once. The state legislatures are mostly now in session and many have big good roads programmes in hand but this push from Washington would stimulate all and give Washington the credit for a great deal which will be done.

3)     The Secretary of Agriculture might find it desirable to call to Washington all the secretaries of agriculture of the different states and talk over with them various small and big enterprises which would result in the giving of employment in different sections.

4)     It might be well for the President to invite the Governors of the different states to come to Washington to sit down with him in the White House to discuss projects of various kinds in their states. The Governors would learn what others are doing or contemplate doing in other states and by example and exchange of information and ideas, cause many things to be done in many states which would give a great deal of employment. The publicity which would grow out of such a conference would encourage municipalities to find various public operations which could be begun and furnish work. Everything possible should be undertaken so as to create a demand for all sorts of building supplies and other material. The inauguration of a national movement to start work and furnish employment would bring tremendous results in the aggregate.

Visionary and uncertain schemes should be left for the future. Only obviously practical efforts should be undertaken.

Washington is now dead and down—entirely relaxed. It should be galvanized into rushing action. It is almost as important to get a move on as it was in war times.

There should be a sensible reorganization of the personnel with the idea of getting a lot of hustlers on the job. This is necessary because many men now here are tired out and new blood is needed,

---

[2] Logan Waller Page, late director of the United States Office of Public Roads. Page had died on December 9, 1918. The acting director of the agency at this time was its chief engineer, Philip St. Julien Wilson.

but even more essential is the necessity of convincing the country that the President means business and is getting new workers to get results, regardless of politics or personal relationship.

When you return on the GEORGE WASHINGTON, it might be desirable for you to invite all correspondents who desire to return to ride with you. It would do you incalculable benefit to visit with these men, socially and informally, for half a dozen days. The friendly intercourse would have good effect through the trying months to come.

5)    Have some one like John D. Ryan come to Washington a day or two after your return, and frankly discuss the commercial situation of the country and make suggestions as to things he thinks should be done. Have him followed by others. Let some publicity be given to their visits so that the country will understand that the President is taking counsel with the best men of the country to guide him in administering for its welfare.

Ask Mr. Ryan or some suitable person of the same standing and character to associate with him in an informal way—men like Mr. Gary and others (Mr. Gary I suggest because he has made most helpful statements since you have been away)—to co-operate with Washington in carrying out schemes for readjustment. This will not only accomplish much good but will make a good impression on the country which will see the President working hand in hand with able business men in supporting and strengthening commercial affairs in this emergency.

There should be a proper regard for the possible criticism that you are deferring too much to financial men who have their own games to play. Plenty of publicity will take care of this.

6)    The labor employing department of the Department of Labor should be urged to the greatest and most comprehensive activity. Great publicity should be given to its efforts.

If there is a separate labor supply division in the Department of Agriculture, ditto for its activity.

7)    Men who earned promotion for bravery or efficient service in the War should be given their promotions, regardless of previous bung[l]ing.

8)    An investigation should be made of the Pay Department, quiet but effective, to determine why the soldiers have been paid so carelessly. Nothing should protect the guilty ones from the President's just wrath. Hit them quick and hit them hard.

9)    Report should be had from Secretary Daniels as to the number of vessels used for war that can be converted to peace craft. If there are any, the conversion should be begun at once as the vessels are needed. His report should be [c]omprehensive. For instance, what

is being done with the Eagle boats?[3] Torpedo chasers will not be needed for some time and these might make good canal barges.

The names for the President's consideration on return as suitable for various jobs should be carefully made up so that he can pick out ambassadors to enemy countries, cabinet ministers and first-class hustling men for minor places. "Lame ducks" unless the dead ones should have obvious qualifications for hard work and getting things done, should have short sh[r]ift.

It is quite likely that the period of industrial and commercial relaxation, necessary while inevitable readjustments are being made, will not last very long. These energetic measures suggested will help to make the time of strain and worry shorter. They will leave with the country the impression that you have aided tremendously in restoring prosperous peace conditions. It will particularly please the country if you should return from your great task in Europe and instantly set in motion forceful measures to promote and safe-guard our domestic affairs.

In short, my idea is that the President ought to get on the job in these matters with both feet, as soon as possible.

Sincerely yours,   Tumulty

TLS (WP, DLC).

[3] The "Eagle boats" were small antisubmarine ships equipped with radio listening devices, small guns, and depth charges. Henry Ford had contracted in January 1918 to build one hundred of the vessels at his River Rouge automobile plant in Detroit. By the time of the Armistice, seven Eagle boats had been completed, but none saw service until after that date. The original order for one hundred of the ships was later reduced to sixty. See Frank A. Cianflone, "The Eagle Boats of World War I," *United States Naval Institute Proceedings*, XCIX (June 1973), 76-80.


# From Frank Lyon Polk

Washington, January 30th, 1919.

For the President.

Our 366, January 22nd addressed to you giving substance of Oil Leasing Bill was sent by Scott Ferris and not by Secretary of the Interior. Regret error.

In response to your 454,[1] I have asked the Attorney General and Secretary of the Navy for their views and will cable you immediately.

Polk.

T telegram (WP, DLC).

[1] RL to FLP, Jan. 26, 1919.

## From Carter Glass

Washington January 30, 1919.

For the President from Glass.

Food Relief Bill as reported by conferees passed both Houses before receipt of your cable.[1] As agreed to, it permits the Relief to which your cable makes reference.                    Polk.

T telegram (WP, DLC).
  [1] That is, WW to C. Glass, Jan. 28, 1919.

## From Bainbridge Colby

Washington Received 30 January, 1919.

Senate resolution of December fifth copy of which Chairman Hurley has directed Shipping Board to report what legislation should be enacted for maintaining and developing of American merchant marine. Discussions of board have not reached any agreement as to recommendations to be made. Neither Douglas nor Page[1] are in affirmation for following plans but are not agreed on any alternative plan. Proposal having most support contemplating marking down cost and sale of ships to individuals on easy terms of initial payment and fifteen to eighteen years for completion of purchase price. Result of suspense of judgement is that request from Senate is without answer from the board and end of session is approaching. I purpose to avoid charging [charge] of disrespect to Senate and with assent of colleagues to make report as individual members but desire that report be in no way inconsistent with your ideas on this subject. I do not offer plan with any confidence in its merit but feel it rational and that it will clarify the discussion. It is desirable that one great company be organized to combine and consolidate with ships now owned by the government and all ships of American overseas transportation company. This organization to be owned and managed by private interests but financially backed and supervised by government. Such a company would enable our nation to compete with others in the carrying trade of the world. First object of such an organization would be building up of American foreign commerce. Incidentally should be a paying investment as a business enterprise. Such a company would be able to maintain shipping office in every important port abroad and the personnel of offices would be engaged both in securing cargo for American ships and primarily in promoting American commerce. Such a proposition would be much more satisfactory than a number of small competing companies with inadequate financial strength. Substantial economy could be made in overhead charges and in arrangement of voyages. This proposition has merit of utilizing to the best advantage the great fleet of ships constructed for the war emergency which otherwise must be sold at a tremendous loss.

It would enable the government to give indispensable back[ing] to upbuilding of our marine without running counter to the strong prejudice against log roll evil of subsidies. It also recognizes public interest in the subject without establishing government ownership and operation as to which there is much honest skepticism and at the moment a very strong adverse prejudice. I propose unless you disapprove to report to Congress my opinion such corporations should be chartered by Act of Congress with a capital stock sufficient to take over at fair valuation all ships and ship facilities we now have, also all ships and other property of American companies engaged in oversea transportation. For all the property acquired capital stock should be issued carrying a government guarantee of a minimum dividend of say four per cent. Stock issued for property which we now own at least a majority and perhaps whole be sold to the public so the corporation would be privately owned and managed with rights of stockholders to have whatever dividends might be earned except that balance above say eight or ten per cent be divided between stockholders and government. The charter should reserve to government rights to take all ships on equitable terms in case national emergency and the rights in peace time to establish steamship lines for the promotion of American commerce which in the first instance might not be profitable as a business enterprise. The loss caused by the establishment of such lines to be absorbed by the government. Government directors have authority to fix the rates of charge for transportation American goods, to establish lines to promote American commerce, to protect American shippers against discriminatory foreign rates and prevent payment of excess salaries or dealings which might result in private profit. Charter should contain restrictions against foreign owners ships or stocks and require at all time a full supply of ships. I do not attempt to state proposition in full details all of which should have careful consideration. Urgency arises especiall[y] because we have acquired or contracted for property some three billion dollars which must be disposed of according to law within a six months after end of war. All power of Shipping Board and Fleet Corporation as delegates of presidential authority absolutely expires at that time. An attempt to dispose of such a vast amount of property within such a period could be done only at tremendous sacrifice. I ask Hurley to consider this proposition hoping it will have his approval as a constructive suggestion for founding an American merchant marine. I assume he will give his own view of subject. Mr. Whipple approves plan here outlined. Only other plan suggested is to sell or lease all government vessels either by private agreement or auction to enable private and competing companies to engage more extensively in the transportation of foreign commerce. Can not agree to this proposition because it involves unnecessary sacrifice of government investments because it will at once be antagonize[d] by public opinion seeking to impute to the administration a willingness to distribute public property amongst favored receivers and the field of such allocation is necessarily narrow unless the government takes great chances of the management and [by] resulting deterioration of public property it will deprive government of means of sustained patronage without which American marine can not be carried through the difficulty the losing year of its establishment. I do not believe small companies would be capable of holding own against the concentrated national competition of greater maritime nations and the plan as whole not commensurate with public expectation and the scale of our efforts and out of laying out [our outlay?]. I regret to intrude this subject upon your attention at this time but knowing how important you deem it to be I am anxious to make no move and express no opinion might cause possible embar[r]assment.

T telegram (WP, DLC).
¹ He meant John A. Donald and Charles R. Page.


## From Grant Squires

My dear Mr. President                    New York. January 30 1919

I thank you for your letter of January 13, acknowledging mine of a month ago, with its wishes for the New Year. It was very kind of you in the stress of your manifold occupations in which you are now so worthily engaged to send me any word of acknowledgment at all, and I appreciate it.

The matters which have occupied me here during the last six months still continue to do so, and I confess to some alarm at the continued signs of unrest on the part of those who have been under observation.

Without doubt it is only another manifestation continued after the war by those in behalf of Germany, clearly supported by German bankers here who are far from being without funds to continue the propaganda in behalf of their fatherland, which they did so unblushingly during active hostilities.

I think our people are too ready to conclude that with the signing of the armistice it was tantamount to peace itself. I am sure you and I feel differently. The friends of unrest, disorder and revolution hold meetings here almost nightly. Some in the interest of advanced socialism parading for the moment to catch the support of their ignorant followers under the name of Bolshevik. Others in behalf of Free Ireland, and all denunciatory of the present Government at Washington, yourself and your cabinet not being spared in being held up to the most vicious characterization. Of course a man with a power of oratory in times like these will find an audience but if it was confined to that, we should not so much fear as we do their secret plottings for the overthrow of the Government. That is exactly what is doing here more than I have ever known it in the past, and in many ways quite as dangerous as any of the bloody acts committed in Russia and in Germany.

To cap the climax, not that I am personally any longer concerned but because of its [the] significance of the channels through which the enemy works, last week the Bureau with which I had been associated was placed in a false position by an official statement from Washington called forth by the testimony given before Senator Overman's Judiciary Committee charged with investigating Hearst and German propaganda generally.[1]

Against our wishes and quite unexpectedly, several of us who were familar with these two subjects of enquiry were subpoenaed to tell what we knew to this Committee.[2] One witness went so far at the demand of Senator Nelson and Senator Overman to give a list of some citizens who had been active in various movements during the last year and a half in the country and the result you will see from the clippings enclosed.[3] All efforts on the part of the Government to keep posted about the present day activities of Bolshevik and anarchist have been halted and it is doubtful if the effect has not been just the reverse of what your own good judgment would have ordered done had you been present. I wonder if you would approve, had you been present, of the removal of all the official records, files and information gained by Military Intelligence during the war in Washington from a fireproof building to a fire-trap, which I am told was done last week, to save three thousand dollars. It is not pleasant to contemplate what some of those in our midst would not cheerfully pay to have this evidence go up in smoke some day against its further use by the Government when a time of need arises.

The discharge last week from confinement at Fort Leavenworth of the one hundred and thirteen conscientious objectors has been the signal for a great outcry in the press,[4] and not restricted to the middle West, against the official laudation that accompanied their discharge from confinement and from Army service! This was further accentuated by the announcement that they were handed full Army pay for the full period for which they did no service, with mileage to their respective homes and a new suit of civilian clothing.

The average citizen could not see wherein these patriots did not realize by this treatment from their Government quite as much in the material way as did those uncompromising fighters who exposed themselves to the enemy's pitiless attacks in France.

Pardon this long letter. It may arrive in time for you to read on your voyage home, where you will be warmly welcomed and where the value of your services to not alone your own country but to the world at large is sure to be worthily judged.

Sincerely yours   Grant Squires.

TLS (WP, DLC).
¹ The Senate, on September 19, 1918, had debated and passed S. Res. 307, which directed the Senate Committee on the Judiciary, or a subcommittee thereof, to investigate the widely alleged connection between American brewing and liquor interests and German propaganda efforts in the United States both before and after American intervention in the war. A subcommittee consisting of Senators Lee S. Overman (the chairman), William H. King, Josiah O. Wolcott, Knute Nelson, and Thomas Sterling began hearings on September 27, 1918, and concluded them on February 11, 1919. The resulting testimony and many related documents are printed in U. S. Senate, *Brewing and Liquor Interests and German Propaganda: Hearings Before a Subcommittee of the Committee on the Judiciary, Sixty-Fifth Congress, Second Session, Pursuant to S. Res. 307* (2 vols., Washington, 1919), a standard source for German propaganda and espionage activity in the United States during the First World War.

Archibald Ewing Stevenson, a lawyer of New York who claimed to be associated with the Military Intelligence Division of the Army, testified before the subcommittee on January 21-23, 1919 (*ibid.*, II, 2690-2720, 2729-44, 2751-85). He supplied information primarily about various American socialist and pacifist organizations, many of which even he conceded had little or no direct relationship to either brewing and liquor interests or German propaganda efforts. However, he considered the activities of these organizations, many of whom he connected with the Russian Bolsheviks, to be the greatest menace facing postwar America. He concluded his testimony by presenting to the subcommittee a list of sixty-two prominent Americans whom he believed to be identified with the organizations he had been discussing. The list included such persons as Jane Addams, Emily Greene Balch, Roger N. Baldwin, Charles A. Beard, Elizabeth Gurley Flinn, Thomas Cuming Hall, Morris Hillquit, Frederic C. Howe, David Starr Jordan, Eugene V. Debs, Amos R. E. Pinchot, Norman M. Thomas, Oswald G. Villard, and Lillian D. Wald. *Ibid.*, 2782-85.

Newton D. Baker on January 27 issued the following statement: "I am receiving telegrams and letters with regard to a list of persons handed to the Senate committee by Mr. Archibald Stevenson, who is represented in newspaper accounts as a member of the Military Intelligence Division of the War Department. Mr. Stevenson has never been an officer or an employee of the Military Intelligence Division of the War Department.

"I am told that he and a number of associates have, throughout the war, sought to analyze books and newspaper contributions with a view to determining the opinions of their writers toward the war. I personally have no sympathy with the publication of lists of persons classified with reference to their supposed opinions and grouped under general designations such as 'pacifists,' which may mean any one of a dozen things, some of them quite consistent with the finest loyalty to the country, and some of them inconsistent with such loyalty. As a matter of fact, the War Department does not undertake to censor the opinions of the people of the United States. It has no authority to classify such opinions.

"In the particular list accredited to Mr. Stevenson there are names of people of great distinction, exalted purity of purpose, and life-long devotion to the highest interests of America and of mankind. Miss Jane Addams, for instance, lends dignity and greatness to any list in which her name appears." *Official Bulletin*, III (Jan 28, 1919), 2.

Senator Overman on January 28 presented in the Senate correspondence with the New

York branch of the Military Intelligence Division which indicated that Stevenson had in fact been associated with the "propaganda section" of that branch, though the exact nature of his association remained obscure. *Cong. Record*, 65th Cong., 3d sess., pp. 2187-88.

² Squires testified before the subcommittee on January 15. His remarks are printed in U. S. Senate, *Brewing and Liquor Interests* . . . , II, 2512-21.

³ Eleven newspaper clippings (WP, DLC) pertaining to the testimony discussed in n. 1 above and the subject discussed in n. 4 below.

⁴ Newton D. Baker had ordered Peyton C. March on January 16 to initiate the release of 113 conscientious objectors, specifically named in his memorandum, who had been imprisoned at Fort Leavenworth. The key sentence of the memorandum stated that the objectors were to "be extended clemency in the form of remission of the unexecuted portions of the sentences of the offenders, honorable restoration to duty, and their immediate discharge from the United States Army." Baker's order was made public on January 23. *Official Bulletin*, III (Jan. 23, 1919), 1-3. The discharge of the objectors began on January 27. The statement in Squires' letter about their receiving back pay, mileage, and a new suit of clothing is correct. *New York Times*, Jan. 28, 1919. However, they received no "official laudation," unless the portion of the key sentence quoted above could be construed as such.

## Joseph Clark Grew to Gilbert Fairchild Close, with Enclosure

My dear Mr. Close:                              Paris, January 30, 1919.

I am enclosing a copy of a telegram which has been received at the Commission in regard to an invitation to President Wilson to receive the freedom of the City of Dublin, and asking the President to receive a deputation from Dublin.

The Department of Indexing and Files reports that there is no record in the correspondence of the Commission of the letter of January 4th or telegram of the 21st[1] to which reference is made.

Sincerely yours,   J. C. Grew

TLS (WP, DLC).

¹ H. Campbell to GFC, Jan. 4, 1919, TLS, and Jan. 21, 1919, T telegram, both in WP, DLC. Grew did not have a record of these communications, because they were sent not to the A.C.N.P. but to the American embassy in Paris. About this matter, see also WW to RL, Jan. 24, 1919 (second letter of that date).

### E N C L O S U R E

Dublin January 28, 1919.

No reply received to my letter of 4th January or my telegram of 21st, inviting President Wilson to receive the freedom of the City of Dublin, and asking the President to receive a deputation from the Corporation of Dublin. Will you kindly state when it will be convenient for the President to meet the deputation?

Town Clerk,   Dublin.[1]

T telegram (WP, DLC).

¹ That is, Henry Campbell.

## From Margaret Woodrow Wilson

Bruxelles [Jan.] 30 [1919]

Must change program here because of little cold. Nothing serious. When do you advise my coming to Paris to spend a few days with you?                    Love   Margaret Wilson

T telegram (WP, DLC).

## To Walter Stowell Rogers

My dear Rogers:                    Paris, 31 January, 1919.

I value very highly your letter of yesterday about the Island of Yap. Will you not add to the service you have done in calling attention to its significance by drawing up for me a brief outline of the way in which you think it would be best to solve the communication problem of the Pacific, possibly under International supervision?[1]

Cordially and sincerely yours,   Woodrow Wilson

TLS (received from Mrs. William S. Bellamy).
  [1] Rogers' reply may have been his "MEMORANDUM ON WIRE AND RADIO COMMUNICATIONS . . . , PARIS 12 February, 1919," T MS (WP, DLC). However, this memorandum is twenty-six pages long and deals with the communications problem on a worldwide basis. As for the German cables in the Pacific Ocean which the Japanese had seized, Rogers recommended international ownership and operation as part of an international "TransPacific cable system."

## From Robert Lansing, with Enclosure

Dear Mr. President:                    Paris. January 31, 1919.

I am convinced from remarks made to me by members of the Council of Ten that they do not expect or believe it possible to reach a definite agreement on the League of Nations for some time and that no plan could be in shape to submit to the Plenary Conference before your return to the United States and Mr. Lloyd George's departure for London. I am disposed to think that this postponement will be very acceptable to certain governments and that they will seek to delay rather than hasten an agreement.

The consequence of this would be that you would return to Washington without a definite accomplishment or at least without one which could be made public. Certainly this would be unfortunate since it would be most disappointing to the peoples of all countries and would doubtless arouse criticism at home and encourage your opponents to renewed hostility.

The only way that I see to avoid going home apparently empty handed would be to have the Plenary Conference adopt a resolution embodying the salient features of the League of Nations, which resolution could be in the nature of an instruction to the Committee on the League in guiding their deliberations. With that idea I enclose a suggestion for a resolution. It has been hastily drawn and can I know be greatly improved.

The process of action through resolutions is not a good one, but I am sure that it will be continued and that unless we draft them some others will. The British are fertile in producing them, particularly Sir Maurice Hankey, who is writing them constantly during our meetings. There appears, therefore, no other course of procedure unless it is wiser to amend the British proposals.

Faithfully yours,   Robert Lansing.

TLS (WP, DLC).


ENCLOSURE

REDRAFT OF RESOLUTION OF JANUARY 23, 1919.

January 30, 1919.

The Conference, in order that the Committee appointed to work out the details of the constitution and functions of a League of Nations may be guided in the consideration and preparation of its report, makes the following declarations:

That it is a fundamental principle of international peace that all nations are equal in the rights of undisturbed possession of their respective territories, of independent exercise of their respective sovereignties, and of free use of the high seas as the common property of all peoples;

That the members of the League of Nations should by mutual covenants undertake—

(1) To refrain from invading and to protect from invasion the sovereign rights and territories of one another;

(2) To submit to international arbitration all disputes of a justiciable nature which have failed of diplomatic settlement;

(3) To submit to investigation by the League of Nations all other disputes which have failed of diplomatic settlement;

(4) To refrain from hostile acts or the employment of force pending the arbitration or investigation of a dispute;

(5) To abide in good faith by an arbitral award and to respect a report by the League of Nations upon a dispute submitted to it for investigation;

That the League of Nations should have authority to appoint mandatories and to empower them to exercise, under such conditions as it may deem just, sovereign rights over the territories which were formerly the colonial possessions of Germany and also over such new states erected by the Treaty of Peace as are declared to be international protectorates, it being understood that the interests and wishes of the inhabitants of the territories affected are primarily to be considered in the selection of mandatories and the provisions of the mandates issued, and that in the case of new states the mandates shall provide for the gradual assumption of complete independence.

That the League of Nations should be charged with the consideration and formulation of a plan for a general reduction of national armaments on land and sea and in the air, including therein restrictions upon compulsory military service and upon the manufacture and sale of arms and munitions of war.

T MS (WP, DLC).

# From Henry White, with Enclosure

CONFIDENTIAL

Dear Mr. President:                    [Paris] 31 January 1919

I deem it proper to transmit to you the enclosed brief memorandum of a conversation which I have just had with Mr. Venizelos. I may add that General Bliss tells me he is not aware of any such request, as that attributed by Mr. Venizelos to Mr. Clemenceau, ever having been made by the Supreme War Council at Versailles.
                    Yours very sincerely,   Henry White

TLS (WP, DLC).

E N C L O S U R E

CONFIDENTIAL MEMORANDUM:                    31 January 1919

Mr. Venizelos has just (midday) been to see me to express the hope if, as he had read in the newspapers this morning, it is proposed by the Supreme War Council to take into consideration the question of sending Allied troops to Turkey and a quota to be supplied by each nation, that a certain number of Greek troops would be included. He stated that Greece could furnish three Divisions, and he would like particularly to be able to have a representation of the Greek Army included among the troops to be sent to Turkey, for the reason that about six weeks ago Mr. Clemenceau had requested Greece to send troops to the Ukraine. He added that the request had not been made to him directly but that General Franchet d'Esperay[1] had been instructed by his Government to request the Commander of the Greek Army[2] to send the Greek troops in question to the Ukraine.[3] The Greek Commander-in-Chief, of course, referred the matter to Mr. Venizelos, who, being in Paris, asked Mr. Clemenceau for what purpose these troops were desired in the Ukraine. Whereupon, according to Mr. Venizelos, the French President of the Council rather lost his temper, and, without giving the explanations desired, said to Mr. Venizelos that of course if he did not wish to send Greek troops to the Ukraine he need not do so, but intimated that the request had been made at the instance of the Supreme War Council at Versailles and that the position of Greece would not be sympathetic to the Allies, were she to decline to comply therewith.

Mr. Venizelos said, furthermore, that one Greek Division is now on its way to the Ukraine, and that two others are shortly to follow. He stated, that his reason for making the suggestion in respect to the sending of Greek troops with others of the Allied nations to Turkey is that it would strike the Greek nation as somewhat extraordinary, and not at all favorably, that a portion of the Greek Army should be sent to the Ukraine, in which there are practically no Greek inhabitants—certainly no considerable body of such inhabitants—and that none should accompany the troops of the Allies to Turkey, in which Greek interests are very large and Greek inhabitants exceedingly numerous.

I lost no time in communicating this information to General Bliss.

T MS (WP, DLC).

[1] That is, Franchet d'Esperey.

[2] Gen. Leonidas Paraskevopoulos.

[3] Actually, the French government had first suggested that Greek troops should join the French army in anti-Bolshevik operations in the Ukraine in early November 1918. After extensive negotiations, the Greek government had reluctantly agreed to the proposal in early December. Approximately 3,600 Greek troops had arrived in Odessa on January 20, 1919. Some 23,000 Greek soldiers ultimately participated in the unsuccessful French campaign in the Ukraine. See N. Petsalis-Diomidis, "Hellenism in Southern Russia and the Ukrainian Campaign: Their Effect on the Pontus Question (1919)," *Balkan Studies*, XIII (1972), 221-63, especially pp. 233-41.

# From William Shepherd Benson, with Enclosure

Paris 31 January, 1919.

MEMORANDUM FOR THE PRESIDENT:

In presenting the enclosed paper I desire to invite your attention particularly to one of the principal features involved in maritime international law, namely: that *in this paper the State is held responsible at all times, particularly in time of war, for the conduct of its citizens.*[1]

This principle, if adopted and logically carried out, it seems to me would eliminate many of the troubles that have been encountered in the past in dealing with neutral shipping, and in many ways would simplify the whole subject of international maritime law and many other questions involved in the principle of the freedom of the seas. I realize that it is a complete reversal of the old system, but, nevertheless, I am a firm believer in its adoption.

Sincerely,   W. S. Benson

TLS (WP, DLC).
[1] Italics WW's.

E N C L O S U R E

CONFIDENTIAL

U.S. NAVAL ADVISORY STAFF, PARIS.

SUBJECT: QUESTION XI AND RECOMMENDATIONS.

On what principle should the freedom of neutral shipping on the High Seas during war be founded? What should be the general rules governing the application of the principle?

*Copies to*:
Mr. Lansing
Colonel House
General Bliss
Mr. White
Navy Dept.
Files.

10 January, 1919.

CONFIDENTIAL.

U. S. NAVAL ADVISORY STAFF, PARIS.

*Subject*: Question XI and Recommendations.

I.

On what principle should the freedom of neutral shipping on the High Seas during war be founded?

II.

What should be the general rules governing the application of the principle?

### As to I.

Governmental responsibility under definite sanctions for all violations of neutrality committed by vessels authorised to fly the national flag.

### As to II.

(a) The following cases are in violation of neutrality when committed by a vessel that is lawfully under the flag of a neutral nation:

1. To take direct part in hostilities.
2. To be under the orders or control of a belligerent agent.
3. To be in the employment of a belligerent.
4. To transmit military intelligence concerning belligerents whether by radio or otherwise.
5. To transport belligerent subjects on the High Seas except under regulations agreed upon in time of peace.
6. Breach of blockade by use of papers showing a false destination.
7. To carry contraband to a belligerent port, or to a port occupied by a belligerent.

*General Rule Regarding Contraband.*

(b) It is a violation of neutrality for any neutral government to permit, or to fail to prevent, the passage of contraband articles from its territory to the adjoining territory of a belligerent, or to a vessel of a belligerent nationality, or to any vessel clearing for a belligerent port; but it is no violation of neutrality for neutrals to trade freely between themselves in articles on the contraband list.

*Rights and Immunities of Neutrals.*

(c) Neutral vessels are subject to the belligerent right of visit for the sole purpose of determining nationality and destination as shown by the ship's papers.

(d) No neutral vessel shall be subject to capture except for breach of blockade, or taking direct part in hostilities.

(e) Neutral vessels may carry contraband freely to any neutral port.

(f) Neutral vessels may carry enemy goods not contraband of war.

(g) Neutral cargoes, not contraband of war, on belligerent vessels shall not be subject to condemnation.

(h) No merchant vessel, neutral or enemy, shall be destroyed.

*Rights of Belligerents.*

(i) Vessels of belligerents shall be liable to enemy capture and condemnation.

(j) Belligerent vessels of war shall have the right to visit all merchantmen on the High Seas to determine their nationality and their destination.

(k) Belligerents shall have the right to use force against or to seize a neutral vessel taking direct part in hostilities, and to seize a vessel violating or attempting to violate a blockade.

*General Rules.*

(l) There shall be but one class of contraband—consisting of articles on the list of contraband.

(m) The list of contraband shall be fixed by general agreement in time of peace, and shall not be subject to additions in war by the action of any belligerent power.

(n) It shall not be unlawful for neutral vessels to clear for blockaded ports, provided the true destination is set forth in the ship's papers.                                    W. S. Benson,
                                    Admiral, U.S. Navy.[1]

TS MS (WP, DLC).
    [1] Benson also enclosed an "appendix" which elaborated upon this memorandum.


## From Herbert Bayard Swope

Dear Mr. President:                          [Paris, c. Jan. 31, 1919]

I had intended writing this before but you have been so busy I rather feared I might be intruding. Even if I am, I will take the liberty of saying that your speech on Saturday[1] was the *greatest* you ever made. It was so true, so fine and so wide as to make it stand out in all the big things you have said. It combined the best of everything with the inspiration of the occasion, to which you rose in such a way as to make us proud and glad.

                                    Sincerely   Swope

ALS (WP, DLC).
    [1] That is, Wilson's speech to the Plenary Session of the peace conference on January 25. See the Protocol printed at that date.


## From William Bramwell Booth[1]

Dear Mr President                      London [Jan.] 31 [1919]

The immense moral influence you have exercised upon the present situation in Europe leads me to hope that before you leave Paris you will secure some decision as to the supply with as little delay as possible of food for the industrial areas of Germany and Austria. Large sections of the population are I have good reason to know suffering acute distress and the prospect of improvement is slight now that the military forces of the Central Powers are defeated. It must be the highest wisdom to promote such efforts as are likely to induce friendly relations with the people generally. Proper regard must of course be had to the claims of justice upon wrongdoers but a special blessing attaches to the merciful. With the assurance of my highest esteem I am yours faithfully.

W Bramwell Booth

T telegram (WP, DLC).
  [1] General of the Salvation Army since 1912.

## From the Diary of Colonel House

January 31, 1919.

We had a most successful meeting in my rooms[1] between the President, General Smuts, Lord Robert Cecil and myself. David Miller was the only other person present. We discussed our difficulties regarding the League and brought them nearly to a vanishing point. We decided that Miller, representing us, and Hurst,[2] representing the British, should draft a new form of Covenant based upon the one which the President and I jointly prepared. I had arranged for Cecil and Smuts to leave at ten o'clock as the President I knew would wish to leave at that time. However, the President himself took the initiative a few minutes before ten, but he remained behind for a quarter of an hour in order to talk and felicitate with me over the successful outcome of the evening's conference.

I took occasion to tell him that he should devote just as much time to the League of nations before he left for home as was necessary; that the relative importance of the League and the others [other] things that were being done at the Quai d'Orsay were not to be compared. In the one instance, the world was being turned upside down and a new order was being inaugurated. In the other instance, it was simply a question of boundaries and what not, which had been the subject matter of peace conferences since time immemorial. I urged him, therefore, to put his back under the League and make it his main effort during the Conference. I thought he had a great opportunity to make himself the champion of peace and to change the order of things throughout the world.

The President asked what I thought he should talk about at the reception which the Chamber of Deputies is to give him on Monday afternoon at five o'clock. I thought if he would speak on the League of Nations and say that France had really made its birth possible because of the position she has been forced into by Germany, and the obvious necessity of such a war never again being possible. He seemed pleased with the suggestion.

We arranged to have the meeting of the full Drafting Committee for the League of Nations in my rooms at 2.30 on Monday—the President to preside. He asked me to write a form of invitation and send them for him to sign, which I did this morning.

¹ In the Hôtel Crillon.
² That is, Cecil James Barrington Hurst, legal adviser to the British delegation.

## From the Diary of Lord Robert Cecil

January 31 [1919].

We then went down to see the President and House with Miller, a lawyer there. The President, like our Prime Minister, had read nothing, but he did know something about the subject, though not perhaps very much. He discussed the question of what representation was to be given to minor Powers, but ultimately agreed to try my plan of an executive committee of the Great Powers, with guarantees that any minor Power whose interests are affected shall become an *ad hoc* member of the committee, and also have power in certain cases to demand that the business shall be transferred from the executive committee to the Conference of the whole League.

## To Josephus Daniels

My dear Daniels:                    Paris, 31 January, 1919.

Thank you for your letter about Homer Cummings.¹ You may be sure I will keep it in mind. Commissions such as you have in thought, are, I take it for granted, quite certain to be set up at some stage of our processes over here, but that stage has not yet been reached and therefore I am unable to look forward to any definite prospect in the matter. It would not be wise therefore to speak to Cummings about it because I might not find anything suitable.

I am taking it for granted that Cummings is to be the new chairman of the National Committee. If that is the case, would it or would it not be a mistake to withdraw him over here for a task which might last a good many months?

Thank you for the cheering sentences about the confidence of the people in me. It is hard to tell from this distance how far the malicious partisan attacks that are constantly being made reflect any considerable volume of public opinion, and such assurances as your letter brings are therefore the more cheering and delightful. We all unite in the most cordial messages.

Affectionately yours,   Woodrow Wilson

TLS (J. Daniels Papers, DLC).
  [1] JD to WW, Jan. 10, 1918 [1919], ALS (WP, DLC). Daniels suggested that Wilson appoint Homer S. Cummings to an international commission "to study some phases of the final settlement." Such an appointment, Daniels said, would give Cummings "recognition," which would aid him in a projected election bid in 1920 for the Senate seat of Frank B. Brandegee.

## To Franklin Knight Lane, William Cox Redfield, and William Bauchop Wilson

[Paris] January 31, 1919.

511. Your 381.[1] For Secretaries Lane, Redfield and Wilson from the President.

The situation with reference to the export of copper is as follows: Copper may be exported in unlimited amounts to all countries except enemy countries and to neutrals contiguous thereto. Such neutrals may, however, import copper in amounts sufficient to meet their full needs, increased rations to be announced about February 1st. The only further relaxation possible is therefore exports of copper to or for account of enemy. This involves the following considerations which are given great weight by the Allies, and though they do not entirely meet with our judgment, we cannot but give a serious hearing to their views, particularly as under the terms of the armistice blockade conditions were to remain:

ONE: To what extent shall enemy commercial and industrial interests be allowed to revive through imports of raw material prior to agreement as to reparation and acceptance of other terms of peace which we may desire to impose? Foch regards it as of most serious military importance that Germany be not permitted to obtain at this time materials useful for war purposes.

TWO: Shall enemy be allowed to revive industries prior to rehabilitation of corresponding industries of areas devastated by the enemy?

THREE: Is it desirable to permit enemy to utilize foreign credits for purchase of raw materials, which credits might otherwise in the opinion of the Allies be used to produce a greater reparation?

We have, however, submitted a memorandum[2] to British and French Governments urging the immediate granting to the enemy of a limited ration on certain raw materials, which might include copper, in an amount sufficient to permit moderate revival of industry and diminution of non-employment in enemy countries but not in amount sufficient to permit any active revival of industry in competition with corresponding industries of associated countries. Such relaxation we regard as peculiarly applicable to Southern Europe.

I fully appreciate the importance of providing markets for our products and shall embrace every opportunity to do so consistent with the military situation, our peace objectives and the maintenance of accord with Associated Governments.

                                                          Ammission.

T telegram (WP, DLC).
    ¹ FKL, WCR, and WBW to WW, Jan. 23, 1919, T telegram (WP, DLC).
    ² The Editors have been unable to find this document.


## To Joseph Patrick Tumulty

                    Paris (Received 7:30 p.m., January 31, 1919).

My own thought turned to Mitchell Palmer as successor to Gregory, but that appointment is much against Gregory's judgment and this disturbs me, and it also disturbs me that, beginning at the bottom of the ladder years ago in the Department of Justice, Todd worked his way to the top and earned every step.

I wonder if you have any further advice as to this appointment.
                                                    Woodrow Wilson.

T telegram (J. P. Tumulty Papers, DLC).


## To Margaret Woodrow Wilson

                                        Paris, 31 January, 1919.

Very much distressed to hear you are not well and beg most earnestly that you will take the utmost care of yourself. Come here any time that it is safe for you to come. We seem absolute fixtures because of the continuous demands of the conference business upon me and you can therefore count on finding us where you left us. All join with me in the most loving and solicitous messages.
                                                    Woodrow Wilson.

T telegram (WP, DLC).

## From Josephus Daniels

Washington. January 31, 1919.

House Committee unanimously reports bill for three year programme[1] with limitation according to the approval in your cable.[2] It is a notable and remarkable victory. It would be fine if you felt disposed to send PADGETT a telegram of appreciation.

Josephus Daniels.[3]

T telegram (J. Daniels Papers, DLC).
   [1] The House Committee on Naval Affairs had voted unanimously on January 31 to report out the naval appropriation bill (H.R. 15539) which incorporated the three-year shipbuilding program recommended by the Wilson administration. The bill as reported included an amendment which stated that the President might suspend the building program if at any time before the contracts had been awarded a "tribunal or tribunals competent to secure peaceful determination of international disputes, and which shall render unnecessary the maintenance of competitive armaments" should have been established and that, in any event, no contracts were to be entered into before February 1, 1920. *New York Times*, Feb. 1, 1919. For a summary of the building program as submitted to Congress in the appropriation bill on February 1, 1919, see 65th Cong., 3d sess., House Report No. 1024, p. 3.
   [2] See G. F. Close to W. S. Benson, Jan. 27, 1919.
   [3] This telegram had to be repeated and was received in Paris on February 3, 1919.

## From Charles Williston McAlpin

My dear President Wilson:        New York City January 31, 1919.

I want to send you just a line to congratulate you on the masterly way in which you are dealing with all the problems that are arising in connection with the Peace Conference. The way in which you carry conviction to the hearts of the delegates reminds me of the old days at Princeton when you knew what was right and were never afraid to express your sentiments in words which no one was able to controvert.

I thank God daily that you are where you are for without your guidance there would have been nothing but confusion.

May God bless you abundantly is the fervent prayer of

Your sincere friend,   C W McAlpin

TLS (WP, DLC).

## Robert Lansing to Frank Lyon Polk

Paris, January 31st, 1919.

521. VERY CONFIDENTIAL. Department 391, January 24th, 3 p.m. and Department 392, January 24th, 4 p.m.

The subject of these cables has received the careful consideration of Secretary Lansing and McCormick and the latter has discussed

the matter fully with the President who approves and authorizes
the following procedure:

You are requested to ask for a secret hearing before such committee or committees of Congress as you think best. At this hearing
you will state that it is the President's wish that the Siberian situation and the activities of the Administration in relation thereto
be made known fully and frankly, though in strict confidence, to
the members of these committees. You will then develop the strategic importance both from the point of view of Russia and of the
United States of the Trans-Siberian Railway as being a principal
means of access to and from the Russian people and as affording
an opportunity for economic aid to Siberia where the people are
relatively friendly and resistant to Bolshevik influence and where
there are large bodies of Czecho-Slovaks who rely upon our support,
as well as large numbers of enemy prisoners of war whose activities
must be watched and if necessary controlled. The potential value
of this railroad as a means for developing American Commerce,
particularly from the West Coast of the United States to Russia
might be mentioned. You may then narrate in considerable detail
the difficulties which we have had with Japan with reference to
this railway and in particular the action of Japan in practically
seizing the Chinese Eastern Railway, thereby in effect controlling
all intercourse to and from Russia via the Pacific. You may refer to
the number of troops sent by Japan for this purpose and point out
that such number was far in excess of that contemplated by the
arrangement under which troops of the Associated Governments
were landed in Siberia. The nature of the activities of Japan including disposition of their troops and Japanese commercial activities should then be referred to followed by a statement of the efforts
of the Government of the United States to restore the railroad to a
condition where it would not be exclusively dominated by any one
power such as Japan. The conversations of the President and Secretary of State with the Japanese Ambassador, the negotiations of
Ambassador Morris under instructions from the Department and
the economic pressure applied by the War Trade Board may be
referred to. You should then describe the successful conclusion of
these efforts of the United States as evidenced by the arrangements
for administration of the Railway by Stevens as a Russian employee
and the withdrawl of substantial numbers of Japanese troops.[1] We
feel that these proceedings and their conclusion can properly be
described as a very important and constructive achievement which
may be of inestimable value to the people of Russia and to the
United States as well as the world in general, provided they are
followed through, thereby giving practical effect to the principle of

the open door. You will then point out that in order to give substance and permanence to the arrangement which has been reached it will be necessary to devise a plan for the financing of the railway and that it is the view of the President that this financing should be regarded as a joint obligation of the interested Governments and that the President is prepared to propose and endeavor to secure agreement on such a plan provided it seem probable that Congress will be prepared to appropriate the funds necessary to permit the Government of the United States to carry out its proportional share of any financing agreed to. You may add that if the disposition of the Committees whom you will be addressing is favorable to such a plan, the President will as a provisional measure and as indicated in American [Ammission] 376, January 21st,[2] arrange through the Russian Bureau, Incorporated, or through his special fund, for a limited temporary advance to support Stevens, pending the submission to Congress of a definite financial plan provided one can be agreed to. The consequence of failure to support Stevens, as indicated by Departments 113, January 6th,[3] should be developed and the responsibility of Congress in connection therewith made clear. It is felt that it may be desirable that Woolley appear with you and state to the members of the Committees the purposes and activities of the War Trade Board Russian Bureau Incorporated, pointing out that these purposes and activities have from time to time been publicly announced and that the corporation does not constitute a secret instrumentality.

The foregoing is designed to indicate the spirit in which the President wishes the Siberian situation to be handled and you should not consider yourself bound to follow literally the suggestions made. It is desired that you treat the matter with the utmost frankness, giving all information at your disposal under of course a pledge of confidence.

It is desired that you cable as promptly as possible the attitude of the Congressional Committees and pending our hearing from you on this subject you are requested to hold in abeyance the giving of instructions to General Graves and the advance of money by War Trade Board Corporation as suggested by Ammission 376, January 21.

We feel that it may be a wise practise to take Congress more into the confidence on such matters and we at least desire to make the experiment in this case.                                   Lansing.

T telegram (WP, DLC).
   [1] About this agreement, see FLP to RL, Jan. 6, 1919 (third telegram of that date), Vol. 53.
   [2] RL to FLP, Jan. 21, 1919, about which, see WW to RL, Jan. 20, 1919, n. 1.
   [3] See the telegram cited in n. 1 above.

## From the Diary of Edith Benham

January 31, 1919

I am glad to have a chance to write down directly after luncheon what I heard. The President spoke of a curious lack of ingenuousness on Foch's part—whether intentional or not he could not decide. Together the British, French and United States forces number 1,500,000. Opposite them he stated are 37 German Divisions so the German Commander Winterfeld had stated. Pershing who was not present when Foch made the statement, but to whom the President sent the memorandum, wrote back and said very politely and indirectly that Foch has misinformed the President.[1] That what Winterfeld had said was that there were five German Divisions on the bridge heads and thirty-two on the way home. The President was wondering the reason for this deliberate misstatement. The fear of the Germans is a perfect mania here even now that they are practically impotent, and then I think the French are trying to make us do the main part of police duty. One instance the President had cited was with Poland. They, the Poles, are hemmed about with unfriendly people and I suppose their affairs are turbulent, too, so the suggestion was calmly made that the British and French each send a regiment and the Americans a Division! It is on a par with what Ned Bun,[2] who is passing through on his way home (lucky soul) said, that we are being done at every turn and the French are trying to work off old gassed horses on us. The President said whenever the French called a meeting of the Supreme War Council he found it was to put over some scheme though he usually found that Foch was certainly on the surface very straightforward. Someone asked him about the English and he said he found them very honest and straightforward as far as they were allowed to be. Their problems are difficult ones and I think ours are, too. In Mesopotamia and Arabia they have over a million men and must keep them to preserve order. The whole of the United Kingdom is calling for demobilization of all save the regular army and that could not police those countries. They want us to be the mandatory for them and we should be, but he said he had to tell them he could not promise such a thing until he had gone home, had gone on a speech making tour and educated the United States to the point of taking the trusteeship of any European or Asiatic country, for the proposal is for the United States to be the mandatory for Constantinople, too. He has been speaking of abolishing compulsory military training in other countries and said last night he suggested to Orlando compulsory training as they wish to continue it, but to have equipment for 700,000 men or less. He has some rather nebulous ideas now about free industrial training with a certain amount of military training added. He said frankly he had not thought out that idea at all fully and would have to have the advice of experts to suggest how these industrial schools which incidentally would teach English to our foreign born could be established and made practical. The suggestions he has had from the Army officers would only lead to the establishment of a Prussian military system. I had said I hoped the necessity of something of the kind—military training of some sort—could be made a national consciousness such as we had never had until this war. He agreed to the value of the national spirit and also spoke of the great spread of the ideas of sanitation and consequent better health of the population.

[1] See J. J. Pershing to WW, Jan. 25, 1919.
[2] Unidentified.

## From the Diary of Dr. Grayson

Saturday, February 1, 1919.

In the afternoon, we attended the conference session at the Quai D'Orsay when the question of inviting the Russians to participate in the Prince's Islands' Conference was taken up. Clemenceau opposed it, but the President and Lloyd George insisted. Finally the plan originated by the President was adopted and the invitation was sent by wireless to the various Russian factions.

## Hankey's Notes of a Meeting of the Council of Ten[1]

Quai d'Orsay, February 1, 1919, 3 P.M.

BC-20

1. PRESIDENT WILSON asked permission to communicate to the Conference the gist of a telegram, which he had received from M. Tchicherin, the Commissioner for Foreign Affairs of the Bolshevik Government. In this telegram M. Tchicherin said that he had seen in the Press some reference to the summoning of a Conference of Russian Delegates at Prinkipo, and he asked for an official invitation.[2] He, (President Wilson), wished to know what action should be taken. To send an official communication would be tantamount to a recognition of the Bolshevik Government.

MR. LLOYD GEORGE expressed the view that M. Tchicherin had received his notice like everybody else.

[1] The complete text of these notes is printed in *PPC*, III, 835-55.
[2] See G. V. Chicherin to WW, Jan. 29, 1919.

PRESIDENT WILSON pointed out that a notification had been made to the Press and not in a direct manner. He was quite willing to ignore M. Tchicherin's request, but the Great Powers were anxious to get these delegates together, and perhaps an answer should be sent to take away the excuse that they had received no invitation to attend the meeting. Apparently M. Tchicherin wanted a personal invitation.

(It was decided to adjourn the question for further consideration.)

2. M. CLEMENCEAU handed in the following document representing the final agreement reached between the Czechs and the Poles regarding the occupation of the Principality of Teschen:[3]

"The Representatives of the Great Powers, having been informed of the conflict which has arisen between the Czechs and Poles in the Principality of Teschen, in consequence of which the mining district of Ostrawa-Karwin and the railway from Oderberg to Teschen and Jablunkau has been occupied by the Czechs, have declared as follows:

In the first instance they think it necessary to remind the nationalities who have engaged to submit the territorial questions which concern them to the Peace Conference, that they are, pending its decision, to refrain from taking as a pawn or from occupying the territories to which they lay claim.

The representatives take note of the engagement by which the Czech Delegates have declared that they were definitely stopping their troops on the line of the railway which runs from Oderberg to Teschen-Jablunkau.

Pending the decisions of the Peace Conference Congress as to the definitive assignment of the territories that part of the railway line to the North of Teschen and the mining regions will remain in the occupation of Czech troops while the southern section of the line starting from and including the town of Teschen down to Jablunkau will be entrusted to the military supervision of the Poles.

The undersigned consider it indispensable that a Commission of Control should be immediately sent to the spot to avoid any conflict between the Czechs and Poles in the region of Teschen. This Commission, apart from the measures that it will have to prescribe, will proceed to an enquiry on the basis of which the Peace Conference may form its decision in fixing definitely the respective frontiers of

[3] The Council of Ten, on the previous day, January 31, had accepted the recommendation by the Commission on Poland that Czechoslovak and Polish troops, respectively, should occupy the northern and southern parts of Teschen, and that a Commission of Control should be sent there to find a basis on which the peace conference might fix definitely "the respective frontiers of the Czechs and Poles in the contested area." Wilson had been present but had taken little part in the discussion. For the record of this meeting, see PPC, III, 813-34.

the Czechs and Poles in the contested zone. The seat of this Commission will be situated in the town of Teschen.

In order to seal the Entente between two friendly nations which should follow a policy in full accord with that of the Allied and Associated Powers, the representatives of the Great Powers register the promise of the Czech representatives that their country will put at the disposition of the Poles all its available resources in war material and will grant to them every facility for the transit of arms and ammunition.

The exploitation of the mines of the Karwin-Ostrawa district will be carried out in such a way as to avoid all infraction of private property while reserving any police measures which the situation may require. The Commission of Control will be empowered to supervise this and if necessary to secure to the Poles that part of the output which may be equitably claimed by them to meet their wants.

It is understood that the local administration will continue to function in accordance with the conditions of the pact of the 5th November, 1918, and that the rights of minorities will be strictly respected.

Pending the decision of the Peace Congress, political elections and military conscription will be suspended in the Principality of Teschen.

No measure implying annexation of all or of a part of the said Principality either to the territory of Poland or of Czecho-Slovakia taken by interested parties shall have binding force.

The Delegates of the Czech Nation engage to release immediately with their arms and baggage the Polish prisoners taken during the recent conflict."

On the proposal of Mr. Lloyd George and General Botha—

It was agreed that the document should first be signed by the representatives of the Great Powers and subsequently by the Czech and Pole delegates and by the members of the Commission for Poland.

3. M. CLEMENCEAU read the following reply received from the Military Representatives of the Supreme War Council, Versailles, with reference to the Resolution passed by the Delegates of the Five Great Powers at the Conversation held at the Quai d'Orsay on the 30th January, 1919 (see I.C. 128),[4] on the subject of the proper distribution of the Allied military forces required for the maintenance of order in the Turkish Empire and in Trans-Caucasia:

[4] That is, the minutes of the Council of Ten printed at Jan. 30, 1919, 3:30 p.m. The resolution referred to is the one in the final paragraph of these minutes.

The Military Representatives consider it necessary for them to be further advised on the three following subjects:

1. The territories to be occupied in view of the fact that certain parts of the Ottoman Empire are not at the present time occupied.

2. The total number of troops required to maintain order in these territories as estimated by the local military commanders.

3. Whether a joint occupation of these territories is intended, or whether definite zones are to be attributed to the interested Powers, who would be designated by the Great Powers.

M. CLEMENCEAU said that the Conference had put certain definite questions to the Military Representatives, who had merely asked the same questions in reply.

MR. LLOYD GEORGE expressed the view that it was the duty of the Military Representatives to reply to the questions put to them. The first question put by the Military Representatives was perhaps only partly a military question, but the second was wholly a military one. It was one of the very questions the Military Representatives themselves had been asked, and, in his opinion, they should certainly give an answer. The third question was one which the Conference could perhaps, and, indeed, ought to answer.

PRESIDENT WILSON said that the answer to the last question would be that definite zones would be allotted to particular Powers, and there would be no joint occupation.

After some further discussion, it was agreed to transmit the following reply to the Military Representatives of the Supreme War Council at Versailles through the Secretaries:

1. The Conference does not contemplate a joint occupation of any territories.

2. The Conference did not contemplate the military occupation of any territories other than those already occupied, unless the Military Representatives think that the occupation of additional territory is desirable.

3. The Military Representatives should themselves obtain and submit estimates regarding the number of troops required for the maintenance of order in the occupied territories.

4. The Minutes of the Meeting of the 30th January, 1919, relating to the question under reference, shall be supplied to the Military Representatives of the Supreme War Council at Versailles.

4. M. CLEMENCEAU said that he would next ask the Conference to give their formal approval to the Instructions for the Delegates of the Allied Governments to Poland.

On the proposal of PRESIDENT WILSON it was agreed, after some discussion, that the following clause should be added to the Instructions for the Delegates of the Allied Governments to Poland:

"Marshal Foch is requested to inform the German military authorities that the Associated Powers are sending to Poland a commission which is fully empowered to compose all disturbances there so far as possible, and instructed, for that purpose, to insist that the Polish authorities refrain from all use of force against the German forces, and the Marshal is requested to convey to the German authorities in German Poland the demand of the Associated Powers that they altogether refrain from the further use of force in that province and from interference with the life of the people there pending the conclusion of the Peace Conference."[5]

GENERAL BOTHA then proposed the addition of the following final clause of the Instructions:

"Where matters within the scope of these instructions require the making of special arrangements for their immediate disposition, the delegates are authorised and empowered to make such necessary and provisional arrangements, which shall be binding upon all parties concerned unless and until disapproved by the four Powers concerned."

(This was agreed to.)

GENERAL BOTHA pointed out that the Delegates would have to deal with the neighbours of Poland. One of these neighbours would be the Bolsheviks. He enquired whether the Delegates were authorised to enter into negotiations with the Bolshevik representatives.

PRESIDENT WILSON expressed the view that it was almost an inevitable part of their duties as Commissioners to endeavour to bring about an armistice between the Poles and the Bolsheviks.

MR. LLOYD GEORGE said that there would be no objection to the Delegates seeing the leaders of the Bolshevik Armies. But it would obviously not be necessary for them to meet either M. Trotski or M. Lenin.

M. CLEMENCEAU thought the sense of the meeting would be that the Delegates could meet whoever they liked, provided they did not ask for definite permission to meet particular individuals to be named.

(The following text of Final Instructions for the Delegates of the Allied Governments in Poland was then formally accepted:

"It will be the business of the Delegates of the Allied Governments to convey as early as possible information to their Governments on the present situation in Poland. The Military question and the Food question are the most urgent, but reports on the political and social conditions of the country should be sent without unnecessary delay.

The Polish Government should be warned against adopting a

[5] There is a WWhw MS of this resolution in WP, DLC.

policy of an aggressive character. Any appearance of attempting to prejudge the decisions of the Conference will have the worst possible effect. The Delegates should invite the most earnest consideration of the Polish Government to the declaration recently made on this subject by the representatives of the Powers at Paris.

Every effort should be made to bring to an end the hostilities which are now taking place between the Poles and neighbouring peoples. Armistices should be arranged wherever possible and the Delegates should use their good offices to bring them about.

In this connection it should be noted that the invasion by the Poles of German territory tends to restore the German military spirit and to delay the breakup of the German Army; and it has the further disadvantage of complicating the arrangements for German disarmament which the Allies desire to carry out with the least possible delay.

The Delegates should enquire how far the Polish Government possess the means to maintain order within their existing territory and of preserving it from external aggression whether carried out by Bolshevists or any other forces and they should study and report on the measures necessary to supply any deficiencies which may be found to exist.

The food question will require their earnest attention and they should co-operate with the Mission about to be despatched to Poland by the Supreme Council of Supply and Relief. In order to secure this cooperation the principal Delegates of the Supreme Council of Supply and Relief should be attached to the Delegation whenever questions of food supply have to be dealt with.

Marshal Foch is requested to inform the German military authorities that the Associated Powers are sending to Poland a Commission which is fully empowered to compose all disturbances there so far as possible, and instructed, for that purpose, to insist that the Polish authorities refrain from all use of force against the German forces, and the Marshal is requested to convey to the German authorities in German Poland the demand of the Associated Powers that they altogether refrain from the further use of force in that province and from interference with the life of the people there pending the conclusion of the Peace Conference.

Where matters within the scope of these instructions require the making of special arrangements for their immediate disposition, the Delegates are authorised and empowered to make such necessary and provisional arrangements, which shall be binding upon all parties concerned unless and until disapproved by the four Powers concerned.")

5. M. ORLANDO invited attention to the fact that the period granted

for the submission of documents relating to territorial claims would expire on that date. He wished to enquire whether this period was to be rigidly applied. He had been informed by M. Dutasta that, up to yesterday, no documents had been received by the Secretariat General, except a part of the Greek case and a report by the Czecho-Slovak Delegates.

MR. BALFOUR expressed the view that a time limit having been granted, the Conference could now proceed with their business. Should any of the Delegations object, the obvious reply would be that the Delegations themselves were to blame for not having submitted their reports in due time. On the other hand, the Conference should not refuse to accept any documents which might be sent in hereafter.

[6. It was agreed that the members of the Commission for Teschen might be either military or civil, and that their names should be handed in Monday morning, February 3, 1919.]

7. At this stage M. Bratiano and M. Misu, members of the Roumanian Delegation to the Peace Conference, accompanied by their experts, MM. A. Lapedatu and Constantine Bratiano,[6] were admitted to the Conference.

M. CLEMENCEAU asked M. Bratiano to put forward the Roumanian case.[7]

[Bratiano described Rumania's services to the Entente; the Treaty of Alliance of August 17, 1916, between the Allies and Rumania, and the Military Convention of the same date; the collapse of the Russian military efforts against Germany and its effect on Rumania; and the treaty of peace between Rumania and the Central Powers, May 7, 1918, which he characterized as "a lull in a conflict which was to be resumed." Bratiano then set forth Rumania's claims to Transylvania, Bukovina, and Bessarabia, which "only represented the manifestation of the national aspirations of the people and the desire of the Roumanians to be once more united on the ethnical territory assigned to them by history." He asked authority for Rumania to occupy all the territories it claimed, and he requested that the Banat and Dobruja be occupied by Allied and not Serbian troops. Clemenceau thanked Bratiano for his statement, and the Rumanian delegates withdrew.]

MR. LLOYD GEORGE said that, speaking for himself and for many

[6] Ion I. C. Brătianu, Prime Minister and Minister of Foreign Affairs of Rumania; Nicolae Mişu, Rumanian Minister to Great Britain; Alexandru Lăpedatu, historian and expert on ethnographical and geographical questions; and Constantin Brătianu, secretary general of the Rumanian delegation.

[7] The statement by Ion I. C. Brătianu was in part a continuation of his remarks to the Council of Ten on the previous day, January 31, when he and Vesnić had presented the conflicting claims of Rumania and Serbia to the Banat. Wilson had been present but had taken no part in the discussion.

of those whom he had been able to consult, it was extremely difficult to decide questions of boundaries on statements, however lucid, made in the course of a Conversation. He wished, therefore, to propose that in the first place experts of the five Great Powers should examine such questions, and, if possible, make a unanimous recommendation. It is quite possible that on many of the questions to be considered, the experts would agree. Naturally, these experts could not decide the problem, but they could clear the ground, and, in cases of disagreement, the representatives of the Great Powers would be compelled to argue out the case there in Council Chamber. But there were many questions regarding which the Great Powers were perfectly impartial. For instance, they were quite impartial regarding the Roumanian claims on Hungary, to an exposé of which they had listened that day. He thought, therefore, that if a preliminary investigation was carried out by experts, it would greatly assist. He fully admitted that this procedure could not be introduced as a permanent arrangement, or be accepted as a precedent for universal application; but in the particular case of the Roumanian claims, in order to arrive at a decision, he hoped the experts would be allowed to examine the ground in the first instance, and the representatives of the Great Powers would eventually decide the question. He wished, therefore, to move the following Resolution:

"It is agreed that the questions raised in M. Bratiano's statement on the Roumanian territorial interests in the Peace Settlement shall be referred for examination in the first instance by an expert Committee composed of two representatives each of the United States of America, the British Empire, France and Italy.

It shall be the duty of the Committee to reduce the questions for decision within the narrowest possible limits, and to make recommendations for a just settlement.

The Committee is authorised to consult the representatives of the peoples concerned."

PRESIDENT WILSON expressed the view, which he felt sure was shared by the mover of the Resolution, that only those aspects of the question, which did not touch the purely political side of the problem, should be examined by the experts. All other questions requiring the exercise of tact and compromise must necessarily be reserved to the representatives of the Great Powers, including the protection of minorities, etc. The experts, therefore, should merely consider the territorial and racial aspects of the case.

MR. BALFOUR thought that strategical questions might also be considered by the experts.

M. ORLANDO said he had a statement to make in reference to a matter of individual conscience, which he did not wish to force on his colleagues. But he felt himself bound to Roumania by a Treaty. In his opinion, the laws relating to public and civil rights only became valid after their promulgation. He did not wish to defend secret treaties which, indeed, were now out of fashion; but a treaty having been signed by Italy, France and Great Britain, he could make no distinction between a secret treaty and a public treaty.

M. CLEMENCEAU drew the attention of M. Orlando to the fact that the Roumanian Treaty had, by the common assent of the representatives of the Great Powers there in that room, been cancelled. It had been agreed that Roumania should, for reasons given, have proper representation at the Peace Conference; but, it was distinctly understood that the grant of representation would not renew every clause of the Treaty, which she had broken by going out of the war. (I.C. 104.)[8]

MR. LLOYD GEORGE also pointed out that Roumania was now claiming more than she had been granted by the secret treaty.

M. ORLANDO said he had no recollection of the incident quoted. But, in any case, the treaty of 1916 between Roumania and the Allies having been signed, did that fact tend to invalidate the Peace Treaty subsequently signed by Roumania with the Central Powers at Bucarest? If so, the previous treaty with the Allies was *ipso facto* annulled. In his opinion, Roumania was forced to sign the Peace Treaty with the Central Powers, and she had not been a free agent. Consequently, he did not consider the latter treaty to be valid, no more than he would consider himself bound by an agreement signed whilst a pistol was being held at his head.

M. CLEMENCEAU remarked that he did not think such an argument really helped the case of the Roumanians.

M. ORLANDO said that, at any rate, he had given expression to a matter which had lain on his conscience. He turned now to Mr. Lloyd George's proposal and was glad to find that it was not to form a precedent. Therefore, some of his objections would fall to the ground. But, as regards the application of the proposal to the case under consideration, the decisive question to be settled was wholly and solely a political one. Being exclusively political, the whole responsibility for the settlement must rest with the representatives of the Great Powers.

Mr. Lloyd George's resolution said that specialists would be appointed. What kind of specialists? If it was intended to appoint specialists on the Roumanian question, he himself had none; and

---

[8] That is, the minutes of the Council of Ten printed at Jan. 12, 1919, 4 p.m. The specific reference was to the paragraphs of those notes relating to the representation of Rumania at the peace conference.

they would be difficult to find. But even then, he would ask: What branch of the Roumanian question should these specialists represent? Should they be geographical, historical, strategical or ethnographical specialists? The question was a very complex and mixed one, and its various aspects could not be separately examined. Consequently, the specialists who might be appointed though knowing their particular subject could not give good assistance in the final solution of the problem. Further, the resolution said that the Committee would consult the representatives of the people concerned. The experts would thus, in fact, become examining magistrates. Mr. Lloyd George's proposal thus became a very serious one, since the experts would constitute the Court of First Instance and the delegates of the Great Powers, the Final Court of Appeal. He failed to see how such a procedure would expedite matters. In his opinion, it necessarily meant delay, especially if the experts decided that the enquiry must take place *in situ*. His proposals might not be acceptable to his colleagues: but he had felt obliged to put forward his views though he did not wish to press them. In his opinion, the procedure proposed by Mr. Lloyd George in this case had great inconveniences, and, if accepted, he noted with pleasure that it would not form a precedent.

M. SONNINO expressed the view that the experts might find themselves compelled to go to the spot to consult the representatives of the people concerned.

MR. LLOYD GEORGE explained that the experts would carry out their work in exactly the same matter as their Committee on Teschen had done.

M. SONNINO replied that unfortunately in the case of the Roumanian claims, the representatives of the minorities, (Hungarians, Ukrainians, Bolshevists), would have to be consulted, and they had no representatives here in Paris. He did not see why the representatives of the Great Powers themselves should not first discuss the question with their own experts, and afterwards consult the delegates of the countries concerned, who could give the most expert information available.

PRESIDENT WILSON agreed that perhaps it might be wise to omit the clause of the resolution which authorised the experts to consult the representatives of the people concerned. Ever since the United States of America had entered the war, he had had a body of scholars continuously studying such questions of fact as racial aspects, historical antecedents, and economic and commercial elements: the two latter being of very great importance in many of the questions under dispute, as had been realised in the case of the Banat. Furthermore, it must be remembered that however complete their confidence might be in the delegates of Roumania, Serbia, and other countries, who would present claims; these delegates were merely advocates, and they made opposite claims as to the right inferences to be drawn from facts. They did not represent their facts in the same way, and there would always be something that was not quite clear. As the United States of America were not bound by any of the treaties in question, they were quite ready to approve a settlement on a basis of facts. But the claimants did not always restrict themselves even to the limits set by Treaties and their claims frequently exceeded what was justified by the Treaties.

MR. LLOYD GEORGE, in this connection, drew attention to the Roumanian claims on the Banat. The Roumanians now claimed the whole of the Banat, whereas the Treaty only gave them a part.

PRESIDENT WILSON, continuing, said that he was seeking enlightenment, and this would no doubt be afforded by a convincing presentation by the experts. If the resolution proposed by Mr. Lloyd George did not receive acceptance, he would find himself compelled to fight the question merely on the views expressed by the American experts; but he would prefer that these conclusions should be corrected by the views of the French, British and Italian experts.

M. CLEMENCEAU enquired from M. Orlando whether he still objected to the resolution.

M. ORLANDO said that he had already expressed his willingness to accept the resolution, provided it was not to create a precedent.

(It was agreed that the questions raised in M. Bratiano's statement on the Roumanian territorial interests in the Peace settlement should be referred for examination in the first instance by an expert committee, composed of two representatives each of the United States of America, the British Empire, France and Italy.

It shall be the duty of this Committee to reduce the questions for decision within the narrowest possible limits, and to make recommendations for a just settlement.

The Committee is authorised to consult the representatives of the peoples concerned.)

8. It was decided that the Naval Peace Terms Committee should forthwith meet to draft the Naval clauses to be introduced in the Peace Treaty with Germany.

(The Meeting adjourned to 11 o'clock on Monday, the 3rd February, 1919.)

T MS (SDR, RG 256, 180.03101/27, DNA).

## To Lord Robert Cecil

My dear Lord Robert:                    Paris, February 1, 1919.

I take pleasure in inviting you to attend a meeting of the Drafting Committee for a League of Nations on Monday afternoon at half past two o'clock, in room 355, third floor of the Hotel Crillon.

Cordially and sincerely yours,   [Woodrow Wilson][1]

CCL (WP, DLC).
[1] Wilson sent this same letter, *mutatis mutandis*, to Jan C. Smuts, Léon Bourgeois, Fernand Larnaude, Vittorio E. Orlando, Vittorio Scialoja, Sutemi Chinda, Kentaro Otchiai, Paul Hymans, Ku Wei-chün (V. K. Wellington Koo), Milenko R. Vesnić, Senator Epitacio Pessoa of Brazil, and Jayme Batalha Reis, Portuguese Minister to Russia.

## To Robert Lansing, with Enclosure

My dear Mr. Secretary:                  Paris, 1 February, 1919.

It would be very unfortunate to make a blunder by treating our Socialists differently from the way in which the Socialists of other countries are being handled, and I hope that you have by this time received an answer to your inquiry about this passport business.

Cordially and sincerely yours,   [Woodrow Wilson]

CCL (WP, DLC).

### E N C L O S U R E

Chicago [received Feb. 1, 1919]

State Department refuses answer to Socialist party delegates application for passports to international socialist and labor congress. Why this discrimination?                    Adolph Germer

T telegram (WP, DLC).

## To Henry White

My dear Mr. White:                      Paris, 1 February, 1919.

What Mr. Venizelos has in mind[1] is evidently the resolution taken the other day at the Quai D'Orsay to ask for the advice of the military advisors of the Supreme War Council with regard to a possible redistribution of the military burden of occupying the various territories in the Near East which are now held chiefly, I believe, by British troops.

Personally I should think it a bit dangerous to send Greek troops to any part of Asia Minor for example because Greece makes claims

to certain coast regions there, but of course any claims to participation that they may have ought to be considered. I would be very
much obliged if you would let General Bliss see this.

   Cordially and faithfully yours, Woodrow Wilson

TLS (H. White Papers, DLC).
 [1] See H. White to WW, Jan. 31, 1919, and the Enclosure thereto.

## To Herbert Bayard Swope

My dear Swope:      Paris, 1 February, 1919.

 You have frequently made me a debtor to you for the best kind
of encouragement and your little note about my speech introducing
the resolution on the League of Nations at the Conference a week
ago certainly adds greatly to the debt, because I often feel highly
in need of just that kind of cheer. The battle for some things is a
bit lonely, though I can honestly say that I believe great progress
is being made in establishing at any rate sound principles as the
basis of our action. Thank you with all my heart.

   Cordially and faithfully yours, [Woodrow Wilson]

CCL (WP, DLC).

## From Alfred George Gardiner

Dear Mr. President,    London, E.C. Feb. 1/19

 You were good enough to say, in giving me a copy of the Covenant,[1] that you would welcome any comments that might suggest
themselves to me. I have read the document very carefully & to
my lay mind it seems to meet the requirements with completeness,
foresight & wisdom. My disposition would be to say that I have no
criticisms to offer, but in obedience to your request I make the
following comments:

 Art. 4. The principle of disarmament, it appears to me, might be
made an essential condition of accepting the League, so that any
Nation which joined, by the act of joining, agreed to disarm. This
article provides that the plan for disarmament is to be binding only
when unanimously approved, although in the subsequent paragraph some of the main provisions are treated as essential conditions of the League itself. I would respectfully suggest the omission
of the last two lines of the first paragraph of the article & the addition
of a provision for the inspection by the delegates of the League of
all armament factories. If the armaments are to be required only
(a) for the maintenance of internal order (b) as partly the common

stock of the world's provisions for maintaining international peace, trade secrets ought not to exist & no trade rivalry or jealousy need interfere with examination of munitions industries.

Art. 6. Would it not be as well expressly to provide that, in the event there mentioned, the vessels of any power disregarding the Covenant which may be in the harbours of the contracting parties, shall instantly be arrested? This may be [intended?] in the general words, but the mention of the specific power is, I think, of service.

Art. 13. Might it not be well to provide, not merely that no power shall enter into engagements inconsistent with the terms of the Covenant, but that all agreements of international character—other than financial & commercial—shall be submitted for approval? This may be too far-reaching, but Art. 13 leaves open the question whether a treaty obligation is or is not inconsistent with the terms of the Covenant, & the question may be very difficult to solve.

Many of the supplementary provisions, it seems to me, might well be incorporated in the main body of the Covenant. They may be a mere matter of form, but they have the character of essential conditions rather than of supplementary provisions.

If there should be anything in these few comments that you find deserving of consideration I shall be deeply gratified.

In sending them, I should like to express my sense of the distinguished courtesy you & Mrs. Wilson showed me in Paris & my sincere hope that your labours for the settlement of this disturbed world may be crowned with enduring success.

With profound respect, I am, dear Mr. President

Yours Sincerely   A. G. Gardiner.

ALS (WP, DLC).
    ¹ When they met in the Palais Murat on January 21. See the extract from the Grayson Diary printed at that date.


## From Joseph Patrick Tumulty

Washington, February 1 [1919]

No. 30. Frankly, our party here is greatly dispirited and needs stimulation. Todd's selection would be depressing and without value, seriously affecting the morale of our party. Gregory's argument for his promotion will apply to hundreds of deserving Democrats and Republicans in Government service. It would apply to the case of Adee and others who have worked their way to high positions. Gregory naturally favors Todd because of association. You are the leader and have the final say. When McReynolds was appointed to the bench and Gregory made his successor, this principle was not applied, and Todd occupied the same position then he occupies now. When Bryan resigned, John Bassett Moore was not appointed Secretary. Neither was the next in command, when McAdoo resigned.

Party service has always been recognized where ability and fitness of candidate was admitted. One of Gregory's own intimates has told me in confidence that Todd's appointment is unwise. While he is a good lawyer, he is not broad-visioned or sympathetic with our Democratic purposes. Frankly, your attitude toward the future of our party will be measured by this appointment. Palmer is young, militant, progressive and fearless, as shown by recent investigation;[1] he stands well with country, Congress, and appeals to young voters; he is effective on the stump. McCormick, Cummings, and whole Democratic Committee is in favor of his selection. Roper, a Southern man, one of our wisest friends, heartily endorses him and says it would be disastrous to appoint another Southern man.

The following is a list of men appointed from Virginia: Comptroller of the Currency, Interstate Commerce Commissioner Woolley, Ambassador to Italy, Ambassador to Spain, Secretary of the Treasury Glass, Marshal of United States Court for C[h]ina, Auditor of the Interior Department, Assistant Commissioner of General Land Office, Assistant Commissioner of Patents, Superintendent of Coast and Geodetic Survey, First Assistant Chief of Bureau of Foreign and Domestic Commerce, Consul General at Athens, Consul General at Manchester, England.

During last month the following names of Southern men were sent to the Senate: Carter Glass, Secretary of the Treasury; John Skelton Williams, Comptroller of the Currency; Walker D. Hines, of Kentucky, Railroad Director; Alexander C. King, of Georgia, Solicitor General of the U. S.

Todd will be rated as another Southern appointment. His appointment would make two Cabinet officers from Virginia. This issue is more acute than you realize. Republicans are taking full advantage. Gregory says Todd is a New York lawyer, although argument he puts forward favoring his selection is that Todd spent his [whole][2] life in Attorney General's Office (Who's Who regards Todd as a Virginia[n]). Newspapers of the country will carry him in their news stories as a Southerner.

The occupant of this office has a great deal of power. We should not trust it to anyone who is not heart and soul with us. I do not mean to criticise Gregory, but no Cabinet officer should be permitted to select his successor, any more than I should select mine.

Our enemies and some of our friends have the feeling that you do not care to recognize the services of those who stood by us in the dark days. The appointment of Todd and the ignoring of men of the high type of Palmer, who have been faithful throughout, will accentuate this feeling. The Democratic party, under your inspiring leadership, by slight changes can be made a great militant organization. I know you will supply us with the [tonic]. Affectionate regards.                    Tumulty.

T telegram (WP, DLC).
    [1] Tumulty must have been referring here either to some private investigation made by Palmer in his capacity of Alien Property Custodian or to a similar investigation made of Palmer's conduct of that office by some outside individual or agency. Some of Palmer's actions as Alien Property Custodian were strongly criticized both at the time and later, but no formal investigations of these actions took place until after Palmer had retired from public office. See Stanley Coben, *A. Mitchell Palmer: Politician* (New York and London, 1963), pp. 140-49.
    [2] Additions from the copy in the J. P. Tumulty Papers, DLC.


## From Charles W. Ervin[1]

New York, 1 Feb. 1919.

While the daily cables report you as fighting in Europe for certain ideals of democracy set forth in your fourteen points among which are free and open discussions on matters vitally affecting the people in the United States the postmaster general is declaring issues of a daily paper engaging in open free and orderly discussion unmailable. The New York Call is fighting for many of the ideals to which you have given public expression as well as fighting for other democratic ideals that you have not as yet championed. Issues of this paper are being thrown out of the mail by order Albert Sidney Burleson in denial of every principle of your stated beliefs and in flagrant defiance of the first amendment to the Constitution of the United States.[2]                    Charles W. Ervin.

T telegram (WP, DLC).
    [1] Editor of the *New York Call*; Socialist candidate for Governor of New York in 1918.
    [2] Burleson had denied second-class mailing privileges to the *New York Call* on November 13, 1917. The *Call* had applied to be reinstated to the second-class mails on January 9, 1919, and its case was now pending before the Post Office Department. See "Burleson and the Call," *New Republic*, XXI (Jan. 7, 1920), 157-58.


## Gilbert Fairchild Close to William Bramwell Booth

My dear Mr. Booth:                    Paris, 1 February, 1919.

The President asks me to acknowledge receipt of your telegram of January 31st and to thank you for your message. He asks me to assure you that the problem which you present is being carefully studied and worked out in the face of a great many serious difficulties.    Cordially and sincerely yours,    [Gilbert F. Close]

CCL (WP, DLC).

## From the Diary of Dr. Grayson

Sunday, February 2, 1919.

The President rested during the morning and had as a luncheon guest, George Creel, who told him his impressions of what he said he saw in the Balkans and Austro-Hungary. In the afternoon, we went for a motor ride. In the evening, the President read aloud to Mrs. Wilson and me a number of chapters from A. G. Gardiner's "Pebbles on the Shore."[1]

[1] Alpha of the Plough [Alfred George Gardiner], *Pebbles on the Shore* (London, 1916).

## From Norman Hezekiah Davis

My dear Mr. President:          Paris, 2nd February, 1919.

From conversations which other Americans and I have had lately with various French, British, and Italian officials there seems to be a concerted movement on foot to obtain directly or indirectly an interlocking of the United States into the whole financial situation in Europe. The question is so frought with complications that I venture to explain the situation as it appears to me. Apparently, the cloak to be used for this purpose is through fa[s]cinating plans for stabilizing international exchange, the pooling of raw materials, and the guarantee of the German undertakings for reparation. I venture to call your attention to this because our participation in any one of these various undertakings would be in effect giving a blank check on the United States. Any agreement on our part to stabilize international exchange would, in effect, not only enable France and Italy to continue to use their banknote printing presses without restraint and put off the day when they must meet their financial problems squarely, but would amount to our making good all the trade balances against them from every quarter of the world and also a great portion of their war expenses before our entry into the war. Such an undertaking would also place and keep the dollar at a discount on the same level as the depreciated European currency. In my opinion, the United States Government should not enter into any general financial or economic arrangements of any kind growing out of this war, but simply should undertake to consider sympathetically on its merits any claims by any individual government for specific assistance on any problem, which can thus be presented to Congress.

I am, my dear Mr. President
Cordially yours,   Norman H. Davis

TLS (WP, DLC).

# From Josephus Daniels

Washington Feb 2 1919

For the President quote I suggest for your serious consideration whether it is not wise to put all matters connected with the Shipping Board and Emergency Fleet under a corporation exactly like the Panama Railroad Corporation. It might be wise for the Sec. of the Navy to bear the same relation to the corporation as the Sec. of War bears to the Panama Railroad Corporation, and to enroll all officers and crews in the Naval Reserve. They would receive the pay they now receive plus a nominal Naval Reserve retainer. I have suggested the Panama Railroad Corporation idea to Baker, Colby and Whipple. The last two are looking into it. There is a conviction here that some change that will secure quick action, cut down expense and aid the world in getting down as near as may be to pre-war ocean rates is much to be desired unquote

Josephus Daniels

I am in sympathy with this. Please ask the Sec'y of the Navy to take it up with Hurley who sails on the Leviathan to-morrow. It is in line with H's own ideas. W.W.

T telegram (W. S. Benson Papers, DLC).

# From the Diary of Edith Benham

February 2, 1919

Sundays are always quiet for us. Mr. Creel came to luncheon and gave an account of a trip he has just completed through Poland, Czechoslovakia, and those other mysterious old-new countries. He brought back some posters and the inscriptions translated read, "We want a Wilson Peace." He went among the poor people who regard the President as a new popular Saint. His pictures hung in many windows and the people told Mr. Creel that they wanted Wilson to reign over them. The President says that such expressions make him very nervous, for he fears the revulsion which is bound to come when they find he can't do all they hope. Such revulsions of popular feeling are dangerous to a degree. Mr. Creel said prices were lower in Vienna than in Paris, and the people looked well fed and the streets were bright. He said that in the less highly civilized communities bathing became a lost art—all he did for his morning ablutions was to apply a bit of snow deftly to his right eyelid and his toilet was completed.

The conversation drifted around to the Jews and the Zionist movement in which the President is much interested. He doesn't expect all the Jews will want to return naturally, but it would give them as a race the same nationality they have lacked for centuries.

He had to go down to the Crillon tonight to go over a paper the Commission had prepared to which he had to make certain changes and came home rather brain weary, so as usual he picked up a book, one of A. G. Gardiner's books of essays, and read aloud for an hour. When he is tired like that to change the current of his thought he often does that, sometimes a poem, sometimes some article he has been sent to read. He reads very well and it is nice to sit around the open fire and listen to good things. You see, we usually dine early at seven, and then go into his sitting room and stay for a time. Often he is busy and works on his typewriter which he has in the study.

## The Hurst-Miller Draft of the Covenant of the League of Nations

[Feb. 2, 1919]

### DRAFT COVENANT.
#### *Preamble.*

In order to secure international peace and security by the acceptance of obligations not to resort to the use of armed force, by the prescription of open, just and honourable relations between nations, by the firm establishment of the understandings of international law as the actual rule of conduct among governments, and by the maintenance of justice and a scrupulous respect for all treaty obligations in the dealings of organised peoples with one another, and in order to promote international co-operation, the Powers signatory to this Covenant adopt this constitution of the League of Nations.

#### ARTICLE I.

The action of the High Contracting Parties under the terms of this Covenant shall be effected through the instrumentality of meetings of Delegates representing the High Contracting Parties, of meetings at more frequent intervals of an Executive Council representing the States more immediately concerned in the matters under discussion, and of a permanent International Secretariat to be established at the capital of the League.

#### ARTICLE 2.

Meetings of the Body of Delegates shall be held from time to time as occasion may require for the purpose of dealing with matters within the sphere of action of the League.

Meetings of the Body of Delegates shall be held at the capital of the League, or at such other place as may be found convenient, and shall consist of not more than two representatives of each of the High Contracting Parties.

An Ambassador or Minister of one of the High Contracting Parties shall be competent to act as its representative.

All matters of procedure at meetings of the Body of Delegates, including the appointment of committees to investigate particular matters, shall be regulated by the Body of Delegates, and may be decided by a majority of those present at the meeting.

### ARTICLE 3.

The representatives of the States, members of the League directly affected by matters within the sphere of action of the League, will meet as an Executive Council from time to time as occasion may require.

The United States of America, Great Britain, France, Italy, and Japan shall be deemed to be directly affected by all matters within the sphere of action of the League. Invitations will be sent to any Power whose interests are directly affected, and no decision taken at any meeting will be binding on a State which was not invited to be represented at the meeting.

Such meetings will be held at whatever place may be decided on, or, failing any such decision, at the capital of the League, and any matter affecting the interests of the League, or relating to matters within its sphere of action or likely to affect the peace of the world, may be dealt with.

### ARTICLE 4.

The permanent Secretariat of the League shall be established at [blank] which shall constitute the capital of the League. The Secretariat shall comprise such secretaries and staff as may be required, under the general direction and control of a Chancellor of the League, by whom they shall be appointed.

The Chancellor shall act as Secretary at all meetings of the Body of Delegates or of the Executive Council.

The expenses of the Secretariat shall be borne by the States members of the League in accordance with the distribution among members of the Postal Union of the expenses of the International Postal Union.

### ARTICLE 5.

Representatives of the High Contracting Parties and officials of the League when engaged on the business of the League shall enjoy diplomatic privileges and immunities, and the buildings occupied by the League or its officials or by representatives attending its meetings shall enjoy the benefits of extraterritoriality.

## ARTICLE 6.

Admission to the League of States who are not signatories of this Covenant requires the assent of not less than two-thirds of the Body of Delegates.

No State shall be admitted to the League except on condition that its military and naval forces and armaments shall conform to standards prescribed by the League in respect of it from time to time.

## ARTICLE 7.

The High Contracting Parties undertake to respect and preserve as against external aggression the territorial integrity and existing political independence of all States members of the League.

## ARTICLE 8.

The High Contracting Parties recognise the principle that the maintenance of peace will require the reduction of national armaments to the lowest point consistent with domestic safety and the enforcement by common action of international obligations; and the Executive Council shall formulate plans for effecting such reduction. It shall also enquire into the feasibility of abolishing compulsory military service, and the substitution therefor of forces enrolled upon a voluntary basis, and into the military and naval equipment which it is reasonable to maintain.

The High Contracting Parties further agree that there shall be full and frank publicity as to all national armaments and military or naval programmes.

## ARTICLE 9.

Any war or threat of war, whether immediately affecting any of the High Contracting Parties or not, is hereby declared a matter of concern to the League, and the High Contracting Parties reserve the right to take any action that may be deemed wise and effectual to safeguard the peace of nations.

It is hereby also declared and agreed to be the friendly right of each of the High Contracting Parties to draw the attention of the Body of Delegates, or of the Executive Council, to any circumstances anywhere which threaten to disturb international peace, or the good understanding between nations upon which peace depends.

## ARTICLE 10.

The High Contracting Parties agree that should disputes arise between them which cannot be adjusted by the ordinary processes of diplomacy, they will in no case resort to armed force without previously submitting the questions and matters involved either to arbitration or to enquiry by the Executive Council, and until three months after the award by the arbitrators, or a recommendation by the Executive Council; and that they will not even then resort to armed force as against a member of the League which complies with the award of the arbitrators, or the recommendation of the Executive Council.

ARTICLE 11.

The High Contracting Parties agree that whenever any dispute or difficulty shall arise between them which they recognise to be suitable for submission to arbitration, and which cannot be satisfactorily settled by diplomacy, they will submit the whole subject-matter to arbitration, and will carry out in full good faith any award or decision that may be rendered.

ARTICLE 12.

The Executive Council will formulate plans for the establishment of a Permanent Court of International Justice, and this Court will be competent to hear and determine any matter which the parties recognise as suitable for submission to it for arbitration under the foregoing Article.

ARTICLE 13.

If there should arise between States members of the League any dispute likely to lead to a rupture, which is not submitted to arbitration as above, the High Contracting Parties agree that they will refer the matter to the Executive Council; either party to the dispute may give notice to the Chancellor of the existence of the dispute, and the Chancellor will make all necessary arrangements for a full investigation and consideration thereof. For this purpose the parties agree to communicate to the Chancellor statements of their case with all the relevant facts and papers.

Where the efforts of the Council lead to the settlement of the dispute, a statement shall be prepared for publication indicating the nature of the dispute and the terms of settlement, together with such explanations as may be appropriate. If the dispute has not been settled, a report by the Council shall be published, setting forth with all necessary facts and explanations the recommendations which the Council think just and proper for the settlement of the dispute. If the report is unanimously agreed to by the members of the Council, other than the parties to the dispute, the High Contracting Parties agree that none of them will go to war with any party which complies with its recommendations. If no such unanimous report can be made, it shall be the duty of the majority to issue a statement indicating what they believe to be the facts and containing the recommendations which they consider to be just and proper.

The Executive Council may in any case under this article refer the dispute to the Body of Delegates. The dispute shall be so referred at the request of either party to the dispute. In any case referred to the Body of Delegates all the provisions of this Article relating to the action and powers of the Executive Council shall apply to the action and powers of the Body of Delegates.

### ARTICLE 14.

Should any of the High Contracting Parties be found by the League to have broken or disregarded its covenants under Article 10, it shall thereby *ipso facto* be deemed to have committed an act of war against all the other members of the League, which shall immediately subject it to the severance of all trade or financial relations, the prohibition of all intercourse between their nationals and the nationals of the covenant-breaking State, and the prevention, so far as possible, of all financial, commercial, or personal intercourse between the nationals of the covenant-breaking State and the nationals of any other State, whether a member of the League or not.

It shall be the duty of the Executive Council in such a case to recommend what effective military or naval force the members of the League shall severally contribute to the armed forces to be used to protect the covenants of the League.

The High Contracting Parties agree, further, that they will mutually support one another in the financial and economic measures which are taken under this article in order to minimise the loss and inconvenience resulting from the above measures, and that they will mutually support one another in resisting any special measures aimed at one of their number by the covenant-breaking State, and that they will afford passage through their territory to the forces of any of the High Contracting Parties who are co-operating to protect the covenants of the League.

### ARTICLE 15.

In the event of disputes between one State member of the League and another State which is not a member of the League, or between States not members of the League, the High Contracting Parties agree that the State or States not members of the League shall be invited to become *ad hoc* members of the League, and upon acceptance of any such invitation, the above provisions shall be applied with such modifications as may be deemed necessary by the League.

Upon such invitation being given the Executive Council shall immediately institute an enquiry into the circumstances and merits of the dispute and recommend such action as may seem best and most effectual in the circumstances.

In the event of a Power so invited refusing to become *ad hoc* a member of the League, and taking any action against a State member of the League, which in the case of a State member of the League would constitute a breach of Article 10, the provisions of Article 14 shall be applicable as against the State taking such action.

If both parties to the dispute when so invited refuse to become *ad hoc* members of the League, the Executive Council may take such action and make such recommendations as will prevent hostilities, and will result in the settlement of the dispute.

### ARTICLE 16.

The High Contracting Parties entrust to the League the general supervision of the trade in arms and ammunition with the countries in which the control of this traffic is necessary in the common interest.

### ARTICLE 17.

The High Contracting Parties agree that in respect of territories which formerly belonged to the German Empire or to Turkey, and which are inhabited by peoples unable at present to secure for themselves the benefits of a stable administration, the well-being of these peoples constitutes a sacred trust for civilisation, and imposes upon the States members of the League the obligation to render help and guidance in the development of the administration. They recognise that all policies of administration or economic development should be based primarily upon the well-considered interests of the peoples themselves, upon the maintenance of the policy of the open door, and of equal opportunity for all the High Contracting Parties in respect of the use and development of the economic resources of the territory. No military or naval forces shall be formed among the inhabitants of the territories in excess of those required for purposes of defence and of internal police.

### ARTICLE 18.

The High Contracting Parties will work to establish and maintain fair hours and humane conditions of labour for all those within their several jurisdictions, and they will exert their influence in favour of the adoption and maintenance of a similar policy and like safeguards wherever their industrial and commercial relations extend. Also they will appoint commissions to study conditions of industry and labour in their international aspects, and to make recommendations thereon, including the extension and improvement of existing conventions.

### ARTICLE 19.

The High Contracting Parties agree that they will make no law prohibiting or interfering with the free exercise of religion, and that they will in no way discriminate, either in law or in fact, against those who practice any particular creed, religion, or belief whose practices are not inconsistent with public order or public morals.

### ARTICLE 20.

The High Contracting Parties will agree upon provisions intended to secure and maintain freedom of transit and just treatment for the commerce of all States members of the League.

### ARTICLE 21.

The High Contracting Parties agree that any treaty or international engagement entered into between States members of the League shall be forthwith registered with the Chancellor, and as soon as possible published by him.

### ARTICLE 22.

The High Contracting Parties severally agree that the present Covenant is accepted as abrogating all obligations *inter se* which are inconsistent with the terms hereof, and solemnly engage that they will not hereafter enter into any engagements inconsistent with the terms hereof.

In case any of the Powers signatory hereto, or subsequently admitted to the League shall, before becoming a party to this Covenant, have undertaken any obligations which are inconsistent with the terms of this Covenant it shall be the duty of such Power to take immediate steps to procure its release from such obligations.

Printed in Miller, *Drafting of the Covenant*, II, 231-37.

## From the Diary of David Hunter Miller

Sunday, February 2nd [-3rd] [1919]

I went to the President's house at 6:15 and left the paper.[1] Mr. Close said that the President was busy and would be unable to see me then as he would probably continue to be busy for some time. Upon returning to the office I had a message a little later, saying that the President was to be at Colonel House's at 8:15 and wished me there.

At the conference this evening nobody was present except the President and Colonel House. I explained to the President what Mr. Hurst had said about Lloyd George's desire for brevity, and described generally how agreement on the paper had been reached. The President said that he did not like the paper very much; that the British seem to have taken a good many things out, some of which he thought were important. He then took the original draft[2] as a basis of discussion and went over it, making certain changes and approving some of the changes which the British had made.[3]

He then asked me if it could be recast with these changes and printed. I told him that this could be done in time for the meeting the next day. I then went back to the office and proceeded to have the work done, and left the printing office with the completed copies at 6 A.M.

Miller, *My Diary at the Conference of Paris*, I, 104-105.
[1] That is, the Hurst-Miller draft of the Covenant.
[2] That is, his second "Paris draft."
[3] In the documents which follow the entry from the McCormick Diary.


## From the Diary of Vance Criswell McCormick

February 2 (Sunday) [1919]

Went to the President's house at 6 o'clock. Got him to present at Supreme War Council tomorrow program for a considerable relaxation of embargo. Discussed Congress' attack upon the Russian Bureau.[1] He approved our proceeding with plans irrespective of attack, as he finds work more necessary now than ever, as the war is not over so far as Russia is concerned and they need our relief. He certainly has courage where criticism of himself is concerned. Discussed work of Reparations Commission and League of Nations as it concerned Economic Control. He seemed in great shape.

[1] See FLP to RL, Jan. 24, 1919 (first telegram of that date), n. 1.

# The First Version of the Third "Paris Draft" of the Covenant of the League of Nations

## COVENANT

**PREAMBLE**

*by the acceptance of obligations not to resort to the use of armed force*

In order to secure international peace and security by the prescription of open, just, and honorable relations between nations, by the firm establishment of the understandings of international law as the actual rule of conduct among governments, and by the maintenance of justice and a scrupulous respect for all treaty obligations in the dealings of organized peoples with one another, and in order to promote international cooperation, the Powers signatory to this covenant and agreement ~~jointly and severally~~ adopt this constitution of the League of Nations.

**ARTICLE I.**

The action of the Signatory Powers under the terms of this covenant shall be effected through the instrumentality of a Body of Delegates which shall consist of the ~~ambassadors and ministers~~ of the contracting Powers accredited to H. and the Minister for Foreign Affairs of H. The meetings of the Body of Delegates shall be held at the seat of government of H. and the Minister for Foreign affairs of H. shall be the presiding officer of the Body.

*diplomatic or special representatives*

Whenever the Delegates deem it necessary or advisable, they may meet temporarily at the seat of government of R. or of E., in which case the Ambassador or Minister to H. of the country in which the meeting is held shall be the presiding officer pro tempore.

It shall be the privilege of any of the contracting Powers to assist its representative in the Body of Delegates by any method of conference, counsel, or advice that may seem best to it, and also to substitute upon occasion a special representative for its regular diplomatic representative accredited to H.

**ARTICLE II.**

The Body of Delegates shall regulate their own procedure and shall have power to appoint such committees as they may deem necessary to inquire into and report upon any matters that lie within the field of their action.

It shall be the right of the Body of Delegates, upon the initiative of any member, to discuss, either publicly or privately as it may deem best, any matter lying within the jurisdiction of the League of Nations as defined in this covenant, or any matter likely to affect the peace of the world; but all actions of the Body of Delegates taken in the exercise of the functions and powers granted to them under this Covenant shall be formulated and agreed upon by an Executive Council, which shall act either by reference or upon its own initiative and which shall consist of the representatives of the Great Powers, together with representatives drawn in annual rotation from two panels, one of which shall be made up of the representatives of the States ranking next after the Great Powers and the other of the representatives of the minor States (a classification which the Body of Delegates shall itself establish and may from time to time alter), such a number being drawn from these panels as will be but one less than the representa-

1

tives of the Great Powers; and three or more negative votes in the Council shall operate as a veto upon any action or resolution proposed.

All resolutions passed or actions taken by the Executive Council, except those adopted in execution of any direct powers herein granted to the Body of Delegates themselves, shall have the effect of recommendations to the several governments of the League.

The Executive Council shall appoint a permanent Secretariat and staff and may appoint joint committees, chosen from the Body of Delegates or consisting of specially qualified persons outside of that Body, for the study and systematic consideration of the international questions with which the Council may have to deal, or of questions likely to lead to international complications or disputes. It shall also take the necessary steps to establish and maintain proper liaison both with the foreign offices of the signatory powers and with any governments or agencies which may be acting as mandatories of the League of Nations in any part of the world.

ARTICLE III.

*undertake to respect and to protect as against external aggression the*

The Contracting Powers ~~unite in guaranteeing to each other~~ political independence and territorial integrity *of all States members of the League* ~~as against external aggression; but it is understood between them that such territorial readjustments, if any, as may in the future become necessary by reason of changes in present racial conditions and aspirations or present social and political relationships, pursuant to the principle of self-determination, and also such territorial readjustments as may in the judgment of three-fourths of the Delegates be demanded by the welfare and manifest interest of the peoples concerned, may be effected if agreeable to those peoples and to the States from which the territory is separated or to which it is added; and that territorial changes may in equity involve material compensation. The Contracting Powers accept without reservation the principle that the peace of the world is superior in importance to every question of Political jurisdiction or boundary.~~

ARTICLE IV.

*Substitute VIII, first paragraph.*

~~The Contracting Powers recognize the principle that the establishment and maintenance of peace will require the reduction of national armaments to the lowest point consistent with domestic safety and the enforcement by common action of international obligations; and the Executive Council is directed to formulate at once plans by which such a reduction may be brought about. The plan so formulated shall be binding when, and only when, unanimously approved by the Governments signatory to this Covenant.~~

~~As the basis for such a reduction of armaments, all the Powers subscribing to the Treaty of Peace of which this Covenant constitutes a part hereby agree to abolish conscription and all other forms of compulsory military service, and also agree that their future forces of defense and of international action shall consist of militia or volunteers, whose numbers and methods of training shall be fixed, after expert inquiry, by the agreements with regard to the reduction of armaments referred to in the last preceding paragraph.~~

The Executive Council shall also determine for the consideration and action of the several governments what direct military equipment and armament is fair and reasonable in proportion to the scale of forces laid down in the programme of disarmament; and these limits, when adopted, shall not be exceeded without the permission of the Body of Delegates.

2

The Contracting Powers further agree that munitions and implements of war shall not be manufactured by private enterprise or for private profit, and that there shall be full and frank publicity as to all national armaments and military or naval programmes.

### ARTICLE V.

The Contracting Powers jointly and severally agree that should disputes or difficulties arise between or among them which cannot be satisfactorily settled or adjusted by the ordinary processes of diplomacy, they will in no case resort to armed force without previously submitting the questions and matters involved either to arbitration or to inquiry by the Executive Council of the Body of Delegates or until there has been an award by the arbitrators or a decision by the Executive Council; and that they will not even then resort to armed force as against a member of the League of Nations who complies with the award of the arbitrators or the decision of the Executive Council.

The Powers signatory to this Covenant undertake and agree that whenever any dispute or difficulty shall arise between or among them with regard to any question of the law of nations, with regard to the interpretation of a treaty, as to any fact which would, if established, constitute a breach of international obligation, or as to any alleged damage and the nature and measure of the reparation to be made therefor, if such dispute or difficulty cannot be satisfactorily settled by the ordinary processes of negotiation, to submit the whole subject matter to arbitration and to carry out in full good faith any award or decision that may be rendered.

In case of arbitration, the matter or matters at issue shall be referred to three arbitrators, one of the three to be selected by each of the parties to the dispute, from outside their own nations, when there are but two such parties, and the third by the two thus selected. When there are more than two parties to the dispute, one arbitrator shall be named by each of the several parties and the arbitrators thus named shall add to their number others of their own choice, the number thus added to be limited to the number which will suffice to give a deciding voice to the arbitrators thus added in case of a tie vote among the arbitrators chosen by the contending parties. In case the arbitrators chosen by the contending parties cannot agree upon an additional arbitrator or arbitrators, the additional arbitrator or arbitrators shall be chosen by the Executive Council.

On the appeal of a party to the dispute the decision of the arbitrators may be set aside by a vote of three fourths of the Delegates, in case the decision of the arbitrators was unanimous, or by a vote of two-thirds of the Delegates in case the decision of the arbitrators was not unanimous, but unless thus set aside shall be finally binding and conclusive.

When any decision of arbitrators shall have been thus set aside, the dispute shall again be submitted to arbitrators chosen as heretofore provided, none of whom shall, however, have previously acted as arbitrators in the dispute in question, and the decision of the arbitrators rendered in this second arbitration shall be finally binding and conclusive without right of appeal.

If for any reason it should prove impracticable to refer any matter in dispute to arbitration, the parties to the dispute shall apply to the Executive Council to take the matter under consideration for such mediatory action or recommendation as it may deem wise in the circumstances. The Council shall immediately accept the reference and give notice to the parties, and shall make the necessary arrangements for a full hearing, investigation, and consideration. It shall ascertain and as soon as possible

3

make public all the facts involved in the dispute and shall make such recommendations as it may deem wise and practicable based on the merits of the controversy and calculated to secure a just and lasting settlement. Other members of the League shall place at the disposal of the Executive Council any and all information that may be in their possession which in any way bears upon the facts or merits of the controversy; and the Executive Council shall do everything in its power by way of mediation or conciliation to bring about a peaceful settlement. The decisions of the Executive Council shall be addressed to the disputants, and shall not have the force of a binding verdict. Should the Executive Council fail to arrive at any conclusion, it shall be the privilege of the members of the Executive Council to publish their several conclusions or recommendations; and such publications shall not be regarded as an unfriendly act by either or any of the disputants.

Every award by arbitrators and every decision by the Executive Council upon a matter in dispute between States must be rendered within twelve months after formal reference.

### ARTICLE VI.

*be found by the League to have broken or disregarded*

Should any contracting power ~~break or disregard~~ its covenants under ARTICLE V, it shall thereby *ipso facto* be deemed to have committed an act of war against all the members of the League, which shall immediately subject it to a complete economic and financial boycott, including the severance of all trade or financial relations, the prohibition of all intercourse between their subjects and the subjects of the covenant-breaking State, and the prevention, so far as possible, of all financial, commercial, or personal intercourse between the subjects of the covenant-breaking State and the subjects of any other State, whether a member of the League of Nations or not.

It shall be the privilege and duty of the executive Council of the Body of Delegates in such a case to recommend what effective military or naval force the members of the League of Nations shall severally contribute, and to advise, if it should think best, that the smaller members of the League be excused from making any contribution to the armed forces to be used against the covenant-breaking State.

The covenant-breaking State shall, after the restoration of peace, be subject to the regulations with regard to a peace establishment provided for new States under the terms SUPPLEMENTARY ARTICLE IV.

*Insert last paragraph of XIII. of Condensed draft*

### ARTICLE VII.

If any Power shall declare war or begin hostilities, or take any hostile step short of war, against another Power before submitting the dispute involved to arbitrators or consideration by the Executive Council as herein provided, or shall declare war or begin hostilities, or take any hostile step short of war, in regard to any dispute which has been decided adversely to it by arbitrators chosen and empowered as herein provided, the Contracting Powers hereby engage not only to cease all commerce and intercourse with that Power but also to unite in blockading and closing the frontiers of that Power to commerce or intercourse with any part of the world and to use any force that may be necessary to accomplish that object.

### ARTICLE VIII.

Any war or threat of war, whether immediately affecting any of the Contracting Powers or not, is hereby declared a matter of concern to the League of

*a /*

Nations and to all the Powers signatory hereto, and those Powers hereby reserve the right to take any action that may be deemed wise and effectual to safeguard the peace of nations.

It is hereby also declared and agreed to be the friendly right of each of the nations signatory or adherent to this Covenant to draw the attention of the Body of Delegates or of the Executive Council to any circumstances anywhere which threaten to disturb international peace or the good understanding between nations upon which peace depends.

The Delegates and the Executive Council shall meet in the interest of peace whether war is rumored or threatened, and also whether the Delegates of any Power shall inform the Delegates that a meeting and conference in the interest of peace is advisable.

The Delegates may also meet at such other times and upon such other occasions as they shall from time to time deem best and determine.

### ARTICLE IX.

In the event of a dispute arising between one of the Contracting Powers and a Power not a party to this Covenant, the Contracting Power involved hereby binds itself to endeavor to obtain the submission of the dispute to judicial decision or to arbitration. If the other Power will not agree to submit the dispute to judicial decision or to arbitration, the Contracting Power shall bring the matter to the attention of the Executive Council. The Delegates shall in such a case, in the name of the League of Nations, invite the Power not a party to this Covenant to become *ad hoc* a party and to submit its case to judicial decision or to arbitration, and if that Power consents it is hereby agreed that the provisions hereinbefore contained and applicable to the submission of disputes to arbitration or discussion shall be in all respects applicable to the dispute both in favor of and against such Power as if it were to this Covenant.

In case the Power not a party to this Covenant shall not accept the invitation of the Executive Council to become *ad hoc* a party, it shall be the duty of the Executive Council immediately to institute an inquiry into the circumstances and merits of the dispute involved and to recommend such joint action by the Contracting Powers as may seem best and most effectual in the circumstances disclosed.

### ARTICLE X.

If hostilities should be begun or any hostile action taken against the Contracting Power by the Power not a party to this Covenant before a decision of the dispute by arbitrators or before investigation, report and recommendation by the Executive Council in regard to the dispute, or contrary to such recommendation, the Contracting Powers engage thereupon to cease all commerce and communication with that Power and also to unite in blockading and closing the frontiers of that Power to all commerce or intercourse with any part of the world, and to employ jointly any force that may be necessary to accomplish that object. The Contracting Powers also undertake to unite in coming to the assistance of the Contracting Power against which hostile action has been taken, and to combine their armed forces in its behalf.

### ARTICLE XI.

In case of a dispute between states not parties to this Covenant, any Contracting Power may bring the matter to the attention of the Delegates or the Executive Council, who shall thereupon tender the good offices of the League of Nations with a view to the peaceable settlement of the dispute.

5

If one of the states, a party to the dispute, shall offer and agree to submit its interests and cause of action wholly to the control and decision of the League of Nations, that state shall *ad hoc* be deemed a Contracting Power. If no one of the states, parties to the dispute, shall so offer and agree, the Delegates shall, through the Executive Council, of their own motion take such action and make such recommendation to their governments as will prevent hostilities and result in the settlement of the dispute.

### ARTICLE XII.

Any Power not a party to this Covenant, whose government is based upon the principle of popular self-government, may apply to the Body of Delegates for leave to become a party. If the Delegates shall regard the granting thereof as likely to promote the peace, order, and security of the World, they shall act favorably on the application, and their favorable action shall operate to constitute the Power so applying in all respects a full signatory party to this Covenant. This action shall require the affirmative vote of two-thirds of the Delegates.

### ARTICLE XIII.

The Contracting Powers severally agree that the present Covenant and Convention is accepted as abrogating all treaty obligations *inter se* which are inconsistent with the terms hereof, and solemnly engage that they will not enter into any engagements inconsistent with the terms hereof.

In case any of the Powers signatory hereto or subsequently admitted to the League of Nations shall, before becoming a party to this Covenant, have undertaken any treaty obligations which are inconsistent with the terms of this Covenant, it shall be the duty of such Power to take immediate steps to procure its release from such obligations.

### SUPPLEMENTARY AGREEMENTS.

#### I.

In respect of the peoples and territories which formerly belonged to ~~Austria-Hungary, and~~ to Turkey, and in respect of the colonies formerly under the dominion of the German Empire, the League of Nations shall be regarded as the residuary trustee with the right of oversight or administration in accordance with certain fundamental principles hereinafter set forth; and this reversion and control shall exclude all rights or privileges of annexation on the part of any Power.

These principles are, that there shall in no case be any annexation of any of these territories by any State either within the League or outside of it, and that in the future government of these peoples and territories the rule of self-determination, or the consent of the governed to their form of government, shall be fairly and reasonably applied, and all policies of administration or economic development be based primarily upon the well-considered interests of the people themselves.

#### II.

Any authority, control, or administration which may be necessary in respect of these peoples or territories other than their own self-determined and self-organized autonomy shall be the exclusive function of and shall

6

*The provisions of this Article can also be applied in respect of other peoples and territories which are not otherwise disposed of in the treaty of peace of which this Covenant forms a part or are not definitively constituted as autonomous states.*

be vested in the League of Nations and exercised or undertaken by or on behalf of it.

It shall be lawful for the League of Nations to delegate its authority, control, or administration of any such people or territory to some single State or organized agency which it may designate and appoint as its agent or mandatory; but whenever or wherever possible or feasible the agent or mandatory so appointed shall be nominated or approved by the autonomous people or territory.

### III.

The degree of authority, control, or administration to be exercised by the mandatory State or agency shall in each case be explicitly defined by the Executive Council in a special Act or Charter which shall reserve to the League complete power of supervision, and which shall also reserve to the people of any such territory or governmental unit the right to appeal to the League for the redress or correction of any breach of the mandate by the mandatory State or agency or, for the substitution of some other State or agency, as mandatory.

The mandatory State or agency shall in all cases be bound and required to maintain the policy of the open door, or equal opportunity for all the signatories to this Covenant, in respect of the use and development of the economic resources of such people or territory.

The mandatory State or agency shall in no case form or maintain any military or naval force, native or other, in excess of definite standards laid down by the League itself for the purposes of internal police.

Any expense the mandatory State or agency may be put to in the exercise of its functions under the mandate, so far as they cannot be borne by the resources of the people or territory under its charge upon a fair basis of assessment and charge, shall be borne by the several signatory Powers, their several contributions being assessed and determined by the Executive Council in proportion to their several national budgets, unless the mandatory State or agency is willing itself to bear the excess costs; and in all cases the expenditures of the mandatory Power or agency in the exercise of the mandate shall be subject to the audit and authorization of the League.

The object of all such tutelary oversight and administration on the part of the League of Nations shall be to build up in as short a time as possible out of the people or territory under its guardianship a political unit which can take charge of its own affairs, determine its own connections, and choose its own policies. The League may at any time release such a people or territory from tutelage and consent to its being set up as an independent unit. It shall also be the right and privilege of any people or territory to petition the League to take such action, and upon such petition being made it shall be the duty of the League to take the petition under full and friendly consideration with a view to determining the best interests of the people or territory in question in view of all the circumstances of their situation and development.

### IV.

No new State shall be recognized by the League or admitted into its membership except on condition that its military and naval forces and armaments shall conform to standards prescribed by the League in respect of it from time to time.

The League of Nations is empowered, directly and without right of delegation, to watch over the relations *inter se* of all new independent States arising

7

~~or created and shall assume and fulfil the duty of conciliating and composing differences between them with a view to the maintenance of settled order and the general peace.~~

**V.**

The Powers signatory or adherent to this Covenant agree that they will themselves seek to establish and maintain fair hours and humane conditions of labor for all those within their several jurisdictions who are engaged in manual labor and that they will exert their influence in favor of the adoption and maintenance of a similar policy and like safeguards wherever their industrial and commercial relations extend.

*Substitute XVIII of Condensed Draft.*

**VI.**

The League of Nations shall require all new States to bind themselves as a condition precedent to their recognition as independent or autonomous States and the Executive Council shall exact of all States seeking admission to the League of Nations the promise, to accord to all racial or national minorities within their several jurisdictions exactly the same treatment and security, both in law and in fact, that is accorded the racial or national majority of their people.

**VII.**

Recognizing religious persecution and intolerance as fertile sources of war, the Powers signatory hereto agree, and the League of Nations shall exact from all new States and all States seeking admission to it the promise, that they will make no law prohibiting or interfering with the free exercise of religion, and that they will in no way discriminate, either in law or in fact, against those who practice any particular creed, religion, or belief whose practices are not inconsistent with public order or public morals.

**VIII.**

*When the* *Shall have* ~~The~~ rights of belligerents on the high seas outside territorial waters ~~having~~ been defined by international convention, it is hereby agreed and declared as a fundamental covenant that no Power or combination of Powers shall have a right to overstep in any particular the clear meaning of the definitions thus established; but that it shall be the right of the League of Nations from time to time and on special occasion to close the seas in whole or in part against a particular Power or particular Powers for the purpose of enforcing the international covenants here entered into.

**IX.**

It is hereby covenanted and agreed by the Powers signatory hereto that no treaty entered into by them, ~~either simply or jointly,~~ shall be regarded as valid, binding, or operative until it shall have been published and made known to all the other ~~signatories.~~

*States members of the League.*

**X.**

It is further covenanted and agreed by the signatory Powers that in their fiscal and economic regulations and policy no discrimination shall be made between one nation and another among those with which they have commercial and financial dealings.

8

Printed copy with WWhw emendations (WP, DLC).

# From David Hunter Miller, with Enclosure

Sir:                                          [Paris] 3 February, 1919.

I have the honor to transmit to you herewith ten texts of a draft of "Covenant," printed this morning. About thirty other texts are available.

In lieu of former Supplementary Articles I, II, and III, there have been inserted, in accordance with my understanding of your direction, the substance of the provisions of the recent resolution regarding mandataries, adding, however, the first and last paragraphs of former Supplementary Article III.

The remaining changes from the former draft include only, I believe, those which were indicated by you, and a few others which followed from the changes so indicated, or which were made for conformity.

I am, Sir, with great respect,
Your obedient servant,   David Hunter Miller

TLS (WP, DLC).

## ENCLOSURE
### COVENANT
#### PREAMBLE

In order to secure international peace and security by the acceptance of obligations not to resort to the use of armed force, by the prescription of open, just and honorable relations between nations, by the firm establishment of the understandings of international law as the actual rule of conduct among governments, and by the maintenance of justice and a scrupulous respect for all treaty obligations in the dealings of organized peoples with one another, and in order to promote international cooperation, the Powers signatory to this Covenant adopt this constitution of the League of Nations.

#### ARTICLE I.

The action of the Contracting Powers under the terms of this Covenant shall be effected through the instrumentality of a Body of Delegates which shall consist of the diplomatic representatives of the Contracting Powers accredited to X. and the Minister of Foreign Affairs of X. The meetings of the Body of Delegates shall be held at the seat of government of X. and the Minister for Foreign Affairs of X. shall be the presiding officer.

Whenever the Delegates deem it necessary or advisable, they

may meet temporarily at the seat of government of Y. or of Z., in which case the diplomatic representative to X. of the country in which the meeting is held shall be the presiding officer *pro tempore*.

It shall be the privilege of any of the Contracting Powers to assist its representative in the Body of Delegates by any method of conference, counsel, or advice that may seem best to it, and also to be represented at any time by a special representative.

ARTICLE II.

The Body of Delegates shall regulate their own procedure and shall have power to appoint such committees as they may deem necesary to inquire into and report upon any matters that lie within the field of their action.

It shall be the right of the Body of Delegates, upon the initiative of any member, to discuss, either publicly or privately as it may deem best, any matter lying within the field of action of the League of Nations as defined in this Covenant, or any matter likely to affect the peace of the world; but all actions of the Body of Delegates taken in the exercise of the functions and powers granted to them under this Covenant shall be formulated and agreed upon by an Executive Council, which shall act either by reference or upon its own initiative and which shall consist of the representatives of the Great Powers, together with representatives drawn in annual rotation from two panels, one of which shall be made up of the representatives of the States ranking next after the Great Powers and the others of the representatives of the minor States (a classification which the Body of Delegates shall itself establish and may from time to time alter), such a number being drawn from these panels as will be but one less than the representatives of the Great Powers; and three or more negative votes in the Council shall operate as a veto upon any action or resolution proposed.

All resolutions passed or actions taken by the Body of Delegates or by the Executive Council, except those adopted in execution of any specific powers herein granted, shall have the effect of recommendations to the several governments of the League.

The Executive Council shall appoint a permanent Secretariat and staff and may appoint joint committees, chosen from the Body of Delegates or consisting of other specially qualified persons, for the study and systematic consideration of the international questions with which the Council may have to deal, or of questions likely to lead to international complications or disputes. The Executive Council shall also take the necessary steps to establish and maintain proper liaison both with the foreign offices of the Contracting Powers and with any governments or agencies which may be acting as mandataries of the League in any part of the world.

### ARTICLE III.

The Contracting Powers undertake to respect and to protect as against external aggression the political independence and territorial integrity of all States members of the League.

### ARTICLE IV.

The Contracting Powers recognize the principle that the maintenance of peace will require the reduction of national armaments to the lowest point consistent with domestic safety and the enforcement by common action of international obligations; and the Executive Council shall formulate plans for effecting such reduction. It shall also require [inquire] into the feasibility of abolishing compulsory military service and the substitution therefor of forces enrolled upon a voluntary basis and into the military and naval equipment which it is reasonable to maintain.

### ARTICLE V.

The Contracting Powers agree that should disputes or difficulties arise between or among them which cannot be satisfactorily settled or adjusted by the ordinary processes of diplomacy, they will in no case resort to armed force without previously submitting the questions and matters involved either to arbitration or to inquiry by the Executive Council and until there has been an award by the arbitrators or a recommendation by the Executive Council; and that they will not even then resort to armed force as against a member of the League of Nations who complies with the award of the arbitrators or the recommendation of the Executive Council.

The Contracting Powers agree that whenever any dispute or difficulty shall arise between or among them with regard to any question of the law of nations, with regard to the interpretation of a treaty, as to any fact which would, if established, constitute a breach of international obligation, or as to any alleged damage and the nature and measure of the reparation to be made therefor, if such dispute or difficulty cannot be satisfactorily settled by the ordinary processes of negotiation, to submit the whole subject matter to arbitration and to carry out in full good faith any award or decision that may be rendered.

In case of arbitration, the matter or matters at issue shall be referred to arbitrators, one of whom shall be selected by each of the parties to the dispute from outside their own nationals, when there are but two such parties, and a third by the two thus selected. When there are more than two parties to the dispute, one arbitrator shall be named by each of the several parties and the arbitrators thus named shall add to their number others of their own choice, the number thus added to be limited to the number which will suffice to give a deciding vote to the arbitrators thus added in case of a division among the arbitrators chosen by the contending parties. In case the arbitrators chosen by the contending parties cannot agree upon an additional arbitrator or arbitrators, the additional arbitrator or arbitrators shall be chosen by the Executive Council.

On the appeal of a party to the dispute the decision of said arbitrators may be set aside by a vote of three-fourths of the Delegates, in case the decision of the arbitrators was unanimous, or by a vote of two-thirds of the Delegates in case the decision of the arbitrators was not unanimous, but unless thus set aside shall be finally binding and conclusive.

When any decision of arbitrators shall have been thus set aside, the dispute shall again be submitted to arbitrators chosen as heretofore provided, none of whom shall, however, have previously acted as arbitrators in the dispute in question, and the decision of the arbitrators rendered in this second arbitration shall be finally binding and conclusive without right of appeal.

If for any reason it should prove impracticable to refer any matter in dispute to arbitration, the parties to the dispute shall apply to the Executive Council to take the matter under consideration for such mediatory action or recommendation as it may deem wise in the circumstances. The Council shall immediately accept the reference and give notice to the parties, and shall make the necessary arrangements for a full hearing, investigation and consideration. The Council shall ascertain and as soon as possible make public all the facts involved in the dispute and shall make such recommendation as it may deem wise and practicable based on the merits of the controversy and calculated to secure a just and lasting settlement. Other members of the League shall place at the disposal of the Executive Council any and all information that may be in their possession which in any way bears upon the facts or merits of the controversy; and the Executive Council shall do everything in its power by way of mediation or concilation to bring about a peaceful settlement. The recommendation of the Executive Council shall be addressed to the disputants. Should the Executive Council fail to arrive at any conclusion, it shall be the privilege of the members of the Executive Council to publish their several conclusions or recommendations; and such publications shall not be regarded as an unfriendly act by any of the disputants.

The Executive Council may in any case refer the consideration of a dispute to the Body of Delegates. The consideration of the dispute shall be so referred at the request of either party to the dispute. In any case referred to the Body of Delegates all the provisions of this Article relating to the action and powers of the Executive Council shall apply to the action and powers of the Body of Delegates.

## ARTICLE VI.

Should any Contracting Power be found by the League to have broken or disregarded its covenants under ARTICLE V, it shall thereby *ipso facto* be deemed to have committed an act of war against all the members of the League, which shall immediately subject it to a complete economic and financial boycott, including the severance of all trade or financial relations, the prohibition of all intercourse between their nationals and the nationals of the covenant-breaking State, and the prevention, so far as possible, of all financial, commercial, or personal intercourse between the nationals of the covenant-breaking State and the nationals of any other State, whether a member of the League or not.

It shall be the duty of the Executive Council in such a case to recommend what effective military or naval force the members of the League shall severally contribute, and to advise, if it should think best, that the smaller members of the League be excused from making any contributions to the armed forces to be used against the covenant-breaking State.

The covenant-breaking State shall, after the restoration of peace, be subject to the regulations with regard to a peace establishment provided for new States under the terms SUPPLEMENTARY ARTICLE IV.

## ARTICLE VII.

If any Contracting Power shall be found by the League to have declared war or to have begun hostilities or to have taken any hostile step short of war, against another Contracting Power before submitting the dispute involved to arbitrators or consideration by the Executive Council as herein provided, or to have declared war or to have begun hostilities or to have taken any hostile step short of war, in regard to any dispute which has been decided adversely to it by arbitrators the Contracting Powers hereby engage not only to cease all commerce and intercourse with that Power but also to unite in blockading and closing the frontiers of that Power to commerce or intercourse with any part of the world and to use any force which may be agreed upon to accomplish that object.

## ARTICLE VIII.

Any war or threat of war, whether immediately affecting any of the Contracting Powers or not, is hereby declared a matter of concern of the League and to all the Contracting Powers, and the Contracting Powers hereby reserve the right to take any action that may be deemed wise and effectual to safeguard the peace of nations.

It is hereby also declared and agreed to be the friendly right of each of the Contracting Powers to draw the attention of the Body of Delegates or of the Executive Council to any circumstances anywhere which threaten to disturb international peace or the good understanding between nations upon which peace depends.

The Body of Delegates and the Executive Council shall meet in the interest of peace whenever war is rumored or threatened, and also whenever the representative of any Power shall inform the Body of Delegates that a meeting and conference in the interest of peace is advisable.

The Body of Delegates may also meet at such other times and upon such other occasions as they shall from time to time deem best and determine.

### ARTICLE IX.

In the event of a dispute arising between one of the Contracting Powers and a power not a party to this Covenant, the Contracting Power shall bring the matter to the attention of the Executive Council. The Executive Council shall in such a case, in the name of the League, invite the Power not a party to this Covenant to become *ad hoc* a party, and if that Power consents it is hereby agreed that the provisions hereinbefore contained and applicable to the submission of disputes to arbitration or to consideration shall be in all respects applicable to the dispute both in favor of and against such Power as if it were a party to this Covenant.

In case the Power not a party to this Covenant shall not accept the invitation of the Executive Council to become *ad hoc* a party, it shall be the duty of the Executive Council immediately to institute an inquiry into the circumstances and merits of the dispute involved and to recommend such joint action by the Contracting Powers as may seem best and most effectual in the circumstances disclosed.

### ARTICLE X.

If hostilities should be begun or any hostile action taken against the Contracting Power by the Power not a party to this Covenant before a decision of the dispute by arbitrators or before investigation, report and recommendation by the Executive Council in regard to the dispute, or contrary to such recommendation, the Contracting Powers engage thereupon to cease all commerce and communication with that Power and also to unite in blockading and closing the frontiers of that Power to all commerce or intercourse with any part of the world, and to employ jointly any force which may be agreed upon to accomplish that object. The Contracting Powers also undertake to unite in coming to the assistance of the Contracting Power against which hostile action has been taken, and to combine their armed forces in its behalf.

## ARTICLE XI.

In case of a dispute between states not parties to this Covenant, any Contracting Power may bring the matter to the attention of the Body of Delegates or the Executive Council, who shall thereupon tender the good offices of the League with a view to the peaceable settlement of the dispute.

If one of the states, a party to the dispute, shall offer and agree to submit its interests and cause of action wholly to the control and decision of the League, that state shall *ad hoc* be deemed a Contracting Power. If no one of the states, parties to the dispute, shall so offer and agree, the Body of Delegates shall through the Executive Council or of its own motion take such action and make such recommendation to the governments as will prevent hostilities and result in the settlement of the dispute.

## ARTICLE XII.

Any Power not a party to this Covenant, whose government is based upon the principle of popular self-government, may apply to the Body of Delegates for leave to become a party. If the Body of Delegates shall regard the granting thereof as likely to promote the peace, order, and security of the World, they shall act favorably on the application, and their favorable action shall operate to constitute the Power so applying in all respects a full signatory party to this Covenant. This action shall require the affirmative vote of two-thirds of the Body of Delegates.

## ARTICLE XIII.

The Contracting Powers severally agree that the present Covenant is accepted as abrogating all treaty obligations *inter se* which are inconsistent with the terms hereof, and solemnly engage that they will not enter into any engagements inconsistent with the terms hereof.

In case any of the Powers signatory hereto or subsequently admitted to the League shall, before becoming a party to this Covenant, have undertaken any treaty obligations which are inconsistent with the terms of this Covenant, it shall be the duty of such Power to take immediate steps to procure its release from such obligations.


## SUPPLEMENTARY AGREEMENTS.
### I.

To the colonies formerly part of the German Empire, and to those territories formerly belonging to Turkey which include Armenia, Kurdestan, Syria, Mesopotamia, Palestine and Arabia, which are inhabited by peoples not able to stand by themselves under the strenuous conditions of the modern world, there should be applied the principle that the well-being and development of such peoples form a sacred trust of civilization and that securities for the performance of this trust should be embodied in the constitution of the League.

The best method of giving practical effect to this principle is that the tutelage of such peoples should be entrusted to advanced nations who by reason of their resources, their experience or their geographical position, can best undertake this responsibility, and that this tutelage should be exercised by them as mandatories on behalf of the League.

The character of the mandate must differ according to the stage of development of the people, the geographical situation of the territory, its economic conditions and other similar circumstances.

## II.

Certain communities formerly belonging to the Turkish Empire have reached a stage of development where their existence as independent nations can be provisionally recognized subject to the rendering of administrative advice and assistance by a mandatory power until such time as they are able to stand alone. The wishes of these communities must be a principal consideration in the selection of the mandatory power.

Other peoples, especially those of Central Africa, are at such a stage that the mandatory must be responsible for the administration of the territory subject to conditions which will guarantee the prohibition of abuses such as the slave trade, the arms traffic and the liquor traffic, and the prevention of the establishment of fortifications or military and naval bases and of military training of the natives for other than police purposes and the defense of territory, and will also secure equal opportunities for the trade and commerce of other members of the League.

There are territories, such as South-West Africa and certain of the Islands in the South Pacific, which, owing to the sparseness of their population, or their small size, or their remoteness from the centres of civilization, or their geographical contiguity to the mandatory state, and other circumstances, can be best administered under the laws of the mandatory state as if integral portions thereof, subject to the safeguards above-mentioned in the interests of the indigenous population.

## III.

In every case of mandate, the mandatory state shall render to the League an annual report in reference to the territory committed to its charge.

The degree of authority, control, or administration to be exercised by the mandatory State or agency shall in each case be explicitly defined by the Executive Council in a special Act or Charter which shall reserve to the League complete power of supervision, and which shall also reserve to the people of any such territory or governmental unit the right to appeal to the League for the redress or correction of any breach of the mandate by the mandatory State or agency or for the substitution of some other State or agency, as mandatory.

The object of all such tutelary oversight and administration on the part of the League of Nations shall be to build up in as short a time as possible out of the people or territory under its guardianship a political unit which can take charge of its own affairs, determine its own connections, and choose its own policies. The League may at any time release such people or territory from tutelage and consent to its being set up as an independent unit. It shall also be the right and privilege of any people or territory to petition the League to take such action, and upon such petition being made it shall be the duty of the League to take the petition under full and friendly consideration with a view of determining the best interests of the people or territory in question in view of all circumstances of their situation and development.

### IV.

No new State shall be recognized by the League or admitted into its membership except on condition that its military and naval forces and armaments shall conform to standards prescribed by the League in respect of it from time to time.

### V.

The Contracting Powers will work to establish and maintain fair hours and humane conditions of labor for all those within their several jurisdictions and they will exert their influence in favor of the adoption and maintenance of a similar policy and like safeguards wherever their industrial and commercial relations extend. Also they will appoint Commissions to study conditions of industry and labor in their international aspects and to make recommendations thereon, including the extension and improvement of existing conventions.

### VI.

The League shall require all new States to bind themselves as a condition precedent to their recognition as independent or autonomous States and the Executive Council shall exact of all States seeking admission to the League, the promise to accord to all racial or national minorities within their several jurisdictions exactly the same treatment and security, both in law and in fact, that is accorded the racial or national majority of their people.

## VII.

Recognizing religious persecution and intolerance as fertile sources of war, the Contracting Powers agree, and the League shall exact from all new States and all States seeking admission to it the promise that they will make no law prohibiting or interfering with the free exercise of religion, and that they will in no way discriminate, either in law or in fact, against those who practice any particular creed, religion, or belief whose practices are not inconsistent with public order or public morals.

## VIII.

When the rights of belligerents on the high seas outside territorial waters shall have been defined by international convention, it is hereby agreed and declared as a fundamental Covenant that no Power or combination of Powers shall have a right to overstep in any particular the clear meaning of the definitions thus established; but that it shall be the right of the League from time to time and on special occasion to close the seas in whole or in part against a particular Power or Powers for the purpose of enforcing the international Covenants here entered into.

## IX.

It is hereby covenanted and agreed by the Contracting Powers that no treaty entered into by them shall be regarded as valid, binding, or operative until it shall have been published and made known to all the other States members of the League.

## X.

It is further covenanted and agreed by the Contracting Powers that in their fiscal and economic regulations and policy no discrimination shall be made between one nation and another among those with which they have commercial and financial dealings.

Printed copy (WP, DLC).


## To David Hunter Miller

My dear Mr. Miller:                    Paris, 3 February, 1919.

Thank you for the copies of the revised "Covenant." I am deeply indebted to you for a highly serviceable and extraordinarily prompt piece of work and I hope with all my heart that it will serve as the basis of the work of the Drafting Commission.

Cordially and sincerely yours,   Woodrow Wilson

TLS (D. H. Miller Papers, DLC).

## From the Diary of Dr. Grayson

Monday, February 3, 1919.

The President attended the initial conference of the League of Nations Committee, which began its work of framing the league constitution. He made a long speech dealing with the subject.[1] Leaving the conference we proceeded to the Chamber of Deputies, where the President was given a reception and made a speech. This was a very formal function and was very largely attended.

[1] The Editors have not found a copy of this speech.


## From the Diary of Colonel House

February 3, 1919.

I had my usual call from Wiseman. He said Lord Robert was greatly perturbed when he heard that the President, Miller and I had gotten together last night and revamped our own Covenant of the League of Nations. Miller, the President and I worked from a little after eight until after ten o'clock. I tried to get the President to accept the draft which had been agreed upon Friday night which Cecil, Smuts, he and I had prepared.[1] He said the document had "no warmth or color in it" and he very much preferred the one which we already had. I agreed with him, and yet I knew the wisest thing to do was to accept the other as a basis for our discussions today. After we revamped our own, Miller remained up the entire night supervising the printing of it and had it ready for us by breakfast this morning. Sir William thought it would be exceedingly unwise to let Lord Robert come into the general meeting of the Committee this afternoon feeling as he did, and asked what suggestions I had to make. I told him to have Cecil come a quarter of an hour before the meeting and I would undertake to have the President here and we would see what could be done.

I telephoned the President and told him we were making a mistake in not keeping Lord Robert Cecil in harmony with us. That he was the only one connected with the British Government who really had the League of Nations at heart. Lloyd George and others were for it because of the pressure of public opinion, but if we had Cecil with us, Lloyd George would either have to agree or Cecil would make a fight in Parliament which George would not wish.

The three of us met promptly at 2.15 in my study. The meeting bade fair to be stormy for the first seven or eight minutes. After that, things went better and the President finally decided to do what I advised him to do last night, that is, to take the joint draft of Miller and Hirst and use it as a basis for discussion. After that, everything went smoothly.

The full Committee of fifteen met in one of my salons and all during the discussion Lord Robert was on our side. I think the President was quite content that he had yielded the point. We did not get very far because we did not have the Covenant translated into French. It was agreed we should do this and present it to the delegates tomorrow morning, and that tomorrow night we should again meet here at 8.30 for a detailed discussion of the Articles.

The President, I thought, showed considerable nervousness both during the conversation with Lord Robert Cecil and afterward in the general meeting over which he presided. I sat between him and Lord Robert. I did no talking, but prompted first one and then the other. Orlando, I placed at the President's right. The others I had sit wherever they desired. I had placed in the room a great round table, about which the fifteen of us sat. I could not help thinking that perhaps this room would be the scene of the making of the most important human document that has ever been written. It certainly will be the greatest if we do our work well.

¹ That is, the Hurst-Miller draft.

## From the Diary of Lord Robert Cecil

February 3 [1919].

Just after I had seen Loudon¹ I suddenly heard that the President intended to reject the re-draft of his proposals made by Hurst and Miller and revert to his own old form, which filled me with consternation. After one or two agitated interviews with Wiseman, Smuts and others, I went down at 2.15 to the Crillon to meet House and the President. I did not conceal my severe disappointment at this new change, and pointed out that it would inevitably mean very long delay; that Bourgeois would be certain to ask for a translation of the document; and that it would expose us to very elaborate and detailed amendments. After some little discussion the President, who was a little apologetic in manner, agreed to present the Hurst-Miller draft as a skeleton, reserving to himself the right to clothe it with flesh and blood, as he put it. The incident is exceedingly characteristic of the great tenacity of his mind, and his incapacity for cooperation resulting from a prolonged period of autocratic power. I do not think that he had the least idea that he had taken any unusual course in abruptly tearing up a draft which we had jointly agreed to have prepared as our working text. He was mildly surprised that I should resent it, and when House interjected that Miller had sat up for two nights drafting and redrafting to please the President the latter took very little interest in the observation.

We then went into the Committee itself, and as he had met me so nobly I supported all his most tyrannical proposals, coercing poor Bourgeois into discussing the draft which he saw for the first time, with only twenty four hours' delay for it to be translated and considered. However, there really is very little to say in the committee, since we are, except on a few points, all agreed—at least I hope so.

¹ That is, John Loudon, the former Dutch Foreign Minister.

# From the Peace Conference Diary of Sir William Wiseman

February 3rd, 1919. (Monday).

NOTE ON LEAGUE OF NATIONS.

After much difficulty CECIL persuaded the PRESIDENT to let HURST and MILLER re-write the President's draft-treaty and cut it down to a small and really legal document. This was ready on Sunday, and the first meeting of the Committee of the League of Nations was fixed for Monday at 2.30. On Sunday night, however, the President went through the Miller-Hurst draft with HOUSE, and decided to reject it altogether and return to his original draft. This I only learnt early Monday morning, and persuaded House to have a meeting between the President and Cecil at 2.15, or a quarter of an hour before the Committee meeting. CECIL, when I told him, was furious, but HOUSE persuaded the President to revert to the Hurst-Miller draft, and when CECIL got down at 2.15 the PRESIDENT was ready to agree. The PRESIDENT had then to keep the Meeting going with a speech while MILLER went round to his office and got enough copies of the old draft to be handed round.

# Hankey's Notes of a Meeting of the Council of Ten¹

Quai d'Orsay, February 3, 1919, 11 A.M.

BC-21

[Clemenceau opened the meeting with arrangements for appointment of delegates to the Commission for Teschen and the Commission to Rumania. Wilson said that the American delegate to the former had not yet been found; "there were so few available Americans on this side of the water."]

M. CLEMENCEAU said he wished to raise the question of the appointment of additional delegates to represent the Small Powers on the various committees. The number of delegates to form part of each of these committees had been duly agreed upon and were already appointed; but he thought they should if possible, endeavour to meet the special wishes of the Smaller Powers, treating each case on its merits.

First as regards the League of Nations. The Conference had decided that each of the Great Powers should appoint two delegates, and that 5 delegates should be elected to represent the whole of the Smaller Powers.

The Smaller Powers had nominated delegates from Belgium, Serbia, Brazil, China, and Portugal, but they now asked that an additional delegate should be appointed by each of the following countries, namely, Poland, Greece, Czecho-Slovakia, and Rumania.

PRESIDENT WILSON thought that the proposal would have the effect of constituting a very large committee, and the representation of the Smaller Powers would thereby become equal to the representation of the Great Powers. The League of Nations committee, however, was to meet that afternoon, and he proposed that he should be empowered to put the question to the Drafting committee for decision.

[This was agreed to, and the question of appointing supplementary delegates to represent the smaller powers on the Inter-Allied Commission on the International Regime of Ports, Waterways, and Railways was left to that body to decide. Clemenceau then said that the conference had agreed that each of the great powers should have three representatives on the Inter-Allied Commission on Reparation, and that ten seats should be reserved for the smaller powers. Accordingly, two representatives each of Poland, Rumania, Serbia, Greece, and Belgium had been appointed. He continued:] Czecho-Slovakia now also asked to appoint a representative on account of its paramount economic and financial interests in connection with the final liquidation of the Austro-Hungarian Empire, especially as they had agreed to take over part of the Austrian debt. If Czecho-Slovakia were admitted, all the Powers interested in the liquidation of the Austro-Hungarian Empire would be represented, as Poland, Rumania, and Serbia, were duly represented.

MR. LLOYD GEORGE agreed that Czecho-Slovakia had a good case and should be represented.

M. CLEMENCEAU pointed out that Portugal had also put forward claims to a seat.

(After further discussion it was agreed that two additional seats should be granted to Czecho-Slovakia on the Inter-Allied Commission on Reparation.)

[Lloyd George announced that the British Attorney General and Solicitor General would represent their country on the Inter-Allied Commission on Breaches of the Laws of War.]

(At this stage M. Venizelos and M. Politis,[2] members of the Greek Delegation to the Peace Conference, accompanied by their experts M. Speranza and M. Rentis[3] were admitted to the Conference.)

M. CLEMENCEAU asked M. Venizelos to explain the territorial claims of Greece.

M. VENIZELOS said that he came there at the invitation of the Great Powers to put forward the territorial claims of Greece, and he proposed to divide the subject into the following chapters:

<table>
<tr><td>N. Epirus;</td><td>Thrace;</td></tr>
<tr><td>The Isles;</td><td>Asia Minor.</td></tr>
</table>

[He discussed the first three "chapters" in great detail. Wilson did not participate in the discussion.]

(It was decided that M. Venizelos should put forward the claims of Greece to Asia Minor on the following day.)

(The meeting adjourned to 11 o'clock on Tuesday, the 4th of February, 1919.)

T MS (SDR, RG 256, 180.03101/28, DNA).
  [1] The complete text of these notes is printed in *PPC*, III, 856-66.
  [2] Nicholas Politis, Minister of Foreign Affairs.
  [3] N. Speranza, a director in the Greek Ministry of Foreign Affairs; Constantine Rentis, or Rendis, a chief of section in the Greek Ministry of Foreign Affairs.

# Minutes of a Meeting of the Commission on the League of Nations

FIRST MEETING.

HELD AT THE HOTEL CRILLON, FEBRUARY 3, 1919, AT 2:30 P.M.
President WILSON *in the Chair.*

Present:

| | |
|---|---|
| President Wilson<br>Colonel House | } United States of America. |
| Lord Robert Cecil<br>Lieutenant General J. C. Smuts | } British Empire. |
| Mr. Léon Bourgeois<br>Mr. Larnaude | } France. |
| Mr. Orlando<br>Senator Scialoja | } Italy. |
| Baron Makino<br>Viscount Chinda | } Japan. |
| Mr. Hymans | Belgium. |
| Mr. Epitacio Pessoa | Brazil. |

Mr. V. K. Wellington Koo          China.
Mr. Jayme Batalha Reis           Portugal.
Mr. Vesnitch                     Serbia.

*The Chairman* laid before the Commission a Draft Covenant, the text of which is contained in Annex 1,[1] which it was agreed should form the basis of the Commission's deliberations. Mr. Léon Bourgeois laid before the Commission the French proposals relating to the creation of a League of Nations (Annex 2).[2] Mr. Orlando laid before the Commission an Italian Draft Scheme (Annex 3).[3]

A general discussion followed dealing with the procedure to be adopted.

*(The meeting adjourned to meet at 8:30 P.M. on the 4th February at the same place.)*

Printed copy (WP, DLC).
[1] The Hurst-Miller draft.
[2] Printed in Miller, *The Drafting of the Covenant*, II, 238-46.
[3] As has been noted, it is printed in *ibid*, pp. 246-55.


# An Address to the French Chamber of Deputies[1]

February 3, 1919

Mr. President: I am keenly aware of the unusual and distinguished honor you are paying me by permitting me to meet you in this place and address you from this historical platform. Indeed, Sir, as day follows day, and week has followed week, in this hospitable land of France, I have felt the sense of comradeship every day become more and more vivid; the thrill of sympathy every day become more and more intimate, and it has seemed to me that the meaning of history was being singularly made clear. We knew before this war began that France and America were united in affection. We knew the occasion which drew the two nations together in those years, which now seem so far away, when the world was first beginning to thrill with the impulse of human liberty, when soldiers of France came to help the struggling little Republic of America to get to its feet and proclaim one of the first victories of freedom.

We had never forgotten that, but we did not see the full meaning of it. A hundred years and more went by, and the spindles were

[1] Delivered at the Palais Bourbon in the early evening. President Poincaré had accompanied Wilson to the palace. Clemenceau and all members of the French ministry were present, as were such distinguished guests as Lloyd George, Balfour, and Lansing. Wilson was greeted in a speech by Paul Eugène Louis Deschanel, the President of the Chamber of Deputies. The audience cheered Wilson for five minutes when he was introduced and remained standing during his speech. *New York Times*, Feb. 4, 1919. An English translation, Hw MS, of Deschanel's remarks is in WP, DLC.

slowly weaving the web of history. We did not see the pattern until the threads began to come together; we did not see it to be complete, the whole art of the designer to be made plain. For look what has happened. In that far off day when France came to the assistance of America, America was fighting Great Britain, and now she is linked as closely to Great Britain as she is to France. We see now how these apparently diverging lines of history are coming together. The nations which once stood in battle array against one another are now shoulder and shoulder facing a common enemy. It was a long time before we saw that, and in the last four years something has happened that is unprecedented in the history of mankind. It is nothing less than this, that bodies of men on both sides of the sea and in all parts of the world have come to realize their comradeship in freedom.

France, in the meantime, as we have so often said, stood at the frontier of freedom. Her lines ran along the very lines that divided the home of freedom from the home of military despotism. Hers was the immediate peril. Hers was the constant dread. Hers was the most pressing necessity of preparation; and she had constantly to ask herself this question, "If the blow falls, who will come to our assistance?" And the question was answered in the most unexpected way. Her allies came to her assistance, but many more than her allies. The free peoples of the world came to her assistance. And then America paid her debt of gratitude to France by sending her sons to fight upon the soil of France. She did more. She assisted in drawing the forces of the world together in order that France might never again feel her isolation, in order that France might never again feel that hers was a lonely peril, would never again have to ask the question who would come to her assistance.

For the alternative is a terrible alternative for France. I do not need to point out to you that east of you in Europe the future is full of questions. Beyond the Rhine, across Germany, across Poland, across Russia, across Asia, there are questions unanswered, and they may be for the present unanswerable. France still stands at a frontier. France still stands in the presence of these threatening and unanswered questions—threatening because unanswered—stands waiting for the solution of matters which touch her directly and intimately and constantly. And if she must stand alone, what must she do? She must be constantly armed. She must put upon her people a constant burden of taxation. She must undergo a sacrifice that may become intolerable. And not only she, but the other nations of the world, must do the like. They must stand armed cap-a-pie. They must be ready for any terrible incident of injustice. The thing is not conceivable. I visited the other day a portion of the devastated regions of France. I saw the noble city of Rheims in ruin, and I could not help saying to myself, "Here is where the blow fell, because the rulers of the world did not sooner see how to prevent it." The rulers of the world have been thinking of the relations of governments and forgetting the relations of peoples. They have been thinking of the maneuvers of international dealings, when what they ought to have been thinking of was the fortunes of men and women and the safety of homes, and the care that they should take that their people should be happy because they were safe. They now know that the only way to do it is to make it certain that the same thing will happen always that happened this time, that there shall never be any doubt or waiting or surmise, but that whenever France or any other free people is threatened the whole world will be ready to vindicate its liberty.

It is for that reason, I take it, that I find such a warm and intelligent enthusiasm in France for the society of nations. The society of nations France, with her keen vision, France with her prophetic vision, sees to be not only the need of France, but the need of mankind. And she sees that the sacrifices which are necessary for the establishment of the society of nations are not to be compared with the sacrifices that will be necessary if she does not have the society. A little abatement of independence of action is not to be compared with the constant dread of another catastrophe.

The whole world's heart has bled that the catastrophe should have fallen on the fair cities and areas of France. There was no more beautiful country. There was no more prosperous country. There was no more free-spirited people in it. All the world admired France, and none of the world grudged France her greatness and her prosperity, except those who grudged her her liberty. And it profited us, terrible as the cost has been, to witness what has happened, to see with the physical eye what has happened because injustice was wrought. The President of the Chamber has pictured, as I cannot picture, the appalling sufferings, the terrible tragedy of France, but it is a tragedy which need not be repeated. As the pattern of history has disclosed itself, it has disclosed the hearts of men drawing towards one another. Comradeships have become vivid. The purpose of association has become evident. The nations of the world are about to consummate a brotherhood which will make it unnecessary in the future to maintain those crushing armaments which make the peoples suffer almost as much in peace as they suffer in war.

When the soldiers of America crossed the ocean, they did not bring with them merely their arms. They brought with them a very vivid conception of France. They landed upon the soil of France with quickened pulses. They knew that they had come to do a thing which the heart of America had long wished to do. When General Pershing stood at the tomb of Lafayette and said, "Lafayette, we are here," it was as if he had said, "Lafayette, here is the completion of the great story whose first chapter you assisted to write." The world has seen the great plot worked out, and now the people of France may rest assured that their prosperity is secure, because their homes are secure; and men everywhere not only wish her safety and prosperity, but are ready to assure her that with all the force and wealth at their command they will guarantee her security and safety. So, as we sit from day to day at the Quai d'Orsay I think to myself, "We might, if we could gain audience of the free peoples of the world, adopt the language of General Pershing and say, 'Friends, men, humble women, little children, we are here; we are here as your friends, as your champions, as your representatives. We have come to work out for you a world which is fit to live in and in which all countries can enjoy the heritage of liberty for which France and America and England and Italy have paid so dear.' "[2]

T MS (WP, DLC).

[2] There is a two-page WWT outline of this address, with the composition date of Feb. 1, 1919, in WP, DLC.

## To Herbert Clark Hoover

My dear Mr. Hoover:                               Paris, 3 February, 1919.

I dare say it would be serviceable to discuss these matters with the press as you suggest,[1] but how can you when the French press is so carefully censored by the Government that everything is excluded which they do not wish to have published. You could probably get it in the English and the American papers but could you get publicity for it anywhere else?

I am returning the papers marked "A" and "B" herewith[2] because your letter does not show clearly whether they are merely memoranda for my eye or whether they are papers which you wish submitted to the Supreme War Council when it meets.

Cordially and faithfully yours,   Woodrow Wilson

TLS (Hoover Archives, CSt-H).

[1] Wilson was responding to HCH to WW, Feb. 1, 1919, printed as an addendum.

[2] See HCH to WW, Feb. 4, 1919, with its Enclosure.

## To Boghos Nubar

My dear Mr. Nubar:                    Paris, 3 February, 1919.

It would give me genuine pleasure to receive you and see you personally as you request in your letter of January 29th, but I must be perfectly frank and tell you that it would be a great deal more serviceable if you would send me a written memorandum because in these days of hurry and preoccupation what I am told orally does not, I find, remain in my mind as clearly as I should wish to retain it, and I should have need in any case to ask you for a written memorandum. Will you not be gracious enough to let me have one in order that I may be as serviceable as possible?

Cordially and sincerely yours,   [Woodrow Wilson]

CCL (WP, DLC).

## To Lord Curzon

My dear Lord Curzon:                  Paris, 3 February, 1919.

Your gracious letter of January 23rd[1] reminding me of the honor Oxford University has done me in asking me to deliver the Romanes Lecture for the year 1919 and accept the degree of D.C.L., Honoris Causa, has reached me and given me a great deal of pleasure.

It is clear that I cannot get away from Paris on any errand not connected with the Peace Conference before returning to the United States, I am sorry to say. I am expecting, and I am so hoping, to return after the adjournment of our Congress on the 4th of March but I feel very guilty of keeping you and the other Oxford authorities in doubt as to what they may expect of me, and therefore write to ask if it is not your judgment that I had better abandon the hope of delivering the Romanes Lecture and receiving the degree at the hands of the University. I would personally be quite willing to have the Vice Chancellor issue the statement which you suggest, were it not for the fear in my mind that the work here might develop in such a way as to make it unconscientious for me to withdraw either my presence or my thought from it. My own personal judgment is that I ought in fairness to the University to say that I cannot come. This is a very great disappointment to me but my impression of the engrossing character of what we have undertaken here has been so enhanced by the labors of the past few weeks that I cannot deceive myself about it any longer.

I feel that the University has done all that it could to honor me in proposing these appointments and I beg that you will express to

your colleagues my deep appreciation and my genuine disappointment.    Cordially and sincerely yours,   [Woodrow Wilson]

CCL (WP, DLC).
  ¹ Lord Curzon to WW, Jan. 23, 1919, ALS (WP, DLC).


## From Edward Mandell House

Dear Governor,                                    Paris, [Feb. 3, 1919]
    I believe that what you have said today will hearten the people
of the world as nothing you have said before. It was complete and
satisfying.                                            E.M.H.

ALI (WP, DLC).


## From Robert Lansing

My dear Mr. President:                       Paris. February 3, 1919.
    I am deeply interested, as you know, in the constitution and
procedure of international courts of arbitrations, and having participated in five proceedings of this sort I feel that I can speak with
a measure of authority.
    In the first place let me say that a tribunal, on which represent-
atives of the litigants sit as judges, has not proved satisfactory even
though the majority of the tribunal are nationals of other countries.
However well prepared from experience on the bench to render
strict justice, the litigants' arbitrators act in fact as advocates. As
a consequence the neutral arbitrators are decidedly hampered in
giving full and free expression to their views and there is not that
frank exchange of opinion which should characterize the conference of judges. It has generally resulted in a compromise, in which
the nation in the wrong gains a measure of benefit and the nation
in the right is deprived of a part of the remedy to which it is entitled.
In fact an arbitration award is more of a political and diplomatic
arrangement than it is a judicial determination. I believe that this
undesirable result can be in large measure avoided by eliminating
arbitrators of the litigant nations. It is only in the case of monetary
claims that these observations do not apply.
    Another difficulty has been the method of procedure before in-
ternational tribunals. This does not apply to monetary claims, but
to disputes arising out of boundaries, interpretation of treaties, national rights, &c. The present method of an exchange of cases and
of countercases is more diplomatic than judicial, since it does not

put the parties in the relation of complainant and defendant. This relation can in every case be established, if not by mutual agreement, then by some agency of the League of Nations charged with that duty. Until this reform of procedure takes place there will be no definition of issues and arbitration will continue to be the long and elaborate proceeding it has been in the past.

There is another practical obstacle to international arbitration as now conducted which ought to be considered, and that is the cost. This obstacle does not affect the wealthy nations but it does prevent small and poor nations from resorting to it as a means of settling disputes. Just how this can be remedied I am not prepared to say, although possibly the international support of all arbitral tribunals might be provided. At any rate I feel that something should be done to relieve the great expense which now prevents many of the smaller nations from resorting to arbitration.

I would suggest, therefore, that the Peace Treaty contain a provision directing the League of Nations to hold a conference or summon a conference to take up this whole matter and draft an international treaty dealing with the constitution of arbitral tribunals and radically revising the procedure.

On account of the difficulties of the subject, which do not appear on the surface but which experience has shown to be very real, I feel that it would be impracticable to provide in the Peace Treaty too definitely the method of constituting arbitral tribunals. It will require considerable thought and discussion to make arbitration available to the poor as well as the rich, to make an award a judicial settlement rather that a diplomatic compromise, and to supersede the cumbersome and prolonged procedure with its duplication of documents and maps by a simple method which will settle the issues and materially shorten proceedings which now unavoidably drag along for months, if not for years.

Faithfully yours,   Robert Lansing.

TLS (WP, DLC).


# From George Creel

My dear Mr. President:                    Paris, 3 February, 1919.

As I told you yesterday, I was tremendously impressed with Karolyi[1], the new President of Hungary, and I feel intensely that his government is worth saving. He demobilized his army, as you know, and from that very day every provision of the armistice has been violated by the Allies.

The two things that can save him are:

(1) The Peace Commission's insistence upon the integrity of the armistice provisions;

(2) A note to Karolyi, at the earliest possible date, asking him to send a delegation to present the case of Hungary.

I also urge, as a matter of real importance, that you see the correspondents of the American daily papers between now and Saturday, and once again before you sail. Have the invitation confined to the daily papers, one representative from each paper, and in this way only about twenty men will attend. The interview will not be for publication, but simply for their guidance. I am convinced that it will make for splendid feeling, and be of the greatest advantage.

I would also like to suggest that you give ten minutes, some time before Saturday, to General Kernan. He goes to Poland next Saturday.[2] He is a pretty big man, very wise and very able, but utterly in the dark as to what he is to do when he gets to Poland.

Believe me,　　　　　Very respectfully,　George Creel

TLS (WP, DLC).
[1] About Mihály Karolyi, see the Enclosure with RL to WW, Nov. 9, 1918, Vol. 53.
[2] Maj. Gen. Francis Joseph Kernan, at this time a technical adviser on military questions to the American Commission to Negotiate Peace, and Robert H. Lord had been nominated as the American members of the Inter-Allied Commission to Poland, about which see the minutes of the Supreme War Council, Jan. 22, 1919, 11 a.m.

# From Joseph Patrick Tumulty

[The White House] February 4 [3], 1919

No. 31. Conferees after six (?) years of controversy have agreed on oil leasing bill. Ferris said all members of conference committee, numbering ten, agreed to report, with the exception of Smoot, who wishes to postpone action until next session so that Republicans can propose unworkable bill, thus inviting Presidential veto for use to alienate West. Ferris says bill protects every right of Government, but fears Gregory may try to block passage and suggests that you cable Gregory telling him that opposition, in view of full agreement, is unwise.

We are trying to force action on water power legislation, suffrage, and appropriations so as to obviate necessity for extra session; make another attempt [making progress].[1]

Am still in bed but keeping in touch with things.

Tumulty.

T telegram (WP, DLC).
[1] Correction from the copy in the Tumulty Papers, DLC.

## From William Levi Hutcheson[1]

Indianapolis, Ind. Feb. 3 [1919]

During the period in which our country was engaged in active conflict of war with the enemy the workers responded nobly to their countrys needs and while there were some difficulties and misunderstandings between workers and their employers the workers showed their Americanism by responding and conforming to the methods of adjustment as made by the various instrumentalities of the Government one of which was the national war labor board. Since the signing of the armistice there have been occasions when the war labor board made findings as affecting the workers on work being done under supervision of the war department. On several of these occasions the war department has refused to be bound by the awards of the board. I would respectfully request that you notify the war department to comply with and observe awards as made by the war labor board and that they submit to the jurisdiction of the board matters that cannot be settled between the war department and the workmen as their attitude at the present time is constructing [obstructing] the progress of our country and they as well as other departments of our Government should be helpful.

Wm. L. Hutcheson.[2]

T telegram (WP, DLC).
[1] President of the United Brotherhood of Carpenters and Joiners of America and a member of the National War Labor Board.
[2] Wilson sent a copy of this telegram to Baker and asked for his advice. WW to NDB, Feb. 5, 1919, T telegram (WP, DLC).

## Frank Lyon Polk to Robert Lansing

Washington. February 3, 1919.

552. URGENT For the Secretary of State.

There is pending in the Foreign Relations Committee a resolution of sympathy for Irish freedom. One proposal goes as far as requesting the President to instruct the Peace Delegates to present the matter for consideration in Paris. I have been able to delay the matter in committee for over a month but I understand it may be forced out this week unless I can tell committee the President would prefer to have it held in committee. Both sides are playing politics with the resolution in order to get the Irish vote and I hesitate to recommend that the President interfere. I, however, feel that I should ask you to lay the matter before him and request that you give me at earliest possible moment his views.

The Irish Party here are shortly to hold a convention and intend to select delegates to go to Paris to present the Irish cause. Ex-Senator O'Gorman, Bourke Cochrane and others of that caliber mentioned as delegates. I think I have been able to discourage this movement but any prophecy in regard to an Irish meeting is dangerous. If the question of passports for the delegates does not come up now it is reasonably certain to come up later and I suggest that this matter should also be given consideration.          Polk.

T telegram (WP, DLC).

## From the Diary of Dr. Grayson

Tuesday, February 4, 1919.

The President put in a fifteen-hour day today.[1] He had conferences in the morning with Colonel House, who talked with him about the general aspirations of the French, and with Secretary of State Lansing, who told him about his various conferences.

In the afternoon the President conferred with Dr. Wellington Koo, the Chinese Minister to the United States, and also met Premier Delacroix, of Belgium.

After dinner he went to the Crillon Hotel, where he presided over a meeting of the League of Nations Committee. This committee had a distinctly lively session, as the French were explaining the necessity of giving the League, when created, a General Staff of an Army and Navy to enforce its decrees. Of course, the President was opposed to this, but Bourgeois made several long-winded speeches, and it was very late before the President went back to the Murat Palace and to bed.

[1] For one thing, he attended a meeting of the Council of Ten at eleven o'clock in the morning, where Vénisélos presented Greece's claims to western Asia minor. Wilson made only two brief comments. Minutes of this meeting are printed in PPC, III, 867-75.

## To Oscar Otto[1]

My dear Mr. Otto:                    Paris, February 4, 1919.

I have learned of the very late hours you have been keeping in order to print important documents, which it has been necessary for me to have with the least possible delay in connection with my work in the Peace Conference.

Your enthusiasm and spirit in this work has contributed in a real way in assisting me, and I am personally grateful to you for your help.      Cordially and sincerely yours,   Woodrow Wilson

TLS (received from O. Otto).
    ¹ A private in the army with the printing unit of the American Commission to Negotiate
Peace. Wilson wrote the same letter, *mutatis mutandis*, on February 4 to Sergeants
Jerome V. O'Hara and John J. Brady and Privates Edward McNulty, John J. Farrell,
Harry Brown, and Frank Fox, all CCL (WP, DLC).

## From Robert Lansing

My dear Mr. President:                    Paris February 4, 1919.

The Chinese Commission on the day following the presentation
of their rights to Shan-Tung informed me that they greatly feared
the Japanese would attempt to intimidate the Peking Government,
and persuade that Government to disown Doctor Koo's representation here. Their fears appear to have been well grounded. General
Churchill¹ has today received two telegrams from the Assistant
Military Attache at Peking showing that the Japanese Government
is attempting this very thing. I enclose copies of the telegrams.²
The reference in the first telegram to a statement by Premier Clemenceau is confirmed by a statement made to me by Doctor Koo
a few days ago that M. Clemenceau had made the same statement
to him.                    Faithfully yours,   Robert Lansing.

CCLS (R. Lansing Papers, DLC).
    ¹ That is, Brig. Gen. Marlborough Churchill.
    ² Capt. Hallet R. Robbins to M. Churchill, Feb. 3, 1919, two T telegrams (R. Lansing
Papers, DLC). The first telegram reported that Japanese officials had been making
unofficial representations to Chinese officials "looking toward demand that Chinese
Government disavow action of their delegates at Paris and submit to Japanese dictation
in the presentation of China's case before the Peace Conference." The Japanese, the
telegram continued, "threaten military intervention and to retain Kiao-Chou and the
whole of Shang-Tung permanently, also the immediate withdrawal of all financial support." The second telegram stated that the Japanese Minister to China, Torikichi Obata,
had formally presented this demand to the Chinese Acting Foreign Minister, Ch'en Lu,
on February 2 and had indeed "threatened military force." Robbins also noted that
Clemenceau had told the Chinese Minister to France, Hu Wei-te, on December 30,
1918, that he would like to "help China" but could not do so because of a secret treaty
between France and Japan. Robbins concluded with the remark that the President of
China, Hsü Shih-ch'ang, and Ch'en Lu were not disposed to yield to the Japanese
demand but feared that China would be "sold out by the Allies."

## From Frank Lyon Polk

                    Washington, February 4, 1919.

Urgent. 561. February 4th, 4:00 P.M. Important, confidential for
the attention of the President and the Secretary.

The following telegram received from Peking.

"February 3, 1:00 a.m. Your cipher telegram of January 31, 5:00
p.m.¹

*Strictly confidential.* I had a conversation with the acting Minister for Foreign Affairs² today shortly after the Japanese minister

had seen him. The latter remonstrated, declaring that his Government was greatly displeased with the statement of Minister Koo to the effect that the Chinese Government had no objection to making known the secret agreements. This ought not to be done without in each case first obtaining the consent of the Japanese Government. He then queried as to whom China is to rely upon, stating that England has her hands full with internal difficulties, while Japan has five hundred thousand tons naval vessels, and an army of one million men waiting. He also brought up the matter of the unpaid portion of the Japanese military loan, suggesting that, as the name of the War Participation Bureau has been changed to National Defense Bureau, it would be necessary for the Chinese Government specifically to ask for the continuance of name under this loan. As the Chinese Government is in no way seeking foreign military protection, and as the military party which controls the cabinet feels dependent on continued Japanese financial support, the inference from the above two statements is unmistakable.

Japanese Minister asked whether the Chinese Government wanted to publish the agreement of September 24th. This relates to the Shantung Railway and admits the succession of Japan to German rights in Shantung. It was negotiated by the Minister of Railways, Tsao,[3] and signed by Chinese Minister at Tokyo,[4] but never ratified. Reported to Department from fragmentary evidence in number 2361. (This will be forwarded to you shortly) Acting Minister for Foreign Affairs opposes ratification.

In reply to my question he said that the Government has already wired the Chinese delegation in appreciation of its action, but that the representations of the Japanese Minister would be taken up by the President and Premier[5] tomorrow. He stated that he was opposed to tying hands of the delegation. The latter understands that any point of information which may be asked by the American delegation with respect to treaties or otherwise is to be supplied. Acting Minister stated that copies of all treaties had been taken a[long] by Minister Lu.[6] I doubt that they have everything as some arrangements seem to have been made without knowledge of Foreign Office. If Chinese delegation has all the texts I shall urge Foreign Office again to telegraph them. Acting Minister also informed me that he felt much concerned because the French Premier had stated to Minister Lu that he should be glad to support China in the matter of Shantung, but was (?) by an existing agreement with Japan. What is this agreement? Acting Minister agreed that the case of China probably stood well in the public opinion of the world, but expressed fear that [if] bargaining like the above should succeed, China would be sacrificed. Veiled threats of the

Japanese Minister did not seem to frighten him unduly as he realized that military coercion at this time scarcely feasible. But he felt great concern about possible support of Japanese pretentions by certain foreign powers as well as about the aspirations of the Japanese supported military clique which is trying to render abortive Shanghai Peace Conference[7] and may succeed unless friendly powers supply sound guarantee of Chinese finance without delay. When I suggested joint proposal of President and Shanghai conference on this subject would probably receive favorable consideration, he said but time is everything in this matter."

Polk, Acting

T telegram (WP, DLC).

[1] FLP to P. S. Reinsch, Jan. 31, 1919, T telegram (SDR, RG 59, 793.94/762, DNA). This telegram was sent in response to RL to FLP, Jan. 30, 1919, T telegram (SDR, RG 59, 793.94/762, DNA). Lansing had informed Polk that the Japanese delegation at the peace conference had presented a claim to the unconditional cession to Japan by Germany of the leased territory of Kiaochow, the railways, and other rights in Shantung Province. The Chinese delegation had stated that these rights should be returned to China and that the Sino-Japanese conventions of 1915 should be subject to revision at the peace conference. The Chinese presentation of their case had made "an excellent impression," Lansing commented, and, unless "some false move" was made at Peking, China had a good chance to recover its rights in Shantung. "The Chinese delegates," he continued, "fear some Japanese intrigue at Peking to bring pressure to bear here. I suggest you repeat the foregoing to Peking and instruct the Legation to keep the Commission and the Department fully informed. The Japanese delegates made a qualified promise to produce the text of all secret agreements with China relating to this subject. The Chinese would do well to telegraph promptly frankly and fully the texts of all such agreements."

Polk repeated Lansing's message verbatim to Reinsch. He suggested in addition that Reinsch express to the Chinese Foreign Ministry the hope that it would not submit to Japanese pressure and that it would give its delegates at the peace conference a free hand. He warned that the situation required "the most delicate and skillful diplomatic treatment" to avoid giving offense to the Japanese.

[2] Ch'en Lu.

[3] Ts'ao Ju-lin, Chinese Minister of Communications.

[4] Chang Tsung-hsiang.

[5] That is, Hsü Shih-ch'ang and Ch'ien Neng-hsun.

[6] That is, Lu Cheng-hsiang.

[7] Efforts had been under way since November 1918 to organize a peace conference to bring an end to the military and political conflict between two rival Chinese governments based at Peking and Canton which had originated from a splitting off of southern members of the Chinese Parliament in 1917. For a brief discussion of the very complicated factional struggle in China in these years, see John K. Fairbank, Edwin O. Reischauer, and Albert M. Craig, *East Asia: The Modern Transformation* (Boston, 1965), pp. 654-55. After long delay, much of it inspired by various factions on both sides who wanted no peace negotiations at all, the conference of delegates from the northern and southern governments assembled at Shanghai on February 20. It adjourned on February 28, reconvened on April 7, and continued until May 15, when it broke up over irreconcilable differences. Although efforts to revive the conference continued as late as October 1919, it never met again. For discussions of the origins, objectives, and course of the peace conference, see the American legation's reports on the general political situation and economic conditions in China for the quarters ended December 31, 1918; March 31, 1919; June 30, 1919; September 30, 1919; and December 31, 1919. The relevant portions are printed in *FR 1919*, I, 270-74, 359-60, 375-76, and 396-97, respectively. For the date of the first meeting of the conference, see T. Sammons to P. S. Reinsch, Feb. 21, 1919, *ibid.*, p. 299.

## From William Shepherd Benson

My dear Mr. President: Paris 4 February 1919.

In Paper No. 11, "On What Principle Should the Freedom of Neutral Shipping on the High Seas During War be Founded? What Should Be the General Rules Governing the Application of the Principle?,"[1] you will possibly recall that the fundamental principle is that in time of war the neutral state be held responsible for the acts of its citizens upon the high seas. In our study of this question we have been more and more impressed with its force and adaptibility.

Some of my Advisory Section in discussing this question informally with some of our British colleagues, have found the British at first entirely opposed to the principle, but upon further discussion they show an inclination to take our view. I consider that before allowing the Advisory Section on Naval Matters to discuss this subject any further, it is quite necessary that we have your views on the subject, or at least your approval before continuing the discussion.

My reason for troubling you with memoranda of this character is due to my anxiety to be absolutely sure that all action taken is in full accord with your views and wishes.

Very sincerely yours, W. S. Benson.

Dear Admiral,

I entirely approve a continuation of the discussion in order fully to develop the British view. I am very much interested, but must let the matter clear up for a while in my own mind.

W.W.

TLS (W. S. Benson Papers, DLC).
[1] See W. S. Benson to WW, Jan. 31, 1919, with Enclosure.

## From Herbert Clark Hoover, with Enclosure

Dear Mr. President: Paris, 4 February 1919.

An error in the enclosure sent to you in my letter of yesterday[1] with respect to the relaxation of blockade has, I am sorry to say, confused your mind on the matter. I enclose herewith the resolution drafted by Mr. McCormick and myself, which we are anxious to get through the Supreme War Council. It has three main purposes:

FIRST. There is no right in the law of God or man that we should longer continue to starve neutrals now that we have a surplus of food. That is the object of the first part of the first resolution.

SECOND. The French, by obstruction of every financial measure that we can propose to the feeding of Germany in the attempt to compel us to loan money to Germany for this purpose, have defeated every step so far for getting them the food which we have been promising for three months. The object of the second part of the first resolution and of the second resolution is to at least find some channel by which the Germans can help themselves by trade with neutrals and South America.

THIRD. The object of the third resolution is to allow the people bordering on the Mediterranean to get into production and trade with all their might and by so doing not only revive their commercial life but also to a large degree supply themselves with food and other commodities and thus take a large part of the burden of relief from the back of our government.

There is no possibility that with all the restrictions on trade taken off that the old Empire of Austria could ever resurrect any military importance. At the present time, we are actually furnishing food to points in Austria at the expense of governments that could be taken care of by private individuals if they could revive their foreign credits without enemy trade restrictions, blockade and censorship, etc., on commercial transactions. Of importance also in the longer view is that the Southwestern area of Europe simply cannot be fed with any governmental resources that either the Allies or ourselves can produce over the next six months, unless they be allowed to get into the production of exportable commodities at the earliest possible moment.

I have worked consistently since arriving in Europe on the 25th day of November to secure these objects and I have to confess that although they have been accepted in principle in first one department and one government after another, they are constantly defeated by one bureaucratic and special self-interest after another of various governments, and I can assure you that the blockade against neutrals and the Southwest is being used today for purely economic ends, when its sole justification was for the protection and furtherance of military operations, which justification is now gone.

I realize that there is still some political importance in maintaining the blockade against Germany within certain limits, but it does not apply to the rest of Europe. I can see no hope of securing the removal of these restrictions except by a direct and strong intervention through yourself and mandatory orders given by the Supreme War Council.

Any reference to a given department in any government will in many cases receive a negative opinion from individuals, simply because of interest in the self-perpetuation of bureaucracy or special interests of government or trade in a desire to continue the use of this weapon for aims entirely apart from the war. I am confident that no action is possible except of a mandatory character from the top. Faithfully yours, Herbert Hoover

TLS (WP, DLC).
[1] Actually, HCH to WW, Feb. 1, 1919.

### E N C L O S U R E

#### PROPOSED RESOLUTION
#### TO BE PRESENTED BY THE PRESIDENT TO SUPREME WAR COUNCIL.

The Supreme War Council at the present time sees no military objection to certain relaxations of economic control of the enemy and approves and recommends the following relaxation in existing export and import control:

1. Norway, Sweden, Denmark, Holland and Switzerland to be allowed to import unlimited amounts of foodstuffs and to be permitted to re-export foodstuffs to Germany subject to the control of the Associated Governments, the aggregate amount of such re-exports with other imports of foodstuffs by Germany, not to exceed the amount of foodstuffs which the Supreme War Council may, from time to time, have agreed to permit to be imported into Germany.

2. Residents of Germany to be permitted, in such manner and through such agency as may be approved by the Supreme Council of Food and Supply, to communicate with persons in foreign countries relative to the purchase of such amounts of foodstuffs as the Supreme War Council may have agreed shall be imported into Germany.

3. All commodities to be allowed to be imported into or exported from South Europe and countries bordering on the Mediterranean without limit as to amount and without guarantee against re-export of imports.

T MS (WP, DLC).

## Two Letters from Bernard Mannes Baruch

My dear Mr. President: Paris, February 4, 1919

When I left Washington I was told not to bring anyone with me,[1] consequently I am without sufficient men to cover the field. May I not now ask the privilege of bringing over the men that are necessary, which will be not more than ten? All of these men were associated with me in the work of the War Industries Board, have gained the confidence of the business world, and are especially fitted to meet the conditions that we have to face here. They were all volunteer workers, and doubtless they would be very glad to continue on that basis, but I should like to be able to pay their expenses here, if you think that proper, and I should like to know through what fund that would be done. Many of the war activities are ceasing, and I should like to have some additional space allotted outside the Crillon in which these men could do their work. All I need is your authorization.

I find on every side the tendency to force the United States into a position in which it will be assuming a larger part of the indebtedness incurred in the war. They are approaching this through several avenues: through the endeavor to guarantee the reparation assessed against Germany, which they intend to force through the League of Nations; another way by obtaining loans from us on a plea of inability to finance themselves in any other way, until we shall be in the position where we shall have practically assumed a larger share of the war debt. Another way in which they are approaching it is through the internationalization of exchange, which means the breaking down of our credit to their level, instead of letting the law of supply and demand work through the ordinary channels of trade.     Very truly yours,   Bernard M Baruch

TLS (WP, DLC).
   [1] Ammission to FLP, Dec. 18, 1918, reproduced in the Diary of G. Auchincloss, CtY, Dec. 19, 1918.


My dear Mr President,                           [Paris, c. Feb. 4, 1919]
   May I suggest that Dr Garfield would be of valuable assistance here. He has good sense, courage and the right viewpoint.
                              Sincerely   Bernard M Baruch

ALS (WP, DLC).


## Ignace Jan Paderewski to Edward Mandell House

[Warsaw] Feb. 4 1919.

Surrounded by enemy from all sides Danzig being in German hands Poland cannot communicate with civilized world. To our Commission and delegates about thirty people carrying important documents and material for Peace Conference unable to leave Warsaw. The Polish Government respectfully asks Peace Conference to deliver safe conducts for this Commission. Invasion of Polish South Galicia territory continues.[1] Several important positions and villages have been occupied by their troops. Their patrols have been already seen in our oil districts. Six hundred prominent citizens all leaders of Silesian peoples arrested and deported. College students mere children hanged.[2] Tcheque minister Foreign Affairs Shehla[3] affirmed in Parliament that occupation of Silesia took place with approval of Polish Government and with consent of entente powers and United States. The first assertion is untrue. The Government as Government considers the second equally false but public opinion greatly alarmed and concerned. People cannot conceive why at this moment of ever growing Eastern danger no assistance is being given and General Hallers Army[4] is detained in France while the Tcheques are allowed to make war on us because we possess what they would like to have. Kindly forgive my troubling you again and help before it is too late.                               J. Paderewski.

T telegram (WP, DLC).
  [1] A reference to the continuing conflict between Polish and Ukrainian military forces for control of the former Austro-Hungarian imperial province of Galicia, centering upon its capital of Lvov, or Lemberg. See Oleksa Horbač, "The Ukrainian-Polish War in Galicia," in Volodymyr Kubijovyč, ed., *Ukraine: A Concise Encyclopaedia* (2 vols., Toronto, 1963-71), I, 781-87.
  [2] The Editors have found no reference to these alleged events. More generally, Paderewski here referred to the seizure of Teschen by Czechoslovakian troops on January 23. For the background of this action, see Piotr S. Wandycz, *France and Her Eastern Allies, 1919-1925; French-Czechoslovak-Polish Relations from the Paris Peace Conference to Locarno* (Minneapolis, Minn., 1962), pp. 75-89.
  [3] Actually, Antonín Svehla, Minister of Home Affairs and acting Prime Minister at this time.
  [4] That is, the Polish army in France under the command of Gen. Józef Haller. For the lengthy negotiations among the United States, France, Great Britain, the Pilsudski government in Poland, and the Polish National Committee in Paris as to when and how Haller's army should return to Poland, see Lundgreen-Nielsen, *The Polish Problem at the Paris Peace Conference*, pp. 125-31, 136-61.


# Minutes of a Meeting of the Commission on the League of Nations

SECOND MEETING, FEBRUARY 4, 1919, AT 8:30 P.M.
President WILSON *in the Chair.*

The Commission entered upon the consideration of the Draft Covenant.[1]

The Preamble was provisionally passed, subject to the understanding, arrived at on the motion of Mr. Bourgeois, that it would be open to the Commission to reconsider it later after the Articles had been examined; and subject also to an amendment, proposed by Lord Robert Cecil and accepted by the Commission, to transfer the words, "In order to promote international co-operation" to the beginning of the Preamble as follows: "In order to promote international co-operation and to secure international peace. * * *"

A discussion followed on the title of the international body to be established; various preferences were expressed for the words, "Society," "Union," "League," "States," and "Nations" respectively.

*Mr. Pessoa* remarked that the word "Society" had a special meaning and belonged to the domain rather of private law than of international law. He preferred "League" or "Union." He also preferred the use of the word "State" to that of the word "Nation"; the "person" whose juridical life is the subject matter of international law is the State, not the nation. The phrase "League of States" or "Union of States" should therefore be used.

It was generally agreed that there was no object to be gained by altering the formula endorsed by popular usage in each language.

*Mr. Hymans* brought forward the request made for representation on the Commission of four other Powers, Greece, Poland, Roumania, and the Czecho-Slovak Republic, which had been referred to the Commission by the Conference. After discussion it was agreed that the new members should be admitted, and President Wilson undertook to convey this decision to the Conference.

*Mr. Batalha Reis* said that he considered it necessary to settle what language should be adopted for the authoritative text of the Covenant.

This question was left to be dealt with later by the Conference.

The Commission then proceeded to the discussion of the Articles of the Draft.

### ARTICLE I.

After some discussion on the point raised by Mr. Bourgeois as to whether the meetings of the Body of Delegates should be periodical or permanent, Article 1 was adopted, subject to the omission of the words "Representing the States more immediately concerned in the matters under discussion."

### ARTICLE 2.

The following amendments, proposed by *Lord Robert Cecil*, were adopted:

In the second paragraph for the words from "Not more than two representatives" down to the end of the third paragraph, substitute the words "The Ambassadors or Ministers of the High Contracting Parties at [blank], unless other representatives are specially appointed for this purpose."

After the words "Body of Delegates" in the fourth paragraph, insert in each case the words "Or the Executive Council."

In the same paragraph for the words "Those present," substitute the words "The States represented."

On the motion of *President Wilson*, the words "At stated intervals and" were added after the word "held" in the first line of the Article.

Before proceeding to the consideration of Article 3, *Lord Robert Cecil* asked that the question of the representation of the British Dominions should be reserved for subsequent discussion.

ARTICLE 3.

A prolonged discussion took place regarding the representation of Powers other than the Great Powers on the Executive Council of the League.

*Mr. Pessoa* said that, according to Article 3, the Five Great Powers would have permanent representatives on the Executive Council, whereas the other Powers would be represented on it only when their interests were directly affected. But seeing that, in this case, the small Powers interested would not be able to take part in the deliberations—as being parties to the dispute—it followed that all decisions would be taken by the Great Powers. The Council would be, therefore, not an organ of the "League of Nations" but an organ of "Five Nations," a kind of tribunal to which everyone would be subject. The original scheme was more liberal. It gave all the Powers permanent representatives, and he did not see why this principle was abandoned.

Mr. Hymans, Mr. Vesnitch, Mr. Koo, and Mr. Reis also emphasised the claims of the smaller Powers to adequate representation on the Council, and these claims were endorsed by Mr. Bourgeois and Mr. Orlando.

*Lord Robert Cecil* doubted the advisability of enlarging the membership of the Executive Council, but proposed that, as the consensus of opinion on the Commission was against him, the discussion should be adjourned until the next meeting, when a new draft of Article 3 could be presented for the consideration of the Commission.

The text of the Preamble and of Articles 1 and 2, as adopted, is contained in the Annex.

*(The Commission accordingly adjourned, the next meeting being fixed for the following evening at 8:30 P.M.)*

*Annex to Minutes of Second Meeting.*

DRAFT AS PROVISIONALLY APPROVED.

COVENANT.

*Preamble.*

In order to promote international co-operation and to secure international peace and security by the acceptance of obligations not to resort to the use of armed force, by the prescription of open, just, and honourable relations between nations, by the firm establishment of the understandings of international law as the actual rule of conduct among Governments, and by the maintenance of justice and a scrupulous respect for all treaty obligations in the dealings of organised peoples with one another, the Powers signatory to this Covenant adopt this constitution of the League of Nations.

### ARTICLE I.

The action of the High Contracting Parties under the terms of this Covenant shall be effected through the instrumentality of meetings of Delegates representing the High Contracting Parties, of meetings at more frequent intervals of an Executive Council, and of a permanent international Secretariat to be established at the Capital of the League.

### ARTICLE 2.

Meetings of the Body of Delegates shall be held at stated intervals and from time to time as occasion may require for the purpose of dealing with matters within the sphere of action of the League. Meetings of the Body of Delegates shall be held at the Capital of the League or at such other place as may be found convenient, and shall consist of the Ambassadors or Ministers of the High Contracting Parties at [blank], unless other representatives are specially appointed for this purpose.

All matters of procedure at meetings of the Body of Delegates or Executive Council, including the appointment of Committees to investigate particular matters, shall be regulated by the Body of Delegates or the Executive Council and may be decided by a majority of the States represented at the meeting.

Printed copy (WP, DLC).
[1] That is, of the Hurst-Miller draft.


## From the Diary of Colonel House

February 4, 1919.

We made considerable progress in the meeting of the Committee on the League of Nations. I will not go into these meetings in detail since there will be minutes taken. After all, the results are the important things. Hymans, Cecil, the President and Bourgeois did most of the talking. The Japs never speak. General Smuts speaks so seldomly that it is practically not at all. My province is to prompt the President on the one side, and Lord Robert on the other, and to keep things running smoothly. I try to find in advance where trouble lies and to smooth it out before it goes too far. In this way, we have gotten over some pretty bad hurdles.

Cecil and I do nearly all the difficult work between the meetings of the Committee and try to have as little fraction [friction] at the meetings as possible. The President often tells me that under no circumstances will he do a certain thing and a few hours later, consents. I generally approve of what is finally done and not what he says he will or will not do. . . .

Baron Makino and Viscount Chinda came for advice concerning what Japan had best do regarding the race question. There is a demand in Japan that the Peace Conference through the League of Nations should express some broad principle of racial equality. Chinda and Makino do not desire to bring it up themselves if they can avoid doing so. I advised them to prepare two resolutions, one which they desired, and another which they would be willing to accept in lieu of the one they prefer. I promised I would then see what could be done.

I was interested to hear Chinda and Makino say: "On July 8th at Magnolia you expressed to Viscount Ishii sentiments which pleased the Japanese Government, therefore we look upon you as a friend, and we have come for your advice."[1]

I took occasion to tell them how much I deprecated race, religious or other kinds of prejudice. I insisted, however, that it was not confined to any one country or against any particular class of people. I found prejudice existing among the Western peoples against one another as well as against Eastern peoples. I cited the contempt which so many Anglo Saxons have for the Latins, and vice versa. I thought this was one of the serious causes of international trouble, and should in some way be met.

[1] About this conversation, which actually took place on July 6, see EMH to WW, July 6, 1918 (first letter of that date), Vol. 48.

## Two Telegrams from Joseph Patrick Tumulty

Washington [Feb. 4, 1919].

Number 33. Republican Senators refuse to confirm Williams at this session[1] and threaten filibuster on all appointments after this session. If you have any appointments in mind, I would suggest you forward them at once.

Postmaster General in long talk with me today confirms all I said to you in my dispatch about the advisability of appointing Palmer.[2] I made no suggestion to him in the matter. His support of Palmer is based on his own conviction [investigation]. He says that he has been on the outs with Palmer of late but considers him the best man for this place, saying he would be of great service to the party and administration. He asked me to cable you this.

Tumulty

[1] Carter Glass had announced on January 16 that he would recommend that Wilson reappoint John Skelton Williams as Comptroller of the Currency when his current term expired on February 2. The New York Times, January 22, 1919, reported that Republican

members of the Senate planned to oppose his confirmation. Williams' nomination was formally submitted to the Senate on February 3, and the Senate Banking and Currency Committee began its confirmation hearings on February 11. The hearings revealed that at least some bankers were strongly opposed to Williams' reappointment. The committee, by a strict party vote of nine to four, recommended confirmation on February 24. However, the Senate failed to act in the matter before the final adjournment of the Sixty-fifth Congress on March 4. Glass announced on March 6 that Williams would continue in his office under a Treasury Department appointment. Despite objections to this procedure from members of Congress, Williams held his office until the end of the Wilson administration. See the *New York Times*, Jan. 17 and 22, Feb. 12, 21, 22, and 25, March 5 and 7, 1919, and *Cong. Record*, 65th Cong., 3d sess., p. 2611.
  ² See JPT to WW, Feb. 1, 1919.

The White House February 4, 1919

No. 34. Bill introduced by Senator Phelan providing for enlargement of National Park in California and naming it Roosevelt National Park has passed Senate. Senator Phelan thinks expression from you to Ferris, favoring bill, would put it through House. Would be generous tribute. Hope you will cable Ferris.

Tumulty.

T telegrams (WP, DLC).

# Frank Lyon Polk to Robert Lansing and Vance Criswell McCormick

Washington, February 4, 1919.

SPECIAL CIPHER

568 Very confidential, for the Secretary of State and McCormick:
Your 521 January thirty-first eight p.m.

I have given the suggestion made by you most careful consideration, have taken advice of the men in the Department, and then brought the question up at Cabinet today. Everyone is of the same mind that it would be very inadvisable for me to go to Congress at this time with any plan, one, of acquiring money to be expended abroad or, two, having anything to do with Russia. In regard to the first objection, having just been through the fight to obtain the money for the one hundred million dollar fund for feeding Europe, I am convinced that I would not be given any consideration whatever, in view of the fact our plans in regard to the railroad—as to who are to contribute and how much it would cost—are so absolutely indefinite. In the Committee on Appropriations, the whole fight made on the Food Bill by the opponents and the criticisms made even by our friends was that they did not have information enough. The information in the case of the Food Bill was so much more than anything I could offer at present, I am advised by everyone that an attempt to get any agreement from committee would be hopeless.

In regard to the second objection, the first question to be asked would be what is the Russian policy. If no answer could be given, the reasons for not being able to give an answer would have no weight. Senator Johnson is demanding that troops be withdrawn from Archangel, and there is considerable support of his position on the ground that our men are being killed and no one knows why they are still there. Of course these criticisms are unjust, but they carry more or less weight. Any attempt to commit Congress to a definite policy on the Siberian railroad, which is only a part of the whole Russian problem, would be hopeless unless some definite information could be given them on the whole subject. The Vice President said that if the Russian question were thrown into Congress at this time, it would probably jeopardize all the appropriation bills.

In view of the unanimous opinion of all who have been consulted, I think it would be wiser for me not to approach them for money for this purpose. It seems to me that it has to be settled now whether we will accept the compromise arrangement for operating railroad and then take our chance later on being able to get Congress to assume the responsibility. If Congress then refuses to accept a carefully worked out plan that shows how much money will be required and how much each Government will contribute, then the responsibility will be on Congress, but to get Congress to commit itself to any proposal for financing the railroad—in its present mood when it is badly frightened over the amount of money we are spending and when it is so completely at sea as to what should be done in Russia—would be hopeless.

Shall I give formal approval. Japanese pressing for answer.

Polk Acting

TS telegram (SDR, RG 59, 861.77/655, DNA).

## Edith Bolling Galt Wilson to Her Family

Dearest Ones:　　　　　　　　　　　　　　Paris Feb. 4, 1919

... Yesterday W. was received by the Chamber of Deputies—at the old Palais de Bourbon—& afterwards there was a Reception to us both. I know you read all of this in the papers so long before this reaches you that it almost seems foolish to repeat it. But it was another of those gorgeous Ceremonials where the stage is set with such splendor & color that the picture stands out vividly in your memory. The great flagged court yard in which the motor halts after passing through massive gates & stone archways, the "Republican Guard" in white britchs, Crimson Coats & shining Brass Helmets from which long black horse tails fall all drawn up in way [here a small sketch] on either side of a broad door way—the steps covered with crimson carpet and the buglers & drummers heralding our approach

The Building is gorgeously decorated & the Chamber of Deputies a very handsome room. I sat with Madame Poincareé & the wife of the President of the Chamber,[1] in a box, & it was a beautiful scene before us. The speech was enthusiastically received and applauded. Of course I thought it was splendid

The Reception, afterwards, was deadly (as all French Receptions on this order are) for no one introduces any one else, & dense crowds of people surround & examine you as though you were something from a strange planet.

Then everyone scrambles for food, which is abundant & varied on a highly decorated table running the length of the room. This feat accomplished the staring begins again—often through glasses— & one is free to depart. But it is evidently the custom of the Country & no one minds. . . .        Love to each one Fondly   Edith

ALS (EBW Papers, DLC).
[1] That is, Henriette Benucci Poincaré and Germaine Brice Deschanel.


## From Frederic Yates

Dear Mr. President,

Nursing home. London,
4 Feb. 1919.

We so much regretted—my wife and Mary and I—that we could not see you when you came to Carlisle and Manchester. I was too poorly,—having had some mysterious ailment—which X Rays now have discovered and in about an hour I shall be in the hands of the surgeon. My wife and Mary are brave and I have only to go through with it and be worthy of them. My house is in order,— bills all paid, my will made, and Mary taking on the duties should anything occur.[1]

I want to give you my love and reverence. You have lifted us all up, dear Great Man. I send this to Washington so as not to disturb you by even adding one feather weight to your cares.

I know you love us,            Your friend,   Fred Yates.

I am reading Lord Charnwood's "Lincoln"[2] in my bed—if all goes well I get out in a month. I have the best surgeon there is—Gordon Taylor.[3]

ALS (WP, DLC).
[1] Yates died on February 11.
[2] Godfrey Rathbone Benson, 1st Baron Charnwood, *Abraham Lincoln* (London and New York, 1916).

[3] William Gordon Taylor, who later changed his name to Gordon Gordon-Taylor, was at this time assistant surgeon to the Middlesex Hospital, London. Taylor had recently returned from military service in France.

## From the Diary of Edith Benham

February 4, 1919

The speeches are historical and I don't attempt to describe them. The President's was not delivered with the usual facility for he was very tired from a long conference he had about the League. He says he believes Leon Bourgeois has been instructed by Clemenceau to delay and obstruct proceedings just as much as possible. He has information that that is Clemenceau's game. He was very tired when he got in the car and just sat back in the seat with her [Mrs. Wilson's] hand in his trying to remember what he had planned to say for the continued trouble at the Crillon had driven away all his ideas. After the whole thing when we were driving home he asked if he had not wandered a great deal. He did hesitate a little, a very unusual thing for him, but otherwise nothing was noticeable. He also said he had not delivered the speech he had intended— not absolutely—deviating in certain points. Old Mr. Henry White told me that Deschanel who really made a wonderful speech, had been rehearsing his for weeks and had sent for Jusserand to confer with him over one sentence in which the "re" sound occurred twice! I was sure he had been busy over the diction, etc., because every gesture was finished. I was sorry to see the greatest applause, and the President said he was, too, coming from the left where the socialists sit.

## From the Diary of Dr. Grayson

Wednesday, February 5, 1919.

The President conferred this morning with Lloyd George and Balfour at the Murat Palace. The British leaders explained the problems which had developed in connection with the Australian objections to the mandatory system that was to be made a part of the administration of the captured German Colonies under the auspices of the League of Nations.

In the afternoon the President went back to the Quai D'Orsay to attend a meeting of the Supreme War Council, where the Russian situation was again under consideration.

There was another night conference of the committee on the League of Nations, which began at 8:30 P.M., and lasted until after midnight.

# Hankey's Notes of a Meeting of the Council of Ten[1]

Quai d'Orsay, February 5, 1919, 3 P.M.

BC-23

[The names were announced of the members of the Commission on Greek and Albanian Affairs.[2]]

(At this stage Dr. Kramartz[3] and M. Benes and the technical advisers entered the room.)

M. BENES said that, before beginning to expound the Czecho-Slovak problem, he would like to declare what were the principles guiding Czecho-Slovak policy. The movement culminating in the formation of an independent Czecho-Slovak State had begun 3½ years ago. The agitation had been carried on by scattered exiles in the various Allied countries. There was, at that time, no Government and no organised political body. In 3 years these exiles had succeeded, with the help of the population remaining at home, in putting up a Central Government and a political organisation which was vital, and, with the help of the Allies, three armies in the field.

Before dealing with the question of the future frontiers of this new State, he would like to recall that the Czecho-Slovak people had shown a practical sense of politics which had won for them the recognition of the Allies. He would also like to recall that, in all these years, the Nation had been entirely united. It had never hesitated to side with the Allies in the interests of democracy. It had not fought for territory, but for the same principles as the Allied Nations. It had risen against a mediaeval Dynasty backed by bureaucracy, militarism, the Roman Catholic Church, and, to some extent, by high finance. The Nation has plunged into this struggle without asking for any guarantees or weighing the probabilities of success. All the Nation wanted was to control its own destinies. The Nation felt itself to be a European Nation and a member of the Society of the Western States.

In seeking now to shape the Czecho-Slovak State, the very same principles would be their guide. They would adopt the European and human point of view, and base their claims on the very principles the Conference was assembled to establish.

The Nation, after 300 years of servitude and vicissitudes which had almost led to its extermination, felt that it must be prudent, reasonable and just to its neighbours; and that it must avoid pro-

[1] The complete text of these minutes is printed in PPC, III, 876-87.
[2] William L. Westermann and Clive Day for the United States; Sir Robert Borden and Sir Eyre Crowe for the British Empire; Jules Cambon and Jean Étienne Paul Gout, chief of the Asiatic section of the Ministry of Foreign Affairs, for France; and Giacomo de Martino, Secretary General of the Ministry of Foreign Affairs, and Col. Fortunato Castoldi, technical expert on political and diplomatic questions, for Italy.
[3] That is, Karel Kramář.

voking jealousy and renewed struggles which might again plunge it into similar danger. It was in this spirit that he wished to explain the territorial problem.

M. BENES, continuing, said that the first territorial question was that of the four provinces, Bohemia, Moravia, Austrian Silesia and Slovakia. These territories were claimed for ethnographical reasons. They contained 10 millions of the Nation.

The first three had been one State from the sixth Century. The Czech Dynasty had lasted until 1747, when a unitary form of government had prevailed against federalist and national tendencies. In 1526, the Hapsburgs had been elected Kings of Bohemia, and, though, up to the present time they had *de jure* recognised Czech Institutions, they had begun from that date to centralize power. Czech independence might be said to have lasted until 1747. Since then, though the Juridicial existence of the State continued to be acknowledged, it had no practical significance. Hence the Czech Insurrection in 1848 and that which had coincided with the beginning of this war.

Historical considerations, though not the predominant factor at the present time, must be accorded some weight, in as much as they very deeply affected public opinion. It was these old historical causes that armed the Czech people against the Germanic masses around them. Three times the Czech people had rebelled, not merely against Germanism but against a system of aristocratic and Roman Catholic privilege; three times the nation had been overwhelmed by the superior numbers of the German peoples. At the end of the 17th Century, after the great battle of the White Mountain, the Czech people had practically ceased to exist. It was reanimated only at the end of the 18th Century by the French Revolution. Since then the Nation had worked so hard that, at the beginning of the 20th century, it was industrially, intellectually and politically, the most developed community in Central Europe. Throughout the 19th Century whenever the Czech people had attempted to free themselves it was always the appeal to history that had inspired them.

M. Benes said that he must draw attention to the exposed situation of the Czecho-Slovak nation. It was the advanced guard of the Slav world in the West, and therefore constantly threatened by German expansion. The Germanic mass, now numbering some 80 millions, could not push westwards as its road was blocked on that side by highly developed nations. It was, therefore, always seeking outlets to the south and to the east. In this movement it found the Poles and the Czechs in its path. Hence the special importance of the Czecho-Slovak frontiers in Central Europe. It might be hoped that the Germans would not again attempt forcible invasions, but they had done so in the past so often that the Czechs had always felt they had a special mission to resist the Teutonic flood. Hence the fanatical devotion of the Czechs which had been noticed by all in this war. It was due to the constant feeling of the Czechs that they were the protectors of democracy against Germanism, and that it was their duty at all times to fight the Germans.

The first territorial claim of the Czechs was to Bohemia, Moravia and Austrian Silesia, which formed a geographical and ethnographical whole. However, there were some 2,400,000 Germans in Bohemia according to Austrian official statistics. The presence of these Germans was the result of centuries of infiltration and colonisation. The statistics, however, were official statistics drawn up with a deliberate political purpose. It was easy to prove their mendacity. The Czech figures showed that the Austrian census exaggerated the number of Germans in Bohemia by 800,000 or a million. The Czech statistics had been very carefully made. When the Austrian census in 1910 was under preparation, State and Municipal authorities sent to each village in the mixed districts warnings that the census would be established on the lines of spoken language not of mother tongue. If, therefore, a workman conversed in German with his employer, he was set down as a German, under pain of losing his employment and of being evicted from his home. The same method had been employed in the territories of other mixed populations in the Austro-Hungarian Kingdom. According to Czech calculations there were about 1,500,000 Germans in Bohemia.

MR. LLOYD GEORGE asked when the previous census had taken place.

M. BENES replied that it had been in 1900, and that the same methods had been employed and the same results obtained.

PRESIDENT WILSON asked how many Czechs there were in Bohemia.

M. BENES replied that in Bohemia itself there were 4,500,000. He wished to add that in the Bohemian territory represented as German there was also an autochthonous Czech population representing about one-third of the whole. To this must be added the fluctuations of the industrial population. He explained by the help of a map the progress of the German encroachments on Bohemia. Four distinct spheres could be distinguished, and it was noticeable that the greatest German advance had always taken place after the defeat of the Czech nation. The most notable encroachment had occurred at the end of the 17th and during the 18th Centuries. The progress had been checked in the 19th Century and in the 20th a beginning of the reversal of the process had been noticeable.

It was on these considerations that the Czechs founded their claim to the restoration of the land taken from them.

The best argument, however, on which to establish the rights of the Czechs was of an economic order. The Czecho-German parts of Bohemia contained nearly the whole of the industries of the country. Bohemia as a whole was the strongest industrial portion of Austria-Hungary. It possessed 93% of the sugar industry (it was the fourth sugar producing country in the world). The whole of the glass works of Austria-Hungary were on Czecho-Slovak territory. It possessed 70% of the textile industry, 70% of the metal industry, 55% of the brewing, and 60% of the alcohol production. Nearly all these industries were on the confines of Bohemia in the mixed territory. Without the peripheral areas Bohemia could not live. The centre of the country was agricultural, and the two parts were so interdependent that neither could exist without the other. If the Germans were to be given the outer rim of Bohemia they would also possess the hinterland. Most of the workmen on which these industries depended were of Czech nationality. In particular, the mining regions attracted large numbers of Czechs. The whole country was really homogeneous, and must remain united.

[Here follows a discussion of Czechoslovakia's boundary claims during which Wilson and Lansing asked one question each.]

(The following resolution was then adopted: That the questions raised in the statement by M. Benes on the Czecho-Slovak territorial interests in the Peace Settlement shall be referred for examination in the first instance to an expert Committee composed of two representatives each of the United States of America, the British Empire, France and Italy.

It shall be the duty of this Committee to reduce the questions for decision within the narrowest possible limits and make recommendations for a just settlement.

The Committee is authorised to consult representatives of the peoples concerned.)

(The Meeting then adjourned.)

T MS (SDR, RG 256, 180.03101/30, DNA).

## To Norman Hezekiah Davis

My dear Mr. Davis:                    Paris, 5 February, 1919.

Thank you for your letter of the 2nd about the concerted movement which is on foot to obtain an interlocking of the United States with the continental governments in the whole financial situation. I was already aware of the effort and on my guard against it, but

I should greatly value unanimous cooperation on the subject. You have been at close quarters with these efforts and I would be very much obliged if you would let Mr. Baruch, Mr. McCormick, the Shipping Board men and the members of the Peace Commission know what you know.

Cordially and sincerely yours,   [Woodrow Wilson]

CCL (WP, DLC).


## To Bernard Mannes Baruch

My dear Mr. Baruch:                    Paris, 5 February, 1919.

Thank you for your letter of yesterday. I am perfectly willing that you should bring over eight or ten of the men you have in mind to assist you and hope that if necessary you will secure quarters for them outside the Crillon. I think the best way to handle the expense would be through the Peace Commission by an extra allotment from the fund at my disposal, though I am a bit startled to find how low that fund is running.

I realize the efforts that are being made to tie us to the shaky financial structure of Europe and am counting upon your assistance to defeat the efforts. I have asked Mr. Norman Davis to tell you the things that he knows, though I have no doubt that he has already told you most of it.

Cordially and sincerely yours,   [Woodrow Wilson]

CCL (WP, DLC).


## From Edward Mandell House

Dear Governor:                    Paris, February 5th, 1919.

I enclose two papers which I think you should have before the meeting tonight.

The first is a draft of the Preamble and Articles One and Two as provisionally adopted last night.[1]

The second is Article Three as drafted at a meeting I had this morning at which Lord Robert Cecil, General Smuts, Orlando and Mr. Koo were present.[2] I tried to get Bourgeois but he could not be reached.

Tonight Orlando will propose the adoption of Article Three as drafted.

You will note that the next to the last paragraph of Article Three is the same as the last paragraph of Article Two in the Provisional

Draft. If Article Three is adopted as drafted the last paragraph of Article Two will be left out.

Affectionately yours, [E. M. House]

CCL (E. M. House Papers, CtY).
[1] These enclosures are missing in the Wilson and House Papers; however, they are printed in Miller, *My Diary at the Conference of Paris*, V, 85-86.
[2] As the minutes of the League of Nations Commission of February 4, 1919, and Miller, *The Drafting of the Covenant*, I, 146-48, reveal, the delegates of the small powers insisted upon representation of those powers on the Executive Council of the League of Nations, from which they were excluded in Article 3 of the Hurst-Miller draft, and that the commission go back to what these delegates called "the American plan," or the plan embodied in Wilson's first, second, and third "Paris" drafts of the Covenant. In all of these drafts, as the reader will recall, Wilson provided for four small-power representatives on the Council, to be chosen by the Body of Delegates in such manner as it saw fit.
This question was referred to the drafting committee, which met in Colonel House's suite in the Crillon in the morning of February 5. Cecil and House were still strongly opposed to the representation of the small powers, and House said that he was not willing to have more than two such representatives on the Council. However, at this meeting House did present a new draft of Article 3 based upon Wilson's earlier provision. This draft is printed in Miller, *My Diary at the Conference of Paris*, V, 88, and in Miller, *The Drafting of the Covenant*, I, 154. The documents do not reveal the authorship of this draft. The drafting committee's new version of Article 3 provided for only two small-power representatives on the Council. It is printed in *ibid.*, pp. 154-55. Orlando introduced this version at the meeting of the commission on the same day, February 5.

## From Robert Lansing

My dear Mr. President: Paris. 5th February, 1919.

I have received a letter from Mr. Whitlock at Brussels stating that at an audience with the King of Belgium the Minister read that portion of a personal letter from you in which you asked him to present your greetings to Their Majesties.[1]

Mr. Whitlock asks me to inform you that the King was greatly pleased and took a copy of the message saying that he would keep it "as a precious souvenir."

Faithfully yours, Robert Lansing

TLS (WP, DLC).
[1] See WW to B. Whitlock, Jan. 10, 1919, Vol. 53.

## Minutes of a Meeting of the Commission on the League of Nations

THIRD MEETING, FEBRUARY 5, 1919, AT 8:30 P.M.
President WILSON *in the chair*

*President Wilson* reported that, pursuant to the decision of the Commission and of the Conference at the Quai D'Orsay, he would invite the representatives of Greece, Poland, Roumania, and the

Czecho-Slovak Republic, to associate themselves with the Commission.

The Commission continued their discussion of the Covenant.

*Mr. Orlando* moved the adoption of the redraft of Article 3.

Discussion centred upon the question of the number of representatives to be accorded in the Executive Committee to Powers other than the United States of America, Great Britain, France, Italy, and Japan.

*Mr. Hymans* proposed five Delegates, in order that these Powers might be represented on an equality with the first.

*Mr. Vesnitch* proposed four Delegates, and in this he was supported by *Mr. Bourgeois*.

*Mr. Pessoa* accepted in principle Mr. Hymans' proposition, but preferred Mr. Vesnitch's proposal as to the selection of the Delegates. He did not see why the Great Powers should choose their own representatives, while those of the small Powers were chosen by the Assembly.

Upon a motion by *Lord R. Cecil*, the redraft of this article was adopted, with the exception of the specific figure of their representation, on the understanding that the Commission would determine this later.

The Article so adopted included the last paragraph of Article 2, from which it was therefore omitted.

Upon the motion of *Mr. Bourgeois*, it was agreed to adopt the word "seat" instead of "capital" in this Article and throughout the draft.

*President Wilson* expressed his thanks to the Commission for the provision of the last paragraph, that the first meeting of the General Assembly and the Executive Committee should be summoned by the President of the United States; making the observation, however, that this suggestion did not emanate from the United States Delegation.

### ARTICLE 4.

This article was adopted with the following amendment:

In the first paragraph, for the words "by whom they shall be appointed" substitute the words "chosen by the Executive Council, by whom they shall be appointed, subject to confirmation by the Executive Council."

Further verbal amendment was made:

Strike out the word after "members" in the third paragraph of the article and insert "of the Universal Postal Union of the expenses of the International Bureau of the Universal Postal Union."

*Mr. Hymans* voiced the desire of the Belgian Government and of a large number of Belgian organisations that Brussels should be the Seat of the League.

*President Wilson* stated that the Commission had listened to this proposal with sympathy, but that a decision on the subject would be taken later.

### ARTICLE 5.

This Article was adopted without discussion.

### ARTICLE 6.

*President Wilson* proposed the following amendment:

To add at the beginning of the second paragraph the words "only self-governing States shall be admitted to membership in the League; Colonies enjoying full powers of self-government may be admitted; but no State, &c.," the rest of the paragraph remaining the same.

Mr. Bourgeois stated that the only condition of admission provided for in the present text was a vote of two-thirds of the Body of Delegates without taking into consideration the moral conditions set forth in President Wilson's first draft. To his mind these conditions, which were mentioned in the French and Italian drafts, had reference to the reparations to be required from Germany before admitting her into the League.

*Lord Robert Cecil* proposed the following amendment:

In the second paragraph to substitute after the word "Delegates" the words "and by a like majority the League may impose on any States seeking admission such conditions as it may think fit."

Lord Robert Cecil emphasised the special position of India.

As regards the conditions as to their form of government to be required from the States which shall subsequently be admitted to the League, *Mr. Bourgeois* stated, by way of example, the form of the French draft, which contained the following definition: "Nations having representative institutions of such nature that they be considered as themselves responsible for the acts of their government."

It was agreed that the question of a definitive formula on this point should be further considered.

With this exception the wording of Article 6 was held to be provisionally adopted, retaining the amendment proposed by President Wilson, as above set forth.

*Lord Robert Cecil* declared that he accepted this decision on the understanding that, as a matter of fact, India would in any case be included in the League by virtue of the signature of the Covenant by the representatives of the British Empire, and in view of the hope expressed by President Wilson that India would be a member of the League. . . .

The text of Articles 3-6 of the draft, as adopted by the third meeting of the Commission, is contained in the Annex.

*(The Commission adjourned until the next evening, 6th February, at 8:30.)*

## Annex to Minutes of Third Meeting.

### ARTICLE 3.

The Executive Council shall consist of the representatives of the United States of America, the British Empire, France, Italy, and Japan, together with [blank] representatives of the other States, members of the League, appointed by the Body of Delegates on such principles and in such manner as they think fit. Pending the appointment of these representatives of the other States, representatives of [blank] and [blank] shall be members of the Executive Council.

Meetings of the Council shall be held from time to time as occasion may require, and at least once a year at whatever place may be decided on or, failing any such decision, at the Seat of the League, and any matter within the sphere of action of the League or affecting the peace of the world may be dealt with at such meetings.

Invitations shall be sent to any Power to attend a meeting of the Council at which matters directly affecting its interests are to be discussed and no decision taken at any meeting will be binding on such Power unless so invited.

All matters of procedure at meeting of the body of Delegates or the Executive Council including the appointment of Committees to investigate particular matters shall be regulated by the Body of Delegates or the Executive Council, and may be decided by a majority of the States represented at the meeting.

The first meeting of the Body of Delegates and of the Executive Council shall be summoned by the President of the United States of America.

### ARTICLE 4.

The permanent Secretariat of the League shall be established at [blank] which shall constitute the Seat of the League. The Secretariat shall comprise such secretaries and staff as may be required, under the general direction and control of a Chancellor of the League, chosen by the Executive Council, by whom they shall be appointed, subject to confirmation by the Executive Council.

The Chancellor shall act as Secretary at all meetings of the Body of Delegates, or of the Executive Council.

The expenses of the Secretariat shall be borne by the States members of the League in accordance with the distribution among members of the Universal Postal Union of the expenses of the International Bureau of the Universal Postal Union.

### ARTICLE 5.

Representatives of the High Contracting Parties and officials of the League when engaged on the business of the League shall enjoy diplomatic privileges and immunities, and the buildings occupied by the League, or its officials, or by representatives attending its meetings shall enjoy the benefits of extraterritoriality.

### ARTICLE 6.

Admission to the League of States who are not signatories of this Covenant requires the assent of not less than two-thirds of the Body of Delegates.

Only self-governing States shall be admitted to membership in the League; Colonies enjoying full powers of self-government may be admitted; but no State shall be admitted to the League except on condition that its military and naval forces and armaments shall conform to standards prescribed by the League in respect of it from time to time.

Printed copy (WP, DLC).

## From the Diary of Colonel House

February 5, 1919.

General Bliss told me of the meeting of the Military part of the Supreme War Council at Versailles.[1] He, the President and I had this under discussion last night, and the President directed Bliss not to force the Germans to make radical changes in the Armistice to the advantage of the Allies. Bliss strongly recommended this position and the President accepted it—a position I heartily approve. It is unfair and is not worthy of the Allied Governments.

At the meeting, the British represented by General Wilson, and the Italians represented by General Diaz, voted for further encroachment on German territory. Bliss was outvoted two to one. Foch said nothing and did not indicate his mind. However, he asked Bliss to remain behind and they discussed the question together for three quarters of an hour. Foch told Bliss that he was in thorough sympathy with the American position and that the position taken by the British and Italians might bring a clash, and then everything would flame up again. The Armistice would be a thing of the past, and war of a certain sort, would be one [on]. Much to my surprise, Foch expressed the opinion that an immediate peace should be made with Germany so that the wheels of industry should be started in motion throughout the world. This has been my contention all the time. He thought the situation full of peril for us all. He told Bliss that if his Government insisted upon his carrying out the military program that he, Foch, would send in his resignation.

I asked the President to come down in advance of the meeting of the Committee on the League of Nations in order to tell him of the conversation between Bliss and myself. I suggested that before this matter was passed upon at the meeting of the Supreme War Council day after tomorrow, that he either see Foch or get permission to use what he said to Bliss when he argued the matter with Clemenceau, Lloyd George and Orlando.

I showed the President the draft that Baron Makino and Viscount Chinda had brought this afternoon. The resolution they wanted we discarded at once,[2] but the resolution which they had prepared as a compromise the President thought might do by making a slight change which he did in his own handwriting.[3] Both copies of these proposed articles are attached. Later in the evening, I showed Chinda what we had prepared and he seemed to think it would be satisfactory. He wished to first discuss it with his colleagues.

[1] See the report printed as Appendix B to the minutes of the Council of Ten printed at Feb. 7, 1919.
[2] The Editors have been unable to find this resolution.
[3] It is printed as the following document.


## A Draft of an Article for the Covenant[1]

[Feb. 5, 1919]

The equality of nations being a basic principle of the League, the H.C.P. agree that concerning the aliens in their territories, they will accord them, ⟨as far as it is in their legitimate power,⟩ *so soon and so far as practicable*, equal treatment and rights in law and in fact, without making any distinction on account of their race or nationality.

T MS (E. M. House Papers, CtY).
[1] Words in angle brackets deleted by Wilson; words in italics WWhw.


## To Joseph Patrick Tumulty

Paris, 5 February, 1919.

Do not think it would be possible to have the meeting of governors on the labor employment matter referred to in your number thirty two[1] a part of the programme of my arrival at home because I must hurry to Washington, but would be willing to attend such a meeting if possible before returning to Europe as I fear I must do after

Congress adjourns. I realize the interest and importance of the whole matter. Sorry to hear you are still in bed. Hope that you are not attempting too much. Affectionate messages from us all.

Woodrow Wilson.

T telegram (WP, DLC).
¹ JPT to WW, Feb. 3, 1919, CCS telegram (WP, DLC). Tumulty informed Wilson that the Labor Department, on December 23, 1918, had requested the governors and governors-elect of all the states and the mayors of principal cities to incorporate in their annual messages to the legislatures and city councils "a recommendation that they encourage a public building program and the stimulation of construction in all needed public improvements as a stabilizing industrial influence." Practically all of the governors, according to Tumulty, had responded enthusiastically. More recently, "Senators and others" had suggested that Tumulty, on behalf of Wilson, call a conference of governors "to intensify further the interest along these lines." It had been further suggested that this meeting take place in New York and that it coincide with Wilson's arrival there from Europe, in the hope that Wilson would speak before the conference. Tumulty requested immediate instruction in the matter.

## To Lemuel Phillips Padgett

Paris, 5 February, 1919.

May I not express my gratification and gratitude and congratulations at the unanimous report of the three year Naval programme?

Woodrow Wilson.

T telegram (WP, DLC).

## From Carter Glass

Washington February 5, 1919.

For the President from Glass:

Conferees have agreed on provisions of revenue bill. Report will probably be approved by Senate and House this week. Bill is great improvement over 1917 act structurally as well as from standpoint of administrative practicability. It will supersede several existing income tax laws and consolidates in one measure all income tax provisions. Practically all provisions for administrative relief in unusual cases are incorporated as urged by the Treasury Department. Normal income tax rate of twelve percent alike for individuals and corporations with six percent only upon first four thousand of taxable income of individuals eight percent and four percent respectively prescibed after nineteen eighteen with ten percent upon corporations. Surtax rates for individuals range from one percent of amount by which net income exceeds five thousand and does not exceed six thousand to 65 percent of amount by which net income exceeds one million.

War profits tax of eighty percent imposed for 1919 with alternative excess profits tax of 30 percent upon profits between eight percent and twenty percent of invested capital and 65 percent upon profits exceeding 20 percent of invested capital. In general war profits tax ceases after 1918 but excess profits tax continued at rates of 20 percent and 40 percent, and 1918 rates of war and excess profits taxes are continued with respect to profits derived during 1918 from government contract made between April 6th, 1917 and November 11th, 1918. War profits and excess profits taxes do not apply to individuals and partnerships but amount of tax upon small corporations is limited and 1917 corporations are treated like partnerships. Adequate relief provisions are adopted but do not apply to profits derived on cost plus basis from Government contracts made between above dates.

Measure contains provisions for continuing with changes in rates and objects of taxes now imposed on sales of commodities by manufacturers, importers and producers upon transportation of passengers, freight and express upon policies of insurance upon admissions and dues, telegraph and telephones upon transfer and net estates of decedents. Measure will also contain provision for so called luxury taxes, tax being based on amount in excess of stated amounts paid by certain wearing apparel and articles of personal adornment or comfort and articles of household decoration and use. Floor taxes are levied upon tobacco and tobacco manufacturers and upon distilled spirits held for sale by dealers on the date the new law becomes effective.

Income and war profits and excess profits taxes payable in four installments, March 15th, June 15th, September 15, and December 15th. Because of imperative need of funds for redemption outstanding obligations becoming due March 15th, Department plans no general extension of time. Filing returns and paying first installment of taxes on March 15th despite extremely brief period for equipping administrative machinery for this work. Vitally important that bill become law at earliest possible date to insure collection maximum floor taxes and allow greatest possible time for income tax returns and payment before March 15th. Large revenue dependent upon early approval inasmuch as new rates of most excise taxes become operative upon passage of the law. While bill is not satisfactory to Treasury in all its important aspects it is best can be obtained and I shall recommend your approval. Because of short interval before fiscal installment date I shall proceed upon assumption you will approve measure.

What is your wish with respect to despatch of measure for your approval.                                                    Polk, Acting.

T telegram (WP, DLC).

## To Thomas Watt Gregory

Paris, 5 February, 1919.

For Attorney General Gregory. Understand that the conferees on the oil leasing bill have come to an agreement and think it unwise in the circumstances to attempt further guidance in the matter.

To insist upon alteration now would throw the matter into the next Congress where much less favorable action would be certain with perhaps serious consequences to the country.

Woodrow Wilson.

T telegram (WP, DLC).

## From Thomas Watt Gregory

Washington February 5, 1919

Following for the President from the Attorney General:

"In accordance with your request submitted through Polk, I submit views on oil relief embodied in the proposed conference report. After discussing with you the oil relief measures, and in view of your expressed convictions as to the limit of liberality to which you were willing to go in dealing with the oil claimants, I agreed that I would not object to a bill which contained the following salient features:

1st. Where the validity of the claim was questioned on behalf of the United States the President was authorized within 12 months after approval of the act to direct a compromise of the controversy to be carried out by exchange or division of lands or proceeds of operation, this to apply to land within as well as outside of naval reserve.

2nd. Upon relinquishment, within 90 days after the approval of the act, of claims to lands outside of naval reserves, which claims would be valid but for withdrawal order September 27, 1909, and upon payment of amount to value at time of production of not less than one-eighth of oil produced from said land, claimants should be entitled to lease of one half of said land claimed for period of twenty years at royalty of one-half net proceeds.

3rd. No fraudulent claimant was to be entitled to such lease, but before bona fide purchaser without our knowledge of the fraud was not chargeable therewith.

4th. Leases were to be made by the Secretary of the Interior under appropriate rules and regulations. Bill now proposed and agreed to by conferees but not yet reported incorporated 1st, 3rd, and 4th general features as above set out, but radically changes the 4th feature in following particulars:

First: It allows claimants 6 months within which to relinquish claims instead of 90 days, and provides for payment to unlimited flat rate of one-eighth for past production instead of minimum of one-eighth. This means that those parties who deliberately trespassed upon public domain after withdrawal order was upheld by Supreme court February 23rd 1915 would in many instances be granted large rewards for willful trespasses.

Second: The claimant is to be leased entire area claimed instead of one-half thereof. The object of limiting the lease of claimant to one-half of land was in order that the general public might have right by competition along with claimants to secure leases for other one-half. This change means that public is cut off from a chance to secure lease of any of the land.

Third. Instead of a royalty of one-half of net proceeds for future production, proposed bill changes royalty to a minimum of one-eighth of net proceeds.

Fourth: Proposed Bill provides for leasing existing wells in naval reserves together with sufficient land for operation thereof upon same terms and royalties for past and future production as provided for leased claims outside of naval reserves. The objections set out above as to royalties on leased claims apply to royalties on leased wells with additional objection that much of naval reserve number two[1] is already intensively drilled, and contemplated well leases thereon seized.

Speaking broadly, proposed conference report impresses me as giving to oil claimants as much as or more than any compromise measure these claimants have heretofore suggested. The demand for large production which has heretofore seemed to justify some sacrifice of Government's interest does not now seem to exist.

In view of drastic and radical departure from provisions to which you have hitherto assented, I cannot approve the bill as agreed to by the conferees, and respectfully recommend that it be not acquiesced in. Secretary Daniels authorizes me to say that as far as interests of the Navy are concerned he concurs on above. Excuse some delay arising from inability to secure prompt conference."

Polk, Acting.

T telegram (WP, DLC).
[1] The area in California known as Buena Vista Hills.

# From the Diary of Dr. Grayson

Thursday, February 6, 1919.

In the morning the President held a conference at the Murat Palace with Samuel Gompers, and later talked over the Italian problems with Premier Orlando.

In the afternoon he attended another session of the Supreme War Council.

# Hankey's Notes of a Meeting of the Council of Ten[1]

Quai d'Orsay, February 6, 1919, 3 P.M.

BC-24

1. M. CLEMEMCEAU, in opening the meeting, said that before beginning the business of the day he wished to make mention of a matter previously decided. He referred to the destruction of German submarines. He had understood that the decision had been that only submarines under construction should be destroyed. On referring to the Minutes, however, he saw that destruction of those handed over complete was also included. This decision was not that which he thought had been reached. He would, therefore, advise that before this decision was carried out, the advice of the Naval Commission concerning the fate of all the captured ships in Allied hands, should be awaited.

MR. LLOYD GEORGE thought that it would be better to destroy as many of these pests as possible.

M. CLEMENCEAU said that some had been assigned to France and some to Italy. He thought it was wrong that some should be destroyed while others were given away.

BARON MAKINO said that seven had been given to Japan.

MR. BALFOUR said that he understood M. Clemenceau to desire a uniform policy.

M. CLEMENCEAU said that that was exactly his meaning. (It was agreed that further information as to what steps had been taken should be obtained, and that the question should be decided later.)

2. (At this stage the Delegates for the Hedjaz and their technical advisers[2] entered the room.)

EMIR FEISAL said that

In his memorandum of January 29th to the Peace Conference,[3]

---

[1] The complete text of these minutes is printed in PPC, III, 888-94.

[2] The plenipotentiary delegates were Prince Faisal and Rustum Haidar. The technical advisers were Col. Thomas E. Lawrence, Gen. Nuri al-Sa'id, and Awni Abd al-Hadi, the secretary general of the delegation.

[3] Prince Faisal, "Territorial Claims of the Government of the Hedjaz," Jan. 29, 1919, printed in Miller, *My Diary at the Conference of Paris*, IV, 300.

he had asked for the independence of all the Arabic speaking peoples in Asia, from the line Alexandretta-Diarbekir[4] southward.

He based his request on the following points:

(i) This area was once the home of important civilisations, and its people still have the capacity to play their part in the world.

(ii) All its inhabitants speak one language—Arabic.

(iii) The area has natural frontiers which ensure its unity and its future.

(iv) Its inhabitants are of one stock—the Semitic. Foreigners do not number 1% among them.

(v) Socially and economically it forms a unit. With each improvement of the means of communication its unity becomes more evident. There are few nations in the world as homogeneous as this.

(vi) The Arabic speaking peoples fought on the side of the Allies in their time of greatest stress, and fulfilled their promises.

(vii) At the end of the war the Allies promised them independence.[5] The Allies had now won the war, and the Arabic speaking peoples thought themselves entitled to independence and worthy of it. It was in accord with the principles laid down by President Wilson and accepted by all the Allies.

(viii) The Arab army fought to win its freedom. It lost heavily: some 20,000 men were killed. Allenby acknowledged its services in his despatches. The army was representative of Arab ideals and was composed of young Syrians, Lebanese, Hejazis, Mesopotamians, Palestinians, and Yemenis.

(ix) The blood of Arab soldiers, the massacres among the civil populations, the economic ruin of the country in the war, deserved recognition.

(x) In Damascus, Beyrout, Tripoli, Aleppo, Latakia, and the other districts of Syria, the civil population declared their independence and hoisted the Arab flag before the Allied troops arrived. The Allied Commander in Chief[6] afterwards insisted that the flag be lowered to install temporary Military Governors. This he explained to the Arabs was provisional, till the Peace Conference settled the future of the country. Had the Arabs known it was in compliance with a secret treaty[7] they would not have permitted it.

[4] That is, Diyarbakir, a city in eastern Turkey on the Tigris River.

[5] This Anglo-French declaration of November 1918 is printed in R. Cecil to C. A. de R. Barclay, Oct. 31, 1918, n. 2, Vol. 51, and in the minutes of the Council of Ten printed at Feb. 13, 1919, 3 p.m.

[6] Gen. Sir Edmund Henry Hynman Allenby, commander of the Egyptian Expeditionary Force.

[7] The Sykes-Picot Agreement of 1916, which provided for the partition of the Ottoman Empire into colonies and spheres of influence under the control of Great Britain, France, and Russia. The agreement also stated that the three nations were "prepared to recognize and protect an independent Arab State or a Confederation of Arab States . . . under the suzerainty of an Arab chief" in a carefully delimited area of the former Ottoman possessions. See A. J. Balfour to WW, May 18, 1917, n. 1, Vol. 42.

(xi) The Syrians who joined the Northern Army were recognised by the Allies as Belligerents. They demand through this delegation their independence.

His Father[8] did not risk his life and his Kingdom by joining in the war at its most critical time to further any personal ambitions. He was not looking for an Empire. He rose up to free all the Arabic provinces from their Turkish Masters. He did not wish to extend the boundaries of the He[d]jaz Kingdom a single inch.

His ideal was the ideal of all Arabic patriots. He could not believe that the Allies would run counter to their wishes. If they did so the consequences would be grave. The Arabs were most grateful to England and France for the help given them to free their country. The Arabs now asked them to fulfil their promises of November 1918. It was a momentous decision the Conference had to take, since on it depended the life of a nation inhabiting a country of great strategic importance between Europe and Asia.

The greatest difficulty would be over Syria. Syria claimed her unity and her independence, and the rest of the Arabic liberated areas wished Syria to take her natural place in the future confederation of liberated Arabic speaking Asia, the object of all Arab hopes and fears.

Some of the people of the present province of Lebanon were asking for French guarantees. Some of them did not wish to sever their connection with Syria. He was willing to admit their independence, but thought it essential to maintain some form of economic union in the interest of mutual development. He hoped nothing would be done now to render the admission of the Lebanon to the future confederation impossible, if it desired admission.

For the moment also the inhabitants of the rest of Syria hoped that the Lebanon people would of their own accord decide for federal union with themselves in Syria.

The Arabs realised how much their country lacked development. They wanted it to be the link between the East and West, to hand on Western civilisation to Asia. They did not wish to close their doors to civilised people; on the contrary, as rulers of their own country, in their zeal for their country's betterment, they wanted to seek help from everyone who wished them well; but they could not sacrifice for this help any of the independence for which they had fought, since they regard it as a necessary basis of future prosperity. They must also guard their economic interests, as part of their duty as Governors. He hoped no Power imagined that it had the right to limit the independence of a people because it had material interests in their country.

---

[8] Hussein (or Husayn) ibn Ali al-Hashimi, Sharif of Mecca and Medina and King of the Hedjaz.

Arab religious differences were being exploited. These had been triumphed over in the Hedjaz army, in which all creeds co-operated to free their country. The first efforts of the Arab Government would be to maintain this welding of the faiths, in their common service of the principle of nationality.

Palestine, for its universal character, he left on one side for the mutual consideration of all parties interested. With this exception he asked for the independence of the Arabic areas enumerated in his memorandum.

When this principle was admitted, he asked that the various Provinces, on the principle of self-determination, should be allowed to indicate to the League of Nations the nature of the assistance they required. If the indications before the Conference in any one case were not conclusive as to their wishes for their complete independence or for their mandatory power, he suggested that an international inquiry, made in the area concerned, might be a quick, easy, sure and just way of determining their wishes.

3. MR. LLOYD GEORGE asked how many troops the Hedjaz had put into the field.

EMIR FEISAL replied that it was impossible to give the exact figure; but, including the Hedjaz Army, the Arabs had put about 100,000 men into the field. There was, in addition, a considerable number of Irregulars who were not on his registers. He thought he could assert that every man of fighting age in possession of a rifle between Mecca and Aleppo had joined the Arab standards. How many that might have been it was difficult to say, as he had no figures of the population. There remained four Divisions of Regulars as the standing army: the Irregulars had dispersed to their own homes.

He wished to explain that the Arab Government had been organised, as it were, in the firing line. It had been born after the outbreak of war and was not yet regularly constituted. Hence the difficulty of producing exact figures. Medina had only surrendered a few days ago.

MR. LLOYD GEORGE asked whether the Arab troops had taken any part on the Mesopotamian front.

EMIR FEISAL replied that all their operations outside the Hedjaz had been in Syria. In Mesopotamia there had been no need for an independent Arab movement and no scope for one in that region. Five of his Commanding Officers, however, and many of his men came from Mesopotamia. They had fought in his army to vindicate their rights to self-government.

4. PRESIDENT WILSON asked the Emir whether, seeing that the plan of mandatories on behalf of the League of Nations had been adopted, he would prefer for his people a single mandatory, or several.

EMIR FEISAL said that he would not like to assume towards his people the responsibility of giving an answer to this question. It must be for the Arab people to declare their wishes in respect to a mandatory authority. Neither he, nor his father, nor, he thought, any person now living, would be ready to assume the responsibility of deciding this question on behalf of the people. He was here to ask for the independence of his people and for their right to choose their own mandatory.

PRESIDENT WILSON said that he understood this perfectly, but would like to know the Emir's personal opinion.

EMIR FEISAL said that personally he was afraid of partition. His principle was Arab unity. It was for this that the Arabs had fought. Any other solution would be regarded by the Arabs in the light of a division of spoils after a battle. The Arabs had fought a hard fight to achieve unity. He hoped the Conference would regard them as an oppressed nation which had risen against its masters. The Arabs asked for freedom only and would take nothing less. He thought the Conference would be of the opinion that the Arab revolt had been as well conducted as any rebellion of an oppressed people in recent memory. The Arabs were an ancient people, civilised and organised at a time when the nations represented in this room were unformed. They had suffered centuries of slavery and had now seized the chance of emancipation. He hoped that the Conference would not thrust them back into the condition from which they had now emerged. The Arabs had tasted slavery: none of the nations gathered in the room knew what that meant. For 400 years the Arabs had suffered under a violent military oppression, and as long as life remained in them, they meant never to return to it. . . .

T MS (SDR, RG 256, 180.03101/31, DNA).


# Minutes of a Meeting of the Commission on the League of Nations

FOURTH MEETING, FEBRUARY 6, 1919, AT 8:30 P.M.
President WILSON *in the chair*.

Mr. Veniselos, Mr. Dmowski, Mr. Diamandy,[1] and Mr. Kramar, representing Greece, Poland, Roumania, and the Czecho-Slovak Republic respectively, took their seats as members of the Commission, in accordance with the desire expressed by the meeting of Powers with special interests held on January 27, 1919.

Before proceeding to a consideration of Article 7 the Commission was reminded by *Mr. Bourgeois* that he had reserved the right to

[1] That is, Count Constantin J. Diamandi.

return later to the question of further amendments to Article 6, in regard to the conditions to be fulfilled by States seeking admission to the League.

### ARTICLE 7.

*Lord Robert Cecil* proposed the omission of the words "and preserve as against external aggression."

*Mr. Larnaude* proposed to abbreviate the article as follows: "The High Contracting Parties undertake to respect and preserve as against all external aggression the States members of the League."

After prolonged discussion he proposed a new drafting as follows: "The High Contracting Parties undertake mutually to respect and preserve against all aggression the States members of the League, according to the provisions of the following Article." (Article 8.)

*President Wilson* then proposed the following amendment to the original Article: "In case of any such aggression the Executive Council shall advise the plan and the means by which this obligation shall be fulfilled."

President Wilson's amendment was adopted.

It was agreed to postpone the consideration of Lord Robert Cecil's suggestion to insert a provision for the periodical revision of international obligations.

### ARTICLE 8.

*Mr. Bourgeois* pointed out the inability of France to agree to the abolition of compulsory military service, which appeared to France to be a fundamental issue of democracy, and was a corollary of universal suffrage.

After remarks by Mr. Orlando and Mr. Larnaude, *President Wilson* proposed to delete the last clause of the first paragraph relative to the possibility of abolishing compulsory military service and to substitute for it the following: "The Executive Council shall also determine for the consideration and action of the several Governments what military equipment and armament is fair and reasonable in proportion to the scale of forces laid down in the programme of disarmament; and these limits, when adopted, shall not be exceeded without the permission of the Body of Delegates."

This amendment was adopted.

Upon the proposal of *President Wilson*, which was likewise accepted, the last paragraph of this article was changed as follows: "The High Contracting Parties further agree that munitions and implements of war should not be manufactured by private enterprise, and direct the Executive Council to advise how this practice can be dispensed with; and further agree that there shall be full and frank publicity as to all national armaments and military or naval programmes."

*Baron Makino* proposed that in the first clause of this Article, in the third line, the words "national safety" should be substituted for the words "domestic safety."

This suggestion was adopted.

Article 8, as amended, was adopted.

### ARTICLE 9.

This Article was adopted without amendment.

### ARTICLE 10.

*Mr. Bourgeois* pointed out that situations might arise in which the responsibilities of the members of the League under this Article might be doubtful as the draft now stood. A note was taken of this point for further consideration. The question raised by this observation would be considered more carefully in a discussion of Article 13.

*Mr. Orlando* observed that a good deal of the strength of the project was contained in this Article, inasmuch as the League of Nations should above all else be supported by public opinion. Intentionally moderate as it might be, he approved of the draft, reserving the right in connection with the discussion of Article 13 to suggest such amendments as might be advisable.

*Lord Robert Cecil* pointed out that no time limit was provided for within which an award of arbitration or recommendation of the Executive Council must be made. It was agreed that the Secretaries should be instructed to draft an amendment stipulating, in the case of arbitration, an award within a reasonable period, and in the case of consideration by the Executive Council, a recommendation within six months.

### ARTICLE 11.

This Article was considered as closely connected with Article 10.

*Lord Robert Cecil* proposed the following new paragraph as an amendment:

"For this purpose the court of arbitration to which the case is referred shall be the court agreed on by the parties, or stipulated in any Convention existing between them."

This amendment was accepted.

### ARTICLE 12.

President Wilson's proposal to substitute the word "shall" for the word "will" throughout the article was adopted; likewise the addition of the words "when established" after the second "shall."

*Mr. Bourgeois* made note of the fact that the draft made no mention of the Permanent Court of Arbitration at The Hague, established at the Conference of 1907 with the joint approval of all the Delegates of the countries represented on the Commission. He reminded the Commission of the services rendered by bodies established at The Hague, notably the Commission of Inquiry at Hull in the Doggerbank incident,[2] and the arbitration in the Casablanca, Carthage, and Manouba incidents.[3]

*Mr. Batalha Reis* expressed his entire agreement with Mr. Bourgeois' observations.

Note was made of this observation.

*President Wilson* added that unquestionably, in the creation of a permanent court of international justice, consideration would be given to the existence of and the services rendered by the Permanent Court of Arbitration at The Hague.

A provisional agreement having been reached upon the draft of these last three articles the Commission decided to take up at its next session the consideration of the next succeeding articles.

The text of Articles 7-12, as provisionally adopted, is given in the annex.

*(The Commission adjourned until 8:30 P.M. on the following evening.)*

### Annex to Minutes of Fourth Meeting.

#### ARTICLE 7.

The High Contracting Parties undertake to respect and preserve as against external aggression the territorial integrity and existing political independence of all States members of the League. In case of any such aggression, the Executive Council shall advise the plan and the means by which this obligation shall be fulfilled.

#### ARTICLE 8.

The High Contracting Parties recognise the principle that the maintenance of peace will require the reduction of national armaments to the lowest point consistent with national safety and the enforcement by common action of international obligations; and the Executive Council shall formulate plans for effecting such reduction. The Executive Council shall also determine for the consideration and action of the several governments what military equipment and armament is fair and reasonable in proportion to the scale of forces laid down in the programme of disarmament; and these limits, when adopted, shall not be exceeded without the permission of the Body of Delegates.

The High Contracting Parties further agree that munitions and implements of war should not be manufactured by private enterprise, and direct the Executive Council to advise how this practice

---

[2] About this affair, see n. 3 to the Enclosure printed with WW to RL, Dec. 27, 1915, Vol. 35.
[3] For extensive summaries of and the decisions reached in these cases, see George Grafton Wilson, ed., *The Hague Arbitration Cases* (Boston and London, 1915), pp. 82-101 and 326-71.

can be dispensed with; and further agree that there shall be full and frank publicity as to all national armaments and military or naval programmes.

### ARTICLE 9.

Any war or threat of war, whether immediately affecting any of the High Contracting Parties or not, is hereby declared a matter of concern to the League, and the High Contracting Parties reserve the right to take any action that may be deemed wise and effectual to safeguard the peace of nations.

It is hereby also declared and agreed to be the friendly right of each of the High Contracting Parties to draw the attention of the Body of Delegates or of the Executive Council to any circumstances anywhere which threaten to disturb international peace or the good understanding between nations upon which peace depends.

### ARTICLE 10.

The High Contracting Parties agree that, should disputes arise between them which cannot be adjusted by the ordinary processes of diplomacy, they will in no case resort to armed force without previously submitting the questions and matters involved either to arbitration or to inquiry by the Executive Council, and until three months after the award by the arbitrators or a recommendation by the Executive Council; and that they will not even then resort to armed force as against a member of the League which complies with the award of the arbitrators or the recommendation of the Executive Council.

### ARTICLE 11.

The High Contracting Parties agree that whenever any dispute or difficulty shall arise between them which they recognise to be suitable for submission to arbitration, and which cannot be satisfactorily settled by diplomacy, they will submit the whole subject matter to arbitration, and will carry out in full good faith any award or decision that may be rendered.

For this purpose the Court of arbitration to which the case is referred shall be the Court agreed on by the parties or stipulated in any Convention existing between them.

### ARTICLE 12.

The Executive Council shall formulate plans for the establishment of a Permanent Court of International Justice, and this Court shall, when established, be competent to hear and determine any matter which the parties recognise as suitable for submission to it for arbitration under the foregoing article.

Printed copy (WP, DLC).

## From the Diary of Lord Robert Cecil

Feb. 6 [1919]

In the evening at the Commission I struggled to persuade the President not to insist on guaranteeing the territorial integrity of all the members of the League, but, supported by the smaller Powers, who seem singularly perverse, he insisted on doing so. I am afraid there will be trouble with the Dominions, who do not appreciate the idea of having to fight for the integrity of Bohemia, or some such place. However, we softened it down a little by requiring the Executive Council to draw up a plan of operations if the guarantee came into effect. It was rather annoying to find all the foreigners quite keen for the guarantee, though almost openly expressing the view that it would not be kept, as a kind of demonstration. Beyond that we had a word or two about the private manufacture of armaments, the prohibition of which I did not openly oppose because my sympathies are so strongly in favour of the prohibition, though I see only too clearly the difficulties which it may land us in. However, in effect the matter was referred to the Executive Council for action, so that I do not suppose very much will be done if the case against it is really as strong as the soldiers and sailors protest.

Now that I have sat for two or three days with the President I am coming to the conclusion that I do not personally like him. I do not know quite what it is that repels me: a certain hardness, coupled with vanity and an eye for effect. He supports idealistic causes without being in the least an idealist himself, at least so I guess, though perhaps I misjudge him. I still like House very much. The President is exceedingly courteous to me, and I think listens to me more than he does to any other member of the Commission; also in 99 cases out of 100 we are agreed, but all the same I do not like him.

## From Tasker Howard Bliss

Paris, February 6th, 1919.

MEMORANDUM FOR THE PRESIDENT.

General Bliss radically disagreed with the Committee and declined to accept the report.[1]

He approves of securing every advantage that we can by *negotiation* with Germany.

He disapproves introducing into the renewed Armistice a *sine quâ non* condition which, in case of refusal to accept by the Germans, makes resumption of the war by the Allies necessary.

He thinks that the introduction of such demands into the renewed Armistice, accompanied by threat to use force, is dishonorable; that it is not necessary; and that it may mean the resumption of the war.                                           Tasker H. Bliss.

TS MS (WP, DLC).
  [1] It is printed as Appendix B to the minutes of the Supreme War Council printed at Feb. 7, 1919.


# From Herbert Clark Hoover

Dear Mr. President:                                 Paris, 6 February 1919.

The Military Council in Germany appointed to look after Russian prisoners, upon which General Harries[1] represents us, has made an appeal to the Supreme Food Council and many other bodies for supplies for these prisoners. It appears that the British Red Cross have contributed about $2,500,000 and the American Red Cross is contributing $1,000,000, and these two organizations are prepared to furnish the necessary machinery for distribution. The total cost of the necessary food supplies, in addition to the above assistance, amounts to about $700,000 a month.

We have no American funds under the law that are available for this purpose. On the other hand, it appears that the object of taking care of these prisoners is to prevent them from going back to Russia in the middle of the winter and joining in the Bolshevik army, and therefore is solely a military purpose. Is it not, therefore, the proper duty of the American army to furnish supplies for the American contribution to this end? If you are inclined to this view, it would seem to me desirable to give some indication to General Pershing of authority for the American army to supply say one-third of the foodstuffs to be supplied, leaving two-thirds to the English and French to supply from their military stores. If the Americans took such a proportion it might be interpreted into American commodities, amounting to say 350 tons of flour per month, leaving to the other Allies a larger proportion of the commodities of non-American origin to furnish. If either the American Red Cross or the Army were to give the 350 tons of flour a month through General Harries, he could no doubt carry out the necessary distribution.

I would be glad indeed to have your views upon the matter and, if you approve my suggestion, if you would communicate it to General Pershing.                 Faithfully yours,   Herbert Hoover

TLS (WP, DLC).
  [1] Brig. Gen. George Herbert Harries.

## From Boghos Nubar

Mr. President,                          Paris, le 6 Février 1919

I beg to tender to you my heartiest thanks for your very kind letter and in reply I hasten to remit to you the Memorandum[1] you are good enough to ask for.

In order not to take unduly your valuable time, I have tried to make it as short as possible. Thus, I evaded to recount over again the massacres and sufferings which the Turks inflicted upon the Armenians. You are already so well aware of those facts as to have signed, with your great heart, a moving appeal for help on behalf of Dr. Barton's Committee. For that act, I must express to you, Mr. President, in the name of all Armenians and my own, our heartfelt gratitude.

I have equally evaded to make a historical sketch of all the circumstances which today render utterly impossible any thought of maintaining even the vestige of the Turkish yoke over our christian nation, the most civilized of all Asiatic Turkey. The Peace Conference has already come to a decision which frees us from that nightmare.

Our scheme, which the National Delegation has persistently followed since the beginning of this War, may be summed up into the following three points:

I°—Liberation of Armenian provinces from the Turkish yoke;

2°—Union of those liberated provinces, with the Armenian Republic in the Caucasus, in order to form one whole Armenian democratic independent State, placed under the guarantee of the League of Nations;

3°—A Mandate to be given by the League of Nations to one of the Powers for the purpose of assisting the new Armenian State, for a temporary period, in the task of its resurrection and reconstruction.

Of the above programme the first point is an accomplished fact today. The victory of the United States and the Allies, by whom the Armenians stood throughout the War, has definitely liberated them from all & any Ottoman domination.

The second item of our programme will equally be realized, as the Peace Conference has just ruled that the emancipated peoples of Asiatic Turkey, therefore the Armenians, shall be placed under the protection and control of the League of Nations.

The third and last point has also been adopted by the Peace Conference in its principles of Mandatory Powers. There thus remains, in order to fulfil entirely our programme, only the nomination of Armenia's Mandatory Power by the League of Nations.

In this respect, it is vital to examine a very delicate point, viz:— the utterly unjustifiable and unwarrantable pretensions of the Paris Syrian Committee, who wish to swallow our Cilicia by adding it to Syria, as shown on the annexed maps which have been published by the Syrian Committee.

Armenians are uneasy about this point, because the Syrian Committee's pretensions may, in case admitted, detach Cilicia from integral Armenia and attach it to Syria, the mandate whereof will most probably be handed over to France. I must say that Cilicia is an essentially Armenian province; it was during four centuries the seat of the last Armenian Kingdom; and there even are some regions, such as Zeitoun, etc, wherein Armenians have up to our present day enjoyed semi-independence under Armenian Rulers. And from immemorial times to this day the Catholicos of Cilician Armenians has had his Pontiff's Seat in Sis, capital of Cilicia. Among the population in Cilicia, before the war, the Syrians were only 20,000 as against more than 200,000 Armenians. To hand Cilicia over to Syria would therefore mutilate Armenia, in violation of the principle of Nationalities; it would strangle Armenia amidst her mountainous regions; and it would further paralize and kill her economic life, by isolating her from the Mediterranean. The attached Memorandum gives ampler information on that topic.

That is the reason why I feel bound to invite your close attention to this aspect of the Armenian problem, in order that you may, by your intervention at the Peace Conference, prevent an injustice being committed and in order to definitely solve the Armenian problem by deciding upon the establishment of an Integral Independent Armenia. That State to be composed, as aforesaid, of all the Turkish Armenian provinces, of Cilicia, and also of the Caucasian Armenian provinces, already an Independent Republic, & to be placed under the guarantee of the League of Nations, and assisted by that League's Mandatory Power during a temporary period.

The wish of all Armenians of Turkey, whom I have the honour to represent, and that of all Armenians of the Republic in the Caucasus, whose chief representative, Mr. Aharonian,[2] ex-President, actually in Paris, works in perfect harmony with us, is that the United States of America undertake the Mandate for assistance to Armenia.

The great American democracy, by granting her assistance to our new State, can of all Nations, by her disinterestedness, give confidence to the Armenians about the future of their Motherland. That would be an act worthy of the great American people who joined this War for the sake of their ideals.

You will gather, Mr. President, the reasons which had so far hindered us from officially expressing our wish, not knowing whether it would be favorably received. We now profoundly trust that the United States, which has at all times come to our aid in our misfortunes, will not leave its work unfinished, and that it will, at this supreme moment, grant us the assistance which is indispensable for the re-birth of the Armenian people.

May I be permitted to add that, according to my information, it is only the officials at the Quai d'Orsay who have some designs upon Cilicia and who encourage the Syrian Committee. But I have reasons to believe that Mr. Clemenceau faces the question with a liberal spirit, more according to the principles which you have proclaimed, and that, if you would kindly talk the matter over with him, I do think he would disagree with the pretensions of the Syrians, and second any solution giving full satisfaction to the Armenians, of whom he has always been a friend and a staunch champion.

Believe me, Mr. President,
          Most faithfully and sincerely yours.    Boghos Nubar

TLS (WP, DLC).
    [1] B. Nubar, "Brief Statement of the Armenian National Claims," n.d., TS MS (WP, DLC).
    [2] Avetis Aharonian, novelist and socialist politician, leader of the delegation of the Republic of Armenia attending the peace conference. There had been some friction between Aharonian's delegation, which represented the republic formed largely from that portion of Armenia formerly part of the Russian Empire, and Nubar's Armenian National Delegation, which represented the interests primarily of that portion of Armenia formerly part of the Ottoman Empire. See Richard G. Hovannisian, *The Republic of Armenia* (2 vols. to date, Berkeley and Los Angeles, 1971-82), I, 257-60.

## Gilbert Fairchild Close to the Marquis de Chambrun

My dear Marquis de Chambrun:          Paris, 6 February 1919.

The President was very much pleased to learn that you had offered to take him out to the home of the Marquis LaFayette and he wishes very much that it were possible for him to take advantage of your courtesy. His duties in connection with the Peace Conference make it necessary for him to forego pleasures of this kind, at any rate for the present, and he asks me to express to you his deep appreciation and his sincere regret that he cannot take advantage of this very delightful suggestion.

                              Sincerely yours,    [Gilbert F. Close]

CCL (WP, DLC).

## From Joseph Patrick Tumulty

[The White House, Feb. 6, 1919]

Number 36. Since you have been away, Hitchcock has been your main defender, making very strong and admirable speeches. Democratic caucus last night on suffrage; no actual result except best information that Pollock[1] will vote for suffrage. One vote more necessary. Arthur Mullen, National Committeeman, Nebraska, formerly opposed to suffrage, has written Hitchcock strong letter. Know how you feel toward Hitchcock, but suffrage situation so desperate, would you not be justified in cabling him asking for his support for suffrage?                                                Tumulty

T telegram (WP, DLC).
 [1] That is, Senator William Pegues Pollock, Democrat of South Carolina.

## From Newton Diehl Baker

Washington. February 6th [1919]

CONFIDENTIAL. FOR THE PRESIDENT:

I appreciate your transmitting to me Mr. Hucheson's cable regarding Carpenters' controversy.[1] On November 11th Daniels, Hurley, and I issued orders eliminating overtime on all government work to avoid unnecessary additional expense incident thereto. Union Carpenters on army base, Brooklyn, immediately struck for restoration of overtime. Subsequently changed their demands to increase in pay from five dollars and fifty cents per day to six dollars and fifty cents per day. Entire building program of War Department since June 1917 has been carried through under the agreement between Mr. Gompers and me providing that department will pay prevailing union scale in the vicinity of its work and providing a commission of three persons represent[ing] Labor, Army and Public to pass upon all controversies arising. Organized Labor has cooperated loyally with the Department throughout the War and has in every case until signing of Armistice accepted decision this commission. Commission passed on Carpenters' case in December and decided unanimously against them. Mr. Gompers then brought matter to my personal attention and the papers which he submitted indicated clearly that New York Union Carpenters were under agreement with their employers for five dollars and fifty cents per day and that they had struck in violation of this written agreement. I determined that War Department was clearly paying prevailing union rate and advised Mr. Gompers that the only remedy for the men was to return to work and request a rehearing. The men refused to return to work but at my direction the matter has been re-investigated. Report clearly establishes that the Department is still paying prevailing union rate in New York City.

Subparagraph A. Mr. Hucheson personally does not recognize the validity of agreement between Mr. Gompers and me. This agreement has been followed, however, by all building trades throughout the War and has been record for efficiency by agreement by Carpenters on numerous occasions. I have told Mr. Gompers that until the agreement with him was abrogated controversies must continue to be passed upon by the commission established by him and me and not by the War Labor Board. The matter is not a serious one. It has received my personal attention and should, I believe, be handled in accordance with the uniform procedure in such case.

Subparagraph B. If you find yourself in disagreement with me I shall, of course, be very glad to adopt any suggestions which you may make. The matter, however, can easily await your return, before which time it is likely that it will be adjusted.

Baker.

T telegram (WP, DLC).
¹ W. L. Hutcheson to WW, Feb. 3, 1919.


## From William Cox Redfield

[Washington] February 6, 1919

Quote Due to governmental control over industry during the war and the measures taken to stimulate production and the conversion of factories to war purposes and general disorganizing influences of war upon peace time pursuits prices were inflated from fifty to two hundred and fifty per cent above pre-war levels stop These high prices still remain stop Business has become stagnant, industrial activity has slackened because of lack of orders from consumers who are buying merest necessities waiting for prices to fall stop As a result the number of unemployed already large is increasing rapidly stop If this condition continues, social disturbances will result and financial failures sufficient to induce a condition of panic may be expected stop I believe and the opinion is shared by Secretary Glass and the Cabinet generally and by my industrial advisors, formerly division heads of the War Industries Board, that the Department of Commerce should do all in its power to secure by voluntary action the establishment of a reduced level of prices at which the Railroad Administration and other government agencies would be justified in buying freely stop If this reduction were made and announced the public would enter freely upon general purchases and take up new enterprizes and new construction stop All agree that there is adequate latent buying power which only requires satisfactory prices to become active and effective stop Many industries express willingness to cut prices to a basis which would stimulate activity but fear charges of unfair competition with less efficient competitors if action were taken independently stop I am convinced that stimulation of the volume of sales is the vital need for both high and low cost producers, as well as for labor and interests of whole Nation stop Following approval at conference at Treasury Monday and in discussion in Cabinet Tuesday full and very representative meeting my office of public officers and private parties Wednesday urged that I seek your approval to the appointment of a committee[1] composed of persons formerly heads divisions of War Industries Board, including a representative of labor and Railroad Administration to deal with the problem under the control of Department Commerce stop The meeting Wednesday showed gratifying recognition of the necessity of capital absorbing the first shock of readjustment and agreed labor should not be reduced except as actual reduction of cost of living shall make possible a reduction in money wages without any reduction in relative wages stop I am satisfied that the committee proposed will adopt a liberal attitude toward labor stop Committee proposed to consist of Peek, Chairman, Ritter, Bush, Scott, Frayne, Powell[2] stop In consultation Glass, Burleson, Lane, Wilson, Woolley, Meyer of War Finance Corporation, Miller of Federal Reserve Board, have expressed warm approval, in fact no opposition. Awaiting reply (signed) Redfield unquote                                        Tumulty

T telegram (WP, DLC).
[1] That is, the so-called Industrial Board of the Department of Commerce. For a detailed discussion of the board's activities and the controversy surrounding them, see E. Jay Howenstine, Jr., "The Industrial Board, Precursor of the N.R.A.: Price-Reduction Movement after World War I," *Journal of Political Economy*, LI (June 1943), 235-50, and Robert F. Himmelberg, "Business, Antitrust Policy, and the Industrial Board of the Department of Commerce, 1919," *Business History Review*, XLII (Spring 1968), 1-23.
[2] That is, George Nelson Peek, William McClellan Ritter, Samuel Prescott Bush, Frank Augustus Scott, Hugh Frayne, and Thomas Carr Powell.

# From the Diary of Edith Benham

February 6, 1919

There are very few happenings these days for the poor President is so tired he doesn't do much talking about anything. Very glad, I imagine, to get away from all discussions. With all his fatigue and these crushing responsibilities he is never too tired to be kind and gentle and considerate to every one of us and I have never heard one impatient word from him. The only thing which really worries him is to have anyone late or to be detained when he has an appointment. I don't mean late for meals or anything like that, but when he is going anywhere he likes one to be ready and started at the hour agreed. Mrs. Wilson is very punctual and I am, too, so we don't ruffle him, but Margaret has an awful time getting ready when she is going with him, for she is usually late and it is pretty hard changing the habits of a lifetime. He is working hard even when he is home redrafting the League of Nations. Yesterday he said Sir Robert Cecil for whom I don't think he cares very much, was delegated to write a draft of the League. It was more a digest of the proceedings and when he presented it every bit of life had been taken out of it and it was absolutely unrepresentative of the proceedings as a whole. So the Committee called for the original American draft. Quite a triumph, wasn't it?[1]

[1] Miss Benham was confused. Cecil had not written a new draft of the Covenant; Wilson was of course referring to the Hurst-Miller draft. The "triumph" of which Miss Benham wrote, really belonged to the representatives of the small powers, who had Bourgeois' support and Wilson's also. The drafting committee itself conceded the principle of small-power representation and, in Wilson's own words, the right of the small powers to elect their own members of the Council. Moreover, by leaving open the number of small-power representatives, the commission opened the way for the small-power members, on February 13, to achieve their goal of four representatives on the Council. See the minutes of the League of Nations Commission printed at that date. Needless to say, the "triumph" changed the fundamental character of the League of Nations.
For a contrary view of Wilson's role in this discussion and decision, see George W. Egerton, *Great Britain and the Creation of the League of Nations: Strategy, Politics, and International Organization, 1914-1919* (Chapel Hill, N. C., 1978), pp. 129-31.

## Tasker Howard Bliss to Robert Lansing[1]

Paris, February 7, 1919.

CONFIDENTIAL MEMORANDUM FOR MR. LANSING.

1. The one thing that all the American advisers of President Wilson are especially concerned in is that nothing be done, at their suggestion or by lack of their suggestion, that at any time could with any justice be alleged to impugn his good faith.

At no moment should the following be lost from consideration. When Germany made her final appeal to the President, he replied, enunciating certain general terms and principles which would be acceptable to him, and said that he would refer the whole matter to the European Allies associated with him in the war and that he would be guided by their views. The heads of the Allied European governments met in Paris and, after prolonged and careful consid-

[1] There is a copy of this memorandum in the T. H. Bliss Papers, DLC. See Frederick Palmer, *Bliss, Peacemaker: The Life and Letters of General Tasker Howard Bliss* (New York, 1934), p. 371.

eration, drew up the terms on acceptance of which they would be willing to grant an armistice to Germany. These terms were finally accepted in solemn conference at Versailles and were telegraphed to the President in Washington with the declaration that he could inform Germany that if the latter would accept them they would unite with the President in negotiating peace with Germany on the basis of the President's fourteen declarations. Germany accepted these terms and signed the conditions of the Armistice on November 11, 1918. From that moment all that every conscientious adviser of the President hopes is that no step may be taken that can now or subsequently, when all passions cool down, be justly charged as a breach of faith.

2. There are certain things which were not demanded of Germany in the original Armistice of November 11. They were not demanded at the time because of the belief that Germany would continue fighting rather than accede to the demand. They are things that all of us would now like to have done. They are things that could have been demanded before November 11 because, had we believed that we could obtain them, all that would have been necessary would have been to continue the then existing state of active war until Germany consented. But it was not so done. Among those who now desire to have these things done, the only difference of opinion is as to how we can secure their being done without a resumption of the war. Whatever we may say, the world in general regarded the war as brought to a practical termination by the Armistice of November 11th last. If the Allies now, in attempting to secure these things, bring on a renewal of the war, the dissolution of the Peace Conference, and the wiping out of all of the conditions under which the terms of peace are now being considered,—they will have to render a severe account to the world for that result.

And so, the only real difference among those who believe that there are certain desirable things still to be secured from Germany in the prolongation of the Armistice, is as to how they can be secured without the danger of a rupture of the present existing unofficial peace without having the blame justly laid upon the Allies.

In granting an Armistice to a defeated enemy, the conqueror may, for any reason that seems good to him, leave in the possession of the former a certain amount of war materiel and a certain personnel. But the conqueror, at any subsequent stage of the Armistice, may properly demand such reasonable information as to the general location and use of such materiel and personnel as will satisfy him that they are not liable to be used in the resumption of hostilities against himself.

If, therefore, the conqueror's sole object is to be guaranteed against the resumption of hostilities by his enemy (in the Treaty of Peace he may impose whatever permanent terms he can secure), he can feel quite safe if he has in the enemy's territory a body of properly qualified inspectors who will report to him as often as he may require exactly what the enemy may be doing with the respect to personnel and materiel. These inspectors will inform him of all movements of troops; of the strength and composition of these troops; whether demobilization has stopped or is still continuing; whether new troops are being raised; whether military stores are being issued from the depots, parks or arsenals; what is the rate of production of the various kinds of materiel. At any moment it is competent for the conqueror to say, in respect to any one of these things, that what is being done is regarded by him as an intent to resume hostilities and must be instantly stopped or it will be re-garded as a practical resumption of hostilities and action will be taken by the conqueror accordingly.

It may be objected to the foregoing suggestion that a refusal on the part of the Germans would lead to the use of force quite as much as would the proposed additional clause to be inserted in the renewal of the Armistice and which is to the effect that Germany must surrender certain materiel and give us control of certain man-ufacturing facilities under the threat of war. But there is an essential difference between the two cases. The conqueror, who has granted terms to his adversary with a view to preventing resumption of hostilities while peace is being negotiated, has a right to assure himself that those things which, in his mercy, he has left with his adversary are not being prepared for use in this very resumption of hostilities. A demand for the surrender of war materiel, which was omitted to be taken by the original Armistice, would be justified if reasonable evidence was presented that this materiel is being prepared for use in a resumption of hostilities. No such evidence has been presented or exists so far as is now known, but we have a right, not now to seize this materiel, but to see that there is no evidence of intent to use it for resuming hostilities, and our right then to seize it would be created as a result of our knowledge of this intent. The demand for an efficient system of inspection to guard us against a misuse of the materiel left in the hands of Germany is a demand which the common people of Germany (and it is with them that we now have to deal) are more likely to accept than any other one because it does not involve anything necessarily humiliating. It is a demand which the Allies can justify for them-selves. A more drastic demand may cause such a popular upheaval in Germany as might wreck the present Constituent Assembly and bring on all of the evil conditions in Germany which the entire world has every reason to avoid.

3. If the Supreme War Council, without having received any evidence of an intent on the part of the Germans to use materiel left in their hands for the resumption of hostilities, and contrary to the advice of the American military advisors, are still determined to demand a further surrender of war materiel and the control of manufacturing facilities, it can impose one or another of varying conditions.

a) It can impose the demands of the Loucheur Commission, from which General Bliss dissented.

b) It can demand the surrender of all material listed by the Loucheur Commission, to be delivered to a neutral, such as Denmark or Holland or both. It can also impose on the plants manufacturing war materiel and on the accumulations of war materials a system of inspection outlined in Paragraph 2.

c) It could demand the delivery to a neutral of all surplus heavy guns, field guns and machine guns.

d) It would make the Allies quite safe if under "c)" only the heavy artillery and machine guns were required to be delivered.

e) Finally, it could demand the delivery of materiel under "c)" and "d)" into the hands of the Allies.

f) Under any of the foregoing combinations, a proper system of inspection should be required in order to ascertain what they are doing with the materiel which is still left to them and also the rate at which they may be producing new materiel.

4. It would seem to make little difference which of the foregoing combinations be used in formulating the new demands upon Germany because any one of them should render her practically helpless, in the military sense, during any possible period of peace negotiations.

T MS (WP, DLC).

# Hankey's Notes of a Meeting of the Supreme War Council[1]

Quai d'Orsay, February 7, 1919, 3:30 p.m.

BC-25, SWC-3

1. M. CLEMENCEAU, having declared the meeting opened, stated that the question of the occupation of the enemy's territory by the forces of the Allied and Associated Powers had been studied by a Committee, with M. Loucheur as Chairman, and by Marshal Foch. Their reports were now ready, and he asked Marshal Foch to make a statement in this regard.

[1] The complete text of these minutes, including appendixes and annexes, is printed in PPC, III, 895-925.

MARSHAL FOCH read the following note:

"The meeting of the Commanders in Chief at Marshal Foch's, which was ordained by the Supreme Council of the Allies on January 24th,[2] was held on January 26th. The object of this meeting was to determine, with the greatest possible accuracy, the situation of the Allied Armies on March 31st 1919, such as will result from the measures taken by each Government for demobilisation and repatriation, and also to consider what further provisions could be made, given these measures.

*The French Army*, on April 5th, will still have under the colours 2,267,000 men, of which 1,350,000 in the Armies of the North and North-East. It will comprise a minimum of 46 divisions, each with 4 regiments up to fighting strength, (and sufficient men in reserve for their maintenance during 3 to 4 months of operations) and 6 Cavalry Divisions.

No measure has yet been decided upon to be carried out after this date (April 5).

*The British Army*, according to the measures decided upon by the British Government on January 23rd, will comprise 900,000 men for the whole of the Empire.

The arrangements made will render it possible to have in France, on April 1st, 10 strong divisions and 2 cavalary divisions, (Infantry divisions up to 10 battalions of 900 men). To this should be added, for an indefinite period, 2 or 3 divisions from the Dominions.

These forces in France amount to a total of 552,000 men, the fighting force of which will be 212,000 men.

It will be possible to maintain this situation for a period of several months.

*The American Army*, on April 1st, will have in France:

15 Divisions in the zone of the armies,

5 Divisions near the embarkation ports.

Those forces amount from 1,380,000 to 1,400,000 men, with a fighting strength of 680,000.

*On May 1st*, the American Army in France will comprise:

10 Divisions in the zone of the Armies,

5 Divisions near the embarkation ports.

If, on this date, the Peace Preliminaries are not signed, the American Command considers, *but without making any definite agreement on the subject*, that during May and June sufficient troops and war material will be left in France to provide for home transportation, and this without encroaching upon the above mentioned 10 divisions, in such a way that on July 1st, there may remain in France 10 divisions amounting to 380,000 men.

[2] See the minutes of a meeting of the Supreme War Council printed at Jan. 24, 1919.

*The Italian Army* has actually, in the war zone in Italy, 1,540,000, with a fighting strength of 1,020,000 men. Up to April 1st, four classes (each of 100,000 men) will probably be mustered out, that is to say a total of 400,000 men, 225,000 of which from the war zone, 1,315,000 men will therefore remain in the war zone.

On April 1st, the Italian Army will comprise:

   31 Divisions (including those of Dalmatia, but exclusive of the two divisions forming the 2nd Army Corps),
   3 divisions in Albania,
   1 division in the Balkans.

The table, given in Appendix "A"[3] summarizes the situation of the Allied Armies facing Germany on April 1st.

This situation shows that there are sufficient resources to oppose Germany up to April 1st on the Western Front.

It also shows that after this date, and if the Peace Preliminaries are not signed, the Future can only be ensured by maintaining the above mentioned resources in stopping the process of demobilization."

M. LOUCHEUR then gave a summary of the report of the Commission appointed by the Supreme War Council at the meeting of the 24th January, 1919. (For full text of report, see Appendix "B," with its annexures 1 to 5 inclusive.)

M. Loucheur added that his Committee considered that the control over the manufacture of arms and munitions in Germany could be easily established with a force of 200 officers, and that this control could be in operation by the end of March, provided the proposed new Armistice clauses were duly signed on 20th February next, on which date the present Armistice period would expire. Moreover, by April 5th, sufficient *materiel* would have been surrendered to justify the continuance of demobilisation, if Germany carried out her agreement with sufficient good-will. According to Marshal Foch's estimate, there would still be 51 Divisions and 10 cavalry divisions in the French Army.

PRESIDENT WILSON said that he understood the proposal to contemplate very serious and extensive additions to the original armistice conditions. Whenever this was attempted it was always possible that the armistice would not be renewed, and if renewed, that the Allies would be prepared to enforce the new conditions. He would like to ask Marshal Foch two questions, namely, whether in the latter's opinion these new conditions would be accepted, and, if so, whether it would be necessary to undertake any serious measures to ensure their enforcement.

[3] This chart, "Allied Forces Still Confronting Germany at Combat Strength on April 1, 1919," is printed in *PPC*, III, 909.

MARSHAL FOCH replied that he did not think the Germans would accept the new conditions without pressure. When he met the German delegates he would say: "Accept these conditions or the armistice will be broken." He could not enter into negotiations with the Germans.

As to the second question, it would evidently be necessary to take measures to insure fulfillment of the new condition, and to establish control. Whether the control proposed would be effective he did not know; but it did not guarantee anything. The officers who went to Germany would only see what they were allowed to see, and if later they discovered that the terms of the armistice had been violated they would so report; but meanwhile demobilisation would have progressed. The demobilisation was to progress on the assurance given by this control, and if the terms agreed to were violated, it would then be too late to do anything about it. He, therefore, thought it futile to base the demobilisation plans on promises of this kind, fulfilment of which could not be insured.

M. CLEMENCEAU then inquired if Marshal Foch could suggest any more effective method of control.

MARSHAL FOCH said they might occupy all the factories, but he considered that to be an impracticable solution. Or, they might occupy one or two factories, such as Essen; but to occupy Essen alone it was estimated seven divisions would be required, so that the burden to be borne would be enhanced thereby rather than diminished. The hoped-for relief would in reality merely mean an additional burden.

M. CLEMENCEAU asked whether Marshal Foch had any other suggestion to make.

MARSHAL FOCH replied in the negative. It would be impossible to prevent a country like Germany from doing what she wished at home. She would always be able to manufacture arms. The Allies could not stop all their industries.

PRESIDENT WILSON expressed his appreciation of the clear and frank reply made by Marshal Foch, and he called attention to the fact that what was desired was to find means for reducing the Allied forces; while it seemed that the occupation of the factories might call for a further increase.

MR. LLOYD GEORGE enquired whether the application of that part of M. Loucheur's report which demanded the surrender of guns, rifles and machine guns, would not make Germany impotent, at least during the duration of the armistice.

MARSHAL FOCH agreed that it would weaken Germany, but by how much and for how long he did not know; nor did he know how long the armistice would last.

MR. LLOYD GEORGE expressed the view that it would take a certain period of time to replace all the equipment Germany was to be asked to surrender, and he enquired from M. Loucheur whether he could say what that period would probably be.

M. LOUCHEUR replied that with all her available resources it would take Germany at least two years.

MR. LLOYD GEORGE next enquired whether Germany could manufacture all those arms unless the Allies allowed the necessary raw material to go through to Germany.

M. LOUCHEUR replied that the producing power of Germany in iron and steel had already been reduced 40% by the occupation of Alsace-Lorraine by Allied troops.

MR. LLOYD GEORGE said it would therefore take Germany more than two years to turn out the immense armament proposed to be surrendered; and he certainly did not think that it could be manufactured without the knowledge of the Allies' inspecting officers who would be present in the country.

M. LOUCHEUR agreed that this would be quite impossible, and he was prepared to take full responsibility for this statement.

MR. LLOYD GEORGE thought that if Germany were told that unless she assented to these terms, the supply of raw materials and needed food would be refused, that she would undoubtedly consent. It would also be advantageous to Germany to reduce her army to the maximum figure required for the maintenance of order, if by so doing she assured a proportionate reduction of the armies of the allies.

M. LOUCHEUR and MARSHAL FOCH agreed.

MR. LLOYD GEORGE, continuing, said: "Supposing the disarmament of Germany were made one of the conditions of peace," (and he could not conceive the omission of such a condition), "would it be easier to impose this condition at that time, say in July, rather than now?"

MARSHAL FOCH did not know what peace conditions would be imposed; but the question now before the Conference relating to the surrender of the armament still possessed by Germany was so vague and indeterminate that the experts themselves had never been able to agree on the number of guns Germany still possessed. The experts had only been able to say that Germany should surrender various items of war material in excess of certain given figures.

M. LOUCHEUR said that his Committee had in their report adopted the figures supplied by the Intelligence Services of the different armies, and it had called for the surrender of three-fourths of the total number given.

MARSHAL FOCH interposed that he could not assume any responsibility for those figures—they were necessarily unreliable.

PRESIDENT WILSON asked what the Allies would do if Germany promised the surrender of these materials and did not give them up. How would they get them?

MARSHAL FOCH replied that there would be only one way, viz: "By War." But, instead of pursuing a question so indeterminate as the size of Germany's armaments, which could never be accurately known, there were other methods of exercising pressure, which should be considered. Besides the resumption of hostilities by means of the Armies of Occupation, there were the maintenance of the blockade and the stoppage of supplies. Germany needed food and raw materials, and if those three instruments (Armies of Occupation, supplies, blockade), were centralised under a single military control, with powers to open and close the channels of supply according to the observance of Germany, he thought that the fulfilment of the conditions which it was proposed to impose could be attained.

MR. LLOYD GEORGE asked whether Marshal Foch could doubt that, if the surrender of these guns were made a condition for the renewal of the armistice, Germany would not do so rather than renew hostilities.

MARSHAL FOCH replied that he did not know, but, if the proposition were made and refused, the armistice would have to be broken.

MR. LLOYD GEORGE enquired whether the Germans would face a continuance of the blockade rather than surrender their guns, which after all were not of the slightest use to them except for offensive purposes.

MARSHAL FOCH thought it would be unwise to speculate on the answer to that question.

MR. LLOYD GEORGE asked M. Loucheur if, in his opinion, it would be necessary to occupy all the factories. On a previous occasion he (M. Loucheur) had stated that there were two or three essential factories, which, if taken over, would practically mean the disarmament of Germany.

M. LOUCHEUR replied that if the factories in the area of Westphalia, such as Essen, Bochum up to Duisburg were held, it would mean a diminuition of 75% of the effective means of production of Germany.

(At this stage the military, naval and technical advisers withdrew.)

PRESIDENT WILSON said that the last time the armistice conditions had been discussed, he had thought it his duty to oppose any addition to the armistice terms. He thought that the Council should have known what it was doing when the armistice was drawn up, and that it was not sportsmanlike to attempt to correct now the errors that had then been made. It was quite clear to him that the Allies were running a grave risk of bringing about a situation when, having made a threat, they might be challenged to carry it out. He understood that the Allies already controlled in the occupied districts of Germany 26,000,000 out of 32,000,000 tons of the iron production of Germany. He was afraid that the control of the factories by officers, as proposed, would prove insufficient, and that it would become necessary to occupy more territory, with the result that the military commanders would require more troops. It had already been suggested by Mr. Lloyd George that, as Germany was paying for the Army of Occupation, it would clearly be to her interest to reduce this burden. It must also be remembered that if the demobilisation of the German Army were imposed on a large scale, Germany would have forced on her a large body of unemployed, who would add to the element of unrest and be a danger to Germany and to the Allies. It was, therefore, to the interest of the latter to give Germany the means of renewing her economic life, not only for the purpose of reducing the number of unemployed, but also to enable her to pay the reparations which the Allies had a right to expect. He, therefore, proposed the institution of a civil commission to meet a similar German commission, to negotiate with them and to say—that if Germany would reduce her forces and yield a proper proportion of her mischievous equipment, the Allies would reduce their army of occupation, reducing the charges therefor; they would at the same time relax the blockade to allow the passage of sufficient raw materials, except for armaments, to enable her to renew her economic life.

He thought in that way the Allies would avoid doing the improper thing of exacting terms, without running the risk of renewing war and of bringing about an intolerable state of affairs.

MR. LLOYD GEORGE said that he did not think they were necessarily bound either as an obligation of honour, or as sportsmen, to renew the Armistice for ever or on exactly the same terms. He did not know how long the Armistice would last, but he felt that he and his colleagues were under obligation to the world and to their people to protect them against a renewal of hostilities. The terms of the Armistice did not contain any undertaking either to feed Germany or to furnish raw materials; but these things were now being considered. The alterations were not, therefore, all on one side; and if the terms could be changed in favour of the Germans, they could also be changed in favour of their own people. He had been very much impressed by a conversation he had held with Sir Douglas Haig. Field Marshal Haig had expressed views similar to those held by President Wilson, namely, that the number of infantry did not matter. But he had also called attention to the fact that Germany still had the materiel and armament, which would enable her within a short period of time to call back three or four million men, fully equipped for war. By that time most of the American and British troops would have gone home and be out of reach, and the French would have scattered over the country. If Germany should therefore mean mischief, she could call together millions of well-trained men, with full complement of officers and non-commissioned officers, thousands of the best guns in the world, and fifty thousand machine guns. A fit of anger might come over her. It was impossible to say how long the present government would last, and a change of government might mean a change of policy. A tailor named Ebhardt [Ebert] was Chancellor, Scheidemann was one of the leaders; but neither were men of real power. It was impossible to say who would be on top in six weeks' time. Germany herself was being endangered by having this temptation left at her door. Consequently, nothing unfair would be done by imposing the proposed conditions. The only question to be settled was how those conditions should be imposed. It might be fair to do this on the lines suggested by President Wilson by making clear that the Allies would not help Germany unless these conditions were accepted. Nothing with reference to the supply of food and raw materials appeared in the Armistice. Consequently, they were fully entitled to refuse to supply these things to Germany. He thought there was a good deal to be said in favour of appointing a civilian commission; but the question would have to be settled at the time of the renewal of the Armistice. This arrangement would be best both for the Germans and for the Allies.

PRESIDENT WILSON agreed that the Allies were under no moral obligations to furnish food. He was proud as a moral man that on humane grounds it was not intended to let the people of Germany starve. There was also no obligation to furnish raw materials, and the price which the Allies had in their mind to exact for these concessions was not extravagant. But, if they were prepared to assist Germany to renew her commercial life, they had a right to ask guarantees for their own safety: and it would be both honourable and reasonable to impose such conditions. He thought that there would be a great moral advantage in approaching the German delegates through a civilian commission, which would not threaten them. He would also like to see the negotiations begun immediately so as to be completed before the date fixed for the renewal of the Armistice.

MR. LLOYD GEORGE pointed out that he had forgotten to mention one most important point. According to Marshal Foch's report, the Allied forces would by April next be very greatly reduced. At the present moment sufficient men were available and, therefore, the question should, he thought, be discussed at once before further demobilisation took place.

M. CLEMENCEAU regretted that he was not in accord with President Wilson in this matter. France would be placed in a position of great danger if a firm attitude were not adopted. When the terms of the Armistice had been discussed he had said that only what was necessary should be inserted, in order not to risk a refusal of the terms. But, each time it had been agreed to renew the Armistice for a period of one month only, and this was done with the express object of having an opportunity of imposing new terms, adapted to the changing situation. The right to impose new terms, or new conditions, could not therefore be contested either on juridicial or any other grounds; and the Germans themselves had made no objection to the occupation of Kehl and other places. But he had one other thing to say. The present moment was decisive, not because it was a question of winning the war, but because there was danger of losing the fruits of victory. It was essential to act quickly. The forces at the call of the Allies had not yet diminished appreciably. In the last few weeks the Germans had become insolent, and recently an incident had occurred. Marshal Foch had been forced to use constraint to bring the German delegates to a meeting. If now ambassadors were to be sent and negotiations were to be begun, much valuable time would be lost; and April would come and find our forces partially scattered. The American and Australian troops would have returned to their homes, and France and Great Britain would be left alone to face the Germans, who, seeing the Allies always giving way, would in turn become more arrogant. He knew the German people well. They became ferocious when any one retires before them. Was it forgotten that they were still at war; that the Armistice was a status of war? The Germans had not forgotten it. He called attention to the case of Poland. The Poles had stopped the further advance of their troops at the request of the Allies; but the Germans had treated a similar request with a blank refusal. The terms of the refusal were well-known. The Allies would be exposed to great danger unless they menaced the Germans now. There was need of a strong Poland. Furthermore, President Wilson had, as one of his fourteen points, assumed the obligation of reconstituting Poland. The League of Nations was a very fine conception, but it could not be constituted without nations. As one of the nations concerned, Poland was most necessary as a buffer on the East just as France formed a buffer on the West. If the Germans were formally told that any attack by them on the East would mean an advance by the Allies on the West, he knew that such language would be understood by the Germans and would command immediate compliance. Instead of this, it was proposed to buy the good will of the Germans by offering them food and raw materials. A state of war still existed, and any appearance of yielding would be construed as an evidence of weakness. At any rate, personally he could not accept President Wilson's proposition. He did not wish to starve the Germans, but the blockade must be maintained. If he so far forgot the interests of his country and of Europe as to consent to this proposal, the Chamber would undoubtedly dismiss him, and it would be acting right in doing so.

MR. LLOYD GEORGE said that he had never suggested raising the blockade. It had but [been?] agreed to let some food through, and the question of permitting the passage of some raw materials was being considered. But it would not be to the interest of the Allies to starve Germany, or to have Germany completely unemployed—a pool breeding infection throughout Europe. He therefore proposed the following resolution.

"The Supreme War Council agree—

(1) That a civilian commission shall be appointed at once to negotiate an agreement with the Germans on the following lines: that food and raw materials, other than those required for the manufacture of material of war, shall be allowed to enter Germany on the following conditions: (M. Loucheur's Committee to insert the conditions in their report.)

(2) That the Commission shall be instructed to complete the negotiations before the next renewal of the Armistice in order that if necessary, Marshal Foch may put pressure on the enemy to comply as a condition of the renewal of the Armistice.

(3) That the Commission be authorised by Marshal Foch to commence the negotiations at once and to complete them before the next renewal of the Armistice in order that, if necessary, Marshal Foch may put pressure on the enemy to secure compliance."

M. CLEMENCEAU expressed his inability to accept this proposal. He objected to it after long reflection. He had no objection to offer to civilians being attached to Marshal Foch's Commission; but he felt convinced that as long as a state of war existed it was for soldiers to confer with soldiers. He proposed that a new clause should be drafted to be included in the Armistice, reversing the sequence of ideas contained in Mr. Lloyd George's proposal. Their demands should, in the first place, be stated, followed if necessary by a statement to the effect that the Allies would be ready, as an act of grace, to consider the question of relaxing the blockade with a view to the supply of certain quantities of food and raw materials.

PRESIDENT WILSON wished respectfully to submit that M. Clemenceau's proposal was open to strong objection. A demand was first put forward, and then followed an offer of concession. He thought, the concession would nullify the threat. M. Clemenceau had said that Germans could be handled only by threats, and he might be right. But, if what they wanted could be got by negotiations, with the idea in the mind of the Germans that a threat might follow, threats could still ultimately be resorted to. But if they began with threats and then offered concessions, the force of the threat would be reduced.

MR. LLOYD GEORGE said that he had tried in drafting his resolution to reconcile the ideas of President Wilson and M. Clemenceau. As a matter of fact, his sympathies were entirely with M. Clemenceau. It would be impossible to reduce the allied forces until the conditions now proposed had been accepted. On the other hand, the Allies could not continue to maintain their big forces until peace was signed.

PRESIDENT WILSON reminded his colleagues that as far as Marshal Foch's opinion was concerned, it would not be possible before April to know whether the conditions, if accepted, were being carried out, and there would be no safety in reducing the Allied forces between now and April. No Government was going to reduce its forces below the point of safety. Certainly the United States would not do so. If he saw any good prospect of bringing about a reduction of forces by the proposals made, he would be more impressed by them, but it seemed to be Marshal Foch's opinion that those forces could not safely be reduced until peace was signed.

MR. LLOYD GEORGE said that he saw no safety even then, unless the Germans were compelled to surrender these thousands of guns. The situation on the signing of peace would be the same as now.

M. CLEMENCEAU said that Marshal Foch was not a military Pope; he was sometimes mistaken. He was a great General and all were prepared to do him honour as such; but as a matter of fact he had always been opposed to the idea of imposing disarmament on Germany. When asked what means could be taken to enforce disarmament he had proposed strengthening the blockade. In this he was directly opposed by President Wilson. He (M. Clemenceau) was as deeply impressed as anyone by the seriousness of the situation, and dreaded as much as anyone a renewal of the war. But he knew the Germans; and today they must be spoken to firmly. The German people wanted economic advantages, and he did not object to their being eventually granted. But it was a *sine qua non* that they should in the first place accept the Allies' demand as a matter of right. He would not consent to Ambassadors being sent to Germany to negotiate with offers of concessions when the Allies had a right to demand. He felt confident this was wholly a psychological question. He would merely ask the Council to consider the Germans' reply to the Allies' request for a cessation of hostilities against the Poles. The German reply would have to be answered. Should the answer be: "If you stop attacking Poland, we will give you bread, sugar and other supplies?" No. The Germans must be told that if they attacked the Poles, the Allied troops would march into Germany. That argument would appeal to the Germans and, after due compliance with the Allies' demands, sugar, butter and supplies could then be granted.

BARON SONNINO thought that Marshal Foch's statement had not been quite correctly interpreted. The Marshal had concurred in the opinion that the disarmament of Germany would be advantageous. He merely did not consider that disarmament would by itself give complete assurance of safety.

M. ORLANDO thought that Marshal Foch had a basic idea, which explained any inconsistencies in his statements. He wanted to have at his disposal the greatest number of troops he could get. His idea was a sound one, for he could count on the troops under his orders, but he could make no certain estimate of the strength of the enemy's forces. On the other hand, civilians were obliged to consider things in a more complicated manner. This question of demobilisation was a difficult one. President Wilson had said, that should the necessity arise American troops would be retained, and Italy, no doubt, would be prepared to do the same. But demobilisation once begun was very difficult to stop. Italy's soldiers had now been under arms for four years and were tired. The progress of demobilisation could be slowed down, but it could not be stopped. It is for that political reason that it would be impossible to count on being able to stop demobilisation. It could be done; but it would be most undesirable to have to do so. At a previous meeting it had been decided that it would be more difficult to stop demobilisation than to insist upon a reduction in the enemies' force. The present proposal was a consequence of the decision then taken.

In regard to President Wilson's contention that they were under an obligation not to insert new conditions on renewal of the armistice, he thought that M. Clemenceau's point was just, namely, that the armistice had deliberately been made renewable at given intervals of time so that new conditions might be made, if necessary. The Allies had signed two important armistices—one with Austria which was for an indefinite period; the other with Germany which provided periodic renewals, and so implied the possibility of changes and additions. As far as the psychological question was concerned, he begged President Wilson to believe that he also knew the Germans well. If the Allies were willing to accept less than was contained in M. Loucheur's report, let them reduce their demands; but whatever was wanted must be demanded in the form of an order and in a loud tone of voice. If a German thought that the one having the mastery showed any signs of hesitation, or failed to look him straight in the eyes, he would concede nothing. The victors must speak to the Germans as to the vanquished. It would be undesirable to have to face a refusal. Therefore, if necessary, the conditions might be reduced, but whatever was agreed to must be demanded as an order.

M. CLEMENCEAU said that the present moment was particularly favourable because there was practically no government in Germany now. In three months' time the situation might be quite different and unfavourable to the Allies.

MR. LLOYD GEORGE said that he was anxious for a unanimous decision. All he wanted was to get the guns away from the Germans, so that it might not be necessary to maintain huge armies. He did not contemplate making Europe an armed camp for ever, and the way to prevent this was to disarm Germany. If it was possible to blend President Wilson's suggestions with the French proposals and get the guns, concerted action might become possible. With this object in view he offered the following draft resolution:

The Supreme War Council agree:

(1) That a Civilian Commission of the Allied and Associated Powers shall be attached to Marshal Foch on the occasion of the next renewal of the Armistice and in connection with the Marshal's negotiations shall endeavour to arrange with the Germans that controlled quantities of food and raw materials other than those required for the manufacture of material of war shall be allowed to reach Germany. That it shall be an essential part of the above arrangement that the demands set forth in M. Loucheur's Report be complied with.

M. CLEMENCEAU regretted that he could not accept this resolution. He had two objections to it. First, he could not take any obligation in the matter of supplies without having consulted his experts. Secondly, this proposal had the vice of first discussing the reward, while in his opinion the demand should be made first. Otherwise, there would be endless discussion about the kinds and classes of supplies required. The discussions would last for months and the favourable moment would be lost. He wanted the military conditions agreed to first, and the diplomatic negotiations might then follow.

PRESIDENT WILSON considered the recommendation contained in the Loucheur report to be a panic programme. The report not only called for the surrender of big guns, which in his opinion should be given up, but it also went into details of aircraft and factory production. He was in favour of controlling factories by regulating the raw material that went to them; but he thought that if officers were sent there they would get into trouble and would have to be supported by military forces.

MR. LLOYD GEORGE agreed, but thought that the output of factories must be supervised.

M. SONNINO thought that the Allies' demands could be reduced to three or four important items, such as big guns and machine guns.

LORD MILNER agreed. In his opinion if the demands were reduced as suggested by M. Sonnino, and a certain number of factories were watched, the desired result would be obtained.

MR. LLOYD GEORGE suggested that a Committee be appointed consisting of one member representing each of the Great Powers having armies on the Western Front, to examine and determine the items of war material to be surrendered by Germany with a view to her disarmament.

This was agreed to. The following representatives were nominated:

United States of America    Mr. Lansing
Great Britain                     Lord Milner
France                             M. Tardieu

It was further agreed that the report should be submitted at the next meeting to be held on Saturday, February 8th, at 3.30 p.m.

Appendix B

Report by the Committee appointed by the
SUPREME WAR COUNCIL at the Meeting
of the 24th January, 1919, (MORNING).

The Committee consisting of

Monsieur Loucheur   as President                    (France)
Marshal Foch         Commander-in-Chief of the Allied Forces.
General Bliss                                           (America)
General Sir Henry Wilson                          (Great Britain)
    (acting for Mr. Winston Churchill)

General Sir Frederick Sykes                    (Royal Air Force)
H. E. General Diaz    Chief of the Staff, Italian Army.
assembled on the 27th January, 2nd and 5th February.

From an examination of the Reports made by the Sub-Committees and from the discussion which followed it appeared that—

1. There is some uncertainty regarding the strength of the existing German Army, and the resources in war material of all kinds at its disposal, but both are still considerable.

2. There is similar uncertainty regarding the war material and stocks of munitions in the interior of Germany, both in proof and in course of manufacture, also regarding the means of production of such materials, but these stocks and the means of production also are certainly still considerable in quantity.

Any serious reduction in the effective strength of the Allied Army of Occupation must depend on the carrying out of certain necessary measures, the execution of which must be controlled. To this end the Committee recommends the following arrangements:

*War material actually in possession of the German Armies.*

An approximate estimate of such war material is set forth in Annex No. 1.

The Committee therefore considers that the Allied Governments should fix definitely the number of troops and the amount of war material of certain categories to be left in the hands of the German Armies, which it proposes should be reduced to a strength of 25 Infantry Divisions and 5 Cavalry Divisions, and recommends that all material in excess should be handed over.

All the war material to be surrendered by the Germans, all stock of asphyxiating gas and gas masks, must be given up at places selected by agreement, to Committees of Allied officers who will carry out the removal, or the destruction, or the putting out of action of the surrendered war material, according to circumstances.

As regards destruction and putting out of action, certain detailed measures have been considered; these will be carried out by the above mentioned Allied officers if the general principles are accepted.

### Manufacture of War Material.

Similarly it is necessary that the German Government should pledge itself not to continue the manufacture of war material during the period of the armistice, in order that she may not rearm in secrecy.

The most certain method of ensuring the correct execution of the above undertaking would consist in controlling certain German munition factories but not necessarily all of them and in removing or destroying special machinery as indicated in the Report of the

Technical Sub-Committee (Annex 2). This control could be exercised by a comparatively small number of Allied experts.

It is, however, necessary to provide for the possibility that, after the Allies have reduced the Army of occupation, Germany may put obstacles in the way of such control and resume the production of war material.

The Committee, therefore, calls attention to the fact that a form of guarantee less comprehensive, but sufficiently efficacious, provided that the delivery of existing material has taken place, could be found in the establishment of absolute control by military occupation of the area extending to the east of the Rhine for an average depth of about 50 kilometres from Cologne to 15 kilometres to the north of Duisburg, in such a way as to embrace Essen and the principal Krupp establishments, the greater part of the Rheinish-Westphalian coal-fields, and the metallic industries which depend on these. A map has been sent to Marshal Foch showing this zone.

The importance of this region from the point of view of war industries is so great that it would be practically impossible for Germany once disarmed to take up arms if she had not free disposal of it.

Further, the prevention of exportation to the unoccupied German territories of the general products of this area, would have the most serious consequences from an economic point of view. If the general munition control is interfered with or if unauthorised production is found to be going on, trade between the occupied territory and the unoccupied territory would be prohibited.

These results can be looked for as a consequence of negotiating with the enemy, or they can be enforced upon him as a condition of the renewal of the armistice. In the latter case the text of the agreement might be that of the appended draft.

General Bliss has drawn up a Note (Annex 3) dealing with certain reservations he wishes to make on the subject matter of the above paragraphs.

General Diaz brought to notice the importance, in case German Austria should be joined to Germany, of foreseeing the necessity of taking analogous measures as regards factories in which war material is manufactured in that region, where there are many of importance.

(Attached is an additional clause to the Armistice conditions compiled in accordance with the above mentioned idea.)

To this Report are annexed the following documents:

*Annex 1.* Report dated 1st February, 1919, of the Military Sub-Committees.

*Annex* 2. Report dated 2nd February, 1919 of the Technical Sub-Committee.

*Annex* 3. Memorandum by General Bliss, United States Army.

*Annex* 4. Paper by General Groves[4] devoted to aeronautics.

*Annex* 5. Normal allowance of arms for German units.[5]

ADDITIONAL CLAUSE TO THE ARMISTICE CONDITIONS

1. It is hereby agreed that provided Germany renounces definitely any intention to resume hostilities and carries out the following conditions as a guarantee of such renunciation, the Allied and Associated Governments will reduce the financial burden imposed upon Germany by the Allied occupation.

2. The reduction of the burden of occupation must be preceded by the adoption of the measures mentioned below, the execution of which will show clearly the wish of Germany not to resume hostilities and to cease the manufacture of war material.

3. Germany undertakes to reduce the effective personnel of her Armies to such numbers as are strictly necessary for the garrison of their frontier and the maintenance of order in the interior, that is to say

  25 Divisions*

   5 Cavalry Divisions*

4. Germany consequently undertakes to reduce the quantity of war material to be maintained to the following figures:

NOTE General Weygand wishes to give further consideration to these figures before accepting them.

| | |
|---|---|
| Heavy Guns | 1,000 |
| Field Guns | 1,575 |
| Machine Guns | 3,825 |
| Automatic Rifles | 4,500 |
| Rifles | 412,500 |
| Aeroplanes | see para: 5 bis. |
| Trench Mortars | 1,400 |

5. Consequently all war material of the above natures in excess of these figures will be delivered at places to be fixed by agreement, either in occupied or non-occupied portions of Germany or outside Germany, to Commissions of Allied officers who will be appointed for this purpose. These surrenders will apply to the whole of the war material existing either with the Armies or in the interior in parks, depots, factories, etc., whether finished, under proof or in course of construction or repair. The Allied officers will carry out

---

* The establishment of a Division is shown in Annex 5.

4 Brig. Gen. Robert Marsland Groves, Deputy Chief of the British Air Staff.

5 Only Annex 3 of the above printed here.

according to circumstances the removal or the destruction or the putting out of action of the war material so surrendered.

5. bis. *Aircraft*. With regard to Aircraft, Germany to surrender the following:

(a) 5,000 engines of types to be selected by the Allies.

(b) 450 German marine aircraft (i.e. Aeroplanes, seaplanes and flying boats) to be selected by the Allies.

(c) 15 Airships to be selected by the Allies.

(d) All aircraft will be complete with all war equipment and armament and to be flown by German personnel to places to be specified by the Allies before a date to be fixed by the Allies.

(e) 6 rigid airship sheds over 800 feet long, with the complete hydrogen-producing plant for each of the airship-sheds, will also be surrendered in an efficient condition.

NOTE It is considered important that the question of the ultimate destination or destruction of all aircraft and aircraft material surrendered by Germany shall be settled by the Supreme War Council when a decision as to the amount to be delivered has been arrived at.

6. All tanks, (all gas masks) and stocks of mustard and arsenical gases with projectors and cylinders will be surrendered.

7. Germany will, in addition, bind herself expressly to stop all manufacture of war material of every kind, except that strictly necessary for the upkeep of material of which the existence is authorised.

8. To ensure the loyal and complete execution of the pledges undertaken by Germany as laid down in paras. 1, 3, 4, 5, 5 bis, 6 and 7, the Allied Governments will maintain in Germany a Mission of technical experts and officers who will control the factories, workshops and building yards engaged in the manufacture of the classes of war material mentioned in pars. 4, 5 bis, and 6 and munition parks and magazines of all kinds.

This mission shall be authorised to inspect factories and to remove or destroy such specialised machinery engaged in the production of the above mentioned claims of war material as they may consider necessary to ensure the cessation of output as aforesaid.

The civil and military German authorities will supply these experts with the whole of the information which they will need to carry out their mission and will furnish them with all the necessary material means, and all the necessary authorisations to complete it, without allowing any obstacle to be placed in their way.

9. In the event of Germany not agreeing to the foregoing proposals, or in the event of her not carrying them out after having

agreed to them the Allied Governments will proceed to the military occupation of the Westphalian basin on the right bank of the Rhine, the territory painted red on the map which is annexed.

General [blank]

C.I.G.S.

MILITARY SECTION, BRITISH DELEGATION. 5TH FEBRUARY 1919.

### ANNEX III

#### MEMORANDUM

The report of the Committee is based on the assumption that any serious reduction in the effective strength of the Allied Army of Occupation calls for:

1. The fixing of the strength of the German Army.

2. The surrender of all war materials in Germany not required by the German Army whose size is thus regulated.

3. The control of all factories, shops, building yards, engaged in the manufacture of war material.

Under (1) the strength recommended for the German Army is 25 divisions of infantry and 5 cavalry divisions, it being assumed that these divisions are sufficient for the garrisoning of the frontiers and the maintenance of order in the interior. The infantry and cavalry divisions would be organised and armed as at present. The total arms needed for this force is given as:

| Heavy guns | 1,000 |
| Field guns | 1,575 |
| Machine guns | 3,825 |
| Automatic rifles | 4,500 |
| Rifles | 412,000 |

Under (2) it is proposed that Germany turn over to the Allies everything in excess of the war material listed in the above paragraph. Subtracting the above amounts from the material listed in the report of the sub-committee, it would appear that the following would be turned over to the Allies:

| Heavy Guns | 1,500 |
| Field Guns | 6,425 |
| Machine Guns | 41,675 |
| Rifles | 838,000 |

In addition to the above the report calls for the surrender of all war material in the interior of Germany both in proof and in course of manufacture, including all stocks of asphyxiating gas and gas masks. The amount of this material is unknown, but it is believed to be considerable in amount.

[6] *Sic.*

Under (3) it is proposed that the Allies maintain in Germany technical experts and officers who will control the factories, workshops, and building yards engaged in the making of the war material discussed above.

It is proposed in the new armistice terms (para 9) "in the event of Germany not agreeing to the foregoing proposals or in the event of her not carrying them out after having agreed to them, the Allies will proceed to the military occupation of the Westphalian Basin on the right bank of the Rhine."

The paragraph quoted above (para 9) negatives in a large degree the idea that the Allies by negotiation reach an agreement with Germany in regard to the above demands.

Previous to the negotiation of the original armistice with Germany my position was that Germany should be required to completely demobilise except such forces as were needed for the maintenance of order and to surrender her arms. These terms were at the time considered too harsh, and milder terms were offered Germany which she accepted in the original armistice conditions. I do not find it consistent with my sense of right to go beyond the terms of the original armistice agreement except as a penalty for Germany's wilful failure to comply with these conditions. To my mind to proceed now to a military occupation of the Westphalian basin on the right bank of the Rhine in the event of Germany not agreeing to the foregoing new proposals would be on the part of the Allies and the United States a breaking of the Armistice agreement. If it did not lead to a resumption of hostilities the Allies could be readily accused of violating their own agreement and justly so. If it led to the grave consequence of the resumption of the war due to this act the responsibility would belong to the Allied Governments and the Government of the United States.

I regret that I find myself unable to agree to the report of this Committee to the Supreme War Council recommending the addition of clauses to the original armistice agreement which are based on the threat of forcible occupation of further German territory unless our proposals are agreed to.

APPENDIX "C" TO SWC-3.

No. 956. From ALLIED GENERAL HEADQUARTERS, February 3, 1919. Marshal Foch, Commander-in-Chief of the Allied Armies, to the President of the Council, Minister for War

In continuation of the letter from the Secretary-General of the Peace Conference, dated February 1st, which you transmitted to me in Schedule No. 1561.D., and received by me on February 2nd at Noon, I have the honour to inform you that I have addressed to

General Nudant,[6] President of the International Armistice Commission, the following telegram:

"Please to make the following communication without delay, to the High German Command:

"Marshal Foch informs the German Military Authorities that the Associated Powers are sending to Poland a Commission which has full powers to allay all disorders there in so far as is possible. For this purpose the Commission has been instructed to urge the Polish Authorities to abstain altogether from the use of force against the German forces. The Marshal is communicating to the German Authorities in German Poland the injunction of the Associated Powers that they should henceforward abstain from any use of force in that province and from all interference in its public life, pending the completion of the labours of the Peace Conference."

I enclose herein copy of the telegram which I have received on this subject from General Nudant.          (sgd) Foch.

Telegram From General Nudant to Marshal Foch. February 3rd, 1919. 2.45 p.m.

No. 431. PG.

(1) I communicated this morning to the German Commission telegram No. 934 of February 2nd, in regard to the despatch of an Inter-Allied Commission to Poland.

(2) The President of the German Commission immediately asserted the absolute right of the German Government to ensure the protection of their subjects within their own territory. He added that present events necessitated a rapid intervention so as to re-establish order in view of the assassination of German subjects and of Pogroms against the Jews. This point of view will undoubtedly be confirmed to me shortly by the German delegates.

T MS (SDR, RG 256, 180.03101/32, DNA).
[6] Gen. Alphonse Pierre Nudant.

# Minutes of a Meeting of the Commission on the League of Nations

FIFTH MEETING, FEBRUARY 7, 1919, AT 8:30 P.M.
President WILSON *in the Chair.*

The Commission proceeded to the consideration of Article 13.

The following two amendments to the article were adopted.

On the motion of *Mr. Vesnitch*, after the word "Chancellor" in the seventh line were inserted the words "as promptly as possible."

On the motion of *Lord Robert Cecil*, at the end of the first paragraph were inserted the words "and the Executive Council may forthwith direct the publication thereof."

Following a remark by Senator Scialoja concerning the exercise of this right, it was understood that the Council should decide what documents, if any, were to be published, without affecting the right of the parties to publish whatever documents they themselves might think pertinent to the dispute.

Upon the motion of *President Wilson*, the words "and the privilege of the minority" were added after the words "the duty of the majority."

*Mr. Hymans* then proposed the following amendments:

For the words in the second paragraph "if the report is unanimously agreed to by the members" substitute the words "if the report is agreed to by the majority of the members," and for the last sentence of the paragraph substitute the words "if the report is unanimously agreed to by the members of the Council other than the parties to the dispute, the High Contracting Parties agree that they will carry out in full good faith the decision that has been rendered."

These proposals were discussed at length. Mr. Hymans' view was supported by the French delegates and by Mr. Vesnitch, but Lord Robert Cecil raised doubts as to the desirability of giving mandatory effect to the decisions of a majority of the Council, and President Wilson shared these doubts. Mr. Veniselos in agreement with Mr. Bourgeois urged that as regards the second amendment proposed by Mr. Hymans the Council should have some right to secure the satisfaction of the claims of the injured party to a dispute in cases where the Council had unanimously reported in favour of those claims. He also suggested that as regards the first amendment proposed by Mr. Hymans some mandatory effect might safely be given to the decisions of a large majority of the Council, for instance, a majority of four out of the five Great Powers and three out of four small Powers, assuming that representatives of four small Powers are included in the Council. Finally, Mr. Veniselos pointed out that some time limit should be put to the right of either party to a dispute to refer the dispute from the Council to the Body of Delegates, and this point was generally agreed to by the Commission.

It was finally decided that a Sub-Committee consisting of Mr. Hymans, Mr. Bourgeois, Lord Robert Cecil, and Mr. Veniselos should undertake the drafting of amendments to the Article in the sense of the Commission's discussion.

Article 13 was therefore passed by for the time being on the understanding that the main principles embodied in it were agreed to.

ARTICLE 14.

On the motion of *Lord Robert Cecil* the words at the beginning, "to be found by the League to have broken or disregarded," were altered to "break or disregard."

On the motion of *President Wilson* it was agreed to strike out the words "which shall immediately subject it," and insert instead the words "which already undertake immediately to subject it."

*Mr. Hymans* raised the point whether Articles 7, 11, and 13 should not be added to Article 10 in the second line of this Article, in order that the sanctions provided in this Article might operate equally in respect of the situations contemplated in Articles 7, 10, 11, and 13.

After discussion, it was generally agreed that a reference to Article 7 might be ambiguous, and that it was not really necessary to provide a sanction, especially by such summary procedure as that provided for in Article 14, to enforce the agreement embodied in Article 11. It was thought, however, that some sanction might perhaps be provided in the case of an unanimous report by the Executive Council under Article 13, and this question was likewise referred to the Sub-Committee above mentioned.

Subject to the above amendments, Article 14 was provisionally passed.

ARTICLE 15.

*Lord Robert Cecil* proposed to insert after the words "*ad hoc* members of the League" the words "upon such conditions as the Executive Council may deem just."

This amendment was adopted.

*Mr. Orlando* pointed out that the words "become *ad hoc* members of the League" were not really accurate, and in this he was supported by the French delegates. It was therefore agreed to refer this passage in the article to the Sub-Committee above mentioned, who should be asked to recommend another expression.

With this exception, no objection was raised to the draft of Article 15, which was therefore considered provisionally adopted subject to reconsideration in connection with the recommendations of the Sub-Committee.

In regard to the general scope of these three articles, *Mr. Bourgeois* expressed the hope that a clearer statement might be made of the cases in which the sanctions of the League would be applied, as he did not consider that the wording of Articles 10, 13, and 14 when taken together were sufficiently explicit.

(*The Commission adjourned until* 10:.30 *A.M. on the following day.*)

*Annex to Minutes of Fifth Meeting.*

### ARTICLE 14.

Should any of the High Contracting Parties break or disregard its covenants under Article 10, it shall thereby *ipso facto* be deemed to have committed an act of war against all the other members of the League, which hereby undertake immediately to subject it to the severance of all trade or financial relations, the prohibition of all intercourse between their nationals and the nationals of the covenant-breaking State, and the prevention, so far as possible, of all financial, commercial, or personal intercourse between the nationals of the covenant-breaking State and the nationals of any other State, whether a member of the League or not.

It shall be the duty of the Executive Council in such a case to recommend what effective military or naval force the members of the League shall severally contribute to the armed forces to be used to protect the covenants of the League.

The High Contracting Parties agree, further, that they will mutually support one another in the financial and economic measures which are taken under this article in order to minimise the loss and inconvenience resulting from the above measures, and that they will mutually support one another in resisting any special measures aimed at one of their number by the covenant-breaking State, and that they will afford passage through their territory to the forces of any of the High Contracting Parties who are co-operating to protect the covenants of the League.

Printed copy (WP, DLC).

## To Robert Lansing

My dear Lansing: Paris, 7 February, 1919.

I recognize the seriousness of this matter,[1] and think that it might be well for you to send a message to Reinsch, telling him to advise the Chinese Government to stand firm, and a message to Morris in Tokyo instructing him to have a friendly conversation with the Minister of Foreign Affairs about this matter and disclose our knowledge of what is going on in Peking, and express our distress that there should be these indications that the Japanese Government is not willing to trust to the fairness and justness of the Peace Conference.

Koo might be advised in the meantime to follow the course that he thinks right.

Cordially and faithfully yours, Woodrow Wilson

TLS (R. Lansing Papers, DLC).
[1] See FLP to WW, Feb. 4, 1919.

## Robert Lansing to Frank Lyon Polk

[Paris, c. Feb. 7, 1919]

Confidential

Your 561 of February 4th four p.m.

The President joins me in asking you please to instruct Minister Reinsch to take occasion to impress upon the Chinese Government discreetly and orally the importance of standing firm. Please also instruct Ambassador Morris to find opportunity to have a friendly conversation about the matter with the Japanese Minister for Foreign Affairs. Disclose our knowledge of what is taking place in Peking and express our distress that such indications are given of Japan's unwillingness to trust the fairness and justness of the Peace Conference.

Hw telegram (R. Lansing Papers, DLC).

## To Norman Hezekiah Davis

My dear Mr. Davis: Paris, 7 February, 1919.

I am returning this letter[1] in order to express the hope that you will fully acquaint the Treasury Department, if you have not done so already, with the various plans by means of which the effort is being made to tie our finances up with the necessities of the governments on this side.

Cordially and sincerely yours, [Woodrow Wilson]

CCL (WP, DLC).
[1] That is, N. H. Davis to WW, Feb. 2, 1919.

## To Herbert Clark Hoover

My dear Hoover: Paris, 7 February, 1919.

It goes against every instinct of charity and prudence for me to be obliged to say so, but I do feel obliged to say that I do not think we would be justified in making this use of Army supplies, and there is no fund at my disposal which could be used for this purpose.[1] I am afraid we shall have to rest satisfied with what the British and American Red Cross can do in this distressing and important matter.

Cordially and sincerely yours, Woodrow Wilson

CCL (WP, DLC).
[1] See HCH to WW, Feb. 6, 1919.

## To Brand Whitlock

My dear Whitlock:                    Paris, 7 February, 1919.

I am genuinely distressed to find that I cannot, before going back home, leave Paris long enough to make a visit to Brussels such as I would wish to make; indeed, not long enough to make any sort of visit. My duties here exact every hour of me and, I hope, will be very much more helpful to Belgium than any visit I could make would be. But, as I said to Mr. Hymans the other night, I have really set my heart on coming to Brussels, and I would be obliged if you would be kind enough to see the King and tell him of my genuine distress that I cannot come now and of my hope that upon my return I shall be able to do so.

For it does now seem as if it would be necessary for me to come back after the adjournment of Congress, and I cannot believe that some interval will not occur when I do return that I can get away from Paris.

Please present my warm regards to the King, with an expression of my highest esteem and my genuine interest in all that affects Belgium.

You have been very kind to my little girl,[1] and you may be sure that we all appreciate it very deeply. She was extremely fortunate to be in such hands when her cold came upon her. We are all very grateful to you.

With warmest regards,
Cordially and sincerely yours,   Woodrow Wilson

TLS (received from Jerome Shestack).
[1] Margaret Wilson had arrived in Brussels on January 27, where she was a guest of the Whitlocks. A Brussels newspaper, *L'Étoile Belge*, reported on February 1 that she was suffering from influenza. *New York Times*, Jan. 29 and Feb. 2, 1919.


## To Herbert Bayard Swope

*Confidential*

My Dear Swope:                    Paris, 7 February, 1919

I am sure I need not tell you that I would grant an interview to you if I granted it to anybody,[1] but there is not only the usual difficulty which stands in the way of granting an interview to one and denying it to others, but there is this additional and very great difficulty: that an interview by myself at this time would seem to me very dangerous. I mean that if I gave you an interview, I would have to deal with you, of course, with the utmost frankness and say something and not talk in generalities, and it is very important just now that I should not say anything. I am surrounded by intrigue here, and the only way I can succeed is by working silently, saying nothing in public unless it becomes necessary to bring about an open contest.

I am sure that with your knowledge of the world and your experience you will appreciate how imperative this consideration is.

I appreciate very warmly your generous desire to help and am sure you are helping in your dispatches, though I do not have the opportunity to see them.

Cordially and faithfully yours,   [Woodrow Wilson]

CCL (WP, DLC).
[1] Wilson was replying to H. B. Swope to WW, Feb. 5, 1919, ALS (WP, DLC).


## From Howard Sweetser Bliss[1]

My dear President Wilson:      Paris, France, February 7th, 1919.

Having just come from Syria and from seeing many Syrians in Egypt, I beg to state to you how earnestly and even passionately the people of Syria are depending upon your twelfth point and upon the Anglo-French Declaration of November 1918.[2]

They crave a fair opportunity to express their own political aspirations and they claim that this craving is justified by the above mentioned documents.

And such an opportunity they have not had. The censorship of the Press and Post Office and the difficulty of holding private and public gatherings have prevented it. They are discouraged and timid.

For they have seen a pro-French delegation, *which they believe does not represent either Lebanon or Syria*, slip away from Beirut, by the help of the local French authorities, on their way to Paris, while they themselves are not permitted to discuss with any freedom their political future. They believe this to be unfair and wrong.

I understand that this delegation from the Lebanon is soon to have a hearing before the Peace Congress. I earnestly hope that their declarations will be sifted by the Peace Commissioners and that their supposed mandate and the method of their departure from Syria will be closely investigated.

I have heard with satisfaction that an American Commission is soon to be sent out from here in order to give a hearing to the Syrians. If such a commission is adequately backed by the French and British authorities at home *and in Syria* the result of their investigations ought to be helpful. In my opinion an international Commission would have certain marked advantages over a purely American Commission and perhaps the change will still be made. I believe that the report of any commission, made up of fair, wide-minded and resourceful men, would show that the Syrians desire the erection of an independent state or states under the care, for the present, of a Power or of the "League of Nations." I believe the Power designated by the people would be America, for the Syrians believe in American disinterestedness; or England, for the people trust her sense of Justice and believe in her capacity. I believe that French guardianship would be rejected for three reasons: Serious-minded men in Syria fear that the people of Syria would imitate France's less desirable qualities; they do not consider the French to be good administrators; they believe that France would exploit the country for her own material and political advantage. They do not trust her.

If America should be indicated as the Power desired I earnestly hope that she will not decline.

Any information I may possess, is of course, at your disposal.

Yours very truly,   Howard S. Bliss

TLS (WP, DLC).
    [1] President of the Syrian Protestant College of Beirut (later the American University of Beirut).
    [2] Again, see R. Cecil to C. A. de R. Barclay, Oct. 31, 1918, n. 2, Vol. 51, and the minutes of the Council of Ten printed at Feb. 13, 1918, 3 p.m.

## Gilbert Fairchild Close to Joseph Clark Grew

My dear Mr. Grew:                    Paris, 7 February, 1919.

The President asks me to tell you, in reply to your letter of January 30th enclosing the telegram from the Town Clerk of Dublin, that he intends to write to the Dublin people at once. He hopes that the suggestion of a deputation will be discouraged.

Sincerely yours,   Gilbert F. Close

TLS (WP, DLC).

## From William Shepherd Benson

[Paris] 7 February, 1919.

MEMORANDUM FOR THE PRESIDENT

SUBJECT:   Comments on proposed Naval clauses to be inserted in the preliminaries of the peace with Germany.[1]

*Paragraph No. 1* (a) No comments.
                (b) No comments.
                (c) The intention here is that the material resulting from breaking up the submarines mentioned in paragraph

(b) above may be used by the Germans themselves and not to be delivered to the Allies.

*Paragraph No. 2* (Surface Vessels.)

It is very important that the phrase in this paragraph which provides that these vessels are to be destroyed or demolished should remain, as by retaining it in the final terms all of the powers are committed to the destruction of these vessels. It was necessary this morning for me to insist upon this point. The French are very reluctant to agree to destruction and this morning exhibited for the first time a marked tendency towards the distribution of these vessels for the purpose of increasing Naval armaments of the allies. Although the British did not concur in the French proposal their attitude was not one of marked opposition. The Naval interest of the United States demands that no one of the vessels taken from Germany shall remain in existence.

*Paragraph No. 3*

The same comments apply as in paragraph No. 2.

*Paragraph No. 4*

No comments.

[12] *Paragraph No. 5* (Heligoland).

The original form of this paragraph provided that the United States should assist in the control of the destruction of Heligoland. I am not in accord with the idea of this destruction, and especially of the destruction of the harbor works, but I consented to let the paragraph stand if the participation of the United States in the demolition was not required. Heligoland is essentially a defensive rather than an offensive position, especially since Germany is to be left without a Navy.

[2] *Paragraph No. 6*

The original paragraph provided that the control of the demolition of the fortifications should be participated in by the United States, but upon my request all mention of the United States was omitted. Attention is invited to the fact that this paragraph requires demolition of all German fortifications in the Baltic as far as Longitude 16 east. It leaves the eastern entrance of the Kiel Canal and Germany's naval post at Kiel wholly undefended.

[3] *Paragraph No. 7* (Kiel Canal)

During the discussion it was generally admitted that in time of war, in which Germany was a belligerent, that Germany would exercise the complete control over the Kiel Canal, and that no provision which we might make, short of military occupation, could prevent her from so doing.

[4] *Paragraph No. 8*

This article was inserted because of the importance to navies of outlying naval bases. To deprive Germany of all her naval bases, or all places where she can establish naval bases, is equivalent to depriving her of ability to exercise whatever naval power she may have away from her own coast.

5 *Paragraph No. 9* (Submarine Cables.)

The original proposition was that these cables should be taken from Germany without compensation. In the discussion I pointed out that this would be contrary to international law and contrary to American interests; that our interest required that we have free communication in time of peace with all countries and that it was not to our interest that our communications with the central powers should be monopolized by other powers. Upon my suggestion the entire matter was left to the decision of the prize courts. I believe that these prize courts will not condemn the cables mentioned.

*Paragraph No. 10*

This paragraph was originally worded so as to include our two ex-German auxiliary cruisers; DEKALB and VON STEUBEN. I declined to discuss the paragraph until the names of those cruisers had been excluded from the appendix, maintaining that sovereignty over them had passed absolutely and that it was not now a subject for discussion. My view was accepted.

*Paragraph No. 11* and No. 11 (Bis)

No comments.

*Paragraph No. 12*

No comments.

*Paragraph No. 13*

No comments.

[W. S. Benson]    Admiral, U.S. Navy.

CC MS (W. S. Benson Papers, DLC).
[1] Benson below comments upon and explains a slightly different version of the document printed as Appendix D to the minutes of the Supreme War Council printed at Feb. 8, 1919, which Benson enclosed with his memorandum.
[2] Wilson's numbering.

## To Joseph Patrick Tumulty

Paris, February 7, 1919.

Will be glad to have you say to Ferris that I hope the bill providing for park in honor of Roosevelt will be passed, but I do not think it advisable for me to appear in the matter publicly because I would be suspected of insincerity.[1]

My stay in Washington will be so short that I do not think I ought to sanction an elaborate public reception. I hope you will explain to Mr. Harper[2] that I think my stay ought to be as quiet and business-like as possible.

Would be glad to know if you still favor my landing in Boston rather than New York.

Please convey the following to Sherley: "Hear that you are again endeavoring to work out a budget plan. I hope sincerely that you will succeed."[3]                                        Woodrow Wilson

T telegram (J. P. Tumulty Papers, DLC).
 [1] Wilson was responding to JPT to WW, Feb. 4, 1919 (second telegram of that date).
 [2] Robert Newton Harper, president of the District National Bank of Washington. Wilson was here responding to JPT to WW, Feb. 5, 1919, T telegram (WP, DLC).
 [3] Wilson was here responding to JPT to WW, Feb. 5, 1919, T telegram (WP, DLC).


## To Carter Glass

Paris, 7 February 1919.

Thank you for your telegram about the Revenue Bill.[1] You may take my approval for granted and my only suggestion about actually signing the bill is that I shall be leaving here probably by the fifteenth and it is possible that the bill might not be able to reach this side before I was on my way to that side. Congratulations.
                                        Woodrow Wilson.

T telegram (WP, DLC).
 [1] C. Glass to WW, Feb. 5, 1919.


## Three Telegrams from Joseph Patrick Tumulty

The White House, 7 February, 1919.

[No. 37] Vote on suffrage Monday. *This is our last chance.* Will you cable Trammell and Overman. There is a real chance here and with Williams too I know. Please do not fail us.    Tumulty.


The White House, 7 February 1919.

[No. 39] Censorship of mails causing great disturbance to business here. Postmaster General thinks it ought to be removed. Cause of great criticism.                                        Tumulty.


The White House, February 8 [7], 1919.

No. 42. Williams a real possibility. His wife[1] intimated to a friend that the Senator really distracted and wishes to please you. A little friendly cable note from you to him will help. Wolcott and Trammel[1] on fence. A little push from you will help.

Tumulty.

T telegrams (WP, DLC).
[1] Elizabeth Dial Webb (Mrs. John Sharp) Williams.

## From William Cox Redfield

Washington, 7 Feb. 1919.

Number forty. Secretary Redfield requests me send following quote

"Referring cablegram yesterday kindly urge Baruch release Peek for purpose explained stop. This deemed essential to full success plan stop. Procedure suggested yesterday meets general approval unquote." Tumulty.

T telegram (WP, DLC).

## From the Peace Conference Diary of Sir William Wiseman

February 7th, 1919. (Friday).

HOUSE told me of a letter WHITE had received from LODGE saying that in his (LODGE'S) personal opinion it would be right for the President to commit the American people to manage Constantinople as mandatories.

# ADDENDA

## A Memorandum by Thomas Garrigue Masaryk

[June 19, 1918]

I spoke with the President from five to five forty-five.[1] The main subject of the discussion has been the question of intervention in Russia, whether the Japanese could intervene in Siberia and organize Siberia, and whether our Bohemian troops could be used to that end. I explained my view on the matter, that I am not in favor of a so-called intervention, because I do not see what it would bring about. But I would be in favor of renewing the war upon Germany by the whole Japanese army. The President was very well informed about the number of Japanese troops available, and we agreed that there are many difficulties, above all the question of how to pay the Japanese. Then the President asked my opinion about a propaganda work which the United States could easily start, to send business men with goods, conducting a barter, because the Russians would not accept money for their grain and the goods they have to exchange. The question of this barter has been studied for the President by the Secretary of Commerce, Mr. Redfield, and perhaps tomorrow the President will hear his report. Then the Y.M.C.A. would be sent to Russia and the Red Cross. It seems the President has already chosen a man not a business man who would control this whole work. He did not give me the name of the man. to France. The political effect of our troops fighting in France is very great, it being the most effective anti-Austrian propaganda among all non-German and non-Magyar nations in Austria. On this occasion I emphasized the necessity of dismembering Austria if the war should be won. The President accepted this view and consented. I explained to him that there is a great propaganda conducted from Rome, and finally I urged him to help Italy: she deserves it for her loyalty and, militarily speaking, Italy, strengthened by American troops, could invade Austria and that would shorten the war. The President seemed to realize all this.

We parted. He was very friendly indeed, and asked me to come and give my opinion on points which he will submit to me.

T MS (R. Crane Papers, DGU).
[1] About this meeting, see WW to C. R. Crane, June 11, 1918, and WW to RL, June 19, 1918, n. 1, Vol. 48.

## From Herbert Clark Hoover

My Dear Mr. President:                    Paris, 1 February 1919.

Mr. McCormick will be sending to you the three resolutions which we are most anxious should be gotten through the Supreme War Council at its meeting on Monday or Tuesday. As you know, I have been advocating these points now for nearly two months and, from selfish or bureaucratic obstruction, we have as yet no results, and I see no hope of attaining any such results except through strong intervention on your part.

Our merchants are in extreme jeopardy from their surplus supplies of food, which the British now repudiate as to purchase but which they obstruct to a wider freedom of market. The French obstruct the notion of neutrals trading with Germany, although it would alleviate both the financial problem and distress. We have no justification in humanity or politics in debarring neutrals from buying all the food they wish for their own consumption now that we have ample supplies. The blockade on Mediterranean countries has no purpose whatever, except to serve detailed selfish interests. All these measures impose a much larger burden on relief than would be necessary if all these people could produce and trade where they may in food.

There is so much obstruction that I despair even getting it past the Supreme War Council unless some great world opinion is brought to bear, and I would like to have you advise me whether you do not think it is desirable for me to disclose the nature of these resolutions that you will propose, to the press at once, and I am sure there will be a reaction from the whole neutral world and a reaction from the United States in your support, and the very nature of this reaction will expedite acceptance of the principles.

Faithfully yours,   Herbert Hoover

TLS (Hoover Archives, CSt-H).

# INDEX

## NOTE ON THE INDEX

THE alphabetically arranged analytical table of contents at the front of the volume eliminates duplication, in both contents and index, of references to certain documents, such as letters. Letters are listed in the contents alphabetically by name, and chronologically within each name by page. The subject matter of all letters is, of course, indexed. The Editorial Notes and Wilson's writings are listed in the contents chronologically by page. In addition, the subject matter of both categories is indexed. The index covers all references to books and articles mentioned in text or notes. Footnotes are indexed. Page references to footnotes which place a comma between the page number and "n" cite both text and footnote, thus: "418,n1." On the other hand, absence of the comma indicates reference to the footnote only, thus: "59n1"—the page number denoting where the footnote appears.

The index supplies the fullest known form of names and, for the Wilson and Axson families, relationships as far down as cousins. Persons referred to by nicknames or shortened forms of names can be identified by reference to entries for these forms of the names.

All entries consisting of page numbers only and which refer to concepts, issues and opinions (such as democracy, the tariff, the money trust, leadership, and labor problems), are references to Wilson's speeches and writings. Page references that follow the symbol Δ in such entries refer to the opinions and comments of others who are identified.

Three cumulative contents-index volumes are now in print: Volume 13, which covers Volumes 1-12, Volume 26, which covers Volumes 14-25, and Volume 39, which covers Volumes 27-38. Volume 52, covering volumes 40-51, is in preparation.

# INDEX

*Abraham Lincoln* (Charnwood), 488,n2

A.C.N.P.: *see* American Commission to Negotiate Peace

Adalia, district, 350

*Addresses of President Wilson on First Trip to Europe December 3, 1918 to February 24, 1919,* 156n, 273n, 310n

Adee, Alvey Augustus, 428

Ador, Gustave, 233-34, 302

Adriatic question, 134-35; and the press, 112,n3, 123

Africa, 249, 250, 252-54, 318-22; *see also* under the names of the individual political units, such as South Africa, Union of; South-West Africa

*African Origins of the Mandates Idea* (Louis), 311n2

agriculture: use of cereals for beverages, 193-94; Tumulty on employment ideas in, 391

Aharonian, Avetis, 517,n2

Albania, 490,n2, 527

Albert I (King of the Belgians), 495, 550

Albrecht-Carrié, René, 135n3

Aleppo, 506

Algeria, 368

Alien Property Custodian, 429n1

Allen, William G., 380n3

Allenby, Edmund Henry Hynman, 506,n6

Allied Maritime Transport Council, 30

Allied Supreme Council for Supply and Relief: *see* Supreme Council for Supply and Relief

Allies: and war expenses, 196; agree on commemorative medal for all soldiers, 246-47; *see also* under the names of the individual countries

Alsace-Lorraine, 285, 299, 529

American Commissioners to Negotiate Peace, 3-4, 55, 84-88, 134-35, 304

American Commission to Negotiate Peace (A.C.N.P.), 7n1, 180, 399n1, 471n2, 473,n1; photograph of, *illustration section*

American Federation of Labor, 309

American Jewish Congress, 258n1

American Red Cross, 102, 103n7, 515, 549

American Red Cross Commission to Russia, 181n6

American University of Beirut, 551n1

*A. Mitchell Palmer: Politician* (Coben), 429n1

Anatolia, 350

Anderson, George Weston, 58,n2

Anglo-American relations: *see* Great Britain and the United States

Appropriations, Committee on (House of Reps.), 486

Arabia, 350, 360, 414, 455

Arabs: Prince Faisal's claims for, 506-509

Archangel, Russia: *see* Russia—Murmansk and Archangel, intervention in

Armenia and Armenians, 225, 330, 360, 370, 371, 455; and representation at Paris Peace Conference, 226,n2, 346; Nubar on claims of, 516-18

Armistice: Foch on renewal terms, 7,n3; Supreme War Council on, 7-12; Germany signs, 108, 121, 172,n3; Great Britain and Italy want more German territory, U.S. opposed to further encroachment, 499-500; Bliss on, 514, 522-25; and Loucheur Report, 527, 538-45; WW on not altering terms but setting up commission to negotiate, 530-31, 532-33; Lloyd George on not being bound to renew on same terms, 531-32, 533; additional clauses to conditions, 541; Benson on naval clauses, 552-54

Armistice Commission at Spa, 9,n5, 10, 214, 219

arms limitation, 140, 189,n5, 218-21, 226, 238-46, 264, 402, 427-28, 451, 510, 512

Army (U.S.): *see* United States Army

Arnold, Matthew, 309

Asia Minor, 463, 473n1

Asquith, Herbert Henry, 177

Associated Press, 60

Association of State Farmers' Unions Presidents, 228n1

Atwater, Caleb Huntington, 383,n1

Auchincloss, Gordon, 151,n2

Australia, 379; and representation at Paris Peace Conference, 14, 44, 65; territorial claims and mandatory issue, 250, 251, 251-52, 289, 299-300, 308, 312, 325, 333, 348, 351, 358, 363, 366, 489

Austria, 170

Austria-Hungary, 51, 303

Awni Abd al-Hadi, 505,n2

Baker, Newton Diehl, 55, 227, 432; on pork industry and food relief, 105-106; on investigation of German propaganda in the U.S., 397n1; discharge of conscientious objectors, 397-98,n4; on carpenters' controversy, 519-20

Baker, Ray Stannard: on publicity, 59, 189-91, 191-92

Baku, Russia, 372n7

Balch, Emily Greene, 397n1

Baldwin, Roger Nash, 397n1

Balfour, Arthur James, 173, 464n1; and Supreme War Council meetings, 5, 9, 10, 37, 201; and Council of Ten meetings, 16-17, 19, 20, 24, 47, 66, 70, 74, 76, 110, 114, 116, 117-18, 119, 182, 184-85, 187, 189, 209, 211, 222, 284, 285-86, 287, 288-89, 289, 311, 323-24, 343, 345, 352, 374, 375, 376-77, 377-78, 421, 422, 505; on press leaks and WW's meeting on Adriatic question, 123; Seymour on, 384; WW meets with, 489; photograph of, *illustration section*

Balkan states, 527

*Balkan Studies,* 403n3

Baltic provinces, 92, 94, 103n7

Banat, The, 421n7, 424, 425

Banking and Currency Committee (Senate), 485n1